THE MEANING OF DIFFERENCE

THE MEANING OF DIFFERENCE

American Constructions of Race, Sex and Gender, Social Class, and Sexual Orientation

A Text/Reader
FOURTH EDITION

Karen E. Rosenblum

George Mason University

Toni-Michelle C. Travis

George Mason University

Mc Graw Hill

Boston   Burr Ridge, IL   Dubuque, IA   Madison, WI   New York   San Francisco   St. Louis
Bangkok   Bogotá   Caracas   Kuala Lumpur   Lisbon   London   Madrid   Mexico City
Milan   Montreal   New Delhi   Santiago   Seoul   Singapore   Sydney   Taipei   Toronto

The McGraw·Hill Companies

Higher Education

THE MEANING OF DIFFERENCE: AMERICAN CONSTRUCTIONS OF RACE, SEX AND GENDER, SOCIAL CLASS, AND SEXUAL ORIENTATION

1 2 3 4 5 6 7 8 9 0 DOC/DOC 0 9 8 7 6 5

ISBN 0-07-299746-X

Editor in Chief: *Emily Barrosse*
Publisher: *Phillip A. Butcher*
Sponsoring Editor: *Sherith H. Pankratz*
Developmental Editor: *Katherine Blake*
Senior Marketing Manager: *Daniel M. Loch*
Managing Editor: *Jean Dal Porto*
Project Manager: *Ruth Smith*
Associate Designer: *Marianna Kinigakis*
Cover and Interior Design: *Kay Fulton*
Cover Credit: *#91 by Karen Deicas DePodesta, 2002; Art For After Hours/SuperStock, Inc.*
Photo Research Coordinator: *Natalia C. Peschiera*
Senior Media Project Manager: *Nancy Garcia*
Production Supervisor: *Janean A. Utley*
Permissions Editor: *Frederick T. Courtright*
Composition: *by Cenveo*
Printing: *45 # New Era Matte Plus, R.R. Donnelley and Sons, Inc./Crawfordsville, IN.*

Library of Congress Cataloging-in-Publication Data
Rosenblum, Karen, E.
The meaning of difference : American constructions of race, sex and gender, social class,
    and sexual orientation : a text/reader / Karen E. Rosenblum, Toni-Michelle C. Travis [editors]. — 4th ed.
        p. cm.
    Includes index
    ISBN 0-07-299746-X (softcover : alk. paper)
    1. United States—Social conditions—1980- 2. Pluralism (Social sciences)—United States.
  I. Rosenblum, Karen Elaine. II. Travis, Toni-Michelle, 1947-
  HN59.2.M44 2006
  306'.0973—dc22

                                                2005043763

The Internet addresses listed in the text were accurate at the time of publication. The inclusion of a website does not indicate an endorsement by the authors of McGraw-Hill, and McGraw-Hill does not guarantee the accuracy of the information presented at these sites.

www.mhhe.com

ABOUT THE AUTHORS

KAREN E. ROSENBLUM is associate professor of sociology at George Mason University in Fairfax, Virginia. She has served as the university's Vice President for University Life and as director of the Women's Studies Program. Professor Rosenblum received her Ph.D. in sociology from the University of Colorado, Boulder. Her areas of research and teaching include sex and gender, language, and deviance.

TONI-MICHELLE C. TRAVIS is associate professor of government and politics at George Mason University in Fairfax, Virginia. She is a faculty member in Women's Studies and also Director of the African American Studies program. Professor Travis received her Ph.D. in political science from the University of Chicago. Her areas of research and teaching include race and gender dimensions of political participation, urban politics, and American government. She has served as the president of the National Capital Area Political Science Association and the Women's Caucus of the American Political Science Association. A political analyst, she is a frequent commentator on Virginia and national politics.

CONTENTS

SECTION IV—BRIDGING DIFFERENCES

PREFACE

The Meaning of Difference is an effort to understand how *difference* is constructed in contemporary American culture: How do categories of people come to be seen as "different"? How does being "different" affect people's lives? What does difference mean at the level of the individual, social institution, or society? What difference does "difference" make? Focusing on the most significant categories of difference in America—race, sex/gender, sexual orientation, social class, and disability—what is *shared* across these categories? What can be learned from their commonalities? That *The Meaning of Difference* is now in its fourth edition makes us hopeful that this comparative approach can be useful in understanding American conceptions and constructions of difference.

ORGANIZATION AND CONCEPTUAL FRAMEWORK

The Meaning of Difference is divided into four sections. Each section includes an opening Framework Essay and a set of readings, with the Framework Essay providing the conceptual structure by which to understand the readings. Thus, the Framework Essays are not simply introductions to the readings; they are the "text" portion of this **text/reader.**

The first section's Framework Essay and readings describe how categories of difference are *created;* the second considers the *experience* of difference; the third examines the *meanings* assigned to difference by law, politics, public policy, the economy, science, popular culture, and language; and the fourth describes what people can do to *challenge and change these constructions* of difference.

Each of the readings included in the volume have been selected by virtue of their applicability to multiple categories of difference. For example, F. James Davis's conclusions about the construction of race (Reading 1), could be applied to a discussion of sexual identity or disability. How much of "x" does it take to locate someone as gay or straight, abled or disabled? Ira

Berkow's description of the experience of a white quarterback on the football team of a black university (Reading 27) might make one curious about others' experience of being the "only one" in a particular setting. Similarly, Beverly Daniel Tatum's discussion of the development of racial identity (Reading 26) inevitably makes us think about the development of all the other identities so important to people's lives. In all, our aim has been to select readings that help identify both what is unique and what is shared across our experiences of difference.

DISTINGUISHING FEATURES

Four features make *The Meaning of Difference* distinctive:

- First, it offers a conceptual framework by which to understand the commonalities among these categories of difference. This encompassing conceptual approach makes *The Meaning of Difference* unique.
- Second, no other book provides an accessible and historically grounded discussion of the Supreme Court decisions critical to the creation of these differences.
- Third, *The Meaning of Difference* has been designed with an eye toward the pedagogic difficulties that often accompany this subject matter. Our experience has been that when the topic is *simultaneously* race, sex and gender, social class, sexual orientation, and disability no one group can be easily cast as victim or victimizer.
- Finally, no other volume offers a detailed discussion and set of readings on how to challenge and change the constructions of difference. This is a new section in the book, responding to the needs expressed by instructors and students.

CHANGES IN THE FOURTH EDITION

The fourth edition includes **39** *new* **readings** and an entirely **new section entitled "Bridging Differences."** Addressing the sense of powerlessness that often accompanies the study of difference, this section describes steps that students can take to move beyond that feeling and proceed with the work of social change.

Also, in this edition, there are:

- more readings on the **impact of race on Latino identities;**
- more readings on **popular culture;**
- all new readings in the sections on **sex and gender, sexual orientation, the economy,** and **science;**
- a more **accessible layout** of the readings in Section II, Experiencing Difference;
- coverage of the **2003 Supreme Court decision on the University of Michigan's** use of race in admissions to the undergraduate and law school programs;

- coverage of the **2003 Supreme Court decision on disabled people's access to public buildings;**
- **discussion questions** for each reading;
- four new **Personal Accounts;**
- a **more detailed index** of the topics in the readings and framework essays.

This edition covers **many new and important topics,** including:

- The re-segregation of American public schools, despite the landmark 1954 *Brown v. Board of Education* Supreme Court ruling (Reading 43)
- The experience of multi-racial families (Reading 6) and multi-racial individuals (Reading 23)
- The movement to compel states to provide adequate funding for all public schools (Reading 46)
- Race and ethnic ambiguity as a fashion trend in advertising (Reading 53 and 54)
- How inequalities affect health and even mortality rates (Reading 52)
- Whether it is time for all sexual identity categories to disappear (Reading 20)
- The stigma faced by young girls whose breasts develop early (Reading 31)
- The social consequences of an American economy that offers both economic growth and job insecurity (Reading 15)
- The Cold War impetus behind America's minority rights revolution (Reading 44)
- The 2003 Supreme Court decision on the University of Michigan's use of race-based admissions (Reading 41)
- The 2003 Supreme Court decision on disabled people's access to public buildings (Reading 41)
- Life as a low-wage worker (Reading 16)
- How those with privilege and power can be allies to those facing discrimination (Readings 61, 62, 63, and 64)
- Media depictions of black men (Reading 56)
- The features of the workplace that continue to contribute to sex discrimination (Reading 47)
- How substantial racial inequalities could remain despite decades of civil rights law (Reading 48)
- The nature and consequences of the myth of Asian Americans as the model minority (Reading 49)
- The impact of the images of masculinity on young boys (Reading 32)
- Popular culture's "race is over" theme (Reading 55)
- The images of Native Americans conveyed by the names of sports teams (Reading 59)
- The impact of race on Latino identities (Readings 5 and 24)
- Determining who is "really" a Native American (Reading 4)
- How to pursue "everyday activism" (Reading 61)
- Racial identity development in adolescence (Reading 26)

- Being "the only one": the experience of a white quarterback on the football team of a black university (Reading 27)
- How the children of lesbian and gay couples react to the prospect of their parents' marriage (Reading 35)
- Trying to get around if you are disabled: cabs and mass transit experiences (Reading 39)

HIGHLIGHTS IN THE FOURTH EDITION

Several readings from the previous edition have been retained not only because of their wide popularity among students and faculty, but also because they have become classics in the field. Foremost in this category is **F. James Davis**'s, "Who is Black? One Nation's Definition" and two articles by **Marilyn Frye,** "Oppression" and "To Be and Be Seen: The Politics of Reality." "Asian American Panethnicity," by **Yen Le Espiritu** and "Whiteness as an 'Unmarked' Category," by **Ruth Frankenberg** hold this rank as well. Certainly, **John Larew**'s "Why Are Droves of Unqualified, Unprepared Kids Getting into our Top Colleges" has been eye-opening for students trying to understand affirmative action policies. **Robert Moore**'s "Racism in the English Language" paints a vivid, and still relevant, picture of the values embedded in the language of color; **Laurel Richardson Walum** accomplishes the same for gender in her article, "Gender Stereotyping in the English Language."

Every section of the fourth edition also includes new readings, and some sections have been entirely revised. There are several new readings that we think have the potential to become classics. One is "Why Are All the Black Kids Sitting Together in the Cafeteria," which is a chapter from **Beverly Daniel Tatum**'s national bestseller. "The Minority Quarterback," by **Ira Berkow,** was part of the 2001 *New York Times* Pulitzer-Prize-winning series "How Race is Lived in America." Both **Barbara Ehrenreich**'s "Nickel and Dimed: On (Not) Getting By in America" and **Bert Archer**'s "The End of Gay (and the Death of Heterosexuality)" are extracts from books that have received significant comment and praise. "A World of Their Own," by **Liza Mundy** was included in Oliver Sack's edition, *Best American Science Writing of 2003.*

SUPPLEMENTS

Instructor's Manual/Test Bank

Jamey Piland, a colleague at Trinity College in Washington, D.C., has used *The Meaning of Difference* in several interdisciplinary courses and, from that experience, has produced a thoughtful Instructor's Manual that focuses especially on how to teach this material. Few instructors have had the experience of teaching *all* of these topics—let alone all of them in a single course—as Professor Piland has. Andrea Herrera at the University of Colorado, Colorado Springs, did an excellent job revising Jamey's work for this new edition.

New for the fourth edition is the addition of a Test Bank that will be combined with the Instructor's Manual. The Test Bank, developed by Susan Weldon of Eastern Michigan University, includes multiple-choice and true-false questions for the Framework Essays and each of the 64 readings. Susan also developed the Website practice tests for students' use.

Race/Class/Gender/Sexuality SuperSite

This companion Website provides information about the book, including an overview, summaries of key features and what's new in the third edition, information about the authors, and Practice Test Questions.

Non-text-specific content on this site includes an annotated list of Weblinks to useful sites; a list of professional resources (e.g., professional journals); links to Websites offering Census 2000 information; a glossary; flashcards; and a comprehensive list (annotated and listed by category) of films and videos in the areas of race, class, gender, ethnicity, and sexuality.

Visit the SuperSite by going to either

www.mhhe.com/rosenblum

or

www.mhhe.com/raceclassgender

ACKNOWLEDGMENTS

Many colleagues and friends have helped us clarify the ideas we present here. David Haines has been unfailingly available to help Karen think through conceptual, technical, and ethical dilemmas. She could not imagine a colleague more supportive or wise. Theodore W. Travis provided insight on Supreme Court decisions, their relationship to social values, and their impact on American society. As always, this edition has benefited enormously from the comments of our colleagues at George Mason. Since this project first emerged over a decade ago, Victoria Rader has been generous in sharing her insights as a teacher and writer. Her wisdom especially guided our development of the book's new section, "Bridging Differences." Two other colleagues—Rose Pascarell and Jamey Piland—merit special thanks both for their feedback and the good work they accomplish with students. As a friend and friendly editor, none could be better than Sheila Barrows. Finally, we owe special thanks to our students at George Mason University for sharing their experiences with us.

For this edition, we again convey our appreciation to Joan Lester and the Equity Institute of Emeryville, California, for their understanding of the progress that can be made through a holistic analysis.

Kathy Blake of McGraw-Hill shepherded this volume to completion with the same good organization and insight she provided on previous editions.

And, as in previous editions, McGraw-Hill proved itself committed to a thorough review process by putting together a panel of accomplished scholars with broad expertise. All offered detailed, insightful, and invaluable critiques, and we are much in their debt:

Edward Jankowski, William Paterson University

Andrea O'Reilly Herrera, University of Colorado at Colorado Springs

Henry M. Codjoe, Dalton State College

Blanche M. Hughes, Colorado State University

Dan Pence, California State University, Chico

Juliet C. Rothman, University of California, Berkeley

Karen Rosenblum
Toni-Michelle Travis
George Mason University

THE MEANING OF DIFFERENCE

CONSTRUCTING CATEGORIES OF DIFFERENCE

FRAMEWORK ESSAY

This book considers how *difference* is constructed in contemporary American society. It explores how categories of people are seen as significantly different from one another and how people's lives are affected by these conceptions of difference. The four sections of this book have been organized around what we consider to be the key questions about difference: how it is constructed, how it is experienced by individuals, how meaning is attributed to difference, and how differences can be bridged.

We believe that race, sex, social class, sexual orientation, and disability are currently the primary axes of difference in American society—they are also what social scientists would call *master statuses*. In common usage, the term *status* means prestige or esteem. But for social scientists, the term describes positions in a social structure. In this sense, statuses are like empty slots (or positions) that individuals fill. The most obvious kinds of statuses are kinship and occupational; for example, uncle, mother-in-law, cousin, office manager, paramedic, disk jockey. At any point in time, an individual holds multiple statuses—kinship, occupational, religious—as well as race, sex, social class, sexual orientation, and ability/disability statuses.

This latter set of statuses—the ones we focus on in this book—are significantly more powerful than most other social statuses. Social scientists refer to these as *master* statuses because they so profoundly affect a person's life. The *Oxford Dictionary of Sociology* defines master statuses as those that "in most or all social situations will overpower or dominate all other statuses. . . . Master status influences every other aspect of life, including personal identity" (Marshall, 1994:315). This does not mean, however, that people always understand the impact of the master statuses they occupy—indeed much of this book is about recognizing that impact.

We plan to explore similarities in the operation of these master statuses. While there are certainly differences of history, experience, and impact, we believe that similar processes are at work when we "see" differences of color, sex and gender, social class, sexual orientation, and disability, and we believe that there are similarities in the consequences of these master statuses for individuals' lives.

In preparing this volume, we noticed that talk about racism, sexism, homophobia,[1] and class status seemed to be everywhere—film, music, news reports, talk shows, sermons, and scholarly publications—and that the topics carried considerable intensity. These are controversial subjects; thus, readers may have strong reactions to these issues. Two perspectives—essentialism and constructionism—are core to this book and should help you understand your own reaction to the material.

---

[1]The term *homophobia* was coined in 1971 by psychologist George Weinberg to describe an irrational fear of, or anger toward, homosexuals. While the psychological application has disappeared, the word remains in common use to describe a strong opposition to or rejection of same-sex relationships. Two alternative words are emerging: *antigay* and *heterosexism*. Heterosexism is the presumption that all people are heterosexual and that heterosexuality is the only acceptable form of sexual expression.

The Essentialist and Constructionist Orientations

The difference between the *constructionist* and *essentialist* orientations is illustrated in the tale of the three umpires, first apparently told by social psychologist Hadley Cantril:

> Hadley Cantril relates the story of three baseball umpires discussing their profession. The first umpire said, "Some are balls and some are strikes, and I call them as they are." The second replied, "Some's balls and some's strikes, and I call 'em as I sees 'em." The third thought about it and said, "Some's balls and some's strikes, but they ain't nothing 'till I calls 'em." (Henshel and Silverman, 1975:26)

The first umpire in the story can be described as an essentialist. In arguing that "I call them as they are," he indicates his assumption that balls and strikes are entities that exist in the world independently of his perception of them. For this umpire, balls and strikes are easily identified, and he is merely a neutral observer of them. This umpire "regards knowledge as objective and independent of mind, and himself as the impartial reporter of things 'as they are' " (Pfuhl, 1986:5). For this essentialist umpire, balls and strikes exist in the world; he simply observes their presence.

Thus, the essentialist orientation presumes that items in a category all share some "essential" quality, their "ball-ness" or "strike-ness." For essentialists, the categories of race, sex, sexual orientation, and social class identify significant, empirically verifiable differences among people. From the essentialist perspective, racial categories exist apart from any social processes; they are objective categories of real difference among people.

The second umpire is somewhat removed from pure essentialism. His statement, "I call 'em as I sees 'em," conveys the belief that while an independent, objective reality exists, it is subject to interpretation. For him the world contains balls and strikes, but individuals may have different perceptions about which is which.

The third umpire, who says "they ain't nothing 'till I calls 'em," is a constructionist. He operates from the belief that "conceptions such as 'strikes' and 'balls' have no meaning except that given them by the observer" (Pfuhl, 1986:5). For this constructionist umpire, reality cannot be separated from the way a culture makes sense of it; strikes and balls do not exist until they are constructed through social processes. From this perspective, difference is created rather than intrinsic to a phenomenon. Social processes, such as those in political, legal, economic, scientific, and religious institutions, create differences, determine that some differences are more important than others, and assign particular meanings to those differences. From this perspective, the way a society defines difference among its members tells us more about that society than the people so classified. *The Meaning of Difference* operates from the constructionist perspective, since it examines how we have arrived at our race, sex, sexual orientation, and social class categories.

Few of us have grown up as constructionists. More likely, we are essentialists who believe that master statuses such as race or sex entail clear-cut, unchanging, and in some way meaningful differences. Still, not everyone is an essentialist. Those from mixed racial or religious backgrounds are familiar with the ways in which identity is not clear-cut. They grow up understanding how definitions of self vary with the context; how others try to define one as belonging in a particular category; and how, in many ways, one's very presence calls prevailing classification systems into question. For example, the experience Jelita McLeod describes in Reading 23 of being asked "What are you?" is a common experience for biracial people. Such experiences make evident the social constructedness of racial identity.

Most of us are unlikely to be exclusively essentialist or constructionist. As authors we take the constructionist perspective, but we have still relied on essentialist terms we find problematic. The irony of questioning the idea of race but still talking about "blacks," "whites," and "Asians," or of rejecting a dualistic approach to sexual identity while still using the terms *gay* and *straight*, has not escaped us. Indeed, throughout our discussion we have used the currently favored essentialist phrase "sexual orientation" over the more constructionist "sexual preference."[2]

Further, there is a serious risk that a text such as this falsely identifies people on the basis of *either* their sex, race, sexual orientation, or social class, despite the fact that master statuses are not parts of a person that can be broken off from one another like the segments of a Tootsie Roll (Spelman, 1988). All of us are always *simultaneously* all of our master statuses, and it is that complex package that exists in the world. While Section I of the readings may make it seem as if these were separable statuses, they are not. Indeed, even the concept of master status could mislead us into thinking that there could be only one dominating status in one's life.

Both constructionism and essentialism can be found in the social sciences. Indeed, essentialism has been the basis of probability theory and statistics (Hilts, 1973), and it forms the bedrock for most social scientific research. Both perspectives also are evident in social movements, and those movements sometimes shift from one perspective to the other over time. For example, some feminists and most of those opposed to feminism have held the essentialist belief that women and men are inherently different. The constructionist view that sexual identity is chosen dominated the gay rights movement of the 1970s (Faderman, 1991), but today most members of that movement take the essentialist approach that sexual identity is something one is born with. By contrast, those opposed to gay relationships take the constructionist view that it is chosen. In this case, language often signals which perspective is being used. For example, sexual *preference* conveys active, human decision making with the possibility of change (constructionism), while sexual *orientation* implies something fixed and inherent to a person (essentialism). As evidence that an essentialist approach to sexual identity is becoming more prevalent, Gallup polls show that an increasing percentage of Americans believe homosexuality is a genetic trait. In 1977, 13 percent indicated they believed that to be the case; in 2004, 37 percent agreed with that statement (Moore, 2004).

This example from journalist Darryl Rist shows the appeal essentialist explanations might have for gay rights activists:

---

[2]The term "sexual identity" seems now to be replacing "sexual orientation." It could be used in either an essentialist or a constructionist way.

[Chris Yates's parents were] Pentecostal ministers who had tortured his adolescence with Christian cures for sexual perversity. Shock and aversion therapies under born-again doctors and gruesome exorcisms of sexual demons by spirit-filled preachers had culminated in a plan to have him castrated by a Mexican surgeon who touted the procedure as a way to make the boy, if not straight, at least sexless. Only then had the terrified son rebelled.

Then, in the summer of 1991, the journal *Science* reported anatomical differences between the brains of homosexual and heterosexual men. . . . The euphoric media—those great purveyors of cultural myths—drove the story wildly. Every major paper in the country headlined the discovery smack on the front page. . . . Like many others, I suspect, Chris Yates's family saw in this newly reported sexual science a way out of its wrenching impasse. After years of virtual silence between them and their son, Chris's parents drove several hundred miles to visit him and ask for reconciliation. Whatever faded guilt they might have felt for the family's faulty genes was nothing next to the reassurance that neither by a perverse upbringing nor by his own iniquity was Chris or the family culpable for his urges and actions. "We could never have condoned this if you could do something to change it. But when we finally understood that you were *born* that way, we knew we'd been wrong. We had to ask your forgiveness." (Rist, 1992:425–26)

Understandably, those under attack would find essentialist orientations appealing, just as the expansiveness of constructionist approaches would be appealing in more tolerant eras. Still, either perspective can be used to justify discrimination, since people can be persecuted for the choices they make as well as for their genetic inheritance.

Why have we spent so much time describing the essentialist and constructionist perspectives? Discussions about race, sex, sexual orientation, and social class generate great intensity partly because they involve the clash of essentialist and constructionist assumptions. Essentialists are likely to view categories of people as "essentially" different in some important way; constructionists are likely to see these differences as socially created and arbitrary. An essentialist asks what causes people to be different; a constructionist asks about the origin and consequence of the categorization system itself. While arguments about the nature and cause of racism, sexism, homophobia, and poverty are disputes about power and justice, from the perspectives of essentialism and constructionism they are also disputes about what differences in color, sexuality, and social class *mean*.

The constructionist approach has one clear advantage, however. It is from that perspective that one understands that all the talk about race, sex, sexual orientation, and social class has a profound significance. Such talk is not simply *about* difference; it is itself the *creation* of difference. In the sections that follow, we examine how categories of people are named, dichotomized, and stigmatized—all toward the construction of difference.

Naming

Difference is constructed first by naming categories of people. Therefore, constructionists pay special attention to the names people use to refer to themselves and others—the times at which new names are asserted, the negotiations that surround the use of particular names, and those occasions when people are grouped together or separated out.

Asserting a Name   Both individuals and categories of people face similar issues in the assertion of a name. A change of name involves, to some extent, the claim of a new identity. For example, one of our colleagues wanted to be called by her full first name rather than by its shortened version because that had come to seem childish to her. It took a few times to remind people that this was her new name, and with most that was adequate. One colleague, however, argued that he could not adapt to the new name; she would just have to tolerate his continued use of the nickname. This was a small but public battle about who had the power to name whom. Did she have the power to enforce her own naming, or did he have the power to name her despite her wishes? Eventually, she prevailed.

A more disturbing example was a young woman who wanted to keep her "maiden" name after she married. Her fiancé agreed with her decision, recognizing that he would be reluctant to give up his name were the tables turned. When his mother heard of this possibility, however, she was outraged. In her mind, a rejection of her family's name was a rejection of her family. She urged her son to reconsider getting married. We do not know how this story ended.

Thus, asserting a name can create social conflict. On both a personal and societal level, naming can involve the claim of a particular identity and the rejection of others' power to impose a name. For example, is one Native American, American Indian, or Sioux; African American or black; girl or woman; Asian, Asian American, Korean, or Korean American; gay or homosexual; Chicano, Mexican American, Mexican, Latino or Hispanic? And

> Just who is Hispanic? The answer depends on whom you ask.
>
> The label was actually coined in the mid-1970s by federal bureaucrats working under President Richard M. Nixon. They came up with it in response to concerns that the government was wrongly applying "Chicano" to people who were not of Mexican descent, and otherwise misidentifying and underserving segments of the population by generally classifying those with ancestral ties to the Spanish cultural diaspora as either Chicano, Cuban, or Puerto Rican.
>
> Nearly three decades later, the debate continues to surround the term Hispanic and its definition. Although mainly applied to people from Latin American countries with linguistic and cultural ties to Spain, it also is used by the U.S. government to refer to Spaniards themselves, as well as people from Portuguese-speaking Brazil.
>
> Especially on college campuses, a sizable and growing minority of people prefer "Latino," which does not have the same association with Spanish imperialism. That term is controversial as well, however, mainly because it stems from the term Latin America and wrongly implies ties to ancient Rome. (Schmidt, 2003)

Deciding what name to use for a category of people is not easy. It is unlikely that all members of the category use the same name; the name members use for one another may not be acceptable for outsiders to use; nor is it always advisable to ask what name a person prefers. We once saw an old friend become quite angry when asked whether he preferred the term *black* or *African American.* "Either one is fine with me," he replied, "*I* know what *I* am." To him, the question meant that he was being seen as a member of a category, not as an individual.

Because naming may involve a redefinition of self, an assertion of power, and a rejection of others' ability to impose an identity, social change movements often claim a new name, while opponents may express opposition by continuing to use the old name. For example, *black* emerged in opposition to Negro as the Black Power movement sought to distinguish itself from the Martin Luther King–led moderate wing of the civil rights movement. The term *Negro* had itself been put forward by influential leaders such as W. E. B. Du Bois and Booker T. Washington as a rejection of the term "colored" that had dominated the mid- to late 19th century. "[D]espite its association with racial epithets, 'Negro' was defined to stand for a new way of thinking about Blacks" (Smith, 1992:497–98). Similarly, in 1988 Ramona H. Edelin, president of the National Urban Coalition, proposed that *African American* be substituted for *black*. Now both terms are about equally in use (Smith, 1992; Gallup, 2003)[3] Ironically, *colored people* used to be a derogatory reference to African Americans, but *people of color* is now a common reference to all nonwhites.

Each of these name changes—from *Negro* to *black* to *African American*—was first promoted by activists as a way to demonstrate their commitment to a new order. A similar theme is reflected in the history of the terms *Chicano* and *Chicanismo*. Although the origin of the terms is unclear, the principle was the same. As reporter Ruben Salazar wrote in the 1960s, "a Chicano is a Mexican-American with a non-Anglo image of himself" (Shorris, 1992:101). ("Anglo" is a colloquialism for white used in the southwestern and western United States.)

Similarly, the term *homosexual* was first coined in 1896 by a Hungarian physician hoping to decriminalize same-sex relations between men. It was incorporated into the medical and psychological literature of the time, which depicted nonprocreative sex as pathological. Sixty years later, activists rejected the pathological characterization and the name associated with it and began substituting *gay* for homosexual. Presently *gay* is used both as a generic term encompassing men and women and as a specific reference to men.[4] The 1990s activist group, Queer Nation, may have started a rejection of the word, however, with its name and slogan: "We're here. We're queer. Get used to it." Once an epithet, "queer" now seems to be on its way toward acceptability, if only as demonstrated in the success of the cable television show, *Queer Eye for the Straight Guy.*

Just as each of these social movements has involved a public renaming that proclaims pride, the women's movement has asserted *woman* as a replacement for *girl*. A student who described a running feud with her roommate illustrates the significance of these two terms. The student preferred the word *woman,* arguing that the word *girl* when applied to females past adolescence was insulting. Her female roommate just as strongly preferred the term *girl* and regularly applied it to the females

---

[3]Thus, one can find Black Studies, Afro-American Studies, and African American Studies programs in universities across the country.

[4]In the 17th century, *gay* became associated with an addiction to social pleasure, dissipation, and loose morality, and was used to refer to female prostitutes (e.g., "gay girl"). The term was apparently first used in reference to homosexuality in 1925 in Australia. "It may have been both the connotations of femininity and those of immorality that led American homosexuals to adopt the title 'gay' with some self-irony in the 1920s. The slogan 'Glad to Be Gay,' adopted by both female and male homosexuals, and the naming of the Gay Liberation Front, which was born from the Stonewall resistance riots following police raids on homosexual bars in New York in 1969, bear witness to a greater self-confidence" (Mills, 1989:102).

she knew. Each of them had such strong feelings on the matter that it was apparent they would not last as roommates.

How could these two words destroy their relationship? It appears that English speakers use the terms *girl* and *woman* to refer to quite different qualities. *Woman* (like *man*) is understood to convey adulthood, power, and sexuality; *girl* (like *boy*) connotes youth, powerlessness, and irresponsibility (Richardson, 1988). Thus, the two roommates were asserting quite different places for themselves in the world. One claimed adulthood; the other saw herself as not having achieved that yet. This is the explanation offered by many females: It is not so much that they like being *girls,* as that they value youth and/or do not yet feel justified in calling themselves *women.* Yet this is precisely the identity the women's movement has asserted: "We cannot be girls anymore, we must be women."

Creating Categories of People   While individuals and groups may assert names for themselves, governments also have the power to create categories of people. The history of the race and ethnicity questions asked in the U.S. census illustrates this process.

Every census since the first one in 1790 has included a question about race. By 1970, the options for race were white, Negro or black, American Indian (with a request to print the name of the enrolled or principal tribe), Japanese, Chinese, Filipino, Hawaiian, Korean, and Other (with the option of specifying). Reading 2 charts the evolution of the census's race categories. The 1970 census began the practice of allowing the head of the household to identify the race of household members: before that, the census taker had made that decision based on the appearance of the family. Thus, the Census Bureau began treating race as primarily a matter of *self*-identification. Still, it was assumed that a person could only be a member of *one* racial group, so respondents were allowed only one option for each household member.

The 1970 census also posed the first ethnicity question, asking whether the individual was of Hispanic or non-Hispanic ancestry, and providing four checkoff categories with space to fill in other possibilities. (Ethnicity, which generally refers to national ancestry, is a subject we will return to shortly.) The Hispanic/non-Hispanic question was added at the recommendation of the Census Bureau's Hispanic Advisory Committee as a way to correct for the *differential undercount* of the Hispanic population. A differential undercount means that more people are undercounted in one category than in another; for example, the census yields a larger undercount of those who rent their homes than of those who own them. Undercounting primarily affects the data on low-income residents of inner cities. This is the case because the poor often move and are thus difficult to contact, are more likely to be illiterate or non-English speakers (there was no Spanish-language census form until 1990), and are more likely to be illegal immigrants afraid to respond to a government questionnaire. (The Constitution requires a count of *all* the people in the United States, not just those who are citizens or legal residents.) Because census data affect the distribution of billions of dollars of federal aid, as well as voting rights and civil rights enforcement, undercounting has a significant impact. Indeed, the bureau's Census 2000 FAQ Web page notes that $182 billion will be distributed annually to state, local, and tribal governments based on formulas using Census 2000 data.

Census data had always been critical to the functioning of American government: the apportionment of seats in the U.S. House of Representatives and the distribution of federal funding to states and localities are based on census data. However, by the 1970s information on race was increasingly needed to document and eliminate discrimination. Such data, the newly formed U.S. Commission on Civil Rights argued, was necessary to monitor equal access in housing, education, and employment.

> There were the civil rights movement and its offshoots such as the Mexican-American Brown Power movement. In addition, the federal government initiated the War Against Poverty and the Great Society programs. These movements and programs stated clearly that poor minority groups had a legitimate claim to better conditions in cities. Several of the social welfare programs of President Johnson's Great Society distributed dollars by means of statistically driven grant-in-aid formulas. The proliferation of federal grants programs and the cities' increasing dependence upon them tended to heighten the political salience of census statistics. Such formulas often incorporated population size, as measured or estimated by the Census Bureau, as a major factor. By 1978 there were more than one hundred such programs, covering a wide range of concerns, from preschool education (Headstart) to urban mass transportation (U.S. Congress, 1978).... [T]he single most commonly used data source was the decennial census. (Choldin, 1994:27–8)

In all, the census offered an important source of information for the courts, Congress, and local entities to gauge the extent of discrimination and monitor civil rights enforcement. Data on race allowed the monitoring of the Voting Rights Act, equal employment opportunity programs, and racial disparities in health, birth, and death rates. As John Skrentny describes in Reading 45, a remarkable bipartisan consensus supported these initiatives.

To improve the collection of race data, in the 1970s the Commission on Civil Rights reviewed the race categorization practices of federal agencies and concluded that while "the designations do not refer strictly to race, color, national or ethnic origin," the categories were nonetheless what the general public understood to be *minority groups* (U.S. Commission on Civil Rights, 1973:39). "The federal emphasis was clearly on minority status in a legal sense. Minority group status did not derive from a specific race or ethnicity *per se,* but on the treatment of race and ethnicity to confer a privileged, disadvantaged, or equitable status and to gauge representation and under-representation" (Tamayo Lott, 1998:37). The aim of data collection was to pinpoint the extent of discrimination, not to identify all population categories.

Thus, in 1977 on the recommendation of the Civil Rights Commission, the Office of Management and Budget (OMB) issued Statistical Directive No. 15, "Race and Ethnic Standards for Federal Statistics and Administrative Reporting," which established standard categories and definitions for all federal agencies, including the Bureau of the Census. Directive No. 15 defined four racial and one ethnic category: American Indian or Alaskan Native, Asian or Pacific Islander, Negro or Black, White, and Hispanic.

> The choice of four racial categories and one ethnic category [Hispanic] redefined the United States beyond a White and non-White classification and even beyond a White and Black classification. The new classification facilitated the enumeration of a multiracial and

multicultural population. . . . The particular status of Hispanics was recognized in two ways. Hispanic was the only choice for the ethnic category. Furthermore . . . Black and White Hispanics were enumerated as Hispanics. To avoid duplicated counts, the Black and White categories excluded Hispanics. (Tamayo Lott, 1998:54)

The racial and ethnic diversity of the United States is more complex now than it was in the 1970s. Reading 3 provides the first 17 questions of the "long" version of the 2000 census. The long form is distributed to one in six households; the "short" form goes to all other households. Both short and long versions ask for the name of each person in the household and their sex, age, race, and whether they are of Spanish/Hispanic/Latino ancestry—which means that these are the only questions asked of *all* those who take the census. The long form asks additional questions on the social and economic characteristics of householders (including their ethnicity, as in question 10), and on the physical and financial characteristics of their housing.

Certainly, the most notable change in the 2000 census was its recognition that a person may identify himself or herself as being a member of more than one racial group. For the first time in its 210-year history, the census's race question (question 6 on the long form) provided for the identification of mixed lineage—though it did not offer a category called *multiracial.* This change was one outcome of a comprehensive review and revision of OMB's Directive No. 15 that included public hearings, sample surveys of targeted populations, and collaboration among the more than 30 federal agencies that collect and use data on race and ethnicity. While this change was spurred by activists who identified themselves as mixed-race, the bureau's pretesting also indicated that less than 2 percent of respondents would mark more than one race for themselves, and thus the historical continuity with previous censuses would not be compromised. The bureau's expectation was close to the mark—2.4 percent of the population, almost 7 million people, marked two or more races for themselves in the 2000 census.

One change that was not made in the 2000 census, however, was inclusion of a race category called *Arab* or *Middle Eastern* because public comment did not indicate agreement on a definition for this category. Thus, in the 2000 census Arab or Middle Eastern peoples continue to be categorized as white.

As in previous censuses, undercounting remains an important fiscal and political issue, given the disproportionate undercounting of people of color. Still, gay couples may well be the most undercounted population. Since the 1990 census, the form has provided "unmarried partner" as a possible answer to the question of how the people in the household are related to one another. The number of gay couples (not gay people) increased more than 300 percent between the 1990 and 2000 censuses, to 594,391 couples, but that number is probably less than a complete count because of respondents' reluctance to report (Cohn, 2001). Overall, however, the Census Bureau contends that the net *national* undercount for the 2000 census was smaller than it had been in 1990 (down to 0.06 percent from 1.6 percent) (U.S. Department of Commerce, October 18, 2001).

We end this phase of our discussion with two cautions. First, on a personal level, many of us find census categorizations objectionable. But as *citizens,* we still seek the benefits and protections of policies based on these data—and as citizens we share the goal of eliminating discriminatory practices.

[R]eliable racial data are crucial to enforcing our basic laws against intentional racial discrimination, which enjoy broad public support. For example, in order to demonstrate that an employer is engaging in a broad based "pattern or practice" of discrimination in violation of the Civil Rights Act of 1964, a plaintiff must rely on statistical proof that goes beyond the plight of an individual employee. Supreme Court precedent in such cases requires plaintiffs to show a statistically significant disparity between the proportion of qualified minorities in the local labor market and the proportion within the employer's work force. A disparity of more than two standard deviations creates a legal presumption that intentional discrimination is occurring, since a disparity of that magnitude almost never occurs by accident.

Demographic information, in other words, provides the "big picture" that places individual incidents in context. Voting rights cases require similar proof, as do many housing discrimination cases and suits challenging the discriminatory use of federal funds. Without reliable racial statistics, it would be virtually impossible for courts or agencies to detect institutional bias, and antidiscrimination laws would go unenforced. More fundamentally, we simply cannot know as a society how far we've come in conquering racial discrimination and inequality without accurate information about the health, progress and opportunities available to communities of different races. (Jenkins, 1999:15–16)

Second, when considering official counts of the population, we must be careful not to assume that what is counted is real. While census data contribute to the essentialist view that the world is populated by distinct, scientifically defined categories of people, this brief history demonstrates that not even those who collect the data make that assumption; rather, census categories have been based on constructionist premises. As OMB warns,

The racial and ethnic categories set forth in the standards should not be interpreted as being primarily biological or genetic in reference. Race and ethnicity may be thought of in terms of social and cultural characteristics as well as ancestry. (Office of Management and Budget, 1997:2)

There are no clear, unambiguous, objective, generally agreed-upon definitions of the terms "race" and "ethnicity." Cognitive research shows that respondents are not always clear on the differences between race and ethnicity. There are differences in terminology, group boundaries, attributes and dimensions of race and ethnicity....

[The Directive No. 15 categories] do not represent objective "truth" but rather are ambiguous social constructs and involve subjective and attitudinal issues. (Office of Management and Budget, 1995:44680)

Aggregating and Disaggregating   The federal identification policies we have been describing collapsed various national-origin groups into four categories: Hispanics, Native Americans, Blacks, and Asian or Pacific Islanders. This process *aggregated* categories of people; that is, it combined, or "lumped together," different groups. In the census, Puerto Ricans, Mexicans, Cubans, and others from Central and South America all became "Hispanic" in some sense. While *Latino* and *Hispanic* remain commonly used aggregate terms, the diversity of this population has increased dramatically. Data from the 2000 census show that the number of respondents identifying as "Other Spanish/Hispanic/Latino"—that is, who are neither Mexican, Mexican American, Chicano, Puerto Rican, or Cuban—has doubled from 5 million to 10 million since the 1990 census. "Other Spanish/Hispanic/Latino" is now the fastest growing group in the Spanish/Hispanic/Latino category (Population Reference Bureau, 2001).

The groups that are now lumped together have historically regarded one another as different, and thus in people's everyday lives the aggregate category is likely to *disaggregate,* or fragment, into its constituent national-origin elements. For example, one might think that *Latino* or *Asian American* are terms used for self-identification, but this is rarely the case. In the United States, "Mexicans, Puerto Ricans, and Cubans have little interaction with each other, most do not recognize that they have much in common culturally, and they do not profess strong affection for each other" (de la Garza et al., 1992:14). Thus, it is not surprising that a survey of the Latino population concludes that "respondents do not primarily identify as members of an Hispanic or Latino community. . . . [Rather, they] overwhelmingly prefer to identify by national origin . . . " (de la Garza et al., 1992:13).

> The difficulty with determining who counts as Hispanic is that Hispanics do not appear to share any properties in common. Linguistic, racial, religious, political, territorial, cultural, economic, educational, social class, and genetic criteria fail to identify Hispanics in all places and times. . . .
>
> [Nonetheless], we are treated as a homogeneous group by European Americans and African Americans; and even though Hispanics do not in fact constitute a homogeneous group, we are easily contrasted with European Americans and African Americans because we do not share many of the features commonly associated with these groups. (Gracia, 2000: 204–205)

In short, the category *Latino/Hispanic* exists primarily, but not exclusively, from the perspective of non-Latinos.

Like all the differences masked by the terms *Latino* and *Hispanic,* among those sharing the *Asian Pacific American* or *Asian American* are groups with different languages, cultures, and religions and sometimes centuries of hostility. Like *Hispanic/Latino,* the category *Asian American* is based more on geography than on any cultural, racial, linguistic, or religious commonalities. "Asian Americans are those who come from a region of the world that *the rest of the world* has defined as Asia" (Hu-Dehart, 1994).[5]

---

[5]In census classification, the category *Asian* includes Asian Indian, Chinese, Filipino, Japanese, Korean, Vietnamese; *Other Asian* includes Bangladeshi, Bhutanese, Burmese, Cambodian, Hmong, Indo-Chinese, Indonesian, Iwo Jiman, Laotian, Malaysian, Maldivian, Mongolian, Nepalese, Okinawan, Pakistani, Singaporean, Sri Lankan, Thai, and Taiwanese. The category *Pacific Islander* includes Native Hawaiian, Guamanian or Chamorro, Samoan; *Other Pacific Islander* includes Carolinian, Chuukese, Fijian, Kirabati, Kosraean, Mariana Islander, Marshallese, Melanesian, Micronesian, New Hebridian, Palauan, Papua New Guinean, Pohnpeian, Polynesian, Saipanese, Solomon Islander, Tahitian, Tokelauan, Tongan, and Yapese (U.S. Census Bureau, 2001).

In 1980, Asian Indians successfully lobbied to change their census classification from white to Asian American by reminding Congress that historically immigrants from India had been classed as Asian. With other Asians, those from India had been barred from immigration by the 1917 Immigration Act, prohibited from becoming naturalized citizens until 1946, and denied the right to own land by the 1920 Alien Land Law. Indeed, in 1923 the U.S. Supreme Court (in *Thind*) ruled that Asian Indians were non-white, and could therefore have their U.S. citizenship nullified (Espiritu, 1992:124–25). Thus, for most of their history in the United States, Asian Indians had been classed as Asian.

Collective classifications such as Latino or Asian American were not simply the result of federal classifications, however. Student activists inspired by the Black Power and civil rights movements first proposed the terms. As Yen Le Espiritu describes in Reading 7, college students coined the identifier *Asian American* in response to "the similarity of [their] experiences and treatment." *Asian American, Hispanic,* and *Latino* are examples of *panethnic* terms, that is, classifications that span national-origin identities. Panethnicity is "the development of bridging organizations and solidarities among subgroups of ethnic collectivities that are often seen as homogeneous by outsiders. . . . Those. . . . groups that, from an outsider's point of view, are most racially homogeneous are also the groups with the greatest panethnic development" (Lopez and Espiritu, 1990:219–20).

Panethnicity is useful but unstable. "The elites representing such groups find it advantageous to make political demands by using the numbers and resources panethnic formations can mobilize. The state, in turn, can more easily manage claims by recognizing and responding to large blocs as opposed to dealing with the specific claims of a plethora of ethnically defined interest groups" (Omi, 1996:180). At the same time, competition and historic antagonisms make such alliances unstable. "At times it is advantageous to be in a panethnic bloc, and at times it is desirable to mobilize along particular ethnic lines" (Omi, 1996:181).

The terms *Native American* and *African American* are also aggregate classifications, but in this case they are the result of conquest and enslavement.

> The "Indian," like the European, is an idea. The notion of "Indians" was invented to distinguish the indigenous peoples of the New World from Europeans. The "Indian" is the person on shore, outside of the boat. . . . There [were] hundreds of cultures, languages, ways of living in Native America. The place was a model of diversity at the time of Columbus's arrival. Yet Europeans did not see this diversity. They created the concept of the "Indian" to give what they did see some kind of unification, to make it a single entity they could deal with, because they could not cope with the reality of 400 different cultures. (Mohawk, 1992: 440)[6]

Conquest made "Indians" out of a heterogeneity of tribes and nations that had been distinctive on linguistic, religious, and economic grounds. It was not only that Europeans had the unifying concept of "Indian" in mind—after all, they were sufficiently aware of cultural differences to generate an extensive body of specific treaties with individual tribes. It was also that conquest itself—encompassing as it did the appropriation of land, the forging and violation of treaties, and the implementation of forced relocation policies—structured the lives of Native Americans along common lines. While contemporary Native Americans still identify themselves by tribal

---

[6]The idea of "Europe" and the "European" is also a constructed, aggregate category. "Physically, Europe is not a continent. Where is the water separating Europe from Asia? It is culture that separates Europe from Asia. Western Europe roughly comprises the countries that in the Middle Ages were Latin Christendom, and Eastern Europe consists of those countries that in the Middle Ages were Eastern Orthodox Christendom. It was about A.D. 1257 when the Pope claimed hegemony over the secular emperors in Western Europe and formulated the idea that Europeans, that Christians, were a unified ethnicity even though they spoke many different languages" (Mohawk, 1992:439–40).

ancestry, just as those called Asian American and Latino identify themselves by national origin, their shared experience of conquest also forged the common identity reflected in the collective name, *Native American.*

Similarly, the capture, purchase, and forced relocation of Africans, and their experience of forcibly being moved from place to place as personal property, created the category now called *African American.* This experience forged a single people from a culturally diverse group; it produced an "oppositional racial consciousness," that is, a unity-in-opposition (Omi and Winant, 1994). "Just as the conquest created the 'native' where once there had been Pequot, Iroquois, or Tutelo, so too it created the 'black' where once there had been Asante or Ovimbundu, Yoruba or Bakongo" (Omi and Winant, 1994:66).

Even the categories of gay and straight, male and female, and poor and middle class are aggregations that presume a commonality by virtue of shared master status. For example, the category *gay and lesbian* assumes that sharing a sexual orientation binds people together despite all the issues that might divide them as men and women, people of different colors, or people of different social classes. And, just as in the cases we have previously discussed, alliances between gays and lesbians will depend on the circumstances and specific issues.

Still, our analysis has so far ignored one category of people. From whose perspective do the categories of Native American, Asian American, African American, and Latino/Hispanic exist? Since "difference" is always "difference *from*," from whose perspective is "difference" determined? Who has the power to define "difference"? If "we" are in the boat looking at "them," who precisely are "we"?

Every perspective on the social world emerges from a particular vantage point, a particular social location. Ignoring who is in the boat treats that place as if it were just the view "anyone" would take. Historically, the people in the boat were European; contemporarily, they are white Americans. As Ruth Frankenberg frames it in Reading 8, in America "whites are the nondefined definers of other people," "the unmarked marker of others' differentness." Failing to identify the "us" in the boat means that "white culture [becomes] the unspoken norm," a category that is powerful enough to define others while itself remaining invisible and unnamed. Indeed, Frankenberg argues that those with the most power in a society are best positioned to have their own identities left unnamed, thus masking their power.

The term *androcentrism* describes the world as seen from a male-centered perspective. By analogy, one may also describe a *Eurocentric* and *heterocentric* perspective. To some extent, regardless of their sex, race, or sexual orientation, all Americans operate from an andro-, Euro-, and heterocentric perspective since these are the guiding assumptions of the culture. Recognizing these perspectives as historically and culturally located makes it possible to evaluate their adequacy.

Dichotomizing

Many forces promote the construction of aggregate categories of people. Frequently, these aggregates emerge as *dichotomies.* To dichotomize is not only to divide something into two parts; it is also to see those parts as mutually exclusive and in opposition. Dichotomization encourages the sense that there are only two categories, that everyone fits easily in one or the other, and that the categories stand in opposition to each other. In contemporary American culture, we appear to treat the master statuses of race, sex, class, and sexual orientation as if each embodied "us" and "them"—as if for each master status people could be easily sorted into two mutually exclusive, opposed groupings.[7]

Dichotomizing Race   The clearest example of dichotomization is provided by the "one-drop rule" discussed by F. James Davis in Reading 1. Despite the increasing number of people who are biracial, many popular autobiographies by bi- and mixed-race people, and the census's introduction of the multiple checkoff for race, American social practices apparently remain governed by the "rule" that a person with any traceable African heritage is black. Indeed, one piece of evidence that the rule persists is the fact that only about 5 percent of African Americans used the 2000 census to identify themselves as being of multiple races—even though a large portion would have Native American and/or white ancestry. This compares to the 14 percent of Asian and 40 percent of American Indian respondents who classified themselves as of more than one race. While in other cultures people of mixed racial ancestry might be defined as *mixed,* American culture does not so far provide that option, and it especially does not provide it to those of African ancestry. As Davis makes clear, this practice is strongly supported by both blacks and whites.

Considering the census, one must look to those 18 or younger for a sign that the one-drop rule is losing its hold: For both Hispanics and non-Hispanics, "people who reported more than one race [in the 2000 census] were more likely to be under age 18 than those reporting only one race. Of the 6.8 million people in the two or more races population, 42 percent were under 18. . . . Among the 2.2 million Hispanics who reported more than one race, 43 percent were under 18" (Jones and Smith, 2001:9). More generally, perhaps the popularity of bi- and multiracial celebrities, such as Jasmine Guy, Jennifer Beals, Halle Berry, Derek Jeeter, Lenny Kravitz, Mariah Carey, Greg Louganis, and Tiger Woods, and the emergence of the ethnically ambiguous advertising described by Ruth La Ferla in Reading 55 bode well for the unraveling of the one-drop rule.

The black/white dichotomy has been an abiding and rigidly enforced one, but different regions and historical periods have also produced their own two-part distinctions. In the Southwest the divide has been between Anglos and Latinos, and on parts of the West Coast it is between Asian Americans and whites. Each of these variations, however, is an instance of America's more encompassing and historic dichotomization: that of whites and nonwhites.

While three racial categories—*white, Negro,* and *Indian*—were identified throughout the 19th century (Omi and Winant, 1994), all were located within the white/non-white dichotomy. In 1854, the California Supreme Court in *People v. Hall* held that blacks, mulattos, Native Americans, and Chinese were "not white" and therefore could not testify for or against a white man in court (Takaki, 1993:205–6). (Hall, a

---

[7]Springer and Deutsch (1981) coined the term *dichotomania* to describe the current belief that there are male and female sides of the brain. We think that term also fits our discussion.

white man, had been convicted of killing a Chinese man on the testimony of one white and three Chinese witnesses; the Supreme Court overturned the conviction.) Mexican residents of the southwest territories ceded to the United States in the 1848 Treaty of Guadalupe Hidalgo, however, "were defined as a white population and accorded the political-legal status of 'free white persons'" (Omi and Winant, 1994). European immigrants such as the Irish were initially treated as nonwhite, or at least not-yet-white. In turn, they lobbied for their own inclusion in American society on the basis of the white/nonwhite distinction.

> [Immigrants struggled to] equate whiteness with Americanism in order to turn arguments over immigration from the question of who was foreign to the question of who was white. . . . Immigrants could not win on the question of who was foreign. . . . But if the issue somehow became defending "white man's jobs" or "white man's government" . . . [they] could gain space by deflecting debate from nativity, a hopeless issue, to race, an ambiguous one. . . . After the Civil War, the new-coming Irish would help lead the movement to bar the relatively established Chinese from California, with their agitation for a "white man's government," serving to make race, and not nativity, the center of the debate and to prove the Irish white. (Roediger, 1994:189–90)

Historically, *American* has meant white, as many Americans of Asian ancestry learn when they are complimented on their English—a compliment that presumes that someone who is Asian could not be a native-born American.[8] A story from the 1998 Winter Olympics illustrates the same point. At the conclusion of the figure skating competition, MSNBC posted a headline that read "American Beats Out Kwan for Women's Figure Skating Title." The reference was to Michelle Kwan, who won the silver medal, losing the gold to Tara Lapinsky. But both Kwan and Lapinsky are Americans. While Kwan's parents immigrated from Hong Kong, she was born and raised in the United States, is a U.S. citizen, and was a member of the U.S. team. The network attributed the mistake to overworked staff and apologized. But for Asian American activists, this was an example of how people of Asian descent have remained perpetual foreigners in American society.

African American novelist Toni Morrison would describe this as a story about "how *American* means *white*":

> Deep within the word "American" is its association with race. To identify someone as South African is to say very little; we need the adjective "white" or "black" or "colored" to make our meaning clear. In this country it is quite the reverse. American means white, and Africanist people struggle to make the term applicable to themselves with . . . hyphen after hyphen after hyphen. (Morrison, 1992:47)

Because *American* means *white*, those who are not white are presumed to be recent arrivals and often told to go "back where they came from." Thus, we appear to operate within the dichotomized *racial* categories of American/non-American—these are racial categories, because they effectively mean white/nonwhite.

---

[8]Since the historic American ban on Asian immigration remained in place until 1965, it is the case that a high proportion of Asian Americans are foreign-born, though there is considerable variation within that category. For example, among Japanese Americans, only 32 percent were foreign-born, while that was the case for 83 percent of Vietnamese Americans (Hirschman, 1996).

But what exactly *is* race? First, we need to distinguish *race* from *ethnicity*. Social scientists define *ethnic groups* as categories of people who are distinctive on the basis of national origin or heritage, language, or cultural practices. "Members of an ethnic group hold a set of common memories that make them feel that their customs, culture, and outlook are distinctive" (Blauner, 1992). Thus, racial categories encompass different ethnic groups. For example, the American racial category *white* includes ethnic groups such as Irish, Italian, and Polish Americans. Unfortunately, many fail to recognize ethnic distinctions among people of color. For example, not all blacks in the United States are African American; some are Haitian, Jamaican, or Nigerian.

The term *race* first appeared in the Romance languages of Europe in the Middle Ages to refer to breeding stock (Smedley, 1993). A "race" of horses described common ancestry and a distinctive appearance or behavior. *Race* appears to have been first applied to New World peoples by the Spanish in the 16th century. Later it was adopted by the English, again in reference to people of the New World, and generally came to mean "people," "nation," or "variety." By the late 18th century, "when scholars became more actively engaged in investigations, classifications, and definitions of human populations, the term 'race' was elevated as the one major symbol and mode of human group differentiation employed extensively for non-European groups and even those in Europe who varied in some way from the subjective norm" (Smedley, 1993:39).

Though elevated to the level of science, the concept of race continued to reflect its origins in animal breeding. Farmers and herders had used the concept to describe stock bred for particular qualities; scholars used it to suggest that human behaviors could also be inherited. "Unlike other terms for classifying people . . . the term 'race' places emphasis on innateness, on the inbred nature of whatever is being judged" (Smedley, 1993:39). Like animal breeders, scholars also presumed that appearance revealed something about potential behavior. Just as the selective breeding of animals entailed the ranking of stock by some criteria, scholarly use of the concept of race involved the ranking of humans. Differences in skin color, hair texture, and the shape of head, eyes, nose, lips, and body were developed into an elaborate hierarchy of merit and potential for "civilization."

The idea of race emerged among all the European colonial powers, although their conceptions of it varied. However, only the British in colonizing North America and South Africa constructed a system of rigid, exclusive racial categories and a social order *based on race,* a "racialized social structure" (Omi and Winant, 1994). "[S]kin color variations in many regions of the world and in many societies have been imbued with some degree of social value or significance, but color prejudice or preferences do not of themselves amount to a fully evolved racial worldview" (Smedley, 1993:25).

This racialized social structure—which in America produced a race-based system of slavery and subsequently a race-based distribution of political, legal, and social rights—was a historical first. "Expansion, conquest, exploitation, and enslavement have characterized much of human history over the past five thousand years or so, but none of these events before the modern era resulted in the development of ideologies or social systems based on race" (Smedley, 1993:25, 15). While differences of color had long been noted, societies had never before been built on those differences.

As scientists assumed that race differences involved more than simply skin color or hair texture, they sought the biological distinctiveness of racial categories—but with little success. In the early 20th century, anthropologists looked to physical features such as height, stature, and head shape to distinguish the races, only to learn that these are affected by environment and nutrition. Soon the search turned to genetics, only to find that those cannot be correlated with conventional racial classifications. Even efforts to reach a consensus about how many races exist or what specific features distinguish one from another are problematic. As one anthropologist has put it, "Classifying people by color is very much like classifying cars by color. Those in the same classification look alike . . . but the classification tells you nothing about the hidden details of construction or about how the cars or people will perform" (Cohen, 1998:12).

> If our eyes could perceive more than the superficial, we might find race in chromosome 11: there lies the gene for hemoglobin. If you divide humankind by which of two forms of the gene each person has, then equatorial Africans, Italians and Greeks fall into the "sickle-cell race"; Swedes and South Africa's Xhosas (Nelson Mandela's ethnic group) are in the healthy hemoglobin race. Or do you prefer to group people by whether they have epicanthic eye folds, which produce the "Asian" eye? Then the !Kung San (Bushmen) belong with the Japanese and Chinese. . . . [D]epending on which traits you pick, you can form very surprising races. Take the scooped-out shape of the back of the front teeth, a standard "Asian" trait. Native Americans and Swedes have these shovel-shaped incisors, too, and so would fall in the same race. Is biochemistry better? Norwegians, Arabians, north Indians and the Fulani of northern Nigeria . . . fall into the "lactase race" (the lactase enzyme digests milk sugar). Everyone else—other Africans, Japanese, Native Americans—form the "lactase-deprived race" (their ancestors did not drink milk from cows or goats and hence never evolved the lactase gene). How about blood types, the familiar A, B, and O groups? Then Germans and New Guineans, populations that have the same percentages of each type, are in one race; Estonians and Japanese comprise a separate one for the same reason. . . . The dark skin of Somalis and Ghanaians, for instance, indicates that they evolved under the same selective force (a sunny climate). But that's all it shows. It does *not* show that they are any more closely related in the sense of sharing more genes than either is to Greeks. Calling Somalis and Ghanaians "black" therefore sheds no further light on their evolutionary history and implies—wrongly—that they are more closely related to each other than either is to someone of a different "race." . . . If you pick at random any two "blacks" walking along the street, and analyze their 23 pairs of chromosomes, you will probably find that their genes have less in common than do the genes of one of them with that of a random "white" person. (Begley, 1995:67, 68)

The "no-race" theory is now widely accepted in physical anthropology and human genetics (Cohen, 1998). This perspective argues that "(1) Biological variability exists but this variability does not conform to the discrete packages labeled races. (2) So-called racial characteristics are not transmitted as complexes. (3) Races do not exist because isolation of groups has been infrequent; populations have always interbred" (Lieberman, 1968:128). Still, few scholars outside of anthropology seem to take this perspective into account.

[I]t does not appear that this debate [about the existence of race] has had widespread impact on professionals in the fields of medicine, psychology, sociology, history, or political science. . . . [I]t will suffice to point out that virtually all scholars who write about "race and intelligence" assume that the "races" which they study are distinguished on the basis of biologically relevant criteria. So accepted is this fact that most scholars engaged in such research never consider it necessary to justify their assignment of individuals to this or that "race." . . . [Thus], the layman who reads the literature on race and racial groupings is justified in assuming that the existent typologies have been derived through the application of theories and methods current in disciplines concerned with the biological study of human variation. Since the scientific racial classifications which a layman finds in the literature are not too different from popular ones, he can be expected to feel justified in the maintenance of his views on race. (Marshall, 1993:117, 121)

In all, "race is a biological fiction, but a social fact" (Rubio, 2001: xiv). Its primary significance is as a *social* concept. We "see" race, we expect it to tell us something significant about a person, and we organize social policy, law, and the distribution of wealth, power, and prestige around it. From the essentialist position, race is assumed to exist independently of our perception of it; it is assumed to significantly distinguish one group of people from another. From the constructionist perspective, race exists because we have created it as a meaningful category of difference among people.

Dichotomizing Sexual Orientation   Many similarities exist in the construction of race and sexual orientation categories. First, both are often dichotomized—into black/white, white/nonwhite, or gay/straight—and individuals are expected to fit easily into one category or the other. While the term *bisexual* has become increasingly common, and one of the readings included here declares the end of *both* gay and straight identities (Bert Archer in Reading 20), we see the assumption that people are either gay or straight as still culturally dominant.

For example, scientists continue to seek biological differences between gay and straight people just as they have looked for such differences between the "races." But here as well, the research is intrinsically suspect, since we are unlikely to find any biological structure or process that *all* gay people share but *no* straight people have (Sherman Heyl, 1989). Still, the conviction that such differences must exist propels the search and leads to the popularization of questionable findings.

Dean Hamer first published his findings about the relationship of genes to sexuality in *Science* and, a little later, in a popular book called *The Science of Desire*. In both report and book, Hamer made clear that he did not figure he'd found a gay gene. He'd found a conspicuous concurrence of a specific genetic marker among self-declared homosexuals. The findings were statistically significant, but the relationship of the genetic marker to the behavior was as yet undetermined. None of which stopped the newspapers from using the euphonic "gay gene" in their headlines, nor other interested parties from citing this fantastic discovery as further proof of the firmly rooted, unchangeable nature of homosexuality. (Archer, 2002:135)

As with race, sexual orientation appears more straightforward than it really is. Because sexuality encompasses physical, social, and emotional attraction, as well as fantasies, self-identity, and actual sexual behavior over a lifetime (Klein, 1978), determining one's sexual orientation may involve emphasizing one of these features over the others. Just as the system of racial classification asks people to pick *one* race, the sexual orientation system requires that all the different aspects of sexuality be distilled into two possible choices.

For example, an acquaintance described the process by which he came to self-identify as gay. In high school and college he had dated and been sexually active with women, but his relations with men had always been more important to him. He looked to men for emotional and social gratification, as well as for relief from "gender games" he felt required to play with women. He had been engaged to be married, but when that ended, he spent his time exclusively with other men. Eventually he established a sexual relationship with another man and came to identify himself as gay. His experience reflects the varied dimensions of sexuality and shows the resolution of those differences by choosing a single sexual identity. Rather than say "I used to be straight but I am now gay," he described himself as always "really" having been gay.

Alfred Kinsey's landmark survey of American sexual practices showed that same-sex experience was more common than had been assumed, and that sexual practices could change over the lifespan. Kinsey suggested that instead of thinking about "homosexuals" and "heterosexuals" as if these were two discrete categories of people, we should recognize that sexual behavior exists along a continuum from those who are exclusively heterosexual to those who are exclusively gay.

Further, there is no necessary correspondence between identity and sexual behavior. Someone who self-identifies as gay is still likely to have had some heterosexual experience; someone who self-identifies as straight may have had some same-sex experience; and even those who have had *no* sexual experience may lay claim to being gay or straight. Identity is not always directly tied to behavior. Indeed, a person who self-identifies as gay may have had *more* heterosexual experience than someone who self-identifies as straight. This distinction between identity and experience was underscored by the results of a 1994 survey, the most comprehensive American sex survey since Kinsey's. Only 2.8 percent of the men and 1.4 percent of the women identified themselves as gay, but an additional 7.3 percent and 7.2 percent, respectively, reported a same-sex experience or attraction (Michael, 1994).

One last analogy between the construction of race and sexual orientation bears discussion. Most Americans would not question the logic of this sentence: "Tom has been married for 30 years and had a dozen children, but I think he's *really* gay." In a real-life illustration of the same logic, a young man and woman were often seen kissing on our campus. When this became the subject of a class discussion, a suggestive ripple of laughter went through the room: Everyone "knew" that the young man was really gay.

How could they "know" that? For such conclusions to make sense, we must believe that someone could be gay irrespective of his or her actual behavior. Just as it is possible in this culture for one to be "black" even if one looks "white," apparently one may be gay despite acting straight. Just as "black" can be established by any African heritage, "gay" is apparently established by displaying any behavior thought to be associated with gays. Indeed, "gay" can be "established" by reputation alone, by a failure to demonstrate heterosexuality, or even by the demonstration of an overly aggressive heterosexuality. Therefore, "gay" can be assigned no matter what one actually does. In this sense, gay can function as an *essential identity* (Katz, 1975), that is, an identity assigned to an individual *irrespective of his or her actual behavior,* as in "I know she's a genius even though she's flunking all her courses." Because no behavior can ever conclusively prove one is *not* gay, this label is an extremely effective mechanism of social control.

In all, several parallels exist between race and sexual orientation classifications. With both, we assume there are a limited number of possibilities—usually two, but no more than three—and we assume individuals can easily fit into one or the other option. We treat both race and sexual orientation categories as encompassing populations that are internally homogeneous and profoundly dissimilar from each other. For both, this presumption of difference has prompted a wide-ranging search for the biological distinctiveness of the categories. Different races or sexual orientations are judged superior and inferior to one another, and members of each category historically have been granted unequal legal and social rights. Finally, we assume that sexual orientation, like skin color, tells us something meaningful about a person.

Dichotomizing Class   Any discussion of social class in the United States must begin with the understanding that Americans "almost never speak of themselves or their society in class terms. In other words, class is not a central category of cultural discourse in America" (Ortner, 1991:169). Indeed, considering the time and attention Americans devote to sexual orientation, sex/gender, or race, it is hard not to conclude that social class is a taboo subject in our culture (Fussell, 1983). Because social class is so seldom discussed, the vocabulary for talking about it is not well developed.

Yet despite its relative invisibility, as Michael Zweig notes in Reading 13, social class operates in ways quite similar to race and sex. That is, just as American culture offers interpretations of what differences in color or sex mean, it also provides interpretations about what differences in income, wealth, or employment status might mean. As is the case with the other master status categories, social class is also often dichotomized, usually into those called "poor" and those called "middle class."

This social class dichotomization is particularly interesting in that it reflects an actual polarization of income and wealth among Americans, although not one accurately captured by the dichotomy "poor and middle class." As Nancy Wiefek describes in Reading 15, since 1970 the distribution of wealth and income among Americans has become much more unequal, with an increasing gap between rich and poor and a declining number of families in the middle class. So the real social class division would appear to between rich and poor. Still, it seems to us that Americans are more likely to assume the country is divided between the poor and middle class, as if those in the highest brackets were "really just like the rest of us."

Further, Americans often construct this poor/middle class distinction as if it reflected an individual's merit as a person. More often than people of other nationalities, Americans explain success and failure in terms of *individual merit* rather than economic or social forces (Morris and Williamson, 1982)—we even sometimes forget the inherited wealth behind "self-made" billionaires, as Dusty Horwitt describes in Reading 17. Yet in the early part of the 20th century, those who were poor were understood to be "hardworking, low-wage workers, a group of people who in the public mind were at once numerous (perhaps the majority), the least well-off, economically productive, and impeded by socially contrived barriers to their advancement" (Cohen 1995 in Arrow, Bowles, and Durlauf, 2000:x). Today, however, "many of the least well off are not regarded as productive in any respect, and widespread understandings of their actions now serve more often to disqualify than to entitle them to a larger share of the social product" (Arrow et al., 2000:x). Now an emphasis on individual values, attributes, and lifestyle—rather than unemployment, discrimination, or a changing economy—characterizes popular opinion and social science research on social class (Kahlenberg, 1997; Mincy, 1994). Americans are prone to think that those who succeed financially do so on the basis of their own merit, and that those who don't succeed have failed because they *lack* merit. Indeed many talk about social class as if it were just the result of personal values or attitudes. Surveys indicate that over half of the American public believe "that lack of effort by the poor was the principal reason for poverty, or a reason at least equal to any that was beyond a person's control. . . . Popular majorities did not consider any other factor to be a very important cause of poverty—not low wages, or a scarcity of jobs, or discrimination, or even sickness" (Schwarz and Volgy, 1992:11).

This attribution of poverty and wealth to individual merit hides the complex reality of American social class. It ignores those who work but earn less than the poverty line—a group estimated to be between 7 and 9 million workers (Kim, 1999). Although Americans are aware of a broad range of social class differences (Jackman and Jackman, 1983; Vanneman and Cannon, 1987), the widespread conviction that one's station in life reflects one's ability and effort in many ways overshadows this awareness. In all, social class standing is taken to reveal one's core worth—a strikingly essentialist formulation.

Dichotomizing Sex First, to distinguish the terms *sex* and *gender, sex* refers to females and males—that is, to chromosomal, hormonal, anatomical, and physiological differences—and *gender* describes the socially constructed roles associated with each sex. Gender is learned; it is the culturally and historically specific acting out of "masculinity" and "femininity." The term is often used erroneously as being synonymous with biological sex. For example, newspapers describe what are really sex differences in voting as "gender differences," and the recent ability to select the sex of a baby is called "gender selection." In these Framework Essays, however, the distinction between the two terms will be maintained.

Even sex can be understood as a socially created dichotomy much like race, sexual orientation, or gender, although that approach can be unsettling. Readings 9 and 10 by developmental geneticist Anne Fausto-Sterling and anthropoligist Walter Williams describe the belief in Western culture that there are two, and only two, sexes and that all individuals can be clearly identified as one or the other (Kessler and McKenna, 1978). But like sexual orientation, sex refers to a complex set of attributes—anatomical, chromosomal, hormonal, physiological—that may sometimes be inconsistent with one another or with individuals' sense of their own identity. This situation was illustrated by a Spanish athlete who is anatomically female, but in a pregame genetic test was classified as male. On the basis of that test, she was excluded from the 1985 World University Games. She was then reclassified as female in 1991, when the governing body for track-and-field contests abandoned genetic testing and returned to physical inspection. As the gynecologist for the sports federation noted, "about 1 in 20,000 people has genes that conflict with his or her apparent gender" (Lemonick, 1992).

Just as with race and sexual orientation, people are assigned to the categories of male or female irrespective of inconsistent or ambiguous evidence. In order to achieve consistency between the physical and psychological, some people are propelled into sex change surgery as they seek to produce a body consistent with their self-identities. Others will pursue psychotherapy to find an identity consistent with their bodies. In either case, it makes more sense to some people to use surgery and therapy to create consistency than to accept inconsistency: a man who feels like a woman must become a woman rather than just being a man who feels like a woman.

The Social Construction of Disability

Our discussion of race, sexual orientation, sex and gender, and social class has emphasized that each of these categories encompasses a continuum of behavior and characteristics rather than a finite set of discrete or easily separated groupings. It has also stressed that difference is a social creation—that differences of color or sex, for example, have no meaning other than what is attributed to them.

Can the same be said about ability and disability, which also qualify as master statuses? It is often assumed that people are easily classed as able-bodied or disabled, but that is no more true in this case than it is for the other master statuses. The comments of sociologist Irving Zola show how our use of statistics contributes to the misconception of ability/disability as fixed and dichotomous.

> The way we report statistics vis-à-vis disability and disease is generally misleading. If we speak of ratio figures for a particular disease as 1 in 8, 1 in 14, etc., we perpetuate what Rene Dubos (1961) once called "The Mirage of Health." For these numbers convey that if 1 person in 10 does get a particular disease, that 9 out of 10 do not. This means, however, only that those 9 people do not get that particular disease. It does not mean that they are disease-free, nor are they likely to be so. . . .
>
> Similarly deceptive is the now-popular figure of "43 million people with a disability" . . . for it implies that there are over 200 million Americans without a disability. . . . But the metaphor of being but a banana-peel slip away from disability is inappropriate. The issue of disability for individuals . . . is not *whether* but *when*, not so much *which one* but *how many* and *in what combination.* (Zola, 1993:18)

However, recognizing that the ability/disability dichotomy is illogical may be easier than understanding the case that disability is socially constructed. That point, which has emerged in the disability rights movement, is made by Michael Oliver in Reading 53. Rather than treating disability as a defect within an individual, this approach argues that disability is created by physical and social environments.

For example, in the case below, disability is created by environments that lack the physical design or social supports that would make life worth living.

Larry McAfee was aged 34 when a motorcycle accident resulted in complete paralysis and the need to use a ventilator. His insurance benefit (of $1 million) enabled him to employ personal care attendants in his own home for a period after his accident but when this ran out he was forced to enter a nursing home. He decided life wasn't worth living and tried turning his respirator off but couldn't cope with the feeling of suffocation. So he petitioned the courts to be allowed to be sedated while someone else unplugged his breathing apparatus. . . .

Yet when, as a result of the publicity, McAfee received an outpouring of support from disability activists, he decided to delay the decision to take his own life. What he really wanted was to live in his own home and get a job. . . .

It is not the physical disability itself but the social and economic circumstances of the experience which can lead to a diminished quality of life. (Morris, 1991:40–41)

Not only can disability be understood as the result of disabling environments, but also the categories of disability are themselves socially constructed. "Epilepsy, illness, disease, and disability are not 'givens' in nature. . . . but rather *socially constructed* categories that emerge from the interpretive activities of people acting together in social situations" (Schneider, 1988:65). Learning disabilities are an example of this process.

Before the late 1800s when observers began to write about "word blindness," and, more significantly, before the mid-1960s when educators and others began to popularize learning disability, it did not exist. Learning disability did not exist as a means for making sense of difficulties people experienced in learning groups (Coles, 1987). Even the human variation (i.e., the learning difficulties) to which it refers has not existed for most of human history. However, today almost 2 million students are served as learning disabled, more than are served through any other disability category (U.S. Department of Education, 1990:12). (Higgins, 1992:9)

While both abled and disabled individuals participate in the social construction of disability, they do not do so on an equal basis. Cultural concepts such as dependence and independence—which bear heavily on judgments about what constitutes a disability—are most often imposed on disabled people by those not so identified.

In terms of the physical world, none of us—whether disabled or not—is completely independent in the sense that we rely on nothing and nobody. However, the meaning of our dependence on others and on the physical world is determined by both its socio-economic and ideological context. For example, we all depend on water coming out of the tap when we turn it on, while a disabled person depends on someone to help her get dressed in the morning. However, when non-disabled people talk about water coming out of the tap, the issue is whether the water company is reliable; when they talk about [a disabled person] being dependent on an assistant, the issue for them is what they see as her helplessness created by her physical limitations. (Morris, 1991:137–38)

In both these ways—physical and conceptual—we create disability.

Through our beliefs and our behaviors, through our policies and our practices, we make disability (Albrecht, 1981:275; Ferguson, 1987). Through interpersonal, organizational, and social activities, we make disability (Bogdan and Biklen, 1977). In all areas of social life we make and remake disability. (Higgins, 1992:6)

Constructing the "Other"

We have seen how the complexity of a population may be reduced to aggregates and then to a simplistic dichotomy. Aggregation assumes that those who share a master status are alike in "essential" ways. It ignores the multiple and conflicting statuses an individual inevitably occupies. Dichotomization especially promotes the image of a mythical *Other* who is not at all like "us." Whether in race, sex, sexual orientation, social class, or disability, dichotomization yields a vision of "them" as profoundly different. Ultimately, dichotomization results in stigmatizing those who are less powerful. It provides the grounds for whole categories of people to become the objects of contempt.

Constructing "Others" as Profoundly Different   The expectation that Others are profoundly different can be seen most clearly in the significance that has been attached to sex differences. In this case, biological differences between males and females have been the grounds from which to infer an extensive range of nonbiological differences. Women and men are assumed to differ from each other in behavior, perception, and personality, and such differences are used to argue for different legal, social, and economic roles and rights. The expectation that men and women are not at all alike is so widespread that we often talk about them as members of the "opposite" sex; indeed, it is not unusual to talk about the "war" between the sexes.

While this assumption of difference undergirds everyday life, few significant differences in behavior, personality, or even physical ability have been found between men and women of any age. Indeed, there are more differences within each sex than between the sexes. Susan Basow illustrates this point in the following:

> The all-or-none categorizing of gender traits is misleading. People just are not so simple that they either possess all of a trait or none of it. This is even more true when trait dispositions for groups of people are examined. Part a of Figure 1 illustrates what such an all-or-none distribution of the trait "strength" would look like: all males would be strong, all females weak. The fact is, most psychological and physical traits are distributed according to the pattern shown in Part b of Figure 1 with most people possessing an average amount of that trait and fewer people having either very much or very little of that trait.
>
> To the extent that females and males may differ in the average amount of the trait they possess (which needs to be determined empirically), the distribution can be characterized by *overlapping normal curves,* as shown in Part c of Figure 1. Thus, although most men are stronger than most women, the shaded area indicates that some men are weaker than some women and vice versa. The amount of overlap of the curves generally is considerable. Another attribute related to overlapping normal curves is that differences within one group are usually greater than the differences between the two groups. Thus, more variation in strength occurs within a group of men than between the average male and the average female. (Basow, 1992:8)

This lack of difference between women and men is especially striking given the degree to which we are all socialized to produce such differences. Thus, while boys and girls, and men and women, are often socialized to be different as well as treated differently, this does not mean they inevitably *become* different. Even though decades of

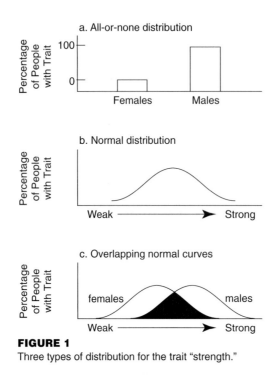

FIGURE 1
Three types of distribution for the trait "strength."

research have confirmed few sex differences, the search for difference continues and some suggest may even have been intensified by the failure to find many differences.

The same expectation that the Other differs in personality or behavior emerges in race, class, and sexual orientation classifications. Race differences are expected to involve more than just differences of color, those who are "gay" or "straight" are expected to differ in more ways than just their sexual orientation, and the poor and middle class are expected to differ in more than just economic standing. In each case, scientific research is often directed toward finding such differences.

Sanctioning Those Who Associate with the "Other"　　There are also similarities in the sanctions against those who cross race, sex, class, or sexual orientation boundaries. Parents sometimes disown children who marry outside of their racial or social class group, just as they often sever connections with children who are gay. Those who associate with the Other are also in danger of being labeled a member of that category.

For example, during the Reconstruction period following the Civil War, the fear of invisible black ancestry was pervasive among southern whites, because that heritage would subject them to nascent segregation. "Concern about people passing as white became so great that even behaving like blacks or willingly associating with them were often treated as more important than any proof of actual black ancestry" (Davis, 1991:56). Thus, southern whites who associated with blacks ran the risk of being defined as black.

A contemporary parallel can be found in gay/straight relations. Those who associate with gays and lesbians or defend gay rights are often presumed—by gays and straights alike—to be gay. Many men report that when they object to homophobic remarks, they simply become the target of them. Indeed, the prestige of young men in fraternities and other all-male groups often rests on a willingness to disparage women and gays (Sanday, 1990).

Similarly, few contemporary reactions are as strongly negative as that against men who appear feminine. Because acting like a woman is so disparaged, boys learn at an early age to control their behavior or suffer public humiliation. This ridicule has its greatest effect on young men; the power and prestige usually available to older men reduces their susceptibility to such accusations. There is a long list of behavior young men must avoid for fear of being called feminine or gay: Don't be too emotional, watch how you sit, don't move your hips when you walk, take long strides, don't put your hands on your hips, don't talk too much, don't let your voice show emotion, don't be too compliant or eager to please, etc.

Because effeminate men are often assumed to be gay, they become targets for verbal and physical abuse. Indeed, as Laura Sessions Stepp describes in Reading 35, even elementary school boys are subject to this abuse. The popular linkage of effeminate behavior with a gay sexual orientation is so strong that it may be the primary criterion most Americans use to decide who is gay: A "masculine" man must be straight; a "feminine" man must be gay. But gender and sexual orientation are *separate* phenomena. Knowing that someone is a masculine man or a feminine woman does not tell us what that person's sexual orientation is—indeed, our guesses are most likely to be "false negatives"; that is, we are most likely to falsely identify someone as straight. Because we do not know who among us is gay, we cannot accurately judge how gay people behave.

In the world of mutual Othering, being labeled one of "them" is a remarkably effective social control mechanism. Boys and men control their behavior so that they are not called gay. Members of racial and ethnic groups maintain distance from one another to avoid the criticism that might be leveled by members of their own and other groups. These social controls are effective because all parties continue to enforce them.

Stigma

In the extreme, those depicted as Other may be said to be *stigmatized*. Whole categories of people have been stigmatized as a result of the outcome of large-scale social and historical processes.

The term *stigma* comes from ancient Greece, where it meant a "bodily sign designed to expose something unusual and bad about the moral status of [an individual]" (Goffman, 1963:1). Such signs were "cut or burnt into the body to advertise that the bearer was a slave, a criminal, or a blemished person, ritually polluted, to be avoided, especially in public places" (Goffman, 1963:1). Stigmatized people are those "marked" as bad, unworthy, and polluted because of the category they belong to, for example, their race, sex, sexual orientation, or social class category. The core assumption behind stigma is that internal merit is revealed through external features—for the Greeks, that a brand or a cut showed the moral worth of the person. This is not an unusual linkage; for example, physically attractive people are often assumed to possess a variety of positive attributes (Adams, 1982). We assume that people who look good must *be* good.

Judgments of worth based on membership in certain categories have a self-fulfilling potential. Those who are judged superior by virtue of their membership in some acceptable category are given more opportunity to prove themselves; those who are judged less worthy by virtue of membership in a stigmatized category have difficulty establishing their merit no matter what they do. For example, social psychology data indicate that many whites perceive blacks as incompetent, regardless of evidence to the contrary: White subjects were "reluctant or unable to recognize that a black person is higher or equal in intelligence compared to themselves" (Gaertner and Dovidio, 1986:75). This would explain why many whites react negatively to affirmative action programs. If they cannot conceive of black applicants as being *more* qualified than whites, they will see such programs as only mandates to hire the less qualified.

Stigma involves objectification as well as devaluation. *Objectification* means treating people as if they were objects, members of a category rather than possessors of individual characteristics. In objectification, the "living, breathing, complex individual" ceases to be seen or valued (Allport, 1958:175). In its extreme, those who are objectified are "viewed as having no other noteworthy status or identity. When that point is reached a person becomes *nothing* but 'a delinquent,' 'a cripple,' 'a homosexual,' 'a black,' 'a woman.' The indefinite article 'a' underlines the depersonalized nature of such response" (Schur, 1984:30–31).

Examples of Stigmatized Master Statuses: Women and the Poor   Sociologist Edwin Schur argues that because women are subject to both objectification and devaluation, they are discredited, that is, stigmatized. First, considering objectification, Schur argues that women are seen

> as all alike, and therefore substitutable for one another; as innately passive and objectlike; as easily ignored, dismissed, trivialized, treated as childlike, and even as a non-person; as having a social standing only through their attachments to men (or other non-stigmatized groups); and as a group which can be easily victimized through harassment, violence, and discrimination. (Schur, 1984:33)

Objectification occurs when women are thought of as generally indistinguishable from one another; for example, when someone says, "Let's get the woman's angle on this story." It also occurs when women are treated as nothing more than their body parts. This is what Emily White describes in Reading 32—young girls who are assumed to be "sluts" because they are big-breasted. They are nothing more than their cup size; they are objects.

African Americans, Latinos, Asian Americans, and gay/lesbian people are often similarly treated as indistinguishable from one another. Indeed, hate crimes have been defined by this quality of interchangeability, such as an attack on any black family that moves into a neighborhood or the assault of any woman or man who looks gay. Hate crimes are also marked by excessive brutality and personal violence rather than property destruction—all of which indicate that the victims have been objectified (Levin and McDevitt, 1993).

Some members of stigmatized categories objectify themselves in the same ways that they are objectified by others. Thus, women may evaluate their own worth in terms of physical appearance. In the process of self-objectification, a woman "joins the spectators of herself"; that is, she views herself as if from the outside, as if she were nothing more than what she looked like (Berger, 1963:50). This sense of making an object of oneself was captured several years ago in a cereal commercial where a bikini-clad woman posed before a mirror. She had lost weight for an upcoming vacation and was imagining herself as a stranger on the beach might see her. Thus, she succeeded in making an object of herself. While physical appearance is also valued for men, it rarely takes precedence over all other qualities. Rather, men are more likely to be objectified in terms of wealth and power.

In addition to being objectified, there is a strong case that American women as a category remain devalued, a conclusion drawn from the characteristics most frequently attributed to men and women. Research conducted over the last 40 years has documented a remarkable consistency in those attributes. Both sexes are described as possessing valued qualities, but the characteristics attributed to men are more valued in the culture as a whole. For example, the female-valued characteristics include being talkative, gentle, religious, aware of the feelings of others, security oriented, and attentive to personal appearance. Male-valued traits include being aggressive, independent, unemotional, objective, dominant, active, competitive, logical, adventurous, and direct (Basow, 1992; Baron and Byrne, 2004).[9] (Remember that these attributes are only people's *beliefs* about sex differences.)

In many ways, the characteristics attributed to women are inconsistent with core American values. While American culture values achievement, individualism, and action—all understood as male attributes—women are expected to subordinate their personal interests to the family and to be passive and patient (Richardson, 1977). Therefore, "women are asked to become the kind of people that this culture does not value" (Richardson, 1977:11). Thus, it is more acceptable for women to display masculine traits, since these are culturally valued, than it is for men to display less-valued feminine characteristics. Men who are talkative, gentle, religious, aware of the feelings of others, security oriented, and attentive to personal appearance are much maligned. In contrast, women may be independent, unemotional, objective, dominant, active, competitive, logical, adventurous, and direct with fewer negative consequences. The characteristics we attribute to women are not valued for everyone, unlike the characteristics attributed to men.

---

[9]"Compared with White women, Black women are viewed as less passive, dependent, status conscious, emotional and concerned about their appearance. . . . Hispanic women tend to be viewed as more 'feminine' than White women in terms of submissiveness and dependence. . . . [A] similar stereotype holds for Asian women, but with the addition of exotic sexuality. . . . Native-American women typically are stereotyped as faceless . . . drudges without any personality. . . . Jewish women are stereotyped as either pushy, vain 'princesses' or overprotective, manipulative 'Jewish mothers' . . . working-class women are stereotyped as more hostile, confused, inconsiderate and irresponsible than middle-class women . . . and lesbians are stereotyped as possessing masculine traits" (Basow, 1992:4).

Much of what we have described about the stigmatization of women applies to the poor as well. Indeed, being poor is a much more obviously shameful status than being female. The category *poor* is intrinsically devalued. At least in contemporary American culture, it is presumed there is little commendable to be said about poor people; "they" are primarily constructed as a "problem." Poor people are also objectified; they are described as "*the* poor," as if they were all alike, substitutable for and interchangeable with one another.

> Most of the writing about poor people, even by sympathetic observers, tells us that they are different, truly strangers in our midst: Poor people think, feel, and act in ways unlike middle-class Americans. . . .
>
> We can think about poor people as "them" or as "us." For the most part, Americans have talked about "them." Even in the language of social science, as well as in ordinary conversation and political rhetoric, poor people usually remain outsiders, strangers to be pitied or despised, helped or punished, ignored or studied, but rarely full citizens, members of a larger community on the same terms as the rest of us. They are . . . "those people," objects of curiosity, analysis, prurience, or compassion, not subjects who construct their own lives and history. Poor people seem cardboard cutouts, figures in single dimension, members of inferior categories, rarely complex, multifaceted, even contradictory in the manner of other persons. (M. Katz, 1989:6, 126)

And, like women, poor people are not expected to display attributes valued in the culture as a whole.

Stereotypes about People in Stigmatized Master Statuses   Finally, in an effort to capture the general features of what "we" say about "them," let us consider five common stereotypes about individuals in stigmatized master statuses.

First, they are presumed to lack the values the culture holds dear. Neither women nor those who are poor, gay, black, Asian American, or Latino are expected to be independent, unemotional, objective, dominant, active, competitive, logical, adventurous, or direct. Stigmatized people are presumed to lack precisely those values that nonstigmatized people are expected to possess.

Second, stigmatized people are likely to be seen as a problem (Adam, 1978; Wilson and Gutierrez, 1985). Certainly black, Latino, and Native American men and women, gay and lesbian people of all colors, white women, and people living in poverty are constructed as *having* problems and *being* problems. Often the implication is that they are also responsible for many of our national problems. While public celebrations often highlight the historic contributions of such groups to the culture, little in the public discourse lauds their current contributions. Indeed, those in stigmatized categories are often constructed as *nothing but a problem,* as if they did not exist apart from those problems. This was illustrated by a black student who described her shock at hearing white students describe her middle-class neighborhood as a "ghetto."

Ironically, this depiction of stigmatized people as nothing but a problem is often accompanied by the trivialization of those problems. For example, a 2002 Gallup poll showed 34 percent of men very satisfied with the way women are treated in society, compared to only 18 percent of women. In 2002, while men were more likely than in 1976 to believe that women have equal opportunities on the job, women were less likely to believe that than in 1975 (Brooks, 2004). Similarly, despite the participation of thousands of people in annual Gay Pride marches throughout the country, television footage typically trivializes that population by focusing on the small number in drag. Whites' opinion that blacks prefer welfare to supporting themselves similarly trivializes the experience of poverty (Thornton and Whitman, 1992). Thus, the problems that stigmatized categories of people create for those in privileged statuses are highlighted, while the problems they experience are discounted.

Third, people in stigmatized master statuses are stereotyped as lacking self-control; they are characterized as being lustful, immoral, and carriers of disease (Gilman, 1985, 1991). Currently, such accusations hold center stage in the depictions of gay men, but historically such charges have been leveled at African American, Latino, and Asian American men (e.g., Chinese immigrants in the late 19th century). Poor women and women of color have been and continue to be depicted as promiscuous, while poor men and women are presumed to be morally irresponsible.

Fourth, people in stigmatized categories are often marked as having too much or too little intelligence, and in either case as tending to deception or criminality. Many stigmatized categories of people have been assumed to use their "excessive" intelligence to unfair advantage. This was historically the case for Jews, and now appears to be the case for Asian American college students.

> [T]he educational achievement of Asian American students was, and continues to be, followed by a wave of reaction. The image of Asian Americans as diligent super-students has often kindled resentment in other students. Sometimes called "damned curve raisers," a term applied first to Jewish students at elite East Coast colleges during the 1920s and 1930s, Asian American students have increasingly found themselves taking the brunt of campus racial jokes. (Takagi, 1992:60)

Fifth, people in stigmatized categories are depicted as both childlike and savagely brutal. Historically, characterizations of Native Americans, enslaved Africans, and Chinese immigrants reflected these conceptions. Currently, the same is true for the poor in their representation as both pervasively violent and irresponsible. A related depiction of women as both "virgins and whores" has been well documented in scholarship over time.

Perhaps because people in stigmatized master statuses are stereotyped as deviant, it appears that those who commit violence against them are unlikely to be punished. For example, "most murders in the USA are intra-racial, that is, the alleged perpetrator and the victim are of the same race. . . . Yet of the 845 prisoners executed between 17 January 1977 and 10 April 2003, 53 percent were whites convicted of killing whites and 10 percent were blacks convicted of killing blacks" (Amnesty International, 2003). While a number of factors are operating here, one conclusion is that stigmatized minority victims are valued less than white victims. The same conclusion could be reached in terms of the punishment meted out to those accused of sexual assault. "Major offenses *against* women, which we *profess* to consider deviant, in practice have been responded to with much ambivalence" (Schur, 1984:7). Indeed, one way to recognize a stigmatized category of people is that the violence directed at them is not treated seriously (Schur, 1984).

Overall, individuals in stigmatized master statuses are represented as not only physically distinctive but also the antithesis of the culture's desired behaviors and attributes. They are seen as not operating from cultural values. They are problems; they are immoral and disease ridden; their intelligence is questionable; they are childlike and savage. Such characterizations serve to dismiss claims of discrimination and unfair treatment, affirming that those in stigmatized categories deserve such treatment, that they are themselves responsible for their plight. Indeed, many of these stereotypes are also applied to teenagers, whom the media depict as violent, reckless, hypersexed, ignorant, out of control, and the cause of society's problems (Males, 1994).

A Final Comment

It is disheartening to think of oneself as a member of a stigmatized group, just as it is disheartening to think of oneself as thoughtlessly perpetuating stigma. Still, there are at least two important points of hopefulness here. First, the characteristics attributed to stigmatized groups are similar across a great variety of master statuses. Thus, there is the relief of impersonality because the stigmatized characteristics are not tied to the actual characteristics of any particular group. Second, people who are stigmatized have often formed alliances with those who are not stigmatized to successfully lobby against these attributions.

As we said at the outset of this essay, our hope is to provide you with a framework by which to make sense of what sex, race, social class, and sexual orientation mean in contemporary American society. Clearly, these categorizations are complex; they are tied to emotionally intense issues that are uniquely American; and they have consequences that are both mundane and dramatic. From naming, to aggregating, to dichotomizing, and ultimately to stigmatizing, difference has a meaning for us. The readings in Section I explore the construction of these categorizations; the readings in Section II examine how we experience them; the readings in Section III address the meaning that is attributed to difference; and the readings in Section IV describe how we can bridge these differences.

KEY CONCEPTS

aggregate To combine or lump together (verb); something composed of different elements (noun). (pages 11–14)

-centrism or –centric Suffix meaning centered around, focused around, taking the perspective of. Thus, **androcentric** means focused around or taking the perspective of men; **heterocentric** means taking the perspective of heterosexuals; and **eurocentric** means having a European focus. (page 14)

constructionism The view that reality cannot be separated from the way a culture makes sense of it—that meaning is "constructed" through social, political legal, scientific, and other practices. From this perspective, differences among people are created through social processes. (pages 3–5)

dichotomize To divide into two parts and to see those parts as mutually exclusive. (pages 14–23)

differential undercount In the census, undercounting more of one group than of another. (pages 8–11)

disaggregate To separate something into its constituent elements. (pages 11–14)

essential identity An identity that is treated as core to a person. Essential identities can be attributed to people even when they are inconsistent with actual behavior. (page 21)

essentialism The view that reality exists independently of our perception of it, that we perceive the meaning of the world rather than construct that meaning. From this perspective, there are real and important (essential) differences among categories of people. (pages 3–5)

ethnic group, ethnicity An ethnic group is composed of people with a shared national origin or ancestry and shared cultural characteristics, such as language. For example, Polish Americans, Italian Americans, Chinese Americans, and Haitian Americans are ethnic groups. "African American" can be considered a racial category, but also an ethnicity (given the shared history of slavery). (page 17)

gender Masculinity and femininity; the acting out of the behaviors thought to be appropriate for a particular sex. (page 22)

heterosexism The presumption that all people are heterosexual (in this sense, synonymous with heterocentric); the presumption that heterosexuality is the only acceptable form of sexual expression. (page 2)

master status A status that has a profound effect on one's life, that dominates or overwhelms the other statuses one occupies. In contemporary American society, race, sex, sexual orientation, social class, and ability/disability function as master statuses, but other statuses—such as religion—do not. For example, race strongly affects occupational status, income, health, and longevity. Religion may have a similar impact in other cultures. (page 2)

objectification Treating people as if they were objects, as if they were nothing more than the attributes they display. (page 28)

Other A usage designed to refer to those considered profoundly unlike oneself. (page 25)

panethnic An ethnic classification that spans national-origin identities. (page 13)

race The conception that people can be classified into coherent groups based on skin color, hair texture, shape of head, eyes, nose, and lips. (pages 15–19)

sex The categories of male and female. (page 22)

status A position in society. Individuals occupy multiple statuses simultaneously, such as occupational, kinship, and educational statuses. (page 2)

stigma An attribute for which someone is considered bad, unworthy, or deeply discredited. (pages 27–32)

REFERENCES

Adam, Barry. 1978. *The Survival of Domination.* New York: Elsevier.

Adams, Gerald R. 1982. Physical Attractiveness. *In the Eye of the Beholder: Contemporary Issues in Stereotyping,* edited by A. G. Miller, 253–304. New York: Praeger.

Albrecht, Gary L. 1981. Cross-National Rehabilitation Policies: A Critical Assessment. *Cross-National Rehabilitation Policies: A Sociological Perspective,* edited by G. Albrecht, 269–77. Beverly Hills, CA: Sage.

Allport, Gordon. 1958. *The Nature of Prejudice.* Garden City, NY: Doubleday Anchor.

Amnesty International. 2003. Death by Discrimination: The Continuing Role of Race in Capital Cases. http://web.amnesty.org/library/print/ENGAMR510462003.

Archer, Bert. 2002. *The End of Gay (and the Death of Heterosexuality).* New York: Thunder's Mouth Press.

Arrow, Kenneth, Samuel Bowles, and Steven Durlauf. 2000. Introduction. *Meritocracy and Economic Inequality,* edited by Kenneth Arrow, Samuel Bowles, and Steven Durlauf, ix–xv. Princeton, NJ: Princeton University Press.

Baron, Robert A., and Donn Byrne. 2004. *Social Psychology.* Boston: Pearson.

Basow, Susan A. 1992. *Gender: Stereotypes and Roles.* 3d ed. Pacific Grove, CA: Brooks/Cole Publishing.

Begley, Sharon. 1995. Three Is Not Enough. *Newsweek,* February 13, 67–69.

Berger, Peter L. 1963. *Invitation to Sociology: A Humanistic Perspective.* Garden City, NY: Doubleday Anchor.

Blauner, Robert. 1992. Talking Past Each Other: Black and White Languages of Race. *The American Prospect,* 10.

Bogdan, Robert, and Douglas Biklen. 1977. Handicapism. *Social Policy,* 7:14–19.

Brooks, Deborah Jordan. 2002. Job Equality Views: Gender Gap Still Wide. *Gallup Poll News Service.* August 27.

Choldin, Harvey M. 1986. Statistics and Politics: The "Hispanic Issue" in the 1980 Census. *Demography,* 23:403–18.

———. 1994. *Looking for the Last Percent: The Controversy over Census Undercounts.* New Brunswick, NJ: Rutgers University Press.

Cohen, G. 1995. *Self, Ownership, Freedom, and Equality.* Cambridge: Cambridge University Press.

Cohen, Mark Nathan. 1998. *Culture of Intolerance: Chauvinism, Class, and Racism in the United States.* New Haven, CT: Yale University Press.

Cohn, D'Vera. 2001. Counting of Gay Couples Up 300%. *Washington Post,* August 22, A.

Coles, Gerald. 1987. *The Learning Mystique: A Critical Look at "Learning Disabilities."* New York: Pantheon.

Conrad, Peter, and Joseph W. Schneider. 1980. *Deviance and Medicalization: From Badness to Sickness.* Philadelphia: Temple University Press.

Davis, F. James. 1991. *Who Is Black? One Nation's Rule.* University Park, PA: Pennsylvania State University Press.

de la Garza, Rudolfo O., Louis DeSipio, F. Chris Garcia, John Garcia, and Angelo Falcon. 1992. *Latino Voices: Mexican, Puerto Rican, and Cuban Perspectives on American Politics.* Boulder, CO: Westview Press.

Dubos, Rene. 1961. *Mirage of Health.* Garden City, NY: Anchor Books.

Espiritu, Yen Le. 1992. *Asian American Panethnicity: Bridging Institutions and Identities.* Philadelphia: Temple University Press.

Faderman, Lillian. 1991. *Odd Girls and Twilight Lovers: A History of Lesbian Life in Twentieth-Century America.* New York: Penguin Books.

Ferguson, Philip M. 1987. The Social Construction of Mental Retardation. *Social Policy,* 18:51–52.

Fussell, Paul. 1983. *Class.* New York: Ballentine Books.

Gaertner, Samuel L., and John F. Dovidio. 1986. The Aversive Form of Racism. *Prejudice, Discrimination, and Racism,* edited by John F. Dovidio and Samuel L. Gaertner, 61–89. Orlando, FL: Academic Press.

Gallup Organization, Gallup Poll News Service. 2003. Q&A: Black-White Relations in the U.S.

Gilman, Sander. 1991. *The Jew's Body.* New York: Routledge.

———. 1985. *Difference and Pathology: Stereotypes of Sexuality, Race, and Madness.* Ithaca, NY: Cornell University Press.

Goffman, Erving. 1963. *Stigma: Notes on the Management of Spoiled Identity.* Englewood Cliffs, NJ: Prentice-Hall.

Gordon, Margaret T., and Stephanie Riger. 1989. *The Female Fear.* New York: The Free Press.

Gracia, Jorge J. E. 2000. Affirmative Action for Hispanics? Yes and No. *Hispanics/Latinos in the United States: Ethnicity, Race, and Rights,* edited by Jorge J. E. Gracia and Pablo De Greiff, 201–222. New York: Routledge.

Henshel, Richard L., and Robert A. Silverman. 1975. *Perceptions in Criminology.* New York: Columbia University Press.

Higgins, Paul C. 1992. *Making Disability: Exploring the Social Transformation of Human Variation.* Springfield, IL: Charles C. Thomas.

Hilts, V. 1973. Statistics and Social Science. *Foundations of Scientific Method in the Nineteenth Century,* edited by R. Giere and R. Westfall, 206–33. Bloomington, IN: Indiana University Press.

Hirschman, Charles. 1996. Studying Immigrant Adaptation from the 1990 Population Census: From Generational Comparisons to the Process of "Becoming American." *The New Second Generation,* edited by A. Portes, 54–81. New York: Russell Sage Foundation.

Hu-Dehart, Evelyn. 1994. Asian/Pacific American Issues in American Education. Presentation at the 7th Annual National Conference on Race and Ethnicity in American Higher Education, Atlanta, sponsored by The Southwest Center for Human Relations Studies, University of Oklahoma, College of Continuing Education.

Jackman, Mary R., and Robert W. Jackman. 1983. *Class Awareness in the United States.* Berkeley, CA: University of California Press.

Jenkins, Alan. 1999. See No Evil. *The Nation,* June 28:15–19.

Jones, Nicholas A., and Amy Symens Smith. 2001. *The Two or More Races Population: 2000.* November. Census 2000 Brief: U.S. Census Bureau.

Kahlenberg, Richard D. 1997. *The Remedy: Class, Race, and Affirmative Action.* New York: Basic Books.

Katz, Jack. 1975. Essences as Moral Identities: Verifiability and Responsibility in Imputations of Deviance and Charisma. *American Journal of Sociology,* 80:1369–90.

Katz, Michael B. 1989. *The Undeserving Poor: From the War on Poverty to the War on Welfare.* New York: Pantheon Books.

Kessler, Suzanne J., and Wendy McKenna. 1978. *Gender: An Ethnomethodological Approach.* New York: John Wiley & Sons.

Kim, Marlene. 1999. The Working Poor: Lousy Jobs or Lazy Workers. *A New Introduction to Poverty: The Role of Race, Power, and Politics,* edited by Louis Kushnick and James Jennings, 307–19. New York: New York University Press.

Kinsey, Alfred, Wardell Pomeroy, and Clyde Martin. 1948. *Sexual Behavior in the Human Male.* Philadelphia: W. B. Saunders.

Klein, Fritz. 1978. *The Bisexual Option.* New York: Arbor House.

Lemonick, Michael. 1992. Genetic Tests under Fire. *Time,* February 24, 65.

LeVay, Simon. 1991. A Difference in Hypothalmic Structure between Heterosexual and Homosexual Men. *Science,* 253:1034–37.

Levin, Jack, and Jack McDevitt. 1993. *Hate Crimes.* New York: Plenum Press.

Lieberman, Leonard. 1968. A Debate over Race: A Study in the Sociology of Knowledge. *Phylon,* 29:127–41.

Lopez, David, and Yen Espiritu. 1990. Panethnicity in the United States: A Theoretical Framework. *Ethnic and Racial Studies,* 13:198–224.

Males, Mike. 1994. Bashing Youth: Media Myths about Teenagers. *Extra!* March/April, 8–11.

Marshall, Gloria. 1993. Racial Classifications: Popular and Scientific. *The "Racial" Economy of Science: Toward a Democratic Future,* edited by Sandra Harding, 116–27. Bloomington, IN: Indiana University Press (Originally published 1968).

Marshall, Gordon. 1994. *The Concise Oxford Dictionary of Sociology.* Oxford: Oxford University Press.

Michael, Robert T. 1994. *Sex in America: A Definitive Survey.* Boston: Little, Brown.

Mills, Jane. 1989. *Womanwords: A Dictionary of Words about Women.* New York: Henry Holt.

Mincey, Ronald B. 1994. *Confronting Poverty: Prescriptions for Change.* Cambridge: Harvard University Press.

Mohawk, John. 1992. Looking for Columbus: Thoughts on the Past, Present and Future of Humanity. *The State of Native America: Genocide, Colonization, and Resistance,* edited by M. Annette Jaimes, 439–44. Boston: South End Press.

Moore, David W. 2004. Modest Rebound in Public Acceptance of Homosexuals. *Gallup Poll News Service,* May 20.

Morris, Jenny. 1991. *Pride against Prejudice: Transforming Attitudes to Disability.* Philadelphia: New Society Publishers.

Morris, Michael, and John B. Williamson. 1982. Stereotypes and Social Class: A Focus on Poverty. *In the Eye of the Beholder,* edited by Arthur G. Miller, 411–65. New York: Praeger.

Morrison, Toni. 1992. *Playing in the Dark.* New York: Vintage.

Office of Management and Budget. 1995. Standards for the Classification of Federal Data on Race and Ethnicity Notice. *Federal Register* 60:44674–693.

———. October 1997. *Revisions to the Standards for the Classification of Federal Data on Race and Ethnicity.* Washington, DC: U.S. Government Printing Office.

Omi, Michael. 1996. Racialization in the Post–Civil Rights Era. *Mapping Multiculturalism,* edited by A. Gordon and C. Newfield, 178–85. Minneapolis: University of Minnesota Press.

———, and Howard Winant. 1994. *Racial Formation in the United States.* New York: Routledge.

Ortner, Sherry B. 1991. Reading America. Preliminary Notes on Class and Culture. *Recapturing Anthropology: Working in the Present,* edited by Richard G. Fox, 163–89. Santa Fe, NM: School of American Research Press.

Pfuhl, Erdwin H. 1986. *The Deviance Process.* 2d ed. Belmont, CA: Wadsworth.

Population Reference Bureau. 2001. Increasing Diversity in the U.S. Hispanic Population. www.prb.org.

Richardson, Laurel. 1977. *The Dynamics of Sex and Gender: A Sociological Perspective.* New York: Harper and Row.

———. 1988. *The Dynamics of Sex and Gender: A Sociological Perspective.* 3d ed. New York: Harper and Row.

Rist, Darrell Yates. 1992. Are Homosexuals Born That Way? *The Nation,* 255:424–29.

Roediger, David. 1994. *Towards the Abolition of Whiteness.* London: Verso.

Rubio, Philip F. 2001. *A History of Affirmative Action: 1619–2000.* Jackson: University of Mississippi Press.

Sanday, Peggy Reeves. 1990. *Fraternity Gang Rape.* New York: New York University Press.

Schmidt, Peter. 2003. The Label "Hispanic" Irks Some, but Also Unites. *The Chronicle of Higher Education,* November 23, A9.

Schneider, Joseph W. 1988. Disability as Moral Experience: Epilepsy and Self in Routine Relationships. *Journal of Social Issues,* 44:63–78.

Schur, Edwin. 1984. *Labeling Women Deviant: Gender, Stigma, and Social Control.* New York: Random House.

Schwarz, John E., and Thomas J. Volgy. 1992. *The Forgotten Americans.* New York: W. W. Norton.

Sherman Heyl, Barbara. 1989. Homosexuality: A Social Phenomenon. *Human Sexuality: The Societal and Interpersonal Context,* edited by Kathleen McKinney and Susan Sprecher, 321–349. Norwood, NJ: Ablex.

Shipman, Pat. 1994. *The Evolution of Racism: Human Differences and the Use and Abuse of Science.* New York: Simon and Schuster.

Shorris, Earl. 1992. *Latinos: A Biography of the People.* New York: W. W. Norton.

Smedley, Audrey. 1993. *Race in North America: Origin and Evolution of a Worldview.* Boulder, CO: Westview Press.

Smith, Tom W. 1992. Changing Racial Labels: From "Colored" to "Negro" to "Black" to "African American." *Public Opinion Quarterly,* 56:496–514.

Spelman, Elizabeth. 1988. *Inessential Woman.* Boston: Beacon Press.

Springer, S. P., and G. Deutsch. 1981. *Left Brain, Right Brain.* San Francisco: Freeman.

Steinberg, Stephen. 1989. *The Ethnic Myth: Race, Ethnicity, and Class in America.* Boston: Beacon Press.

Takagi, Dana Y. 1992. *The Retreat from Race: Asian-American Admission and Racial Politics.* New Brunswick, NJ: Rutgers University Press.

Takaki, Ronald. 1990. *Iron Cages: Race and Culture in 19th-Century America.* New York: Oxford University Press.

———. 1993. *A Different Mirror.* Boston: Little Brown.

Tamayo Lott, Juanita. 1998. *Asian Americans: From Racial Category to Multiple Identities.* Walnut Creek, CA: Altamira Press.

Thornton, Jeannye, and David Whitman. 1992. Whites' Myths about Blacks. *U.S. News and World Report,* November 9:41–44.

U.S. Census Bureau. 2001. *Census 2000 Summary File 2, Technical Documentation:* September 2001, SF2/01:G39-G41.

U.S. Commission on Civil Rights. 1973. *To Know or Not to Know: Collection and Use of Racial and Ethnic Data in Federal Assistance Programs.* Washington, DC: U.S. Government Printing Office.

U.S. Department of Commerce. 2001. Census Bureau Says No to Adjustment: Review Finds Duplicates Wipe Out Most of Net Undercount. *United States Department of Commerce News,* October 18.

———. 2001. People Who Reported Two or More Races Are Young and Tend to Live in the West. *United States Department of Commerce News,* November 29.

U.S. Department of Education, 1990. *To Assure the Free Appropriate Public Education of All Handicapped Children: Twelfth Annual Report to Congress on the Implementation of the Education of the Handicapped Act.* Washington, DC: U.S. Government Printing Office.

Vanneman, Reeve, and Lynn Weber Cannon. 1987. *The American Perception of Class.* Philadelphia: Temple University Press.

Weinberg, George. 1973. *Society and the Healthy Homosexual.* Garden City, NY: Anchor.

Wilson, II, Clint, and Felix Gutierrez. 1985. *Minorities and the Media.* Beverly Hills, CA: Sage.

Zola, Irving K. 1993. Disability Statistics, What We Count and What It Tells Us: A Personal and Political Analysis. *Journal of Disability Policy Studies,* 4:10–37.

WHAT IS RACE?

Who Is Black? One Nation's Definition

F. James Davis

In a taped interview conducted by a blind, black anthropologist, a black man nearly ninety years old said: "Now you must understand that this is just a name we have. I am not black and you are not black either, if you go by the evidence of your eyes. . . . Anyway, black people are all colors. White people don't look all the same way, but there are more different kinds of us than there are of them. Then too, there is a certain stage [at] which you cannot tell who is white and who is black. Many of the people I see who are thought of as black could just as well be white in their appearance. Many of the white people I see are black as far as I can tell by the way they look. Now, that's it for looks. Looks don't mean much. The things that makes us different is how we think. What we believe is important, the ways we look at life" (Gwaltney, 1980:96).

How does a person get defined as a black, both socially and legally, in the United States? What is the nation's rule for who is black, and how did it come to be? And so what? Don't we all know who is black, and isn't the most important issue what opportunities the group has? Let us start with some experiences of three well-known American blacks—actress and beauty pageant winner Vanessa Williams, U.S. Representative Adam Clayton Powell, Jr., and entertainer Lena Horne.

For three decades after the first Miss America Pageant in 1921, black women were barred from competing. The first black winner was Vanessa Williams of Millwood, New York, crowned Miss America in 1984. In the same year the first runner-up—Suzette Charles of Mays Landing, New Jersey—was also black. The viewing public was charmed by the television images and magazine pictures of the beautiful and musically talented Williams, but many people were also puzzled. Why was she being called black when she appeared to be white? Suzette Charles, whose ancestry appeared to be more European than African, at least looked like many of the "lighter blacks." Notoriety followed when Vanessa Williams resigned because of the impending publication of some nude photographs of her taken before the pageant, and Suzette Charles became Miss America for the balance of 1984. Beyond the troubling question of whether these young women could have won if they had looked "more black," the publicity dramatized the nation's definition of a black person.

Some blacks complained that the Rev. Adam Clayton Powell, Jr., was so light that he was a stranger in their midst. In the words of Roi Ottley, "He was white to all appearances, having blue eyes, an aquiline nose, and light, almost blond, hair" (1943:220), yet he became a bold, effective black leader—first as minister of the Abyssinian Baptist Church of Harlem, then as a New York city councilman, and finally as a U.S. congressman from the state of New York. Early in his activist career he led 6,000 blacks in a march on New York City Hall. He used his power in Congress to fight for civil rights legislation and other black causes. In 1966, in Washington, D.C., he convened the first black power conference.

In his autobiography, Powell recounts some experiences with racial classification in his youth that left a lasting impression on him. During Powell's freshman year at Colgate University, his roommate did not know that he was a black until his father, Adam Clayton Powell, Sr., was invited to give a chapel talk on Negro rights and problems, after which the roommate announced that because Adam was a Negro they could no longer be roommates or friends.

Another experience that affected Powell deeply occurred one summer during his Colgate years. He

---

F. James Davis is professor emeritus of sociology at Illinois State University.

was working as a bellhop at a summer resort in Manchester, Vermont, when Abraham Lincoln's aging son Robert was a guest there. Robert Lincoln disliked blacks so much that he refused to let them wait on him or touch his luggage, car, or any of his possessions. Blacks who did got their knuckles whacked with his cane. To the great amusement of the other bellhops, Lincoln took young Powell for a white man and accepted his services (Powell, 1971:31–33).

Lena Horne's parents were both very light in color and came from black upper-middle-class families in Brooklyn (Horne and Schickel, 1965; Buckley, 1986). Lena lived with her father's parents until she was about seven years old. Her grandfather was very light and blue-eyed. Her fair-skinned grandmother was the daughter of a slave woman and her white owner, from the family of John C. Calhoun, well-known defender of slavery. One of her father's great-grandmothers was a Blackfoot Indian, to whom Lena Horne has attributed her somewhat coppery skin color. One of her mother's grandmothers was a French-speaking black woman from Senegal and never a slave. Her mother's father was a "Portuguese Negro," and two women in his family had passed as white and become entertainers.

Lena Horne's parents had separated, and when she was seven her entertainer mother began placing her in a succession of homes in different states. Her favorite place was in the home of her Uncle Frank, her father's brother, a red-haired, blue-eyed teacher in a black school in Georgia. The black children in that community asked her why she was so light and called her a "yellow bastard." She learned that when satisfactory evidence of respectable black parents is lacking, being light-skinned implies illegitimacy and having an underclass white parent and is thus a disgrace in the black community. When her mother married a white Cuban, Lena also learned that blacks can be very hostile to the white spouse, especially when the "black" mate is very light. At this time she began to blame the confused color line for her childhood troubles. She later endured much hostility from blacks and whites alike when her own second marriage, to white composer-arranger

Lennie Hayton, was finally made public in 1950 after three years of keeping it secret.

Early in Lena Horne's career there were complaints that she did not fit the desired image of a black entertainer for white audiences, either physically or in her style. She sang white love songs, not the blues. Noting her brunette-white beauty, one white agent tried to get her to take a Spanish name, learn some Spanish songs, and pass as a Latin white, but she had learned to have a horror of passing and never considered it, although Hollywood blacks accused her of trying to pass after she played her first bit part in a film. After she failed her first screen test because she looked like a white girl trying to play black-face, the directors tried making her up with a shade called "Light Egyptian" to make her look darker. The whole procedure embarrassed and hurt her deeply. . . .

Other light mulatto entertainers have also had painful experiences because of their light skin and other caucasoid features. Starting an acting career is never easy, but actress Jane White's difficulties in the 1940s were compounded by her lightness. Her father was NAACP leader Walter White. Even with dark makeup on her ivory skin, she did not look like a black person on the stage, but she was not allowed to try out for white roles because blacks were barred from playing them. When she auditioned for the part of a young girl from India, the director was enthusiastic, although her skin color was too light, but higher management decreed that it was unthinkable for a Negro to play the part of an Asian Indian (White, 1948:338). Only after great perseverance did Jane White make her debut as the educated mulatto maid Nonnie in the stage version of Lillian Smith's *Strange Fruit* (1944). . . .

THE ONE-DROP RULE DEFINED

As the above cases illustrate, to be considered black in the United States not even half of one's ancestry must be African black. But will one-fourth do, or one-eighth, or less? The nation's answer to the question "Who is black?" has long been that a black is any person with *any* known African black ancestry

(Myrdal, 1944:113–18; Berry and Tischler, 1978:97–98; Williamson, 1980:1–2). This definition reflects the long experience with slavery and later with Jim Crow segregation. In the South it became known as the "one-drop rule," meaning that a single drop of "black blood" makes a person a black. It is also known as the "one black ancestor rule," some courts have called it the "traceable amount rule," and anthropologists call it the "hypo-descent rule," meaning that racially mixed persons are assigned the status of the subordinate group (Harris, 1964:56). This definition emerged from the American South to become the nation's definition, generally accepted by whites and blacks alike (Bahr, Chadwick, and Stauss, 1979:27–28). Blacks had no other choice. This American cultural definition of blacks is taken for granted as readily by judges, affirmative action officers, and black protesters as it is by Ku Klux Klansmen.

Let us not be confused by terminology. At present the usual statement of the one-drop rule is in terms of "black blood" or black ancestry, while not so long ago it referred to "Negro blood" or ancestry. The term "black" rapidly replaced "Negro" in general usage in the United States as the black power movement peaked at the end of the 1960s, but the black and Negro populations are the same. The term "black" is used [here] for persons with any black African lineage, not just for unmixed members of populations from sub-Saharan Africa. The term "Negro," which is used in certain historical contexts, means the same thing. Terms such as "African black," "unmixed Negro," and "all black" are used here to refer to unmixed blacks descended from African populations.

We must also pay attention to the terms "mulatto" and "colored." The term "mulatto" was originally used to mean the offspring of a "pure African Negro" and a "pure white." Although the root meaning of mulatto, in Spanish, is "hybrid," "mulatto" came to include the children of unions between whites and so-called "mixed Negroes." For example, Booker T. Washington and Frederick Douglass, with slave mothers and white fathers, were referred to as mulattoes (Bennett, 1962:255). To whatever extent their mothers were part white,

these men were more than half white. Douglass was evidently part Indian as well, and he looked it (Preston, 1980:9–10). Washington had reddish hair and gray eyes. At the time of the American Revolution, many of the founding fathers had some very light slaves, including some who appeared to be white. The term "colored" seemed for a time to refer only to mulattoes, especially lighter ones, but later it became a euphemism for darker Negroes, even including unmixed blacks. With widespread racial mixture, "Negro" came to mean any slave or descendant of a slave, no matter how much mixed. Eventually in the United States, the terms mulatto, colored, Negro, black, and African American all came to mean people with any known black African ancestry. Mulattoes are racially mixed, to whatever degree, while the terms black, Negro, African American, and colored include both mulattoes and unmixed blacks. These terms have quite different meanings in other countries.

Whites in the United States need some help envisioning the American black experience with ancestral fractions. At the beginning of miscegenation between two populations presumed to be racially pure, quadroons appear in the second generation of continuing mixing with whites, and octoroons in the third. A quadroon is one-fourth African black and thus easily classed as black in the United States, yet three of this person's four grandparents are white. An octoroon has seven white great-grandparents out of eight and usually looks white or almost so. Most parents of black American children in recent decades have themselves been racially mixed, but often the fractions get complicated because the earlier details of the mixing were obscured generations ago. Like so many white Americans, black people are forced to speculate about some of the fractions—one-eighth this, three-sixteenths that, and so on. . . .

PLESSY, PHIPPS, AND OTHER CHALLENGES IN THE COURTS

Homer Plessy was the plaintiff in the 1896 precedent-setting "separate-but-equal" case of

Plessy v. Ferguson (163 U.S. 537). This case challenged the Jim Crow statute that required racially segregated seating on trains in interstate commerce in the state of Louisiana. The U.S. Supreme Court quickly dispensed with Plessy's contention that because he was only one-eighth Negro and could pass as white he was entitled to ride in the seats reserved for whites. Without ruling directly on the definition of a Negro, the Supreme Court briefly took what is called "judicial notice" of what it assumed to be common knowledge: that a Negro or black is any person with any black ancestry. (Judges often take explicit "judicial notice" not only of scientific or scholarly conclusions, or of opinion surveys or other systematic investigations, but also of something they just assume to be so, including customary practices or common knowledge.) This has consistently been the ruling in the federal courts, and often when the black ancestry was even less than one-eighth. The federal courts have thus taken judicial notice of the customary boundary between two sociocultural groups that differ, on the average, in physical traits, not between two discrete genetic categories. In the absence of proof of a specific black ancestor, merely being known as a black in the community has usually been accepted by the courts as evidence of black ancestry. The separate-but-equal doctrine established in the Plessy case is no longer the law, as a result of the judicial and legislative successes of the civil rights movement, but the nation's legal definition of who is black remains unchanged.

State courts have generally upheld the one-drop rule. For instance, in a 1948 Mississippi case a young man, Davis Knight, was sentenced to five years in jail for violating the antimiscegenation statute. Less than one-sixteenth black, Knight said he was not aware that he had any black lineage, but the state proved his great-grandmother was a slave girl. In some states the operating definition of black has been limited by statute to particular fractions, yet the social definition—the one-drop rule—has generally prevailed in case of doubt. Mississippi, Missouri, and five other states have had the criterion of one-eighth. Virginia changed from one-fourth to one-eighth in 1910, then in 1930 forbade white intermarriage with a person with any black ancestry. Persons in Virginia who are one-fourth or more Indian and less than one-sixteenth African black are defined as Indians while on the reservation but as blacks when they leave (Berry, 1965:26). While some states have had general race classification statutes, at least for a time, others have legislated a definition of black only for particular purposes, such as marriage or education. In a few states there have even been varying definitions for different situations (Mangum, 1940:38–48). All states require a designation of race on birth certificates, but there are no clear guidelines to help physicians and midwives do the classifying.

Louisiana's latest race classification statute became highly controversial and was finally repealed in 1983 (Trillin, 1986:77). Until 1970, a Louisiana statute had embraced the one-drop rule, defining a Negro as anyone with a "trace of black ancestry." This law was challenged in court a number of times from the 1920s on, including an unsuccessful attempt in 1957 by boxer Ralph Dupas, who asked to be declared white so that a law banning "interracial sports" (since repealed) would not prevent him from boxing in the state. In 1970 a lawsuit was brought on behalf of a child whose ancestry was allegedly only one two-hundred-fifty-sixth black, and the legislature revised its law. The 1970 Louisiana statute defined a black as someone whose ancestry is more than one thirty-second black (La. Rev. Stat. 42:267). Adverse publicity about this law was widely disseminated during the Phipps trial in 1983 (discussed below), filed as *Jane Doe v. State of Louisiana*. This case was decided in a district court in May 1983, and in June the legislature abolished its one thirty-second statute and gave parents the right to designate the race of newborns, and even to change classifications on birth certificates if they can prove the child is white by a "preponderance of the evidence." However, the new statute in 1983 did not abolish the "traceable amount rule" (the one-drop rule), as demonstrated by the outcomes when the Phipps decision was appealed to higher courts in 1985 and 1986.

The history in the Phipps (Jane Doe) case goes as far back as 1770, when a French planter named Jean Gregoire Guillory took his wife's slave, Margarita, as his mistress (Model, 1983:3–4). More than two centuries and two decades later, their great-great-great-great-granddaughter, Susie Guillory Phipps, asked the Louisiana courts to change the classification on her deceased parents' birth certificates to "white" so she and her brothers and sisters could be designated white. They all looked white, and some were blue-eyed blonds. Mrs. Susie Phipps had been denied a passport because she had checked "white" on her application although her birth certificate designated her race as "colored." This designation was based on information supplied by a midwife, who presumably relied on the parents or on the family's status in the community. Mrs. Phipps claimed that this classification came as a shock, since she had always thought she was white, had lived as white, and had twice married as white. Some of her relatives, however, gave depositions saying they considered themselves "colored," and the lawyers for the state claimed to have proof that Mrs. Phipps is three thirty-seconds black (Trillin, 1986:62–63, 71–74). That was more than enough "blackness" for the district court in 1983 to declare her parents, and thus Mrs. Phipps and her siblings, to be legally black.

In October and again in December 1985, the state's Fourth Circuit Court of Appeals upheld the district court's decision, saying that no one can change the racial designation of his or her parents or anyone else's (479 So. 2d 369). Said the majority of the court in its opinion: "That appellants might today describe themselves as white does not prove error in a document which designates their parents as colored" (479 So. 2d 371). Of course, if the parents' designation as "colored" cannot be disturbed, their descendants must be defined as black by the "traceable amount rule." The court also concluded that the preponderance of the evidence clearly showed that the Guillory parents were "colored." Although noting expert testimony to the effect that the race of an individual cannot be determined with scientific accuracy, the court said the law of racial designation is not based on science, that "individual race designa-

tions are purely social and cultural perceptions and the evidence conclusively proves those subjective perspectives were correctly recorded at the time the appellants' birth certificates were recorded" (479 So. 2d 372). At the rehearing in December 1985, the appellate court also affirmed the necessity of designating race on birth certificates for public health, affirmative action, and other important public programs and held that equal protection of the law has not been denied so long as the designation is treated as confidential.

When this case was appealed to the Louisiana Supreme Court in 1986, that court declined to review the decision, saying only that the court "concurs in the denial for the reasons assigned by the court of appeals on rehearing" (485 So. 2d 60). In December 1986 the U.S. Supreme Court was equally brief in stating its reason for refusing to review the decision: "The appeal is dismissed for want of a substantial federal question" (107 Sup. Ct. Reporter, interim ed. 638). Thus, both the final court of appeals in Louisiana and the highest court of the United States saw no reason to disturb the application of the one-drop rule in the lawsuit brought by Susie Guillory Phipps and her siblings.

CENSUS ENUMERATION OF BLACKS

When the U.S. Bureau of the Census enumerates blacks (always counted as Negroes until 1980), it does not use a scientific definition, but rather the one accepted by the general public and by the courts. The Census Bureau counts what the nation wants counted. Although various operational instructions have been tried, the definition of black used by the Census Bureau has been the nation's cultural and legal definition: all persons with any known black ancestry. Other nations define and count blacks differently, so international comparisons of census data on blacks can be extremely misleading. For example, Latin American countries generally count as black only unmixed African blacks, those only slightly mixed, and the very poorest mulattoes. If they used the U.S. definition, they would count far more blacks than they do, and if

Americans used their definition, millions in the black community in the United States would be counted either as white or as "coloreds" of different descriptions, not as black.

Instructions to our census enumerators in 1840, 1850, and 1860 provided "mulatto" as a category but did not define the term. In 1870 and 1880, mulattoes were officially defined to include "quadroons, octoroons, and all persons having any perceptible trace of African blood." In 1890 enumerators were told to record the *exact* proportion of the "African blood," again relying on visibility. In 1900 the Census Bureau specified that "pure Negroes" be counted separately from mulattoes, the latter to mean "all persons with some trace of black blood." In 1920 the mulatto category was dropped, and black was defined to mean any person with any black ancestry, as it has been ever since.

In 1960 the practice of self-definition began, with the head of household indicating the race of its members. This did not seem to introduce any noticeable fluctuation in the number of blacks, thus indicating that black Americans generally apply the one-drop rule to themselves. One exception is that Spanish-speaking Americans who have black ancestry but were considered white, or some designation other than black, in their place of origin generally reject the one-drop rule if they can. American Indians with some black ancestry also generally try to avoid the rule, but those who leave the reservation are often treated as black. At any rate, the 1980 census count showed that self-designated blacks made up about 12 percent of the population of the United States.

No other ethnic population in the nation, including those with visibly non-caucasoid features, is defined and counted according to a one-drop rule. For example, persons whose ancestry is one-fourth or less American Indian are not generally defined as Indian unless they want to be, and they are considered assimilating Americans who may even be proud of having some Indian ancestry. The same implicit rule appears to apply to Japanese Americans, Filipinos, or other peoples from East Asian nations and also to Mexican Americans who have

Central American Indian ancestry, as a large majority do. For instance, a person whose ancestry is one-eighth Chinese is not defined as just Chinese, or East Asian, or a member of the mongoloid race. The United States certainly does not apply a one-drop rule to its white ethnic populations either, which include both national and religious groups. Ethnicity has often been confused with racial biology and not just in Nazi Germany. Americans do not insist that an American with a small fraction of Polish ancestry be classified as a Pole, or that someone with a single remote Greek ancestor be designated Greek, or that someone with any trace of Jewish lineage is a Jew and nothing else.

It is interesting that, in *The Passing of the Great Race* (1916), Madison Grant maintained that the one-drop rule should be applied not only to blacks but also to all the other ethnic groups he considered biologically inferior "races," such as Hindus, Asians in general, Jews, Italians, and other Southern and Eastern European peoples. Grant's book went through four editions, and he and others succeeded in getting Congress to pass the national origins quota laws of the early 1920s. This racist quota legislation sharply curtailed immigration from everywhere in the world except Northern and Western Europe and the Western Hemisphere, until it was repealed in 1965. Grant and other believers in the racial superiority of their own group have confused race with ethnicity. They consider miscegenation with any "inferior" people to be the ultimate danger to the survival of their own group and have often seen the one-drop rule as a crucial component in their line of defense. Americans in general, however, while finding other ways to discriminate against immigrant groups, have rejected the application of the drastic one-drop rule to all groups but blacks.

UNIQUENESS OF THE ONE-DROP RULE

Not only does the one-drop rule apply to no other group than American blacks, but apparently the rule is unique in that it is found only in the United States and not in any other nation in the world. In fact, definitions of who is black vary quite sharply from country to country, and for this reason people in other countries often express consternation about our definition. James Baldwin relates a revealing incident that occurred in 1956 at the Conference of Negro-African Writers and Artists held in Paris. The head of the delegation of writers and artists from the United States was John Davis. The French chairperson introduced Davis and then asked him why he considered himself Negro, since he certainly did not look like one. Baldwin wrote, "He *is* a Negro, of course, from the remarkable legal point of view which obtains in the United States, but more importantly, as he tried to make clear to his interlocutor, he was a Negro by choice and by depth of involvement—by experience, in fact" (1962:19).

The phenomenon known as "passing as white" is difficult to explain in other countries or to foreign students. Typical questions are: "Shouldn't Americans say that a person who is passing as white is white, or nearly all white, and has previously been passing as black?" or "To be consistent, shouldn't you say that someone who is one-eighth white is passing as black?" or "Why is there so much concern, since the so-called blacks who pass take so little negroid ancestry with them?" Those who ask such questions need to realize that "passing" is so much more a social phenomenon than a biological one, reflecting the nation's unique definition of what makes a person black. The concept of "passing" rests on the one-drop rule and on folk beliefs about race and miscegenation, not on biological or historical fact.

The black experience with passing as white in the United States contrasts with the experience of other ethnic minorities that have features that are clearly non-caucasoid. The concept of passing applies only to blacks—consistent with the nation's unique definition of the group. A person who is one-fourth or less American Indian or Korean or Filipino is not regarded as passing if he or she intermarries and joins fully the life of the dominant community, so the minority ancestry need not be hidden. It is often suggested that the key reason for this is that the physical differences between these other groups and whites are less pronounced than the physical differences between African blacks and whites, and therefore are less threatening to whites. However, keep in mind that the one-drop rule and anxiety about passing originated during slavery and later received powerful reinforcement under the Jim Crow system.

For the physically visible groups other than blacks, miscegenation promotes assimilation, despite barriers of prejudice and discrimination during two or more generations of racial mixing. As noted above, when ancestry in one of these racial minority groups does not exceed one-fourth, a person is not defined solely as a member of that group. Masses of white European immigrants have climbed the class ladder not only through education but also with the help of close personal relationships in the dominant community, intermarriage, and ultimately full cultural and social assimilation. Young people tend to marry people they meet in the same informal social circles (Gordon, 1964:70–81). For visibly non-caucasoid minorities other than blacks in the United States, this entire route to full assimilation is slow but possible.

For all persons of any known black lineage, however, assimilation is blocked and is not promoted by miscegenation. Barriers to full opportunity and participation for blacks are still formidable, and a fractionally black person cannot escape these obstacles without passing as white and cutting off all ties to the black family and community. The pain of this separation, and condemnation by the black family and community, are major reasons why many or most of those who could pass as white choose not to. Loss of security within the minority community, and fear and distrust of the white world are also factors.

It should now be apparent that the definition of a black person as one with any trace at all of black African ancestry is inextricably woven into the history of the United States. It incorporates beliefs once used to justify slavery and later used to buttress the castelike Jim Crow system of segregation. Developed in the South, the definition of "Negro" (now black) spread and became the nation's social and legal definition. Because blacks are defined according to the one-drop rule, they are a socially constructed category in which there is wide variation in racial traits and therefore not a race group in the scientific sense. However, because that category has a definite status position in the society it has become a self-conscious social group with an ethnic identity.

The one-drop rule has long been taken for granted throughout the United States by whites and blacks alike, and the federal courts have taken "judicial notice" of it as being a matter of common knowledge. State courts have generally upheld the one-drop rule, but some have limited the definition to one thirty-second or one-sixteenth or one-eighth black ancestry, or made other limited exceptions for persons with both Indian and black ancestry. Most Americans seem unaware that this definition of blacks is extremely unusual in other countries, perhaps even unique to the United States, and that Americans define no other minority group in a similar way. . . .

DISCUSSION QUESTIONS

1. Is black a color category or a status?
2. Do you think passing still occurs?

REFERENCES

Bahr, Howard M., Bruce A. Chadwick, and Joseph H. Stauss. 1979. *American Ethnicity.* Lexington, MA: D.C. Heath & Co.

Baldwin, James. 1962. *Nobody Knows My Name.* New York: Dell Publishing Co.

Bennett, Lerone, Jr. 1962. *Before the Mayflower: A History of the Negro in America 1619–1962.* Chicago: Johnson Publishing Co.

Berry, Brewton. 1965. *Race and Ethnic Relations.* 3rd ed. Boston: Houghton Mifflin Co.

Berry, Brewton, and Henry L. Tischler. 1978. *Race and Ethnic Relations.* 4th ed. Boston: Houghton Mifflin Co.

Buckley, Gail Lumet. 1986. *The Hornes: An American Family.* New York: Alfred A. Knopf.

Gordon, Milton M. 1964. *Assimilation in American Life.* New York: Oxford University Press.

Grant, Madison. 1916. *The Passing of the Great Race.* New York: Scribner.

Gwaltney, John Langston. 1980. *Drylongso: A Self-Portrait of Black America.* New York: Vintage Books.

Harris, Melvin. 1964. *Patterns of Race in the Americas.* New York: W. W. Norton.

Horne, Lena, and Richard Schickel. 1965. *Lena.* Garden City, NY: Doubleday & Co.

Mangum, Charles Staples, Jr. 1940. *The Legal Status of the Negro in the United States.* Chapel Hill: University of North Carolina Press.

Model, F. Peter, ed. 1983. "Apartheid in the Bayou." *Perspectives: The Civil Rights Quarterly* 15 (Winter– Spring), 3–4.

Myrdal, Gunnar, assisted by Richard Sterner and Arnold M. Rose. 1944. *An American Dilemma.* New York: Harper & Bros.

Ottley, Roi. 1943. *New World A-Coming.* Cleveland: World Publishing Co.

Powell, Adam Clayton, Jr. 1971. *Adam by Adam: The Autobiography of Adam Clayton Powell, Jr.* New York: Dial Press.

Preston, Dickson J. 1980. *Young Frederick Douglass: the Maryland Years.* Baltimore: Johns Hopkins University Press.

Trillin, Calvin. 1986. "American Chronicles: Black or White." *New Yorker,* April 14, 1986, pp. 62–78.

White, Walter. 1948. *A Man Called White: The Autobiography of Walter White.* New York: Viking Press.

Williamson, Joel. 1980. *New People: Miscegenation and Mulattoes in the United States.* New York: The Free Press.

The Evolution of Identity

Decade to decade, the U.S. census has changed its classifications of race and ethnicity. Partially, this reflects the growing diversity of the country. It also reveals the nation's evolving politics and social mores. When the first census was taken in 1790, enumerators classified free residents as white or "other"; while slaves were counted separately. By 1860, residents were classified as white, black or mulatto. Hispanic origin first became a category in 1970. Here are the categories used in the decennial counts from 1860 to 2000, as presented by AmeriStat (www.ameristat.org).

1860	1870	1880	1890¹	1900²	1910	1920	1930	1940	1950	1960	1970	1980	1990	2000
White	White	White	White	White	White	White	White	White	White	White	White	White	White	White
Black	Black	Black	Black	Black (Negro descent)	Black	Black	Black	Black	Negro	Negro	Negro or Black	Black or Negro	Black or Negro	Black, African American or Negro
Mulatto	Mulatto	Mulatto	Mulatto		Mulatto	Mulatto								
	Chinese	Chinese	Chinese	Chinese	Chinese	Chinese	Chinese	Chinese	Chinese	Chinese	Chinese	Chinese	Chinese	Chinese
	Indian	Indian	Indian	Indian	Indian	Indian	Indian	Indian	Amer. Indian	Amer. Indian	Indian (Amer.)	Indian	Indian (Amer.)	Amer. Indian or Alaska Native
			Quadroon											
			Octoroon											
			Japanese	Japanese	Japanese	Japanese	Japanese	Japanese	Japanese	Japanese	Japanese	Japanese	Japanese	Japanese
						Filipino	Filipino	Filipino	Filipino	Filipino	Filipino	Filipino	Filipino	Filipino
						Hindu	Hindu	Hindu						
						Korean	Korean	Korean			Korean	Korean	Korean	Korean
												Asian Indian	Asian Indian	Asian Indian
							Mexican							
										Aleut		Aleut	Aleut	
										Eskimo		Eskimo	Eskimo	
										Hawaiian	Hawaiian	Hawaiian	Hawaiian	Native Hawaiian
										Part Hawaiian				
												Vietnamese	Vietnamese	Vietnamese
												Guamanian	Guamanian	Guamanian or Chamorro
												Samoan	Samoan	Samoan
													Other Asian Pacific Islander	**Other Asian** / **Other Pacific Islander**
					Other	Other	Other	Other	Other	Other	Other	Other	Other race	Some other race

ETHNICITY

											1970	1980	1990	2000
											Mexican	Mexican, Mexican Amer.	Mexican, Mexican Amer.	Mexican, Mexican Amer.
											Puerto Rican Central/So. American	**Chicano** Puerto Rican	Chicano Puerto Rican	Chicano Puerto Rican
											Cuban Other Spanish (None of these)	Cuban Other Spanish/ Hispanic Not Spanish/ Hispanic	Cuban Other Spanish/ Hispanic Not Spanish/ Hispanic	Cuban Other Spanish/ Hispanic/Latino Not Spanish/ Hispanic/Latino

1 In 1890, mulatto was defined as a person who was three-eighths to five-eighths black. A quadroon was one-quarter black and an octoroon one-eighth black.

2 American Indians have been asked to specify their tribe since the 1900 Census.

Bold letters indicate first usage since 1860.

NOTE: Before the 1970 Census, enumerators wrote in the race of individuals using the designated categories. In subsequent censuses, respondents or enumerators filled in circles next to the categories with which the respondent identified. Also beginning with the 1970 Census, people choosing American Indian, other Asian, other race, or for the Hispanic question, other Hispanic categories, were asked to write in a specific tribe or group. Hispanic ethnicity was asked of a sample of Americans in 1970 and all Americans beginning with the 1980 Census.

Sources: AmeriStat, "200 Years of U.S. Census Taking: Population and Housing Questions 1790–1990," U.S. Census Bureau. FROM: *The Washington Post*, Federal Page, August 13, 2001.

Census 2000: Seventeen Questions from the Long Form

Person 1

Your answers are important! Every person in the Census counts.

1 **What is this person's name?** *Print the name of Person 1 from page 2.*

Last Name

First Name   MI

2 **What is this person's telephone number?** *We may contact this person if we don't understand an answer.*

Area Code + Number

3 **What is this person's sex?** *Mark ⊠ ONE box.*

☐ Male
☐ Female

4 **What is this person's age and what is this person's date of birth?**

Age on April 1, 2000

Print numbers in boxes.

Month   Day   Year of birth

➡ NOTE: Please answer BOTH Questions 5 and 6.

5 **Is this person Spanish/Hispanic/Latino?** *Mark ⊠ the "No" box if not Spanish/Hispanic/Latino.*

☐ **No**, not Spanish/Hispanic/Latino
☐ Yes, Mexican, Mexican Am., Chicano
☐ Yes, Puerto Rican
☐ Yes, Cuban
☐ Yes, other Spanish/Hispanic/Latino — *Print group.*

6 **What is this person's race?** *Mark ⊠ one or more races* to indicate what this person considers himself/herself to be.

☐ White
☐ Black, African Am., or Negro
☐ American Indian or Alaska Native — *Print name of enrolled or principal tribe.*

☐ Asian Indian   ☐ Native Hawaiian
☐ Chinese   ☐ Guamanian or Chamorro
☐ Filipino
☐ Japanese   ☐ Samoan
☐ Korean   ☐ Other Pacific Islander —
☐ Vietnamese   *Print race.*
☐ Other Asian — *Print race.*

☐ Some other race — *Print race.*

7 **What is this person's marital status?**

☐ Now married
☐ Widowed
☐ Divorced
☐ Separated
☐ Never married

8 **a. At any time since February 1, 2000, has this person attended regular school or college?** *Include only nursery school or preschool, kindergarten, elementary school, and schooling which leads to a high school diploma or a college degree.*

☐ No, has not attended since February 1 → *Skip to 9*
☐ Yes, public school, public college
☐ Yes, private school, private college

☞ Question is asked of all persons on the short (100-percent) and long (sample) forms.

2043

Form D-61B

46

Person 1 (continued)

8 **b. What grade or level was this person attending?**
Mark ☒ ONE box.

☐ Nursery school, preschool
☐ Kindergarten
☐ Grade 1 to grade 4
☐ Grade 5 to grade 8
☐ Grade 9 to grade 12
☐ College undergraduate years (freshman to senior)
☐ Graduate or professional school *(for example: medical, dental, or law school)*

9 **What is the highest degree or level of school this person has COMPLETED?** *Mark ☒ ONE box.*
If currently enrolled, mark the previous grade or highest degree received.

☐ No schooling completed
☐ Nursery school to 4th grade
☐ 5th grade or 6th grade
☐ 7th grade or 8th grade
☐ 9th grade
☐ 10th grade
☐ 11th grade
☐ 12th grade, **NO DIPLOMA**
☐ **HIGH SCHOOL GRADUATE** — high school DIPLOMA or the equivalent *(for example: GED)*
☐ Some college credit, but less than 1 year
☐ 1 or more years of college, no degree
☐ Associate degree *(for example: AA, AS)*
☐ Bachelor's degree *(for example: BA, AB, BS)*
☐ Master's degree *(for example: MA, MS, MEng, MEd, MSW, MBA)*
☐ Professional degree *(for example: MD, DDS, DVM, LLB, JD)*
☐ Doctorate degree *(for example: PhD, EdD)*

10 **What is this person's ancestry or ethnic origin?**

(For example: Italian, Jamaican, African Am., Cambodian, Cape Verdean, Norwegian, Dominican, French Canadian, Haitian, Korean, Lebanese, Polish, Nigerian, Mexican, Taiwanese, Ukrainian, and so on.)

11 **a. Does this person speak a language other than English at home?**

☐ Yes
☐ No → *Skip to 12*

b. What is this language?

(For example: Korean, Italian, Spanish, Vietnamese)

c. How well does this person speak English?

☐ Very well
☐ Well
☐ Not well
☐ Not at all

12 **Where was this person born?**

☐ In the United States — *Print name of state.*

☐ Outside the United States — *Print name of foreign country, or Puerto Rico, Guam, etc.*

13 **Is this person a CITIZEN of the United States?**

☐ Yes, born in the United States → *Skip to 15a*
☐ Yes, born in Puerto Rico, Guam, the U.S. Virgin Islands, or Northern Marianas
☐ Yes, born abroad of American parent or parents
☐ Yes, a U.S. citizen by naturalization
☐ No, not a citizen of the United States

14 **When did this person come to live in the United States?** *Print numbers in boxes.*
Year

15 **a. Did this person live in this house or apartment 5 years ago (on April 1, 1995)?**

☐ Person is under 5 years old → *Skip to 33*
☐ Yes, this house → *Skip to 16*
☐ No, outside the United States — *Print name of foreign country, or Puerto Rico, Guam, etc., below; then skip to 16.*

☐ No, different house in the United States

Person 1 (continued)

15 **b. Where did this person live 5 years ago?**

Name of city, town, or post office

Did this person live inside the limits of the city or town?

☐ Yes
☐ No, outside the city/town limits

Name of county

Name of state

ZIP Code

16 **Does this person have any of the following long-lasting conditions:**

	Yes	No
a. Blindness, deafness, or a severe vision or hearing impairment?	☐	☐
b. A condition that substantially limits one or more basic physical activities such as walking, climbing stairs, reaching, lifting, or carrying?	☐	☐

17 **Because of a physical, mental, or emotional condition lasting 6 months or more, does this person have any difficulty in doing any of the following activities:**

	Yes	No
a. Learning, remembering, or concentrating?	☐	☐
b. Dressing, bathing, or getting around inside the home?	☐	☐
c. (Answer if this person is 16 YEARS OLD OR OVER.) Going outside the home alone to shop or visit a doctor's office?	☐	☐
d. (Answer if this person is 16 YEARS OLD OR OVER.) Working at a job or business?	☐	☐

DISCUSSION QUESTIONS READING 2

1. What assumptions are made about American society when there are only three racial categories?
2. Did "the other" become a larger or smaller category over time?
3. What is the impact of immigration on the creation of new categories?

DISCUSSION QUESTIONS READING 3

1. How might the government use social characteristics data?
2. What does census data tell us about America's changing demographics?

Real Indians: Identity and the Survival of Native America

Eva Marie Garroutte

The most common tribal requirement for determining citizenship concerns "blood quantum," or degree of Indian ancestry. . . . About two-thirds of all federally recognized tribes of the coterminous United States specify a minimum blood quantum in their legal citizenship criteria, with one-quarter blood degree being the most frequent minimum requirement.[1] (In the simplest instance, an individual has a one-quarter blood quantum if any one of her four grandparents is of exclusively Indian ancestry and the other three are non-Indian.) The remaining one-third of Indian tribes specify *no* minimum blood quantum. They often simply require that any new enrollee be a lineal (direct) descendant of another tribal member. . . .

Legal definitions of tribal membership regulate the rights to vote in tribal elections, to hold tribal office, and generally to participate in the political, and sometimes also the cultural, life of the tribe. One's ability to satisfy legal definitions of identification may also determine one's right to share in certain tribal revenues (such as income generated by tribally controlled businesses). Perhaps most significantly, it may determine the right to live on a reservation or to inherit land interests there.

The tribes' power to determine citizenship allows them to delimit the distribution of certain important resources, such as reservation land, tribal monies, and political privileges. But this is hardly the end of the story of legal definitions of identity. The federal government has many purposes for which it, too, must distinguish Indians from non-Indians, and it uses its own, separate legal definition for doing so. More precisely, it uses a whole array of legal definitions. Since the U.S. Constitution uses the word "Indian" in two places but defines it nowhere, Congress has made its own definitions on an ad hoc basis.[2] A 1978 congressional survey discovered no less than *thirty-three* separate definitions of Indians in use in different pieces of federal legislation.[3] These may or may not correspond with those any given tribe uses to determine its citizenship.

Most federal legal definitions of Indian identity specify a minimum blood quantum—frequently one-quarter but sometimes one-half—but others do not. Some require or accept tribal citizenship as a criterion of federal identification, and others do not. Some require reservation residency, or ownership of land held in trust by the government, and others do not. Other laws affecting Indians specify *no* definition of identity, such that the courts must determine to whom the laws apply.[4] Because of these wide variations in legal identity definitions and their frequent departure from the various tribal ones, many individuals who are recognized by their tribes as citizens are nevertheless considered non-Indian for some or all federal purposes. The converse can be true as well.[5]

There are a variety of contexts in which one or more federal legal definitions of identity become important. The matter of economic resource distribution—access to various social services, monetary awards, and opportunities—probably comes immediately to the minds of many readers. The legal situation of Indian people, and its attendant opportunities and responsibilities, are the result of historic negotiations between tribes and the federal government. In these, the government agreed to compensate tribes in various ways for the large amounts of land and other resources that the tribes had surrendered, often by force.[6] Benefits available to those who can satisfy federal definitions of Indian identity are administered through a variety of agencies, including the Bureau of Indian Affairs, the Indian Health Service, the Department of Agriculture, the Office of Elementary and Secondary Education, and the Department of Labor, to name a few.[7]

Eva Marie Garroutte is a professor of Sociology at Boston College.

Legal definitions also affect specific economic rights deriving from treaties or agreements that some (not all) tribes made with the federal government. These may include such rights as the use of particular geographic areas for hunting, harvesting, fishing, or trapping. Those legally defined as Indians are also sometimes exempted from certain requirements related to state licensure and state (but not federal) income and property taxation.[8] . . .

"IF HE GETS A NOSEBLEED, HE'LL TURN INTO A WHITE MAN"

North American Indians who successfully negotiate the rigors of legal definitions of identity at the federal level can achieve what some consider the dubious distinction of being a "card-carrying Indian." That is, their federal government can issue them a laminated document (in the United States, a CDIB; in Canada an Indian status card) that certifies them as possessing a certain "degree of Indian blood."

. . . Canadian-born country music singer Shania Twain has what it takes to be a card-carrying Indian: she is formally recognized as an Anishnabe (Ojibwe) Indian with band membership in the Temagami Bear Island First Nation (Ontario, Canada). More specifically, she is legally on record as possessing one-half degree Indian blood. Given this information, one might conclude that Twain's identity as an Indian person is more or less unassailable. It's not.

Controversy has engulfed this celebrity because of an anonymous phone call to a Canadian newspaper a few years ago that led to the disclosure of another name by which Shania was once known: Eileen Regina Edwards. Eileen/Shania was adopted by a stepfather in early childhood and took the surname of Twain at that time. So far well and good— except for one thing. Both sides of her *biological* family describe themselves not as Indian but as white. It is only Jerry Twain, her late stepfather, who was Indian.

As the adopted child of an Anishnabe man, Shania Twain occupies an unusual status. Though the U.S. government allows for the assignment of blood quantum only to biological descendants of Indian people, Canada allows for the naturalization of non-Native children through adoption.[9] Although Twain has stated that her white mother (now deceased) had told her, in childhood, that her biological father (also deceased) had some Indian heritage, his family denies the suggestion entirely. They say they are French and Irish. Ms. Twain explains: "I don't know how much Indian blood I actually have in me, but as the adopted daughter of my father Jerry, I became legally registered as 50-percent North American Indian. Being raised by a full-blooded Indian and being part of his family and their culture from such a young age is all I've ever known. That heritage is in my heart and my soul, and I'm proud of it."[10]

Twain has been sharply criticized, in both the United States and Canada, for not making the full details of her racial background clearer, especially to awards-granting agencies such as the First Americans in the Arts (FAITA), which honored her in February 1996 as a Native performer. FAITA itself has made no such complaint. The group states that it is satisfied that "Ms. Twain has not intentionally misrepresented herself." And more importantly, her adopted family defends her. An aunt observes: "She was raised by us. She was accepted by our band. If my brother were alive, he'd be very upset. He raised her as his own daughter. My parents, her grandparents, took her into the bush and taught her the [Native] traditions."[11]

Twain's case shows with uncommon clarity that legal and biological definitions are conceptually distinct. . . .

In their modern American construction, at least, biological definitions of identity assume the centrality of an individual's genetic relationship to other tribal members. Not just any degree of relationship will do, however. Typically, the degree of closeness is also important. And this is the starting point for much of the controversy that swirls around issues of biological Indianness. . . .

Sociologist Eugeen Roosens summarizes such common conceptions about the importance of blood quantum for determining Indian identity:

There is . . . [a] principle about which the whites and the Indians are in agreement. . . . People with more Indian blood . . . also have more rights to inherit what their ancestors, the former Indians, have left behind. In addition, full blood Indians are more authentic than half-breeds. By *being* pure, they have more right to respect. They *are,* in all aspects of their being, more *integral.*[12]

Biological ancestry can take on such tremendous significance in tribal contexts that it overwhelms all other considerations of identity, especially when it is constructed as "pure." As Cherokee legal scholar G. William Rice points out, "Most [people] would recognize the full-blood Indian who was enrolled in a federally recognized tribe as an Indian, even if the individual was adopted at birth by a non-Indian family and had never set foot in Indian country nor met another Indian."[13] Mixed-race individuals, by contrast, find their identity claims considerably complicated. Even if such an individual can demonstrate conclusively that he has *some* Native ancestry, the question will still be raised: Is the *amount* of ancestry he possesses "enough"? Is his "Indian blood" sufficient to distinguish him from the mixed-blood individual spotlighted by an old quip: "If he got a nosebleed, he'd turn into a white man"?

Members of various tribes complain of factionalism between these two major groups—full bloods and mixed bloods—and they suggest that the division arose historically because of mixed bloods' greater access to the social resources of the dominant society and their enhanced ability to impose values and ideas upon others.[14] As Julie M., a citizen of the United Keetowah Band of Cherokee Indians, says: "For the Cherokee people, there's been this mixed blood/full blood kind of dynamic going from before the removal [in 1838, also known as the Trail of Tears]. . . . It's kind of like us-and-them. . . . It's almost been like a *war* in some cases. . . . It's a 'who's-really-going-to-be-in-control-of-the-tribe?' kind of thing." Many historians have similarly found it logical that political allegiances would tend to shift for those Indian people who formed alliances, through intermarriage, with members of the dominant society, and

that this has made the division between full bloods and mixed bloods politically important.[15]

Modern biological definitions of identity, however, are much more complicated than this historical explanation can account for. This complexity did not originate in the ideas and experiences of Indian tribes. Instead, they closely reflect nineteenth- and early-twentieth-century theories of race introduced by Euro-Americans. These theories (of which there were a great many) viewed biology as definitive, but they did not distinguish it from culture. Thus, blood became quite literally the vehicle for the transmission of cultural characteristics. "'Half-breeds' by this logic could be expected to behave in 'half-civilized,' i.e., partially assimilated, ways while retaining one half of their traditional culture, accounting for their marginal status in both societies."[16]

These turn-of-the-century theories of race found a very precise way to talk about *amount* of ancestry in the idea of blood quantum, or degree of blood. The notion of blood quantum as a standard of Indianness emerged with force in the nineteenth century. Its most significant early usage as a standard of identification was in the General Allotment (Dawes) Act of 1887, which led to the creation of the Dawes Rolls [the "base roll" or written record of tribal membership in a specific year]. It has been part of the popular—and legal and academic—lore about Indians ever since.

Given this standard of identification, full bloods tend to be seen as the "really real," the quintessential Indians, while others are viewed as Indians in diminishing degrees. The original, stated intention of blood quantum distinctions was to determine the point at which the various responsibilities of the dominant society to Indian peoples ended. The ultimate and explicit federal intention was to use the blood quantum standard as a means to liquidate tribal lands and to eliminate government trust responsibility to tribes, along with entitlement programs, treaty rights, and reservations. Through intermarriage and application of a biological definition of identity Indians would eventually become citizens indistinguishable from all other citizens.[17]

Degree of blood is calculated, with reference to biological definitions, on the basis of the immediacy of one's genetic relationship to those whose bloodlines are (supposedly) unmixed. As in the case with legal definitions, the initial calculation for most tribes' biological definitions begins with a base roll, a listing of tribal membership and blood quanta in some particular year. These base rolls make possible very elaborate definitions of identity. For instance, they allow one to reckon that the offspring of, say, a full-blood Navajo mother and a white father is one-half Navajo. If that half-Navajo child, in turn, produces children with a Hopi person of one-quarter blood degree, those progeny will be judged one-quarter Navajo and one-eighth Hopi. Alternatively, they can be said to have three-eighths general Indian blood.

As even this rather simple example shows, over time such calculations can become infinitesimally precise, with people's ancestry being parsed into so many thirty-seconds, sixty-fourths, one-hundred-twenty-eighths, and so on.…

For those of us who have grown up and lived with the peculiar precision of calculating blood quantum, it sometimes requires a perspective less influenced by the vagaries of American history to remind us just how far from common sense the concepts underlying biological definitions of identity are. I recall responding to an inquiry from a Southeast Asian friend about what blood quantum was and how it was calculated. In mid-explanation, I noticed his expression of complete amazement. "That's the dumbest thing I ever heard," he burst out. "Who ever thought of *that?*"

The logic that underlies the biological definition of racial identity becomes even more curious and complicated when one considers the striking difference in the way that American definitions assign individuals to the racial category of "Indian," as opposed to the racial category "black." As a variety of researchers have observed, social attributions of black identity have focused (at least since the end of the Civil War) on the "one-drop rule," or rule of hypodescent.[18] …

Far from being held to a one-drop rule, Indians are generally required—both by law and by popular opinion—to establish rather *high* blood quanta in order for their claims to racial identity to be accepted as meaningful, the individual's own opinion notwithstanding. Although people must have only the slightest trace of "black blood" to be *forced* into the category "African American," modern American Indians must (1) formally produce (2) strong evidence of (3) often rather substantial amounts of "Indian blood" to be *allowed* entry into the corresponding racial category. The regnant biological definitions applied to Indians are simply quite different than those that have applied (and continue to apply) to blacks. Modern Americans, as Native American Studies professor Jack Forbes (Powhatan/Lenape/Saponi) puts the matter, "are *always finding 'blacks'* (even if they look rather un-African), and … *are always losing 'Indians.'*"[19]

BIOLOGICAL DEFINITIONS: CONTEXTS AND CONSEQUENCES

Biological definitions of Indian identity operate, in short, in some curious and inconsistent ways. They are nevertheless significant in a variety of contexts. And they have clear relationships, both direct and indirect, to legal definitions. The federal government has historically used a minimum blood quantum standard to determine who was eligible to receive treaty rights, or to sell property and manage his or her own financial affairs.[20] Blood quantum is *one* of the criteria that determines eligibility for citizenship in many tribes; it therefore indirectly influences the claimant's relationship to the same kinds of rights, privileges, and responsibilities that legal definitions allow.[21]

But biological definitions of identity affect personal interactions as well as governmental decisions. Indian people with high blood quanta frequently have recognizable physical characteristics. As Cherokee Nation principal tribal chief Chad Smith observes, some people are easily recognizable as Indians because they pass "a brown paper bag test," meaning that their skin is "darker than a #10 paper sack." It is these individuals who are often most closely associated with negative racial stereotypes in the larger society. Native American Studies professor Devon Mihesuah makes a point about Indian women that is really applicable to either gender: "Appearance is the most visible aspect of one's race; it determines how Indian women define themselves and how others define and treat them. Their appearance, whether Caucasian, Indian, African, or mixed, either limits or broadens Indian women's choices of ethnic identity and ability to interact with non-Indians and other Indians."[22]

Every day, identifiably Indian people are turned away from restaurants, refused the use of public rest rooms, ranked as unintelligent by the education system, and categorized by the personnel of medical, social service, and other vital public agencies as "problems"—all strictly on the basis of their appearance. As Keetoowah Band Cherokee full-blood Donald G. notes, a recognizably Indian appearance can be a serious detriment to one's professional and personal aspirations: "It seems the darker you are, the less important you are, in some ways, to the employer. . . . To some, it would be discouraging. But I am four-fourths [i.e., full-blood] Cherokee, and it doesn't matter what someone says about me. . . . I feel for the person who doesn't like my skin color, you know?"

There are circumstances, however, in which it is difficult for the victims of negative racial stereotyping to maintain an attitude as philosophical as this. In one interview, a Mohawk friend, June L., illustrated the potential consequences of public judgments based on skin color. She reminded me of a terrifying episode that had once unfolded while I was visiting at her house. Our conversation was interrupted by a phone call informing this mother of five that her college-student son, who had spent the summer day working on a roof, had suddenly become ill while driving home. Feeling faint, he had pulled up to a local convenience store and made his way inside, asking for a drink of water. The clerk refused. Dangerously dehydrated, the young man collapsed on the floor from sunstroke. "The worst thing about it," June recalled, "was that I have to keep wondering: What was the reason for that? Did that clerk refuse to help my son because she was just a mean person? Or was it because she saw him stumble into the store and thought, 'Well, it's just some

drunken Indian'?" Anxiety about social judgments of this kind are a fact of daily life for parents of children whose physical appearance makes their Indian ancestry clearly evident.

At the same time, June's remarks showed the opposite side to the coin of physical appearance. In some contexts, not conforming to the usual notions of "what Indians look like" can also be a liability:

> My aunt was assistant dean at a large Ivy League university. One day she called me on the phone. She had one scholarship to give out to an Indian student. One of the students being considered was blonde-haired and blue-eyed. The other one was black-haired and dark-skinned, and she looked Indian. The blonde girl's grades were a little better. My aunt didn't know what to do. She said to me, "Both these girls are tribal members. Both of them are qualified [for the scholarship]. They're sitting outside my office. What would *you* do?" I told her that, as an Indian person, there was only one thing I *could* say. Which was to give the money to the one with the dark skin. As Indian people, we *do* want to have Indian people that *look* like they're Indian to represent us.

Readers may be surprised by such a candid statement. But June's pragmatic reasoning takes account of certain historical realities. As she explained further, "We like people to *know* who's doing those accomplishments, like getting scholarships. We want them to know this is an Indian person doing this. Because I come from a background where if you looked Indian, you were put in special education because the schools said you couldn't learn. And it wasn't true. We need Indian people today who look Indian to show everyone the things we can do."

A physical appearance that is judged insufficiently "Indian" can also act as a barrier to participation in certain cultural activities. Bill T., a Wichita and Seneca minister in his midfifties, recalls that, in his youth, he witnessed light-skinned individuals who attempted to participate in powwow dances being evicted from the arena. "That kind of thing is still happening today," he added sadly, and other respondents readily confirmed this observation. A more unusual instance of the relevance of physical appearance to cultural participation was volunteered by Frank D., a Hopi respondent. His tribe's ceremonial dances feature the appearance of powerful spirit beings called kachinas, which are embodied by masked Hopi men. Ideally, the everyday, human identity of the dancers remains unknown to observers. Frank commented on the subject of tribal members whose skin tone is noticeably either lighter or darker than the norm:

> **Frank D.:** Say, for instance, if a Hopi marries a black person . . . [and] you get a male child . . . it's gonna be darker skinned. It might even be black. A black kachina just wouldn't fit out here [at Hopi]. You see, everybody'd know who it is. He'd be very visible [in the ceremonial dances]. . . . It'd be very hard on that individual. Kids don't work the other way, too—if they're real light. . . . Kachinas gotta be *brown.*
> **Author:** So there are certain ceremonial roles that people could not fill because of their appearance?
> **Frank D.:** Well, they *could,* but it would be awful tough. A lot of these [ceremonial] things are done with secrecy. No one knows who the kachinas are. Or at least, the kids don't. And then, say you get somebody who really stands out, then everybody knows who that [dancer] is, and it's not good. For the ceremony—because everybody knows who that person is. And so the kids will start asking questions—"How come that kachina's so dark, so black?" or "How come that kachina's white?" They start asking questions and it's really hard. So I think, if you're thinking about kids, it's really better if kachinas are brown.

Finally, the physical appearance borne by mixed bloods may not only create barriers to tribal cultural participation; it may also offer an occasion for outrightly shaming them. Cornelia S. remembers her days at the Eufala Indian School:

> You *had* to be Indian to be [allowed admission] there. . . . But . . . if [certain students] . . . didn't look as Indian as we did, or if they looked like they were white, they were kind of looked down upon, like treated differently because [people would say] "oh, that's just a white person." . . . They just [would] tease 'em and stuff. Say "oh, whatcha doin' white boy" or "white girl"—just stuff like that.

Nor is the social disapproval of light-skinned mixed bloods strictly the stuff of schoolyard teasing. The same respondent added that even adults confront questions of blood quantum with dead seriousness:

> Us Indians, whenever we see someone else who is saying that they're Indian . . . or trying to be around us Indians, and act like us, and they don't look like they're Indian and we know that they're not as much Indian as *we* are, yeah, we look at them like they're not Indian and, ya know, don't really like why they're acting like that. . . . But you know, I'm not *that* far off . . . into judging other people and what color [they are].

The late author Michael Dorris, a member of the Modoc tribe (California), has written that humiliations related to his appearance were part of his daily experience. He describes (in his account of his family's struggle with his son's fetal alcohol syndrome, *The Broken Cord*) an encounter with a hospital admissions staff, to whom he had just identified himself and his son as Indians. "They surveyed my appearance with curiosity. It was an expression I recognized, a reaction, familiar to most people of mixed-blood ancestry, that said, 'You don't *look* like an Indian.' No matter how often it happened, no matter how frequently I was blamed by strangers for not resembling their image of some Hollywood Sitting Bull, I was still defensive and vulnerable. 'I'm part Indian,' I explained."[23]

Even his tragic death has not safeguarded Dorris from insinuations about inadequate blood quantum. Shortly after his 1997 suicide, a story on his life and death in *New York* magazine reported that the author's fair complexion had always caused some observers to wonder about his racial identity and archly repeated a rumor: "It is said he . . . [eventually] discovered tanning booths."[24]

In short, many Indian people, both individually and collectively, continue to embrace the assumption that close biological connections to other Indian people—and the distinctive physical appearance that may accompany those connections—imply a stronger claim on identity than do more distant ones. As Potawatomi scholar of Native American Studies Terry Wilson summarizes, "Few, if any, Native Americans, regardless of upbringing in rural, reservation, or urban setting, ignore their own and other Indians' blood quantum in everyday life. Those whose physical appearances render their Indian identities suspect are subject to suspicious scrutiny until precise cultural explanations, especially blood quantum, are offered or discovered."[25]

DISCUSSION QUESTIONS

1. As Garroutte describes them, what are the various ways that one might be defined as a "real" Indian? When might these different definitions of "Indianness" conflict?

2. Thinking about June's description of her son being refused a drink of water and her advice about who should receive the Indian scholarship, do you see any consistencies or inconsistencies in her approach?

3. Garroutte notes that turn-of-the century race theorists treated blood as the "vehicle for the transmission of cultural characteristics." Can you give some specific examples of what this might mean? Do you think contemporary American social practices operate from the same premise?

NOTES

1. Thornton surveyed 302 of the 317 tribes in the lower forty-eight states that enjoyed federal acknowledgment in 1997. He found that 204 tribes had some minimum blood quantum requirement, while the remaining 98 had none. Russell Thornton, "Tribal Membership Requirements and the Demography of 'Old' and 'New' Native Americans," *Population Research and Policy Review* 16 (1997): 37.

2. The two mentions of "Indians" in the Constitution appear in passages regarding the regulation of commerce and the taking of a federal census. The word "tribe" also appears once in the Constitution, in the Commerce Clause.

3. Sharon O'Brien, "Tribes and Indians: With Whom Does the United States Maintain a Relationship?" *Notre Dame Law Review* 66 (1991): 1481.

4. One particularly important law that provides no definition of "Indian" is the Major Crimes Act of 1885 (23 Stat. 385, U.S.C. Sec. 1153). It subjects reservation Indi-

ans to federal prosecution for certain offenses for which non-Indians would face only state prosecution.

5. For a detailed discussion of legal cases bearing on the definition of "Indian," see Felix S. Cohen, *Handbook of Federal Indian Law* (Charlottesville, Va.: Michie/Bobbs-Merrill, 1982).

6. Wilcomb E. Washburn, *Red Man's Land/White Man's Law: A Study of the Past and Present States of the American Indian* (New York: Charles Scribner's Sons, 1971).

7. These agencies administer resources and programs in areas such as education, health, social services, tribal governance and administration, law enforcement, nutrition, resource management, tribal economic development, employment, and the like. The most recently published source describing various programs and the requirements for participation is Roger Walk, *Federal Assistance to Native Americans: A Report Prepared for the Senate Select Committee on Indian Affairs of the US Senate* (Washington, D.C.: Government Printing Office, 1991). In fiscal year 2001, recognized tribes and their members had access to approximately four billion dollars of federal funding for various social programs. U.S. Government Accounting Office, *Indian Issues: Improvements Needed in Tribal Recognition Process,* Report to Congressional Requesters, Washington D.C.: Government Printing Office, November 2001.

8. Non-Indian students in my classes sometimes tell me that Indians also regularly receive such windfalls as free cars and monthly checks from the government strictly because of their race. It is my sad duty to puncture this fantasy; there is no truth in it. The common belief that Indians receive "free money" from the government probably stems from the fact that the government holds land in trust for certain tribes. As part of its trust responsibility, it may then lease that land, collect the revenue, and distribute it to the tribal members. Thus, some Indians do receive government checks, but these do not represent some kind of manna from heaven; they are simply the profits derived from lands which they own. For details on the special, political-economic relationship of Indians to the federal government in relation to taxation and licensure, see Gary D. Sandefur, "Economic Development and Employment Opportunities for American Indians," in *American Indians: Social Justice and Public Policy,* ed. Donald E. Green and Thomas V. Tonneson, Ethnicity and Public Policy Series, vol. 9 (Milwaukee: University of Wisconsin System Institute on Race and Ethnicity, 1991), 208–22.

9. Aside from the issue of adopted children, the legal requirements for establishing legal status as Indian in Canada have been even more complicated and peculiar than the U.S. ones, and the tensions related to them even more severe. Until 1985, a Canadian Indian woman who married a legally non-Indian man lost her legal status as

an Indian, and her children (who might have a blood quantum of one-half) could never be recognized as Indian under Canadian law. A non-Indian woman who married an Indian man, however, gained Indian status for herself and her children. Men could neither gain nor lose Indian status through marriage. When a 1985 bill amended the Indian Act, which governed such matters, the issue of "real Indianness" came to a head. Many Canadian Indian women and children sought and received Indian legal status, but when they attempted to return to the reservations, they often got a chilly welcome from Indian communities already overburdened with financial obligations to their existing population. Like their American counterparts, Canadian Indian bands continue to struggle with the issue of how to conceive the boundaries of their membership. For a good discussion of Canadian Indian identification policies, see Eugeen Roosens, *Creating Ethnicity: The Process of Ethnogenesis* (Newbury Park, Calif.: Sage, 1989).

10. Shania Twain quoted in Jackie Bissley, "Country Star Shania Twain's Candor Is Challenged," *Indian Country Today,* 9–16 April 1996.

11. Quoted in Jackie Bissley, "Country Singer Says Stories Robbing Her of Her Native Roots," *Indian Country Today,* 16–23 April 1996. Even Twain's unusual situation does not exhaust the intricate aspects of the Canadian legal system as it struggles with matters of Indian identity. Roosens describes other fine points of Indian identity in force north of the border over a period of several decades:

Since 1951, to be registered as an Indian one has to be the legitimate child of an Indian father. The ethnic origin of the mother is irrelevant. . . . Furthermore, if the grandmother on the Indian side of a mixed marriage (the father's mother) is a non-Indian by descent, then the grandchild loses his or her status at the age of 21. Thus, one can be officially born an Indian and lose this status at the age of maturity. (Roosens, *Creating Ethnicity,* 24)

12. Roosens, *Creating Ethnicity,* 41–42. Roosens is discussing the situation of Canadian Indians, but the same remarks apply to American Indians.

13. G. William Rice, "There and Back Again—An Indian Hobbit's Holiday: Indians Teaching Indian Law," *New Mexico Law Review* 26, no. 2 (1996): 176.

14. Melissa L. Meyer, "American Indian Blood Quantum Requirements: Blood Is Thicker than Family," in *Over the Edge: Remapping the American West,* ed. Valerie J. Matsumoto and Blake Allmendiger (Berkeley: University of California Press, 1999).

15. Historians such as Grace Steele Woodward and Marion Starkey have made this argument. But see also Julia Coates, "None of Us Is Supposed to Be Here" (Ph.D. diss., University of New Mexico, 2002) for a revisionist understanding of Cherokee history.

16. C. Matthew Snipp, "Who Are American Indians? Some Observations about the Perils and Pitfalls of Data for Race and Ethnicity," *Population Research and Policy Review* 5 (1986): 249. For excellent and intriguing discussions of the evolution of ideas about blood relationships among European and Euro-American peoples over several centuries, and transference of these ideas into American Indian tribal populations, see Meyer, "Blood Quantum Requirements," and Circe Sturm, *Blood Politics: Race, Culture, and Identity in the Cherokee Nation of Oklahoma* (Berkeley: University of California Press, 2002). See further Peggy Pascoe, "Miscegenation Law, Court Cases, and Ideologies of 'Race' in Twentieth Century America," *Journal of American History* 83, no. 1 (June 1996): 44–69. For the processes by which some of these theories were rejected by scientists, see Elazar Barkan, *Retreat of Scientific Racism: Changing Concepts of Race in Britain and the United States between the World Wars* (Cambridge: Cambridge University Press, 1992).

17. Thomas Biolsi, "The Birth of the Reservation: Making the Modern Individual among the Lakota," *American Ethnologist* 22, no. 1 (February 1995): 28–49; Patrick Limerick, *The Legacy of Conquest: The Unbroken Past of the American West* (New York: W. W. Norton, 1988).

18. Naomi Zack, "Mixed Black and White Race and Public Policy," *Hypatia* 10, 1 (1995): 120–32; Ariela J. Gross, "Litigating Whiteness: Trials of Racial Determination in the Nineteenth-Century South," *Yale Law Journal* 108 (1998): 109–88.

19. Jack D. Forbes, "The Manipulation of Race, Caste, and Identity: Classifying AfroAmericans, Native Americans and Red-Black People," *Journal of Ethnic Studies* 17, no. 4 (1990): 24; original emphasis. Indians are "lost," in Forbes' sense, both to black *and* to white racial classifications, but at differing rates. Popular conventions of racial classification in America tend to prevent individuals with any discernible black ancestry from identifying themselves as Indians. As an interview respondent quoted by anthropologist Circe Sturm observes, "This is America, where being to any degree Black is the same thing as being to any degree pregnant." Sturm, *Blood Politics,* 188.

By contrast, individuals with discernible white ancestry are *sometimes* allowed by others to identify as Indian. In their case the legitimacy of their assertion is likely to be evaluated with reference to the *amount* of white ancestry, and with beliefs about whether that amount is enough to merely *dilute* or to entirely *compromise* Indian identity. Other factors, such as culture and upbringing, may also be taken into account. People of partial white ancestry, in other words, are typically somewhat more free (although not entirely free) to ne-gotiate a legitimate identity as Indian than are people of partial black ancestry.

20. For further details on the historical impact of blood quantum on individuals' legal rights, see Felix S. Cohen, *Cohen's Handbook of Federal Indian Law* (Char-lottesville, Va.: Michie/Bobbs-Merrill, 1982).

21. For a listing of the blood quantum requirements that different tribes require for tribal citizenship, see Edgar Lister, "Tribal Membership Rates and Requirements," unpublished table (Washington, D.C.: Indian Health Service, 1987). An edited version of the table appears in C. Matthew Snipp, *American Indians: The First of This Land* (New York: Russell Sage Foundation, 1989), appendix.

22. Devon A. Mihesuah, "Commonality of Difference: American Indian Women and History," in *Natives and Academics: Researching and Writing about American In-dians,* ed. Devon A. Mihesuah (Lincoln: University of Nebraska Press, 1998), 42. For a fascinating and detailed discussion of the significance of appearance among contemporary Cherokees in Oklahoma, see Sturm, *Blood Politics,* 108–15.

23. Michael Dorris, *The Broken Card* (New York: Harper Perennial, 1990), 22.

24. Eric Konigsberg, "Michael Dorris's Troubled Sleep," *New York Magazine,* 16 June 1997, 33. For a related article, see Jerry Reynolds, "Indian Writers: The Good, the Bad, and the Could Be, Part 2: Indian Writers: Real or Imag-ined," *Indian Country Today,* 15 September 1993.

25. Terry P. Wilson, "Blood Quantum: Native American Mixed Bloods," in *Racially Mixed People in America,* ed. Maria P. P. Root (Newbury Park, Calif.: Sage, 1992), 109.

READING 5

Latinos and the U.S. Race Structure

Clara E. Rodríguez

According to definitions common in the United States, I am a light-skinned Latina, with European features and hair texture. I was born and raised in New York City; my first language was Spanish, and I am today bilingual. I cannot remember when I first

Clara E. Rodríguez is a professor of sociology at Fordham Uni-versity's College at Lincoln Center.

realized how the color of one's skin, the texture of one's hair, or the cast of one's features determined how one was treated in both my Spanish-language and English-language worlds. I do know that it was before I understood that accents, surnames, resi-dence, class, and clothing also determined how one was treated.

Looking back on my childhood, I recall many in-stances when the lighter skin color and European features of some persons were admired and terms such as "pelo malo" (bad hair) were commonly used to refer to "tightly curled" hair. It was much later that I came to see that this Eurocentric bias, which favors European characteristics above all others, was part of our history and cultures. In both Americas and the Caribbean, we have inherited and continue to favor this Eurocentrism, which grew out of our history of indigenous conquest and slavery (Shohat and Stam 1994).

I also remember a richer, more complex sense of color than this simple color dichotomy of black and white would suggest, a genuine esthetic appre-ciation of people with some color and an equally genuine valuation of people as people, regardless of color. Also, people sometimes disagreed about an individual's color and "racial" classification, espe-cially if the person in question was in the middle range, not just with regard to color, but also with regard to class or political position.[1]

As I grew older, I came to see that many of these cues or clues to status—skin color, physical features, accents, surnames, residence, and other class char-acteristics—changed according to place or situa-tion. For example, a natural "tan" in my South Bronx neighborhood was attractive, whereas down-town, in the business area, it was "otherizing." I also recall that the same color was perceived differently in different areas. Even in Latino contexts, I saw some people as lighter or darker, depending on cer-tain factors, such as their clothes, occupations, and families.[2] I suspect that others saw me similarly, so that in some contexts, I was very light, in others darker, and in still others about the same as every-one else. Even though my color stayed the same, the perception and sometimes its valuation changed.

I also realize now that some Latinos' experiences were different from mine and that our experiences affect the way we view the world. I know that not all Latinos have multiple or fluctuating identities. For a few, social context is irrelevant. Regardless of the context, they see themselves, and/or are seen, in only one way. They are what the Census Bureau refers to as *consistent;* that is, they consistently answer in the same way when asked about their "race." Often, but not always, they are at one or the other end of the color spectrum.

My everyday experiences as a Latina, supplemented by years of scholarly work, have taught me that certain dimensions of race are fundamental to Latino life in the United States and raise questions about the nature of "race" in this country. This does not mean that that all Latinos have the same experiences, but that for most, these experiences are not surprising. For example, although some Latinos are consistently seen as having the same color or "race," many Latinos are assigned a multiplicity of "racial" classifications, sometimes in one day! I am reminded of the student who told me after class one day, "When people first meet me, they think I'm Italian, then when they find out my last name is Mendez, they think I'm Spanish, then when I tell them my mother is Puerto Rican, they think I'm nonwhite or Black." Although he had not changed his identity, the perception of it changed with each additional bit of information.

Latino students have also told me that non-Latinos sometimes assume they are African American. When they assert they are not "Black" but Latino, they are either reproved for denying their "race" or told they are out of touch with reality. Other Latinos, who see Whites as Other-than-me are told by non-Latinos, "But you're white." Although not all Latinos have such dramatic experiences, almost all know (and are often related to) others who have.

In addition to being reclassified by others (without their consent), some Latinos shift their own self-classifications during their lifetime. I have known Latinos, who became "black," then "white," then "human beings," and finally "Latino"—all in a relatively short time. I have also known Latinos for whom the sequence was quite different and the time period longer. Some Latinos who altered their identities came to be viewed by others as legitimate members of their new identity group. I also saw the simultaneously tricultural, sometimes trilingual, abilities of many Latinos who manifested or projected a different self as they acclimated themselves to a Latino, African American, or White context (Rodríguez 1989:77).

I have come to understand that this shifting, context-dependent experience is at the core of many Latinos' life in the United States. Even in the nuclear family, parents, children, and siblings often have a wide range of physical types. For many Latinos race is primarily cultural; multiple identities are a normal state of affairs; and "racial mixture" is subject to many different, sometimes fluctuating, definitions.

Some regard *racial mixture* as an unfortunate or embarrassing term, but others consider the affirmation of mixture to be empowering. Lugones (1994) subscribes to this latter view and affirms "mixture," *mestizaje,* as a way of resisting a world in which purity and separation are emphasized, and one's identities are controlled: "Mestizaje defies control through simultaneously asserting the impure, curdled multiple state and rejecting fragmentation into pure parts . . . the mestiza . . . has no pure parts to be 'had,' controlled." (p. 460) Also prevalent in the upper classes is the hegemonic view that rejects or denies "mixture" and claims a "pure" European ancestry. This view also is common among middle- and upper-class Latinos, regardless of their skin color or place of origin. In some areas, people rarely claim a European ancestry, such as in indigenous sectors of Latin America, in parts of Brazil and in some coastal areas in Colombia, Venezuela, Honduras, and Panama (see, for e.g., Arocha 1998; De la Fuente 1998). Recently, some Latinos have encouraged another view in which those historical components that were previously denied and denigrated, such as indigenous and African ancestry, were privileged (see, e.g., Moro; *La Revista de Nuestra Vida* [Bogota, Colombia, September 1998]; *La Voz del Pueblo Taino*

[The Voice of the Taino People], official newsletter of the United Confederation of Taino People, U.S. regional chapter, New York, January 1998).

Many people, however—mostly non-Latinos—are not acquainted with these basic elements of Latino life. They do not think much about them; and when they do, they tend to see race as a "given," an ascribed characteristic that does not change for anyone, at any time. One is either white or not white. They also believe that "race" is based on genetic inheritance, a perspective that is just another construct of race.

Whereas many Latinos regard their "race" as primarily cultural, others, when asked about their race, offer standard U.S. race terms, saying that they are White, Black, or Indian. Still others see themselves as Latinos, Hispanics, or members of a particular national-origin group *and* as belonging to a particular race group.[3] For example, they may identify themselves as Afro-Latinos or white Hispanics. In some cases, these identities vary according to context, but in others they do not.

I have therefore come to see that the concept of "race" can be constructed in several ways and that the Latino experience in the United States provides many illustrations of this. My personal experiences have suggested to me that for many Latinos, "racial" classification is immediate, provisional, contextually dependent, and sometimes contested. But because these experiences apply to many non-Latinos as well, it is evident to me that the Latino construction of race and the racial reading of Latinos are not isolated phenomena. Rather, the government's recent deliberations on racial and ethnic classification standards reflect the experiences and complexities of many groups and individuals who are similarly involved in issues pertaining to how they see themselves and one another (U.S. Dept. of Commerce 1995; U.S. Office of Management and Budget 1995, 1997a, 1997b, 1999).

Throughout my life, I have considered racism to be evil and I oppose it with every fiber of my being. I study race to understand its influence on the lives of individuals and nations because I hope that honest, open, and well-meaning discussions of race and ethnicity and their social dynamics can help us appreciate diversity and value all people, not for their appearance, but for their character.

It was because of my personal experiences that I first began to write in this area and that I was particularly sensitive to Latinos' responses to the census' question about race. The U.S. Census Bureau's official position has been that race and ethnicity are two separate concepts. Thus, in 1980 and in 1990, the U.S. census asked people to indicate their "race"—white, black, Asian or Pacific Islander, American Indian or "other race"—and also whether or not they were Hispanic. Latinos responded to the 1990 census' question about race quite differently than did non-Latinos. Whereas less than 1% of the non-Hispanic population reported they were "other race," more than 40% of Hispanics chose this category. Latinos responded similarly in the previous decennial census (Denton and Massey 1989; Martin, DeMaio, and Campanelli 1990; Rodríguez 1989, 1990, 1991; Tienda and Ortiz 1986). Although the percentages of different Hispanic groups choosing this category varied, all chose it more than did non-Hispanics.

In addition, the many Hispanics who chose this category wrote—in the box explicitly asking for race—the name of their "home" Latino country or group, to "explain" their race—or "otherness."[4] The fact that these Latino referents were usually cultural or national-origin terms, such as Dominican, Honduran, or Boricua (i.e., Puerto Rican) underscores the fact that many Latinos viewed the question of race as a question of culture, national origin, and socialization rather than simply biological or genetic ancestry or color. Indeed, recent studies have found that many Latinos understand "race" to mean national origin, nationality, ethnicity, culture (Kissam, Herrera, and Nakamoto 1993), or a combination of these and skin color (Bates et al 1994:109; Rodríguez 1991a, 1992, 1994; Rodríguez and Cordero-Guzmán 1992). For many Latinos, the term *race* or *raza* is a reflection of these understandings and not of those often associated with "race" in the United States, e.g., defined by hypodescent.[5] Studies have found that Latinos also tend to see race along a continuum and not as a dichotomous variable in which individuals are either white or black (Bracken and de Bango 1992; Rodríguez and Hagan 1992; Romero 1992).

This does not mean that there is one Latino view of race. Rather, there are different views of race within different countries, classes, and even families. Latinos' views of race are dependent on a complex array of factors, one of which is the racial formation process in their country of origin. Other variables also influence their views of race, for example, generational differences, phenotype, class, age, and education. But even though there is not just one paradigm of Latin American race, there are some basic differences between the way that Latinos view race and the way that race is viewed overall in the United States.

In the United States, rules of hypodescent and categories based on presumed genealogical-biological criteria have generally dominated thinking about race. Racial categories have been few, discrete, and mutually exclusive, with skin color a prominent element. Categories for mixtures—for example, mulatto—have been transitory. In contrast, in Latin America, racial constructions have tended to be more fluid and based on many variables, like social class and phenotype. There also have been many, often overlapping, categories, and mixtures have been consistently acknowledged and have had their own terminology. These general differences are what Latinos bring with them to the United States, and they influence how they view their own and others' "identity."

Although Latinos may use or approach "race" differently, this does not mean that "race" as understood by Latinos does not have overtones of racism or implications of power and privilege—in either Latin America or the United States. The depreciation and denial of African and Amerindian characteristics are widespread.[6] Everywhere in Latin America can be found ". . . a pyramidal class structure, cut variously by ethnic lines, but with a local, regional and nation-state elite characterized as 'white.' And white rules over color within the same class; those who are lighter have differential access to some dimensions of the market" (Torres and Whitten 1998:23).

Suffice it to say at this point that in my many years of research in this area, I have noticed in my and oth-

ers' work that "race" is a recurring, sometimes amusing and benign, and sometimes conflictual issue.[7] For Latinos' responses to questions of race are seldom as simple and straightforward as they tend to be for most non-Hispanic Whites (Rodríguez et al 1991).

In the past, new immigrants immediately underwent a racialization process, which conveyed an implicit hierarchy of color and power. The two elements of this racialization process were (1) the acceptance of and participation in discrimination against people of color (Bell 1992; Du Bois 1962:700 ff; Morrison 1993) and (2) negotiations regarding the group's placement in the U.S. racial-ethnic queue (Jacobson 1998; Rodríguez 1974; Smith 1997; Takaki 1994). Immigrants undergoing this racialization process discriminated implicitly or explicitly against others because of their color and status. Indeed, some immigrants realized that one way to become "White," or more acceptable to Whites, was to discriminate against others seen as "nonwhite" (Ignatiev 1995; Kim 1999; Loewen 1971). Kim (1999) reviewed the historical experience of Asian Americans being triangulated with Blacks and Whites through a simultaneous process of valorization and ostracism. This racial triangulation continued to reinforce White racial power and insulate it from minority encroachment or challenge.

Some immigrants discriminated against Blacks and/or other depreciated minorities, by not living with "them," not hiring "them" in enclave economies, or articulating prejudices against "them." Institutionalized discrimination and normative behavior aided racialization so that, for example, it became difficult to rent or sell to members of certain groups because of exclusionary practices. Nearly all immigrant groups experienced this seldom-mentioned, but indisputable dimension of the Americanization process. Critical to the racialization process was the belief that there is always some "other" group to which one is superior. Indeed, this process has been an effective means of protecting the status quo because it made it difficult to understand and pursue areas of common interest and resulted in divide-and-conquer outcomes.

Latinos—and many other groups—come to the United States with different views on race and with their own racial hierarchies. The relation of these people's racialization to their hierarchies in the United States has not been widely studied. But it is clear that when they arrive, they too become part of a racialization process in which they are differentiated according to the official perception of their race, which may or may not be the same as their own perception. This racial reclassification immerses immigrants in a social education process in which they first learn—and then may ignore, resist, or accept—the state-defined categories and the popular conventions about race (particularly one's own) (Rodríguez 1994a).

The racialization process also includes contradictory views of the way that Hispanics are generally regarded. At one extreme, Hispanics are a Spanish-speaking white ethnic group, who are simply the most recent in the continuum of immigrant groups and are expected to follow the traditional path of assimilation. Another view holds that the term *Hispanic*—which has generally not been unknown to new immigrants from Latin America—is subtly "colored" by negative and racial associations. For example, the stereotyped image (for both Hispanics and non-Hispanics) of a Hispanic is "tan." Within this perspective, Hispanics are often referred to as "light skinned," not as white. Yet, many Hispanics would be seen as White, Black, or Asian if it were not known that they were Hispanic. But seeing Hispanics/Latinos as "light" clearly restricts their "Whiteness" and thus makes them nonwhite by default, but not a member of other race groups. Thus, many Hispanics entering this country become generically "nonwhite" to themselves, or to others, regardless of their actual phenotype or ancestry.

The United States' racialization process affects all groups' sense of who they are, and how they are seen, in regard to color and race. There are few studies of this concerning Latinos, but some autobiographies suggest that the racialization process has had a significant impact (see, e.g., Rivera 1983; Rodríguez 1992; Santiago 1995; Thomas 1967). Whether this has been a dissonant impact and has affected Latinos' mobility and the quality of life has not yet been determined.

Some Latinos, influenced by movements such as the Black Power movement, Afrocentrism, pan-Africanism and African diaspora philosophies, and the celebration of negritude, have come to see themselves, and sometimes their group, as Black. Terms like *Afro-Latino, black Cuban,* and *black Panamanian* are now common, and some Latinos celebrate their African roots. Others focus on their Amerindian or indigenous component, while still others see themselves only as white or mixed or identify themselves only ethnically.

A Dominican student of mine told me that each of her and her husband's children claimed a different identity. So they had one Black child, one White child, and one Dominican child. Each of the children had different friends and tastes. Many variables contribute to and interact with the racialization process to determine how individuals decide on their group affiliation. Generation, phenotype, previous and current class position, and the size and accessibility of one's cultural or national-origin group, as well as the relative size of other groups, all affect how individual Latinos identify themselves.

My own life experiences have demonstrated the social constructedness of race, and subsequent research has shown that "race" is not fixed, is imperfectly measured, is at variance with scientific principles, is often conflated with the concept of "ethnicity," and is under increasing scientific criticism and popular interrogation. Nonetheless, race is still real; it still exists.[8] We may question its necessity, the right of anyone to establish such markers, and its validity as a scientific concept. We may see it as unjust and want to change it. But we must acknowledge its significance in our lives. It can be deconstructed, but it cannot be dismissed.

DISCUSSION QUESTIONS

1. What do you think Rodríguez means when she says that for Latinos, race is "cultural"?
2. What do you think is the impact of American racial constructions on immigrant Latino Americans?

NOTES:

1. In her study of Spanish speaking Caribbeans, Dominguez states that "An individual may be identified as *indio, trigueno, blanco, prieto,* or whatever in different contexts by different people or even by the same person" (1986:275).
2. Except when specifically referring to women, I use the word *Latino* to refer to both women and men. At the descriptive level, my analyses of how Latinas and Latinos classify themselves racially have not revealed significant differences. But under more controlled conditions, some labor market differences by race and gender have been noted (Gómez n.d.; Rodríguez 1991a).
3. I use both *Hispanic* and *Latino,* in part because both terms are used in the literature and I've tried to use those of the authors I cite when discussing their work. Works based on census material, for example, tend to use the term *Hispanic,* mainly because this is the category under which the data were collected. Other works refer to surveys employing the term *Latino.* See the following for different arguments concerning the preferred term: Gimenez 1989; Hayes-Bautista and Chapa 1987; Oboler 1998; Treviño 1987.
4. According to Jorge del Pinal, 42.7% percent of the Hispanics who chose the "other race" category in the 1990 census gave a Latino referent. However, 94.3% of "other race" persons who provided a write-in gave a Latino referent. (Personal communication, July 30, 1999.) In addition, two-thirds of all those who did not specify their race wrote in their Hispanic ethnicity (U.S. Office of Management and Budget 1995:44689).
5. *Hypodescent* is also referred to as the "one-drop rule," in which "one drop" of "nonwhite or Black blood" determines a person's "race."
6. The degree to which racism is perceived and experienced within the Latino framework may be related to phenotype. Consequently, those farthest from either the local mean or the ideal European model may be those most subject to, and therefore most aware of, racism and discrimination. In the dominant United States framework, those farthest from the stereotype "Latin look" may be those who are most acutely aware of, or in the best position to observe, discrimination.
7. See Davis, et. al. (1998a:III-22-23) for light and humorous discussions of skin color in cognitive interviews.
8. Marks (1994) maintains that folk concepts of race—flawed and scientifically deficient as they may be—are passed down from generation to generation, just as genetic material is inherited. This is part of what keeps the concept of "race" real.

REFERENCES

Alocha, Jaime. 1998. "Inclusion of Afro-Colombians: Unreachable National Goal?" *Latin American Perspectives* 25 (3) (May):70–89.

Bates, Nancy A., Manuel de la Puente, Theresa J. DeMaio, and Elizabeth A. Martin. 1994. "Research on Race and Ethnicity: Results from Questionnaire Design Tests." Paper presented at the U.S. Census Bureau's annual research conference, March 20–23, Rosslyn, VA.

Bell, Derrick. 1992. *Faces at the Bottom of the Well: The Permanence of Racism.* New York: Basic Books.

Bracken, Karen, and Guillermo de Bango. 1992. "Hispanics in a Racially and Ethnically Mixed Neighborhood in the Greater Metropolitan New Orleans Area." *Ethnographic Evaluation of the 1990 Decennial Census Report* 16. Prepared under Joint Statistical Agreement 89–45 with Hispanidad '87, Inc. Washington, DC: U.S. Bureau of the Census.

Davis, Diana K., Johnny Blair, Howard Fleischman, and Margaret S. Boone. 1998a. *Cognitive Interviews on the Race and Hispanic Origin Questions on the Census 2000 Dress Rehearsal Form.* Report prepared by Development Associates, Inc., Arlington, VA, under contract from the U.S. Census Bureau, Population Division, May 29.

De La Fuente, Alejandro. 1998. "Race, National Discourse, and Politics in Cuba: An Overview." *Latin American Perspectives* 25 (3) (May): 43–69. Issue 100 entitled "Race and National Identity in the Americas" and edited by Helen Safa.

Denton, N. A., and D. S. Massey. 1989. "Racial Identity among Caribbean Hispanics: The Effect of Double Minority Status on Residential Segregation." *American Sociological Review* 54:790–808.

Domínguez, Virginia R. 1986. *White by Definition: Social Classification in Creole Louisiana.* New Brunswick, NJ: Rutgers University Press.

Du Bois, W. E. B. 1962. *Black Reconstruction in America, 1860–1880.* Cleveland: World Publishing.

Gimenez, Martha. 1989. "Latino/'Hispanic'—Who Needs a Name? The Case against a Standardized Terminology." *International Journal of Health Services* 19 (3): 557–571.

Gómez, Christina. n.d. "The Continual Significance of Skin Color: An Exploratory Study of Latinos in the Northeast." *Hispanic Journal of Behavioral Sciences,* currently under review.

Hayes-Bautista, D. E., and J. Chapa. 1987. "Latino Terminology: Conceptual Basis for Standardized Terminology." *American Journal of Public Health* 77: 61–68.

Ignatiev, Noel. 1995. *How the Irish Became White.* New York: Routledge & Kegan Paul.

Jacobson, Mathew. 1998. *Becoming Caucasian: Whiteness and the Alchemy of the American Melting Pot.* Cambridge, MA: Harvard University Press.

Kim, Claire Jean. 1999. "The Racial Triangulation of Asian Americans." *Politics and Society* 27(1)(March):105–138.

Kissam, Edward, Enrique Herrera, and Jorge M. Nakamoto. 1993. "Hispanic Response to Census Enumeration Forms and Procedures." Task order no. 46-YABC-2-0001, contract no. 50-YABC-2-66027, submitted by Aguirre Inter-

What's in a Name?

What is in a name? For children, the letters of their name can be a doorway that leads to discovering elements for reading and writing. For some adults, names may represent personal traits or values. They may remind one of places or trades, and even hold personal messages. This has been my experience also, as my full name unveils many different aspects of my identity and heritage.

My first name is Ruth. I identify myself as Jewish. My second name, Carina, reflects my Latina background. I was born and raised in Buenos Aires, Argentina. My surname, Feldsberg, is the name of the city located on the border between Austria and the Czech Republic. But mainly, my last name carries the memories of my father, who was among the fortunate who saw the writing on the wall, and left Nazi-occupied Austria as a refugee. He lived in the Netherlands, Ecuador, and finally settled in Buenos Aires. There he married my mother, Edith Altschul, an Argentine Jew of Czech descent.

I grew up bilingual, speaking Spanish and German at school and at home. I practiced Argentine, European traditions and also observed the Jewish holidays. But the knowledge that we were the only family in the neighborhood to celebrate certain holidays made me feel isolated. Besides religion, I also felt different in terms of ethnicity and the language spoken at home. And although my mother was Argentine, her family's Czech origin also separated me from most of the children my age.

Argentina's middle class is largely formed by Italian or Spanish immigrants, and the official religion is Catholicism. I knew that I could not share my background and felt alienated because others could not relate to my experience. Growing up, I learned to keep a low profile, to be cautious, and not to unveil my identity. I would listen and constantly evaluate whether or not it was safe for me to speak. As I entered adolescence, my own identity became a puzzle even to myself as I began to pose "existential" questions. Who am I really? Latina? Jewish? European? Where do I want to live? These questions ultimately motivated me to explore my roots, travel in Europe, and live in Latin America, the Middle East, and, finally, in the United States. Presently, I live in California, and I am not sure that I have been able to completely answer all those questions. I can relate to discrimination against Latinos, because being Jewish, I learned early on about discrimination. Yet not having been the target of racial or social class oppression, I can be a strong ally. If I heard a pejorative comment about Latinos, without feeling touched, I could quickly dismiss it and see it as lack of knowledge about the complexities, beauty, and diversity among Latinos. The place I still struggle and feel more vulnerable is in my Jewish heritage. I may have become what people call a citizen of the world, and I can live everywhere, but never feel truly at home anywhere.

Ruth C. Feldsberg

national, 411 Borel Ave., Suite 402, San Mateo, CA 94402, to U.S. Bureau of the Census, Center for Survey Methods Research, March.

Lugones, María. 1994. "Purity, Impurity, and Separation." *Signs* 19 (2) (Winter): 459–479.

Marks, Jonathan. 1994. "Black, White, Other: Racial Categories Are Cultural Constructs Masquerading as Biology." *Natural History,* December, pp. 32–35.

Martin, E., T. J. DeMaio, and P. C. Campanelli. 1990. "Context Effects for Census Measures of Race and Hispanic Origin." *Public Opinion Quarterly* 54 (4): 551–566.

Morrison, Tony. 1993. "On the Backs of Blacks." *Time,* special issue (Fall), p, 57.

Oboler,, Suzanne. 1995. *Ethnic Labels/Latino Lives: Identity and the Politics of (Re) Presentation in the United States.* Minneapolis: University of Minnesota Press.

Rivera, Edward. 1983. *Family Installments: Memories of Growing up Hispanic.* New York: Penguin Books.

Rodríguez, Clara. 1989. *Puerto Ricans: Born in the USA.* Boston: Unwin Hyman.

———. 1990. "Racial Identification among Puerto Ricans in New York." *Hispanic Journal of Behavioral Sciences* 12 (4) (November): 366–79.

———. 1991a. "The Effect of Race on Puerto Rican Wages." In *Hispanics in the Labor Force: Issues and Policies,* ed. Edwin Meléndez, Clara Rodríguez, and Janice Barry Figueroa. New York: Plenum Press.

———. 1992. "Race, Culture and Latino 'Otherness' in the 1980 Census." *Social Science Quarterly* 73 (4) (December): 930–937.

———. 1994a. "Challenging Racial Hegemony. Puerto Ricans in the United States." In *Race,* ed. R. Sanjek and S. Gregory. New Brunswick, NJ: Rutgers University Press.

Rodríguez, Clara, Aida Castro, Oscar García, and Analisa Torres. 1991. "Latino Racial Identity: In the Eye of the Beholder?" *Latino Studies Journal* 2 (3) (December): 33–48.

Rodríguez, Clara, and Hector Cordero-Guzmán. 1992. "Placing Race in Context." *Ethnic and Racial Studies* 15 (4): 523–542.

Rodríguez, Nestor, and Jacqueline Hagan. 1991. *Investigating Census Coverage and Content among the Undocumented: An Ethnographic Study of Latino Immigrant Tenants in Houston. Ethnographic Evaluation of the 1990 Decennial Census Report* 3. Prepared under Joint Statistical Agreement 89-34 with the University of Houston, U.S. Bureau of the Census, Washington, DC.

Romero, Mary. 1992. *Ethnographic Evaluation of Behavioral Causes of Census Undercount of Undocumented Immigrants and Salvadorans in the Mission District of San Francisco, California. Ethnographic Evaluation of the 1990 Decennial Census Report* 18. Prepared under Joint Statistical Agreement 89-41 with the San Francisco State University Foundation, U.S. Bureau of the Census, Washington, DC.

Santiago, Roberto. 1995. "Black and Latino." In *Boricuas: Influential Puerto Rican Writings, an Anthology,* ed. Roberto Santiago. New York: Ballantine Books.

Shohat, Ella, and Robert Stam. 1994. *Unthinking Eurocentrism: Multiculturalism and the Media.* New York: Routledge & Kegan Paul.

Smith, Rogers M. 1997. *Civic Ideals: Conflicting Visions in U.S. History.* New Haven, CT: Yale University Press.

Takaki, Ronald. 1994. *From Different Shores: Perspectives on Race and Ethnicity in America.* 2d ed. New York: Oxford University Press.

Thomas, Piri. 1967. *Down These Mean Streets.* New York: Knopf.

Tienda, M., and V. Ortiz. 1986. "'Hispanicity' and the 1980 Census." *Social Science Quarterly* 67 (March): 3–20.

Torres, Arlene, and Norman E. Whitten Jr., eds. 1998. *Blackness in Latin America and the Caribbean.* Vol. 2. Bloomington: Indiana University Press.

Treviño, F. M. 1987. "Standardized Terminology for Standardized Populations." *American Journal of Public Health* 77: 69–72.

U.S. Department of Commerce. 1995. "1996 Race and Ethnic Targeted Test; Notice." *Federal Register.* 60:231:62010-62014. December 1. Washington, DC: U.S. Government Printing Office.

U.S. Office of Management and Budget (OMB). 1995. "Standards for the Classification of Federal Data on Race and Ethnicity; Notice." *Federal Register,* part 6, vol. 60, no. 166, pp. 44674–44693, August 28.

———. 1997a. "Recommendations from the Interagency Committee for the Review of the Racial and Ethnic Standards to the Office of Management and Budget Concerning Changes to the Standards for the Classification of Federal Data on Race and Ethnicity; Notice." *Federal Register,* 62:131:36874–36946, July 9.

———. 1997b. "Revisions to the Standards for the Classification of Federal Data on Race and Ethnicity; Notices." *Federal Register,* 62:210:58782-58790, October 30.

———. 1999. "Provisional Guidance on the Implementation of the 1997 Standards for the Collection of Federal Data on Race and Ethnicity." Prepared by Tabulation Working Group, Interagency Committee for the Review of Standards for Data on Race and Ethnicity, Washington, DC, February 17.

READING 6

Tripping on the Color Line: Black-White Multiracial Families in a Racially Divided World

Heather M. Dalmage

About mid-semester during one of the introductions to sociology courses I teach, two of my cousins decided to sit in on the class. This was my first semester teaching in Chicago, and they wanted to see their "cuz" in action. At the next class meeting the students and I were sitting in a circle discussing some sociological point when the question came up: "Professor, what are you? I was talking to some people about this class, and they asked me what you are, you know, racially. I told them I wasn't sure." Another student joined in: "Yeah, what are you?"

The question is loaded. More than five hundred years' worth of socially, politically, economically, and culturally created racial categories rest in the phrase "what are you." People seeing me in the street would have little doubt that I was a white woman. Yet the cousins who sat in on my class are mixed Korean and Filipino, my aunt is Filipino, my uncle is Korean, my nieces are mixed Indonesian and white, my in-laws are Jamaican, my husband is black. What does that make me? The quick answer is "a white woman from a multiracial family." Nevertheless, the quick answer cannot address more than five hundred years of racial baggage. In a sociology course we can delve into some of this baggage and begin to address race on a more complex level. In day-to-day living, however, race is often used as a clear-cut, unambiguous way of categorizing human

Heather M. Dalmage is a professor of sociology at Roosevelt University.

beings. Those of us who do not come from or live in single-race families must daily negotiate a racialized and racist system that demands we fit ourselves into prescribed categories.

When I decided to begin the research [on this topic], I knew few people in my shoes. My husband (a black man) and I (a white woman) had been together for nearly a decade. I had heard the question "What about the children?" so many times that I finally decided to explore the question myself. I began speaking with multiracial adults about their lives. As I listened to and talked with these individuals, I began to recognize some similarities between their experiences as multiracial people and my own as an interracially married white woman. At the same time I was participating in an adoption reading group and spending a great deal of time researching, discussing, and writing about families created through transracial adoption. It was becoming clear that multiracial people, transracially adopted people, and all members of first-generation multiracial families share many experiences in a racially unjust and segregated society. It further became evident that *family* has been a primary means through which a racially divided and racist society has been maintained. . . .

How do any of us know what to call ourselves racially? Many people will say, "I am what my parents are and what their parents were before them and so on." In short, a popular ideology is that we know our race by our family tree. Of course, this family tree does not grow in thin air. It grows in a society that defines race in particular ways. For many years, the concept of family was legally used to maintain white supremacy by drawing a strict line between white families and all other families. In *Race and Mixed Race,* Naomi Zack argues that "the concept of race has to do with white families— more precisely, with how white family is conceptualized."[1] The traditionally enforced ideology is that a white person is pure so long as he or she has no known relatives or ancestors of color. The flip side is that having one known black ancestor makes you black.[2] The two definitions seem to account for everyone. You are white or not, black or not; there is no in between. Antimiscegenation laws (those ban-

ning marriage between whites and blacks) were set up to maintain the myth of white racial purity and superiority. While laws banning interracial marriage varied from state to state, interracial marriage has been illegal for a good part of our history. Not until 1967, buttressed by the strength of the civil rights movement, did the U.S. Supreme Court strike down antimiscegenation laws as unconstitutional.[3]

In light of the history of race and family, blacks and whites respond very differently to contemporary discussions of multiracialism in the United States. Unlike many whites, most black Americans are aware of the history of the one-drop rule and the myth of white purity. Thus, blacks generally respond more guardedly to claims of multiracialism. For instance, when I talk about my research with black friends and colleagues, many tell me: "All African Americans are multiracial. Why do you want to create and give meaning to a separate category?" And, "I can trace my ancestry. I know which great-grandmothers were raped by white men, and I know who those white men were. But I'm still black." And, "Most African Americans are multiracial, but it is not something we like to talk about or want to celebrate. For us it is a painful history of rape, rejection, and exploitation."

Just the other day I was talking with a colleague who asked, "Do you believe there is a difference between being multiracial and being black?" I said yes.

"But," he contested, "black families and black people are multiracial, so how can you make such a distinction?"

I gave him my standard response: "Most multiracial families today are not created through rape and exploitation. Instead, we come together out of mutual respect, love, and admiration. We choose to be together, and some make great sacrifices to be together. Because of who we are in relation to each other racially, we have to fight to be a family. Larger rules of race work to divide us. Besides, our day-to-day experiences are different from the experiences of people who come from families that define themselves monoracially."

He replied, "I still think y'all just want to separate yourselves from black folks. . . . You want to say you're better than blacks."

I understood my colleague's argument. According to the traditional definition of *white family,* multiracial families and people are not considered white. So why are we trying to muddy the waters and claim that our experiences are different? Should we stake a claim on the side of justice and define ourselves as black families?

If the story ended there, life for multiracial family members would not be much different from the lives of families who consider themselves black. But the story does continue. Black Americans have not passively received the abuses of white supremacy. Instead, they have struggled to unify themselves and fight the injustices of a racist society. By unifying, they have drawn boundaries. A black professor in a local university explained to me one day: "See, the black community wants your husband and your children. We don't have any use for you." In short, the one-drop rule is a downward principle; it does not move upward or across. A white parent or partner is not considered black by most in the black community because he or she has no ancestral claim to blackness. That person can walk away at any time. Yet many whites see the white partner or parent, especially if she is a white woman, as no longer white. At the same time, African Americans may view the entire multiracial family with suspicion, even disdain. By disregarding the rules of race and claiming respect for our multiracial families, we are perceived as race traitors and wishy-washy crossovers. . . .

The percentage of interracial marriages, particularly between blacks and whites, remains low. Fewer than 1 percent of whites and 3 percent of blacks are in black-white marriages. Despite their small albeit growing numbers, however, black-white multiracial families receive more attention than do other multiracial families. The fact that black-white families receive disproportionate attention speaks to the seemingly immutable connection between the one-drop rule, the myth of white racial purity, and the construction of race and family in the United States. . . .

Multiracial family members occupy a unique place in our racialized society. Whether by birth, adoption, or marriage, they are at some point challenged to think about race in their relationships with themselves and others. The way in which many of them articulate race reflects both the pervasiveness and strength of racial essentialism and color-blind thinking. The complexities of race cause many family members to shift perspective. They envision and call on competing color lines as they attempt to understand their lives, sense of community(ies), identity(ies), and politics.

Three primary themes [emerge, especially in black-white multiracial families]: the hurtfulness (and, for whites, the invisibility) of whiteness and racism; the lack of language available to describe multiracial experiences in positive terms; and the individual and institutional demands constantly placed on multiracial family members to conform to a racially divided (and racist) system. . . .

TRIPPING ON THE COLOR LINE

tripping (trip-ping), v.i. [trip, trippin, tripped out] 1. physical and emotional response to a mind-blowing idea or experience. 2. a. having fun at someone else's expense; b. overreacting; presenting oneself in an inappropriate manner. 3. a stumbling over words; misspeaking or stuttering. b. stumbling or falling physically. SYN.—trip, a journey.

The closer individuals live to the color line, the more often they are forced to contend with the changing dynamics of race. Multiracial family members live so close to the line—it weaves through their families—that they are daily contending with the ambiguities and contradictions of race. People who spend their leisure and family time in single-race interactions often take racial categories for granted. They may think of race as a simple concept. Those individuals who live close to the line, however, know that race is anything but simple. They are challenged to question what it means to be black or white. On a day-to-day level, race can get very confusing. They stumble, fumble, act inappropriately, and sometimes feel blown away. They may trip in all kinds of ways. Race itself is a trip, a journey. They travel through hardship, anger, solidarity, unity, hostility, terror, growth, happiness, fear, and uncertainty. Sometimes elusive, always present, race is a social construct that guides the journey of human growth and community. . . .

***Tripping* (trip-ping) 1. physical and emotional response to a mind-blowing idea or experience**

In *Crossing the Color Line,* Maureen Reddy talks about her "mind-blowing" discovery of racism in society through her interracial marriage. "Something inside her snapped" one day when she and her husband were attempting to rent a motel room; she physically attacked a racist and antagonistic motel clerk.[4] At other times she verbally assaulted overt racists. She explains, "I started to feel like a maniac, unable to control myself and my new-found propensity for violence, a sort of Dr. Jekyll and Ms. Hyde for the twentieth century."[5] During the sixties we might have said that her late-in-life discovery of racism was making her trip, that these incidents were blowing her mind.

In my travels among multiracial families I have come across many white interracial parents and partners who share Reddy's sense of tripping. Interracially married whites who grew up in single-race families and segregated neighborhoods had world views that were radically challenged once they became involved with their black partners. Whites, more than other multiracial family members, spoke of being blown away by racism because they were unprepared for the terror and hurt. As whites, they had learned to expect certain privileges—what they considered fair and just practices in society. But once they joined an interracial family, many discovered that the world is neither fair, just, nor equal. The privileges most whites take for granted become glaringly visible. . . .

***Tripping* (trip-ping) 2. a. stumbling over words; misspeaking or stuttering, b. stumbling or falling, physically**

Another way in which we trip on the color line is through our language. We have both competing words and a lack of words to describe race identities and racial experiences, particularly when it comes to multiracialism. Think about all the terms for multiracialism: multiracial, mixed race, biracial, mulatto, interracial, half black, half white, half breed, half caste, half and half, multiethnic, blendo, vanilla swirl, chocolate swirl, black and white, African American and Caucasian, human, zebra, Oreo, sellout, race traitor, yellow boy, red boy, wannabe, white trash, jungle fever, crossover, Cablinasian, new people, beige warriors, gray ladies, wiggers.[6] Some terms are meant to be sensitive, others meant to hurt. All are meant to include every person somewhere in the nation's racial classification system.

Because they do not quite fit into the historically created, officially named, and socially recognized categories, members of multiracial families are constantly fighting to identify themselves for themselves. A difficulty they face is the lack of language available to address their experiences. For example, a few years ago I was invited to speak at Chicago's Expo for Today's Black Woman as a member of a panel exploring multiracialism. The panel consisted of three multiracial women and me. The moderator, a well-known author, asked each panel member to "tell us a bit about your background and how you identify racially."

One woman replied, "My father is white; my mother is black. I grew up with my mother, was not raised to think of myself as multiracial, and so I am black. I do not identify myself as anything other than black."

Another responded, "I cannot deny either one of my parents. They both raised me, and I am here because of them. I identify as multiracial."

Assuming that I had been invited to speak about racial categories in the U.S. census, I had not formulated a response to this question. I began to babble: "Well, it's very complex. Because of my experiences, I no longer claim a white identity."

With an edge in her voice, the moderator asked, "I don't understand. Then what identity do you claim?"

Knowing that the audience of a hundred or so people was likewise baffled by my response I said,

"Well, racial identities are formed in large part through our experiences. As an interracially married woman, my experiences are vastly different from other white women. Things like being seated in the back of restaurants, being denied loans, being steered out of white neighborhoods when we search for housing, being pulled over for no reason, and facing hostility from racist whites are experiences most whites never contend with. Because of my experiences, I no longer take white privilege for granted, and in some cases I am no longer seen as white by other whites."

She pressed, "So what identity do you claim?"

I began struggling for words and found only what seemed to be a confused cop-out: "Well, that's the problem; there is no language to describe it. There is no other racial identity for me to claim. I am still working on that."

A young man in the audience said, "Well, then just say you're black."

I thought for a moment. I was not raised in a black community and did not participate in black culture. I do not want to be disrespectful to those who suffer racist abuse, and I don't want to make cultural claims to which I am not entitled. I recognize that I am granted many privileges based on my skin color. I replied, "People will think I'm a bit nuts. That's not an option in this society." Identities are expressions of our experiences mediated by language. Because essentialist thinking and language is so prevalent, many multiracial family members do not have a language to express various identities. Instead, we find ourselves bound by the color line. . . .

Interracial parents and partners had a particularly difficult time finding language to describe their experiences and racial identities. Often arguments made by and for the recognition of multiracial experiences draw on the idea that individuals possess two or more heritages.[7] Because they cannot claim parents of different heritages, however, interracially married people are left to defend and describe their own shifting identities within a language that connotes race as a biological construct. Self-descriptions may be laced with qualifications and default into either essentialist language

or color-blind rhetoric. For instance, Lionel, a forty-two-year-old black interracially married father living in a middle-class neighborhood in Montclair, New Jersey, is careful to preface how he identifies racially: "I think because of my experiences, although I am not mixed race, I can identify to some degree with a mixed-race person." Likewise, Jane, a sixty-five-year-old white woman living in a poor, predominantly black neighborhood on Chicago's South Side can "identify to some degree." Now widowed, she lives in the same house she and her black husband purchased in the 1950s and in which they raised their three children. She, too, grounds her identity in her experiences and is careful about the wording she chooses to describe herself: "I identify as multiethnic because I feel that in terms of environment I've become multiethnic. I don't want to say multiracial because race involves, or is generally considered to involve, genetic inheritance. I have lived in a black neighborhood for more years than I lived in a white neighborhood—ever since I was married. My experiences are much different than the experiences of white families." Both Lionel and Jane feel the need to qualify their claimed identity in a society that has historically thought of race in biological terms—and continues to do so. . . .

Tripping (trip-ping) 3. a. having fun at someone else's expense; b. overreacting; presenting oneself in an inappropriate manner

Skin color and physical features identify and locate people in a racially divided nation. Single-race people (those who comfortably claim one racial identity and group) may feel confusion, anger, skepticism, concern, pity, hostility, curiosity, or superiority when they meet someone who does not seem to fit neatly into a preset racial category. The way in which they react to members of multiracial families highlights the investment or comfort they have in existing racial categories.

Multiracial people are regularly asked, "What are you?" Those with light skin and European features are often challenged when they claim a black or multiracial identity. Silvia, with her blue eyes, has faced this situation many times: "The thing about my blue eyes, I tell people that I'm mixed and they don't believe me and insist that I'm wrong, which pisses me off more than anything. I say, 'I'm mixed; my father's black.' And they go, 'No, you're not.'" She laughs as she recalls their boldness. "'Yes I am!' I say. Then they say, 'But you have blue eyes.' And I say, 'I don't care what color my eyes are; I'm mixed!'" Still chuckling, she notes that whites tend to have this reaction more than blacks do: "Black people will usually say, 'Oh yeah, I can see it in your lips or hips.' They accept what I am saying. Whites are more likely to argue." With power, privilege, and identity at stake, combined with a general lack of awareness, whites argue with her. But a wide range of appearances in black families helps blacks "see it."

Interracially married people and members of multiracial families who appear to be single race are often assigned to a category and then treated accordingly. All kinds of decisions must be made by multiracial family members about how to respond to essentialist assumptions and demands. There is a pervasive feeling among multiracial family members that most people just don't get it. Instead of considering the color line as a problem, essentialist thinkers often see members of multiracial families as the problem, the mistake. Most people who think in essentialist terms have not had experiences that challenge traditional "stick with your own" racial thinking. Members of multiracial families learn that racial identities are far from static. Brothers and sisters may identify differently, and their identities change over time.[8] The identities they claim and the life experiences they highlight as important change depending on the group they are with, their mood, the larger political and racial climate, their age, and many other factors. Others may decide that multiracial family members are wishy-washy, lack self-esteem, and need therapy. On the contrary, many family members talk about being well grounded and having matured in their understandings of race precisely because of their multiracial experiences. Granted, this can be a difficult concept for people who do not live it to understand. Thus, many multiracial family members have stopped trying to explain or defend themselves and instead "trip on," or have fun at the expense of, people who cling to a belief that the color line is natural and normal and crossing the color line is pathological.

DISCUSSION QUESTIONS

1. How do you think the experience of black-white multiracial families compares to the experience of other multiracial families?
2. Do you think Dalmage's use of the word *tripping* adequately captures the experience of multiracial families and multiracial people?

NOTES

1. Naomi Zack, *Race and Mixed Race* (Philadelphia: Temple University Press, 1994), 22.
2. F. James Davis, *Who Is Black? One Nation's Definition* (University Park, Pa.: Penn State Press, 1991).
3. *Loving v. Virginia,* 388 U.S. 1 (1967).
4. Maureen Reddy, *Crossing the Color Line: Race, Parenting, and Culture* (New Brunswick, N.J.: Rutgers University Press, 1994), 32.
5. Ibid., 33.
6. Golfer Tiger Woods invented the word *Cablinasian to* describe his various claimed heritages.
7. See, for instance, Maria P. P. Root's "Multiracial Bill of Rights," in *The Multiracial Experience*, 3–14.
8. Root, *The Multiracial Experience.*

<hr>

READING 7

Asian American Panethnicity

Yen Le Espiritu

Arriving in the United States, nineteenth-century immigrants from Asian countries did not think of themselves as "Asians." Coming from specific districts in provinces in different nations, Asian immigrant groups did not even consider themselves

Yen Le Espiritu is a professor in the Department of Ethnic Studies at the University of California, San Diego.

PERSONAL ACCOUNT

The Best of Both Worlds

It was the fall of 1988, November 30 to be exact. I had just given birth to a beautiful baby girl six weeks prior. I was getting ready to visit the doctor for a checkup and asked my best friend if she could baby-sit my daughter while I went for my visit to the doctor's office. She was delighted and previously had been begging me to let her watch the baby.

My fiancé was stationed in Saudi Arabia with the U.S. Army. He was a commander in his unit and was a Green Beret. He stayed in Saudi Arabia for seven years during and after the Persian Gulf War.

I guess I need to mention that I am Hispanic, and my daughter is half Hispanic and half African American, which then makes her "biracial" in our country. I had about 45 minutes to get my daughter and the diaper bag ready and make it to my appointment. I was getting nervous on both accounts, leaving my little bundle of joy with my friend and also to go and get a complete physical from the gynecologist.

I heard the phone ring, and I contemplated not answering it in order to save a little time, but I grabbed it. On the other side of the phone, all I could hear was sobbing and gasps of air, and I finally said, "Hello? Who is this?" Then it came: It was my best friend crying her eyes out and confessing that she could not watch my daughter this evening. I asked her "Why?" and much to my surprise, she answered me that her mother would not allow her to watch my daughter because she was half African American and that her mother did not want my daughter in her house.

I stayed on the phone speechless, actually numb. I can't even explain how I felt. All I could do was tell her it was okay, and all she could do was apologize over and over. I knew it wasn't her fault. I cried for hours and canceled my appointment and realized that it had begun. I had been told on every occasion that I would be facing this the minute my little angel came into this world. I denied it but now knew it to be true. How could anyone discriminate against an infant? It was prejudice, ignorance, and just plain unnecessary.

We have both come a long way since that cold, cold autumn day in 1988. My daughter is now 16, a beautiful caramel-colored, young lady with so much to offer the world. She is fluent in English and Spanish and has been in a gifted and talented program since the second grade. She loves the theater and the arts and has read numerous books by famous authors. She has been dancing since she was three and competes in tap and jazz.

Not a day goes by that I don't tell her that she has the best of both worlds and that it will be up to her to utilize it and embrace it. She knows discrimination, and it will be a fight she will have to endure for years to come, but she is ready. She is definitely ready!

Mindy Peral

Chinese, Japanese, Korean, and so forth, but rather people from Toisan, Hoiping, or some other district in Guandong Province in China or from Hiroshima, Yamaguchi, or some other prefecture in Japan. Members of each group considered themselves culturally and politically distinct. Historical enmities between their mother countries further separated the groups even after their arrival in the United States. Writing about early Asian immigrant communities, Eliot Mears (1928:4) reported that "it is exceptional when one learns of any entente between these Orientals." However, non-Asians had little understanding or appreciation of these distinctions. For the most part, outsiders accorded to Asian peoples certain common characteristics and traits that were essentially supranational (Browne

1985:8–9). Indeed, the exclusion acts and quotas limiting Asian immigration to the United States relied upon racialist constructions of Asians as homogeneous (Lowe 1991:28).

Mindful that whites generally lump all Asians together, early Asian immigrant communities sought to "keep their images discrete and were not above denigrating, or at least approving the denigration of, other Asian groups" (Daniels 1988:113). It was not until the late 1960s, with the advent of the Asian American movement, that a pan-Asian consciousness and constituency were first formed. To build political unity, college students of Asian ancestry heralded their common fate—the similarity of experiences and treatment that Asian groups endured in the United States (Omi and Winant

1986:105). In other words, the pan-Asian concept, originally imposed by non-Asians, became a symbol of pride and a rallying point for mass mobilization by later generations. This [discussion] examines the social, political, and demographic factors that allowed pan-Asianism to take root in the 1960s and not earlier.

ETHNIC "DISIDENTIFICATION"

Before the 1960s, Asians in this country frequently practiced ethnic disidentification, the act of distancing one's group from another group so as not to be mistaken and suffer the blame for the presumed misdeeds of that group (Hayano 1981:162). Faced with external threats, group members can either intensify their solidarity or they can distance themselves from the stigmatized segment. Instead of uniting to fight anti-Asian forces, early Asian immigrant communities often disassociated themselves from the targeted group so as not to be mistaken for members of it and suffer any possible negative consequences (Hayano 1981:161; Daniels 1988:113). Two examples of ethnic disidentification among Asians in this country occurred during the various anti-Asian exclusion movements and during World War II. These incidents are instructive not only as evidence of ethnic disidentification but also as documentation of the pervasiveness of racial lumping. Precisely because of racial lumping, persons of Asian ancestry found it necessary to disassociate themselves from other Asian groups.

Exclusion Movements

Beginning with the first student laborers in the late nineteenth century, Japanese immigrants always differentiated themselves from Chinese immigrants. Almost uniformly, Japanese immigrants perceived their Chinese counterparts in an "unsympathetic, negative light, and often repeated harsh American criticisms of the Chinese" (Ichioka 1988:191). In their opinion, the Chinese came from an inferior nation; they also were lower-class laborers, who had not adapted themselves to American society. In 1892, a Japanese student laborer described San

Francisco's Chinatown as "a world of beasts in which . . . exists every imaginable depravity, crime, and vice" (cited in Ichioka 1988:191).

Indeed, the Japanese immigrants were a more select group than their Chinese counterparts. The Japanese government viewed overseas Japanese as representatives of their homeland. Therefore, it screened prospective emigrants to ensure that they were healthy and literate and would uphold Japan's national honor (Takaki 1989:46).

More important, Japanese immigrants distanced themselves from the Chinese because they feared that Americans would lump them together. Aware of Chinese exclusion, Japanese immigrant leaders had always dreaded the thought of Japanese exclusion. To counteract any negative association, Japanese immigrant leaders did everything possible to distinguish themselves from the Chinese immigrants (Ichioka 1988:250). For example, to separate themselves from the unassimilable Chinese laborers, some Japanese immigrant leaders insisted that their Japanese workers wear American work clothes and even eat American food (Ichioka 1988:185). In 1901, the Japanese in California distributed leaflets requesting that they be differentiated from the Chinese (tenBroek, Barnhart, and Matson 1970:23).

However, under the general rubric Asiatic, the Japanese inherited the painful experiences of the Chinese.[1] All the vices attributed to the Chinese were transferred to these newest Asian immigrants (Browne 1985). Having successfully excluded Chinese laborers, organized labor once again led the campaign to drive out the Japanese immigrants. In 1904, the American Federation of Labor adopted its first anti-Japanese resolution. Charging that the Japanese immigrants were as undesirable as the Chinese, the unions' resolution called for the expansion of the 1902 Chinese Exclusion Act to include Japanese and other Asian laborers. By mid-1905, the labor unions of California had joined forces to establish the Asiatic Exclusion League (Hill 1973:52–54; Ichioka 1988:191–192).

Since the Japanese immigrants considered themselves superior to the Chinese, they felt indignant and insulted whenever they were lumped together with them. In 1892, a Japanese immigrant wrote in the *Oakland Enquirer* that he wished "to inveigh with all my power" against American newspapers that compared the Japanese to "the truly ignorant class of Chinese laborers and condemned them as bearers of some mischievous Oriental evils" (cited in Ichioka 1988:192). Instead of joining with the Chinese to fight the anti-Asian exclusion movement, some Japanese leaders went so far as to condone publicly the exclusion of the Chinese while insisting that the Japanese were the equals of Americans (Daniels 1988:113). Above all else, Japanese immigrant leaders wanted Japanese immigration to be treated on the same footing as European immigration (Ichioka 1988:250).

In the end, Japanese attempts at disidentification failed. With the passage of the 1924 Immigration Act, Japanese immigration was effectively halted. This act contained two provisions designed to stop Japanese immigration. The first barred the immigration of Japanese wives even if their husbands were United States citizens. The second prohibited the immigration of aliens ineligible for citizenship. Because the Supreme Court had ruled in 1922 that persons of Japanese ancestry could not become naturalized citizens, this provision effectively closed the door on Japanese and most other Asian immigration (U.S. Commission on Civil Rights 1986:8–9). The Japanese immigrants felt doubly affronted by the 1924 act because it ranked them, not as the equals of Europeans, but on the same level as the lowly Chinese, the very people whom they themselves considered inferior (Ichioka 1988:250). Thus, despite all their attempts to disassociate themselves from the Chinese, with the passage of the act, the Japanese joined the Chinese as a people deemed unworthy of becoming Americans. Little did they foresee that, in less than two decades, other Asian groups in America would disassociate themselves from the Japanese.

World War II and Japanese Internment

Immediately after the bombing of Pearl Harbor, the incarceration of Japanese Americans began. On the night of December 7, the Federal Bureau of Investigation (FBI) began taking into custody persons of Japanese ancestry who had connections to the Japanese government. Working on the principle of guilt by association, the security agencies simply rounded up most of the Issei (first-generation) leaders of the Japanese community. Initially, the federal government differentiated between alien and citizen Japanese Americans, but this distinction gradually disappeared. In the end, the government evacuated more than 100,000 persons of Japanese ancestry into concentration camps, approximately two-thirds of whom were American-born citizens. It was during this period that the Japanese community discovered that the legal distinction between citizen and alien was not nearly so important as the distinction between white and yellow (Daniels 1988:ch. 6).

Like the Japanese, the Chinese understood the importance of the distinction between white and yellow. Fearful that they would be targets of anti-Japanese activities, many persons of Chinese ancestry, especially in the West, took to wearing buttons that proclaimed positively "I'm Chinese." Similarly, many Chinese shopkeepers displayed signs announcing, "This is a Chinese shop." Some Chinese immigrants even joined the white persecution with buttons that added "I hate Japs worse than you do" (Daniels 1988:205; Takaki 1989:370–371). The small Korean and Filipino communities took similar actions. Because of Japan's occupation of Korea at the time, being mistaken as Japanese particularly angered Koreans in the United States. Cognizant of Asian lumping, the United Korean Committee prepared identification cards proclaiming "I am Korean." During the early months of the war, women wore Korean dresses regularly to distinguish themselves from the Japanese (Melendy 1977:158; Takaki 1989:365–366). Similarly, persons of Filipino ancestry wore buttons proclaiming "I am a Filipino" (Takaki 1989:363).

Given the wars between their mother countries and Japan, it is not surprising that the Chinese, Koreans, and Filipinos distanced themselves from the Japanese. But their reactions are instructive not only as examples of ethnic disidentification but also as testimonies to the pervasiveness of racial lumping. Popular confusion of the various Asian groups was so prevalent that it was necessary for Chinese, Filipinos, and Koreans to don ethnic clothing and identification buttons to differentiate themselves from the Japanese. Without these *visible* signs of ethnicity, these three Asian groups would probably have been mistaken for Japanese by anti-Japanese forces. As Ronald Takaki (1989:370) reported, Asian groups "remembered how they had previously been called 'Japs' and how many whites had lumped all Asians together." But there are also examples of how Asian groups united when inter-Asian cooperation advanced their common interests.

Inter-Asian Labor Movements

The most notable example of inter-Asian solidarity was the 1920 collaboration of Japanese and Filipino plantation laborers in Hawaii. In the beginning, plantation workers had organized in terms of national origins. Thus, the Japanese belonged to the Japanese union and the Filipinos to the Filipino union. In the early 1900s, an ethnically based strike seemed sensible to Japanese plantation laborers because they represented about 70 percent of the entire work force. Filipinos constituted less than 1 percent. However, by 1920, Japanese workers represented only 44 percent of the labor force, while Filipino workers represented 30 percent. Japanese and Filipino union leaders understood that they would have to combine to be politically and economically effective (Johanessen 1950:75–83; Takaki 1989:152).

Because together they constituted more than 70 percent of the work force in Oahu, the 1920 Japanese-Filipino strike brought plantation operations to a sudden stop. Although the workers were eventually defeated, the 1920 strike was the "first major interethnic working-class struggle in Hawaii" (Takaki 1989:154).[2] Subsequently, the Japanese Federation of Labor elected to become an interethnic union. To promote a multiethnic class solidarity, the new union called itself the Hawaii Laborers Association (Takaki 1989:154–155).

Although the 1920 strike was a de facto example of pan-Asian cooperation, this cooperation needs to be distinguished from the post-1960 pan-Asian solidarity. The purported unifying factor in 1920 was a common class status, not a shared cultural or racial background (Takaki 1989:154). This class solidarity is different from the large-scale organization of ethnicity that emerged in the late 1960s. For most Asian Americans, the more recent development represents an enlargement of their identity system, a circle beyond their previous national markers of identity. True, like working-class unions, panethnic groups are interest groups with material demands (Glazer and Moynihan 1963; Bonacich and Modell 1980). However, unlike labor unions, panethnic groups couch their demands in ethnic or racial terms—not purely in class terms. In other words, their ethnicity is used as a basis for the assertion of collective claims, many but not all of which are class based.

SOCIAL AND DEMOGRAPHIC CHANGES: SETTING THE CONTEXT

. . . Before 1940, the Asian population in the United States was primarily an immigrant population. Immigrant Asians faced practical barriers to pan-Asian unity. Foremost was their lack of a common language. Old national rivalries were another obstacle, as many early Asian immigrants carried the political memories and outlook of their homelands. For example, Japan's occupation of Korea resulted in pervasive anti-Japanese sentiments among Koreans in the United States. According to Brett Melendy (1977:155), "Fear and hatred of the Japanese appeared to be the only unifying force among the various Korean groups through the years." Moreover, these historical enmities and linguistic and cultural differences reinforced one another as divisive agents.

During the postwar period, due to immigration restrictions and the growing dominance of the second and third generations, American-born Asians outnumbered immigrants. The demographic changes of the 1940s were pronounced. During this decade, nearly twenty thousand Chinese American babies were born. For the first time, the largest five-year cohort of Chinese Americans was under five years of age (Kitano and Daniels 1988:37). By 1960, approximately two-thirds of the Asian population in California had been born in the United States (Ong 1989:5–8). As the Asian population became a native-born community, linguistic and cultural differences began to blur. Although they had attended Asian-language schools, most American-born Asians possessed only a limited knowledge of their ethnic language (Chan 1991:115). By 1960, with English as the common language, persons from different Asian backgrounds were able to communicate with one another (Ling 1984:73), and in so doing create a common identity associated with the United States.

Moreover, unlike their immigrant parents, native-born and American-educated Asians could muster only scant loyalties to old world ties. Historical antagonisms between their mother countries thus receded in importance (Wong 1972:34). For example, growing up in America, second-generation Koreans "had difficulty feeling the painful loss of the homeland and understanding the indignity of Japanese domination" (Takaki 1989:292). Thus, while the older generation of Koreans hated all Japanese, "their children were much less hostile or had no concern at all" (Melendy 1977:156). As a native-born Japanese American community advocate explained, "By 1968, we had a second generation. We could speak English; so there was no language problem. And we had little feelings of historical animosity" (Kokubun interview).

As national differences receded in subjective importance, generational differences widened. For the most part, American-born Asians considered themselves to have more in common with other American-born Asians than they did with foreign-born compatriots.[3] According to a third-generation Japanese American who is married to a Chinese American, "As far as our experiences in America, I have more things in common than differences with a Chinese American. Being born and raised here gives us something in common. We have more in common with each other than with a Japanese from Japan, or a Chinese from China" (Ichioka interview). Much to their parents' dismay, young Asian Americans began

to choose their friends and spouses from other Asian groups. . . .

Before World War II, Asian immigrant communities were quite distinct entities, isolated from one another and from the larger society. Because of language difficulties, prejudice, and lack of business opportunities elsewhere, there was little chance for Asians in the United States to live outside their ethnic enclaves (Yuan 1966:331). Shut out of the mainstream of American society, the various immigrant groups struggled separately in their respective Chinatowns, Little Tokyos, or Manilatowns. Stanford Lyman (1970:57–63) reported that the early Chinese and Japanese communities in the western states had little to do with one another—either socially or politically . . .

Economic and residential barriers began to crumble after World War II. The war against Nazism called attention to racism at home and discredited the notions of white superiority. The fifteen years after the war was a period of largely positive change as civil rights statutes outlawed racial discrimination in employment as well as housing (Daniels 1988:ch. 7). Popular attitudes were also changing. Polls taken during World War II showed a distinct hostility toward Japan: 74 percent of the respondents favored either killing off all Japanese, destroying Japan as a political entity, or supervising it. On the West Coast, 97 percent of the people polled approved of the relocation of Japanese Americans. In contrast, by 1949, 64 percent of those polled were either friendly or neutral toward Japan (Feraru 1950).

During the postwar years, Asian American residential patterns changed significantly. Because of the lack of statistical data,[4] a longitudinal study of the changing residential patterns of Asian Americans cannot be made. However, descriptive accounts of Asian American communities indicate that these enclaves declined in the postwar years. Edwin Hoyt (1974:94) reported that in the 1940s, second-generation Chinese Americans moved out of the Chinatowns. Although they still came back to shop or to see friends, they lived elsewhere. In 1940, Rose Hum Lee found twenty-eight cities with an area called Chinatown in the United States. By 1955, Peter Sih found only sixteen (Sung 1967:143–144). New York's Chinatown exemplifies the declining significance of Asian ethnic enclaves. In 1940, 50 percent of the Chinese in New York City lived in its Chinatown; by 1960, less than one-third lived there (Yuan 1966:331). Similarly, many returning Japanese Americans abandoned their prewar settlement in old central cities and joined the migration to suburbia (Daniels 1988:294). In the early 1970s, Little Tokyo in Los Angeles remained a bustling Japanese American center, "but at night the shop owners [went] home to the houses in the suburbs" (Hoyt 1974:84)....

Moreover, recent research on suburban segregation indicates that the level of segregation between certain Asian American groups is often less than that between them and non-Asians.... Though not comprehensive, these studies together suggest that Asian residential segregation declined in the postwar years.

As various Asian groups in the United States interacted, they became aware of common problems and goals that transcended parochial interests and historical antagonisms. One recurrent problem was employment discrimination. According to a 1965 report published by the California Fair Employment Practices Commission, for every $51 earned by a white male Californian, Japanese males earned $43 and Chinese males $38—even though Chinese and Japanese American men had become slightly better educated than the white majority (Daniels 1988:315). Moreover, although the postwar period marked the first time that well-trained Chinese and Japanese Americans could find suitable employment with relative ease, they continued to be passed over for promotion to administrative and supervisory positions (Kitano and Daniels 1988:47). Asians in the United States began to see themselves as a group that shared important common experiences: exploitation, oppression, and discrimination (Uyematsu 1971).

Because inter-Asian contact and communication were greatest on college campuses, pan-Asianism was strongest there (Wong 1972:33–34). Exposure to one another and to the mainstream society led some young Asian Americans to feel that they were fundamentally different from whites. Disillusioned with the white society and alienated from their traditional communities, many Asian American student activists turned to the alternative strategy of pan-Asian unification (Weiss 1974:69–70).

THE CONSTRUCTION OF PAN-ASIAN ETHNICITY

Although broader social struggles and internal demographic changes provided the impetus for the Asian American movement, it was the group's politics—confrontational and explicitly pan-Asian— that shaped the movement's content. Influenced by the internal colonial model, which stresses the commonalities among "colonized groups," college students of Asian ancestry declared solidarity with fellow Asian Americans—and with other Third World[5] minorities (Blauner 1972:ch. 2). Rejecting the label "Oriental," they proclaimed themselves "Asian American." Through pan-Asian organizations, publications, and Asian American studies programs, Asian American activists built pan-Asian solidarity by pointing out their common fate in American society. The pan-Asian concept enabled diverse Asian American groups to understand their "unequal circumstances and histories as being related" (Lowe 1991:30).

From "Yellow" to "Asian American"

Following the example of the Black Power movement, Asian American activists spearheaded their own Yellow Power movement to seek "freedom from racial oppression through the power of a consolidated yellow people" (Uyematsu 1971:12). In the summer of 1968, more than one hundred students of diverse Asian backgrounds attended an "Are You Yellow?" conference at UCLA to discuss issues of Yellow Power, identity, and the war in Vietnam (Ling 1989:53). In 1970, a new pan-Asian organization in northern California called itself the "Yellow Seed" because "Yellow [is] the common bond between Asian-Americans and Seed symboliz[es] growth as an individual and as an alliance" (Masada 1970). This "yellow" reference was dropped when Filipino Americans rejected the term, claiming that they were brown, not yellow (Rabaya 1971:110; Ignacio 1976:84). At the first Asian American national conference in 1972, Filipino Americans "made it clear to the conferees that we were 'Brown Asians'" by forming a Brown Asian Caucus (Ignacio 1976:139–141). It is important to note, however, that Filipino American activists did not reject the term *yellow* because they objected to the pan-Asian framework. Quite the contrary, they rejected it because it allegedly excluded them from that grouping (Rabaya 1971:110).

. . . Asian American activists also rejected *Oriental* because the term conjures up images of "the sexy Susie Wong, the wily Charlie Chan, and the evil Fu Manchu" (Weiss 1974:234). It is also a term that smacks of European colonialism and imperialism: *Oriental* means "East"; Asia is "east" only in relationship to Europe, which was taken as the point of reference (Browne 1985). To define their own image and to claim an *American* identity, college students of Asian ancestry coined the term *Asian American* to "stand for all of us Americans of Asian descent" (Ichioka interview). While *Oriental* suggests passivity and acquiescence, *Asian Americans* connotes political activism because an Asian American "gives a damn about his life, his work, his beliefs, and is willing to do almost anything to help Orientals become Asian Americans" (cited in Weiss 1974:234).

The account above suggests that the creation of a new name is a significant symbolic move in constructing an ethnic identity. In their attempt to forge a pan-Asian identity, Asian American activists first had to coin a composite term that would unify and encompass the constituent groups. Filipino Americans' rejection of the term *yellow* and the activists' objection to the cliché-ridden *Oriental* forced the group to change its name to Asian American. . . .

Pan-Asian Organizations

Influenced by the political tempo of the 1960s, young Asian Americans began to join such organizations as the Free Speech Movement at the University of California at Berkeley, Students for a Democratic Society, and the Progressive Labor Party. However, these young activists "had no organization or coalition to draw attention to themselves as a distinct group" (Wong 1972:33). Instead, they participated as individuals—often at the invitation of their white or black friends (Chin 1971:285; Nakano 1984:3–4). While Asian American activists subscribed to the integrationist ideology of the 1960s and 1970s social movements, they also felt impotent and alienated. There was no structure to uphold their own identity. As an example, when the Peace and Freedom Party was formed on the basis of black and white coalitions, Asian American activists felt excluded because they were neither black nor white (Wong 1972:34; Yoshimura 1989:107).

In the late 1960s, linking their political views with the growth of racial pride among their ranks, Asian Americans already active in various political movements came together to form their own organizations (Nakano 1984:3–4). Most of the early pan-Asian organizations were college based. In 1968, activists at the University of California, Berkeley, founded one of the first pan-Asian political organizations: the Asian American Political Alliance (AAPA). According to a co-founder of the organization, its establishment marked the first time that the term *Asian American* was used nationally to mobilize people of Asian descent (Ichioka interview). . . .

By the mid-1970s, *Asian American* had become a familiar term (Lott 1976:30). Although first coined by college activists, the pan-Asian concept began to be used extensively by professional and community spokespersons to lobby for the health and welfare of Americans of Asian descent. In addition to the local and single-ethnic organizations of an earlier era, Asian American professionals and community activists formed national and pan-Asian organizations such as the Pacific/Asian Coalition and the Asian American Social Workers (Ignacio 1976:162; Kuo 1979:283–284). Also, Asian American caucuses could be found in national professional organizations such as the American Public Health Association, the American Sociological Association, the American Psychological Association, the American

Psychiatric Association, and the American Librarians Association (Lott 1976:31). Commenting on the "literally scores of pan-Asian organizations" in the mid-1970s, William Liu (1976:6) asserted that "the idea of pan-Asian cooperation [was] viable and ripe for development." . . .

THE LIMITS OF PAN-ASIANISM

Although pan-Asian consolidation certainly has occurred, it has been by no means universal. For those who wanted a broader political agenda, the pan-Asian scope was too narrow and its racial orientation too segregative (Wong 1972:33; Lowe 1991:39). For others who wanted to preserve ethnic particularism, the pan-Asian agenda threatened to remove second- and third-generation Asians "from their conceptual ties to their community" (R. Tanaka 1976:47). These competing levels of organization mitigated the impact of pan-Asianism.

Moreover, pan-Asianism has been primarily the ideology of native-born, American-educated, and middle-class Asians. Embraced by students, artists, professionals, and political activists, pan-Asian consciousness thrived on college campuses and in urban settings. However, it barely touched the Asian ethnic enclaves. When the middle-class student activists carried the enlarged and politicized Asian American consciousness to the ethnic communities, they encountered apprehension, if not outright hostility (Chan 1991:175) Conscious of their national origins and overburdened with their day-to-day struggles for survival, most community residents ignored or spurned the movement's political agenda (P. Wong 1972:34). Chin (1971:287) reported that few Chinatown residents participated in any of the pan-Asian political events. Similarly, members of the Nisei-dominated Japanese American Citizens League "were determined to keep a closed mind and maintain their negative stereotype" of the members of the Asian American Political Alliance (J. Matsui 1968:6). For their part, young Asian American activists accused their elders of having been so whitewashed that they had deleted their experiences of prejudice and discrimination

from their history (Weiss 1974:238). Because these young activists were not rooted in the community, their base of support was narrow and their impact upon the larger society often limited (Wong 1972:37; Nishio 1982:37).

Even among those who were involved in the Asian American movement, divisions arose from conflicting sets of interests as subgroups decided what and whose interests would be addressed. Oftentimes, conflicts over material interests took on ethnic coloration, with participants from smaller subgroups charging that "Asian American" primarily meant Chinese and Japanese American, the two largest and most acculturated Asian American groups at the time (Ignacio 1976:220; Ling 1984:193–195). For example, most Asian American Studies programs did not include courses on other Asian groups, but only on Chinese and Japanese. Similarly, the Asian American women's movement often subsumed the needs of their Korean and Filipina members under those of Chinese and Japanese women (Ling 1984:193–195). Chinese and Japanese Americans also were the instructors of Asian American ethnic studies directors and staff members of many Asian American projects,[6] and advisory and panel members in many governmental agencies (Ignacio 1976:223–224).

The ethnic and class inequality within the pan-Asian structure has continued to be a source of friction and mistrust, with participants from the less dominant groups feeling shortchanged and excluded. The influx of the post-1965 immigrants and the tightening of public funding resources have further deepened the ethnic and class cleavages among Asian American subgroups.

CONCLUSION

The development of a pan-Asian consciousness and constituency reflected broader societal developments and demographic changes, as well as the group's political agenda. By the late 1960s, pan-Asianism was possible because of the more amicable relationships among the Asian countries, the declining residential segregation among diverse

Asian groups in America, and the large number of native-born, American-educated political actors. Disillusioned with the larger society and estranged from their traditional communities, third- and fourth-generation Asian Americans turned to the alternative strategy of pan-Asian unification. Through pan-Asian organizations, media, and Asian American Studies programs, these political activists assumed the role of "cultural entrepreneurs" consciously creating a community of culture out of diverse Asian peoples.[7] This process of pan-Asian consolidation did not proceed smoothly nor did it encompass all Asian Americans. Ethnic chauvinism, competition for scarce resources, and class cleavages continued to divide the subgroups. However, once established, the pan-Asian structure not only reinforced the cohesiveness of already existing networks but also expanded these networks. Although first conceived by young Asian American activists, the pan-Asian concept was subsequently institutionalized by professionals and community groups, as well as government agencies. The confrontational politics of the activists eventually gave way to the conventional and electoral politics of the politicians, lobbyists, and professionals, as Asian Americans continued to rely on the pan-Asian framework to enlarge their political capacities.

DISCUSSION QUESTIONS

1. Why are Asian ethnic enclaves declining in number?
2. Is the term *pan-Asian* still relevant?
3. Who is now considered Asian American?

NOTES

1. On the other hand, due to the relative strength of Japan in the world order, Japanese immigrants at times received more favorable treatment than other Asian immigrants. For example, in 1905, wary of offending Japan, national politicians blocked an attempt by the San Francisco Board of Education to transfer Japanese students from the public schools reserved for white children to the "Oriental" school serving the Chinese (Chan 1991: 59).

2. Although many Korean laborers were sympathetic to the 1920 strike, because of their hatred for the Japanese, they did not participate. As the Korean National Association announced, "We do not wish to be looked upon as strike-breakers, but we shall continue to work in the plantation and we are opposed to the Japanese in everything" (cited in Melendy 1977: 164).

3. The same is true with other racial groups. For example, American-born Haitians are more like their African American peers than like their Haitian parents (Woldemikael 1989: 166).

4. Ideally, residential patterns should be analyzed at the census tract level. However, this analysis cannot be done because Asians were not tabulated by census tracts until the 1980 census.

5. During the late 1960s, in radical circles, the term *third world* referred to the nation's racially oppressed people.

6. For example, the staff of the movement publication *Gidra* were predominantly Japanese Americans.

7. For a discussion of the role of "cultural entrepreneurs," see Cornell (1988b).

REFERENCES

Blauner, Robert. 1972. *Racial Oppression in America.* New York: Harper & Row.

Bonacich, Edna, and John Modell. 1980. *The Economic Basis of Ethnic Solidarity: A Study of Japanese Americans.* Berkeley: University of California Press.

Browne, Blaine T. 1985. "A Common Thread: American Images of the Chinese and Japanese, 1930–1960." Ph.D. dissertation, University of Oklahoma.

Chan, Sucheng. 1991. *Asian Americans: An Interpretive History.* Boston: Twayne.

Chin, Rocky. 1971. "NY Chinatown Today: Community in Crisis." Pp. 282–295 in *Roots: An Asian American Reader,* edited by Amy Tachiki, Eddie Wong, and Franklin Odo. Los Angeles: UCLA Asian American Studies Center.

Cornell, Stephen. 1988a. *The Return of the Native: American Indian Political Resurgence.* New York: Oxford University Press.

————. 1988b. "Structure, Content, and Logic in Ethnic Group Formation." Working Paper series, Center for Research on Politics and Social Organization, Department of Sociology, Harvard University.

Daniels, Roger. 1971. *Concentration Camps USA: Japanese Americans and World War II.* Hinsdale, IL: Dryden Press.

————. 1988. *Asian America: Chinese and Japanese in the United States since 1850.* Seattle: University of Washington Press.

Feraru, Arthur N. 1950. "Public Opinions Polls on Japan." *Far Eastern Survey* 19 (10): 101–103.

I Thought My Race Was Invisible

In a conversation with a close friend, I noticed that I am, to her, a representative of my entire racial category. To put things in perspective, my friend Janet and I have been friends for eight years. During this period, it has come up that I am a third-generation Japanese-American who has no ties to being Japanese other than a couple of sushi dishes I learned how to make from my grandmother. Nonetheless, whenever a question regarding "Asians" comes up, she comes to me as if I can provide the definitive answer to every Asian mystery.

Yesterday Janet asked me if there is a cultural reason why Asians "always drive so slow." Not having noticed that Asians drive slowly (in fact, I have noticed a number of Asians who actually exceed the speed limit), I commented that perhaps they are law-abiding citizens. She said that must explain it: "They are used to following the law." I thought, "Am I one of 'they'?" but didn't comment further. Before we switched subjects, she noted that she "knew there had to be a cultural reason" for their driving.

Janet then told me about a Vietnamese woman at the Hair Cuttery who cut her husband's hair. As is normal, her husband talked to the woman as she worked on his hair; he asked her what she did before working at the Hair Cuttery. She said that she used to work in the fields in California (i.e., she was a field hand). Janet told me of the healthy respect that she and her husband had for a woman who worked in the fields, put herself through cosmetology school, moved East, and became a professional hairstylist. She commented that "Blacks" should follow her example and work instead of complaining of their lot in life.

This conversation was interesting and a bit startling. Janet is a good friend who shares many interests with me. What I realized from this conversation, and in remembering others that were similar, is that she feels that I am a representative of the whole Asian race. Not only is this unrealistic, but it is surprising that she would imagine I could answer for my race given my lack of real cultural exposure. In relaying the story of the Vietnamese woman, I had a sense that she was complimenting me, and my race, for the industriousness "we" demonstrate. It seems to me that she approved of the "typically" Asian way of working (quietly, so as not to insult or offend), even though this woman was probably underpaid and overworked in her field hand job. While she approved of her reticence, Janet did not approve of "Black" complaints.

I realize that to Janet, I will always be Asian. I had not really thought about it before, but I never think of Janet as White; her race is invisible to me. I had thought that my race was invisible too; however, I realize now that I will always be the "marked" friend. This saddens me a bit, but I accept it with the knowledge that she is a close friend. Nonetheless, it is unfortunate to think that even between friends, race is an issue.

Sherri H. Pereira

Glazer, Nathan, and Daniel Patrick Moynihan. 1963. *Beyond the Melting Pot: The Negroes, Puerto Ricans, Jews, Italians, and Irish of New York City.* Cambridge, MA: M.I.T. Press.

Hayano, David M. 1981. "Ethnic Identification and Disidentification: Japanese-American Views of Chinese-Americans." *Ethnic Groups* 3 (2): 157–171.

Hill, Herbert. 1973. "Anti-Oriental Agitation and the Rise of Working-Class Racism." *Society* 10 (2): 43–54.

Hoyt, Edwin P. 1974. *Asians in the West.* New York: Thomas Nelson.

Ichioka, Yuji. 1988. *The Issei: The World of the First Generation Japanese Americans, 1885–1924.* New York: Free Press.

Ignacio, Lemuel F. 1976. *Asian Americans and Pacific Islanders (Is There Such an Ethnic Group?).* San Jose: Filipino Development Associates.

Johanessen, Edward L. H. 1950. *The Labor Movement in the Territory of Hawaii.* M.A. thesis, University of California, Berkeley.

Kitano, Harry H. L., and Roger Daniels. 1988. *Asian Americans: Emerging Minorities.* Englewood Cliffs, NJ: Prentice-Hall.

Kuo, Wen H. 1979. "On the Study of Asian-Americans: Its Current State and Agenda." *Sociological Quarterly* 20 (Spring): 279–290.

Ling, Susie Hsiuhan. 1984. "The Mountain Movers: Asian American Women's Movement in Los Angeles." M.A. thesis, University of California, Los Angeles.

———. 1989. "The Mountain Movers: Asian American Women's Movement in Los Angeles." *Amerasia Journal* 15 (1): 51–67.

Liu, William. 1976. "Asian American Research: Views of a Sociologist." *Asian Studies Occasional Report,* no. 2.

Lott, Juanita Tamayo. 1976. "The Asian American Concept: In Quest of Identity." *Bridge,* November, pp. 30–34.

Lowe, Lisa. 1991. "Heterogeneity, Hybridity, Multiplicity: Marking Asian American Differences." *Diaspora* 1: 24–44.

Lyman, Stanford M. 1970. *The Asian in the West.* Reno and Las Vegas: Desert Research Institute, University of Nevada.

Masada, Saburo. 1970. "Stockton's Yellow Seed." *Pacific Citizen,* 9 October.

Massey, Douglas S., and Nancy A. Denton. 1987. "Trends in the Residential Segregation of Blacks, Hispanics, and Asians, 1970–1980." *American Sociological Review* 52 (December): 802–825.

Matsui, Jeffrey. 1968 "Asian American." *Pacific Citizen,* 6 Setptember.

Mears, Eliot Grinnell. 1928. *Resident Orientals on the American Pacific Coast.* New York: Arno Press.

Melendy, H. Brett. 1977. *Asians in America: Filipinos, Koreans, and East Indians.* Boston: Twayne.

Nakano, Roy. 1984. "Marxist Leninist Organization in the Asian American Community: Los Angeles, 1969–79." Unpublished student paper, UCLA.

Nishio, Alan. 1982. "Personal Reflections on the Asian National Movements." *East Wind,* Spring/Summer, pp. 36–38.

Omi, Michael, and Howard Winant. 1986. *Racial Formation in the United States: From the 1960s to the 1980s.* New York: Routledge and Kegan Paul.

Ong, Paul. 1989. "California's Asian Population: Past Trends and Projections for the Year 2000." Los Angeles: Graduate School of Architecture and Urban Planning.

Rabaya, Violet. 1971. "I Am Curious (Yellow?)." Pp. 110–111 in *Roots: An Asian American Reader,* edited by Amy Tachiki, Eddie Wong, and Franklin Odo. Los Angeles: UCLA Asian American Studies Center.

Sung, Betty Lee. 1967. *Mountain of Gold: The Story of the Chinese in America.* New York: Macmillan.

Takaki, Ronald. 1989. *Strangers from a Different Shore: A History of Asian Americans.* Boston: Little, Brown.

Tanaka, Ron. 1976. "Culture, Communication, and the Asian Movement in Perspective." *Journal of Ethnic Studies* 4 (1): 37–52.

tenBroek, J., E. N. Barnhart, and F. W. Matson. 1970. *Prejudice, War, and the Constitution.* Berkeley: University of California Press.

U.S. Commission on Civil Rights. 1986. *Recent Activities against Citizens and Residents of Asian Descent.* Washington, DC: U.S. Government Printing Office.

Uyematsu, Amy. 1971. "The Emergence of Yellow Power in America." Pp. 9–13 in *Roots: An Asian American Reader,* edited by Amy Tachiki, Eddie Wong, and Franklin Odo. Los Angeles: UCLA Asian American Studies Center.

Weiss, Melford S. 1974. *Valley City: A Chinese Community in America.* Cambridge, MA: Schenkman.

Woldemikael, Tekle Mariam. 1989. *Becoming Black Americans: Haitians and American Institutions in Evanston, Illinois.* New York: AMS Press.

Wong, Paul. 1972. "The Emergence of the Asian-American Movement." *Bridge* 2 (1): 33–39.

Yoshimura, Evelyn. 1989. "How I Became an Activist and What It All Means to Me." *Amerasia Journal* 15 (I): 106–109.

Yuan, D. Y. 1966. "Chinatown and Beyond: The Chinese Population in Metropolitan New York." *Phylon* 23 (4): 321–332.

READING 8

Whiteness as an "Unmarked" Cultural Category

Ruth Frankenberg

America's supposed to be the melting pot. I know that I've got a huge number of nationalities in my blood, but how do I—what do I call myself? And hating this country as I do, I don't like to say I'm an American. Even though it is what I am. I hate identifying myself as only an American, because I have so much objections to Americans' place in the world. I don't know how I felt about that when I was growing up, but I never—I didn't like to pledge allegiance to the flag. . . . Still, at this point in my life, I wonder what it is that somebody with all this melting pot blood can call their own. . . .

Especially growing up in the sixties, when people *did* say "I'm proud to be Black," "I'm proud to be Hispanic," you know, and it became very popular to be proud of your ethnicity. And even feminists, you know, you could say, "I'm a woman," and be proud of it. But there's still a majority of the country that can't say they are proud of anything!

Suzie Roberts's words powerfully illustrate the key themes . . . that stirred the women I interviewed as they examined their own identities: what had formed them, what they counted as (their own or others') cultural practice(s), and what constituted identities of which they could be proud.* This [discussion] explores perceptions of whiteness as a lo-

Ruth Frankenberg is a professor of American studies at the University of California, Davis.
*Between 1984 and 1986 I interviewed 30 white women, diverse in age, class, region of origin, sexuality, family situation and political orientation, all living in California at the time of the interviews.

cation of culture and identity, focusing mainly on white feminist . . . women's views and contrasting their voices with those of more politically conservative women. . . .

[M]any of the women I interviewed, including even some of the conservative ones, appeared to be self-conscious about white power and racial inequality. In part because of their sense of the links and parallels between white racial dominance in the United States and U.S. domination on a global scale, there was a complex interweaving of questions about race and nation—whiteness and Americanness—in these women's thoughts about white culture. Similarly, conceptions of racial, national, and cultural belonging frequently leaked into one another.

On the one hand, then, these women's views of white culture seemed to be distinctively modern. But at the same time, their words drew on much earlier historical moments and participated in long-established modes of cultural description. In the broadest sense, Western colonial discourses on the white self, the nonwhite Other, and the white Other too, were very much in evidence. These discourses produced dualistic conceptualizations of whiteness versus other cultural forms. The women thus often spoke about culture in ways that reworked, and yet remained tied to, "older" forms of racism.

For a significant number of young white women, being white felt like being cultureless. Cathy Thomas, in the following description of whiteness, raised many of the themes alluded to by other feminist and race-cognizant women. She described what she saw as a lack of form and substance:

> . . . the formlessness of being white. Now if I was a middle western girl, or a New Yorker, if I had a fixed regional identity that was something palpable, then I'd be a white New Yorker, no doubt, but I'd still be a New Yorker. . . . Being a Californian, I'm sure it has its hallmarks, but to me they were invisible. . . . If I had an ethnic base to identify from, if I was even Irish American, that would have been something formed, if I was a working-class woman, that would have been something formed. But to be a Heinz 57 American, a white, class-confused American, land of the Kleenex type

American, is so formless in and of itself. It only takes shape in relation to other people.

Whiteness as a cultural space is represented here as amorphous and indescribable, in contrast with a range of other identities marked by race, ethnicity, region, and class. Further, white culture is viewed here as "bad" culture. In fact, the extent to which identities can be named seems to show an inverse relationship to power in the U.S. social structure. The elisions, parallels, and differences between characterizations of white people, Americans, people of color, and so-called white ethnic groups will be explored [here].

Cathy's own cultural positioning seemed to her impossible to grasp, shapeless and unnameable. It was easier to know others and to know, with certainty, what one was *not*. Providing a clue to one of the mechanisms operating here is the fact that, while Cathy viewed New Yorkers and midwesterners as having a cultural shape or identity, women from the East Coast and the Midwest also described or mourned their own seeming lack of culture. The self, where it is part of a dominant cultural group, does not have to name itself. In this regard, Chris Patterson hit the nail on the head, linking the power of white culture with the privilege not to be named:

> I'm probably at the stage where I'm beginning to see that you can come up with a definition of white. Before, I didn't know that you could turn it around and say, "Well what *does* white mean?" One thing is, it's taken for granted. . . . [To be white means to] have some sort of advantage or privilege, even if it's something as simple as not having a definition.

The notion of "turning it around" indicates Chris's realization that, most often, whites are the nondefined definers of other people. Or, to put it another way, whiteness comes to be an unmarked or neutral category, whereas other cultures are specifically marked "cultural."

Many of the women shared the habit of turning to elements of white culture as the unspoken norm. This assumption of a white norm was so prevalent that even Sandy Alvarez and Louise Glebocki, who were acutely aware of racial inequality as well as being members of racially mixed families, referred to "Mexican" music versus "regular" music, and regular meant "white."

Similarly, discussions of race difference and cultural diversity at times revealed a view in which people of color actually embodied difference and whites stood for sameness. Hence, Margaret Phillips said of her Jamaican daughter-in-law that: "She *really* comes with diversity." In spite of its brevity, and because of its curious structure, this short statement says a great deal. It implicitly designates whiteness as norm, and Jamaicans as having or bearing with them "differentness." At the risk of being crass, one might say that in this view, diversity is to the daughter-in-law as "the works" is to a hamburger—added on, adding color and flavor, but not exactly essential. Whiteness, seen by many of these women as boring, but nonetheless definitive, could also follow this analogy. This mode of thinking about "difference" expresses clearly the double-edged sword of a color- and power-evasive repertoire, apparently valorizing cultural difference but doing so in a way that leaves racial and cultural hierarchies intact.

For a seemingly formless entity, then, white culture had a great deal of power, difficult to dislodge from its place in white consciousness as a point of reference for the measuring of others. Whiteness served simultaneously to eclipse and marginalize others (two modes of making the other inessential). Helen Standish's description of her growing-up years in a small New England town captured these processes well. Since the community was all white, the differences at issue were differences between whites. (This also enables an assessment of the links between white and nonwhite "marked" cultures.) Asked about her own cultural identity, Helen explained that "it didn't seem like a culture because everyone else was the same." She had, however, previously mentioned Italian Americans in the town, so I asked about their status. She responded as follows, adopting at first the voice of childhood:

> They are different, but I'm the same as everybody else. They speak Italian, but everybody else in the U.S. speaks English. They eat strange, different food, but I eat the same kind of food as everybody else in the U.S. ... The way I was brought up was to think that everybody who was the same as me were "Americans," and the other people were of "such and such descent."

Viewing the Italian Americans as different and oneself as "same" serves, first, to marginalize, to push from the center, the former group. At the same time, claiming to be the same as everyone else makes other cultural groups invisible or eclipses them. Finally, there is a marginalizing of all those who are not like Helen's own family, leaving a residual, core or normative group who are the true Americans. The category of "American" represents simultaneously the normative and the residual, the dominant culture and a nonculture.

Although Helen talked here about whites, it is safe to guess that people of color would not have counted among the "same" group but among the communities of "such and such descent" (Mexican American, for example). Whites, within this discursive repertoire, became conceptually the real Americans, and only certain kinds of whites actually qualified. Whiteness and Americanness both stood as normative and exclusive categories in relation to which other cultures were identified and marginalized. And this clarifies that there are two kinds of whites, just as there are two kinds of Americans: those who are truly or only white, and those who are white but also something more—or is it something less?

In sum, whiteness often stood as an unmarked marker of others' differentness—whiteness not so much void or formlessness as norm. I associate this construction with colonialism and with the more recent assymetrical dualisms of liberal humanist views of culture, race, and identity. For the most part, this construction views nonwhite cultures as lesser, deviant, or pathological. However, another trajectory has been the inverse: conceptualizations of the cultures of peoples of color as somehow better than the dominant culture, perhaps more natural or more spiritual. These are positive evaluations of a sort, but they are equally dualistic. Many of the women I interviewed saw white culture as less appealing and found the cultures of the "different" people more interesting. As Helen Standish put it:

> [We had] Wonder bread, white bread. I'm more interested in, you know, "What's a bagel?" in other people's cultures rather than my own.

The claim that whiteness lacks form and content says more about the definitions of culture being used than it does about the content of whiteness. However, I would suggest that in describing themselves as cultureless these women are in fact identifying specific kinds of unwanted absences or presences in their own culture(s) as a generalized lack or nonexistence. It thus becomes important to look at what they *did* say about the cultural content of whiteness.

Descriptions of the content of white culture were thin, to say the least. But despite the paucity of signifiers, there was a great deal of consistency across the narratives. First, there was naming based on color, the linking of white culture with white objects—the clichéd white bread and mayonnaise, for example. Freida Kazen's identification of whiteness as "bland," together with Helen Standish's "blah," also signified paleness or neutrality. The images connote several things—color itself (although exaggerated, and besides, bagels are usually white inside, too), lack of vitality (Wonder bread is highly processed), and homogeneity. However, these images are perched on a slippery slope, at once suggesting "white" identified as a color (though an unappealing one) and as an absence of color, that is, white as the unmarked marker.

Whiteness was often signified in these narratives by commodities and brands: Wonder bread, Kleenex, Heinz 57. In this identification whiteness came to be seen as spoiled by capitalism, and as being linked with capitalism in a way that other cultures supposedly are not. Another set of signifiers that constructed whiteness as uniquely tainted by capitalism had to do with the "modern condition": Dot Humphrey described white neighborhoods as "more privatized," and Cathy Thomas used "alienated" to describe her cultural condition. Clare Traverso added to this theme, mourning her own feeling of lack of identity, in contrast with images of her husband's Italian American background (and here, Clare is again talking about perceived differences between whites):

> Food, old country, mama. Stories about a grandmother who can't speak English. . . . Candles, adobe houses, arts, music. [It] has emotion, feeling, belongingness that to me is unique.

In linking whiteness to capitalism and viewing nonwhite cultures as untainted by it, these women were again drawing on a colonial discourse in which progress and industrialization were seen as synonymous with Westernization, while the rest of the world is seen as caught up in tradition and "culture." In addition, one can identify, in white women's mourning over whiteness, elements of what Raymond Williams has called "pastoralism," or nostalgia for a golden era now gone by (but in fact, says Williams, one that never existed).[1]

The image of whiteness as corrupted and impoverished by capitalism is but one of a series of ways in which white culture was seen as impure or tainted. White culture was also seen as tainted by its relationship to power. For example, Clare Traverso clearly counterposed white culture and white power, finding it difficult to value the former because of the overwhelming weight of the latter:

> The good things about whites are to do with folk arts, music. Because other things have power associated with them.

For many race-cognizant white women, white culture was also made impure by its very efforts to maintain race purity. Dot Humphrey, for example, characterized white neighborhoods as places in which people were segregated by choice. For her, this was a good reason to avoid living in them.

The link between whiteness and domination, however, was frequently made in ways that both artificially isolated culture from other factors and obscured economics. For at times, the traits the women envied in Other cultures were in fact at least in part the product of poverty or other dimensions of oppression. Lack of money, for example, often means lack of privacy or space, and it can be valorized as "more street life, less alienation." Cathy Thomas's notion of Chicanas' relationship to the kitchen ("the hearth of the home") as a cultural "good" might be an idealized one that disregards the reality of intensive labor.

Another link between class and culture emerged in Louise Glebocki's reference to the working-class Chicanos she met as a child as less pretentious, "closer to the truth," more "down to earth." And Marjorie Hoffman spoke of the "earthy humor" of Black people, which she interpreted as, in the words of Langston Hughes, a means of "laughing to keep from crying." On the one hand, as has been pointed out especially by Black scholars and activists, the positions of people of color at the bottom of a social and economic hierarchy create the potential for a critique of the system as a whole and consciousness of the need to resist.[2] From the standpoint of race privilege, the system of racism is thus made structurally invisible. On the other hand, descriptions of this kind leave in place a troubling dichotomy that can be appropriated as easily by the right as by the left. For example, there is an inadvertent affinity between the image of Black people as "earthy" and the conservative racist view that African American culture leaves African American people ill equipped for advancement in the modern age. Here, echoing essentialist racism, both Chicanos and African Americans are placed on the borders of "nature" and "culture."

By the same token, often what was criticized as "white" was as much the product of middle-class status as of whiteness as such. Louise Glebocki's image of her fate had she married a white man was an image of a white-collar, nuclear family:

> Him saying, "I'm home, dear," and me with an apron on—ugh!

The intersections of class, race, and culture were obscured in other ways. Patricia Bowen was angry with some of her white feminist friends who, she felt, embraced as "cultural" certain aspects of African American, Chicano, and Native American cultures (including, for example, artwork or dance performances) but would reject as "tacky" (her term) those aspects of daily life that communities of color shared with working-class whites, such as the stores and supermarkets of poor neighborhoods. This, she felt, was tantamount to a selective expansion of middle-class aesthetic horizons, but not to true antiracism or to comprehension of the cultures of people of color. Having herself grown up in a white working-class family, Pat also felt that middle-class white feminists were able to use selective engagement to avoid addressing their class privilege.

I have already indicated some of the problems inherent in this kind of conceptualization, suggesting that it tends to keep in place dichotomous constructions of "white" versus Other cultures, to separate "culture" from other dimensions of daily life, and to reify or strip of history *all* cultural forms. There are, then, a range of issues that need to be disentangled if we are to understand the location of "whiteness" in the terrain of culture. It is, I believe, useful to approach this question by means of a reconceptualization of the concept of culture itself. A culture, in the sense of the set of rules and practices by means of which a group organizes itself and its values, manners, and worldview—in other words, culture as "a field articulating the life-world of subjects . . . and the structures created by human activity"[3]—is an indispensable precondition to any individual's existence in the world. It is nonsensical in terms of this kind of definition to suggest that anyone could actually have "no culture." But this is not, as I have suggested, the mode of thinking about culture that these women are employing.

Whiteness emerges here as inextricably tied to domination partly as an effect of a discursive "draining process" applied to both whiteness and Americanness. In this process, any cultural practice engaged in by a white person that is not identical to the dominant culture is automatically counted as either "not really white"—and, for that matter, not really American, either—(but rather of such and such descent), or as "not really cultural" (but rather "economic"). There is a slipperiness to whiteness here: it shifts from "no culture" to "normal culture" to "bad culture" and back again. Simultaneously, a range of marginal or, in Trinh T. Minh-ha's terminology, "bounded" cultures are generated. These are viewed as enviable spaces, separate and untainted by relations of dominance or by linkage to other structures or systems. By contrast, whiteness is conceived as axiomatically tied to dominance, to economics, to political structures. In this process, both whiteness and nonwhiteness are reified, made into objects rather than processes, and robbed of historical context and human agency. As long as the discussion remains couched in these terms, a critique of whiteness remains a double-edged sword: for one thing, whiteness remains normative because there is no way to name the cultural practices associated with it *as* cultural. Moreover, as I have suggested, whether whiteness is viewed as artificial and dominating (and therefore "bad") or civilized (and therefore "good"), whiteness and all varieties of nonwhiteness continue to be viewed as ontologically different from one another.

A genuine sadness and frustration about the meaning of whiteness at this moment in history motivated these women to decry white culture. It becomes important, then, to recognize the grains of truth in their views of white culture. It is important to acknowledge their anger and frustration about the meaning of whiteness as we reach toward a politicized analysis of culture that is freer of colonial and pastoral legacies.

The terms "white" and "American" as these women used them signified domination in international and domestic terms. This link is both accurate and inaccurate. While it is true that, by and large, those in power in the United States are white, it is also true that not all those who are white are in power. Nor is the axiomatic linkage between Americanness and power accurate, because not all Americans have the same access to power. At the same time, the link between whiteness, Americanness, and power *are* accurate because, as we have seen, the terms "white" and "American" both function discursively to exclude people from normativity—

including white people "of such and such descent." But here we need to distinguish between the fates of people of color and those of white people. Notwithstanding a complicated history, the boundaries of Americanness and whiteness have been much more fluid for "white ethnic" groups than for people of color.

There have been border skirmishes over the meaning of whiteness and Americanness since the inception of those terms. For white people, however, those skirmishes have been resolved through processes of assimilation, not exclusion. The late nineteenth and early twentieth centuries in the United States saw a systematic push toward the cultural homogenization of whites carried out through social reform movements and the schools. This push took place alongside the expansion of industrial capitalism, giving rise to the sense that whiteness signifies the production and consumption of commodities under capitalism.[4] But recognition of this history should not be translated into an assertion that whites were stripped of culture (for to do that would be to continue to adhere to a colonial view of "culture"). Instead one must argue that certain cultural practices replaced others. Were one to undertake a history of this "generic" white culture, it would fragment into a thousand tributary elements, culturally specific religious observances, and class survival mechanisms as well as mass-produced commodities and mass media.

There are a number of dangers inherent in continuing to view white culture as no culture. Whiteness appeared in the narratives to function as both norm or core, that against which everything else is measured, and as residue, that which is left after everything else has been named. A far-reaching danger of whiteness coded as "no culture" is that it leaves in place whiteness as defining a set of normative cultural practices against which all are measured and into which all are expected to fit. This normativity has underwritten oppression from the beginning of colonial expansion and has had impact in multiple ways: from the American pioneers' assumption of a norm of private property used to justify appropriation of land that within their worldview did not have an owner, and the ideological construction of nations like Britain as white,[5] to Western feminism's Eurocentric shaping of its movements and institutions. It is important for white feminists not to continue to participate in these processes.

And if whiteness has a history, so do the cultures of people of color, which are worked on, crafted, and created, rather than just "there." For peoples of color in the United States, this work has gone on as much in the context of relationships to imperialism and capitalism as has the production of whiteness, though it has been premised on exclusion and resistance to exclusion more than on assimilation. Although not always or only forged in resistance, the visibility and recognition of the cultures of U.S. peoples of color in recent times *is* the product of individual and collective struggle. Only a short time has elapsed since those struggles made possible the introduction into public discourse of celebration and valorization of their cultural forms. In short, it is important not to reify any culture by failing to acknowledge its createdness, and not to view it as always having been there in unchanging form.

Rather than feeling "cultureless," white women need to become conscious of the histories and specificities of our cultural positions, and of the political, economic, and creative fusions that form all cultures. The purpose of such an exercise is not, of course, to reinvert the dualisms and valorize whiteness so much as to develop a clearer sense of where and who we are.

DISCUSSION QUESTIONS

1. Why is whiteness considered to be lacking diversity?
2. How would you describe the cultural content of whiteness?
3. Why do some people feel "cultureless"?

NOTES

1. Raymond Williams, *The Country and the City* (New York: Oxford University Press, 1978).
2. The classic statement of this position is W. E. B. Du Bois's concept of the "double consciousness" of Americans of African descent. Two recent feminist statements of similar positions are Patricia Hill Collins, *Black Feminist Thought: Knowledge, Consciousness, and the Politics of Empowerment* (Boston: Unwin Hyman, 1990); and Aida Hurtado, "Relating to Privilege: Seduction and Rejection in the Subordination of White Women and Women of Color," *Signs* 14, no. 4:833–55.
3. Paul Gilroy, *There Ain't No Black in the Union Jack.* London: Hutchinson, 1987.
4. See, for example, Winthrop Talbot, ed., *Americanization* (New York: H. W. Wilson, 1917), esp. Sophonisba P. Breckinridge, "The Immigrant Family," 251–52, Olivia Howard Dunbar, "Teaching the Immigrant Woman," 252–56, and North American Civic League for Immigrants, "Domestic Education among Immigrants," 256–58; and Kathie Friedman Kasaba, " 'To Become a Person': The Experience of Gender, Ethnicity and Work in the Lives of Immigrant Women, New York City, 1870–1940," doctoral dissertation, Department of Sociology, State University of New York, Binghamton, 1991. I am indebted to Katie Friedman Kasaba for these references and for her discussions with me about working-class European immigrants to the United States at the turn of this century.
5. Gilroy, *There Ain't No Black in the Union Jack.*

WHAT IS SEX? WHAT IS GENDER?

The Five Sexes

WHY MALE AND FEMALE ARE NOT ENOUGH

Anne Fausto-Sterling

In 1843 Levi Suydam, a twenty-three-year-old resident of Salisbury, Connecticut, asked the town board of selectmen to validate his right to vote as a Whig in a hotly contested local election. The request raised a flurry of objections from the opposition party, for reasons that must be rare in the annals of American democracy: it was said that Suydam was more female than male and thus (some eighty years before suffrage was extended to women) could not be allowed to cast a ballot. To settle the dispute a physician, one William James Barry, was brought in to examine Suydam. And, presumably upon encountering a phallus, the good doctor declared the prospective voter male. With Suydam safely in their column the Whigs won the election by a majority of one.

Barry's diagnosis, however, turned out to be somewhat premature. Within a few days he discovered that, phallus notwithstanding, Suydam menstruated regularly and had a vaginal opening. Both his/her physique and his/her mental predispositions were more complex than was first suspected. S/he had narrow shoulders and broad hips and felt occasional sexual yearnings for women. Suydam's "feminine propensities, such as a fondness for gay colors, for pieces of calico, comparing and placing them together, and an aversion for bodily labor, and an inability to perform the same, were remarked by many," Barry later wrote. It is not clear whether Suydam lost or retained the vote, or whether the election results were reversed.

Anne Fausto-Sterling is a professor of biology and women's studies at Brown University.

Western culture is deeply committed to the idea that there are only two sexes. Even language refuses other possibilities; thus to write about Levi Suydam I have had to invent conventions—*s/he* and *his/her*—to denote someone who is clearly neither male nor female or who is perhaps both sexes at once. Legally, too, every adult is either man or woman, and the difference, of course, is not trivial. For Suydam it meant the franchise; today it means being available for, or exempt from, draft registration, as well as being subject, in various ways, to a number of laws governing marriage, the family and human intimacy. In many parts of the United States, for instance, two people legally registered as men cannot have sexual relations without violating anti-sodomy statutes.

But if the state and the legal system have an interest in maintaining a two-party sexual system, they are in defiance of nature. For biologically speaking, there are many gradations running from female to male; and depending on how one calls the shots, one can argue that along that spectrum lie at least five sexes—and perhaps even more.

For some time medical investigators have recognized the concept of the intersexual body. But the standard medical literature uses the term *intersex* as a catch-all for three major subgroups with some mixture of male and female characteristics: the so-called true hermaphrodites, whom I call herms, who possess one testis and one ovary (the sperm- and egg-producing vessels, or gonads); the male pseudohermaphrodites (the "merms"), who have testes and some aspects of the female genitalia but no ovaries; and the female pseudohermaphrodites (the "ferms"), who have ovaries and some aspects of the male genitalia but lack testes. Each of those categories is in itself complex; the percentage of male and female characteristics, for instance, can vary enormously among members of the same subgroup. Moreover, the inner lives of the people in each subgroup—their special needs and their problems, attractions and repulsions—have gone unexplored by science. But on the basis of what is known about them I suggest that the three intersexes, herm, merm and ferm, deserve to be considered additional sexes each in its own right. Indeed, I would argue further that sex is a vast, infinitely malleable continuum that defies the constraints of even five categories.

Not surprisingly, it is extremely difficult to estimate the frequency of intersexuality, much less the frequency of each of the three additional sexes: it is not the sort of information one volunteers on a job application. The psychologist John Money of Johns Hopkins University, a specialist in the study of congenital sexual-organ defects, suggests intersexuals may constitute as many as 4 percent of births. As I point out to my students at Brown University, in a student body of about 6,000 that fraction, if correct, implies there may be as many as 240 intersexuals on campus—surely enough to form a minority caucus of some kind.*

In reality though, few such students would make it as far as Brown in sexually diverse form. Recent advances in physiology and surgical technology now enable physicians to catch most intersexuals at the moment of birth. Almost at once such infants are entered into a program of hormonal and surgical management so that they can slip quietly into society as "normal" heterosexual males or females. I emphasize that the motive is in no way conspiratorial. The aims of the policy are genuinely humanitarian, reflecting the wish that people be able to "fit in" both physically and psychologically. In the medical community, however, the assumptions behind that wish—that there be only two sexes, that heterosexuality alone is normal, that there is one true model of psychological health—have gone virtually unexamined.

The word *hermaphrodite* comes from the Greek names Hermes, variously known as the messenger of the gods, the patron of music, the controller of dreams or the protector of livestock, and Aphrodite, the goddess of sexual love and beauty. According to Greek mythology, those two gods parented Hermaphroditus, who at age fifteen became half male and half female when his body fused with the body of a nymph he fell in love with. In some true hermaphrodites the testis and the ovary grow separately but bilaterally; in others they grow together within the same organ, forming an ovo-testis. Not infrequently, at least one of the gonads functions quite well, producing either sperm cells or eggs, as well as functional levels of the sex hormones—androgens or estrogens. Although in theory it might be possible for a true hermaphrodite to become both father and mother to a child, in practice the appropriate ducts and tubes are not configured so that egg and sperm can meet.

In contrast with the true hermaphrodites, the pseudohermaphrodites possess two gonads of the same kind along with the usual male (XY) or female (XX) chromosomal makeup. But their external genitalia and secondary sex characteristics do not match their chromosomes. Thus merms have testes and XY chromosomes, yet they also have a vagina and a clitoris, and at puberty they often develop breasts. They do not menstruate, however. Ferms have ovaries, two X chromosomes and sometimes a uterus, but they also have at least partly masculine external genitalia. Without medical intervention they can develop beards, deep voices and adult-size penises. . . .

Intersexuality itself is old news. Hermaphrodites, for instance, are often featured in stories about human origins. Early biblical scholars believed Adam began life as a hermaphrodite and later divided into two people—a male and a female—after falling from grace. According to Plato there once were three sexes—male, female and hermaphrodite—but the third sex was lost with time.

Both the Talmud and the Tosefta, the Jewish books of law, list extensive regulations for people of mixed sex. The Tosefta expressly forbids hermaphrodites to inherit their fathers' estates (like daughters), to seclude themselves with women (like sons) or to shave (like men). When hermaphrodites menstruate they must be isolated from men (like women); they are disqualified from serving as witnesses or as priests (like women), but the laws of pederasty apply to them.

In Europe a pattern emerged by the end of the Middle Ages that, in a sense, has lasted to the pres-

---

Editors' note: In a 2000 article, Fausto-Sterling revised this estimate to 1.7 percent of births. See "The Five Sexes Revisited" in *The Sciences,* July–August 2000.

ent day: hermaphrodites were compelled to choose an established gender role and stick with it. The penalty for transgression was often death. Thus in the 1600s a Scottish hermaphrodite living as a woman was buried alive after impregnating his/her master's daughter.

For questions of inheritance, legitimacy, paternity, succession to title and eligibility for certain professions to be determined, modern Anglo-Saxon legal systems require that newborns be registered as either male or female. In the U.S. today sex determination is governed by state laws. Illinois permits adults to change the sex recorded on their birth certificates should a physician attest to having performed the appropriate surgery. The New York Academy of Medicine, on the other hand, has taken an opposite view. In spite of surgical alterations of the external genitalia, the academy argued in 1966, the chromosomal sex remains the same. By that measure, a person's wish to conceal his or her original sex cannot outweigh the public interest in protection against fraud.

During this century the medical community has completed what the legal world began—the complete erasure of any form of embodied sex that does not conform to a male–female, heterosexual pattern. Ironically, a more sophisticated knowledge of the complexity of sexual systems has led to the repression of such intricacy.

In 1937 the urologist Hugh H. Young of Johns Hopkins University published a volume titled *Genital Abnormalities, Hermaphroditism and Related Adrenal Diseases.* The book is remarkable for its erudition, scientific insight and open-mindedness. In it Young drew together a wealth of carefully documented case histories to demonstrate and study the medical treatment of such "accidents of birth." Young did not pass judgment on the people he studied, nor did he attempt to coerce into treatment those intersexuals who rejected that option. And he showed unusual even-handedness in referring to those people who had had sexual experiences as both men and women as "practicing hermaphrodites."

One of Young's more interesting cases was a hermaphrodite named Emma who had grown up as a female. Emma had both a penis-size clitoris and a vagina, which made it possible for him/her to have "normal" heterosexual sex with both men and women. As a teenager Emma had had sex with a number of girls to whom s/he was deeply attracted; but at the age of nineteen s/he had married a man. Unfortunately, he had given Emma little sexual pleasure (though he had had no complaints), and so throughout that marriage and subsequent ones Emma had kept girlfriends on the side. With some frequency s/he had pleasurable sex with them. Young describes his subject as appearing "to be quite content and even happy." In conversation Emma occasionally told him of his/her wish to be a man, a circumstance Young said would be relatively easy to bring about. But Emma's reply strikes a heroic blow for self-interest:

> Would you have to remove that vagina? I don't know about that because that's my meal ticket. If you did that, I would have to quit my husband and go to work, so I think I'll keep it and stay as I am. My husband supports me well, and even though I don't have any sexual pleasure with him, I do have lots with my girlfriends.

Yet even as Young was illuminating intersexuality with the light of scientific reason, he was beginning its suppression. For his book is also an extended treatise on the most modern surgical and hormonal methods of changing intersexuals into either males or females. Young may have differed from his successors in being less judgmental and controlling of the patients and their families, but he nonetheless supplied the foundation on which current intervention practices were built.

By 1969, when the English physicians Christopher J. Dewhurst and Ronald R. Gordon wrote *The Intersexual Disorders,* medical and surgical approaches to intersexuality had neared a state of rigid uniformity. It is hardly surprising that such a hardening of opinion took place in the era of the feminine mystique—of the post-Second World War flight to the suburbs and the strict division of family roles according to sex. That the medical consensus was not quite universal (or perhaps that it seemed poised to break apart again) can be gleaned from the near-hysterical tone of Dewhurst and Gordon's book, which contrasts markedly with the calm reason of Young's founding work. Consider their opening description of an intersexual newborn:

> One can only attempt to imagine the anguish of the parents. That a newborn should have a deformity . . . [affecting] so fundamental an issue as the very sex of the child . . . is a tragic event which immediately conjures up visions of a hopeless psychological misfit doomed to live always as a sexual freak in loneliness and frustration.

Dewhurst and Gordon warned that such a miserable fate would, indeed, be a baby's lot should the case be improperly managed; "but fortunately," they wrote, "with correct management the outlook is infinitely better than the poor parents—emotionally stunned by the event—or indeed anyone without special knowledge could ever imagine."

Scientific dogma has held fast to the assumption that without medical care hermaphrodites are doomed to a life of misery. Yet there are few empirical studies to back up that assumption, and some of the same research gathered to build a case for medical treatment contradicts it. Francies Benton, another of Young's practicing hermaphrodites, "had not worried over his condition, did not wish to be changed, and was enjoying life." The same could be said of Emma, the opportunistic hausfrau. Even Dewhurst and Gordon, adamant about the psychological importance of treating intersexuals at the infant stage, acknowledged great success in "changing the sex" of older patients. They reported on twenty cases of children reclassified into a different sex after the supposedly critical age of eighteen months. They asserted that all the reclassifications were "successful," and they wondered then whether reregistration could be "recommended more readily than [had] been suggested so far."

The treatment of intersexuality in this century provides a clear example of what the French historian Michel Foucault has called biopower. The knowledge developed in biochemistry, embryology, endocrinology, psychology and surgery has enabled physicians to control the very sex of the human body. The multiple contradictions in that kind of power call for some scrutiny. On the one hand, the medical "management" of intersexuality

certainly developed as part of an attempt to free people from perceived psychological pain (though whether the pain was the patient's, the parents' or the physician's is unclear). And if one accepts the assumption that in a sex-divided culture people can realize their greatest potential for happiness and productivity only if they are sure they belong to one of only two acknowledged sexes, modern medicine has been extremely successful.

On the other hand, the same medical accomplishments can be read not as progress but as a mode of discipline. Hermaphrodites have unruly bodies. They do not fall naturally into a binary classification; only a surgical shoehorn can put them there. But why should we care if a "woman," defined as one who has breasts, a vagina, a uterus and ovaries and who menstruates, also has a clitoris large enough to penetrate the vagina of another woman? Why should we care if there are people whose biological equipment enables them to have sex "naturally" with both men and women? The answers seem to lie in a cultural need to maintain clear distinctions between the sexes. Society mandates the control of intersexual bodies because they blur and bridge the great divide. Inasmuch as hermaphrodites literally embody both sexes, they challenge traditional beliefs about sexual difference: they possess the irritating ability to live sometimes as one sex and sometimes the other, and they raise the specter of homosexuality.

But what if things were altogether different? Imagine a world in which the same knowledge that has enabled medicine to intervene in the management of intersexual patients has been placed at the service of multiple sexualities. Imagine that the sexes have multiplied beyond currently imaginable limits. It would have to be a world of shared powers. Patient and physician, parent and child, male and female, heterosexual and homosexual—all those oppositions and others would have to be dissolved as sources of division. A new ethic of medical treatment would arise, one that would permit ambiguity in a culture that had overcome sexual division. The central mission of medical treatment would be to preserve life. Thus hermaphrodites would be concerned primarily not about whether they can conform to society but about whether they might develop potentially life-threatening conditions—hernias, gonadal tumors, salt imbalance caused by adrenal malfunction—that sometimes accompany hermaphroditic development. In my ideal world medical intervention for intersexuals would take place only rarely before the age of reason; subsequent treatment would be a cooperative venture between physician, patient and other advisers trained in issues of gender multiplicity.

I do not pretend that the transition to my utopia would be smooth. Sex, even the supposedly "normal," heterosexual kind, continues to cause untold anxieties in Western society. And certainly a culture that has yet to come to grips—religiously and, in some states, legally—with the ancient and relatively uncomplicated reality of homosexual love will not readily embrace intersexuality. No doubt the most troublesome arena by far would be the rearing of children. Parents, at least since the Victorian era, have fretted, sometimes to the point of outright denial, over the fact that their children are sexual beings.

All that and more amply explains why intersexual children are generally squeezed into one of the two prevailing sexual categories. But what would be the psychological consequences of taking the alternative road—raising children as unabashed intersexuals? On the surface that tack seems fraught with peril. What, for example, would happen to the intersexual child amid the unrelenting cruelty of the school yard? When the time came to shower in gym class, what horrors and humiliations would await the intersexual as his/her anatomy was displayed in all its nontraditional glory? In whose gym class would s/he register to begin with? What bathroom would s/he use? And how on earth would Mom and Dad help shepherd him/her through the mine field of puberty?

In the past thirty years those questions have been ignored, as the scientific community has, with remarkable unanimity, avoided contemplating the alternative route of unimpeded intersexuality. But modern investigators tend to overlook a substantial body of case histories, most of them compiled between 1930 and 1960, before surgical intervention became rampant. Almost without exception, those reports describe children who grew up knowing

they were intersexual (though they did not advertise it) and adjusted to their unusual status. Some of the studies are richly detailed—described at the level of gym-class showering (which most intersexuals avoided without incident); in any event, there is not a psychotic or a suicide in the lot.

Still, the nuances of socialization among intersexuals cry out for more sophisticated analysis. Clearly, before my vision of sexual multiplicity can be realized, the first openly intersexual children and their parents will have to be brave pioneers who will bear the brunt of society's growing pains. But in the long view—though it could take generations to achieve—the prize might be a society in which sexuality is something to be celebrated for its subtleties and not something to be feared or ridiculed.

DISCUSSION QUESTIONS

1. Why do you think it has been so important in our culture that individuals be *either* male or female? Or as Fausto-Sterling asks, "Why should we care if there are people whose biological equipment enables them to have sex 'naturally' with both men and women?"
2. If you were the parent of an intersexed infant, what factors would bear on your decision to subject the child to surgical intervention?

READING 10

The Berdache Tradition

Walter L. Williams

Because it is such a powerful force in the world today, the Western Judeo-Christian tradition is often accepted as the arbiter of "natural" behavior of humans. If Europeans and their descendant nations of North America accept something as normal, then

Walter L. Williams is a professor of anthropology and the study of women and men in society at the University of Southern California, Los Angeles.

anything different is seen as abnormal. Such a view ignores the great diversity of human existence.

This is the case for the study of gender. How many genders are there? To a modern Anglo-American, nothing might seem more definite than the answer that there are two: men and women. But not all societies around the world agree with Western culture's view that all humans are either women or men. The commonly accepted notion of "the opposite sex," based on anatomy, is itself an artifact of our society's rigid sex roles.

Among many cultures, there have existed different alternatives to "man" or "woman." An alternative role in many American Indian societies is referred to by anthropologists as *berdache*. . . . The role varied from one Native American culture to another, which is a reflection of the vast diversity of aboriginal New World societies. Small bands of hunter-gatherers existed in some areas, with advanced civilizations of farming peoples in other areas. With hundreds of different languages, economies, religions, and social patterns existing in North America alone, every generalization about a cultural tradition must acknowledge many exceptions.

This diversity is true for the berdache tradition as well, and must be kept in mind. My statements should be read as being specific to a particular culture, with generalizations being treated as loose patterns that might not apply to peoples even in nearby areas.

Briefly, a berdache can be defined as a morphological male who does not fill a society's standard man's role, who has a nonmasculine character. This type of person is often stereotyped as effeminate, but a more accurate characterization is androgyny. Such a person has a clearly recognized and accepted social status, often based on a secure place in the tribal mythology. Berdaches have special ceremonial roles in many Native American religions, and important economic roles in their families. They will do at least some women's work, and mix together much of the behavior, dress, and social roles of women and men. Berdaches gain social prestige by their spiritual, intellectual, or craftwork/artistic contributions, and by their reputation for hard

work and generosity. They serve a mediating function between women and men, precisely because their character is seen as distinct from either sex. They are not seen as men, yet they are not seen as women either. They occupy an alternative gender role that is a mixture of diverse elements.

In their erotic behavior berdaches also generally (but not always) take a nonmasculine role, either being asexual or becoming the passive partner in sex with men. In some cultures the berdache might become a wife to a man. This male-male sexual behavior became the focus of an attack on berdaches as "sodomites" by the Europeans who, early on, came into contact with them. From the first Spanish conquistadors to the Western frontiersmen and the Christian missionaries and government officials, Western culture has had a considerable impact on the berdache tradition. In the last two decades, the most recent impact on the tradition is the adaptation of a modern Western gay identity.

To Western eyes berdachism is a complex and puzzling phenomenon, mixing and redefining the very concepts of what is considered male and female. In a culture with only two recognized genders, such individuals are gender nonconformist, abnormal, deviant. But to American Indians, the institution of another gender role means that berdaches are not deviant—indeed, they do conform to the requirements of a custom in which their culture tells them they fit. Berdachism is a way for society to recognize and assimilate some atypical individuals without imposing a change on them or stigmatizing them as deviant. This cultural institution confirms their legitimacy for what they are.

Societies often bestow power upon that which does not neatly fit into the usual. Since no cultural system can explain everything, a common way that many cultures deal with these inconsistencies is to imbue them with negative power, as taboo, pollution, witchcraft, or sin. That which is not understood is seen as a threat. But an alternative method of dealing with such things, or people, is to take them out of the realm of threat and to sanctify them.[1] The berdaches' role as mediator is thus not just between women and men, but also between the physical and the spiritual. American Indian cultures have taken what Western culture calls negative, and made it a positive; they have successfully utilized the different skills and insights of a class of people that Western culture has stigmatized and whose spiritual powers have been wasted.

Many Native Americans also understood that gender roles have to do with more than just biological sex. The standard Western view that one's sex is always a certainty, and that one's gender identity and sex role always conform to one's morphological sex is a view that dies hard. Western thought is typified by such dichotomies of groups perceived to be mutually exclusive: male and female, black and white, right and wrong, good and evil. Clearly, the world is not so simple; such clear divisions are not always realistic. Most American Indian worldviews generally are much more accepting of the ambiguities of life. Acceptance of gender variation in the berdache tradition is typical of many native cultures' approach to life in general.

Overall, these are generalizations based on those Native American societies that had an accepted role for berdaches. Not all cultures recognized such a respected status. Berdachism in aboriginal North America was most established among tribes in four areas: first, the Prairie and western Great Lakes, the northern and central Great Plains, and the lower Mississippi Valley; second, Florida and the Caribbean; third, the Southwest, the Great Basin, and California; and fourth, scattered areas of the Northwest, western Canada, and Alaska. For some reason it is not noticeable in eastern North America, with the exception of its southern rim. . . .

AMERICAN INDIAN RELIGIONS

Native American religions offered an explanation for human diversity by their creation stories. In some tribal religions, the Great Spiritual Being is conceived as neither male nor female but as a combination of both. Among the Kamia of the Southwest, for example, the bearer of plant seeds and the introducer of Kamia culture was a man-woman spirit named Warharmi.[2] A key episode of the Zuni creation story involves a battle between the kachina spirits of the agricultural Zunis and the enemy hunter spirits. Every four years an elaborate ceremony commemorates this myth. In the story a kachina spirit called *ko'lhamana* was captured by the enemy spirits and transformed in the process. This transformed spirit became a mediator between the two sides, using his peacemaking skills to merge the differing lifestyles of hunters and farmers. In the ceremony, a dramatic reenactment of the myth, the part of the transformed *ko'lhamana* spirit is performed by a berdache.[3] The Zuni word for berdache is *lhamana,* denoting its closeness to the spiritual mediator who brought hunting and farming together.[4] The moral of this story is that the berdache was created by the deities for a special purpose, and that this creation led to the improvement of society. The continual reenactment of this story provides a justification for the Zuni berdache in each generation.

In contrast to this, the lack of spiritual justification in a creation myth could denote a lack of tolerance for gender variation. The Pimas, unlike most of their Southwestern neighbors, did not respect a berdache status. *Wi-kovat,* their derogatory word, means "like a girl," but it does not signify a recognized social role. Pima mythology reflects this lack of acceptance, in a folk tale that explains male androgyny as due to Papago witchcraft. Knowing that the Papagos respected berdaches, the Pimas blamed such an occurrence on an alien influence.[5] While the Pimas' condemnatory attitude is unusual, it does point out the importance of spiritual explanations for the acceptance of gender variance in a culture.

Other Native American creation stories stand in sharp contrast to the Pima explanation. A good example is the account of the Navajos, which presents women and men as equals. The Navajo origin tale is told as a story of five worlds. The first people were First Man and First Woman, who were created equally and at the same time. The first two worlds that they lived in were bleak and unhappy, so they escaped to the third world. In the third world lived two twins, Turquoise Boy and White Shell Girl, who were the first berdaches. In the Navajo language the word for berdache is *nadle,* which means "changing one" or "one who is transformed." It is applied to hermaphrodites—those who are born with the genitals of both male and female—and also to "those who pretend to be *nadle,*" who take on a social role that is distinct from either men or women.[6]

In the third world, First Man and First Woman began farming, with the help of the changing twins. One of the twins noticed some clay and, holding it in the palm of his/her hand, shaped it into the first pottery bowl. Then he/she formed a plate, a water dipper, and a pipe. The second twin observed some reeds and began to weave them, making the first basket. Together they shaped axes and grinding stones from rocks, and hoes from bone. All these new inventions made the people very happy.[7]

The message of this story is that humans are dependent for many good things on the inventiveness of *nadle.* Such individuals were present from the earliest eras of human existence, and their presence was never questioned. They were part of the natural order of the universe, with a special contribution to make.

Later on in the Navajo creation story, White Shell Girl entered the moon and became the Moon Bearer. Turquoise Boy, however, remained with the people. When First Man realized that Turquoise Boy could do all manner of women's work as well as women, all the men left the women and crossed a big river. The men hunted and planted crops. Turquoise Boy ground the corn, cooked the food, and weaved cloth for the men. Four years passed with the women and men separated, and the men were happy with the *nadle.* Later, however, the women wanted to learn how to grind corn from the *nadle,* and both the men and the women had decided that it was not good to continue living separately. So the women crossed the river and the people were reunited.[8]

They continued living happily in the third world, until one day a great flood began. The people ran to the highest mountaintop, but the water kept rising and they all feared they would be drowned. But just in time, the ever-inventive Turquoise Boy found a large reed. They climbed upward inside the tall hollow reed, and came out at the top into the fourth world. From there, White Shell Girl brought another reed, and they climbed again to the fifth world, which is the present world of the Navajos.[9]

These stories suggest that the very survival of humanity is dependent on the inventiveness of berdaches. With such a mythological belief system, it is no wonder that the Navajos held *nadle* in high regard. The concept of the *nadle* is well formulated in the creation story. As children were educated by these stories, and all Navajos believed in them, the high status accorded to gender variation was passed down from generation to generation. Such stories also provided instructions for *nadle* themselves to live by. A spiritual explanation guaranteed a special place for a person who was considered different but not deviant.

For American Indians, the important explanations of the world are spiritual ones. In their view, there is a deeper reality than the here-and-now. The real essence or wisdom occurs when one finally gives up trying to explain events in terms of "logic" and "reality." Many confusing aspects of existence can better be explained by actions of a multiplicity of spirits. Instead of a concept of a single god, there is an awareness of "that which we do not understand." In Lakota religion, for example, the term *Wakan Tanka* is often translated as "god." But a more proper translation, according to the medicine people who taught me, is "The Great Mystery."[10]

While rationality can explain much, there are limits to human capabilities of understanding. The English language is structured to account for cause and effect. For example, English speakers say, "It is raining," with the implication that there is a cause "it" that leads to rain. Many Indian languages, on the other hand, merely note what is most accurately translated as "raining" as an observable fact. Such an approach brings a freedom to stop worrying about causes of things, and merely to relax and accept that our human insights can go only so far. By not taking ourselves too seriously, or overinflating human importance, we can get beyond the logical world.

The emphasis of American Indian religions, then, is on the spiritual nature of all things. To understand the physical world, one must appreciate the underlying spiritual essence. Then one can begin to see that the physical is only a faint shadow, a partial reflection, of a supernatural and extrarational world. By the Indian view, everything that exists is spiritual. Every object—plants, rocks, water, air, the moon, animals, humans, the earth itself—has a spirit. The spirit of one thing (including a human) is not superior to the spirit of any other. Such a view promotes a sophisticated ecological awareness of the place that humans have in the larger environment. The function of religion is not to try to condemn or to change what exists, but to accept the realities of the world and to appreciate their contributions to life. Everything that exists has a purpose.[11]

One of the basic tenets of American Indian religion is the notion that everything in the universe is related. Nevertheless, things that exist are often seen as having a counterpart: sky and earth, plant and animal, water and fire. In all of these polarities, there exist mediators. The role of the mediator is to hold the polarities together, to keep the world from disintegrating. Polarities exist within human society also. The most important category within Indian society is gender. The notions of Woman and Man underlie much of social interaction and are comparable to the other major polarities. Women, with their nurturant qualities, are associated with the earth, while men are associated with the sky. Women gatherers and farmers deal with plants (of the earth), while men hunters deal with animals.

The mediator between the polarities of woman and man, in the American Indian religious explanation, is a being that combines the elements of both genders. This might be a combination in a physical sense, as in the case of hermaphrodites. Many Native American religions accept this phenomenon in the same way that they accept other variations from the norm. But more important is their acceptance of the idea that gender can be combined in ways other than physical hermaphroditism. The physical aspects of a thing or a person, after all, are not nearly as important as its spirit. American Indians use the concept of a person's *spirit* in the way that other Americans use the concept of a person's *character*.

Consequently, physical hermaphroditism is not necessary for the idea of gender mixing. A person's character, their spiritual essence, is the crucial thing.

THE BERDACHE'S SPIRIT

Individuals who are physically normal might have the spirit of the other sex, might range somewhere between the two sexes, or might have a spirit that is distinct from either women or men. Whatever category they fall into, they are seen as being different from men. They are accepted spiritually as "Not Man." Whichever option is chosen, Indian religions offer spiritual explanations. Among the Arapahos of the Plains, berdaches are called *haxu'xan* and are seen to be that way as a result of a supernatural gift from birds or animals. Arapaho mythology recounts the story of Nih'a'ca, the first *haxu'xan*. He pretended to be a woman and married the mountain lion, a symbol for masculinity. The myth, as recorded by ethnographer Alfred Kroeber about 1900, recounted that "These people had the natural desire to become women, and as they grew up gradually became women. They gave up the desires of men. They were married to men. They had miraculous power and could do supernatural things. For instance, it was one of them that first made an intoxicant from rainwater."[12] Besides the theme of inventiveness, similar to the Navajo creation story, the berdache role is seen as a product of a "natural desire." Berdaches "gradually became women," which underscores the notion of woman as a social category rather than as a fixed biological entity. Physical biological sex is less important in gender classification than a person's desire—one's spirit.

The myths contain no prescriptions for trying to change berdaches who are acting out their desires of the heart. Like many other cultures' myths, the Zuni origin myths simply sanction the idea that gender can be transformed independently of biological sex.[13] Indeed, myths warn of dire consequences when interference with such a transformation is attempted. Prince Alexander Maximilian of the German state of Wied, traveling in the northern Plains in the 1830s, heard a myth about a warrior who once tried to force a berdache to avoid women's clothing. The berdache resisted, and the warrior shot him with an arrow. Immediately the berdache disappeared, and the warrior saw only a pile of stones with his arrow in them. Since then, the story concluded, no intelligent person would try to coerce a berdache.[14] Making the point even more directly, a Mandan myth told of an Indian who tried to force *mihdacke* (berdaches) to give up their distinctive dress and status, which led the spirits to punish many people with death. After that, no Mandans interfered with berdaches.[15]

With this kind of attitude, reinforced by myth and history, the aboriginal view accepts human diversity. The creation story of the Mohave of the Colorado River Valley speaks of a time when people were not sexually differentiated. From this perspective, it is easy to accept that certain individuals might combine elements of masculinity and femininity.[16] A respected Mohave elder, speaking in the 1930s, stated this viewpoint simply: "From the very beginning of the world it was meant that there should be [berdaches], just as it was instituted that there should be shamans. They were intended for that purpose."[17]

This elder also explained that a child's tendencies to become a berdache are apparent early, by about age nine to twelve, before the child reaches puberty: "That is the time when young persons become initiated into the functions of their sex. . . . None but young people will become berdaches as a rule."[18] Many tribes have a public ceremony that acknowledges the acceptance of berdache status. A Mohave shaman related the ceremony for his tribe: "When the child was about ten years old his relatives would begin discussing his strange ways. Some of them disliked it, but the more intelligent began envisaging an initiation ceremony." The relatives prepare for the ceremony without letting the boy know of it. It is meant to take him by surprise, to be both an initiation and a test of his true inclinations. People from various settlements are invited to attend. The family wants the community to see it and become accustomed to accepting the boy as an *alyha.*

On the day of the ceremony, the shaman explained, the boy is led into a circle: "If the boy showed a willingness to remain standing in the circle, exposed to the public eye, it was almost certain that he would go through with the ceremony. The singer, hidden behind the crowd, began singing the songs. As soon as the sound reached the boy he began to dance as women do." If the boy is unwilling to assume *alyha* status, he would refuse to dance. But if his character—his spirit—is *alyha*, "the song goes right to his heart and he will dance with much intensity. He cannot help it. After the fourth song he is proclaimed." After the ceremony, the boy is carefully bathed and receives a woman's skirt. He is then led back to the dance ground, dressed as an *alyha,* and announces his new feminine name to the crowd. After that he would resent being called by his old male name.[19]

Among the Yuman tribes of the Southwest, the transformation is marked by a social gathering, in which the berdache prepares a meal for the friends of the family.[20] Ethnographer Ruth Underhill, doing fieldwork among the Papago Indians in the early 1930s, wrote that berdaches were common among the Papago Indians, and were usually publicly acknowledged in childhood. She recounted that a boy's parents would test him if they noticed that he preferred female pursuits. The regular pattern, mentioned by many of Underhill's Papago informants, was to build a small brush enclosure. Inside the enclosure they placed a man's bow and arrows, and also a woman's basket. At the appointed time the boy was brought to the enclosure as the adults watched from outside. The boy was told to go inside the circle of brush. Once he was inside, the adults "set fire to the enclosure. They watched what he took with him as he ran out and if it was the basketry materials, they reconciled themselves to his being a berdache."[21]

What is important to recognize in all of these practices is that the assumption of a berdache role was not forced on the boy by others. While adults might have their suspicions, it was only when the child made the proper move that he was considered a berdache. By doing woman's dancing, preparing a

READING 10: THE BERDACHE TRADITION

meal, or taking the woman's basket he was making an important symbolic gesture. Indian children were not stupid, and they knew the implications of these ceremonies beforehand. A boy in the enclosure could have left without taking anything, or could have taken both the man's and the woman's tools. With the community standing by watching, he was well aware that his choice would mark his assumption of berdache status. Rather than being seen as an involuntary test of his reflexes, this ceremony may be interpreted as a definite statement by the child to take on the berdache role.

Indians do not see the assumption of berdache status, however, as a free will choice on the part of the boy. People felt that the boy was acting out his basic character. The Lakota shaman Lame Deer explained:

> They were not like other men, but the Great Spirit made them *winktes* and we accepted them as such. . . . We think that if a woman has two little ones growing inside her, if she is going to have twins, sometimes instead of giving birth to two babies they have formed up in her womb into just one, into a half-man/half-woman kind of being. . . . To us a man is what nature, or his dreams, make him. We accept him for what he wants to be. That's up to him.[22]

While most of the sources indicate that once a person becomes a berdache it is a lifelong status, directions from the spirits determine everything. In at least one documented case, concerning a nineteenth-century Klamath berdache named Lele'ks, he later had a supernatural experience that led him to leave the berdache role. At that time Lele'ks began dressing and acting like a man, then married women, and eventually became one of the most famous Klamath chiefs.[23] What is important is that both in assuming berdache status and in leaving it, supernatural dictate is the determining factor.

DREAMS AND VISIONS

Many tribes see the berdache role as signifying an individual's proclivities as a dreamer and a visionary. . . .

Among the northern Plains and related Great Lakes tribes, the idea of supernatural dictate through dreaming—the vision quest—had its highest development. The goal of the vision quest is to try to get beyond the rational world by sensory deprivation and fasting. By depriving one's body of nourishment, the brain could escape from logical thought and connect with the higher reality of the supernatural. The person doing the quest simply sits and waits for a vision. But a vision might not come easily; the person might have to wait for days.

The best way that I can describe the process is to refer to my own vision quest, which I experienced when I was living on a Lakota reservation in 1982. After a long series of prayers and blessings, the shaman who had prepared me for the ceremony took me out to an isolated area where a sweat lodge had been set up for my quest. As I walked to the spot, I worried that I might not be able to stand it. Would I be overcome by hunger? Could I tolerate the thirst? What would I do if I had to go to the toilet? The shaman told me not to worry, that a whole group of holy people would be praying and singing for me while I was on my quest.

He had me remove my clothes, symbolizing my disconnection from the material world, and crawl into the sweat lodge. Before he left me I asked him, "What do I think about?" He said, "Do not think. Just pray for spiritual guidance." After a prayer he closed the flap tightly and I was left in total darkness. I still do not understand what happened to me during my vision quest, but during the day and a half that I was out there, I never once felt hungry or thirsty or the need to go to the toilet. What happened was an intensely personal experience that I cannot and do not wish to explain, a process of being that cannot be described in rational terms.

When the shaman came to get me at the end of my time, I actually resented having to end it. He did not need to ask if my vision quest were successful. He knew that it was even before seeing me, he explained, because he saw an eagle circling over me while I underwent the quest. He helped interpret the signs I had seen, then after more prayers and singing he led me back to the others. I felt relieved, cleansed, joyful, and serene. I had been through an experience that will be a part of my memories always.

If a vision quest could have such an effect on a person not even raised in Indian society, imagine its impact on a boy who from his earliest years had been waiting for the day when he could seek his vision. Gaining his spiritual power from his first vision, it would tell him what role to take in adult life. The vision might instruct him that he is going to be a great hunter, a craftsman, a warrior, or a shaman. Or it might tell him that he will be a berdache. Among the Lakotas, or Sioux, there are several symbols for various types of visions. A person becomes *wakan* (a sacred person) if she or he dreams of a bear, a wolf, thunder, a buffalo, a white buffalo calf, or Double Woman. Each dream results in a different gift, whether it is the power to cure illness or wounds, a promise of good hunting, or the exalted role of a *heyoka* (doing things backward).

A white buffalo calf is believed to be a berdache. If a person has a dream of the sacred Double Woman, this means that she or he will have the power to seduce men. Males who have a vision of Double Woman are presented with female tools. Taking such tools means that the male will become a berdache. The Lakota word *winkte* is composed of *win,* "woman," and *kte,* "would become."[24] A contemporary Lakota berdache explains, "To become a *winkte,* you have a medicine man put you up on the hill, to search for your vision. You can become a *winkte* if you truly are by nature. You see a vision of the White Buffalo Calf Pipe. Sometimes it varies. A vision is like a scene in a movie."[25] Another way to become a *winkte* is to have a vision given by a *winkte* from the past.[26] . . .

By interpreting the result of the vision as being the work of a spirit, the vision quest frees the person from feeling responsible for his transformation. The person might even claim that the change was done against his will and without his control. Such a claim does not suggest a negative attitude about berdache status, because it is common for people to claim reluctance to fulfill their spiritual duty no matter what vision appears to them. Becoming any

kind of sacred person involves taking on various social responsibilities and burdens.[27] . . .

A story was told among the Lakotas in the 1880s of a boy who tried to resist following his vision from Double Woman. But according to Lakota informants "few men succeed in this effort after having taken the strap in the dream." Having rebelled against the instructions given him by the Moon Being, he committed suicide.[28] The moral of that story is that one should not resist spiritual guidance, because it will lead only to grief. In another case, an Omaha young man told of being addressed by a spirit as "daughter," whereupon he discovered that he was unconsciously using feminine styles of speech. He tried to use male speech patterns, but could not. As a result of this vision, when he returned to his people he resolved himself to dress as a woman.[29] Such stories function to justify personal peculiarities as due to a fate over which the individual has no control.

Despite the usual pattern in Indian societies of using ridicule to enforce conformity, receiving instructions from a vision inhibits others from trying to change the berdache. Ritual explanation provides a way out. It also excuses the community from worrying about the cause of that person's difference, or the feeling that it is society's duty to try to change him.[30] Native American religions, above all else, encourage a basic respect for nature. If nature makes a person different, many Indians conclude, a mere human should not undertake to counter this spiritual dictate. Someone who is "unusual" can be accommodated without being stigmatized as "abnormal." Berdachism is thus not alien or threatening; it is a reflection of spirituality.

DISCUSSION QUESTIONS

1. What are the defining attributes of the berdache status?
2. What cultural forces or beliefs have supported the berdache tradition in some Native American societies? In what ways are the beliefs of Americans who are not Native American supportive or detrimental to the presence of the berdache tradition?

NOTES

1. Mary Douglas, *Purity and Danger* (Baltimore: Penguin, 1966), p. 52. I am grateful to Theda Perdue for convincing me that Douglas's ideas apply to berdachism. For an application of Douglas's thesis to berdaches, see James Thayer, "The Berdache of the Northern Plains: A Socioreligious Perspective," *Journal of Anthropological Research* 36 (1980): 292–93.

2. E. W. Gifford, "The Kamia of Imperial Valley," *Bureau of American Ethnology Bulletin* 97 (1931): 12.

3. By using present tense verbs in this text, I am not implying that such activities are necessarily continuing today. I sometimes use the present tense in the "ethnographic present," unless I use the past tense when I am referring to something that has not continued. Past tense implies that all such practices have disappeared. In the absence of fieldwork to prove such disappearance, I am not prepared to make that assumption, on the historic changes in the berdache tradition.

4. Elsie Clews Parsons, "The Zuni La' Mana," *American Anthropologist* 18 (1916): 521; Matilda Coxe Stevenson, "Zuni Indians," *Bureau of American Ethnology Annual Report* 23 (1903): 37; Franklin Cushing, "Zuni Creation Myths," *Bureau of American Ethnology Annual Report* 13 (1894): 401–3. Will Roscoe clarified this origin story for me.

5. W. W. Hill, "Note on the Pima Berdache," *American Anthropologist* 40 (1938): 339.

6. Aileen O'Bryan, "The Dine': Origin Myths of the Navaho Indians," *Bureau of American Ethnology Bulletin* 163 (1956): 5; W. W. Hill, "The Status of the Hermaphrodite and Transvestite in Navaho Culture," *American Anthropologist* 37 (1935): 273.

7. Martha S. Link, *The Pollen Path: A Collection of Navajo Myths* (Stanford, CA: Stanford University Press, 1956).

8. O'Bryan, "Dine,'" pp. 5, 7, 9–10.

9. Ibid.

10. Lakota informants, July 1982. See also William Powers, *Oglala Religion* (Lincoln: University of Nebraska Press, 1977).

11. For this admittedly generalized overview of American Indian religious values, I am indebted to traditionalist informants of many tribes, but especially those of the Lakotas. For a discussion of native religions see Dennis Tedlock, *Finding the Center* (New York: Dial Press, 1972); Ruth Underhill, *Red Man's Religion* (Chicago: University of Chicago Press, 1965); and Elsie Clews Parsons, *Pueblo Indian Religion* (Chicago: University of Chicago Press, 1939).

12. Alfred Kroeber, "The Arapaho," *Bulletin of the American Museum of Natural History* 18 (1902–7): 19.

13. Parsons, "Zuni La' Mana," p. 525.

14. Alexander Maximilian, *Travels in the Interior of North America, 1832–1834,* vol. 22 of *Early Western Travels,* ed. Reuben Gold Thwaites, 32 vols. (Cleveland: A. H. Clark, 1906), pp. 283–84, 354. Maximilian was quoted in German in the early homosexual rights book by Ferdinand Karsch-Haack, *Das Gleichgeschlechtliche Leben der Naturvölker* (The same-sex life of nature peoples) (Munich: Verlag von Ernst Reinhardt, 1911; reprinted New York: Arno Press, 1975), pp. 314, 564.

15. Oscar Koch, *Der Indianishe Eros* (Berlin: Verlag Continent, 1925), p. 61.

16. George Devereux, "Institutionalized Homosexuality of the Mohave Indians," *Human Biology* 9 (1937): 509.

17. Ibid., p. 501.

18. Ibid.

19. Ibid., pp. 508–9.

20. C. Daryll Forde, "Ethnography of the Yuma Indians," *University of California Publications in American Archaeology and Ethnology* 28 (1931): 157.

21. Ruth Underhill, *Social Organization of the Papago Indians* (New York: Columbia University Press, 1938), p. 186. This story is also mentioned in Ruth Underhill, ed., *The Autobiography of a Papago Woman* (Menasha, WI: American Anthropological Association, 1936), p. 39.

22. John Fire and Richard Erdoes, *Lame Deer, Seeker of Visions* (New York: Simon and Schuster, 1972), pp. 117, 149.

23. Theodore Stern, *The Klamath Tribe: A People and Their Reservation* (Seattle: University of Washington Press, 1965), pp. 20, 24; Theodore Stern, "Some Sources of Variability in Klamath Mythology," *Journal of American Folklore* 69 (1956): 242ff; Leshe Spier, *Klamath Ethnography* (Berkeley: University of California Press, 1930), p. 52.

24. Clark Wissler, "Societies and Ceremonial Associations in the Oglala Division of the Teton Dakota," *Anthropological Papers of the American Museum of Natural History* 11, pt. 1 (1916): 92; Powers, Oglala Religion, pp. 57–59.

25. Ronnie Loud Hawk, Lakota informant 4, July 1982.

26. Terry Calling Eagle, Lakota informant 5, July 1982.

27. James S. Thayer, "The Berdache of the Northern Plains: A Socioreligious Perspective," *Journal of Anthropological Research* 36 (1980): 289.

28. Fletcher, "Elk Mystery," p. 281.

29. Alice Fletcher and Francis La Flesche, "The Omaha Tribe," *Bureau of American Ethnology Annual Report* 27 (1905–6): 132.

30. Harriet Whitehead offers a valuable discussion of this element of the vision quest in "The Bow and the Burden Strap: A New Look at Institutionalized Homosexuality in Native North America," in *Sexual Meanings,* ed. Sherry Ortner and Harriet Whitehead (Cambridge: Cambridge University Press, 1981), pp. 99–102. See also Erikson, "Childhood," p. 329.

The Gendered Society

Michael S. Kimmel

In no country has such constant care been taken as in America to trace two clearly distinct lines of action for the two sexes, and to make them keep pace with the other, but in two pathways which are always different.

Alexis de Tocqueville
Democracy in America (1835)

Daily, we hear how men and women are different. They tell that we come from different planets. They say we have different brain chemistries, different brain organization, different hormones. They say our different anatomies lead to different destinies. They say we have different ways of knowing, listen to different moral voices, have different ways of speaking and hearing each other.

You'd think we were different species, like, say lobsters and giraffes, or Martians and Venutians. In his best-selling book, pop psychologist John Gray informs us that not only do women and men communicate differently, but they also "think, feel, perceive, react, respond, love, need, and appreciate differently."[1] It's a miracle of cosmic proportions that we ever understand one another!

Yet, despite these alleged interplanetary differences, we're all together in the same workplaces, where we are evaluated by the same criteria for raises, promotions, bonuses, and tenure. We sit in the same classrooms, eat in the same dining halls, read the same books, and are subject to the same criteria for grading. We live in the same houses, prepare and eat the same meals, read the same newspapers, and tune into the same television programs.

Michael S. Kimmel is a professor of sociology at the State University of New York at Stony Brook.

What I have come to call this "interplanetary" theory of complete and universal *gender difference* is also typically the way we explain another universal phenomenon: *gender inequality*. Gender is not simply a system of classification, by which biological males and biological females are sorted, separated, and socialized into equivalent sex roles. Gender also expresses the universal inequality between women and men. When we speak about gender we also speak about hierarchy, power, and inequality, not simply difference.

So the two tasks of any study of gender, it seems to me, are to explain both difference and inequality, or, to be alliterative, *difference* and *dominance*. Every general explanation of gender must address two central questions, and their ancillary derivative questions.

First: *Why is it that virtually every single society differentiates people on the basis of gender?* Why are women and men perceived as different in every known society? What are the differences that are perceived? Why is gender at least one—if not the central—basis for the division of labor?

Second: *Why is it that virtually every known society is also based on male dominance?* Why does virtually every society divide social, political, and economic resources unequally between the genders? And why is it that men always get more? Why is a gendered division of labor also an unequal division of labor? Why are women's tasks and men's tasks valued differently?

It is clear . . . that there are dramatic differences among societies regarding the type of gender differences, the levels of gender inequality, and the amount of violence (implied or real) that is necessary to maintain both systems of difference and domination. But the basic facts remain: *Virtually every society known to us is founded upon assumptions of gender difference and the politics of gender inequality.*

On these axiomatic questions, two basic schools of thought prevail: biological determinism and differential socialization. We know them as "nature" and "nurture," and the question of which is dominant has been debated for a century in classrooms, at dinner parties, by political adversaries, and among friends and families. Are men and women different because they are "hardwired" to be different, or are they different because they've been taught to be? Is biology destiny, or is it that human beings are more flexible, and thus subject to change?

Most of the arguments about gender difference begin . . . with biology. . . . Women and men *are* biologically different, after all. Our reproductive anatomies are different, and so are our reproductive destinies. Our brain structures differ, our brain chemistries differ. Our musculature is different. Different levels of different hormones circulate through our different bodies. Surely, these add up to fundamental, intractable, and universal differences, and these differences provide the foundation for male domination, don't they?

The answer is an unequivocal maybe. Or, perhaps more accurately, yes and no. There are very few people who would suggest that there are no differences between males and females. At least, I wouldn't suggest it. What social scientists call *sex differences* refer precisely to that catalog of anatomical, hormonal, chemical, and physical differences between women and men. But even here, as we shall see, there are enormous ranges of female-ness and male-ness. Though our musculature differs, plenty of women are physically stronger than plenty of men. Though on average our chemistries are different, it's not an all-or-nothing proposition—women do have varying levels of androgens, and men have varying levels of estrogen in their systems. And though our brain structure may be differently lateralized, males and females both do tend to use both sides of their brain. And it is far from clear that these biological differences automatically and inevitably lead men to dominate women. Could we not imagine, as some writers already have, a culture in which women's biological abilities to bear and nurse children might be seen as the expression of such ineffable power—the ability to create life—that strong men wilt in impotent envy?

In fact, in order to underscore this issue, most social and behavioral scientists now use the term *gender* in a different way than we use the word *sex*.

Sex refers to the biological apparatus, the male and the female—our chromosomal, chemical, anatomical organization. Gender refers to the meanings that are attached to those differences within a culture. Sex is male and female; gender is masculinity and femininity—what it means to be a man or a woman. . . . And while biological sex varies very little, gender varies enormously. What it means to possess the anatomical configuration of male or female means very different things depending on where you are, who you are, and when you are living. . . .

The other reigning school of thought that explains both gender difference and gender domination is *differential socialization*—the "nurture" side of the equation. Men and women are different because we are taught to be different. From the moment of birth, males and females are treated differently. Gradually we acquire the traits, behaviors, and attitudes that our culture defines as "masculine" or "feminine." We are not necessarily born different; we become different through this process of socialization.

Nor are we born biologically predisposed toward gender inequality. Domination is not a trait carried on the Y chromosome; it is the outcome of the different cultural valuing of men's and women's experiences. Thus, the adoption of masculinity and femininity implies the adoption of "political" ideas that what women do is not as culturally important as what men do.

Developmental psychologists have also examined the ways in which the meanings of masculinity and femininity change over the course of a person's life. The issues confronting a man about proving himself and feeling successful will change, as will the social institutions in which he will attempt to enact those experiences. The meanings of femininity are subject to parallel changes, for example, among prepubescent women, women in childbearing years, and postmenopausal women, as they are different for women entering the labor market and those retiring from it.

Although we typically cast the debate in terms of *either* biological determinism *or* differential socialization—nature versus nurture—it may be useful to pause for a moment to observe what characteristics they have in common. Both schools of thought share two fundamental assumptions. First, both "nature lovers" and "nurturers" see women and men as markedly different from each other—truly, deeply, and irreversibly different. (Nurture does allow for some possibility of change, but they still argue that the process of socialization is a process of making males and females different from each other—differences that are normative, culturally necessary, and "natural.") And both schools of thought assume that the differences *between* women and men are far greater and more decisive (and worthy of analysis) than the differences that might be observed *among* men or *among* women. Thus, both "nature lovers" and "nurturers" subscribe to some version of the interplanetary theory of gender.

Second, both schools of thought assume that gender domination is the inevitable outcome of gender difference, that difference causes domination. To the biologists, it may be because pregnancy and lactation make women more vulnerable and in need of protection, or because male musculature makes them more adept hunters, or that testosterone makes them more aggressive with other men and with women too. Or it may be that men have to dominate women in order to maximize their chances to pass on their genes. Psychologists of "gender roles" tell us that, among other things, men and women are taught to devalue women's experiences, perceptions, and abilities, and to overvalue men's.

I argue . . . that both of these propositions are false. First, . . . the differences between women and men are not . . . nearly as great as are the differences among women or among men. Many perceived differences turn out to be differences based less on gender than on the social positions people occupy. Second, I . . . argue that gender difference is the product of gender inequality, and not the other way around. In fact, gender difference is the chief outcome of gender inequality, because it is through the idea of difference that inequality is legitimated. As one sociologist recently put it, "The very creation of difference is the foundation on which inequality rests."[2]

Using what social scientists have come to call a "social constructionist" approach, . . . I make the case that neither gender difference nor gender inequality is inevitable in the nature of things, nor, more specifically, in the nature of our bodies. Neither are difference and domination explainable solely by reference to differential socialization of boys and girls into sex roles typical of men and women.

When proponents of both nature and nurture positions assert that gender inequality is the inevitable outcome of gender difference, they take, perhaps inadvertently, a political position that assumes that inequality may be lessened, or that its most negative effects may be ameliorated, but that it cannot be eliminated—precisely because it is based upon intractable differences. On the other hand, to assert, as I do, that the exaggerated gender differences that we see are not as great as they appear and that they are the result of inequality allows a far greater political latitude. By eliminating gender inequality, we will remove the foundation upon which the entire edifice of gender difference is built.

What will remain, I believe is not some nongendered androgynous gruel, in which differences between women and men are blended and everyone acts and thinks in exactly the same way. Quite the contrary, I believe that as gender inequality decreases, the differences among people—differences grounded in race, class, ethnicity, age, sexuality *as well as* gender—will emerge in a context in which each of us can be appreciated for our individual uniqueness as well as our commonality.

MAKING GENDER VISIBLE FOR BOTH WOMEN AND MEN

. . . A dramatic transformation in thinking about gender . . . has occurred over the past thirty years. In particular, three decades of pioneering work by feminist scholars, both in traditional disciplines and in women's studies, has made us aware of the centrality of gender in shaping social life. We now know that gender is one of the central organizing principles around which social life revolves. Until the 1970s, social scientists would have listed only class and race as the master statuses that defined and proscribed social life. If you wanted to study gender in the 1960s in social science, for example, you would have found but one course designed to address your needs—"Marriage and the Family"—which was sort of the "Ladies Auxiliary" of the social sciences. There were no courses on gender. But today, gender has joined race and class in our understanding of the foundations of an individual's identity. Gender, we now know, is one of the axes around which social life is organized and through which we understand our own experiences.

In the past thirty years, feminist scholars properly focused most of their attention on women—on what Catharine Stimpson has called the "omissions, distortions, and trivializations" of women's experiences—and the spheres to which women have historically been consigned, such as private life and the family.[3] Women's history sought to rescue from obscurity the lives of significant women who had been ignored or whose work has been minimized by traditional androcentric scholarship, and to examine the everyday lives of women in the past—the efforts, for example, of laundresses, factory workers, pioneer homesteaders, or housewives to carve out lives of meaning and dignity in a world controlled by men. Whether the focus has been on the exemplary or the ordinary, though, feminist scholarship has made it clear that gender is a central axis in women's lives. . . .

But when we study men, we study them as political leaders, military heroes, scientists, writers, artists. Men, themselves, are invisible *as men*. Rarely, if ever, do we see a course that examines the lives of men as men. What is the impact of gender on the lives of these famous men? How does masculinity play a part in the lives of great artists, writers, presidents, etc. How does masculinity pay out in the lives of "ordinary" men—in factories and on farms, in union halls and large corporations? On this score, the traditional curriculum suddenly draws a big blank. Everywhere one turns there are courses about men, but virtually no information on masculinity.

Several years ago, this yawning gap inspired me to undertake a cultural history of the idea of masculinity in America, to trace the development and shifts in what it has meant to be a man over the course of our history.[4] What I found is that American men have been very articulate in describing what it means to be a man, and in seeing whatever they have done as a way to prove their manhood, but that we haven't known how to hear them.

Integrating gender into our courses is a way to fulfill the promise of women's studies—by understanding men as gendered as well. In my university, for example, the course on nineteenth-century British literature includes a deeply "gendered" reading of the Brontës, that discusses their feelings about femininity, marriage, and relations between the sexes. Yet not a word is spoken about Dickens and masculinity, especially about his feelings about fatherhood and the family. Dickens is understood as a "social problem" novelist, and his issue was class relations—this despite the fact that so many of Dickens's most celebrated characters are young boys without fathers, and who are searching for authentic families. And there's not a word about Thomas Hardy's ambivalent ideas about masculinity and marriage in, say, *Jude the Obscure.* Hardy's grappling with premodernist conceptions of an apathetic universe is what we discuss. And my wife tells me that in her nineteenth-century American literature class at Princeton, gender was the main topic of conversation when the subject was Edith Wharton, but the word was never spoken when they discussed Henry James, in whose work gendered anxiety erupts variously as chivalric contempt, misogynist rage, and sexual ambivalence. James, we're told, is "about" the form of the novel, narrative technique, the stylistic powers of description and characterization. Certainly not about gender.

So we continue to act as if gender applied only to women. Surely the time has come to make gender visible to men. As the Chinese proverb has it, the fish are the last to discover the ocean. . . .

THE CURRENT DEBATE

I believe that we are, at this moment, having a national debate about masculinity in this country—but that we don't know it. For example, what gender comes to mind when I invoke the following current

American problems: "teen violence," "gang violence," "suburban violence," "drug violence," "violence in the schools?" And what gender comes to mind when I say the words "suicide bomber" or "terrorist hijacker"?

Of course, you've imagined men. And not just any men—but younger men, in their teens and twenties, and relatively poorer men, from the working class or lower middle class.

But how do our social commentators discuss these problems? Do they note that the problem of youth and violence is really a problem of young *men* and violence? Do they ever mention that everywhere ethnic nationalism sets up shop, it is young men who are the shopkeepers? Do they ever mention masculinity at all?

No. Listen, for example, to the voice of one expert, asked to comment on the brutal murder of Matthew Shepard, a gay twenty-one-year-old college student at the University of Wyoming. After being reminded that young men account for 80 percent to 90 percent of people arrested for "gay bashing" crimes, the reporter quoted a sociologist as saying that "[t]his youth variable tells us they are working out identity issues, making the transition away from home into adulthood."[5] This "*youth* variable"? What had been a variable about age and gender had been transformed into a variable about age. Gender had disappeared. That is the sound of silence, what invisibility looks like.

Now, imagine that these were all women—all the ethnic nationalists, the militias, the gay bashers. Would that not be *the* story, the *only* story? Would not a gender analysis be at the center of every single story? Would we not hear from experts on female socialization, frustration, anger, PMS, and everything else under the sun? But the fact that these are men earns nary a word.

Take one final example. What if it had been young girls who opened fire on their classmates in West Paducah, Kentucky, in Pearl, Mississippi, in Jonesboro, Arkansas, or in Springfield, Oregon? And what if nearly all the children who died were boys? Do you think that the social outcry would demand that we investigate the "inherent violence" of

Southern culture, or simply express dismay that young "people" have too much access to guns? I doubt it. And yet no one seemed to mention that the young boys who actually committed those crimes were simply doing—albeit in dramatic form at a younger age—what American men have been taught to do for centuries when they are upset and angry. Men don't get mad; they get even. . . .

I believe that until we make gender visible for both women and for men we will not, as a culture, adequately know how to address these issues. That's not to say that all we have to do is address masculinity. These issues are complex, requiring analyses of the political economy of global economic integration, of the transformation of social classes, of urban poverty and hopelessness, of racism. But if we ignore masculinity—if we let it remain invisible—we will never completely understand them, let alone resolve them.

THE PLURAL AND THE POWERFUL

When I use the term *gender,* then, it is with the explicit intention of discussing both masculinity and femininity. But even these terms are inaccurate because they imply that there is one simple definition of masculinity and one definition of femininity. One of the important elements of a social constructionist approach—especially if we intend to dislodge the notion that gender differences alone are decisive—is to explore the differences *among* men and *among* women, since, as it turns out, these are often more decisive than the differences between women and men.

Within any one society at any one moment, several meanings of masculinity and femininity coexist. Simply put, not all American men and women are the same. Our experiences are also structured by class, race, ethnicity, age, sexuality, region. Each of these axes modifies the others. Just because we make gender visible doesn't mean that we make these other organizing principles of social life invisible. Imagine, for example, an older, black, gay man in Chicago and a young, white, heterosexual farm boy in Iowa. Wouldn't they have different definitions of masculinity? Or imagine a twenty-two-year-old wealthy Asian American heterosexual woman in San Francisco and a poor white Irish Catholic lesbian in Boston. Wouldn't their ideas about what it means to be a woman be somewhat different?

If gender varies across cultures, over historical time, among men and women within any one culture, and over the life course, can we really speak of masculinity or femininity as though they were constant, universal essences, common to all women and to all men? If not, gender must be seen as an ever-changing fluid assemblage of meanings and behaviors. In that sense, we must speak of *masculinities* and *femininities,* and thus recognize the different definitions of masculinity and femininity that we construct. By pluralizing the terms, we acknowledge that masculinity and femininity mean different things to different groups of people at different times.

At the same time, we can't forget that all masculinities and femininities are not created equal. American men and women must also contend with a particular definition that is held up as the model against which we are expected to measure ourselves. We thus come to know what it means to be a man or a woman in our culture by setting our definitions in opposition to a set of "others"—racial minorities, sexual minorities. For men, the classic "other" is, of course, women. It feels imperative to most men that they make it clear—eternally, compulsively, decidedly—that they are unlike women.

For most men, this is the "hegemonic" definition—the one that is held up as the model for all of us. It is as Virginia Woolf wrote in 1938, "the quintessence of virility, the perfect type of which all the others are imperfect adumbrations."[6] The hegemonic definition of masculinity is "constructed in relation to various subordinated masculinities as well as in relation to women," writes sociologist R. W. Connell. The sociologist Erving Goffman once described this hegemonic definition of masculinity like this:

> In an important sense there is only one complete unblushing male in America: a young, married, white,

urban, northern, heterosexual, Protestant, father, of college education, fully employed, of good complexion, weight, and height, and a recent record in sports. . . . Any male who fails to qualify in any one of these ways is likely to view himself—during moments at least—as unworthy, incomplete, and inferior.[7]

Women contend with an equally exaggerated ideal of femininity, which Connell calls "emphasized femininity." Emphasized femininity is organized around compliance with gender inequality, and is "oriented to accommodating the interests and desires of men." One sees emphasized femininity in "the display of sociability rather than technical competence, fragility in mating scenes, compliance with men's desire for titillation and ego-stroking in office relationships, acceptance of marriage and childcare as a response to labor-market discrimination against women."[8] Emphasized femininity exaggerates gender difference as a strategy of "adaptation to men's power" stressing empathy and nurturance; "real" womanhood is described as "fascinating" and women are advised that they can wrap men around their fingers by knowing and playing by the "rules." In one research study, an eight-year-old boy captured this emphasized femininity eloquently in a poem he wrote:

> If I were a girl, I'd have to attract a guy
>
> wear makeup; sometimes.
>
> Wear the latest style of clothes and try to be likable.
>
> I probably wouldn't play any physical sports like football or soccer.
>
> I don't think I would enjoy myself around men
>
> in fear of rejection
>
> or under the pressure of attracting them.[9]

GENDER DIFFERENCE AS "DECEPTIVE DISTINCTIONS"

The existence of multiple masculinities and femininities dramatically undercuts the idea that the gender differences we observe are due solely to differently gendered people occupying gender-neutral positions. Moreover, that these masculinities and femininities are arrayed along a hierarchy, and measured against one another, buttresses the argument that domination creates and exaggerates difference.

The interplanetary theory of gender assumes, whether through biology or socialization, that women act like women, no matter where they are, and that men act like men no matter where they are. Psychologist Carol Tavris argues that such binary thinking leads to what philosophers call the "law of the excluded middle," which, as she reminds us, "is where most men and women fall in terms of their psychological qualities, beliefs, abilities, traits and values."[10] It turns out that many of the differences between women and men that we observe in our everyday lives are actually not *gender* differences at all, but differences that are the result of being in different positions or in different arenas. It's not that gendered individuals occupy these ungendered positions, but that the positions themselves elicit the behaviors we see as gendered. The sociologist Cynthia Fuchs Epstein calls these "deceptive distinctions" because, while they appear to be based on gender, they are actually based on something else.[11]

Take, for example, the well-known differences in communication patterns observed by Deborah Tannen in her best-selling book *You Just Don't Understand.* Tannen argues that women and men communicate with the languages of their respective planets—men employ the competitive language of hierarchy and domination to get ahead; women create webs of inclusion with softer, more embracing language that ensures that everyone feels O.K. At home, men are the strong silent types, grunting monosyllabically to their wives, who want to use conversation to create intimacy.[12]

But it turns out that those very same monosyllabic men are very verbal at work, where they are in positions of dependency and powerlessness, and need to use conversation to maintain a relationship with their superiors at work; and their wives are just as capable of using language competitively to maximize their position in a corporate hierarchy. When he examined the recorded transcripts of women's and men's testimony in trials, anthropologist

William O'Barr concluded that the witnesses' occupation was a more accurate predictor of their use of language than was gender. "So-called women's language is neither characteristic of all women, nor limited only to women," O'Barr writes. If women use "powerless" language, it may be due "to the greater tendency of women to occupy relatively powerless social positions" in society.[13] Communication differences turn out to be "deceptive distinctions" because rarely do we observe the communication patterns of dependent men and executive women. . . .

What about those enormous gender differences that some observers have found in the workplace? . . . Men, we hear, are competitive social climbers who seek advancement at every opportunity; women are cooperative team builders who shun competition and may even suffer from a "fear of success." But the pioneering study by Rosabeth Moss Kanter, reported in *Men and Women of the Corporation,* indicated that gender mattered far less than opportunity. When women had the same opportunities, networks, mentors, and possibilities for advancement, they behaved just as the men did. Women were not successful because they lacked opportunities, not because they feared success; when men lacked opportunities, they behaved in stereotypically "feminine" ways.[14]

Finally, take our experiences in the family. . . . Here, again, we assume that women are socialized to be nurturing and maternal, men to be strong and silent, relatively emotionally inexpressive arbiters of justice—that is, we assume that women do the work of "mothering" because they are socialized to do so. And again, sociological research suggests that our behavior in the family has somewhat less to do with gender socialization than with the family situations in which we find ourselves.

Research by sociologist Kathleen Gerson, for example, found that gender socialization was not very helpful in predicting women's family experiences. Only slightly more than half the women who were primarily interested in full-time motherhood were, in fact, full-time mothers; and only slightly more than half the women who were primarily interested in full-time careers had them. It turned out that marital stability, husbands' income, women's work-place experiences, and support networks were far more important than gender socialization in deter-mining which women ended up full-time mothers and which did not.[15]

On the other side of the ledger, research by soci-ologist Barbara Risman found that despite a gender socialization that downplays emotional responsive-ness and nurturing, most single fathers are per-fectly capable of "mothering." Single fathers do not hire female workers to do the typically female tasks around the house; they do those tasks themselves. In fact, Risman found few differences between sin-gle fathers and mothers (single or married) when it came to what they did around the house, how they acted with their children, or even in their children's emotional and intellectual development. Men's parenting styles were virtually indistinguishable from women's, a finding that led Risman to argue that "men can mother and that children are not necessarily better nurtured by women than by men."[16] . . .

Based on all this research, you might conclude, as does Risman, that "if women and men were to experience identical structural conditions and role expectations, empirically observable gender differ-ences would dissipate."[17] I am not fully convinced. There *are* some differences between women and men, after all. Perhaps, as this research suggests, those differences are not as great, decisive, or as im-pervious to social change as we once thought. . . .

THE MEANING OF MEAN DIFFERENCES

Few of the differences between women and men are hardwired into all males to the exclusion of all fe-males, or vice versa. Although we can readily observe differences between women and men in rates of ag-gression, physical strength, math or verbal achieve-ment, caring and nurturing, or emotional expressiveness, it is not true that all males and no fe-males are aggressive, physically strong, and adept at math and science, and all females and no males are caring and nurturing, verbally adept, or emotionally expressive. What we mean when we speak of gender

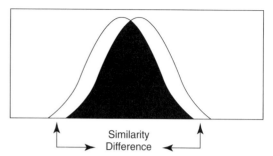

FIGURE 1
Schematic rendering of the overlapping distributions of traits, attitudes, and behaviors by gender. Although mean differences might obtain on many characteristics, these distributions suggest far greater similarity between women and men, and far greater variability among men and among women.

differences are mean differences, differences in the average scores obtained by women and men.

These mean scores tell us something about the differences between the two groups, but they tell us nothing about the distributions themselves, the dif-ferences *among* men or *among* women. Sometimes these distributions can be enormous: There are large numbers of caring or emotionally expressive men, and of aggressive and physically strong women. (See figure 1.) In fact, in virtually all the re-search that has been done on the attributes associ-ated with masculinity or femininity, the differences among women and among men are far greater than the mean differences between women and men. We tend to focus on the mean differences, but they may tell us far less than we think they do.

What we think they tell us, of course, is that women and men are different, from different plan-ets. This is what I . . . call the interplanetary theory of gender difference—that the observed mean dif-ferences between women and men are decisive and that they come from the fact that women and men are biologically so physically different.

For example, even the idea that we are from dif-ferent planets, that our differences are deep and in-tractable, has a political dimension: To call the "other" sex the "opposite" sex obscures the many

PERSONAL ACCOUNT

Basketball

I frequently watch my boyfriend play basketball at an outdoor court with many other males in pick-up games. One time when I was there, there was a new face among the others waiting to play—a female face, and she was not sitting with the rest of the women who were watching. She was dressed and ready to play. I had never seen her in all the time I'd been there before, nor had I ever seen another woman there try to play.

For several games, she did not play. The guys formed teams and she was not asked to join. It was almost like there was a purposeful avoidance of her, with no one even acknowledging that she was there. Finally, she made a noticeable effort, and with some reluctance she was included in the next team waiting to play the winner of the current game. There were whispers and snickers among the guys, and I think it had a lot to do with the perception that she was challenging their masculinity. A "girl" was intruding into their area. My guess is that they were also somewhat nervous about the fact that she really might be good and embarrass some of them.

Anyway, the first couple of times up and down the court she was not given the ball despite the fact that she was wide open. The other guys on the team forced bad shots and tried super hard in what seemed like an effort to prove that she was not needed. The guy who was supposed to guard her on defense really didn't pay her much attention, and that same guy who she was guarding at the other end made sure he drove around her and scored on two occasions.

Finally, one time down the court she called for the ball and sank a shot from at least 16 feet. A huge feeling of relief and satisfaction came over me. Being a basketball player myself, I figured she was probably good or would not be there in the first place, but being a woman I was also happy to see her *first* shot go in. I found out later she had played basketball for a university and she had a great outside shot.

Even after she made one more shot off a rebound that ended up in her hands, she was not given the ball again. I suppose after some of the loud comments from some of the guys on the sidelines, that she was beating the male players out there, she wasn't going to get the ball again. I was kind of shocked that she wasn't *more* accepted even after she showed she was talented. I haven't seen her there since.

Andrea M. Busch

---

ways we are alike. As the anthropologist Gayle Rubin points out:

> Men and women are, of course, different. But they are not as different as day and night, earth and sky, yin and yang, life and death. In fact from the standpoint of nature, men and women are closer to each other than either is to anything else—for instance mountains, kangaroos, or coconut palms. . . . Far from being an expression of natural differences, exclusive gender identity is the suppression of natural similarities.[18]

The interplanetary theory of gender difference is important not because it's right—in fact, it is wrong far more often than it is right—but because, as a culture, we seem desperately to *want* it to be true. That is, the real sociological question about gender is not the sociology of gender differences—explaining the physiological origins of gender difference—but the sociology of knowledge question that explores why gender difference is so important to us, why we cling to the idea of gender difference so tenaciously, why, I suppose, we shell out millions of dollars for books that "reveal" the deep differences between women and men, but will probably never buy a book that says, "Hey, we're all Earthlings!"

That, however, is [my] message. . . . Virtually all available research from the social and behavioral sciences suggests that women and men are not from Venus and Mars, but are both from planet Earth. We're not opposite sexes, but neighboring sexes—we have far more in common with each other than we have differences. We pretty much have the same abilities, and pretty much want the same things in our lives.

DISCUSSION QUESTIONS

1. What do you understand Kimmel to mean when he says that gender inequality produces gender difference? Can you give an example?

2. What is your reaction to Kimmel's position that we are engaged in a national debate about masculinity?
3. In your own words, explain the "deceptive distinctions" aspect of gender.

NOTES

1. John Gray, *Men Are from Mars, Women Are from Venus* (New York: HarperCollins, 1992), 5.
2. Barbara Risman, *Gender Vertigo* (New Haven: Yale University Press, 1998), 25. See also Judith Lorber, *Paradoxes of Gender* (New Haven: Yale University Press, 1994).
3. Catharine Stimpson, *Where the Meanings Are* (New York: Methuen, 1988).
4. See Michael Kimmel, *Manhood in America: A Cultural History* (New York: The Free Press, 1996).
5. Cited in James Brooke, "Men Held in Beatings Lived on the Fringes," *New York Times,* October 16, 1998, A16. Valerie Jenness, the sociologist who was quoted in the story, told me that she was *mis*quoted, and that of course she had mentioned gender as well as age—which suggests that the media's myopia matches that of the larger society.
6. Virginia Woolf, *Three Guineas* [1938] (New York: Harcourt, 1966), 142.
7. R. W. Connell, *Gender and Power* (Stanford: Stanford University Press, 1987), 183; Erving Goffman, *Stigma* (Englewood Cliffs, NJ: Prentice-Hall, 1963), 128.
8. Connell, *Gender and Power,* 183, 188, 187.
9. Cited in Risman, *Gender Vertigo,* 141.
10. Carol Tavris, "The Mismeasure of Woman," *Feminism and Psychology* (1993):153.
11. Cynthia Fuchs Epstein, *Deceptive Distinctions* (New Haven: Yale University Press, 1988).
12. Deborah Tannen, *You Just Don't Understand* (New York: William Morrow, 1991).
13. William O'Barr and Jean F. O'Barr, *Linguistic Evidence: Language, Power and Strategy—The Courtroom* (San Diego: Academic Press, 1995); see also Alfie Kohn, "Girl Talk, Guy Talk," *Psychology Today,* February 1988, 66.
14. Rosabeth M. Kanter, *Men and Women of the Corporation* (New York: Harper and Row, 1977).
15. Kathleen Gerson, *Hard Choices* (Berkeley: University of California Press, 1985); *No Man's Land* (New York: Basic Books, 1993).
16. Risman, *Gender Vertigo,* 70.
17. Risman, *Gender Vertigo,* 21.
18. Gayle Rubin, "The Traffic in Women," in *Toward an Anthropology of Women,* ed. R. R. Reiter, 179–80 (New York: Monthly Review Press, 1975).

READING 12

It's Your Gender, Stupid!

Riki Wilchins

TAKE ME TO YOUR GENDER

Gender. Everyone talks about it, but no one knows what it is or agrees on a definition. Gender *identity?* Gender *expression?* Gender *characteristics?* The gender *system?* A softer synonym for "sex"? *Gender* never stands alone, but always seems to need a noun to refer to.

. . . We assume that it's a common term of meaning, although it appears to be anything but. As with pornography, we may not be able to define it, but we know it when we see it.

The fact that *gender* is used in so many different but related contexts hints that we've touched on something very basic and pervasive in the human condition. So does the fact that we "know it when we see it." But I believe all the confusion surrounding gender means that perhaps just the opposite is the case: that gender is a set of meanings, and so like children learning to tell Daddy from Mommy and little boys from little girls, we see it once we know it.

EARLY MORNING DO

But according to theorist Judith Butler, gender refers not to something we *are* but to something we *do,* which, through extended repetition and because of the vigorous suppression of all exceptions, achieves the appearance of a sort of coherent psychic substance.

In this view, there is no doer behind the deed, no gendered identity behind the acts that we say result from it. The acts are all there is, and it is the strict regulation of these acts within the binary—females must produce feminine behaviors and males

Riki Wilchins is the executive director of GenderPAC, the national gender advocacy group, and cofounder of the Gender Identity Project of New York City's Lesbian and Gay Center.

masculine—that produces the appearance of two coherent and universal genders.

Thus, I don't pull on certain clothes in the morning or style my hair a particular way because of something within me. I do these acts in a manner consistent with either masculine or feminine norms because to do otherwise would render me socially unintelligible. People wouldn't know what I was or how to treat me, and I would be the target of a great deal of hostility.

My achieving a consistent appearance and behavior is then offered as proof of a binary gender inside me.

If my gender is a doing that has to be redone each day just like I pull on those clothes each morning, that would help explain why sometimes my gender "fails": Even though I've felt like a man (and then later like a woman), people didn't always recognize me as such. Even I couldn't always recognize myself as such.

BETTER DEAD THAN READ

If I can "fail" accidentally, maybe there are ways I can fail on purpose that will create room for me to grow, to find new ways of expression that resonate more deeply. If gender is a doing and a reading of that doing, a call-and-response that must be continually done and redone, then it's also unstable, and there are ways I can disrupt it. Maybe universal and binary genders are not so inevitable after all.

This is an attractive line of thinking, especially for anyone who has found themselves transcending narrow, outdated, 20th-century gender norms. . . .

But how do we square this with some of the facts? For instance, transexuality. It is undoubtedly true that some people (the author included) have, or do, feel a profound sense of discomfort at being confined to one sex and gender instead of another. If gender is a *doing*, does that imply that the transexual in distress is somehow reenacting his or her own pain each morning in a repeated series of gendered acts?

And transexuality aside, most people do report experiencing a stable, long-term sense of identifica-

tion with either male or female, man or woman. That would seem to constitute pretty good evidence of gendered identities.

But then again, there are only two types of identities one can report experiencing. For instance, I said, "I feel like a woman trapped in a man's body," and my doctors understood and shipped me off to surgery. But if I'd worn my Intersex Society of North America HERMAPHRODITES WITH ATTITUDE T-shirt and told them, "I feel like a herm trapped in a man's body," they wouldn't have understood and would have shipped me off to a rubber room.

Moreover, paradoxical as it sounds, there is room to question whether any identification, however stable and long-term, actually constitutes *having* an identity. Identification is always an act, a repetition, a name we give to a collection of discrete traits, behaviors, urges, and empathies.

A SYSTEM OF MEANINGS

. . . Gender is a system of meanings and symbols—and the rules, privileges, and punishments pertaining to their use—for power and sexuality: masculinity and femininity, strength and vulnerability, action and passivity, dominance and weakness.

To gender something simply means investing it with one of two meanings. So anything and everything can be gendered, for example: ships, clothing, sexual positions, pens, bowls, hand positions, head tilts, vocal inflections, body hair, and different sports. Indeed, in many romance languages, every object is given a gender (*vive la différence*, Le Monde, *la dolce vita, el toro, el Riki*).

Because being gay itself is a transgression of the rules of gender, because those rules heavily disfavor femininity, gay and feminist (and lately transgendered) critics have tended to focus on gender's many repressive aspects.

The punishments we exact for using the "wrong" words cross from the mundane to the fatal, including hostile stares in the women's room, being humiliated after gym class for being a "sissy" or a "dyke," unfair termination for being a "ball-buster," assault for being a "faggot," arrest for "impersonating a woman," rape for being "too sexy," forced psychiatric treatment for gender identity disorder, genital mutilation for intersexed infants, and, of course, murder.

But like any language, gender's primary effect is not repressive but productive: It produces meanings. These are created through a vast and visible top-down structure: binary birth certificates, restrooms, adoption policies, immigration laws, passports, and marriage laws. But they are also produced and maintained from the bottom up, through thousands of small, everyday acts—interactions that create and destroy gendered meanings in every moment. These microexchanges of meaning—in an elevator, over a meal, while buying a newspaper, when answering the phone—stamp us with our gender, bind us to it, and require us to answer to it in order to interact with other people.

Thus not only does gender restrain us as individuals, but it is through the language of gender that we become who we are, that we come to recognize ourselves—and be recognized by others—as men and women, and only as men and women.

As an academic concept, gender has been remarkably productive. Every year witnesses a new crop of articles, books, and theory about gender. Yet as a civil rights cause, gender is just beginning.

One can see in it the outlines of something that links misogyny, homophobia, transphobia, and the restricted way we raise our youth. Indeed, a widespread understanding of gender would have enormous potential to transform society and remove inequity and violence.

A SEX BY ANY OTHER NAME WOULD STILL SMELL AS SWEET

If gender is a system of meanings, then what are we to make of the recent and remarkable degree to which "gender" is replacing "sex" to refer not only to men and women but also male and female? Perhaps this is only a way to avoid saying the overloaded word "sex," which also means intercourse, in public speech. . . .

The increasing use of gender to replace sex may be an acknowledgment, if only unconsciously, that once you start looking there is nothing, or at least very little, on the far side of language. As an experiment, I recently asked a large group of very hip queer youths to list on a blackboard all the attributes that made up a "real man" and "real woman." Interestingly, on the list beneath "real man" was "has a penis"; the list beneath "real woman" included "doesn't have a penis." Not one person in the entire group thought to list "doesn't have a vagina" or even "has a vagina" as an identifying trait of bodies. I take from this that although the body's moving parts may all be "over there" on the far side of language, nearly everything we make of them to render them meaningful to us is right here, in our laps.

I'D LIKE TO BUY A WOMEN'S DICTIONARY

Gender as a language is at once terribly simple, because it has only two meanings, and terribly complex, because it touches us across the entire plane of contact between our bodies and society. In most languages, words can be used by anyone who can master them. But gender is a language that creates and sustains binary difference. To achieve this, gendered signs must be highly regulated so they don't fall into the wrong hands, as if certain dictionary words were colored blue for boys and pink for girls. Wearing a skirt, smoking a pipe, crying in public, moaning during sex, scratching your crotch, describing anything (but God) as divine: These are some of the signs that may be given by only one half of the population or the other.

20/20 HIND-CITE

. . . For Butler, "successful" genders are those that cite other earlier examples. Thus we learn to become men and women and to be recognized as such by copying other examples. In popular thought, men and women are considered examples of "real" genders, and drag, transexuals, and butch/femme couples are considered copies. Thus drag is to copy as woman is to real. Drag imitates real life.

But if Butler is right, if gender is always an artifice that copies something else, then all gender is a reuse of familiar stereotypes according to the rules for their use. All gender is drag. And those that fail, that are read as "queer," are simply those that break the rules. Thus neither a Streisand drag queen doing "Barbra" nor Barbra herself doing "woman" is any more or less real. There is no real gender to which they might be compared. Both use common symbols to achieve a visual meaning. The drag queen appears "false" because we don't grant her access to those symbols.

Considering gender as a language, I would approach queerness somewhat differently. What did I mean when I told my doctors that I felt "like a woman"? How was it possible for me to feel like anything other than myself? Perhaps I only meant that I was feminine. But although one can be seen as feminine, feel feminine feelings, or to express femininity through our clothing, hairstyle, and posture, can anyone really *be* feminine?

Achieving femininity sounds like a lot of work: how I feel, how I express myself to others, and how they perceive me. It's one thing to feel consistently male or feminine or like a boy, but keeping all that feeling/expressing/being-perceived continuously intact must take a lot of concentration. Having any gender at all is really a sort of accomplishment, a sustained effort.

Genderqueers are people for whom some link in the feeling/expressing/being-perceived fails. For example, a stone butch may feel masculine and embody—in his own mind and behavior— masculinity. Yet because of his sex (the pronoun strains here), she might still be read as womanly, like a girl trying on her boyfriend's clothes, especially if she is large-breasted and large-hipped.

If genderqueer bodies are those that fail because they don't follow the rules, the grammar of gender-as-language, then what are the boundaries of such a term and what are its exclusions? Is a lesbian femme harassed for her miniskirt and fuck-me pumps genderqueer? Is a 3-year-old who tries on his sister's

dress or a 40-year-old who loses a promotion because her boss believes women should be seen but not promoted? What about a football captain who's humiliated by his coach because he wept after a tough loss?

If genderqueerness is not something we do but an identity we are, then none of these people would seem to be candidates. So one of the problems is that a narrow definition will exclude the millions of people who rub up against gender norms but don't step all the way out.

Some feminist theorists have questioned the queerness and radicalness of any sort of gender that doesn't do just that: leave norms behind. They consider transexuals, butch/femmes, and drag queens as not only not genderqueer but actually gender-conforming, because they partake of binary stereotypes. For them, the only "radical" choice is adopting more androgynous genders that fall totally off the binary map.

But how are we to tell someone who faces discrimination or violence that they aren't really queer? Surely their attackers think they are.

Using queerness itself as a category of analysis seems to invite a new round of debate devoted to who is "really queer." A voice that originated from one set of margins begins to create its own marginalized voices. These twin problems of identities—boundaries and hierarchies—emerge whenever we try to base politics on identity.

IT'S NOT ME, I'M JUST ON LOAN

If gender is always a bending of self toward prevailing norms, then gender is always a kind of displacement, from which not even genderqueers are immune.

For instance, Clare Howell recently said to me, "I know I sound like a man." This kind of displacement repositions her voice as coming from somewhere else. This is like the cross-dresser who declares, "I like wearing *women's* clothes." It's safe to say that no cross-dresser ever wore "women's clothes." If the bill came to him, they're his clothes, he bought them: They're obviously *men's clothes.*

The displacement in naming them "women's clothes" prevents us from getting outside the terms of the language, from getting to something new that might redefine skirts or dresses or femininity as being about men.

Many cross-dressers would reply that the point of dressing for them is that these *are* women's clothes. It is the otherness of the clothing, the fact that they are "women's," that is precisely what allows them to feel feminine. But once again, we can't get to someplace new, where femininity might be something about men that is not anchored in Woman (or vice versa).

(I remember telling my therapist one day in what felt like a breakthrough: If I'm a woman and I haven't had surgery, then this must be a woman's penis. Wet dreams must be part of women's experience. However, I would be slow to make this argument at the next feminist conference.)

I don't mean to fall into the familiar trap of criticizing those who want to eat their cake but not have it. Some genderqueers, including cross-dressers, are not interested in that "something new." They will always enjoy appropriation *as* appropriation for its own sake. These strategic displacements renounce ownership and participation. They announce that "this part of my gender isn't me, it belongs to someone else, and I only appropriate/approximate it." They announce an acceptance of a particular gender's rules of access, who "owns" which words and who is allowed to use them. For instance, it's not possible for Clare to declare, "I sound like other men with breasts" or "I sound like other women trapped in male impersonators' bodies" or "I sound like a Clare," because those are not legitimate categories of description. By definition Clare must sound like something else, because her own body is not among the available choices.

Jenell, one of my favorite cross-dressers, always reminds me that hir enjoyment *is* transgression itself. If microminiskirts ever become fashionable for men, she'll have to decamp and find something else that is queer. In this sense, we are working somewhat at cross purposes. We both want to end the intolerable discrimination suffered by those who transcend gender stereotypes. But while I want to empty out those margins and bring queerness into the mainstream, she'd rather keep transgression in place, where s/he can enjoy it, but end its stigmatization. In retrospect, I think we both are right.

YOU MAKE ME FEEL LIKE A NATURAL WOMAN IMPERSONATOR

Why do most genderqueers perceive themselves as falling within a long succession of binaries: female/male, butch/femme, top/bottom, boy/girl? Just as when we were children, we all learned to distinguish binary mommy from binary daddy, brother from sister, and little girls from little boys, it seems that like everyone else, genderqueers see in twos.

It is popular to explain genderqueerness as resulting from a "spectrum of gender" along which all individuals—queer and nonqueer—fall. This is presented as a more enlightened and inclusive approach to bodies. Yet when you look closer, every spectrum turns out to be anchored by the same familiar two poles—male/female, man/woman, gay/straight. The rest of us are just strung out between them, like damp clothes drying on the line. The spectrum of gender turns out to be a spectrum of heterosexual norms, only slightly less oppressive but not less binary than its predecessors. Maybe the problem is that gender is a way of seeing: black-and-white glasses through which we view a Technicolor world. Wherever we look, no matter what is "out there," we see only black and white.

There is an apocryphal story of an American anthropologist who visited a remote island where natives had 17 genders. Upon his return, he reported to the anthropological society that, "like all others we've studied, this culture also has only men and women."

WE ARE MEN WITH BREASTS. WE COME IN PEACE.

I recently spent a week at a large queer activist conference in the Midwest. I was dressed in my best

Banana Republic menswear and looking, if I may say, pretty phat for a woman trapped in a six-foot male impersonator's body. I went across the street to a sports bar to get some change, and when I entered the whole room just seemed to stop: women *and* men turned from the immense TV screen showing the Sunday NFL game to watch me. It was intimidating. I got suddenly very nervous and self-conscious. I knew, for these people, I might just as well have landed from Mars. Before I knew it I was raising my voice, feminizing my stance, and trying to blend in a little.

I try to remind myself that if we can hold our course, it is at precisely such moments that we create a certain kind of freedom. It's a hard thing to keep in mind when you're afraid, that at these times we are doing the best and the most anonymous kind of activism.

What, I always wonder, did those people see? I asked my lover on one such occasion what she thought people were seeing and she replied, "Well, you do look like a man with breasts." Which, fortunately, was exactly the gender I was trying to do that day. As if that were possible. I only wish that option were available. Mostly I think people just try to figure out *what* in the world I am.

DON'T FUCK WITH MOTHER NATURE

But there are lots of things about bodies and genders that don't fit the binary model into which we try to force them, even that most unassailable of binaries: biological sex. Biological sex is considered to be the most basic and natural product of bodies. All creatures reproduce, and to reproduce—unless you're an amoeba—requires two sexes. But consider the lowly seahorse, a creature that is said to "switch sexes." (No, not with the help of a little aquatic seahorse surgeon.) We say it changes "from male to female" because what else could it change from or to?

And the "female" hyena, which not only dominates its species like a male but also has what any decent biologist would admit is a penis. Yet it must be a female, because it bears young. Or the male garter snake, which often morphs into a female after birth to attract male snakes to keep it warm. Something I might try during the next snowstorm.

But what if reproduction doesn't have to include two sexes? Or what if there are other sexes, and they can reproduce as well? But that's not possible, is it? Because any creatures that can reproduce must be either male and female—*by definition.* Hence surgeons' frantic search to locate the "real" sex of intersexed infants before their genitals are cut up to resemble "normal" male or female. The infant's "real sex," *by definition,* cannot be intersex, cannot be whatever it is. Any sex but binary male or female is pathology, unnatural, and unreal, to be discarded and corrected with the knife. We say two sexes is "nature's way." But Man produces this feminine version of Mother Nature—passive, pure, and reserved—when we need her, and then pushes Her aside when the facts don't fit His needs.

The debate over the naturalness of binary sex is circular: Whatever reproduces must be one of two sexes because there are only two sexes to be. Thus it is gender as a system of meaning that produces the "natural" Mother Nature, male and female sexes, and the gender binary that establishes what is genderqueer.

DISCUSSION QUESTIONS

1. Give an example from your own experience of gender producing meaning.
2. What was one point in this article that you found most illuminating and one you found most confusing?
3. How would you define "genderqueers"?
4. Would you agree that violators of the gender binary are "vigorously suppressed"?

WHAT IS SOCIAL CLASS?

What's Class Got to Do with It?

Michael Zweig

Whether in regard to the economy or issues of war and peace, class is central to our everyday lives. Yet class has not been as visible as race or gender, not nearly as much a part of our conversations and sense of ourselves as these and other "identities." We are of course all individuals, but our individuality and personal life chances are shaped—limited or enhanced—by the economic and social class in which we have grown up and in which we exist as adults.

Even though "class" is an abstract category of social analysis, class is real. Since social abstractions can seem far removed from real life, it may help to consider two other abstractions that have important consequences for flesh-and-blood individuals: race and gender. Suppose you knew there were men and women because you could see the difference, but you didn't know about the socially constructed concept of "gender." You would be missing something vitally important about the people you see. You would have only a surface appreciation of their lives. If, based only on direct observation of skin color, you knew there were white people and black people, but you didn't know about "race" in modern society, you would be ignorant of one of the most important determinants of the experience of those white and black people. Gender and race are abstractions, yet they are powerful, concrete influences in everyone's lives. They carry significant meaning despite wide differences in experience within the populations of men, women, whites, blacks.

Similarly, suppose that based on your observation of work sites and labor markets you knew there

Michael Zweig is a professor of economics and director of the Center for Study of Working Class Life at the State University of New York, Stony Brook.

were workers and employers, but you didn't recognize the existence of class. You would be blind to a most important characteristic of the individual workers and employers you were observing, something that has tremendous influence in their lives. Despite the wide variety of experiences and identities among individual workers, capitalists, and middle class people, it still makes sense to acknowledge the existence and importance of class in modern society. In fact, without a class analysis we would have only the most superficial knowledge of our own lives and the experiences of others we observe in economic and political activity. . . .

When people in the United States talk about class, it is often in ways that hide its most important parts. We tend to think about class in terms of income, or the lifestyles that income can buy. . . . [But class can be better understood] as mainly a question of economic and political power. . . .

The working class is made up of people who, when they go to work or when they act as citizens, have comparatively little power or authority. They are the people who do their jobs under more or less close supervision, who have little control over the pace or the content of their work, who aren't the boss of anyone. They are blue-collar people like construction and factory workers, and white-collar workers like bank tellers and writers of routine computer code. They work to produce and distribute goods, or in service industries or government agencies. They are skilled and unskilled, engaged in over five hundred different occupations tracked by the U.S. Department of Labor: agricultural laborers, baggage handlers, cashiers, flight attendants, home health care aides, machinists, secretaries, short order cooks, sound technicians, truck drivers. In the United States, working class people are by far the majority of the population. Over eighty-eight million people were in working class occupations in 2002, comprising 62 percent of the labor force.[1]

On the other side of the basic power relation in a capitalist society is the capitalist class, those most senior executives who direct and control the corporations that employ the private-sector working class. These are the "captains of industry" and finance, CEOs, chief financial officers, chief operating officers, members of boards of directors, those whose decisions dominate the workplace and the economy, and whose economic power often translates into dominant power in the realms of politics, culture, the media, and even religion. Capitalists comprise about 2 percent of the U.S. labor force.

There are big differences among capitalists in the degree of power they wield, particularly in the geographic extent of that power. The CEO of a business employing one hundred people in a city of fifty thousand might well be an important figure on the local scene, but not necessarily in state or regional affairs. On the national scale, power is principally in the hands of those who control the largest corporations, those employing over five hundred people. Of the over twenty-one million business enterprises in the United States, only sixteen thousand employ that many. They are controlled by around two hundred thousand people, fewer than two-tenths of 1 percent of the labor force.

Even among the powerful, power is concentrated at the top. It's one thing to control a single large corporation, another to sit on multiple corporate boards and be in a position to coordinate strategies across corporations. In fact, if we count only those people who sit on multiple boards, so-called interlocking directors, they could all fit into Yankee Stadium. They and the top political leaders in all branches of the federal government constitute a U.S. "ruling class" at the pinnacle of national power.

Capitalists are rich, of course. But when vice-president Dick Cheney invited a select few to help him formulate the country's energy policy shortly after the new Bush administration came into office in 2001, he didn't invite "rich people." He invited people who were leaders in the energy industry, capitalists. The fact that they were also rich was incidental. Capitalists are rich people who control far more than their personal wealth. They control the wealth of the nation, concentrated as it is in the largest few thousand corporations. There is no lobby in Washington

representing "rich people." Lobbyists represent various industries or associations of industries that sometimes coordinate their efforts on behalf of industry in general. They represent the interests that capitalists bring to legislative and regulatory matters.

Something similar operates for the working class. Over thirteen million people are in unions in the United States. Most of these unions—like the United Auto Workers (UAW); the American Federation of State, County, and Municipal Employees (AFSCME); the Carpenters; and the International Brotherhood of Teamsters (IBT)—maintain offices in Washington and in major and even smaller cities where their members work. In addition to engaging in collective bargaining at the workplace, these unions lobby for their members and occasionally coordinate their efforts to lobby for broader working class interests. Sixty-eight unions have joined under the umbrella of the American Federation of Labor, Congress of Industrial Organizations (AFL-CIO) to pool resources and try to advance the interests of working people in general. These organizations represent workers, not "the poor" or "middle-income people," even though some workers are poor and some have an income equal to that of some in the middle class.[2]

In between the capitalist and the working classes is the middle class. The "middle class" gets a lot of attention in the media and political commentary in the United States, but this term is almost always used to describe people in the middle of the income distribution. People sometimes talk about "middle class workers," referring to people who work for a wage but live comfortable if modest lives. Especially in goods-producing industries, unionized workers have been able to win wages that allow home ownership, paid vacations, nice cars, home entertainment centers, and other consumer amenities.

When class is understood in terms of income or lifestyle, these workers are sometimes called "middle class." Even leaders of the workers' unions use the term to emphasize the gains unions have been able to win for working people. "Middle class workers" are supposed to be "most people," those with stable jobs and solid values based in the work ethic, as opposed to poor people—those on welfare or the "underclass"—on one side, and "the rich" on the other. When people think about classes in terms of "rich, middle, and poor," almost everyone ends up in the middle.

Understanding class in terms of power throws a different light on the subject. In this view, middle class people are in the middle of the power grid that has workers and capitalists at its poles. The middle class includes professional people like doctors, lawyers, accountants, and university professors. Most people in the "professional middle class" are not self-employed. They work for private companies or public agencies, receive salaries, and answer to supervisors. In these ways they are like workers.

But if we compare professional middle class people with well-paid workers, we see important differences. A unionized auto assembly worker doing a lot of overtime makes enough money to live the lifestyle of a "middle class worker," even more money than some professors or lawyers. But a well-paid unionized machinist or electrician or autoworker is still part of the working class. Professors and lawyers have a degree of autonomy and control at work that autoworkers don't have. The difference is a question of class.

It is also misleading to equate the working class as a whole with its best-paid unionized members. Only 9 percent of private sector workers belong to unions, and millions of them are low-paid service employees. The relatively well-paid manufacturing industries are not typical of American business, and they are shrinking as a proportion of the total economy.

The middle class also includes supervisors in the business world, ranging from line foremen to senior managers below the top decision-making executives. As with the professional middle class, some people in the supervisory middle class are close to working people in income and lifestyle. We see this mostly at the lower levels of supervision, as with line foremen or other first-level supervisors. They often are promoted from the ranks of workers, continue to live in working class areas, and socialize with working class

friends. But a foreman is not a worker when it comes to the power grid. The foreman is on the floor to represent the owner, to execute orders in the management chain of command. The foreman is in the middle—between the workers and the owners. When a worker becomes a supervisor, he or she enters the middle class. But just as the well-paid "middle class worker" is atypical, so "working class bosses" make up a small fraction of supervisory and managerial personnel in the U.S. economy.

We see something similar with small business owners, the third component of the middle class. Some come out of the working class and continue to have personal and cultural ties to their roots. But these connections do not change the fact that workers aspire to have their own business to escape the regimentation of working class jobs, seeking instead the freedom to "be my own boss." That freedom, regardless of how much it might be limited by competitive pressures in the marketplace and how many hours the owner must work to make a go of it, puts the small business owner in a different class from workers.

At the other end of the business scale, senior managers and high-level corporate attorneys and accountants share quite a bit with the capitalists they serve. They have considerable authority, make a lot of money, and revolve in the same social circles. But they are not the final decision makers. They are at a qualitatively different level in the power grid from those they serve, who pay them well for their service but retain ultimate authority. They, too, are in the middle class.

In all three sections of the middle class—professionals, supervisors, and small business owners—there are fuzzy borders with the working class and with the capitalists. Yet the differences in power, independence, and life circumstances among these classes support the idea of a separate middle class. The middle class is about 36 percent of the labor force in the United States—sizable, but far from the majority, far from the "typical" American.

Like the working class and the capitalists, the middle class is represented in the political process by professional associations and small business groups. There is no "middle-income" lobby, but there are, for example, the Trial Lawyers Association, the American Medical Association, the American Association of University Professors, the National Association of Realtors.

Clearly, classes are not monolithic collections of socially identical people. We have seen that each class contains quite a bit of variation. Rather than sharp dividing lines, the borders between them are porous and ambiguous—important areas to study and better understand. Also, beyond the differences in occupations and relative power within classes, which lead to differences in incomes, wealth, and lifestyles, each class contains men and women of every race, nationality, and creed. Yet, despite these rich internal variations and ambiguous borders, a qualitative difference remains between the life experience of the working class compared with that of the professional and managerial middle class, to say nothing of differences both of these have with the capitalists.

DISCUSSION QUESTIONS

1. How is social class like and also different from race, sex, gender, and sexual orientation?
2. Would you agree with Zweig that "without a class analysis, we would have only the most superficial knowledge of our own lives and the experience of others"?
3. In your own mind, what are the key criteria or concepts Zweig is using to define social class? What is your opinion of his definition of social class?

NOTES

1. For a detailed discussion of the class composition of the United States, on which these and the following findings are based, see Michael Zweig, *The Working Class Majority: America's Best Kept Secret* (Ithaca, NY: Cornell University Press, 2000), chap. 1.
2. Some middle class people are represented by unions, such as university professors in the American Federation of Teachers (AFT) and legal aid attorneys in the UAW. Most union members are in the working class.

READING 14

Getting Ahead
ECONOMIC AND SOCIAL MOBILITY IN AMERICA

Daniel P. McMurrer

Isabel V. Sawhill

The half century since World War II can be divided into two periods. In the first period—from 1947 to 1973—family incomes rose at a healthy clip and the gains were more or less equally shared. Between 1973 and 1994, however, incomes rose more slowly and the gains were heavily tilted toward the top of the distribution (Chart 1).

This part of the story is hardly new. The disappointing rate of economic growth and the growing income gap between rich and poor in recent decades is by now well documented.[1] But there is another chapter in this story.

INEQUALITY AND MOBILITY

Most people would look at the trend depicted in Chart 1 and conclude that America is becoming a bifurcated society. That is too hasty a conclusion. Although the distribution of income among individuals may be unequal in any given year, this does not necessarily mean it is unequal over their lifetimes. For various reasons, many individuals move up in the distribution over time, while many others move down. And the reasons for movement vary. A poor single mother who marries an accountant, for example, may move up substantially in the year of the marriage. A well-to-do farmer whose crop fails may move way down that year. A young computer

Daniel P. McMurrer is a senior researcher specializing in the effects of human capital investments at the American Society for Training and Development in Alexandria, Virginia. Isabel V. Sawhill is vice president and director of economic studies at the Brookings Institution.

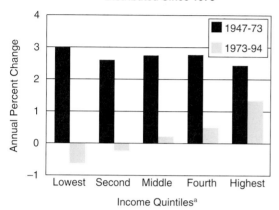

Income Growth Has Been Unequally Distributed Since 1973

Source: Lawrence Mishel and Jared Bernstein, *The State of Working America 1996-97* (Economic Policy Institute, 1997).

[a]The lowest income quintile consists of the 20 percent of all families with the lowest income as measured by the Census Bureau. The second quintile consists of the second-poorest 20 percent, and so forth.

CHART 1

programmer who works hard may move up steadily year by year as she acquires more job experience.

Economic historian Joseph Schumpeter compared the income distribution to a hotel—full of rooms that are always occupied, but often by different people.[2] In order to have an accurate picture of an individual's experience over a lifetime, therefore, we must know not only the size of the different rooms but also the rate at which individuals switch rooms.

This switching goes on all the time and makes it difficult to interpret the standard statistics showing how the top (or bottom) 20 percent of the population has fared over some period of time.

Economists now understand that the amount of mobility is just as important as the distribution of economic rewards in any given year, because it determines the extent to which inequality in the short term translates into inequality over the long term. For example, a very unequal distribution of income in any one year would be of little consequence in a society in which individuals were constantly moving up or down the economic ladder, resulting in

each receiving an equal share of the rewards over a lifetime. Conversely, a society in which there was very little mobility would have a very different character than the previous one—*even if their annual income distributions looked exactly the same.* Thus a crucial question is: How much economic mobility is there?

MOBILITY IN THE UNITED STATES

Much less is known about mobility than about inequality. In recent years, however, a number of studies have used survey data to track the incomes of the same individuals over time.[3] The most commonly used technique for analyzing their mobility is to rank their incomes from highest to lowest in a beginning year. Typically, this ranking breaks the sample into five equal-sized groups (quintiles). This is done again for the incomes of these same individuals in a later year. The percentage of individuals who change income quintiles between these two years is then used as an indicator of mobility. Because the focus is on relative position within the distribution, in order for one individual to move up it is necessary for someone else to move down.[4]

How Much Mobility?

These studies of relative mobility have produced remarkably consistent results, with regard to both the degree of mobility and the extent of changes in mobility over time.[5] Mobility in the United States is substantial, according to this evidence. Large proportions of the population move into a new income quintile, with estimates ranging from about 25 to 40 percent in a single year. As one would expect, the mobility rate is even higher over longer periods—about 45 percent over a 5-year period and about 60 percent over both 9-year and 17-year periods.[6]

Who Moves Up?

Which groups are most likely to be *upwardly* mobile in the income distribution? Evidence suggests that, in recent years, individuals with at least a college education are more likely to move up than any other group (Chart 2).[7] This is a significant change from

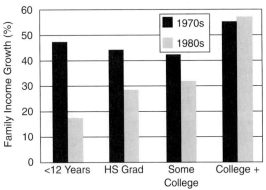

College Graduates Enjoyed the Most Income Growth in the 1980s

Source: Rose (1993), cited in endnote 7. Rose used the Panel Study of Income Dynamics to calculate growth in real family income, after adjusting for family size, for adults ages 22 to 48 at the beginning of each decade.

CHART 2

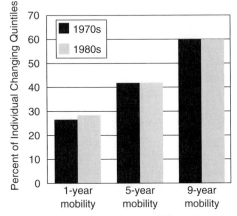

Mobility Rates Have Not Changed

Sources: Data for one-year and five-year mobility are from Burkhauser, Holtz-Eakin, and Rhody (1996), cited in endnote 5; data for nine-year mobility are from Sawhill and Condon (1992), cited in endnote 2. Time periods are slightly different. For one-year and five-year mobility, average rates for 1970–79 and 1980–89 are used; for nine-year mobility, 1967–76 is used for the "1970s" and 1977–86 is used for the "1980s."

CHART 3

the 1970s, when income increases were more evenly distributed across educational levels.

International Comparisons

Although mobility in the United States is substantial, evidence indicates that it is no higher in this country than elsewhere. Indeed, the few studies that have directly compared mobility across countries have concluded that, despite significant differences in labor markets and government policies across countries, mobility rates are surprisingly similar.[8]

Other Measures of Mobility

Two widely reported recent studies of mobility in the United States found extremely high rates of mobility—rates that are much higher than those cited above.[9] This results from differences in analytical approach.[10] Most importantly, these studies examined absolute (rather than relative) mobility.[11] Under this definition of mobility, anyone who moves across a fixed threshold (established in the base year or for the population as a whole) is considered mobile regardless of his or her relative position within the distribution. As a result, factors such as economic growth and the natural tendency of incomes

to increase with age can cause almost everyone to appear mobile.

Mobility over Time

Although mobility in the United States is neither higher than it is in other countries nor as high (in our view) as suggested by studies of absolute mobility, there is nevertheless broad agreement among researchers that the year-by-year movement of individuals between income quintiles is substantial and that lifetime earnings are more evenly distributed than annual earnings. But what about changes in mobility over time? In particular, what has happened to mobility since the early 1970s, when annual inequality began to increase?

The evidence on this point is clear: Mobility has not changed significantly over the last 25 years. Indeed, a number of different studies indicate that relative mobility rates in the United States—both short term and long term—have been remarkably stable (Chart 3 displays the results of two out of six mobility studies cited in endnote 5). Thus, Americans continue to move up and down in the income distribution at the same rate as they did in the past.

As a result, the recent increases in annual inequality have proceeded unchecked by any increase in mobility. An individual's income in any one year is always a poor predictor of lifetime income, but it is not a worse predictor now than it was in the past.

SUMMING UP

The incomes of American families change frequently. Some of the poor get richer, some of the rich get poorer, and for a variety of reasons: accumulation of job skills and experience, marriage and divorce, job change, addition or loss of a second paycheck, and business success or failure.

But despite this churning, overall rates of mobility in the United States have not changed over time. Thus, it is fair to conclude that increases in annual inequality have worsened the distribution of lifetime incomes. Although the disparity in economic rewards has increased, the availability of those rewards—the probability of success or failure—has remained unchanged.

There has been one notable development within this broader picture, however. The mobility of those with little education has declined. Increasingly, a college education is the ticket to upward mobility.

The question of how much inequality is acceptable or appropriate in the United States, as noted earlier, is an issue on which there is no agreement. Still, it is somewhat disturbing to learn that the seemingly relentless growth in the inequality of economic rewards has been unmitigated by any increase in access to those rewards, especially for those with the fewest skills.

CLASS AND OPPORTUNITY

Americans are more likely than individuals in other nations to believe in the importance of talent and effort in shaping a person's life prospects. They are also more likely to reject social class as an acceptable determinant of whether someone succeeds or fails.[12] Given such a strong consensus on the goal of

equal opportunity, the American public has paid remarkably little attention to how close society is to achieving it.

Evidence suggests that family background matters quite a bit—that this society is still far from providing everyone an equal chance to succeed. At the same time, real progress has been made. Inherited advantages of class play a smaller role than they used to in shaping the success of individual Americans, with larger numbers now moving beyond their origins. In this sense, opportunity has increased.

But in another sense, it has not. In the past, the dynamism of the U.S. economy ensured that each generation's prospects were better than those of the last one, irrespective of social origins. Almost all Americans were able to achieve more than their parents. As economic growth has slowed in recent decades, however, so has opportunity. The depressing effect of this growth slowdown has almost completely offset the opportunity gains that have come from the declining importance of class.

Class Still Matters

Opportunity is here defined as the extent to which an individual's economic and social status is determined by his or her own skills and effort rather than by class of origin. It is typically measured as the relationship between parents and their offspring[13] on various indicators of class—occupational status and income are common ones.[14] The more closely the status of individuals reflects the status of their parents, the less opportunity exists in a society and the more class matters. Conversely, the more independent the overall parent-offspring relationship, the less class matters.

In today's America, the socioeconomic class into which individuals are born significantly affects their status as adults. Even in an open, fair, and dynamic society, of course, some relationship between the status of parents and their adult children would be expected.[15] Genetic inheritance alone is likely to account for some of this (although estimates suggest that it would be an extremely small fraction). Further, there will always be a tendency for parents who

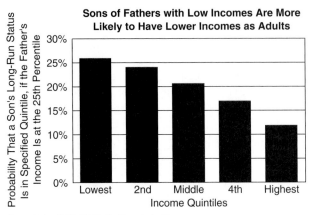

Source: Solon (1989, 1992), cited in endnote 16.
Note: Assumes an intergenerational income correlation of 0.4 and normal income distribution.

CHART 4

occupy positions of high status—whether through their own achievements or for other reasons—to try to extend their advantages to their children. This is a tendency for which public policy can probably never fully compensate as long as children are reared within their own families. Thus, it is almost impossible to imagine a society in which parents' and children's outcomes are completely independent.

The link between the incomes and occupations of parents and offspring in the United States, however, is stronger than would be expected even given these considerations. Recent studies have found an observed correlation between the incomes of fathers and sons of about 0.4.[16] This means, for example, that an adult son whose father's income was a quarter of the way from the bottom of the income distribution (at the 25th percentile) would have a 50 percent chance of having an income in the bottom two-fifths (Chart 4). Conversely, a son whose father's income was at the 95th percentile (not shown) would have a 76 percent chance of being above the median, including a 42 percent chance of being in the top 20 percent.

Occupations are similarly correlated across generations, with children of professionals significantly more likely to become professionals as adults, and children of blue collar workers significantly more likely to work in blue collar occupations (Chart 5).

For example, men with white collar origins are almost twice as likely as those with blue collar origins to end up in upper white collar jobs.

Thus, origins continue to matter. Children from advantaged backgrounds are likely to do well as adults, and children from disadvantaged backgrounds are more likely to do badly. But this is not the end of the story.

Class Matters Less Than Previously

Class may still matter in the United States, but not as much as it used to. The effect of parents' occupational status on that of their offspring declined by about one-third in less than a generation, according to one study.[17] Other studies have confirmed this decline and have shown that it is a continuing one, evident for at least the last three generations and probably longer.[18] One ambitious study finds that the decline dates back to the mid-19th century.[19]

The decline has been driven by the growth of meritocratic practices in the hiring process, the decline of self-employment, and the growing number of Americans with access to higher education. The percentage of adults who are college graduates, for example, increased from 8 percent in 1960 to 23 percent in 1995. Attainment of a college degree has been shown to greatly attenuate the link between occupational origins and occupational destinations.

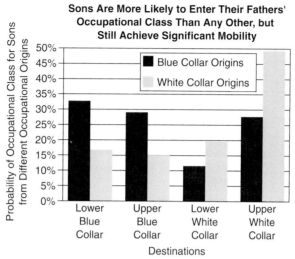

**Sons Are More Likely to Enter Their Fathers'
Occupational Class Than Any Other, but
Still Achieve Significant Mobility**

Source: Authors' calculations of Hout's (1988) data, cited in endnote 17, excluding
farm origins and destinations.

CHART 5

The Offsetting Effect of Slower Economic Growth

The vigorous economic growth that fueled continuing change in the occupational structure of the U.S. economy for most of our history has declined, slowing the pace of occupational change along with it. The economy itself is no longer creating as many chances for individuals to move up the economic ladder as used to be the case—a trend that has largely offset the declining importance of background. One study finds that the two trends have almost completely offset one another, resulting in little overall change in the rates at which individuals move from the class into which they were born.[20] The only difference has come in the composition of upward mobility. A larger proportion of upward mobility across generations is attributable to the declining importance of class and a smaller proportion to economic growth (Chart 6). (If individual opportunity increases in an economy that is not growing at all, intergenerational churning between the socioeconomic classes will increase, but there may be no net improvement for younger generations over their parents.)[21]

This change in the composition of upward mobility—growing individual opportunity and lagging economic growth—is important, because it will be felt differently by different groups, depending on where they start. Everyone is hurt by slower growth. But individuals from more-modest backgrounds will benefit from a more open, less class-based social structure. On balance, according to the data, they should come out ahead. For individuals from more-privileged backgrounds, in contrast, the increased individual "opportunity" implied by the declining importance of class represents an increased likelihood of moving down the social scale. They are more likely than before to experience a drop in status relative to their parents. Both trends (economic growth and individual opportunity) represent losses for them.

Summing Up

The United States remains a society in which class matters. Children who grow up in privileged families are more likely to become highly paid professionals, for example, than are children raised in less-advantaged households. Still, the effects of family background have declined in recent years. Success is less likely to be inherited than it was in earlier years, suggesting that the American playing field is becoming more equal.

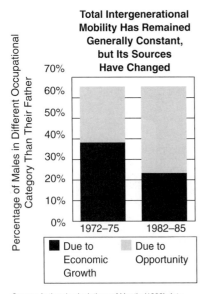

Total Intergenerational Mobility Has Remained Generally Constant, but Its Sources Have Changed

Source: Authors' calculations of Hout's (1988) data, cited in endnote 17, using five occupational categories.

CHART 6

The role of higher education in increasing individual opportunity is notable. Educational attainment in the United States has improved significantly, suggesting that opportunity may continue to grow as a result.

The failure of the economy to grow as rapidly as in the past is equally notable, however. Even as individual opportunity has increased, the slowing of economic growth and the related stagnation of occupational prospects have almost offset this gain. While individuals are increasingly free to move from their roots, fewer destinations represent improvements.

DISCUSSION QUESTIONS

1. In your own words, what are McMurrer and Sawhill's primary conclusions about social mobility in the United States?

2. Based on their conclusions, what predictions would you make about the economic future of your friends compared to their parents? Will the more privileged of them do better, worse, or the same as their parents? And how will the less and moderately privileged of them do compared to their parents?

NOTES

1. Attempts to adjust the data for changes in family size, for different measures of inflation, for the receipt of capital gains, or for income transfers and taxes have not markedly changed the basic trends described above.

2. For further discussion of this analogy, see Isabel V. Sawhill and Mark Condon, "Is U.S. Income Inequality Really Growing? Sorting Out the Fairness Question," Urban Institute, *Policy Bites* 13 (1992).

3. For a more detailed analysis of these studies, see Daniel P. McMurrer and Isabel V. Sawhill, "Economic Mobility in the United States," Research paper 6722 (Washington, DC: Urban Institute, 1996).

4. Thus, if average incomes are increasing over time as a result of economic growth, an individual's income must rise more quickly than the rest of the sample in order to move up to a higher quintile. Movement between quintiles is a relatively crude measure of mobility, as it only roughly captures the magnitude of the change in an individual's income.

5. These studies include Richard V. Burkhauser, Douglas Holtz-Eakin, and Stephen E. Rhody, "Labor Earnings Mobility in the United States and Germany during the Growth Years of the 1980s," mimeograph (Syracuse, NY: Syracuse University, 1996); Mark Condon and Isabel V. Sawhill, "Income Mobility and Permanent Income Inequality," Research paper 6723 (Washington, DC: Urban Institute, 1992); Maury Gittleman and Mary Joyce, "Earnings Mobility in the United States, 1967–91," *Monthly Labor Review,* 3–13 (September 1995); Peter Gottschalk, "Notes on 'By Our Own Bootstraps: Economic Opportunity and the Dynamics of Income Distribution,' by Cox and Alm," mimeograph (Boston: Boston College, 1996); Thomas Hungerford, "U.S. Income Mobility in the Seventies and Eighties," *Review of Income and Wealth,* 403–417 (1993); and Sawhill and Condon (1992).

6. Over any period longer than one year, some individual movement between quintiles is not captured by the analysis. For example, an individual who is in the same quintile in both years examined (say, the first and ninth years) may still have moved between quintiles in the intervening years, although he or she would appear to have been "immobile" over the nine-year period.

7. Stephen Rose, "Declining Family Incomes in the 1980s: New Evidence from Longitudinal Data," *Challenge,* 29–36 (November–December 1993).

8. Rolf Aaberge et al., "Income Inequality and Income Mobility in the Scandinavian Countries Compared to the

Lucky Americans

I identify myself as a biracial, middle/working-class female. My earliest memory of feeling that I was privileged was when I was about six years old, when I first moved to Arlington, Virginia. My parents had just reconciled after being separated, and my siblings and I moved back to Virginia from California. Because my dad had been living on his own, all we had to go back to was a one-bedroom apartment in a moderately rough neighborhood. Many people there were minorities, a large number were immigrants, and many of my peers came from broken homes.

My family and I were not in a better financial situation than other people in the neighborhood, but we were privileged because both my parents had at least a high school education, spoke English, and worked. Others in our neighborhood considered us "lucky," or they thought that we believed we were better than them. Ironically, these feelings often came from people who had fewer children and lived in bigger apartments (there were six of us living in a one bedroom). I realized I was in a "privileged" class because my mom and I often had to translate for our neighbors. We were the Americans "who had it all." I was privileged because I came from a family of natural-born American citizens.

It felt good to know that we had some advantages rather than disadvantages growing up, but I didn't like feeling that our neighbors thought we couldn't relate to them or didn't understand their struggle. My family and I were struggling too, although in a different way. True, we didn't have a language barrier, but my parents were young, with really no trade skills, and on top of that we had no money. I talked to our neighbors but often felt their jealousy and resentment, so I didn't usually feel like being around them.

LeiLani Page

United States," mimeograph, Statistics Norway (1996); Burkhauser et al. (1996); Greg J. Duncan et al., "Poverty Dynamics in Eight Countries," *Journal of Population Economics*, 215–234 (1993).

9. U.S. Department of the Treasury, Office of Tax Analysis, "Household Income Mobility during the 1980s: A Statistical Analysis Based on Tax Return Data" (Washington, DC: U.S. Department of the Treasury, 1992); and W. Michael Cox and Richard Alm, "By Our Own Bootstraps: Economic Opportunity and the Dynamics of Income Distribution," *Federal Reserve Bank of Dallas Annual Report 1995* (Dallas: Federal Reserve Bank of Dallas, 1995).

10. For additional discussion of these methodological questions, see Gottschalk (1996) and Paul Krugman, "The Right, the Rich, and the Facts: Deconstructing the Income Distribution Debate," *American Prospect*, 19–31 (Fall 1992).

11. Absolute mobility is the movement of an individual in relation to an external standard, usually defined by averages among the population as a whole. Thus, it is possible for all individuals in a fixed group to move up in relation to this external standard. Absolute mobility does not measure change in an individual's relative position within a given sample, and is therefore not comparable to relative mobility.

12. See, e.g., Seymour Martin Lipset, *American Exceptionalism* (New York: W.W. Norton, 1996).

13. Because of data limitations, many of the studies in this area have excluded women, focusing on the relationship between fathers and sons.

14. To analyze income relationships, researchers compare the incomes of parents (frequently only fathers) at a certain age with the incomes of their children at a similar age. Analysis of occupational relationships is more complicated. This comparison also requires ranking occupations on a hierarchical scale, which is usually based on a combination of the average income and average years of schooling associated with each occupation.

15. For a more complete discussion of how much opportunity might exist in an open society, see Daniel P. McMurrer, Mark Condon, and Isabel V. Sawhill, "Intergenerational Mobility in the United States," Research paper 6796 (Washington, DC: Urban Institute, 1997).

16. Gary Solon, "Intergenerational Income Mobility in the United States," *American Economic Review* 82:393–408 (1992); Gary Solon, "Intergenerational Income Mobility in the United States," Discussion paper no. 894–89 (Madison, WI: University of Wisconsin Institute for Research on Poverty, 1989); and David J. Zimmerman, "Regression toward Mediocrity in Economic Stature," *American Economic Review* 82:409–429 (1992).

17. Michael Hout, "More Universalism, Less Structural Mobility: The American Occupational Structure in the 1980s," *American Journal of Sociology* 93:1358–1400 (1988).

18. Timothy Biblarz, Vern Bengston, and Alexander Bucur, "Social Mobility across Three Generations," *Journal of Marriage and the Family* 58:188–200 (1996). See also David Grusky and Thomas DiPrete, "Recent Trends in the Process of Stratification," *Demography* 27:617–637 (1990).

19. David Grusky, "American Social Mobility in the 19th and 20th Centuries," Working paper no. 86–28 (Madison, WI: University of Wisconsin Center for Demography and Ecology, 1989).

20. Hout (1988).

21. Different rates of fertility can also affect overall levels of mobility. If less-privileged individuals reproduce more rapidly than the more privileged, more people will be able to experience upward mobility—even in the absence of economic growth.

READING 15

America's Economic Transformation

Nancy Wiefek

THE POST-WORLD WAR II ECONOMY

The American economy grew dramatically during the period following the end of World War II, expanding at an annual rate of 3.5 percent between 1945 and 1970 (Palley 1998, 28; Blumberg 1980, 18). In what economist Frank Levy calls "upward mobility on a rocket ship" (cited in Jost 1993, 634), many incomes doubled in a generation (Levy 1999). This enormous increase in average family income in a generation lifted millions of factory and office workers into a growing middle class and enabled them to sustain a standard of living once thought reserved for the wealthy. Parents who had ended their education in high school or earlier came to expect to send their children to college. Indeed, an entire new working middle-class was created, as

Nancy Wiefek holds a PhD from Pennsylvania State University in political science with a concentration in public opinion research. She is an associate analyst for Lake Snell Perry and Associates in Oakland, California.

blue-collar workers came to enjoy the benefits of home ownership, and high wages gave them the ability to pay for household appliances, new cars, and regular vacations (Palley 1998, 28; Mayer 1963).[1] In the postwar period, the majority of Americans were affluent in the sense that they were in a position to spend money on many things they wanted, desired, or chose to have, rather than on necessities alone. The acquisition of discretion in spending and saving by masses of people represents the essence of the new era that began in the United States in the late 1940s (Katona and Strumpel 1978, 4). However, this rate of growth did not last. The 1970s brought with it wage stagnation for many families and income polarization partly as a result of de-industrialization and globalization of the American economy. In the following sections I will describe these developments and how they relate to America's current economic growth. . . .

INCOME POLARIZATION/THE SHRINKING MIDDLE CLASS

Since 1975, practically all the gains in household income have gone to the top 20 percent of households.

> *Central Intelligence Agency World Fact Book 2001: Profile for the U.S.* (cited in Collins and Yeskel 2000)

The distribution of income among Americans has become dramatically more unequal beginning in the 1970s (Johnston 1999; Wolff 1996; Danziger and Gottschalk 1995; Phillips 1990). The economic growth of the immediate postwar [post-World War II] period contributed to increases in every income group, with even slight declines in the top income group (Palley 1998). But beginning in the 1970s, the income of the bottom 40 percent of families fell; the income of the middle 40 percent stagnated; and the income of the richest 20 percent substantially increased (Whalen 1996; Edmondson 1995; Urban Institute 1992; Krugman 1992).[2] . . .

The Center on Budget and Policy Priorities (CBPP) and the Economic Policy Institute (EPI) released a report in January 2000 covering the ten-year period between 1988 and 1998, analyzing before-tax data from the U.S. Census Bureau adjusted for inflation; they found that earnings for the poorest 20 percent of American families rose less than 1 percent during this period, but jumped 15 percent for the richest fifth. Middle-class incomes grew only 2 percent, while the average income of the top 5 percent grew by 27 percent. Wage growth has been so strong at the high end that the top 1 percent of taxpayers have taken home 94 percent of the growth in total income since 1973 (Krueger, 2002). . . .

While the income gap grew more slowly during the 1990s, the strongest American economy in 30 years did not halt it. Moreover, because census data do not capture income from capital gains, executive bonuses, and other nonwage sources, it is likely that the growth in incomes of top earners, and hence the growth in income inequality, may be even greater than that reflected in the CBPP/EPI study, especially considering the sharp run up in stock-market wealth during the late 1990s (Bernstein et al. 2002; Economic Policy Institute 2000). In fact, a Federal Reserve study shows that stock-option realizations more than doubled between 1996 and 1999, from $50 billion to $116 billion (Hilsenrath 2002). In 1965, U.S. CEOs in major companies earned 26 times more than an average worker; by the end of 2000, the ratio of CEO-to-worker pay had surged to 310 (Economic Policy Institute 2002b; see also, Phillips 2002).

Regardless of the specific definition adopted, the proportion of households with moderate income is diminishing (U.S. Census Bureau 1998; Kacapyr 1996; Greenhouse 1986; Thurow 1984). The wealth held by families in the middle class has decreased since it peaked in 1966 (Levy 1999; Palley 1998; Greenhouse 1986). A study of mobility patterns suggests that those who fall down the income ladder are increasingly outnumbering those who climb it (Duncan, Smeeding, and Rodgers 1991). And this increase in downward mobility continued during the 1990s (Fields 1999).

Overall, the economy has become one in which incomes are more unequal than during the growth period of the immediate postwar period. In addition, it is an economy in which those with more education start out and remain higher earners than those with less education (Rose 1996). Living standards for those without a college degree have deteriorated the most compared to the postwar period (Teixeira and Rogers 1996). For example, between 1976 and 1996 the average 30-year-old male high school graduate saw his income increase only $800 (in 1997 dollars) by the time he reached his 50th birthday (Levy 1999).

Median income plunged by one-half (47%) from 1973 to 1992 for young families with children headed by a high school dropout, and by one-third (37%) for those headed by a high school graduate. Even when the head of the family finished some college (but not a full four years), median family income fell by 22 percent (Children's Defense Fund 1997, 18). The average real incomes of both the bottom quintile and the second-lowest were actually only slightly greater in 1998 than in 1973, even though overall mean income for the entire population had grown over this period (Wolff 2002, 40).

The increase in wealth inequality is even more dramatic. Wealth inequality was at a 70-year high in 1998, with the top 1 percent of wealth-holders controlling 38 percent of total household wealth (Wolff 2002, 8).[3] According to the Federal Reserve Board's triennial survey of consumer finances, the net worth of the median U.S. household (including home equity) in constant dollars declined from $51,640 to $49,900 between 1989 and 1995 because so many Americans had debts growing faster than their assets (Phillips 2002, 107). This wealth inequality is seen in retirement wealth as well. For households that had $1 million in total wealth, retirement wealth grew from 1983 to 1998 by 41 percent in real terms (Economic Policy Institute 2002a).

Importantly, the trends of wage stagnation and increasing income inequality continued throughout the 1990s despite strong national economy growth and corporate profitability. . . . To understand why this is the case, we need to account for changes in the relationship among American workers, employers, and the world economy and how these changes have affected the nature of the workplace.

DE-INDUSTRIALIZATION

One of the most notable transformations in the U.S. labor market since World War II has been the rising share of employment in the low-paying services industry and the declining share in the high-paying manufacturing sectors (Starobin 1995, 2404; Nackenoff 1983).[4] . . . According to the Bureau of Labor Statistics' occupational projections, more than half (54%) of the new jobs created between 1996 and 2006 will be in occupations that pay below the median earning rate—and 40 percent of the new jobs are projected to be in occupations with earnings in the lowest quartile (Economic Policy Institute 1999a).

This shift from the age of steel to the age of the silicon chip is comparable to the transition from farming to factory work in the nineteenth and early twentieth centuries. However, unlike that earlier transition, the disruption is not eased by the availability of relatively unskilled and well-paying jobs (Levy 1999). "The pattern of wages in the old, mill-based economy looked like a normal bell curve. It had a few highly paid jobs at the top, a few low-wage jobs at the bottom, and plenty of jobs in the middle. But in the new services economy, the middle is missing" (Kuttner 1983, 60–63). For services as a whole, employment is concentrated in better-than-average and in poorer-than-average jobs—vastly different from the patterns evidenced in the manufacturing-based economy of the postwar period.

The "new economy" is characterized by a complex of service and information-technology industries (Benner, Brownstein, and Dean 1999, ii). This economy quite naturally produces "an hourglass economy" marked at one end by growth in well-paying, highly skilled professions and, at the other, by the rapid expansion of low-wage jobs requiring only unskilled labor (Benner, Brownstein, and Dean 1999, iii). The jobs that tend to be created in the new economy are distinct from the jobs that tended to be created during the postwar period in crucial ways. In short, for many Americans, the workplace has become a far more capricious place with reductions in real wages, loss of health, pension, and social-safety-net protections, downsizing, outsourcing, and the erosion of job security (Brecher 1997; Rose 1995; Harrison 1994). . . .

While unemployment in earlier decades was often cyclical and temporary, jobs lost to downsizing and restructuring in the new economy are often permanent and frequently occur despite strong corporate earnings. After reviewing dozens of studies, labor economists at the National Bureau of Economic Research (NBER) conclude that, taken as a whole, the literature suggests an increase in involuntary job loss and a modest decline in job stability between the late 1980s and early 1990s (Neumark, Polsky, and Hansen 1999).[5] . . . Edward Wolff of the Jerome Levy Economics Institute stated that the rising duration of unemployment is a fundamental change in the nature of today's labor force. Cyclical fluctuations in the economy cannot alone explain these changes. The average duration of unemployment (the average number of weeks an unemployed person remains unemployed) has nearly doubled. The percentage of unemployed persons who have remained unemployed for 27 weeks or more has almost tripled (Jerome Levy Economics Institute of Bard College 1996, 28). Although college-educated workers have always been much more secure in their jobs than their less-well-educated colleagues, in recent years the gap has slightly closed, according to job-tenure data (Osterman 1999, 48). Job-loss rates among workers with higher levels of education increased in the early 1990s, and by 1997–99 stood at nearly 7 percent, as compared with 5.4 percent for 1987–89 (Farber 2001, cited in Kletzer and Litan 2001). . . .

GLOBALIZATION

. . . While Third World nations have been feeling the effects of globalization for decades, it has only been fairly recently that American workers have felt the full brunt. Similar to the way in which corporations moved from the Snow Belt to the Sun Belt in search of new markets, cheap labor, and unrestricted production sites, multinational corporations can now move production facilities around the world to pursue higher profits through the search for cheaper labor. For example, one-third of U.S. automotive-parts employment migrated south to Mexico between 1978 and 1999, according to Stephen A. Herzenberg, an economist at the Keystone Research Center in Harrisburg, Pennsylvania, resulting in wages in the U.S. automotive-parts industry to decrease by 9 percent after inflation over the same period. Moreover, companies can use the threat of overseas-job shifts against workers who try to unionize and to hold down wages (Berger 2000). According to a 1996 study by Cornell University labor researcher Kate Bronfenbrenner, 62 percent of manufacturers threaten to close plants during union-recruitment drives (cited in Bernstein 2000).

Computer, communication, and transportation technologies have lessened distance as a barrier, making it possible for corporations to "global source"—that is, draw its components and materials from anywhere in the world (Farazmand 1999, 512). Firms can "outsource" throughout the production process, locating low-skill activities in low-wage countries and high-skill activities in high-wage countries (Feenstra and Hanson 2001). These developments, what Bluestone and Harrison (1982) call the hypermobility of capital, have enormous consequences for the American workplace. The workplace that this process facilitates and demands is one characterized by flexibility, constant restructuring, and downsizing (Bernstein 2000; Brecher and Costello 1998).

It is important to note that de-industrialization and globalization were accompanied not just by a change in the nature of employment, but also by an increase in the power of American corporations vis-à-vis workers.[6] In the period following the Second World War, American economic power was at its zenith. American global preeminence produced special characteristics for producers; for example, stability and relative certainty that gave rise to high levels of investment and permanent employment (Madrick 1995, 86). American corporations could "afford" to provide a social contract, and in return they received political peace and labor accord (Aronowitz 1998).[7] On the other side of the equa-

tion, labor strength grew as a result of successful organizing drives within the manufacturing sector. Organizing efforts within the services sector are vastly more difficult and have been much less successful. And as the economy has lost manufacturing jobs by the tens of thousands, union membership continues its twenty-year decline, dropping from 14.1 percent of the workforce in 1997 to 13.9 percent in 1998 (Economic Policy Institute 1999b). At their zenith in 1945, unions represented 35 percent of the private-sector labor force (Osterman 1999, 65). The benefits accorded to all workers from trade-union strength diminished greatly with the shift away from manufacturing, where trade unions were relatively strong, and with the advent of state policies favoring corporations. As Paul Osterman (1999, xii) argues:

> We are witnessing complex transformations in the relationships between American employers and workers, which have resulted in gradual shifts in the balance of power from labor to management. Such changes include the increased willingness of companies to lay off large numbers of workers even during profitable periods, the growing use of labor without perquisites on a "contingent" basis, new organizational strategies that diminish the need for middle managers, technological innovations that strengthen a company's capacity to replace workers, and the eroding threat of union organization.

THE NEW NORMS

There is a general understanding in the United States today that companies are not going to compete for workers by raising wages. And that understanding has become embedded in our social structure.

> David Collander, an economic
> historian at Middlebury College
> (quoted in Uchitelle 2000a)

Particular norms and accepted behaviors develop around particular labor-market structures. Economic transformations necessarily affect these norms and bring about behaviors befitting the new labor-market structure. In order to understand the political impact of anxiety about the new economy it is necessary to understand these new norms. All that occurs within this economy—growth, booms, busts, technological advances—should be viewed within the context of these norms. Osterman (1999) argues that until the last decade or so, the American labor market functioned according to a set of rules and norms the institutional structure of the labor market put into place after the Second World War. For the most part, the behavior of firms was predictable and understandable. He argues that this institutional structure has been destroyed during the past decade, and with it the sense of order that undergirded people's notions of the economy. From this perspective, the loss of order is what explains the unease that persists even in the face of good economic news. There is a greater willingness of firms to lay off employees even when times are good, and, related to this, job security has eroded and the length of time an employee can expect to stay with an employer has shrunk. The rise in contingent employment has made it much less certain what it means to have a "job." Each of the symptoms of labor-market distress—stagnating earnings, heightened insecurity, uncertainty about what it means to hold a job—reflects the collapse of the postwar labor-market institutional structure (Osterman 1999, 32).

Unions, while never representing a majority of the labor force, played an important role in structuring the labor market (Osterman 1999, 30). Many of the practices and norms regarding how employers behaved and what employees could expect were derived from union-management agreements—and the influence of unions extended beyond the firms and industries in which they were strong.[8]

Another important contextual feature of the postwar system was the nature of corporate governance. There is a great deal of evidence that managers placed substantial value on maintaining, indeed, growing employment and on sharing profits not only with stockholders but with the broad employee base (Osterman 1999, 30). One important change during the 1980s was the rise of the leveraged buyout. This new source of finance suddenly made previously seemingly invulnerable firms potential targets for raiders who felt that financial results could be improved by changing management.

Another development was the increased concentration of stock ownership in the hands of institutional investors (public and private pension funds, investment funds, insurance companies). These institutional investors increasingly demanded higher levels of short-term performance and frequently worked as a group to put pressure on managers to deliver (Osterman 1999, 66; Minsky and Whalen 1996–97). Relatedly, the third element in the broader context was the decreased role of government in the regulation of corporations, the enforcement of labor laws, and the increasing of wages.

So we see two developments that, while not being unique in the history of capitalist development, have distinct consequences and occur at a particular point in America's economic history. Technological advances allow corporations to disregard borders, the existence of which used to insulate First World workers from the harshest elements of capitalism's "destructive creativity." Concomitantly, changes in the labor-market institutional structure and the norms of the workplace allow for behaviors among employers and others that are vastly different than what would have been acceptable during the postwar period.[9] Together, these developments have created a new kind of economy in which national economic growth and economic upturns can coexist with job insecurity and economic worries. . . .

UNDERSTANDING THE NEW ECONOMY

What I hear, over and over again, is: Yes, jobs are back. Yes, there are a lot of technological marvels out there. Yes, there's a lot that's good about the economy. But over my kitchen table we worry. It's getting harder to pay the bills.

Robert Reich, former Secretary of Labor
(quoted in Tough 1996, 36)

None of this is to dispute the strength and vitality of the American economy as we enter the twenty-first century. Median family income rose to a record $46,737 in 1998, adjusted for inflation, decisively past the old high of $44,974 in 1989 (Uchitelle 2000a). The standard of living enjoyed by Americans is the envy of virtually all other nations on the globe.

The opportunity of attaining a college education has increased dramatically over the last several decades. Technological advances have literally brought the world, through the Internet, into ordinary Americans' living rooms, and we take our affordable telephone, television, and other consumer goods for granted. The stock market has been vastly opened up as increasing numbers of Americans own stocks.

However, these overall trends can mask some important underlying distinctions. For instance, while more Americans own stock today than ever before, the majority of Americans still do not own any stock in any form, including mutual funds and 401(k)-style pension plans. The top 1 percent of American households captured 42.5 percent of the stock market gains between 1989 and 1997. The next 9 percent of households received 43.3 percent of the total. The remaining 14.2 percent of the benefits of the stock market boom went to the remaining 90 percent of American households (Economic Policy Institute 1999c). "Edward Wolff argues that even among the 49 percent of households that own stock, most own very few shares. He found that among the bottom-three income quintiles of the population, as of 1997, only about 25 percent own any stock at all. And only 6–7 percent of them own more than $10,000" (quoted in Greider 2000, 13). Virtually all of the growth in (marketable) wealth between 1983 and 1998 accrued to the top 20 percent of households. The bottom 40 percent of households saw its wealth decline in absolute terms (Wolff 2002, 67).[10]

Furthermore, while the resources being devoted to human-capital accumulation have increased enormously during the last 15 years, with the share of the workforce with a college degree doubling and the percentage of high school dropouts vastly reduced, if hourly compensation is corrected for the growth of human capital, it becomes negative during the 1980s and 1990s. The typical male college graduate earns 12 percent less today than a male college graduate in 1973. Earnings among workers with a high school diploma are down, as are those of high school dropouts and some workers with college degrees (Jerome Levy Economics Institute of Bard College 1996, 30).

It is not [my purpose] to argue that everyone is suffering or is anxious in the new economy. Those who have the necessary tools, education, skills, and outlook are flourishing. Many individuals relish the freedom that contingent employment offers and are enthused by not knowing where they will be working in five or ten years. Indeed, there have always been groups who benefit more or less from the American economy. However, several distinctions are crucial. First, those who suffer now suffer far more than they would have in the postwar labor-market structure. Second, regardless of current wage and benefit levels, wages and benefits are far lower than they would have been had the trajectory of growth that began in the postwar period continued. Third, the uncertainty of the new economy affects not just those who are always the most vulnerable in the American economy: the postwar era promises of security were heeded by all Americans....

Undoubtedly, the postindustrial economy has the potential for enormous growth and many families are reaping the benefits. In California's Silicon Valley, an average of 63 people hit the millionaire mark during 2000—at the height of the stock market bubble (Nieves 2000). The number of millionaires climbed by 54 percent between 1989 and 1998; the number of "pentamillionaires" ($5,000,000 or more) more than doubled; and the number of "decamillionaires" ($10,000,000 or more) almost quadrupled (Wolff 2002, 16). And, in fact, the security provided to so many during the postwar period certainly constrained the possibility for the exceptional prosperity among the few that we witness in the unfettered "New Economy." As President Clinton remarked at a graduation ceremony at the University of Chicago in 1999, "All of us know that the problem with the new global economy is that it is both more rewarding and more destructive" (Greider 2000, 11)....

DISCUSSION QUESTIONS

1. Thinking about the economic trends Wiefek describes, how have these developments affected your life decisions compared to the decisions your parents or grandparents made at your age?

2. What do you think are some of the consequences of the contemporary coexistence of economic growth and job insecurity?

NOTES

1. Government spending also contributed to the extraordinary economic growth in the post-World War II period; for example, defense expenditures and the Interstate Highway System (Jost 1993, 634; Jackson 1985). Many government programs like the G.I. Bill and low-interest mortgage programs contributed to the relatively egalitarian income-growth patterns evidenced in the postwar period, as did trade-union activism and union membership strength (Aronowitz 1998).

2. More specifically, a period of slow growth and oil shocks (1973 to 1979) was followed by a new pattern of generally slower growth than the immediate postwar period, but with a strong tilt in favor of the top-end of the income distribution (Krugman 1992, 20).

3. Household wealth refers to the net dollar value of the assets less liabilities (or debt) held by the household at one point in time (Wolff 2002, 5).

4. The broad group of service-producing industries include: transportation and public utilities; wholesale trade; retail trade; finance, insurance and real estate; and services. The services industry—the largest share of employment—includes a broad variety of activities such as health care, advertising, computer and data-processing services, personnel supply, private education, social services, legal services, management and public relations, engineering and architectural services, accounting, and recreation (Meisenheimer 1998).

5. There exists much debate about the methodology involved in studies concerning changes in job tenure (see Neumark 2000). Mainstream labor economists are reluctant to conclude that there exists an objective basis for the subjective expressions of insecurity that they acknowledge exist. In the context of this debate, the NBER's conclusions about changes in job tenure are notable.

6. For an analysis of the political activism of business interests beginning in the 1970s, see Akard (1992).

7. For discussions of these developments, see Aronowitz (1998, 9–50) and Blumberg (1980, xii–xiii).

8. It is important to recognize that the decline of unions is also a symptom of this shift. An important component in the decline of unions is the same transformation in attitudes and norms that underlies some of the other changes—namely, that firms are more willing to oppose unions (Osterman 1999, 65).

9. Perhaps the most striking example is President Reagan's firing of 11,000 federally employed air-traffic controllers in the summer of 1981.

10. Marketable wealth (or net worth) is the current value of all marketable or fungible assets ("fungible" assets are defined as liquid assets plus stocks and other equities) less the current value of debts.

REFERENCES

Aiken, Michael, Louis Ferman, and Harold Sheppard. 1968. *Economic Failure, Alienation and Extremism.* Ann Arbor: University of Michigan Press.

Akard, Patrick. 1992. "Corporate Mobilization and Political Power: The Transformation of U.S. Economic Policy in the 1970s." *American Sociological Review* 57:597–615.

Aronowitz, Stanley. 1998. *From the Ashes of the Old.* New York: Houghton Mifflin.

Benner, Chris, Bob Brownstein, and Amy Dean. 1999. *Walking the Lifelong Tightrope: Negotiating Work in the New Economy.* Working Partnerships USA and Economic Policy Institute.

Berger, Suzanne. 2000. "Globalization and Politics." *Annual Review of Political Science* 3:43–62.

Bernstein, Aaron. 2000. "Backlash: Behind the Anxiety over Globalization." *BusinessWeek* (April 24):38–42.

Bernstein, Jared, Heather Boushey, Elizabeth McNichol, and Robert Zahradnik. 2002, April. *Pulling Apart: A State-by-State Analysis of Income Trends.* Center on Budget and Policy Priorities/Economic Policy Institute.

Bluestone, Barry, and Bennett Harrison. 1982. *The Deindustrialization of America.* New York: Basic Books.

Blumberg, Paul. 1980. *Inequality in an Age of Decline.* New York: Oxford University Press.

Brecher, Jeremy. 1997. "American Labor on the Eve of the Millennium." *Z Magazine* (December).

Brecher, Jeremy, and Tim Costello. 1998. *Global Village or Global Pillage: Economic Reconstruction from the Bottom Up.* Cambridge, MA: South End Press.

Centers, Richard. 1949. *The Psychology of Social Classes.* Princeton, NJ: Princeton University Press.

Children's Defense Fund. 1997. *Rescuing the American Dream: Halting the Economic Freefall of Today's Young Families with Children.* Washington, DC: Children's Defense Fund.

Collins, Chuck, and Felice Yeskel. 2000. *Economic Apartheid in America: A Primer on Economic Inequality and Insecurity.* New York: The New Press.

Danziger, Sheldon, and Peter Gottschalk. 1995. *America Unequal.* Cambridge, MA: Harvard University Press.

Duncan, Greg, Timothy Smeeding, and Willard Rodgers. 1991. "Whither the Middle Class? A Dynamic View." Paper prepared for the Jerome Levy Institute Conference on Income Inequality, Bard College, June 18–20.

Economic Policy Institute. 1999a. "Economic Snapshots, February 24." Washington, DC: Economic Policy Institute <http://epinet.org/webfeatures.html>.

———. 1999b. "Economic Snapshots, May 5." Washington, DC: Economic Policy Institute <http://epinet.org/webfeatures.html>.

———. 1999c. "Economic Snapshots, March 17." Washington, DC: Economic Policy Institute <http://epinet.org/webfeatures.html>.

———. 2000. "State Income Inequality Continued to Grow in Most States in the 1990s." Press release, January 18.

———. 2002a. "Economic Snapshots, May 29." Washington, DC: Economic Policy Institute <http://epinet.org/webfeatures.html>.

———. 2002b. "Economic Snapshots, July 24." Washington, DC: Economic Policy Institute <http://epinet.org/webfeatures.html>.

Farazmand, Ali. 1999. "Globalization and Public Administration." *Public Administration Review* 59(6):509–22.

Farber, Henry. 2001. "Job Loss in the United States, 1981–99." Working Paper, Industrial Relations Section, Princeton University <http://www.irs.princeton.edu/farber/working_papers.html>.

Feenstra, Robert, and Gordon Hanson. 2001. "Global Production Sharing and Rising Inequality: A Survey of Trade and Wages." NBER Working Paper No. w8372.

Fields, Gary S. 1999. "Income Mobility: Concepts and Measures," in *New Markets, New Opportunities?: Economic and Social Mobility in a Changing World,* ed. Nancy Birdsall and Carol Graham. Washington, DC: Carnegie Endowment for International Peace/Brookings Institution Press.

Fiorina, Morris. 1978. "Economic Retrospective Voting in American National Elections." *American Journal of Political Science* 22:426–43.

Greenhouse, Steven. 1986. "The Average Guy Takes It on the Chin." *New York Times* (July 13):A1.

Greider, William. 2000. "Unfinished Business: Clinton's Lost Presidency." *The Nation* (February 14).

Harrison, Bennett. 1994. *Lean and Mean: The Changing Landscape of Corporate Power in the Age of Flexibility.* New York: Basic Books.

Hilsenrath, Jon. 2002. "The Economy: Income Gap Narrowed at End of '90s—Study Says Rise in Receipts of U.S.'s Poorest Families Accounted for the Change." *Wall Street Journal* (April 24):A2.

Jackson, Kenneth. 1985. *Crabgrass Frontier: The Suburbanization of the United States.* New York: Oxford University Press.

Jerome Levy Economics Institute of Bard College. 1996. *The Employment Act of 1946: 50 Years Later.* Conference Proceedings produced by the Bard Publications Office (April 25–26).

Johnston, David Cay. 1999. "Gap between Rich and Poor Found Substantially Wider." *New York Times* (September 5):A14.

Jones, F. Arthur, and Daniel Weinberg. 2000, June. "The Changing Shape of the Nation's Income Distribution." *Current Population Reports,* P60–204.

Jost, Kenneth. 1993. "Downward Mobility." *Congressional Quarterly Researcher* 3(27):627–40.

Kacapyr, Elia. 1996. "Are You Middle Class?" *American Demographics* 18(10):30–35.

Katona, George, and Burkhard Strumpel. 1978. *A New Economic Era.* New York: Elsevier.

Kernell, Samuel. 1978. "Explaining Presidential Popularity." *American Political Science Review* 72:506–22.

Kinder, Donald, and Roderick Kiewiet. 1979. "Economic Discontent and Political Behavior: The Role of Personal Grievances and Collective Economic Judgments in Congressional Voting." *American Journal of Political Science* 23:495–527.

Kletzer, Lori G., and Robert E. Litan. 2001. "A Prescription to Relieve Worker Anxiety." *International Economics Policy Briefs.* Institute for International Economics and the Brookings Institution, Washington, DC.

Kramer, Gerald. 1971. "Short-Term Fluctuations in U.S. Voting Behavior, 1896–1964." *American Political Science Review* 65:131–43.

Krueger, Alan. 2002. "When It Comes to Income Inequality, More than Just Market Forces Are at Work." *New York Times* (April 4):C2.

Krugman, Paul. 1992. "The Rich, the Right and the Facts." *American Prospects* 11(fall):19–31.

Kuttner, Robert. 1983. "The Declining Middle." *Atlantic Monthly* (July).

Leggett, John. 1964. "Economic Insecurity and Working-Class Consciousness." *American Sociological Review* 29:226–34.

Levy, Frank. 1999. "Growth Is Not Enough." *Washington Monthly* 31(4):23–24.

Lewis-Beck, Michael S., and Mary Stegmaier. 2000. "Economic Determinants of Electoral Outcomes." *Annual Review of Political Science* 3:183–219.

Madrick, Jeffrey. 1995. *The End of Affluence.* New York: Random House.

Mayer, Kurt. 1963. "The Changing Shape of the American Class Structure." *Social Research* 30:460–68.

Meisenheimer, Joseph, II. 1998. "The Services Industry in the 'Good' Versus 'Bad' Jobs Debate." *Monthly Labor Review* (February).

Minsky, Hyman, and Charles Whalen. 1996–97. "Economic Insecurity and the Institutional Prerequisites for Successful Capitalism." *Journal of Post Keynesian Economics* 19(winter):155–70.

Nackenoff, Carol. 1983. "Economic Dualism and What It Means to American Labor Force Participants." *Journal of Politics* 45:110–42.

Neumark, David. 2000. "Changes in Job Stability and Job Security: A Collective Effort to Untangle, Reconcile, and Interpret the Evidence." NBER Working Paper No. w7472.

Neumark, David, Daniel Polsky, and Daniel Hansen. 1999. "Has Job Security Declined Yet?" *Journal of Labor Economics* 17(4):529–65.

PERSONAL ACCOUNT

I Am a Pakistani Woman

I am a Pakistani woman, raised in the U.S. and Canada, and often at odds with the Western standard of beauty.

As a child in Nova Scotia and later growing up in New York and Indiana, I was proud of my uniqueness. On traditional Pakistani and Muslim holidays, I got to wear bright, fun clothes from my country and colorful jewelry. I had a whole rich tradition of my own to celebrate in addition to Christmas and Easter. However, as I started school, I somehow came to realize that being different wasn't so great—that in other people's viewpoint, I looked strange and acted funny. I learned the importance of fitting in and behaving like the other girls. This involved dressing well, giggling a lot, and having a superior, but flirtatious attitude toward boys. I was very outgoing and had very good grades, so outwardly I was able to "assimilate" with some success. But my sister, who was quiet and reticent, often took the brunt of other children's cruelty. I realize how proud and ashamed I was of my heritage when I look at my relationship with my family.

A lesson I learned early on in the U.S. was that being beautiful took a lot of money. It is painful, as an adult, for me to consider the inexorable, never-ending pressure that my father was under to embody the dominant, middle-class cultural expressions of masculinity, as in success at one's job, making a big salary, and owning status symbols. I resented him so much then for being a poor, untenured professor and freelance writer. I wanted designer clothes, dining out at nice restaurants, and a big allowance. Instead, I had a deeply spiritual thinker, writer, and theologian for a dad. I love(d) him and am so

very grateful for what he's taught me, but as a child I didn't think of him as a success.

The prettiest girls in school all had a seemingly endless array of outfits, lots of makeup and perfume, and everything by the "right" designers. I hated my mom for making many of my clothes and buying things on sale (and my mom was a great seamstress). I hungrily read about Brooke Shields's seemingly perfect life, with her excursions to expensive restaurants and appointments with personal trainers at exclusive spas. I felt a sense of hopelessness that I could never have the resources or opportunities necessary to compete, to be beautiful.

Instead I found safety in conformity. When I was in high school, the WASPy, preppy look was hot; it represented the epitome of success and privilege in America. I worked hard to purchase a wardrobe of clothes with a polo-horse insignia, by many hours at an after-school job. I tried to hide my exotic look behind Khakis, boat shoes, hair barrettes, and pearl studs. There was comfort in conformity. I saw the class "sex symbol" denigrated for wearing tight dresses and having a very well-developed body for a sixteen-year-old, and the more unique dressers dismissed as frivolous, trendy, and more than a little eccentric. You couldn't be too pretty, too ugly, too different—you had to just blend in.

Though I did it well, I perpetually felt like an imposter. This rigidly controlled, well-dressed preppy going through school with good grades in advanced placement classes in no way represented what I felt to be my true essence.

Hoorie I. Siddique

Nieves, Evelyn. 2000. "Many in Silicon Valley Cannot Afford Housing; Even at $50,000 a Year." *New York Times* (February 20):A16.

Osterman, Paul. 1999. *Securing Prosperity: The American Labor Market: How It Has Changed and What to Do about It.* Princeton, NJ: Princeton University Press.

Palley, Thomas. 1998. *Plenty of Nothing: The Downsizing of the American Dream and the Case for Structural Keynesianism.* Princeton, NJ: Princeton University Press.

Peffley, Mark. 1985. "The Voter as Juror: Attributing Responsibility for Economic Conditions," in *Economic Conditions and Electoral Outcomes,* ed. H. Eulau and M. Lewis-Beck. Flemington, NJ: Agathon Press.

Phillips, Kevin P. 1990. *The Politics of Rich and Poor: Wealth and the American Electorate in the Reagan Aftermath.* New York: Random House.

———. 2002. *Wealth and Democracy: A Political History of the American Rich.* New York: Broadway Books.

Rose, Stephen. 1995. "Declining Job Security and the Professionalization of Opportunity." Research Report No. 95-04. Washington, DC: National Commission for Employment Policy.

———. 1996. "The Truth about Social Mobility." *Challenge* 39(3):4–8.

Sears, David, and Carolyn Funk. 1991. "The Role of Self-interest in Social and Political Attitudes." *Advances in Experimental Social Psychology* 24:1–91.

Sniderman, Paul, and Richard Brody. 1977. "Coping: The Ethic of Self-Reliance." *American Journal of Political Science* 21:501–22.

Starobin, Paul. 1995. "The Politics of Anxiety." *National Journal* (September 30): 2402–7.

Street, David, and John Leggett. 1961. "Economic Deprivation and Extremism: A Study of Unemployed Negroes." *American Journal of Sociology* 67:53–57.

Tedin, Kent. 1994. "Self-Interest, Symbolic Values, and the Financial Equalization of the Public Schools." *Journal of Politics* 56(3):628–49.

Teixeira, Ruy, and Joel Rogers. 1996. "Volatile Voters: Declining Living Standards and Non-College-Educated Whites." Economic Policy Institute. Working Paper No. 116.

Thurow, Lester. 1984. "The Disappearance of the Middle Class." *New York Times* (February 5):F3.

Tough, Paul. 1996. "Does America Still Work?" *Harper's* 292(1752):35–38, 45.

Uchitelle, Louis. 2000. "107 Months, and Counting." *New York Times* (January 30):C1.

Urban Institute. 1992. "Is U.S. Income Inequality Really Growing?" *Policy Bites 13.*

U.S. Census Bureau. 1985. *Money Income and Poverty Status of Families and Persons in the United States: 1985, Current Population Report, No. 154.* Washington, DC: U.S. Government Printing Office.

———. 1998. "Income Inequality (Middle Class)" <http://www.census.gov/hhes/income/midclass/midclsan.html>.

Wolff, Edward. 1996/2002. *Top Heavy: The Increasing Inequality of Wealth in America and What Can Be Done about It.* New York: The New Press.

READING 16

Nickel and Dimed

ON (NOT) GETTING BY IN AMERICA

Barbara Ehrenreich

You might think that unskilled jobs would be a snap for someone who holds a Ph.D. and whose normal line of work requires learning entirely new things every couple of weeks. Not so. The first thing I discovered is that no job, no matter how lowly, is truly

Barbara Ehrenreich is the author of 12 books, including *The Worst Years of Our Lives, Blood Rites,* and *Fear of Falling,* which was nominated for a National Book Critics Award.
Editors' note: To learn about the lives of the working poor, professional journalist Barbara Ehrenreich traveled the United States working as a waitress, hotel maid, house cleaner, nursing aid, and Wal-Mart salesperson.

"unskilled." Every one of the six jobs I entered into in the course of this project required concentration, and most demanded that I master new terms, new tools, and new skills—from placing orders on restaurant computers to wielding the backpack vacuum cleaner. None of these things came as easily to me as I would have liked; no one ever said, "Wow, you're fast!" or "Can you believe she just started?" Whatever my accomplishments in the rest of my life, in the low-wage work world I was a person of average ability—capable of learning the job and also capable of screwing up.

I did have my moments of glory. There were days at The Maids when I got my own tasks finished fast enough that I was able to lighten the load on others, and I feel good about that. There was my breakthrough at Wal-Mart, where I truly believe that, if I'd been able to keep my mouth shut, I would have progressed in a year or two to a wage of $7.50 or more an hour. And I'll bask for the rest of my life in the memory of that day at the Woodcrest when I fed the locked Alzheimer's ward all by myself, cleaned up afterward, and even managed to extract a few smiles from the vacant faces of my charges in the process. . . .

But the real question is not how well I did at work but how well I did at life in general, which includes eating and having a place to stay. The fact that these are two separate questions needs to be underscored right away. In the rhetorical buildup to welfare reform, it was uniformly assumed that a job was the ticket out of poverty and that the only thing holding back welfare recipients was their reluctance to get out and get one. I got one and sometimes more than one, but my track record in the survival department is far less admirable than my performance as a jobholder. On small things I was thrifty enough; no expenditures on "carousing," flashy clothes, or any of the other indulgences that are often smugly believed to undermine the budgets of the poor. True, the $30 slacks in Key West and the $20 belt in Minneapolis were extravagances; I now know I could have done better at the Salvation Army or even at Wal-Mart. Food, though, I pretty much got down to a science: lots of chopped meat, beans, cheese, and noodles when I had a kitchen to cook in; otherwise, fast food, which I was able to keep down to about $9 a day. But let's look at the record.

In Key West, I earned $1,039 in one month and spent $517 on food, gas, toiletries, laundry, phone, and utilities. Rent was the deal breaker. If I had remained in my $500 efficiency, I would have been able to pay the rent and have $22 left over (which is still $78 less than the cash I had in my pocket at the start of the month). This in itself would have been a dicey situation if I had attempted to continue for a few more months, because sooner or later I would have had to spend something on medical and dental care or drugs other than ibuprofen. But my move to the trailer park—for the purpose, you will recall, of taking a second job—made me responsible for $625 a month in rent alone, utilities not included. Here I might have economized by giving up the car and buying a used bike (for about $50) or walking to work. Still, two jobs, or at least a job and a half, would be a necessity, and I had learned that I could not do two physically demanding jobs in the same day, at least not at any acceptable standard of performance.

In Portland, Maine, I came closest to achieving a decent fit between income and expenses, but only because I worked seven days a week. Between my two jobs, I was earning approximately $300 a week after taxes and paying $480 a month in rent, or a manageable 40 percent of my earnings. It helped, too, that gas and electricity were included in my rent and that I got two or three free meals each weekend at the nursing home. But I was there at the beginning of the off-season. If I had stayed until June 2000 I would have faced the Blue Haven's summer rent of $390 a week, which would of course have been out of the question. So to survive year-round, I would have had to save enough, in the months between August 1999 and May 2000, to accumulate the first month's rent and deposit on an actual apartment. I think I could have done this— saved $800 to $1,000—at least if no car trouble or illness interfered with my budget. I am not sure, however, that I could have maintained the seven-day-a-week regimen month after month or eluded

the kinds of injuries that afflicted my fellow workers in the housecleaning business.

In Minneapolis—well, here we are left with a lot of speculation. If I had been able to find an apartment for $400 a month or less, my pay at Wal-Mart—$1,120 a month before taxes—might have been sufficient, although the cost of living in a motel while I searched for such an apartment might have made it impossible for me to save enough for the first month's rent and deposit. A weekend job, such as the one I almost landed at a supermarket for about $7.75 an hour, would have helped, but I had no guarantee that I could arrange my schedule at Wal-Mart to reliably exclude weekends. If I had taken the job at Menards and the pay was in fact $10 an hour for eleven hours a day, I would have made about $440 a week after taxes—enough to pay for a motel room and still have something left over to save up for the initial costs of an apartment. But were they really offering $10 an hour? And could I have stayed on my feet eleven hours a day, five days a week? So yes, with some different choices, I probably could have survived in Minneapolis. But I'm not going back for a rematch.

All right, I made mistakes, especially in Minneapolis, and these mistakes were at the time an occasion for feelings of failure and shame. I should have pulled myself together and taken the better-paying job; I should have moved into the dormitory I finally found (although at $19 a night, even a dorm bed would have been a luxury on Wal-Mart wages). But it must be said in my defense that plenty of other people were making the same mistakes: working at Wal-Mart rather than at one of the better-paying jobs available (often, I assume, because of transportation problems); living in residential motels at $200 to $300 a week. So the problem goes beyond my personal failings and miscalculations. Something is wrong, very wrong, when a single person in good health, a person who in addition possesses a working car, can barely support herself by the sweat of her brow. You don't need a degree in economics to see that wages are too low and rents too high.

The problem of rents is easy for a noneconomist, even a sparsely educated low-wage worker, to grasp: it's the market, stupid. When the rich and the poor compete for housing on the open market, the poor don't stand a chance. The rich can always outbid them, buy up their tenements or trailer parks, and replace them with condos, McMansions, golf courses, or whatever they like. Since the rich have become more numerous, thanks largely to rising stock prices and executive salaries, the poor have necessarily been forced into housing that is more expensive, more dilapidated, or more distant from their places of work. . . . In Key West, the trailer park [that was convenient to my hotel job] was charging $625 a month for a half-size trailer, forcing low-wage workers to search for housing farther and farther away in less fashionable keys. But rents were also skyrocketing in the touristically challenged city of Minneapolis, where the last bits of near-affordable housing lie deep in the city, while job growth has occurred on the city's periphery, next to distinctly unaffordable suburbs. Insofar as the poor have to work near the dwellings of the rich—as in the case of so many service and retail jobs—they are stuck with lengthy commutes or dauntingly expensive housing.

If there seems to be general complacency about the low-income housing crisis, this is partly because it is in no way reflected in the official poverty rate, which has remained for the past several years at a soothingly low 13 percent or so. The reason for the disconnect between the actual housing nightmare of the poor and "poverty," as officially defined, is simple: the official poverty level is still calculated by the archaic method of taking the bare-bones cost of food for a family of a given size and multiplying this number by three. Yet food is relatively inflation-proof, at least compared with rent. In the early 1960s, when this method of calculating poverty was devised, food accounted for 24 percent of the average family budget (not 33 percent even then, it should be noted) and housing 29 percent. In 1999, food took up only 16 percent of the family budget, while housing had soared to 37 percent.[1] So the choice of food as the basis for calculating family budgets seems fairly arbitrary today; we might as well abolish poverty altogether, at least on paper, by defining a subsistence budget as some multiple of average expenditures on comic books or dental floss.

When the market fails to distribute some vital commodity, such as housing, to all who require it, the usual liberal-to-moderate expectation is that the government will step in and help. We accept this principle—at least in a halfhearted and faltering way—in the case of health care, where government offers Medicare to the elderly, Medicaid to the desperately poor, and various state programs to the children of the merely very poor. But in the case of housing, the extreme upward skewing of the market has been accompanied by a cowardly public sector retreat from responsibility. Expenditures on public housing have fallen since the 1980s, and the expansion of public rental subsidies came to a halt in the mid-1990s. At the same time, housing subsidies for home owners—who tend to be far more affluent than renters—have remained at their usual munificent levels. It did not escape my attention, as a temporarily low-income person, that the housing subsidy I normally receive in my real life—over $20,000 a year in the form of a mortgage-interest deduction—would have allowed a truly low-income family to live in relative splendor. Had this amount been available to me in monthly installments in Minneapolis, I could have moved into one of those "executive" condos with sauna, health club, and pool.

But if rents are exquisitely sensitive to market forces, wages clearly are not. Every city where I worked in the course of this project was experiencing what local businesspeople defined as a "labor shortage"—commented on in the local press and revealed by the ubiquitous signs saying "Now Hiring" or, more imperiously, "We Are Now Accepting Applications." Yet wages for people near the bottom of the labor market remain fairly flat, even "stagnant." "Certainly," the *New York Times* reported in March 2000, "inflationary wage gains are not evident in national wage statistics."[2] Federal Reserve chief Alan Greenspan, who spends much of his time anxiously scanning the horizon for the slightest hint of such "inflationary" gains, was pleased to inform Congress in July 2000 that the forecast seemed largely trouble-free. He went so far as to suggest that the economic laws linking low unemployment to wage increases may no longer be operative, which is a little like saying that the law of supply and demand has been repealed.[3] Some economists argue that the apparent paradox rests on an illusion: there is no real "labor shortage," only a shortage of people willing to work at the wages currently being offered.[4] You might as well talk about a "Lexus shortage"—which there is, in a sense, for anyone unwilling to pay $40,000 for a car.

In fact, wages *have* risen, or did rise, anyway, between 1996 and 1999. When I called around to various economists in the summer of 2000 and complained about the inadequacy of the wages available to entry-level workers, this was their first response: "But wages are going up!" According to the Economic Policy Institute, the poorest 10 percent of American workers saw their wages rise from $5.49 an hour (in 1999 dollars) in 1996 to $6.05 in 1999. Moving up the socioeconomic ladder, the next 10 percent–sized slice of Americans—which is roughly where I found myself as a low-wage worker—went from $6.80 an hour in 1996 to $7.35 in 1999.[5]

Obviously we have one of those debates over whether the glass is half empty or half full; the increases that seem to have mollified many economists do not seem so impressive to me. To put the wage gains of the past four years in somewhat dismal perspective: they have not been sufficient to bring low-wage workers up to the amounts they were earning twenty-seven years ago, in 1973. In the first quarter of 2000, the poorest 10 percent of workers were earning only 91 percent of what they earned in the distant era of Watergate and disco music. Furthermore, of all workers, the poorest have made the least progress back to their 1973 wage levels. Relatively well-off workers in the eighth decile, or 10 percent–sized slice, where earnings are about $20 an hour, are now making 106.6 percent of what they earned in 1973. When I persisted in my

carping to the economists, they generally backed down a bit, conceding that while wages at the bottom are going up, they're not going up very briskly. Lawrence Michel at the Economic Policy Institute, who had at the beginning of our conversation taken the half-full perspective, heightened the mystery when he observed that productivity—to which wages are theoretically tied—has been rising at such a healthy clip that "workers should be getting much more."[6]

The most obvious reason why they're not is that employers resist wage increases with every trick they can think of and every ounce o£ strength they can summon. I had an opportunity to query one of my own employers on this subject in Maine . . . when Ted, my boss at The Maids, drove me about forty minutes to a house where I was needed to reinforce a shorthanded team. In the course of complaining about his hard lot in life, he avowed that he could double his business overnight if only he could find enough reliable workers. As politely as possible, I asked him why he didn't just raise the pay. The question seemed to slide right off him. We offer "mothers' hours," he told me, meaning that the workday was supposedly over at three—as if to say, "With a benefit like that, how could anybody complain about wages?"

In fact, I suspect that the free breakfast he provided us represented the only concession to the labor shortage that he was prepared to make. Similarly, the Wal-Mart where I worked was offering free doughnuts once a week to any employees who could arrange to take their breaks while the supply lasted. As Louis Uchitelle has reported in the *New York Times,* many employers will offer almost anything—free meals, subsidized transportation, store discounts—rather than raise wages. The reason for this, in the words of one employer, is that such extras "can be shed more easily" than wage increases when changes in the market seem to make them unnecessary.[7] In the same spirit, automobile manufacturers would rather offer their customers cash rebates than reduced prices; the advantage of the rebate is that it seems like a gift and can be withdrawn without explanation.

But the resistance of employers only raises a second and ultimately more intractable question: Why isn't this resistance met by more effective counterpressure from the workers themselves? In evading and warding off wage increases, employers are of course behaving in an economically rational fashion; their business isn't to make their employees more comfortable and secure but to maximize the bottom line. So why don't employees behave in an equally rational fashion, demanding higher wages of their employers or seeking out better-paying jobs? The assumption behind the law of supply and demand, as it applies to labor, is that workers will sort themselves out as effectively as marbles on an inclined plane—gravitating to the better-paying jobs and either leaving the recalcitrant employers behind or forcing them to up the pay. "Economic man," that great abstraction of economic science, is supposed to do whatever it takes, within certain limits, to maximize his economic advantage.

I was baffled, initially, by what seemed like a certain lack of get-up-and-go on the part of my fellow workers. Why didn't they just leave for a better-paying job, as I did when I moved from the Hearthside to Jerry's? Part of the answer is that actual humans experience a little more "friction" than marbles do, and the poorer they are, the more constrained their mobility usually is. Low-wage people who don't have cars are often dependent on a relative who is willing to drop them off and pick them up again each day, sometimes on a route that includes the babysitter's house or the child care center. Change your place of work and you may be confronted with an impossible topographical problem to solve, or at least a reluctant driver to persuade. Some of my coworkers, in Minneapolis as well as Key West, rode bikes to work, and this clearly limited their geographical range. For those who do possess cars, there is still the problem of gas prices, not to mention the general hassle, which is of course far more onerous for the carless, of getting around to fill out applications, to be interviewed, to take drug tests. I have mentioned, too, the general reluctance to exchange the devil you know for one that you don't know, even when the latter is tempting you with a better wage-benefit package. At each new job, you have to start all over, clueless and friendless.

There is another way that low-income workers differ from "economic man." For the laws of economics to work, the "players" need to be well informed about their options. The ideal case—and I've read that the technology for this is just around the corner—would be the consumer whose Palm Pilot displays the menu and prices for every restaurant or store he or she passes. Even without such technological assistance, affluent job hunters expect to study the salary-benefit packages offered by their potential employers, watch the financial news to find out if these packages are in line with those being offered in other regions or fields, and probably do a little bargaining before taking a job.

But there are no Palm Pilots, cable channels, or Web sites to advise the low-wage job seeker. She has only the help-wanted signs and the want ads to go on, and most of these coyly refrain from mentioning numbers. So information about who earns what and where has to travel by word of mouth, and for inexplicable cultural reasons, this is a very slow and unreliable route. Twin Cities job market analyst Kristine Jacobs pinpoints what she calls the "money taboo" as a major factor preventing workers from optimizing their earnings. "There's a code of silence surrounding issues related to individuals' earnings," she told me. "We confess everything else in our society—sex, crime, illness. But no one wants to reveal what they earn or how they got it. The money taboo is the one thing that employers can always count on."[8] I suspect that this "taboo" operates most effectively among the lowest-paid people, because, in a society that endlessly celebrates its dot-com billionaires and centimillionaire athletes, $7 or even $10 an hour can feel like a mark of innate inferiority. So you may or may not find out that, say, the Target down the road is paying better than Wal-Mart, even if you have a sister-in-law working there.

Employers, of course, do little to encourage the economic literacy of their workers. They may exhort potential customers to "Compare Our Prices!" but they're not eager to have workers do the same with wages. . . . The hiring process seems designed, in some cases, to prevent any discussion or even disclosure of wages—whisking the applicant from interview to orientation before the crass subject of money can be raised. Some employers go further; instead of relying on the informal "money taboo" to keep workers from discussing and comparing wages, they specifically enjoin workers from doing so. The *New York Times* recently reported on several lawsuits brought by employees who had allegedly been fired for breaking this rule—a woman, for example, who asked for higher pay after learning from her male coworkers that she was being paid considerably less than they were for the very same work. The National Labor Relations Act of 1935 makes it illegal to punish people for revealing their wages to one another, but the practice is likely to persist until rooted out by lawsuits, company by company.[9]

But if it's hard for workers to obey the laws of economics by examining their options and moving on to better jobs, why don't more of them take a stand where they are—demanding better wages and work conditions, either individually or as a group? This is a huge question, probably the subject of many a dissertation in the field of industrial psychology, and here I can only comment on the things I observed. One of these was the co-optative power of management, illustrated by such euphemisms as *associate* and *team member*. At The Maids, the boss—who, as the only male in our midst, exerted a creepy, paternalistic kind of power—had managed to convince some of my coworkers that he was struggling against difficult odds and deserving of their unstinting forbearance. Wal-Mart has a number of more impersonal and probably more effective ways of getting its workers to feel like "associates." There was the profit-sharing plan, with Wal-Mart's stock price posted daily in a prominent spot near the break room. There was the company's much-heralded patriotism, evidenced in the banners over the shopping floor urging workers and customers to contribute to the construction of a World War II veterans' memorial (Sam Walton having been one of them). There were "associate" meetings that served as pep rallies, complete with the Wal-Mart cheer: "Gimme a 'W,'" etc.

The chance to identify with a powerful and wealthy entity—the company or the boss—is only the carrot. There is also a stick. What surprised and offended me most about the low-wage workplace (and yes, here all my middle-class privilege is on full display) was the extent to which one is required to surrender one's basic civil rights and—what boils down to the same thing—self-respect. I learned this at the very beginning of my stint as a waitress, when I was warned that my purse could be searched by management at any time. I wasn't carrying stolen salt shakers or anything else of a compromising nature, but still, there's something about the prospect of a purse search that makes a woman feel a few buttons short of fully dressed. After work, I called around and found that this practice is entirely legal: if the purse is on the boss's property—which of course it was—the boss has the right to examine its contents.

Drug testing is another routine indignity. Civil libertarians see it as a violation of our Fourth Amendment freedom from "unreasonable search"; most jobholders and applicants find it simply embarrassing. In some testing protocols, the employee has to strip to her underwear and pee into a cup in the presence of an aide or technician. Mercifully, I got to keep my clothes on and shut the toilet stall door behind me, but even so, urination is a private act and it is degrading to have to perform it at the command of some powerful other. I would add pre-employment personality tests to the list of demeaning intrusions, or at least much of their usual content. Maybe the hypothetical types of questions can be justified—whether you would steal if an opportunity arose or turn in a thieving coworker and so on—but not questions about your "moods of self-pity," whether you are a loner or believe you are usually misunderstood. It is unsettling, at the very least, to give a stranger access to things, like your self-doubts and your urine, that are otherwise shared only in medical or therapeutic situations.

There are other, more direct ways of keeping low-wage employees in their place. Rules against "gossip," or even "talking," make it hard to air your grievances to peers or—should you be so daring—to enlist other workers in a group effort to bring about change, through a union organizing drive, for example. Those who do step out of line often face little unexplained punishments, such as having their schedules or their work assignments unilaterally changed. Or you may be fired; those low-wage workers who work without union contracts, which is the great majority of them, work "at will," meaning at the will of the employer, and are subject to dismissal without explanation. The AFL-CIO estimates that ten thousand workers a year are fired for participating in union organizing drives, and since it is illegal to fire people for union activity, I suspect that these firings are usually justified in terms of unrelated minor infractions. Wal-Mart employees who have bucked the company—by getting involved in a unionization drive or by suing the company for failing to pay overtime—have been fired for breaking the company rule against using profanity.[10]

So if low-wage workers do not always behave in an economically rational way, that is, as free agents within a capitalist democracy, it is because they dwell in a place that is neither free nor in any way democratic. When you enter the low-wage workplace—and many of the medium-wage workplaces as well—you check your civil liberties at the door, leave America and all it supposedly stands for behind, and learn to zip your lips for the duration of the shift. The consequences of this routine surrender go beyond the issues of wages and poverty. We can hardly pride ourselves on being the world's preeminent democracy, after all, if large numbers of citizens spend half their waking hours in what amounts, in plain terms, to a dictatorship.

Any dictatorship takes a psychological toll on its subjects. If you are treated as an untrustworthy person—a potential slacker, drug addict, or thief—you may begin to feel less trustworthy yourself. If you are constantly reminded of your lowly position in the social hierarchy, whether by individual managers or by a plethora of impersonal rules, you begin to accept that unfortunate status. To draw for a moment

from an entirely different corner of my life, that part of me still attached to the biological sciences, there is ample evidence that animals—rats and monkeys, for example—that are forced into a subordinate status within their social systems adapt their brain chemistry accordingly, becoming "depressed" in humanlike ways. Their behavior is anxious and withdrawn; the level of serotonin (the neurotransmitter boosted by some antidepressants) declines in their brains. And—what is especially relevant here—they avoid fighting even in self-defense.[11]

Humans are, of course, vastly more complicated; even in situations of extreme subordination, we can pump up our self-esteem with thoughts of our families, our religion, our hopes for the future. But as much as any other social animal, and more so than many, we depend for our self-image on the humans immediately around us—to the point of altering our perceptions of the world so as to fit in with theirs.[12] My guess is that the indignities imposed on so many low-wage workers—the drug tests, the constant surveillance, being "reamed out" by managers—are part of what keeps wages low. If you're made to feel unworthy enough, you may come to think that what you're paid is what you are actually worth.

It is hard to imagine any other function for workplace authoritarianism. Managers may truly believe that, without their unremitting efforts, all work would quickly grind to a halt. That is not my impression. While I encountered some cynics and plenty of people who had learned to budget their energy, I never met an actual slacker or, for that matter, a drug addict or thief. On the contrary, I was amazed and sometimes saddened by the pride people took in jobs that rewarded them so meagerly, either in wages or in recognition. Often, in fact, these people experienced management as an obstacle to getting the job done as it should be done. Waitresses chafed at managers' stinginess toward the customers; housecleaners resented the time constraints that sometimes made them cut corners; retail workers wanted the floor to be beautiful, not cluttered with excess stock as management required. Left to themselves, they devised systems of cooperation and work sharing; when there was a crisis, they rose to it. In fact, it was often hard to see what the function of management was, other than to exact obeisance.

There seems to be a vicious cycle at work here, making ours not just an economy but a culture of extreme inequality. Corporate decision makers, and even some two-bit entrepreneurs like my boss at The Maids, occupy an economic position miles above that of the underpaid people whose labor they depend on. For reasons that have more to do with class—and often racial—prejudice than with actual experience, they tend to fear and distrust the category of people from which they recruit their workers. Hence the perceived need for repressive management and intrusive measures like drug and personality testing. But these things cost money—$20,000 or more a year for a manager, $100 a pop for a drug test, and so on—and the high cost of repression results in ever more pressure to hold wages down. The larger society seems to be caught up in a similar cycle: cutting public services for the poor, which are sometimes referred to collectively as the "social wage," while investing ever more heavily in prisons and cops. And in the larger society, too, the cost of repression becomes another factor weighing against the expansion or restoration of needed services. It is a tragic cycle, condemning us to ever deeper inequality, and in the long run, almost no one benefits but the agents of repression themselves.

But whatever keeps wages low—and I'm sure my comments have barely scratched the surface—the result is that many people earn far less than they need to live on. How much is that? The Economic Policy Institute recently reviewed dozens of studies of what constitutes a "living wage" and came up with an average figure of $30,000 a year for a family of one adult and two children, which amounts to a wage of $14 an hour. This is not the very minimum such a family could live on; the budget includes health insurance, a telephone, and child care at a licensed center, for example, which are well beyond the reach of millions. But it does not include restaurant meals, video rentals, Internet access, wine and liquor, cigarettes and lottery tickets, or even very

much meat. The shocking thing is that the majority of American workers, about 60 percent, earn less than $14 an hour. Many of them get by by teaming up with another wage earner, a spouse or grown child. Some draw on government help in the form of food stamps, housing vouchers, the earned income tax credit, or—for those coming off welfare in relatively generous states—subsidized child care. But others—single mothers for example—have nothing but their own wages to live on, no matter how many mouths there are to feed.

Employers will look at that $30,000 figure, which is over twice what they currently pay entry-level workers, and see nothing but bankruptcy ahead. Indeed, it is probably impossible for the private sector to provide everyone with an adequate standard of living through wages, or even wages plus benefits, alone: too much of what we need, such as reliable child care, is just too expensive, even for middle-class families. Most civilized nations compensate for the inadequacy of wages by providing relatively generous public services such as health insurance, free or subsidized child care, subsidized housing, and effective public transportation. But the United States, for all its wealth, leaves its citizens to fend for themselves—facing market-based rents, for example, on their wages alone. For millions of Americans, that $10—or even $8 or $6—hourly wage is all there is.

It is common, among the nonpoor, to think of poverty as a sustainable condition—austere, perhaps, but they get by somehow, don't they? They are "always with us." What is harder for the nonpoor to see is poverty as acute distress: The lunch that consists of Doritos or hot dog rolls, leading to faintness before the end of the shift. The "home" that is also a car or a van. The illness or injury that must be "worked through," with gritted teeth, because there's no sick pay or health insurance and the loss of one day's pay will mean no groceries for the next. These experiences are not part of a sustainable lifestyle, even a lifestyle of chronic deprivation and relentless low-level punishment. They are, by almost any standard of subsistence, emergency situations. And that is how we should see the poverty of so many millions of low-wage Americans—as a state of emergency.

In the summer of 2000 I returned—permanently, I have every reason to hope—to my customary place in the socioeconomic spectrum. I go to restaurants, often far finer ones than the places where I worked, and sit down at a table. I sleep in hotel rooms that someone else has cleaned and shop in stores that others will tidy when I leave. To go from the bottom 20 percent to the top 20 percent is to enter a magical world where needs are met, problems are solved, almost without any intermediate effort. If you want to get somewhere fast, you hail a cab. If your aged parents have grown tiresome or incontinent, you put them away where others will deal with their dirty diapers and dementia. If you are part of the upper-middle-class majority that employs a maid or maid service, you return from work to find the house miraculously restored to order—the toilet bowls shit-free and gleaming, the socks that you left on the floor levitated back to their normal dwelling place. Here, sweat is a metaphor for hard work, but seldom its consequence. Hundreds of little things get done, reliably and routinely every day, without anyone's seeming to do them.

The top 20 percent routinely exercises other, far more consequential forms of power in the world. This stratum, which contains what I have termed in an earlier book the "professional-managerial class," is the home of our decision makers, opinion shapers, culture creators—our professors, lawyers, executives, entertainers, politicians, judges, writers, producers, and editors.[13] When they speak, they are listened to. When they complain, someone usually scurries to correct the problem and apologize for it. If they complain often enough, someone far below them in wealth and influence may be chastised or even fired. Political power, too, is concentrated within the top 20 percent, since its members are far more likely than the poor—or even the middle class—to discern the all-too-tiny distinctions between candidates that can make it seem worthwhile to contribute, participate, and vote. In all these ways, the affluent exert inordinate power over the

lives of the less affluent, and especially over the lives of the poor, determining what public services will be available, if any, what minimum wage, what laws governing the treatment of labor.

So it is alarming, upon returning to the upper middle class from a sojourn, however artificial and temporary, among the poor, to find the rabbit hole close so suddenly and completely behind me. You were *where,* doing *what?* Some odd optical property of our highly polarized and unequal society makes the poor almost invisible to their economic superiors. The poor can see the affluent easily enough—on television, for example, or on the covers of magazines. But the affluent rarely see the poor or, if they do catch sight of them in some public space, rarely know what they're seeing, since—thanks to consignment stores and, yes, Wal-Mart—the poor are usually able to disguise themselves as members of the more comfortable classes. Forty years ago the hot journalistic topic was the "discovery of the poor" in their inner-city and Appalachian "pockets of poverty." Today you are more likely to find commentary on their "disappearance," either as a supposed demographic reality or as a shortcoming of the middle-class imagination.

In a 2000 article on the "disappearing poor," journalist James Fallows reports that, from the vantage point of the Internet's nouveaux riches, it is "hard to understand people for whom a million dollars would be a fortune . . . not to mention those for whom $246 is a full week's earnings."[14] Among the reasons he and others have cited for the blindness of the affluent is the fact that they are less and less likely to share spaces and services with the poor. As public schools and other public services deteriorate, those who can afford to do so send their children to private schools and spend their off-hours in private spaces—health clubs, for example, instead of the local park. They don't ride on public buses and subways. They withdraw from mixed neighborhoods into distant suburbs, gated communities, or guarded apartment towers; they shop in stores that, in line with the prevailing "market segmentation," are designed to appeal to the affluent alone. Even the affluent young are increasingly unlikely to spend their summers learning how the "other half" lives, as lifeguards, waitresses, or housekeepers at resort hotels. The *New York Times* reports that they now prefer career-relevant activities like summer school or interning in an appropriate professional setting to the "sweaty, low-paid and mind-numbing slots that have long been their lot."[15]

Then, too, the particular political moment favors what almost looks like a "conspiracy of silence" on the subject of poverty and the poor. The Democrats are not eager to find flaws in the period of "unprecedented prosperity" they take credit for; the Republicans have lost interest in the poor now that "welfare-as-we-know-it" has ended. Welfare reform itself is a factor weighing against any close investigation of the conditions of the poor. Both parties heartily endorsed it, and to acknowledge that low-wage work doesn't lift people out of poverty would be to admit that it may have been, in human terms, a catastrophic mistake. In fact, very little is known about the fate of former welfare recipients because the 1996 welfare reform legislation blithely failed to include any provision for monitoring their post-welfare economic condition. Media accounts persistently bright-side the situation, highlighting the occasional success stories and downplaying the acknowledged increase in hunger.[16] And sometimes there seems to be almost deliberate deception. In June 2000, the press rushed to hail a study supposedly showing that Minnesota's welfare-to-work program had sharply reduced poverty and was, as *Time* magazine put it, a "winner."[17] Overlooked in these reports was the fact that the program in question was a pilot project that offered far more generous child care and other subsidies than Minnesota's actual welfare reform program. Perhaps the error can be forgiven—the pilot project, which ended in 1997, had the same name, Minnesota Family Investment Program, as Minnesota's much larger, ongoing welfare reform program.[18]

You would have to read a great many newspapers very carefully, cover to cover, to see the signs of distress. You would find, for example, that in 1999 Massachusetts food pantries reported a 72 percent increase in the demand for their services over the previous year, that Texas food banks were "scrounging" for food, despite donations at or above 1998 levels, as were those in Atlanta.[19] You might learn that in San Diego the Catholic Church could no longer, as of January 2000, accept homeless families at its shelter, which happens to be the city's largest, because it was already operating at twice its normal capacity.[20] You would come across news of a study showing that the percentage of Wisconsin food-stamp families in "extreme poverty"—defined as less than 50 percent of the federal poverty line—has tripled in the last decade to more than 30 percent.[21] You might discover that, nationwide, America's food banks are experiencing "a torrent of need which [they] cannot meet" and that, according to a survey conducted by the U.S. Conference of Mayors, 67 percent of the adults requesting emergency food aid are people with jobs.[22]

One reason nobody bothers to pull all these stories together and announce a widespread state of emergency may be that Americans of the newspaper-reading professional middle class are used to thinking of poverty as a consequence of unemployment. During the heyday of downsizing in the Reagan years, it very often was, and it still is for many inner-city residents who have no way of getting to the proliferating entry-level jobs on urban peripheries. When unemployment causes poverty, we know how to state the problem—typically, "the economy isn't growing fast enough"—and we know what the traditional liberal solution is—"full employment." But when we have full or nearly full employment, when jobs are available to any job seeker who can get to them, then the problem goes deeper and begins to cut into that web of expectations that make up the "social contract." According to a recent poll conducted by Jobs for the Future, a Boston-based employment research firm, 94 percent of Americans agree that "people who work full-time should be able to earn enough to keep their families out of poverty."[23] I grew up hearing over and over, to the point of tedium, that "hard work" was the secret of success: "Work hard and you'll get ahead" or "It's hard work that got us where we are." No one ever said that you could work hard—harder even than you ever thought possible—and still find yourself sinking ever deeper into poverty and debt.

When poor single mothers had the option of remaining out of the labor force on welfare, the middle and upper middle class tended to view them with a certain impatience, if not disgust. The welfare poor were excoriated for their laziness, their persistence in reproducing in unfavorable circumstances, their presumed addictions, and above all for their "dependency." Here they were, content to live off "government handouts" instead of seeking "self-sufficiency," like everyone else, through a job. They needed to get their act together, learn how to wind an alarm clock, get out there and get to work. But now that government has largely withdrawn its "handouts," now that the overwhelming majority of the poor are out there toiling in Wal-Mart or Wendy's—well, what are we to think of them? Disapproval and condescension no longer apply, so what outlook makes sense?

Guilt, you may be thinking warily. Isn't that what we're supposed to feel? But guilt doesn't go anywhere near far enough; the appropriate emotion is shame—shame at our *own* dependency, in this case, on the underpaid labor of others. When someone works for less pay than she can live on—when, for example, she goes hungry so that you can eat more cheaply and conveniently—then she has made a great sacrifice for you, she has made you a gift of some part of her abilities, her health, and her life. The "working poor," as they are approvingly termed, are in fact the major philanthropists of our society. They neglect their own children so that the children of others will be cared for; they live in substandard housing so that other homes will be shiny and perfect; they endure privation so that inflation will be low and stock prices high. To be a member of the working poor is to be an anonymous donor, a nameless benefactor, to everyone else. As Gail, one of my restaurant coworkers put it, "you give and you give."

Someday, of course—and I will make no predictions as to exactly when—they are bound to tire of getting so little in return and to demand to be paid what they're worth. There'll be a lot of anger when that day comes, and strikes and disruption. But the sky will not fall, and we will all be better off for it in the end.

DISCUSSION QUESTIONS

1. Why might the poverty of low-wage workers be invisible to America's middle and upper classes?
2. Ehrenreich describes an American culture of "repressive management," at least in the world of low-wage work. If you have worked in low-wage jobs, has that been your experience?
3. Did it surprise you when Ehrenreich referred to the tax deduction she receives for the interest on her mortgage as a "housing subsidy"? Why or why not?

NOTES

1. Jared Bernstein, Chauna Brocht, and Maggie Spade-Aguilar, "How Much Is Enough? Basic Family Budgets for Working Families," Economic Policy Institute, Washington, D.C., 2000, p. 14.
2. "Companies Try Dipping Deeper into Labor Pool," *New York Times,* March 26, 2000.
3. "An Epitaph for a Rule That Just Won't Die," *New York Times,* July 30, 2000.
4. "Fact or Fallacy: Labor Shortage May Really Be Wage Stagnation," *Chicago Tribune,* July 2, 2000; "It's a Wage Shortage, Not a Labor Shortage," *Minneapolis Star Tribune,* March 25, 2000.
5. I thank John Schmidt at the Economic Policy Institute in Washington, D.C., for preparing the wage data for me.
6. Interview, July 18, 2000.
7. "Companies Try Dipping Deeper into Labor Pool," *New York Times,* March 26, 2000.
8. Personal communication, July 24, 2000.
9. "The Biggest Company Secret: Workers Challenge Employer Practices on Pay Confidentiality," *New York Times,* July 28, 2000.
10. Bob Ortega, *In Sam We Trust,* p. 356; "Former Wal-Mart Workers File Overtime Suit in Harrison County," *Charleston Gazette,* January 24, 1999.
11. See, for example, C. A. Shively, K. Laber-Laird, and R. F. Anton, "Behavior and Physiology of Social Stress and Depression in Female Cynomolgous Monkeys," *Biological Psychiatry* 41:8 (1997), pp. 871–82, and D. C. Blanchard et al., "Visible Burrow System as a Model of Chronic Social Stress: Behavioral and Neuroendocrine Correlates," *Psychoneuroendocrinology* 20:2 (1995), pp. 117–34.
12. See, for example, chapter 7, "Conformity," in David G. Myers, *Social Psychology* (McGraw-Hill, 1987).

13. *Fear of Falling: The Inner Life of the Middle Class* (Pantheon, 1989).
14. "The Invisible Poor," *New York Times Magazine,* March 19, 2000.
15. "Summer Work Is Out of Favor with the Young," *New York Times,* June 18, 2000.
16. The *National Journal* reports that the "good news" is that almost six million people have left the welfare rolls since 1996, while the "rest of the story" includes the problem that "these people sometimes don't have enough to eat" ("Welfare Reform, Act 2," June 24, 2000, pp. 1, 978–93).
17. "Minnesota's Welfare Reform Proves a Winner," *Time,* June 12, 2000.
18. Center for Law and Social Policy, "Update," Washington, D.C., June 2000.
19. "Study: More Go Hungry since Welfare Reform," *Boston Herald,* January 21, 2000; "Charity Can't Feed All while Welfare Reforms Implemented," *Houston Chronicle,* January 10, 2000; "Hunger Grows as Food Banks Try to Keep Pace," *Atlanta Journal and Constitution,* November 26, 1999.
20. "Rise in Homeless Families Strains San Diego Aid," *Los Angeles Times* January 24, 2000.
21. "Hunger Problems Said to Be Getting Worse," *Milwaukee Journal Sentinel,* December 15, 1999.
22. Deborah Leff, the president and CEO of the hunger-relief organization America's Second Harvest, quoted in the *National Journal,* op. cit.; "Hunger Persists in U.S. despite the Good Times," *Detroit News,* June 15, 2000.
23. "A National Survey of American Attitudes toward Low-Wage Workers and Welfare Reform," Jobs for the Future, Boston, May 24, 2000.

READING 17

This Hard-Earned Money Comes Stuffed in Their Genes

Dusty Horwitt

In every age and every nation, the rich and powerful employ new myths to preserve their privileged status. In the 17th and 18th centuries, European

Dusty Horwitt lives in Oakland, California. He has written for several publications including the *Washington Post Magazine, Legal Affairs Magazine,* and *New York Newsday.* This article is the hard-earned product of his labor, and is also due to the influence of his grandfather, father, mother, brother, two aunts, and an uncle, who are all published authors.

monarchs justified their rule through "the divine right of kings," perhaps most famously articulated by Bishop Jacques-Benigne Bossuet, a tutor to Louis XIV's son. "God establishes Kings as his ministers, and reigns through them over the people," Bossuet wrote in a document published posthumously in 1709. . . .

[Similarly,] many wealthy Americans and their political allies have fueled the popular myth that we earn all of our money through individual effort. After all, if our money is fully "hard-earned," the argument goes, it's unfair for the government to take it away—and especially unfair to provide it to the less affluent among us who didn't "earn" their way as we did.

But like the divine right of kings, there is more myth than truth in the phrase "hard-earned" money.

Exhibit A is *Forbes* magazine's list of the 400 wealthiest Americans, which tells the story of a massive redistribution of wealth based more on birth than on hard work.

Among the 100 wealthiest Americans on this year's list, *Forbes* reports that 46, or almost half, owe at least a chunk of their fortunes to inheritance. They include real estate mogul Donald Trump (net worth $2.5 billion), media baron Rupert Murdoch (net worth $7.2 billion) and five heirs to the Wal-Mart fortune Alice, Helen, Jim, John and Robson Walton who are worth $20.5 billion each.

While some people who inherit money work as hard and competently as some who haven't inherited piles of cash, inherited money is not the product of the heir's hard work. Neither is the wealth created by inherited investments.

And inherited money is only one form of unearned wealth. Other types include the businesses, jobs and even access to universities that millions of Americans inherit, at least in part.

Take the case of Fidelity Investments Chairman and CEO Edward C. Johnson III (net worth $4.9 billion) who is described by *Forbes* as "self-made." The magazine doesn't mention that Johnson III took over Fidelity from his father, Fidelity founder Edward C. Johnson II. *Forbes* does note, however, that "self-made" Viacom CEO Sumner Redstone (net worth $9.7 billion) got his start by taking charge of his father's drive-in theater business and that "self-made" financier Charles Bartlett Johnson (net worth $2 billion) and his brother got started by seizing the reins of their father's mutual fund business.

The nation's leading NASCAR dad, Bill France Jr. (net worth $1.2 billion, according to an article in [the *Washington Post*] in 2001), chairman of NASCAR's board of directors, is the son of Bill France Sr., NASCAR's founder. France Jr. has also appointed to NASCAR's board his brother Jim (net worth $1.2 billion), son Brian and daughter Lesa France Kennedy.

The Bush administration has found places for several well-connected offspring including Vice President Cheney's daughter Elizabeth, who until recently was a deputy assistant secretary of state; Supreme Court Justice Antonin Scalia's son Eugene, who formerly served as solicitor of the Labor Department; and Secretary of State Colin Powell's son, Michael, the chairman of the Federal Communications Commission.

Then there are the colleges and universities that give special preferences in the admissions process to children of alumni. Many of the top schools, including Harvard, Princeton, Stanford and the University of Pennsylvania, admit so-called legacies at a rate two to four times that of their overall applicant pool, the *Wall Street Journal* reported [in 2003].

Adam Bellow, author of the recent book *In Praise of Nepotism: A Natural History,* freely acknowledges that he got his publishing job through the connections of his famous father, novelist Saul Bellow. The younger Bellow notes that nepotism benefits Americans of every class, profession and political persuasion—from middle-income firefighters to fantastically wealthy movies stars such as Gwyneth Paltrow to presidential candidates such as Al Gore. (Of course there's a big difference in wealth between landing a job at the fire station and one as a Hollywood star.) As with inherited money, those who receive family help landing a job or a seat at an elite college may be just as hardworking and talented as those who don't. But getting the position in the first place is undeniably a step toward success that is not fully earned.

So what about people like Bill Gates (net worth $46 billion) or Warren Buffett (net worth $36 billion), who seem to have succeeded without significant family help or inheritance? Didn't they earn all of their money? Not according to Buffett.

As the billionaire investor wrote in [the *Washington Post* in 2003], he too, owes much of his wealth to forces outside his control. Buffet explained that he was financially "luckier" than his receptionist of relatively modest means because "I came wired at birth with a talent for capital allocation—a valuable ability to have had in this country during the past half-century. Credit America with most of this value, not me. If the receptionist and I had both been born in, say, Bangladesh, the story would have been far different. There, the market value of our respective talents would not have varied greatly." The same could be said about Bill Gates's lucky mix of talent and timing in the computer world.

Perhaps more obvious is the role of such luck in sports. Michael Jordan undoubtedly worked hard. But he owes much of his wealth to his largely unearned 6-foot-6-inch height and world-class leaping ability (this skill can be modestly improved through effort), not to mention his advertising-friendly good looks and the fact that he came of age at a time of inflated sports salaries. If you don't think timing influences salary, just ask home-run king Hank Aaron who never earned more than $240,000 a season, the same amount that current star, Alex Rodriguez, earns in two games.

Even our hard work itself is not always the result of individual effort. Take the case of Louisiana's boy wonder, Bobby Jindal. Son of Indian immigrants. Rhodes Scholar. Louisiana's secretary for Health and Hospitals at age 24 and near-miss candidate for governor at age 32. Jindal seems like the quintessential Horatio Alger. But like most, if not all, "self-made" individuals, a look beneath the surface reveals a more complex story.

"My dad is from one of those families where if you brought home a grade—a 90—he'd always ask what happened to the other 10 points," [the *Washington Post*] quoted Jindal as saying. Growing up in a family like that, it's fair to say that Jindal's success was not only a product of his hard work or even of his own choice. His parents pushed him to succeed, just as millions of caring parents, including my own, encouraged or required success for their own children.

Would things have turned out less rosy for Jindal or me if we had been born to less worthy parents? Probably. For example, 47 percent of inmates in state prisons have a parent or other close relative who has also been incarcerated, according to the Bureau of Justice Statistics, as reported in the *New York Times*. In addition, half of all juveniles in custody have a father, mother or other close relative who has been in jail or prison. Maybe I'm going out on a limb, but I'm guessing that if these juveniles brought home a grade of 90, their parents didn't ask about the other 10 points.

When you add up the overwhelming influence of inheritance, family connections, God-given talents, timing, government investments, the benefit or burden of being born to a particular set of parents (or maybe just one parent), as well as all the other twists and turns we experience, it's clear that only a portion of our money is hard-earned and probably not

the majority of it. After all, most of us work hard but only 10 percent of Americans control 70 percent of our wealth, while more than 43 million Americans lack something as basic as health insurance. Differences in individual effort cannot explain these disparities. The notion of "hard-earned money" is simplistic at best. What we are given is at least as important to our success as what we earn.

DISCUSSION QUESTIONS

1. Is the belief that we earn all our money by our own effort better described as a myth or an ideology?

2. Do you agree that Warren Buffett and Bill Gates owe their wealth to forces outside their control? Wouldn't they have succeeded anywhere, for example, in Bangladesh?

3. Thinking about the jobs you have held, what portion of your earnings would you attribute to your own "hard-earned effort" versus your connections, timing, government investments, God-given talents, and parental efforts?

WHAT IS SEXUAL ORIENTATION?

The Hazards of Naming Sexual Attraction

Michael R. Kauth

Naming *sexual attraction* entails some risk. First, finding a definition of *sexual attraction* that is valid across cultures is difficult, especially if that definition infers some internal experience. Labeling the

Michael R. Kauth is an independent sexology scholar and the director for education of the South Central Mental Illness Research, Education and Clinical Center, New Orleans Veterans Affairs Medical Center. He is also a clinical assistant professor in the Department of Psychiatry, Tulane University School of Medicine, and in the Louisiana State University School of Medicine.

sexual attraction of someone who is dead or outside our present culture is loaded with risk, as well as possibly arrogant and elitist. Writers who label the sexual attraction of others run the risk of falsely creating eroticism where none existed. Defining *sexual attraction* also sets boundaries that may exclude some erotic experience and present an artificial view of sexual life. On the other hand, studying only sexual behavior tells us what people do but not what they feel sexually, not how they experience their sexual lives, and not how sexual attraction differs from behavior.

Second, language is culture-bound and value-laden. Words have a rich cultural heritage with complex social and political meanings that are transferred, deliberately or inadvertently, to the phenomenon in question. Words are *not* value-free, and the words we choose matter. . . . People today who experience same-sex erotic attraction prefer to label themselves "gay" or "lesbian" rather than "homosexual." The term "homosexual" was adopted in the late 19th century by psychiatrists and medical practitioners to identify a type of psychopathology and, consequently, this term implies sickness, aberrance, and immaturity. Not surprisingly, people for whom this term was applied find it objectionable. The term "gay" has an altogether different history and different meanings, without the taint of psychopathology. Older definitions of "gay" mean happy or joyful, which challenges the image of disease conjured up by the term "homosexual." The term "gay" is also more encompassing. Whereas, "homosexual" refers to a kind of sexual behavior, "gay" implies more pervasive characteristics or a lifestyle.

Because words and ideas have a historical and cultural context, applying terms outside of their context wrongly creates the impression that there is a direct linkage to the past and that a contemporary sense of the idea existed in the past, when in fact it did not. In his book *Christianity, Social Tolerance and Homosexuality,* historian John Boswell (1980) incorrectly used the phrase "gay people" when referring to people in ancient Rome and in the Middle Ages who had same-sex erotic interests. This contemporary verbiage carries with it many assumptions about sexuality, identity, and individuality that did not exist and [had] not coalesced before the late 19th and early 20th centuries. Although the word "gay" predates "homosexual" by several hundred years (Boswell, 1980), until relatively recently it was not associated with sexual attraction. Therefore, Roman male citizens could not be "gay" or "homosexual," although many Roman men had sex with men or boys; sexual attraction and behavior were simply not defined in this way. Sexuality for Roman men was related to their sociopolitical status, not the sex of their partners. As long as they performed the active sexual role, appropriate sexual partners could be women, boys, or men who played the passive role (Cantarella, 1992). For contemporary Western men, however, the sex of one's partners is extremely important and self-defining. . . .

Not only is it a problem to apply contemporary words and ideas to the past, the reverse is also true; unearthing ancient words and concepts and fully grasping their meaning in their original context is a formidable obstacle to modern writers. Beliefs of other cultures often seem strange and irrational, and contemporary values and ideas intrude on their interpretation. . . .

A third caution in naming sexual attraction is related to *who* does the naming. Words and ideas reflect the values and will of the powerful social groups who wield them and alter the way people think about a phenomenon. Words about sexuality such as *homosexual, perversion, promiscuity,* and *contrary to nature* have restricted, regulated, marginalized, and oppressed a particular group of people who were not able to defend themselves (Foucault, 1978/1990). The term "homosexual" still carries many negative associations from the medicopsychiatric practitioners who adopted and popularized the concept during the late 19th and early 20th centuries. The obverse term "heterosexual," meant *normal sexuality* (Freud, 1905/1953, 1920/1953). The adoption of this binary concept of sexual orientation dramatically changed social reality and continues to do so. What is more, physicians' success in authoritatively identifying perverse sexuality established the central and powerful social role of the profession as gatekeeper of psychopathology and regulator of normal sexuality.

Powerful groups other than psychoanalysts and physicians have improved their social position and defined an issue by naming sexual phenomena. Spanish missionaries and conquistadors during the 16th and 17th centuries, for example, saw enormous advantage in naming the sexual behavior of the non-Europeans they encountered. By declaring the indigenous people of the Caribbean and Central and South America to be "sodomites," they redefined social reality (Bleys, 1995). In the Spanish imperialist version of reality, native Indians were barbarian sinners who deserved slavery, rape, wholesale slaughter, the destruction of their culture, and most importantly, the theft of their gold and natural resources. The strength and superior firepower of the Spanish conquistadors and the moral authority of the Catholic missionaries allowed them to reinterpret the meaning of same-sex erotic activities and other sexual behaviors among native Indians and to profit nicely from it. Invading armies, colonists, despots, and other totalitarian regimes gain a great deal by reinterpreting and renaming sexual experience. By approving certain sexual behaviors and labeling other behaviors as immoral, criminal, and intolerable, totalitarian regimes impose control on the sexuality of its citizens, regulate social discourse on sexuality, and increase police power. In 1930s Germany, some of the first and most "effective" acts by Adolf Hitler and his National Socialist Party were the dismissal of women from public office, public encouragement of reproductive (hetero)sexual behavior between Caucasians who were not of Jewish descent, condemnation of non-reproductive sexual activities including masturbation and same-sex erotic behavior, and criminalization of "homosexuals" through a strengthening of Paragraph 175 in 1935. Such actions created the appearance of nationalism, morality, support of (Aryan) marriage and family, and a determined fight against "evil." The Aryan German people were encouraged by the National Socialist Party to think of "homosexuals," Jews, gypsies, and other "undesirable" citizens as subhuman or as diseased persons who had infected the national body and needed to be excised. Naming sexual behavior and people in the manner of the German Nazis made it much easier for ordinary citizens to believe that "homosexuals," Jews, gypsies, and foreigners *should* be deprived of their civil rights, stripped of property, shipped to internment camps, exploited as slave labor, and even murdered. Indeed, naming sexual behavior has significant advantages for those who do the naming.

On a lesser extreme but similarly significant level, modern political parties, elected public officials and political candidates, religious leaders, religious fundamentalists, social conservatives, gay rights activists, feminists, civil rights activists, social liberals, scientists, and social constructionists each gain social power and legitimacy by successfully influencing the naming of sexual behavior and people. At present, these groups are in a battle to determine what particular names and ideas are heard and will be adopted by society. Will people who are attracted to members of the same-sex be viewed by society as *sinners, perverts, criminals,* or as *an oppressed minority?* Will heterosexuality be viewed as a superior social position and exemplary model for society, or will it be seen as only one of many possible ways to structure society? Which (group's) viewpoint will dominate? For the past 20 years, social constructionism has largely dominated the field of sexuality, which was dominated previously by medical science. Gay activists, feminists, gender theorists, sociologists, and university faculty members with a social constructionist perspective have, for better or worse, directed intellectual discourse on sexuality in recent years. As a result, constructionists have benefited directly through journal and book publications, public acceptance of their ideas, public recognition, faculty appointments, and a strong student following. In no small way, the outcome of naming contemporary sexual behavior has real consequences for each group involved in this struggle—including social constructionists—and for all of us.

Finally, social groups also influence social reality by not *correctly* naming a phenomenon and by deliberately *mis*naming it. This may seem to be a subtle or redundant point, but it is not. For many years, *revisionist* historians, scholars, and advocates of popular conventional culture refused to acknowledge the same-sex erotic experiences of prominent historical figures and whole cultures or refashioned those experiences to reflect contemporary "heterosexual" ideals. Before the middle part of the 20th century, American and European anthropologists largely refused to mention the existence of same-sex erotic activities in non-Western cultures (Blackwood, 1993). For those anthropologists who even recognized same-sex erotic behavior, such behavior often escaped objective description and analysis out of embarrassment, disgust, ignorance, fear of promoting such behavior, and fear of personal moral condemnation and academic censure. Anthropologists themselves were not solely responsible for failing to mention same-sex eroticism; pressure from colleagues, academicians, and publishers had a powerful influence on the omission or revision of observations by scholars. The social context of the first half of the 20th century did not permit an open discussion about same-sex eroticism even within academic circles; same-sex erotic behaviors were viewed as perverted, immoral, and contagious. The moralistic Cambridge dean in E. M. Forster's 1913 semiautobiographical novel *Maurice* sharply illustrates this view when he advises a student who translates a portion of Latin text to "omit" a reference to same-sex eroticism, "the unspeakable vice of the Greeks" (1971, p. 51).[1]

One way that historical and cultural references to same-sex erotic attraction have been ignored, omitted, and mislabeled by scholars is by setting impossibly high standards for concluding its existence (Boswell, 1990; Norton, 1997). No such standards are required to conclude other-sex (male-female) eroticism or sexual activity. Scholars readily and eagerly infer and speculate about other-sex erotic attraction and sexual behavior from slim evidence and casual encounters. Yet, in the absence of "hard" proof (and even at times in its obvious presence) of genital-genital contact or orgasm, same-sex eroticism cannot be determined with absolute confidence and, therefore, is not even mentioned. Without evidence of an ejaculating penis or an orgasming vagina, many scholars have claimed that intimate affections, extraordinary violations of social custom, and long-term primary relationships between same-sex partners in the past and in other cultures were *not* sexual, *not* erotic, and merely close friendships. I am not arguing that same-sex eroticism, (perhaps) a statistically less common event than other-sex eroticism, should be read into every same-sex intimate pairing. I do argue, however, that evidence of same-sex erotic attraction and behavior has been ignored because it fails to meet a narrow definition of *sexuality as genitally focused*. The very idea that genital contact is required as evidence of sexual behavior and that sexual behavior, so de-

fined, is required to identify a passionate, romantic relationship is a contemporary Western fiction. In other cultures, and even in our own, genital contact or orgasm need not be present in erotic relationships, which are often characterized by intimate physical contact, preference, altruism, tenderness, emotional support, affection, devotion, fidelity, and jealousy. . . .

While eroticism and sexuality are defined differently by other cultures, these phenomena certainly exist and infuse many relationships. What is more, this scholarly bias against identifying *any* same-sex erotic attraction in pre-industrial non-Western cultures strikes me as parallel to what pro-gay activists do when they see "gay" sexuality in every same-sex encounter or reference.

The outcome of this bias against naming same-sex eroticism in pre-industrial non-Western cultures is a sanitized, de-(homo)sexualized interpretation of history. In such a context, the erotic lives of individuals and cultures in the past are rewritten to conform to contemporary beliefs and ideals. A good example of revisionist biography can be found in Michelangelo the Younger's 1623 collection of his great-uncle's poems. Prior to publication, the great-nephew changed all masculine pronouns in his great uncle's poems to feminine pronouns, creating the false impression that Michelangelo loved women rather than men (Norton, 1997). The deception went undiscovered for almost 250 years. However, in 1863 historian John Addington Symonds found a note written in the margins of the poems by Michelangelo's great-nephew that stated that the poems should not be published in their original form because they expressed *"amor . . . virile."*

Another outrageous example of the heterosexualization of historical figures is the fabrication of Sappho's marriage to Cercylas (Gettone, 1990). What is more, Ovid portrayed Sappho as the lover of the sailor Phaon, a completely fictional character. This fiction of Sappho's romantic relationships with men was repeated and reinforced for centuries. In another infamous case, Vasco da Lucena resexed the eunuch Bagoas, Alexander's male favorite, as a beautiful young woman in his medieval French translation of ancient Roman Quintus Curtius Rufus's *History of Alexander the Great* (Norton, 1997). During that period in France, depicting a great man like Alexander—a model for all men—in an erotic relationship with another man would have been unthinkable; apparently, da Lucena thought that a lie was more acceptable than the truth.

In recent examples of revisionist history, Queen Christina of Sweden, played by woman-loving Greta Garbo, was heterosexualized in the popular 1933 Hollywood film of the same name (Russo, 1981). In the film, despite a fictionalized love affair with the Spanish ambassador, Queen Christina refuses to marry and abdicates her throne. In reality, however, she refused to marry *any* man and was forced to abdicate. Records suggest that Christina loved the countess Ebba Sparre. Similarly, in the 1962 film *Lawrence of Arabia,* Lawrence, played by Peter O'Toole, withstands a fictionalized night of torture at the hands of the evil Turkish bey (Jose Ferrer), although Lawrence himself implied that his experience with the Turkish ruler was sexual and pleasurable rather than abusive (Russo, 1981). The film makes no mention of Lawrence's sexual attraction to or erotic relationships with men. As more recent examples of contemporary heterosexualization, movie studios have often staged public "dates" with beautiful women for their male stars when speculation arose about their homosexuality. . . .

In these few examples, same-sex eroticism is denied and redefined as other-sex eroticism. By not acknowledging and not naming same-sex eroticism, scholars and social groups cover over evidence of same-sex erotic behavior. By renaming same-sex eroticism as other-sex eroticism, scholars and social groups fabricate history, restrict public discussion about same-sex eroticism and drive it underground, and make the public promotion of conventional male-female sexuality a political agenda. . . .

Too often, scientists have failed to consider the implications of naming or not naming erotic experience. The interpretation and presentation of sexuality has political consequences for informants, observers, and historians and should be undertaken with great caution. . . .

DISCUSSION QUESTIONS

1. In your mind, what are the dangers involved in giving a name to sexual attraction?
2. What groups would you identify as currently in control of the sexual attraction–naming process? How do you judge their relative influence?

NOTE

1. Forster wrote *Maurice* in 1913 but left the manuscript unpublished in his desk drawer, fearing negative public reaction to the novel's homoerotic content. *Maurice* was published many years later, posthumously.

REFERENCES

Blackwood, E. (1993). Breaking the mirror: The construction of lesbianism and the anthropological discourse on homosexuality. In L. D. Garnets & D. C. Kimmel (Eds.), *Psychological perspectives on lesbian and gay male experiences* (pp. 297–315). New York: Columbia University Press.

Bleys, R. C. (1995). *The geography of perversion: Male-to-male sexual behaviour outside of the West and the ethnographic imagination, 1750–1918.* New York: New York University Press.

Boswell, J. (1980). *Christianity, social tolerance, and homosexuality: Gay people in Western Europe from the beginning of the Christian era to the fourteenth century.* Chicago: University of Chicago Press.

Cantarella, E. (1992). *Bisexuality in the ancient world.* (C. O'Cuilleanain, Trans.). New Haven and London: Yale University Press. (Original work published 1988).

Forster, E. M. (1971). *Maurice.* New York: Norton.

Foucault, M. (1990). *The history of sexuality. Vol. I: An introduction.* (R. Hurley, Trans.). New York: Vintage Books. (Original work published 1978).

Freud, S. (1953). Leonardo da Vinci and a memory of his childhood. In J. Strachey (Ed.), *The standard edition of the complete psychological works of Sigmund Freud* (Vol. II; pp. 59–138). London: Hogarth Press. (Original work published 1910).

Gettone, E. (1990). Sappho. In W. R. Dynes (Ed.), *Encyclopedia of homosexuality.* Chicago: St. James Press.

Norton, R. (1997). *The myth of the modern homosexual: Queer history and the search for cultural unity.* London: Cassell.

Russo, V. (1981). *The celluloid closet: Homosexuality in the movies.* (Rev. ed.). New York: Harper & Row.

Living Invisibly

For me, coming out is a Sisyphean task. Because of my invisible differences, I constantly have to reveal different parts of my identity. It's not an easy task, either. When I come out as a lesbian/queer woman, people are often surprised because I don't "look" queer. I can count on one hand the number of times I have been recognized by a stranger as part of the LGBT "family." Some people are also surprised to learn that I'm half Taiwanese. I am also half-white, and often assumed to be white, making my race another invisible identity. Because of this, there have been times when people have made racist jokes— either about Asians or other groups—because they thought I was white, and thus thought that these were "acceptable" jokes to tell in my presence.

Invisible identities work differently from other differences. I am lucky not to be harassed on the street because of my race, and since I don't appear queer to your average passerby, I don't usually get harassed for that. I benefit from the privilege of passing as a straight and white, but most days I wish that I could give up that privilege. It is extremely difficult to live your life where some of the most important things about you are hidden. For example, I never know when it is appropriate to come out as queer in class, and almost feel guilty if I never do, even though it may not always be necessary or appropriate. Because I am invisible, I bear the burden of disclosure. When someone assumes that I'm heterosexual, I have to correct her or him (my mother still doesn't believe that I'm queer). When someone assumes that I'm white, I do the same. Regardless, I come out all the time to new people in my life, and each time I do, I hope that they will be able to handle the information with care and respect.

Most people respond well when I come out to them, and I can breathe another sigh of relief when my peers accept me. College, especially, has been a (mostly) safe space for me to be out and proud about my race and sexuality. Living with my multiple invisible identities has taught me to be more assertive in all areas of my life, and I have learned to take risks. I know quite well how privilege works, and how that privilege can be taken away in an instant. I am also proud of all of my identities. The difficulty of coming out is well worth the satisfaction and pride I have of living my life the way that I have always wanted to.

Tara S. Ellison

Is Homosexual a Noun?

Paul R. Abramson

Steven D. Pinkerton

The question that interests us is not whether biology or the environment is the greater contributor to sexual orientation, but how these influences interact in different people to produce the variability in sexual object "choice" evident throughout history, both within and across cultures. The cross-cultural study of sexuality clearly demonstrates that homosexuality is not a unitary phenomenon. . . .

There are at least four distinct conceptualizations to consider: existentialism (homosexuality as a state of being), behaviorism (homosexual acts), self-identification (sexual identity), and sexual orientation (desire, fantasy, etc., as distinct from overt behavior). The question of the relationship among these various aspects is critical to understanding just what it is that should be explained by a biological theory of homosexuality.

To begin with, we need to decide whether *homosexual* is a concrete entity (noun), or merely a descriptor (adjective).[1] In other words, is homosexuality simply a behavior in which certain people occasionally (or consistently) engage, or does it constitute a fundamental characteristic of the self— that of *being* a homosexual? Would we even bother to recognize (or heatedly argue about) homosexuality

Paul R. Abramson is a professor of psychology at the University of California, Los Angeles. Steven D. Pinkerton is a professor of psychiatry and behavioral medicine at the Medical College of Wisconsin.

if society did not pathologize it? In a different context, might it be merely curious, or perhaps even trivially commonplace? And if so, why do we consider it to be a unifying theme of identity? Imagine, that society had instead decided to classify people by the beer that they drink. Such a classification scheme would obviously be trivial because the resulting identities would be based upon an inessential characteristic that reveals little of substance.[2] Similarly, perhaps homosexuality is a biological nonentity that arises as a descriptor merely because society has maligned nonprocreative sex too severely. That is, by making *homosexual behavior* taboo, society may have created *homosexuality* as a cultural entity.

Evidence that this is so may be found in the recent historical record. In the Middle Ages, homosexual acts were condemned by Christians and Jews alike as an "abomination" and a "sin against nature,"[3] yet the performance of a homosexual act did not, in and of itself, brand the sinner as a distinct category of being. Having sex with a same-sex partner no more made one a "homosexual" than coveting a neighbor's wife made one a "coveter."[4] However, with the rise of science, and the psychiatric profession in particular, in the late eighteenth and early nineteenth centuries, homosexual behaviors became pathologized, and those who practiced them became deviants, degenerates, "inverts,"—in other words, "homosexuals."[5] As John De Cecco suggests:

> It was nineteenth-century psychiatry that made homosexual behavior a mental "condition"—either lovesick or gender-sick or both—that enveloped the personality and became its core. The psychiatric name of this mythical state has endlessly changed as new variations arrived at the doctors' consulting room doors, from the original pederasty, contrary sexual feeling, psychic hermaphroditism, sexual inversion, and the lovely Italian *l'amore invertito,* to the less blatant but still pernicious sexual orientation disturbance and egodystonic homosexuality.[6]

Indeed, it was not until 1869 that the German term *homosexualität* was coined for this "condition."[7] In that year, Karl Maria Kertbenny described a "homosexual urge" that "creates in advance a direct horror of the opposite sex, and the victim of this passion finds it impossible to suppress the feeling which individuals of his own sex exercise upon him."[8] Even then, however, homosexuality was typically characterized as predominantly an inversion of gender (masculinity/femininity) rather than of sexual orientation or behavior. This heightened interest in what had hitherto been a stigmatized and often criminalized behavior, but not a defining characteristic of an individual, dovetailed nicely (and certainly not coincidentally) with the nascent social purity movement, which sought to ban prostitution as a means of shoring up the family. In a review of this historical period, John Marshall observes, "the emphasis throughout (and the reason for the link between homosexuality and prostitution) is upon the regulation of male lust and the channeling of sexuality into an institutionalized pattern of 'normal' heterosexual monogamy."[9] The resultant scientific and social scrutiny to which homosexual behaviors and those who practiced them were subjected, in turn, may very well have created the modern homosexual.

All of this illustrates just how complex the issues surrounding homosexuality and sexual orientation really are. There are obviously wide variations in sexual expression, both between individuals and between cultures. Even within an individual there may be discordance between *preference,* which tends to exist as an enduring facet of one's personality (though not always), and *behavior,* which is often situationally determined. Many macho American boys, who grow into macho American men, engage in clandestine homosexual activities as adolescents. And many other men and women suddenly "discover" their "true" homosexual proclivities after years of being happily and heterosexually married:

> Confessions of a false lesbian: I was married to a man when I first came out, and when I fell in love with a woman I searched my past hard and long for evidence that I had "really" "always" been a lesbian. Much more eager to prove to myself that I was a lesbian than to find evidence that I wasn't, I just couldn't say to myself, "I choose to be a lesbian." I was afraid I'd have to be straight unless I could prove I wasn't.[10]

Furthermore, the manner in which people express their sexuality is not necessarily discrete, but is instead embedded in a larger network of cultural meanings. American men who want to try something different rarely engage in same-sex relations, preferring instead to widen their heterosexual repertoires. In America, homosexual diversions are deemed inconsistent with both machismo and, in some interpretations, maleness itself.

. . . The Sambia warriors of Papua New Guinea provide an especially striking example of the transience of "homosexuality."[11] Survival in the forbidding landscape of the New Guinea highlands necessitates that Sambia men be as strong and courageous as possible. To the Sambia, the essence of male masculinity and strength (*jerungdu*) is semen; the more semen, the more macho the man. However, because the "semen organ" is initially "solid and dry" (i.e., incapable of ejaculation), semen is thought to be absent in boys. To masculinize the boys requires some means of infusing them with semen. The Sambia solution is for young "bachelors" to act as donors, providing semen to the preadolescent boys through fellatio. In time, by swallowing adult semen, the boys become men.[12] They can then act as donors themselves, becoming fellatees rather than fellators. Eventually, each Sambia youth finds a wife and begins raising a family (following marriage is a period of bisexual behavior that ends with the arrival of the couple's first child—all homosexual activities cease when a man becomes a father). Thus, *all* boys—who ultimately become husbands, fathers, and fierce warriors—go through a period of exclusive homosexual behavior as a necessary step on the road to manhood.

In stark contrast to the American mythology, the Sambia believe that adolescent homosexuality, and the ingestion of older men's semen, is essential to masculine development and toughness. Both boys (receptive) and men (insertive) participate in these homosexual activities, yet seldom does either have any trouble shifting to his eventual heterosexual role. The homosexual behavior of adolescence and bachelorhood is rarely continued into "adulthood" (i.e., after a man's first child is born). When it is, it typically takes the form of bisexuality, in that the sexual alliances with boys supplement heterosexual contacts with a wife and a full family life. Rarely does a man profess an exclusive preference for boys, for to do so is to invite the scorn of the entire community, and to admit weakness and a lack of *jerungdu,* making one a "rubbish man."[13]

Age-structured homosexuality also challenges a cherished American myth, that of the exclusive homosexual identity. According to this myth, a person either is or isn't a homosexual, and whatever one is, he or she is for life. In America, the alleged incongruence between having a heterosexual identity and participating in homosexual behaviors leads to the further assumption that *any* homosexual activity is, ipso facto, evidence of a homosexual identity. To Americans, it would appear, "you are *who* you do." . . .

The question is, which of the many "homosexualities" are biologists trying to explain? It clearly isn't the situational homosexuality of the prisoner serving a life sentence. It might not even be the life-long homosexuality of the Freudian prototype, unable to disentangle himself from his mother's apron strings. In fact, the targets of biological explanations of sexual orientation—and especially homosexuality—are seldom specified. This uncertainty in the phenomenon being described, it seems to us, casts aspersions on the whole enterprise.

DISCUSSION QUESTIONS

1. What would the authors say were the key factors that turned homosexuality from an adjective to a noun, at least in Western society?
2. Do you envision the possibility of homosexuality becoming an adjective again? Why or why not?

NOTES

1. See also De Cecco (1990), Richardson (1984), and Weinberg (1978).
2. For whatever it's worth, we prefer *Samuel Adam's Boston Lager* (S.P.) and *Mackeson's Stout* (P.A.).

3. The basis of the Judeo-Christian condemnation of (male) homosexual behaviors is God's commandment to Moses, "thou shalt not lie with mankind, as with womankind: It is abomination" (Leviticus 18:22).
4. Boswell (1980).
5. See Foucault (1990); Weeks (1977).
6. De Cecco (1990).
7. Halperin (1989); Herzer (1985).
8. Quoted in Bullough (1967), p. 637.
9. Marshall (1981), p. 139.
10. Whisman (1993), p. 54.
11. Herdt (1981, 1987).
12. The Sambia belief that masculinity can be passed from man to boy through the former's semen bears certain similarities to the Greek pederastic tradition in which sex was "supposed to transmit manly virtues of mind and body from nobleman to young lover" (Karlen, 1980, p. 79).
13. Stoller and Herdt (1985) describe one instance of a "rubbish man." See also Herdt (1987).

REFERENCES

Boswell, J. (1980). *Christianity, Social Tolerance, and Homosexuality.* Chicago: University of Chicago Press.

Bullough, V. L. (1967). *Sexual Variance in Society and History.* New York: Wiley.

De Cecco, J. P. (1990). Confusing the actor with the act: Muddled notions about homosexuality. *Archives of Sexual Behavior, 19,* 409–412.

Foucault, M. (1990). *The History of Sexuality.* New York: Vintage.

Halperin, D. M. (1989). *One Hundred Years of Homosexuality and Other Essays on Greek Love.* New York: Routledge.

Herdt, G. H. (1981). *Guardians of the Flute.* New York: McGraw-Hill.

Herdt, G. H. (1987). *The Sambia: Ritual and Gender in New Guinea.* New York: Holt, Rinehart & Winston.

Herzer, M. (1985). Kertbeny and the nameless love. *Journal of Homosexuality, 12,* 1–26.

Karlen, A. (1980). Homosexuality in history. In J. Marmor (ed.), *Homosexual Behavior: A Modern Reappraisal.* New York: Basic Books.

Marshall, J. (1981). Pansies, perverts and macho men: Changing conceptions of homosexuality. In K. Plummer (ed.), *The Making of the Modern Homosexual.* Totowa, NJ: Barnes & Noble.

Richardson, D. (1984). The dilemma of essentiality in homosexual theory. *Journal of Homosexuality, 9,* 79–90.

Stoller, R. J. & Herdt, G. H. (1985). Theories of origins of male homosexuality. *Archives of General Psychiatry, 42,* 399–404.

Weeks, J. (1977). *Coming Out: Homosexual Politics in Britain from the Nineteenth Century to the Present.* London: Quartet Books.

Weinberg, T. S. (1978). On "doing" and "being" gay: Sexual behavior and homosexual male self-identity. *Journal of Homosexuality, 4,* 143–156.

Whisman, V. (1993). Identity crisis: Who is a lesbian anyway? In A. Stein (ed.), *Sisters, Sexperts, Queers.* New York: Penguin.

READING 20

The End of Gay

(AND THE DEATH OF HETEROSEXUALITY)

Bert Archer

Gay ended for me on a late afternoon in March of 1991 in a men's residence in a small Catholic college in Toronto. It was an inauspicious ending to something that had begun so nobly the century before, that had earned its stripes so bravely on that June New York night in 1969 in front of a little tavern on Christopher Street called Stonewall, and not only survived but flourished through a decade of a plague that any reasonable Bible-literalist could only assume was heaven-sent. Who would have guessed it could be snuffed so easily by some big Italian guy named Vince.

The common room was populated on that day, as it usually was, almost entirely by suburban men in their first and second undergraduate years, sitting around in front of the television flipping through the channels and newspapers, casually meandering in and out of conversations, like the one that was going on around one of the tables about Madonna's "Justify My Love" video, which was get-

Bert Archer is a columnist and reviewer who has written for nerve.com, *Entertainment Weekly, The Bloomsbury Review, POZ, The New York Blade,* and the *Washington Blade.* He is an editor at *eye Weekly.*

ting a lot of play on talk shows and in the news. MTV had refused to run it, and *Entertainment Tonight, Saturday Night Live,* CNN's *Showbiz Today, The Howard Stern Show* and *Nightline* all decided to air it and discuss it and make sure everyone was talking about it.[1] The video was filled with gender-blending images of men kissing women kissing women humping men licking other men, against the backdrop of some breathily erotic throb-pop music. . . .

Madonna was at the height of her celebrity and she had chosen to make a big fat same-sex statement. I remember thinking it was all sorta sexy, the attention and mostly tacit approbation a sign, for sure, of the gaying of the Western Madonna-loving world. I even continued thinking that for a little while after Vince, a first-generation Calabrese-Canadian friend of mine, said, "Y'know, I could see myself doin' a guy. I mean, I'm not a fag or nuthin', but y'know, if I was totally horned up, sure." There were general nods and murmurs from two others (also Italo-Canadesi) around the table, and shocked and guarded silence from the fourth. When I realised it wasn't some sort of entrapment ploy to flush me out (a constant concern of mine at the time), my first thought was, "Whoa, Vince is like this total closet case. Cool." . . .

I was a bit of an outsider in a lot of those common room and dining hall discussions. By this time I'd been sexually and more or less romantically involved with a guy in residence, Mark, for about four years. We'd met in first year, had separate rooms on the same floor of the same residence, and we'd known each other about six months by the time we took a long walk, I think drunken, late one night and he told me that he might not be entirely heterosexual, and wondered about me.

I'd wondered about me too. For the few years leading up to college, and the first months in it, I'd been pretty excited about the whole boy thing. And like many others, I hadn't ever bothered to think of myself as gay because of it. Less, I think, out of any internal homophobia than out of a sense that gays were essentially girls in boys' clothing, readily identifiable creatures that I didn't feel my own fascina-

tion with Jon Griffin's chest in grade eight or Bill Dawson's stomach in grade eleven had much at all to do with. Round about age twelve or thirteen, I started figuring girls' tits were pretty cool, and I had the good fortune to have access to a couple of nice ones, belonging to a sixteen-year-old named Shelley. A couple of years later, in grade eleven and twelve, I had a girlfriend. Pretty in a luscious sort of way, but frustratingly intransigent on the whole sex thing. A familiar story—she was about a year younger, liked the idea of being coyly sexual, but wasn't sure about actually having sex. Not as sure as I was, anyway. Front seats, back seats, ocean-front piers and waterbeds all resulted in bits of exposed flesh, a finger here, a tongue there, tussle, try, tickle, poke, pout, give up, go home.

It was only later, once I'd started something up with Mark, that I looked back and figured that they were anything other than standard, frustrating, exciting, confusing teenage relationships. . . .

By the time of the Vince Incident . . . I was . . . convinced I was gay, though maybe not a fag: I had a boyfriend whom I found sexually interesting and with whom I was thoroughly in love, and had pretty much eliminated women from both my social scene and my sexual prospects. The process had been slow, and since Mark and I had the courage to go to a gay bar precisely once, it had all been pretty petri dish, too.

So I hadn't reached the Doc Martens and slogan T-shirt stage yet (that'd come later), and I did, when I cared to think back, remember more early crushes on girls. But as time went on, I was more and more sure they had been sisterly sorts of things, social attractions to something safe and away from what must have been my more disturbing feelings for boys. Things seemed, in my twenty-second year, pretty much settled, my impression being that girls who had sex with girls and guys who had sex with guys were gay. The ones who did and didn't think they were, were closet cases. Simple. Satisfying.

Then what was up with Vince? I'd never encountered this sort of thing before, never had any of that adolescent sex with otherwise straight boys that might have immunised me against the shock of what Vince said. Sure, I'd heard all about the pubescent sex-play that went on, but I'd obviously been in the wrong scout troop. And I guess I always figured that all the participants, whatever their public identification, were really gay. But as I thought more about it in the days and weeks after the Vince Incident, it became clear that he, for one, wasn't gay. At least not by my working definition. He'd clearly rather have sex with women. But he seemed to have a notion of a sort of interzone I couldn't quite get my head around. It bothered me. . . .

My first reaction, to assume that Vince was gay, was a result of my belief in the binary nature of sexuality. Though there had been times when bisexuality was considered a viable third option, too many of those who ended up gay had gone through a self-professed bisexual period as a way of easing themselves into gay for that to be taken too seriously. But when I realised that whatever sexual possibilities Vince entertained, he was simply not gay, his statement did more for me than imply that straight boys could waver. It eventually resulted in the ungaying of me.

Vince's wasn't a new way of thinking. It was in fact a very old way of thinking, a way of thinking that hadn't been too affected by all the sexual progress made in the name of gay in the almost two decades since my housemates had been born. It was a way of thinking that was once again becoming workable in a North American and Western European context. Madonna had done an end-run around gay, lifted up her dress and flashed everybody in a characteristically rowdy version of what the ancient Greeks called *anasyrma* [a ritual exposing of one's genitals usually associated with religion or art]. And so, though it was odd to encounter these attitudes in a young North American like Vince, it was precisely that (and similar notions and feelings that remained dormant in others of the same generation), when mixed with a sexual culture steeped in fifties bohemianism, soaked in sixties softening, dripping with seventies glam and abandon, and shot through with cold eighties realism culminating in a nineties present represented by Madonna—and Prince and

Morrissey and Rufus Wainwright and Sandra Bernhard and Michael Stipe—that allowed for the beginning of the end of gay and the death of heterosexuality. A process of cultural benediction had begun, and desires, tendencies, ideas that had lain dormant at least since the seventies and eighties were beginning to poke their heads up and find they weren't being instantly lopped off.

I received an alumni newsletter a couple of years ago with a little note in their happy-news column about Vince's marriage. I never had any notion that he'd go off after that table talk and start boffing girls and boys left and right. I even doubted, as I began thinking about him and thinking about using his offhand observation for this book, that he'd remember the afternoon in question, or even recognise his comments in the context I've put them in here. That talk around the table in that upper room was more signifier than signified. It's what alerted me to what was going on, both around me and within me.

It gave me the first hint as to what to think about and what to look for. And as I said, I continued to think about gay and straight and sexual identity in much the same ways that I had for some time, but something had shifted. I realised that Vince and I were on different paths, though they were paths I came to figure would ultimately converge. . . .

I was meanwhile becoming a lot more sexually adventurous. I'd only ever had sex with Mark, and figured it was about time to start using my twenties the way I figured one's twenties ought to be used. And as I started meeting other guys and having sex with a few of them, I started noticing two things. First, that sex could be a lot of fun in all sorts of different ways. And second, that I was having sex with a remarkable number of straight guys.

Now, I'm fully aware of the unreconstructed lust a lot of gay men feel for the mere fact of straightness. All you've got to do is take a look through the personals, or listen in on a cruiseline for a few minutes, and you'll see and hear the deluge of "straight-acting, straight-lookings" and mostly (upon closer inspection) fantastical "straight man looking for same or bi for first-time encounters." And then there's that sub-subgenre of picture books with titles like *Straight Boys.* I do admit to a certain general attraction to that which ought to be, or is at least considered, unattainable. But, being the coy boy I was, in none of these straight-guy incidents did I even come close to initiating things. They all knew I had sex with boys and did the maths themselves. The first time it happened, I figured I was helping some poor soul out of the closet (and felt quite evangelical about it all, frankly). The second time, too. By the third, I started to wonder—two of the three continued to be completely happy, practising straight guys. And by the fourth, when fully half the men I'd had some form of sexual intercourse with identified as straight, I simply had no idea what was going on. . . .

Current common sense would indicate that there was a good deal of repression going on, a good deal of denial, of cognitive dissonance—"I'm doing it, but I'm not that way."

That Way. That Sort. The whole modern gay movement, from mid- to late-Mattachine[2]-style homophilia to Gay Is Good to Queer Nation and OutRage! to *Ellen, Queer as Folk* and beyond, has been a struggle first to define, then to justify and/or celebrate and/or revel in, then to normalise what was still thought of by many as being That Way. And there have been wild successes, genuine victories resulting in real progress being made in very short spans of time in thinking and acting on sexuality and human relationships. But there's a forgotten, ignored, or perhaps never acknowledged baby splashing about in all that bath water the Movement's been sumping: the possibility of a sexual attraction that is neither primarily nor exclusively based in anatomy nor especially relevant to your sense of self. It's an idea that lesbian communities have been dealing with for some time, something about which they have a lot to teach the rest of us.

It's also precisely this idea that was eventually brought home to me by Vince and friends in a what's-old-is-new-again sort of way.

So in my own drawn-out process of trying to figure out what sex was all about, I added [other en-

counters] to what I'd stored away from the Vince Incident and came up with . . . not much. Just a lot of confusion that I was happy to set aside for the time being as I tried to find some sex, and maybe a boyfriend.

What I found instead was my first girlfriend since high school.

I had been thinking about all this stuff, somewhere in the back of my head where most of my really entertaining thinking goes on, and then this woman appeared who was so thoroughly bright and attractive and funny and *interested.* I hesitated briefly, and then dove in. Well, I suppose waded would be an apter metaphor. I liked her, and I liked it (the relationship, the sex, the social possibilities), though I was always at a remove or two when I was with her. Should I be doing this? I wondered as I kissed her. I'm gay, I'd say to myself as I unhooked her bra. Man, I'm fucked up, I'd tentatively conclude as my tongue slid down her stomach.

The relationship didn't last long. And it probably would have been even shorter had she not lived in another city, allowing me to put off what I was quickly concluding was the inevitable. I liked her, I could even foresee loving her, but I figured I was fooling myself, and her. The sex was . . . distant, and I guessed it probably wouldn't get any better. I was gay and she wasn't a guy.

About three months after I ended it I was reading a book—*A Suitable Boy,* I think it was—when it struck me. I lowered the book to my lap and said out loud, "Man, that was stupid," and then raised it again and continued reading. What had struck me fully formed and in a flash was that it didn't matter. Girl, boy—it just didn't matter. The sex wasn't bad because she was a girl, it was bad because I couldn't stop thinking about it, chastising myself for it.[3] Though I hadn't gone looking for it, and though I was not instantly turned on by her the way I was instantly turned on by any number of bike couriers zipping past on any given day, I had been genuinely interested in her physically once we got down to it. Though it seemed counter-intuitive at the time, I really dug the whole vagina thing and got totally turned on by mucking around with it. It was, I discovered, innately sexual, just like a cock, just like an anus (we have just got to find a better word for that). I enjoyed the different ways we positioned ourselves for different aspects of sex, enjoyed how different they were from the ones I used when I was with guys. I noticed some real engineering advantages.

A major factor in my decision to break it off was the reaction of my gay male friends when I told them about her. Without exception (I think I told three or four of them), the first look I got was guarded, the second vaguely angry or frustrated, and the third tutelary.

'You sure you wanna be doing that?' I'd get from one. 'You *are* still gay, right?' from another. 'Man, are you fucked up or what?' from a third. 'You trying to run back into the closet or something? C'mon—are you trying to tell me you're as turned on by her as you are by'—zip—'him? You know as well as I do the pressures that come to bear on us from all corners, and the temptation to recidivism is . . . ' (you get the idea).

There'd be supportive, even curious noises in there too from time to time ('So . . . um . . . what's it . . . like?'), and even, as I brought the subject up in more general terms with others, the occasional 'Oh, yeah, I've done that. It was fine,' but they were always underpinned by a barely contained mixture of offence and defensiveness. In our early twenties many of us were still too close to the then common high-school cover-date experience, that smothering feeling of being forced to date a member of the opposite sex, to pull a pretty comprehensive and usually long-term scam on your date, your peers, and your family to belay fears and suspicions of sexual difference. The whole late eighties and early nineties . . . come-out-come-out-wherever-you-are movement was a reaction against that very thing. We'd all read it, and we were all, to a greater or lesser extent, living it. We certainly all believed it. We were in the middle of a stridently and necessarily monolithic time in the creation of the basic modern homosexual, and challenges to that monolith were met, from within ourselves and without, with condescending and evangelical anger usually reserved for free thinkers during times of war. I didn't, significantly,

take these questions and problems to any of my straight friends (whose numbers were on the wane). I saw myself as a member of a group that had definite image problems it was vigorously trying to resolve, and dissension among the ranks could only vindicate the homophobic presuppositions of the mainstream. One of the most insidious was that gay was a phase in the young, a case of arrested development in the old, and I did not want to give any straight person the impression that I was wavering, that I was coming to the end of my gay phase, which I never really figured I was.

Another question I was asked by most I mentioned this girlfriend quandary to was, did she mean I was bisexual? I assured them I wasn't, as immediately as I'd said I was the first time Mark asked me if I thought I might be gay. I wondered from time to time whether I'd have to reconfigure all this lavish identity construction I'd done over the past couple of years and start looking for a bisexual community to become a part of. New friends, new vocab, a confusing club scene—way too much to handle so soon after such major personal upheavals. And besides, the more I thought about it, the more I was pretty certain that, empirical evidence to the contrary, I wasn't bisexual. I had liked my girlfriend, I was attracted to her on any number of levels—and I liked the sex and in retrospect figured I would have liked it even more as time went on, if I let it (which is how it happens with most of my sex). But I was still gay. I still paid way more attention to Hugh Grant's butt and lips than I did to Elizabeth Hurley's. I still knew Ryan Phillippe's filmography by heart. I still bought underwear for the pretty pictures on the box.

All this of course caused some fissures in my understanding of the terms involved, but I figured I had more important things to worry about and banished them to the back of my head. Well, almost to the back. Those couple of years when I could unabashedly declare myself to be gay were over. I still told people I was, but there was now a nagging little pull inside that kept prompting me to add, 'Well, actually, to be perfectly honest . . . ,' but there was no word for it as far as I could tell, and it would only come out sounding like I was embarrassed to be gay, which wasn't it at all. So I shut that nagging little pulling part of me up; the offending relationship was over and done with, and I doubted, given all the agitation it caused me, that it would be repeated. So I continued having a mostly gay old time. . . .

And then, after I'd finished with the magazine job and begun to think and write on my own full time, when I started really grilling my friends (whose numbers by this time turned to a roughly 70-30 straight-gay split), I found that they, especially the straight women, were right on-side, that it had, in fact, been something a lot of them had thought about but never talked about—not with a guy, anyway. I found many of them either had had some sort of adult sex with another woman or looked forward to someday doing it or didn't rule out the possibility if the right girl and the right circumstances were to present themselves. It was another case of that Starbucks-tramway syndrome. But this time, I just walked right in and ordered a latte to stay. . . .

SEXUAL IDENTITY

Sexual identity—like gender, race, and class—is generally spoken of in either exceedingly measured or exceedingly strident tones; either in academic, theoretical journals and treatises or through megaphones from makeshift podiums in front of government buildings and crowds of unusually dressed (or worse yet, self-consciously normally dressed) people. As a result, and entirely reasonably as far as I'm concerned, most people just tend to turn off when the term comes up. Sexual identity, oppression, rights, blahblahblah—anything else on?

Never has something so big been talked about by so many, so often, to such little intellectual effect. Listen in any local gay café or restaurant and you'll hear, in the background noise, the words 'sex', 'gay', 'out', 'sexuality', 'orientation', 'Ricky Martin and Enrique Iglesias', all indications of conversations on the subject of themselves, of this defining aspect of themselves. But as has been the case with many of the transsexuals I've spoken to, despite the fact of

their self-definition, little progress has been made in the understanding of the issues around which they've centred their lives.

But also like gender, race, and class, sexual identity, and our understanding of it, has a lot to do with our everyday lives and how much happiness we can squeeze out of them. You'd just never know it to listen to the people who tend to talk the most about it.

Dropping sexual identity from our collective psychic wardrobe might at first seem like a big, complicated thing. It certainly seemed that way to many of the sex radicals of the sixties and seventies who figured it was one part of an inexorable path to socialism, or anarchy . . . as it did to the queer theorists who stumbled on the notion again in the eighties. . . . But these days dropping it seems a lot more straightforward. Though it can be explained and bolstered with the use of any number of philosophical and theoretical exoskeletons, when it comes right down to it, it's a simple and—apologies to the poststructuralists—natural thing. Leaving sexual identity behind is simply what happens when our natural instincts to love and to fuck come together with a culture that has brought sexuality in general, not just homosexuality, out of the closet, that has taken it out from under the ever-frowning gaze of religion and removed it from its place as a grim, grey cornerstone of the social order in the formalised shape of marriage.

In a society that has pretty successfully separated sex from reproduction and even, to a large extent, from its role as a stable basis of social propagation, the door's been left open for sex to be a lot more fun than it has been in millennia.

It's in the name of fun that I want to talk about sexuality. And it's tough to talk about sexuality without starting out with gay. Just as there is no nationalism without at least one nation feeling impinged upon by another, no notion of race without at least two races, there is no sexual identity without one group identifying itself as sexually different, making itself heard, and thereby impinging on the rest of us, throwing up this notion that is every bit as amorphous and every bit as enervating as nationalism and race.

Before people came up with the notion that there was such a thing as gay, people were seen, and saw themselves, as pretty much of a piece. And as a result they were. Despite what the nascent gay studies departments tell us, Edward II wasn't gay; he was just a man who seems to have loved Piers more than Isabella. And neither were Michelangelo, Goethe, nor, for that matter, Oscar Wilde. For most of the Christian era in Western Europe and North America, there were those who got married and those who entered religious life. And in both categories, men fell in love with and had sex with men, and women with women, and this said not a thing about what sorts of people they were.

It's pretty clear by now though that sexual identity is a reality. Every time you rebuff a potentially sexual advance by someone of the same sex by saying 'Sorry, I'm not gay' instead of 'Sorry, not interested', you are negatively defining yourself as straight, just as every time you rebuff a potentially sexual advance by someone of the opposite sex by saying 'Sorry, I'm gay' or 'You got a sister?', you're positively identifying as gay. Every time you see a movie on gay themes and think to yourself, 'Well, that's all well and good, but it's not really got much to do with *my* life', you're just as implicated in sexual identity as the person who goes to see that movie expressly because it's about gayness. Gay, in this not so roundabout way, far from involving the 10 percent of us we usually figure (or, if we believe the more recent and no more reliable studies, 1 to 2 percent), actually affects approximately 100 percent of us.

So we're all implicated. So what?

It all comes down to identity, that thing we carry around with us tucked away somewhere near the middle of our brains that enables us to distinguish ourselves from other people. It's part of the same mechanism, the same way we have of understanding ourselves, that allows us to read headlines like 'Crazed Killer on the Loose' and understand it to mean that there are people in this world who are crazed killers and then there are people like us, allowing us in the process a certain degree of comfort in the knowledge that no matter how poorly things

go at work, no matter how loudly that sweet little child screams at us about the mess she's made in her diaper, we will not use this knife gleaming up at us from the counter to do anything about either. It allows us, in short, to imagine there's a connection between action and identity, to imagine an equal sign between the verb 'kill' and the noun 'killer'.

Sexual identity is a new addition to the identity portfolio, and we can see in recent history, and to a large extent even within living memory, the process of its accretion. That's just plain interesting, I think, like being able to watch a pearl form in front of our eyes. Why not take a look, since we're able. It can't help but give us a better, perhaps even a more profound, view of ourselves.

But I'd say it's most important because sexual identity, like that equal sign between verb and noun, is in the end a house built on sand, the living in which makes us, through omission rather than commission, more anxious, less happy people than we might otherwise be. . . .

EX-GAYS

. . . I was once myself convinced that I was utterly unattracted to members of the opposite sex, and further, that I never had been. I remembered my prepubescent relationships with Stacey and Corinne and Kimberly and Susan as being essentially sisterly, or at least lacking the urgency of my equally early relationships with Scott and Michael and Richard and Brent. It was only when I decided that this part of me was worth investigation that I realised, consciously attempting to remove the retrospective filter of a gay identity, that the relationships were pretty much the same; it was only then that I remembered I played prepubescent sex games with Brenda (which I found just as naughtily alluring as learning about erections—in theory—from Kenny), that I had a just-presexual crush on Monica, and that I never played sex games with boys, nor even thought of it. And though I can hear explanations like I must have felt safer playing sex games with girls, in whom I wasn't really interested, than I did with boys, who I thought might be too incriminating, I've heard the opposite reasoning put to work far too often to explain same-sex sex games to put much faith in either scenario. And when, in grade six and seven, I first started feeling those more visceral rumblings sitting beside certain people and not others, even though that dreamy set of Calgarian twins named Christian and Richard were the first to set things in motion, the buxom-before-her-time Jennifer ran a close second. Before I sat down to write this, I had completely forgotten about Jennifer, and about Brenda and Monica.

But enough about me. Let's talk about you.

I think it would be fairly uncontroversial to suggest that your own attractions have changed over time. Perhaps you were once attracted to girls in kilts? Or skaters? Maybe Kurt Cobain or Helena Bonham Carter once did it for you. And now, though you may either retain vestigial attractions for these or have developed a distinct dislike for them, you are perhaps attracted to the lawyer type, or the matronly sort, or maybe you've just moved from Kurt or Helena over to, say, Ewan McGregor or Gwyneth Paltrow. It seems to me that throughout our lives we are continually adding and subtracting attractions as a result of our experiences, of our changes in circumstance, of our aging. Very rarely, I think, do those initial pubescent attractions—to Mister Rogers or Wonder Woman—stick around in anything other than nostalgic or ironic form. All sorts of barriers are crossed in the development of our attractions—when once we were attracted to teenagers we become attracted to adults, when once we were attracted to people because of how they looked we become attracted to them because of how they think. Not everyone undergoes drastic shifts, but we all suffer alterations in the nature of our attractions. ('What did I ever see in her?' is a pretty common sort of thing to ask yourself.) True, sometimes these shifts may be seen as a honing, from Wonder Woman to S/M, from Mister Rogers to daddy types, but the change remains the same. And most people, I'd guess, see this and take it as self-evident that since we don't do this with the sex of those we're attracted to, it's in a different category from, say, superhero outfits. Very few people, they'd

say, go from being attracted to women to being attracted to men.

But since attraction is overdetermined, and since not only aging and financial advancement but also societal pressures and cultural norms all play a role in its development, and since fluidity in the choice of the sex of the sexual object has not been permissible, it has not been an option.

But things have changed, and continue to change. Unrestricted sexual choice, which was once common but unspoken, became less common and more spoken about, then even less common and even more loudly talked about, and is now more universally shouted about than ever and becoming more common once again. In the few years since it has become acceptable to create reasonable portrayals of same-sex attraction in the American and northern European mass media, those who are young enough, independent enough, or sexually introspective enough have started—just started, mind you—to accrete a little less seamlessly. As it becomes obvious through public representation that there are no particular types of people who are either straight or gay, that there are very straight-seeming people who have sex with members of the same sex and very gay-seeming people who have sex with members of the opposite sex,[4] and all sorts of stuff in between and beyond, the connection between act and essence is becoming weaker in people's minds. Echoing my own de-revision (or re-envisioning) of the development of my attractions, Edmund White, one of the most prominent creators of English-language gay literature of the eighties and nineties, said in a review of Marjorie Garber's book on sexuality that reading it had made him realise that he had 'denied the authenticity of my earlier heterosexual feelings in the light of my later homosexual identity'. The same cultural markers that led Garber to write her book and me to write mine are allowing people younger than the fifty-something White to avoid some levels of those original denials and revisions-on-the-run. It's by no means a universal, or even remarkably common, thing for teens and young adults to completely ignore sexual identity and follow less walled-off paths of attraction and relationships. Not yet. But the common teen habit of sexual experimentation, on this far side of gay rights and cultural sexual discourse, has come to mean different things. Experiences that were once singular, or at least confined within age boundaries, are becoming less so. . . .

DISCUSSION QUESTIONS

1. Do you agree with Archer that people born since the 1980's are less committed to sexual identity categories? What evidence would you offer for your position?
2. Is Archer really just bi-sexual?

NOTES

1. *Showbiz Today* got its highest rating of the week running 112 seconds of it, *Saturday Night Live* got its highest rating of the season for the 90-second excerpt it ran, *Nightline* ran it uncensored and got its highest ratings of the year, and *The Howard Stern Show*, which ran it with minor censoring, got its highest rating ever.

2. The Mattachine Society was an early, secretive homosexual rights organisation, founded in 1951 in Los Angeles, a rough equivalent in many ways to other early groups, like the Homophile Association of London, Ontario. Though its founder, Harry Hay, was a devoted Communist, the organisation soon became thoroughly conservative (and Hay left). See *Hay's Radically Gay: Gay Liberation in the Words of its Founder,* edited by Will Roscoe (Boston: Beacon Press, 1996) for the best account I've found of Mattachine and this era in US gay activist thought.

3. Perhaps an opportune moment to point out that I'm a firm subscriber to the Woody Allen School of Qualitative Sexuality—bad sex is a highly relative term in my books, akin to filthy lucre.

4. See, for instance, 'Trials of a Gay-seeming Straight Male' by Leif Ueland on nerve.com, posted 12 June 1998, in which Ueland writes: 'Maybe what my people need is a new definition, a nice user-friendly label. Something that says, "not gay, but not straight in the way to which you're accustomed, and maybe not even willing to rule out the possibility of being gay in the future"'.

EXPERIENCING DIFFERENCE

FRAMEWORK ESSAY

In the first framework essay, we considered the social construction of difference as master statuses were named, aggregated, dichotomized, and stigmatized. Now we turn to *experiencing* these statuses. A story from a friend provides the first illustration of what we mean by this:

> During the summer that my daughter, Jenny, was about eight, her younger brother was visiting his grandparents. My husband and I had a free evening and really wanted to go see *Men in Black.* Normally we would have asked his mother to watch Jenny, but she already had her hands full. Hiring a baby-sitter for the night would have been difficult to arrange and to pay for. We weighed our options and decided that Jenny would be able to handle a PG or PG-13 movie. We watch a lot of movies of all kinds at home, including science fiction and action adventure, and it had seemed that Jenny had a well-developed sense of the difference between real and pretend. We thought that at worst the movie would go over her head, but that she would enjoy the popcorn and soda, not to mention the special status of going to the movies with her parents without her annoying little brother.
>
> Our perception of the movie was that while there was plenty of action, it was definitely a comedy. The "alien monsters" were ridiculous to us, inspiring laughter or mild disgust like that of a yucky bug you find in your bathroom and flush down the toilet. Jenny, however, found the movie to be scary and gross. It was beyond her ability to laugh away as "pretend." She hid her eyes through 90 percent of the movie and did not agree with us that it was funny. She talked for months about how scary it was and chastised us for letting her see it.

This story holds a small lesson about *experiencing* your social status. What we notice in the world depends in large part on the statuses we occupy; in this way we may be said to *experience* our social status. Jenny thought the movie was scary both because of the unique person she is and because of her age, a master status. Her parents did not see the movie that way for the same reasons. All *experienced* the movie through their unique personalities and through the lens of this particular master status.

Although we do not specifically address age in this book, it operates in ways that are analogous to race, sex, class, sexual orientation, and disability. For example, being young affects the way a person is treated in innumerable ways: at a minimum, restrictions on driving, employment, military enlistment, marriage, abortion, admission to movies, and alcohol and cigarette consumption; insurance rates; mandatory school attendance; and "status offenses" (acts that are illegal only for minors). In addition, minors are excluded from voting and exercising other legal rights.

In these ways, those defined as "young" are treated differently from those who are not so defined. Because of that treatment, those who are younger see the world differently from those who are older and no longer operating within these constraints. The young notice things that older people need not notice, because they are not subject to the same rules. Our experiences are tied to the statuses we occupy.

The second example of experiencing one's status comes from the autobiography of one of the first black students in an exclusive white prep school. She recalls what it was like to hear "one [white] girl after another say, 'It doesn't matter to me if somebody's white or black or green or purple. I mean people are just people.'" While she appreciates the girls' intentions, she also hears her own *real* experience being trivialized by comparison to the Muppets. Her status helps to explain what she noticed in these conversations (Cary, 1991:83–84).

In all, you experience your social statuses; you live through them. They are the filters through which you see and make sense of the world, and in large measure they account for how you are treated and what you notice. In the sections that follow, we will focus on the experiences of privilege and stigma associated with master statuses.

THE EXPERIENCE OF PRIVILEGE

Just as status helps to explain what we notice, it also explains what we *don't* notice. In the following classroom discussion between a black and a white woman, the white woman argues that because she and the black woman are both female, they should be allies. The black woman responds,

> "When you wake up in the morning and look in the mirror what do you see?"
>   "I see a woman," replied the white woman.
>   "That's precisely the issue," replied the black woman. "I see a black woman. For me, race is visible every day, because it is how I am *not* privileged in this culture. Race is invisible to you [because it is how you are privileged]." (Kimmel and Messner, 1989:3; emphasis added)

Thus, we are likely to be fairly unaware of the statuses that *privilege* us, that is, provide us with advantage, and acutely aware of those that are the source of trouble—those that yield negative judgments and unfair treatment. The mirror metaphor used by the black woman in this conversation emerges frequently among those who are stigmatized: "I looked in the mirror and saw a gay man." These moments of suddenly realizing your social position with all of its life-shaping ramifications are usually about recognizing how you are stigmatized and underprivileged, but rarely about how you might be privileged or advantaged by the statuses you occupy.

Examples of Privilege

This use of the term *privilege* was first developed by Peggy McIntosh (1988) from her experience teaching women's studies courses. She noticed that while many men were willing to grant that women were disadvantaged (or "underprivileged") because of sexism, it was far more difficult for them to acknowledge that they were themselves advantaged (or "overprivileged") because of it. Extending the analysis to race, McIntosh generated a list of the ways in which she, as a white woman, was overprivileged by virtue of racism. Her list of over 40 white privileges included the following:

> I can turn on the television or open to the front page of the paper and see people of my race widely represented.
>
> When I am told about our national heritage or about "civilization," I am shown that people of my color made it what it is.
>
> I do not have to educate my children to be aware of systemic racism for their own daily protection.
>
> I can worry about racism without being seen as self-interested or self-seeking.
>
> I can think over many options, social, political, imaginative, or professional, without asking whether a person of my race would be accepted or allowed to do what I want to do. (McIntosh, 1988:5–8)

As she talked to people about her list, McIntosh learned about other white privileges: "A black woman said she was glad to hear me 'working on my own people,' because if she said these things about white privilege, she would be seen as a militant." Someone else noted that one privilege of being white was being able to be oblivious to those privileges. "Those in privileged groups are educated [to be oblivious] about what it is like for others, especially for others who have to be in their presence" (McIntosh, 1988).

One feature of privilege is that it makes life easier: it is easier to get around, to get what one wants, and to be treated in an acceptable manner. This is illustrated by the experience of a white newspaper columnist traveling with an African American colleague. Both were using complimentary airline tickets. The white columnist presented his ticket and was assigned a seat; then he watched the same white ticket agent ask his companion for some identification:

> The black man handed over his ticket. The female agent glanced at it and asked, "Do you have some identification?" [The columnist had not been asked for any identification.]
>
> "Yes, I do," the black man said, and he reached for his wallet. "But just out of curiosity, do you mind telling me why you want to see it?"
>
> The agent grinned in embarrassment.
>
> She said nothing in response.
>
> "How about a credit card?" the black man said, and he pulled one out of his wallet.
>
> "Do you have a work ID?" she asked, apparently hoping to see something with the black man's photo on it.
>
> "No," he said, and whipped out another credit card.
>
> "A driver's license would be fine," she said, sounding trapped.
>
> "I don't have my driver's license with me," he said. "I'm taking the plane, not the car. . . ."
>
> "That's fine sir, thank you," the agent finally said, shrinking a bit with each successive credit card. "Enjoy the flight."
>
> The men rode the escalator up to the gate area in silence.
>
> The white man shook his head. "I've probably watched that a hundred times in my life," he said. "But that's the first time I've ever *seen* it."
>
> The black man nodded. He'd seen it more times than he cared to count. "You don't ever need to remind yourself that you're black," he said, "because every day there's somebody out there who'll remind you."
>
> They walked on for a while, and the black man started to laugh to himself. Pirouetting, he modeled his outfit, an Italian-cut, double-breasted suit with a red rose in his lapel for Mother's Day. "I really can't look any better than this," he said sardonically. Then, he looked into his friend's eyes and said, "I had my driver's license. But if I show it, we may as well be in Soweto." (Kornheiser, 1990)

In reading about this exchange, one black student was particularly angered: "Whites will stand by and watch this happen, and either be oblivious to the slight or sympathize with you afterward, but they won't go to the mat and fight for you." While this incident occurred before the 2001 terrorist attacks that made photo-identification a requirement for flying on commercial airlines, its message about privilege remains true. Because drivers licenses can be falsified, African Americans and other passengers of color are still likely to face a higher level of scrutiny than whites by being asked to show more than one form of photo-id.

The columnist noted for the first time a privilege that he had as a middle-class white: he was not assumed to be a thief. By contrast, his black colleague was presumed to have stolen the ticket no matter how upper-class or professional he looked. Similarly, many black and Latino students describe being closely monitored for shoplifting when they are in department stores, just as the students who work for department store security confirm that they are given explicit instructions to watch black and Latino customers more closely. On hearing this, one black student realized why she had the habit of walking through stores with her hands out, palms open, in front of her: it was a way to prove she was not stealing. Oddly, one of the privileges of being white is that shoplifting is easier, since the security people in stores are busy watching the black and Latino customers.

Just as whites are not assumed to be thieves, they are not assumed to be poor. Michael Patrick MacDonald in Reading 37 describes how neither his Irish neighbors in South Boston nor social welfare activists acknowledged the area's poverty, crime, and drugs. "Those were black things that happened in the ghettos of Roxbury. Southie was Boston's proud Irish neighborhood."

But perhaps most important in the realm of white privilege is the presumption that whites are not violent or dangerous to others. This is especially worth noting because if a person or group of people are assumed to be violent, acting against them to preemptively ward off that violence is seen as somehow legitimate. While whites do not generally assume that other whites are a threat, they do assume that of blacks. The percentage appears to be declining, but about half of whites think blacks are aggressive or violent (Smith, 2001). A mundane example of the consequence of this belief is provided by law professor and author Patricia J. Williams:

> My best friend from law school is a woman named C. For months now I have been sending her drafts of this book, filled with many shared experiences, and she sends me back comments and her own associations. Occasionally we speak by telephone. One day, after reading the beginning of this chapter, she calls me up and tells me her abiding recollection of law school. "Actually, it has nothing to do with law school," she says.
>
> "I'll be the judge of that," I respond.
>
> "Well," she continues, "It's about the time I was held at gunpoint by a SWAT team."
>
> It turns out that during one Christmas vacation C. drove to Florida with two friends. Just outside Miami they stopped at a roadside diner. C. ordered a hamburger and a glass of milk. The milk was sour, and C. asked for another. The waitress ignored her. C. asked twice more and was ignored each time. When the waitress finally brought the bill, C. had been charged for the milk and refused to pay for it. The waitress started to shout at her, and a highway patrolman walked over from where he had been sitting and asked what was going on. C. explained that the milk was sour and that she didn't want to pay for it. The highway patrolman ordered her to pay and get out. When C. said he was out of his jurisdiction, the patrolman pulled out his gun and pointed it at her.
>
> ("Don't you think," asks C. when I show her this much of my telling of her story, "that it would help your readers to know that the restaurant was all white and that I'm black?" "Oh, yeah," I say. "And six feet tall.")
>
> Now C. is not easily intimidated and, just to prove it, she put her hand on her hip and invited the police officer to go ahead and shoot her, but before he did so *he* should try to drink the damn glass of milk, and so forth and so on for a few more descriptive rounds. What cut her off was the realization that, suddenly and silently, she and her two friends

had been surrounded by eight SWAT team officers, in full guerrilla gear, automatic weapons drawn. Into the pall of her ringed speechlessness, they sent a local black police-man, who offered her twenty dollars and begged her to pay and be gone. C. describes how desperately he was perspiring as he begged and, when she didn't move, how angry he got—how he accused her of being an outside agitator, that she could come from the North and go back to the North, but that there were those of "us" who had to live here and would pay for her activism.

C. says she doesn't remember how she got out of there alive or why they finally let her go; but she supposes that the black man paid for her. But she does remember returning to the car with her two companions and the three of them crying, sobbing, all the way to Mi-ami. "The damnedest thing about it," C. said, "was that no one was interested in whether or not I was telling the truth. The glass was sitting there in the middle of all this, with the curdle hanging on the side, but nobody would taste it because a black woman's lips had touched it." (Williams, 1991:56–57)

Several front-page cases have shown dramatically how whites' fear of blacks has prompted aggression toward blacks—and then been used after the fact to legitimate the violence.[1] Among the more notorious cases are Bernard Goetz's 1984 New York subway shooting of four unarmed black teenagers (two shot in the back), for which Goetz was found innocent of attempted murder; the 1989 Boston case of Charles Stuart who murdered his pregnant wife but so convinced the police that she had been shot by a black gunman that they failed to pursue an investigation that would have led to the plot hatched by Stuart and his brother; and the 1991 beating of Rod-ney King by several white Los Angeles police officers, all of whom were acquitted. Thus every day, African Americans, especially men, must be vigilant about becom-ing the targets of preemptive violence.

Since the 9/11 attacks on the World Trade Towers and Pentagon, the presumption that a category of people is dangerous and thus appropriately the target of preemp-tive action has been extended to Arab American men or noncitizens from the Mid-dle East. Parallels between the experience of African Americans and those of Middle Eastern origin are especially evident around the topic of *racial profiling* (Harris, 2002). Racial profiling means singling out members of a particular racial group for heightened police surveillance. Since 1996, as a result of a Supreme Court decision in the midst of the so-called War on Drugs (*Whren et al. v. United States*), it has been legal for the police to use traffic stops as an opportunity for an investigation of drugs or other crimes. Motorists pulled over for traffic violations can be asked if they will consent to a search of their car and person. If, in the course of the traffic stop, the of-ficer finds visual evidence of a crime, a search can proceed without the driver's con-sent. Because the number of potential traffic violations is almost limitless, virtually any vehicle can be pulled over anytime.

As a result, a considerable public uproar emerged about police departments across the country disproportionately pulling over black drivers. The phrase "driv-ing while black"—or Latino or Indian—became commonplace. Research by several social scientists confirmed that racial targeting was indeed taking place—for exam-

---

[1]Despite whites' fear of violence at the hands of African Americans, crime is predominately *intra*racial.

ple, state police data in Maryland in the 1990s showed that while 17 percent of drivers on Interstate 95 were black, 70 percent of those stopped and searched were black. Since racial profiling operates from the assumption that people of color are likely to be criminal, those stopped by police are themselves often in danger. For example, in 1998 two New Jersey state troopers fired 11 shots into a van carrying black and Latino men from the Bronx to a basketball camp. Three of the men were wounded. At their sentencing in 2002, the troopers "said their supervisors had trained them to focus on black- and brown-skinned drivers because, they were told, they were more likely to be drug traffickers" (Kocieniewski, 2002). But the research on racial profiling also showed that it was bad police work.

> Does racial profiling in fact help us to catch criminals? [Since African Americans and Latinos are disproportionately arrested and jailed for drug-related crime, doesn't racial profiling] actually "up the odds" of police finding bad guys, guns, or drugs when they make traffic stops and conduct searches? . . .
>
> The answer comes in the form of something called the hit rate: the rate at which police actually find criminals, uncover guns, and confiscate drugs when they perform stops and searches. . . . In just the last couple of years, data have become available in a growing number of jurisdictions that allow us to calculate the hit rate, and to do so separately for blacks, whites, and Latinos. In all of these studies, police stop and search whites not because of race, but because they have observed suspicious behavior. Blacks and Latinos, on the other hand, were stopped not only because of suspicious behavior, but also because of race or ethnic appearance. . . . All of the studies in which the data collected allow for the calculation of hit rates have generated strikingly similar results. All of these studies show higher hit rates not for blacks and Latinos, but for whites. In other words, officers "hit" less often when they use race or ethnic appearance to decide which person seems suspicious enough to merit stops and searches than they do when they use suspicious behavior and not race as their way of selecting suspects. When stops and searches are not racialized, they are more productive. (Harris, 2003:77)

In an effort to stop racial profiling, more than a dozen states passed antiprofiling legislation and hundreds of police departments now collect data on all traffic stops. This emerging consensus against profiling was derailed by 9/11, to the extent that there is now little public objection to racial profiling that targets those of Middle Eastern origin for everything from removal from commercial airlines to investigation and detention. But the targeting of Arab Americans and Middle Eastern noncitizens is susceptible to the same criticism as profiling at traffic stops. "Profiling is a crude substitute for behavior-based enforcement and . . . invites screeners to take a less vigilant approach to individuals who don't fit the profile, even if they engage in conduct that should cause concern" (Carter, 2002:12). In other words, those of us who do not look Middle Eastern have the privilege of not being treated like terrorists, just like those of us who do not look black or Latino have the privilege of not being treated like drug dealers. This could be described as a life-saving privilege.

A different privilege, likely to be invisible to those in single-race families, is the privilege of being recognized as a family. The following account by a mother illustrates how the failure to perceive a family is linked to the expectation of black criminality.

When my son was home visiting from college, we met in town one day for lunch. . . . On the way to the car, one of us thought of a game we'd often played when he was younger.

"Race you to the car!"

I passed my large handbag to him, thinking to more equalize the race since he was a twenty-year-old athlete. We raced the few blocks, my heart singing with delight to be talking and playing with my beloved son. As we neared the car, two young white men yelled something at us. I couldn't make it out and paid it no mind. When we arrived at the car, both of us laughing, they walked by and mumbled "Sorry" as they quickly passed, heads down.

I suddenly understood. They hadn't seen a family. They had seen a young Black man with a pocketbook, fleeing a pursuing middle-aged white woman. My heart trembled as I thought of what could have happened if we'd been running by someone with a gun.

Later I mentioned the incident in a three-day diversity seminar I was conducting at a Boston corporation. A participant related it that evening to his son, a police officer, and asked the son what he would have done if he'd observed the scene.

The answer: "Shot out his kneecaps." (Lester, 1994:56–7)

Turning now from privileges of race to privileges of sexual orientation, the most obvious privilege enjoyed by heterosexuals is that they are allowed to be open about their relationships. From idle conversation and public displays of affection, to the legal and religious approval embodied in marriage, heterosexuals are able to declare that they love and are loved. That privilege is not just denied to lesbians and gays; they are actively punished for such expressions by ostracism, physical assault, unemployment, and even loss of child custody and visitation—not so surprising given the lack of legal recognition of gay families.

Even the ability to display a picture of one's partner on a desk at work stands as an invisible privilege of heterosexuality.

Consider, for example, an employee who keeps a photograph on her desk in which she and her husband smile for the camera and embrace affectionately. . . . [T]he photo implicitly conveys information about her private sexual behavior. [But] most onlookers (if they even notice the photo) do not think of her partner primarily in sexual terms. . . .

[But] if the photograph instead shows the woman in the same pose with a same-sex partner, everyone is likely to notice. As with the first example, the photograph conveys the information that she is in a relationship. But the fact that the partner is a woman overwhelms all other information about her. The *sexual* component of the relationship is not mundane and implicit as with the heterosexual spouse. (Herek, 1992:95–6; emphasis added)

Because heterosexual public affection is so commonplace, it rarely conjures up images of sexual activity. But that is exactly what we may think of when we see a same-sex couple embrace. This is why gay and lesbian people are often accused of "flaunting" their sexuality: *any* display of affection between them is understood by many heterosexuals as virtually a display of the sex act.

In the realm of class privilege, several readings in this text address the considerable differences in health, life span, educational access, and quality of life that accompany American class differences. But these are perhaps the more visible privileges of being middle and upper class. Less apparent is the privilege of being treated as a deserving and competent member of the community. Higher education institutions provide a number of examples of this. One of the boons of the legacy admission system, described by John Larew in Reading 39, is its invisibility. The students admitted to universities this way—who are predominately middle- and upper-class whites—don't have their qualifications questioned by faculty or other students, nor are they likely to agonize about whether they deserved to be admitted.

> Like many children of University of Virginia graduates, Mary Stuart Young of Atlanta, Georgia, wore Cavalier orange and blue long before she took an SAT or mailed an application.
>
> "Coming here just felt right," said Young, 21, who expects to graduate with a religious studies degree in 2004. "This was where I should be."
>
> After all, with two generations of faithful alumni backing her, Young doubled her chances of getting into Thomas Jefferson's university. (Associated Press, 2003)

One of the privileges of being a legacy admission rather than an "affirmative action admit" is that you are treated as a deserving and competent member of the community, rather than someone who doesn't deserve to be there.

The assumption that students are middle or upper class is pervasive within higher education, so working-class students often find schools oblivious or even antagonistic to their needs. Students are presumed to understand how college works, because it is assumed that their parents are college graduates and can advise them: "In an article on working class students in higher education, one student was paraphrased as saying that college is a very unforgiving place. It is unforgiving not of those who don't know the rules, but rather of those who did not know the rules before arriving on campus" (Tokarczyk, 2004:163). Thus, one of the privileges of being a college student from the middle or upper classes is that you come to the university with a good deal of information about how it works.

"Working class students often have difficulty in their studies partially because colleges and universities—elite and nonelite—refuse to recognize that many students must work" (Tokarczyk, 2004:163). For example, schools that require unpaid internships, off-campus experiences, or study abroad trips may forget not only the costs associated with these requirements but also the fact that working-class students may have to quit their jobs to fulfill the requirement. The same is true of faculty office hours—set as if students could easily arrange their schedules to fit the professor's. If working-class students were seen as deserving and competent members of the community, their needs would be factored in automatically, not as a "special favor." The following echoes the experiences Laurel Johnson Black describes in Reading 39:

> Working class students are often an anomaly to their peers. A working class student at Goucher told me that students did not understand her living at home and working three part-time jobs. Because she did not have a car, she had to continually arrange for rides to and from campus. Students just looked at her as though she were strange, so she stopped talking about her situation, stopped trying to make friends, and kept to herself. (Tokarczyk, 2004:164)

In all, one of the privileges of being middle or upper class is that higher education—which is absolutely critical to upward mobility—is in sync with your experience. When you go to a college or university, you can expect to have your life experiences and perspective treated as the norm. The institution will be organized around those experiences in ways large and small, from assuming that everyone should live on campus (and bear the expense of room and board) to assuming you will be able to cover the cost of texts or forgo employment to demonstrate commitment to your studies. In these ways, students from the middle or upper classes have the privilege of feeling like they belong.

Beyond even that, higher education is increasingly becoming available only to those in the middle and upper classes. At the most selective institutions—the top 10 percent of four-year colleges—

> students in the highest economic quartile take up 74 percent of the available slots, while students in the bottom quartile fill just 3 percent. Economically disadvantaged students are 25 times less likely to be found on elite college campuses than economically advantaged students. . . . If low-income students routinely received a break in admissions, as many colleges suggest, we would expect to see them over represented compared with their academic records. . . . But . . . the representation of low-income and working-class students today is actually slightly lower, not higher, than if grades and test scores were the sole basis for admissions. (Kahlenberg, 2004:B11)

As Terry Hartle, senior vice president at the American Council on Education told the *Los Angeles Times,* "Smart poor kids go to college at the same rate as stupid rich kids" (Kirp, 2003:18).

Overall, two privileges shape the experience of all those in nonstigmatized statuses: the privilege of being "unmarked" and the privilege of being seen as "entitled." *Entitlement* is the belief that one has the right to be respected, acknowledged, protected, and rewarded. This is so much taken for granted by those in nonstigmatized statuses that they are often shocked and angered when it is denied them.

> [After the lecture, whites in the audience] shot their hands up to express how excluded they felt because [the] lecture, while broad in scope, clearly was addressed first and foremost to the women of color in the room. . . . What a remarkable sense of entitlement must drive their willingness to assert their experience of exclusion! If I wanted to raise my hand every time I felt excluded, I would have to glue my wrist to the top of my head. (Ettinger, 1994:51)

Like entitlement, the privilege of occupying an "unmarked" status is shared by most of those in nonstigmatized categories. *Doctor* is an *unmarked* status; *woman* doctor is *marked.* Unmarked categories convey the usual and expected distribution of individuals in social statuses—the distribution that does not require any special comment. Thus, the unmarked category tells us what a society takes for granted.

Theoretically, the unmarked category *doctor* might include anyone, but in truth it refers to white males. How do we know that? Because other occupants of that status are usually marked: woman doctor, black doctor, and so on. While the marking of a status signals infrequency—there are few female astronauts or male nurses—it may also imply inferiority. A "woman doctor" or a "black doctor" may be considered less qualified.

Thus, a privilege of those who are not stigmatized is that their master statuses are not used to discount their accomplishments or imply that they serve only special interests. Someone described as "a politician" is presumed to operate from a universality that someone described as "a white male politician" is not. Because white male politicians are rarely described as such, their anchoring in the reality of their own master statuses is hidden. In this way, those in marked statuses appear to be always operating from an "agenda," or "special interest" (e.g., a black politician is often presumed to represent only black constituents), while those in unmarked statuses can appear to be agenda-free. Being white and male thus becomes invisible, since it is not regularly identified as important. For this reason, some recommend identifying *everyone's* race and sex as a way to recognize that we are all grounded in our master statuses.

Marked and unmarked statuses also operate in classroom interactions. At white-dominated universities, white students are unlikely to be asked what white people think or asked to explain the "white experience." In this way, those who are white, male, heterosexual, and middle class appear to have no race, sex, sexual orientation, or social class, and thus have the privilege of escaping classroom discussions about the problems of "their people."

Stigmatized People and Their Experience of Privilege; Privileged People and Their Experience of Stigma

We have described some of the privileges enjoyed by those in nonstigmatized statuses. However, those with stigma also have some experience of privilege—it is just less frequent. For example, the Urban Institute investigated racial discrimination in employment by sending pairs of black and white male college students to apply for jobs in Washington, D.C., and Chicago. The students had been coached to present identical personal styles, dialects, educations, and job histories.

> In 20 percent [of the 576 job applications], the white applicant advanced farther in the hiring process [from obtaining a job application, to interview, to hiring] than his black counterpart, and in 15 percent the white applicant was offered a job while his equally qualified black partner was not. Blacks were favored over comparable white applicants in a much smaller share of cases; in 7 percent of the audits the black advanced farther in the hiring process, and in 5 percent only the black received the job offer. (Turner, Fix, and Struyk, 1991:18)

Black and white applicants both had some experience of preferential hiring, but the white applicant had two to three times more. A similar study of job discrimination against Latino males conducted in Chicago and San Diego indicated an even larger gap between the level of privilege experienced by Anglos and Latinos (Cross, Kenney, Mell, and Zimmermann, 1990).

Thus, concerns about "reverse discrimination" often miss the mark. While blacks, Latinos, Asian Americans, or white women are sometimes favored in hiring, they are not favored as *frequently* as white males. Discrimination continues in its historic direction as evidenced also in the constancy of race differences in income. In 1975, black per capita median annual income was 58.5 percent that of whites; in 1997, it was 60.5 percent; in 2003 it was 58.2 percent. In 1975, the same measure for Latinos was 56.1 percent of whites; in 1997, it was 52.7 percent; in 2003, it was 50.3 percent

(U.S. Department of Commerce, 1993:454; U.S. Bureau of the Census, 1997; U.S. Bureau of the Census, 2003).[2]

Because the focus is so frequently on how stigma affects those who bear it, it is easy to assume that only the targets of racism, sexism, homophobia, or classism are affected by it. But that is not the case. Those who are not themselves the targets of discrimination may still be affected by it. For example,

> Think of white slaveowners and their wives: the meaning of the sexual difference between them was constructed in part by the alleged contrast between them as whites and other men and women who were Black; what was supposed to characterize their relationship was not supposed to characterize the relationship between white men and Black women, or white women and Black men. . . . So even though the white men and women were of the same race, and even though they were not the victims of racism, this does not mean that we can understand the relationship between them without reference to their race and to the racism that their lives enacted. (Spelman, 1988:104–5)

Similarly, interactions between men are affected by sexism, even though the men themselves are not subject to it.

> For example, we can't understand the racism that fueled white men's lynching of Black men without understanding its connection to the sexism that shaped their protective and possessive attitudes toward white women. The ideology according to which whites are superior and ought to dominate Blacks is nested with the ideology according to which white men must protect their wives from attack by Black men. . . . That men aren't subject to sexism doesn't mean sexism has no effect on their relationships to each other. (Spelman, 1988:106)

Similar examples apply to sexual orientation, social class, and disability. Certainly, homophobia shapes heterosexual relations, treatment of those who are disabled affects those who are "temporarily able-bodied," and the stereotypes about poor people affect interactions among those in the middle class. Thus, the most obvious privilege of those in nonstigmatized statuses—that they are not affected by stigma— is not as straightforward as one might think.

Because privilege is usually invisible to those who possess it, they may assume that everyone is treated as they are. When they learn about other instances of discrimination, they may think that the incident was exceptional rather than routine, that the victim was overreacting or misinterpreting, or that the victim must have provoked the encounter. Such responses do not necessarily deny that the incident took place; rather, they deny that the event carries any negative or special meaning.

Through such dismissals, those operating from positions of privilege can deny the experience of those without privilege. For example, college-age students often describe university administrators as unresponsive until they have their parents call to complain. If the parents later said, "I don't know why *you* had such a problem with those people; they were very nice to *me*. Did you do something to antagonize

---

[2]Income figures exclude "money income received before payments for personal income, taxes, Social Security, union dues, Medicare deductions, food stamps, health benefits, subsidized housing, or rent-free housing and goods produced and consumed on the farm" (U.S. Department of Commerce, 1993:425).

them?" that would indicate they were oblivious to their privileged status in the university setting as well as unaware of their student's underprivileged status in it.

Dismissals like these treat the stigmatized person like a child inadequate to judge the world. Often such dismissals are framed in terms of the very stigma about which people are complaining. In this way, what stigmatized people say about their status is discounted precisely because they are stigmatized. The implication is that those who occupy a stigmatized status are somehow the ones *least* able to assess its consequence. The effect is to dismiss precisely those who have had the most experience with the problem.

This process, called *looping* or *rereading,* is described by many who have studied the lives of patients in psychiatric hospitals (Rosenhan, 1973; Schur, 1984; Goffman, 1961, 1963). If a patient says, "The staff here are being unfair to me," and the staff respond, "Of course he would think that—he's crazy," they have reread, or looped, his words through his status. His words have been heard in light of his stigma and dismissed for exactly that reason.

These dismissals serve a function. Dismissing another's experience of status-based mistreatment masks the possibility that one has escaped such treatment precisely because of one's privilege. If we do not acknowledge that *their* status affects *their* treatment, we need not acknowledge that *our* status affects *our* treatment. Thus, we avoid the larger truth that those who are treated well, those who are treated poorly, and all the rest in between are always evaluated both as individuals and as occupants of particular esteemed and disesteemed categories.

Hierarchies of Stigma and Privilege

While it may appear that people can be easily separated into two categories—privileged and stigmatized—every individual occupies several master statuses. The privilege or stigma that might be associated with one status emerges in the context of *all* of one's other statuses. For example, a middle-class, heterosexual Mexican American male may be privileged in terms of class, sex, and sexual orientation, but stigmatized by virtue of being Latino. Given the invisibility of privilege, he is more likely to notice the ways in which his status as Latino stigmatizes him than to notice the privileges that follow from his other statuses. Nonetheless, he is simultaneously all of his statuses; the privileges and disadvantages of each emerge in the context of all the others. An Anglo male and a Latino male may both be said to experience the privilege of sex, but they do not experience the *same* privilege.

While individuals may experience both privilege and stigma, some stigmas are so strong that they cancel out the privileges that one's other statuses might provide. For example, there is much evidence that the stigma of being black in America cancels any privileges that might be expected to follow from being middle-class. For example,

A large body of published research reveals that racial and ethnic minorities experience a lower quality of health services, and are less likely to receive even routine medical procedures than are white Americans. Relative to whites, African Americans—and in some cases, Hispanics—are less likely to receive appropriate cardiac medication or to undergo coronary artery bypass surgery, are less likely to receive hemodialysis and kidney transplantation, and are likely to receive a lower quality of basic clinical services such as intensive care, even when variations in such factors as insurance status, income, age, co-morbid conditions, and symptom expression are taken into account. . . . The majority of studies . . . find that racial and ethnic disparities remain even after adjustment for socioeconomic differences and other healthcare access-related factors. (Institute of Medicine, 2003:1, 2)

Despite the attention given to lending discrimination over the last decade by lenders, financial regulators, federal officials, secondary mortgage market institutions, and community groups, mortgage loan applications from black and Hispanic households are still much more likely to be denied than are applications from whites. For conventional home purchase loans in 2000, blacks were twice as likely as whites to be turned down for a loan. Similarly, the Hispanic/white denial ratio was 1.41. . . . [Mortgage] loan denial rates are higher for black and Hispanic applicants than for white applicants at all income levels. Moreover, for blacks, Hispanics, and Asians, the minority/white denial ratio increases steadily with income. This increase is particularly striking for blacks; the denial ratio is only 1.19 in the lowest income category but climbs to 2.48 in the highest category. (Ross and Yinger, 2002:6, 8)

When indices of racial segregation are computed within categories of income, occupation, or education, researchers have found that levels of Black-White segregation do not vary by social class. Black families annually earning at least $50,000 were just as segregated as those earning less than $2,500. Indeed, Black families annually earning more than $50,000 were more segregated than Hispanic or Asian families earning less than $2,500. In other words, the most affluent Blacks appear to be more segregated than the poorest Hispanics or Asians; and in contrast to the case of Blacks, Hispanic and Asian segregation levels fall steadily as income rises, reaching low or moderate levels at incomes of $50,000 or more. . . . [Contrary to the argument that this residential segregation is self-imposed] most Blacks continue to express strong support for the idea of integration. When asked on opinion polls whether they favor "desegregation, strict segregation, or something in-between," Blacks answer "desegregation" in large numbers. (Massey, 2001:411–412)

To isolate the effect of a criminal record on the job search . . . pairs of young, well-groomed, well-spoken college men with identical résumés [were sent to] apply for 350 advertised entry-level [low-wage] jobs in Milwaukee. The only difference was that one said he had served an 18-month prison sentence for cocaine possession. Two teams were black, two white. For the black testers, the callback rate was 5 percent if they had a criminal record and 14 percent if they did not. For whites, it was 17 percent with a criminal record, and 34 percent without. (Kroeger, 2004)

[As researcher Devah Pager notes] both race and criminal record had a huge effect on the likelihood of receiving a callback from employers. Probably the most surprising finding was that a black applicant with no criminal record was no more likely, in fact even slightly less likely, to receive a callback from employers than was a white applicant with a felony conviction. (Pager, 2003)

College-educated African Americans are having a hard time advancing their careers in the worst turnaround in the labor market in 25 years. Since the economic downturn of 2001, black professionals haven't been able to hold on to highly skilled jobs as they had done in previous recessions, according to the National Urban League's quarterly, *Jobs Report.*

Released 34 months after the recession started, the report notes that African Americans have a higher unemployment rate than whites and remain out of work longer despite the recovery. As of December 2003, the unemployment rate for college-educated whites was 2.6% and the rate for the African American counterparts was 4.1%. By comparison, 34 months into the 1990 recession, the rates for white and African American college graduates were 3.0% and 3.9% respectively. (Hocker, 2004)

Research on the effects of other stigmatized racial statuses has not been as thorough, nor are its findings as consistent, but it is clear that for African Americans, middle-class standing provides little protection against racism.

Does the stigma of being an out-of-the-closet gay or lesbian cause one to lose the privilege that comes from being middle class, white, or both? While the proportion of Americans who believe gays should have equal job opportunities has increased—from 56 percent in 1977 to 89 percent in 2004 (Gallup, 2004)—there is still no federal protection barring discrimination against gays in employment, housing, or health care. In 1998, President Clinton issued an executive order barring federal agencies from such discrimination, but the House of Representatives denied funding to carry out the order (Berke, 1998). Thus, it often seems as though gays are predominately white and at least middle class; in the absence of federal protection, few others can afford to publicly identify themselves as gay (Lester, 1994). While some jurisdictions enact protections, many of those ordinances are later challenged and repealed. At present, it appears that the stigma of being gay often overwhelms the privileges that one's other statuses might afford. The 1998 beating death of gay University of Wyoming student Matthew Shepard, like other hate crimes directed at gays and lesbians, offers horrifying evidence to that effect.

But which status is most important: one's race, sex, sexual orientation, or social class? For the sizable population that occupies multiple stigmatized statuses, it makes little sense to argue which status presents the greatest obstacle since most people live in the *intersection* of their master statuses. That experience is the subtext of many of the readings included in this book. While people are often asked to make alliances based on one status being more significant than another, their real experience is rarely so one-dimensional.

Philosopher Elizabeth Spelman (1988), however, suggests a way to assess the relative priority of each of these statuses. If each master status is imagined as a room we will enter, we can consider which sequential ordering of these rooms most accurately reflects our experience. If the first rooms we encounter are labeled black, white, or Asian, we will find ourselves in a room with those who share our "race" but are different in terms of sex, social class, ethnicity, and sexual orientation. If the second set of rooms is labeled male and female, we will find ourselves with people of the same race and sex. Other rooms might be labeled with sexual orientation or social class categorizations.

Many white feminists have presumed that the first rooms we encounter are sex categorizations, thus arguing that the statuses of female and male have priority over race or class designations; that one is discriminated against first by virtue of one's sex and then by race. Latino, black, and some white feminists have countered that the first rooms are race classifications. In this case, it is argued that racism so powerfully affects people that men and women within racial categories have more in common with one another than they do with those of the same sex but of a different race. Alliances of gay and lesbian people by implication assume that the first doors are marked gay and straight, with sex, race, and class following; disability rights activists would argue that status takes precedence over everything else. In addition to the orderings that correspond to the historical experience of categories of people, each of us likely maintains an ordering based on our personal experience of these statuses.

THE EXPERIENCE OF STIGMA

The previous section considered the privileges conferred by some master statuses; now we examine the stigma conferred by other master statuses.

In his classic analysis of stigma, sociologist Erving Goffman (1963) distinguished between the *discredited,* whose stigma is immediately apparent to an observer (for example, race, sex, some physical disabilities), and the *discreditable,* whose stigma can be hidden (for example, sexual orientation or social class). Since stigma plays out differently in the lives of the discredited and the discreditable, each will be examined separately.

The Discreditable: "Passing"

The discreditable are those who are *passing,* that is, not publicly acknowledging the stigmatized statuses they occupy. (Were they to acknowledge that status, they would become discredited.) The term *passing* comes from "passing as white," which emerged as a phenomenon after 1875 when southern states re-established racial segregation through hundreds of "Jim Crow"[3] laws. At that point, some African Americans passed as a way to get decent jobs.

> [S]ome who passed as white on the job lived as black at home. Some lived in the North as white part of the year and as black in the South the rest of the time. More men passed than women . . . the vast majority who could have passed permanently did not do so, owing to the pain of family separation, condemnation by most blacks, their fear of whites, and the loss of the security of the black community. . . . Passing as white probably reached an all-time peak between 1880 and 1925. (Davis, 1991:56–57)

"Passing as white" is now quite rare and strongly condemned by African Americans, a reaction that "indicate[s] the resolute insistence that anyone with even the slightest trace of black ancestry is black, and a traitor to act like a white" (Davis, 1991:138). We will use the term *passing* here to refer to those who have not made their stigmatized status evident; it is similar to the phrase "being in the closet" which is usually applied to gays. Because passing is now most frequent among gays—as well as most vehemently debated—many of our examples will focus on that stigmatized status.

---

[3]"Jim Crow" was "a blackface, singing-dancing-comedy characterization portraying black males as childlike, irresponsible, inefficient, lazy, ridiculous in speech, pleasure-seeking, and happy, [and was] a widespread stereotype of blacks during the last decades before emancipation . . . " (Davis, 1991:51). "Jim Crow" laws were laws by which whites imposed segregation following the Civil War.

One may engage in passing by chance as well as by choice. For example, the presumption that everyone is heterosexual can have the effect of putting gay people in the closet even when they had not intended to be. During a series of lectures on marriage and the family, one of our faculty colleagues realized that he had been making assignments, lecturing, and encouraging discussion assuming that all of the students in the class had, or wanted to have, heterosexual relationships. Unless his gay and lesbian students specifically countered his assumption, they were effectively passing. His actions forced them to choose between announcing or remaining silent about their status. Had he assumed that students would be involved only with others of the same race, he would have created a similar situation for those in interracial relationships. Thus, assumptions about others' private lives—for example, asking whether someone is married—may have the effect of making them choose between silence or an announcement of something they may consider private.

Since most heterosexuals assume that everyone else is heterosexual, many social encounters either put gay people in the closet or require that they announce their status.

> Every encounter with a new classful of students, to say nothing of a new boss, social worker, loan officer, landlord, doctor, erects new closets [that] . . . exact from at least gay people new surveys, new calculations, new draughts and requisitions of secrecy or disclosure. Even an *out* gay person deals daily with interlocutors about whom she doesn't know whether they know or not [or whether they would care]. . . . The gay closet is not a feature only of the lives of gay people. But for many gay people it is still the fundamental feature of social life; there can be few gay people . . . in whose lives the closet is not a shaping presence. (Sedgwick, 1990:68)

Inadvertent passing is also experienced by those whose racial status is not immediately apparent. An African American acquaintance of ours who looks white is often in settings in which others do not know that she is African American—or in which she does not know if they know. Thus, she must regularly decide how and when to convey that information. This is important to her as a way to discourage racist remarks, since whites often assume it is acceptable to make racist remarks to one another (as men often assume it is acceptable to make sexist remarks to other men, or as straights presume it acceptable to make antigay remarks to those they think are also straight). It is also important to her that others know she is black so that they understand the meaning of her words—so that they will hear her words through her status as an African American woman. Those whose stigma is not apparent must go to some lengths to avoid being in the closet by virtue of others' assumptions. Those with relatively invisible disabilities also face the tension of inadvertent passing. One of our students arrived in class in tears following an encounter with someone she had not realized was disabled. Seeing the young woman trip, the student had asked if she could help—and was angrily rebuffed. The offer to help had been taken as a show of pity.

But passing may also be an intentional choice. For example, one of our students, who was in the process of deciding that he was gay, had worked for many years at a local library, where he became friends with several of his coworkers. Much of the

banter at work, however, involved disparaging gay, or presumably gay, library pa-
trons. As he grappled with a decision about his own sexual identity, his social environment reminded him that being gay is a stigmatized status in American society.
This student did not so much face prejudice personally (since he was not "out" to his
work friends) as he faced an "unwilling acceptance of himself by individuals who are
prejudiced against persons of the kind he can be revealed to be" (Goffman, 1963:42).
Thus, he was not the person his friends took him to be. While survey data indicate
that those who personally know a gay man hold consistently more positive feelings
about gays in general (Herek and Glunt, 1993), the decision to publicly reveal a
stigma that others have gone on record as opposing is not made lightly.

Revealing stigma changes one's interactions with "normals," even with those who
are not particularly prejudiced. Such revelations are likely to alter important relationships. Parents sometimes disown gay children, just as they do children involved
in interracial relationships. Thus, the decision to pass or be "out" is not easily made.
For the discreditable, what Goffman euphemistically described as "information
management" is at the core of one's life. "To tell or not to tell; to let on or not to let
on; to lie or not to lie; and in each case, to whom, how, when, and where" (Goffman,
1963:42). Such choices are faced daily by those who are discreditable—not just those
who are gay and lesbian, but also those who are poor, have been imprisoned, attempted suicide, terminated a pregnancy through abortion, are HIV-positive, are
drug or alcohol dependent, or have been the victims of incest or rape. By contrast,
those who do not occupy stigmatized statuses don't have to invest emotional energy
in monitoring information about themselves; they can choose to talk openly about
their personal history.

Passing has both positive and negative aspects. On the positive side, passing lets the
stigmatized person exert some power over the situation; the person controls the information, the flow of events, and their privacy. By withholding his or her true identity until choosing to reveal it, the person may create a situation in which others'
prejudices are challenged. Passing forces one to be judged as an individual rather than
be discounted by virtue of a stigma. Passing also limits one's exposure to verbal and
physical abuse, allows for the development of previously forbidden relationships, and
improves employment security by minimizing one's exposure to discrimination.

On the negative side, passing consumes a good deal of time, energy, and emotion
in the management of personal information. It introduces deception and secrecy
even into close relationships. Passing also denies others the opportunity to prove
themselves unprejudiced, and it makes one vulnerable to blackmail by those who do
know about one's stigma.

The Discredited: Flaming

While the discreditable face problems of invisibility, *visibility* is the problem for
those who are discredited. Those who are discredited suffer from undue attention
and are subject to being stereotyped.

Being discredited means that one's stigma is immediately apparent to others. As
essayist bell hooks describes below, those who are discredited often have little pa-
tience for those who at least have the option of passing.

Many of us have been in discussions where a non-white person—a black person—struggles to explain to white folks that while we can acknowledge that gay people of all colors are harassed and suffer exploitation and domination, we also recognize that there is a significant difference that arises because of the visibility of dark skin. . . . While it in no way lessens the severity of such suffering for gay people, or the fear that it causes, it does mean that in a given situation the apparatus of protection and survival may be simply not identifying as gay. In contrast, most people of color have no choice. No one can hide, change, or mask dark skin color. White people, gay and straight, could show greater understanding of the impact of racial oppression on people of color by not attempting to make these oppressions synonymous, but rather by showing the ways they are linked and yet differ. (hooks, 1989:125)

For the discredited, stigma is likely to always shape interaction with those who are not stigmatized. However, its effect does not necessarily play out in ways one can easily determine. For those whose stigma is visible, every situation forces them to decide whether the world is responding to them or their stigma. Florynce Kennedy, a black activist in the civil rights and women's movements, once commented that the problem with being black in America was that you never knew whether what happened to you, good or bad, was because of your talents or because you were black (Kennedy, 1976). This situation was described in 1903 by sociologist W. E. B. Du Bois as the "double consciousness" of being black in America. The concept was key to Du Bois's classic, *The Souls of Black Folk,* for which he was rightfully judged "the father of serious black thought as we know it today" (Hare, 1982:xiii). Du Bois described double consciousness this way:

> the Negro . . . [is] gifted with a second-sight in this American world—a world which yields him no true self-consciousness, but only lets him see himself through the revelation of the other world. It is a peculiar sensation, this double consciousness, this sense of always looking at one's self through the eyes of others, of measuring one's soul by the tape of a world that looks on in amused contempt and pity. One ever feels his twoness. . . . (1982:45)

This is the sense of seeing oneself through the eyes of a harshly critical other, and it relates to our discussion of objectification in Framework Essay I. When those who are stigmatized view themselves from the perspective of the nonstigmatized, they have reduced themselves to objects. This theme of double or "fractured" consciousness can also be found in contemporary analyses of women's experience.

The greatest effect of being visibly stigmatized is on one's life chances—literally, one's chances for living. Thus, the readings in this book detail differences in income, employment, health, lifespan, education, targeting for violence, and the likelihood of arrest and imprisonment. In this essay, however, we will consider the more mundane difficulties created by stigmatization, particularly the sense of being "on stage."

The discredited often have the feeling of being watched or on display when they are in settings dominated by nonstigmatized people. For example, when women walk through male-dominated settings, they often feel they are on display in terms of their physical appearance. Asian, black, and Latino students in white-dominated universities often describe a sense of being on display in campus dining facilities. In such cases, the discredited are likely to feel that others are judging them in terms of their stigma.

As sociologist Rosabeth Moss Kanter (1980, 1993) has shown, this impression is probably true. When Kanter studied corporate settings in which one person was visibly different from the others, that person was likely to get a disproportionate share of attention. In fact, people in the setting were likely to closely monitor what the minority person did, which meant his or her mistakes were more likely to be noticed—and the mistakes of those in the rest of the group were more likely to be overlooked, since everyone was watching the minority person. Even in after-work socializing, the minority person was still subject to disproportionate attention.

Kanter also found that the minority person's behavior was likely to be interpreted in terms of the prevailing stereotypes about the members of that category. For example, when there were only a few men in a setting dominated by women, the men were subject to intense observation, and their behavior was filtered through the stereotypes about men. Perceptions were distorted to fit the preexisting beliefs.

Without the presence of a visibly different person, members of a setting are likely to see themselves as different from one another in various ways. Through contrast with the visibly different person, however, they notice their own similarities. In this way, majority group members may construct dichotomies—"us" and "them"—out of settings in which there are a few who are different. It is not surprising that those who are visibly different sometimes isolate themselves in response.

Still, none of this is inevitable. Kanter argues that once minority membership in a setting reaches 15 percent, these processes abate. Until that point, however, those who are in the minority (or visibly stigmatized) are the subject of a good deal of attention. As a consequence, they are often accused of "flaming." *Flaming* refers to behavior that is deliberately outrageous and provocative, behavior that shows off one's opinions, status, etc. Its recent association has been with hostile expression on the Internet, but in the realm of sexual orientation it has long meant being ostentatiously gay. The term probably originated as a criticism of gay men but has since been appropriated more positively by that community. We use the term here to describe an unabashed display of any stigmatized status.

Flaming is a charge that the nonstigmatized often level at those who are stigmatized. Although there are certainly occasions on which the discredited may deliberately make a show of their status, Kanter's work indicates that when their numbers are low in a setting, they are likely to be charged with flaming no matter what they do. When they are subjected to a disproportionate amount of attention and viewed through the lenses of stereotypes, almost anything the discredited do is likely to be noticed and attributed to the category to which they belong. Thus, one charge frequently leveled at those in discredited groups is that they are "so" black, Latino, gay, and so on—that is, that they make too big a show of their status.

This charge may affect those who are visibly stigmatized in various ways. Many are careful to behave in ways contrary to expectations. At other times, however, flaming may be deliberate. In the first session of one class, a student opened his remarks by saying, "Well, you all know I am a gay man, and as a gay man I think. . . ." The buzz of conversation stopped, other students stared at him, and one asked, "How would we know you were gay?" The student pointed to a pink triangle he had pinned to his book bag and explained that he thought they knew that someone wearing it would be gay. (Pink triangles were assigned to gay men during the Nazi era, black triangles to lesbians and other "unwanted" women. Both have been adopted as badges of pride among gay activists. Still, his logic was questionable: Anyone supportive of gay rights might wear the button.)

This announcement—which moved the student from a discreditable to a discredited status—may have been intended to keep his classmates from making overtly antigay comments in his presence. His strategy was designed to counter the negative consequences of passing. To avoid being mistakenly identified as straight, he decided to flame.

Similarly, light-skinned African Americans are required to "flame" as black, lest they be accused of trying to pass. In adolescence, light-skinned black men are often derided by their black and white peers as not "really" black and so they go to great lengths to counter that charge. While many light-skinned black men indicate that, when they are older, their skin color puts them at an advantage in both the black and white communities, in adolescence that is certainly not the case and thus they must flame their identity (Russell, Wilson, and Hall, 1992).

But flaming need not have this tragic side. For example, many bilingual Latino students talk about how much they enjoy a loud display of Spanish when Anglos are present; some Asian American students have described their pleasure in pursuing extended no-English-used card games in public spaces on campus. Black and gay adolescents sometimes entertain themselves by loudly affecting stereotypical behavior and then watching the disapproving looks from observers. Those who do not occupy stigmatized statuses may better appreciate these displays by remembering their experience of deliberate flaming as "obnoxious teenagers" in public settings. Thus, for some flaming may also be fun.

In all, those who are visibly stigmatized—who cannot or will not hide their identity—generate a variety of mechanisms to try to neutralize that stigma. Flaming is one of those mechanisms. It both announces one's stigmatized status and proclaims one's disregard for those who judge it negatively. Flaming neutralizes stigma by denying there is anything to be ashamed of. Thus, it functions as a statement of group pride.

European Ethnic Groups and Flaming

Whites of European ancestry sometimes envy the ethnic "flaming" of African Americans, Hispanics, and Asian Americans. As one student said, "It makes me feel like I just don't have anything." While his ancestry was a mix of Russian Jew, Italian Catholic, and Scotch-Irish Protestant, none of these identities seemed as compelling as the black, Asian, and Hispanic identities he saw around him.

This student's reaction reflects the transformed ethnic identity of the grandchildren and great-grandchildren of people who arrived in the peak immigration period of 1880 to 1920. At that time, Hungarians, Bohemians, Slovaks, Czechs, Poles, Russians, and Italians differed culturally and linguistically from one another and from the Irish, German, Scandinavian, and English immigrants who preceded them. Over the generations—and through intermarriage—this ethnic distinctiveness has been replaced by a socioeconomic "convergence" (Alba, 1990). Among non-Hispanic whites, ethnic ancestry no longer shapes occupation, residence, or political interest, nor is it the basis of the creation of communities of interest.[4] While many enjoy ethnic food and celebrations or have strong feelings attached to stories of immigration, the attachment is not likely to be deep or have much impact on behavior. Ethnic identifications are, instead, likely to be situational and self-selected, for example highlighting the Russian but ignoring the Irish and German sides of the family.

> But what of the consequences of this symbolic ethnicity? Is it a harmless way for Saturday suburban ethnics to feel connected and special? Is it a useful way to unite Americans by reminding us that we are all descended from immigrants who had a hard time and sacrificed a bit? Is it a lovely way to show that all cultures can coexist and that the pluralist values of diversity and tolerance are alive and well in the United States?
>
> The answer is yes and maybe no. Because aside from all of the positive, amusing, and creative aspects to this celebration of roots and ethnicity, there is a subtle way in which this ethnicity has consequences for American race relations. After all, in much of this discussion the implicit and sometimes explicit comparison for this symbolic ethnicity has been the social reality of racial and ethnic identities of America's minority groups. For the ways in which ethnicity is flexible and symbolic and voluntary for white middle-class Americans are the very ways in which it is not so for non-whites and Hispanic Americans.
>
> Thus the discussions of the influence of looks and surname on ethnic choice would look very different if one were describing a person who was one-quarter Italian and three-quarters African American or a woman whose married name changed from O'Connell to Martinez. The social and political consequences of being Asian or Hispanic or black are not symbolic for the most part, or voluntary. (Waters, 1990:155–156)

It is also possible that as ethnic identities disappear for whites, they will be replaced by heightened attention to race. "[M]ost whites do not experience their ethnicity as a definitive aspect of their social identity. . . . The 'twilight of white ethnicity' in a racially defined, and increasingly polarized, environment means that white racial identity will grow in salience" (Omi, 1996:182).

The Expectations of Those Who Share One's Stigma

Stigma also affects interaction among those *within* the stigmatized category. From others in the category one learns a sense of group pride and cues about how to behave, what to expect from those in and outside the category, and how to protect one's self. For those stigmatized by color, sex, or social class, such coping lessons probably come from family members. For those who are gay or lesbian, the lessons are usually provided later in life by members of the gay community.

Particularly for those with visible stigma, there are also frequent reminders that one will be seen as a representative of *all* members of the category. Thus, many in

---

[4]An exception to the process of convergence among European-originated groups may be white, urban, Catholic ethnics. Throughout the 19th century, American Catholic churches were established as specifically ethnic churches (called "nationality churches"). These mostly urban churches were tailored to serve a particular ethnic group, which often included sending a priest from the home country who spoke the immigrants' native language. Thus, within a single urban area one might find separate Irish, Italian, and Polish Catholic churches, as well as effectively separate Catholic schools. The formation of ethnic churches meant that parishes also became ethnically segregated. On occasion, those parishes came to constitute stable, distinctive, working-class ethnic enclaves. In these cases, ethnic identity continues as an active, viable reality.

stigmatized categories must factor in virtually everyone's opinion: What will others in my category think? What will those who are not stigmatized think? Indeed, one may even be criticized for failing to deal with oneself as a stigmatized person—"After all, who do you think you are?" In a sense, members of stigmatized categories may monitor one another much as they are policed by those outside the category, with the difference that those within one's category can at least claim to be operating for one's defense.

This point is illustrated in a story by the late tennis champion Arthur Ashe (1993). Ashe described watching his daughter play with a gift she had just received— a white doll—as they sat in the audience of a televised match in his honor. When the cameras panned his section of seats, he realized that he needed to get the doll away from his daughter or risk the anger of some black viewers who would argue that by letting his child play with a white doll, he appeared to be a bad role model for the black community.

A different example is provided by a Mexican American acquaintance who worked in an office with only a few other Hispanics, most of whom felt that the routes to upward mobility were closed to them. Together they drafted a letter to the firm's president detailing their concerns and seeking some corrective action. Although he had qualms about signing the letter, our acquaintance felt there was no alternative. Because he worked for management, he was then called in to explain his behavior, which his supervisor saw as disloyal. Thus, he was put in the position of having to explain that, as a Chicano, he could not have refused to sign the letter.

Codes of conduct for those in stigmatized categories often require loyalty to the group, a fact of life that in this case the supervisor was unaware of. Indeed, the operating rule for many in stigmatized categories is to avoid public disagreement with one another or public airing of the group's "dirty laundry." Such codes are not trivial, because when the codes are violated, members of stigmatized categories risk ostracism from a critical support network. The reality of discrimination makes it foolhardy to reject those who share one's stigma. What would it have meant to Arthur Ashe to lose the support of other African Americans? To whom would our acquaintance have turned in that organization had he refused to sign the letter? When they are unaware of these pressures, those in privileged categories may make impossible demands of those who are stigmatized; when aware of these pressures, however, such requests are clear tests of loyalty.

POINTS OF CONTENTION, STAGES OF CONTENTIOUSNESS

This essay focused on how privilege and stigma yield different treatment and different world views. In this final section we examine differing conceptions of racism. Then we consider the stages of identity development within which privilege and stigma are experienced.

As we said earlier, flaming sometimes leaves those who are not members of the stigmatized category feeling excluded. For example, when Latino students talked about their pleasure in speaking Spanish, an Anglo friend immediately responded with a description of how excluded she felt on those occasions. While aware of this, the Latino students nonetheless made it clear that they were not willing to forgo these opportunities. Their non-Spanish-speaking friends would just have to understand that it wasn't anything personal. This may well mark the bottom line: Those who are not stigmatized will sometimes feel and be excluded by their friends.

But another question is implied here: If the Hispanics exclude the Anglos, can the Anglos similarly exclude the Hispanics? As a way to approach this, consider the following two statements about gays and straights. In what ways are the statements similar, and in what ways different?

> A heterosexual says, "I can't stand gays. I don't want to be anywhere around them."
>
> A gay says, "I can't stand straights. I don't want to be anywhere around them."

While the statements are almost identical, the speakers come from very different positions of power. The heterosexual could probably structure his or her life so as to rarely interact with anyone gay, or at least anyone self-identified as gay. Most important, however, the heterosexual's attitude is consistent with major social, political, legal, and religious practices. Thus, the heterosexual in this example speaks from a position of some power, if only that derived from alignment with dominant cultural practices.

This is not the case for the gay person in this example, who is unlikely to be able to avoid contact with straights—and who would probably pay a considerable economic cost for self-segregation if that were attempted. There are no powerful institutional supports for hatred of heterosexuals. Similarly, the pleasure of exclusiveness exists against a backdrop of relative powerlessness, discrimination, and stigmatization. The same might be said of men's disparagement of women compared to women's disparagement of men. As one student wrote,

> As a male I have at times been on the receiving end of comments like, "Oh, you're just like all men," or "Why can't men show more emotion?" but these comments or the sentiments behind them do not carry any power to affect my status. Even in the instance of a black who sees me as a representative of all whites, his vision of me does not change my privileged status.

Thus, the exclusiveness of those in nonstigmatized statuses has as its backdrop relative powerfulness, a sense of entitlement, infrequent discrimination based on master status, and a general ability to avoid those who might be prejudiced against people like themselves. The forms of exclusion available to minority group members are unlikely to tangibly affect the lives of those in privileged statuses. Being able to exclude someone from a dance or a club is not as significant as being able to exclude that person from a job, residence, or an educational institution. This is what is meant when it is said that members of stigmatized categories may be prejudiced but not racist or sexist, etc.; they do not have access to the institutional power by which to significantly affect the lives of those in nonstigmatized groups.

The term *racist* also carries different connotations for blacks and whites. For whites, being color conscious is taken as evidence of racism (Blauner, 1992). This understanding of what it means to be a racist has its basis in the civil rights movement. If, as the civil rights movement taught, color should not make a difference in the way people are treated, whites who make a point of *not* noticing race argue that they are being polite and not racist (Frankenberg, 1993).

But given America's historical focus on race, it seems unrealistic for any of us to claim that we are oblivious to it. While many consider it impolite to mention race, differential treatment does not disappear as a consequence. Further, a refusal to notice race conveys that being black, Asian, or Latino is a "defect" that is indelicate (for whites) to mention. Thus, it can be argued that colorblindness is not really a strategy of politeness; rather, it is a strategy of power evasion. Since race clearly makes a difference in people's lives, pretending not to see it is a way to avoid noticing its effect. The alternative would be a strategy of race awareness, that is, of paying systematic attention to the impact of race on oneself and others (Frankenberg, 1993).

Different conceptions of racism also emerge in the course of *racial and ethnic identity development,* which is the "understanding shared by members of ethnic groups, of what it means to be black, white, Chicano, Irish, Jewish, and so on" (White and Burke, 1987:311). In Reading 27, Beverly Daniel Tatum describes black adolescent identity development, but we offer here a brief composite sketch of what appear to be the stages of this development (Cross, 1971, 1978; Hazen, 1992, 1994; Helms, 1990; Morton and Atkinson, 1983; Thomas, 1970; Thomas and Thomas, 1971). This framework might also be extended to the sex, class, disability, and sexual orientation identities we have focused on in this text. One important caution is necessary, however: Not everyone necessarily goes through each of these stages. For example, it is argued that African Americans are rarely found in the first of the stages we detail (Hazen, 1992).

For those in stigmatized statuses, the first stage of identity development involves an internalization of the culture's negative imagery. This stage may include the disparagement of others in one's group and a strong desire to be accepted by dominant group members. For women, this might mean being highly critical of other women. For those who are low income or gay, this stage might entail feelings of shame. For people of color, it might involve efforts to lighten one's skin, straighten one's hair, or have an eye tuck.

In the second stage, anger at the dominant culture emerges, usually as the result of specific encounters with discrimination. Philosopher Sandra Bartky (1990), focusing on women's discovery of the extent of sexism, describes this as a period in which sexism seems to be everywhere. Events and objects that previously had been neutral are discovered to be sexist; it becomes impossible to get through the day without becoming enraged—and the injustices one discovers are communicated to everyone within earshot. One's own behavior is also subject to scrutiny: "Am I being sexist to buy a doll for my niece?" Situations that used to be straightforward become moral tests.

The third stage is sometimes called an immersion stage, because it involves total involvement in one's own culture. In the previous stage, the individual is focused on evaluating and reacting to the dominant culture. In this stage, however, the focus shifts to one's own group. Dominant group members and the dominant group culture become less relevant to one's pursuits. This is often a period of participation in segregated activities and organizations as one seeks distance from dominant group members. While anger is somewhat lessened here, the process of re-evaluating one's old identity continues.

The final stage is described as a period of integration as one's stigmatized status becomes integrated with the other aspects of one's life rather than taking precedence over them. Still, an opposition to prejudice and discrimination continues. At this point, one can distinguish between supportive and unsupportive dominant group members and thus is more likely to establish satisfying relations with them.

For those who do not occupy stigmatized statuses, the first stage of race or ethnic identity development is identified as an unquestioning acceptance of dominant group values. This acceptance might take shape as being oblivious to discrimination or as espousing supremacist ideologies. In Reading 26, Thandeka posits that whiteness is produced when the white child submits to the threats of family members to obey the racial divides.

In the second stage, one becomes aware of stigmatization, often through an eye-opening encounter with discrimination. Such an experience may produce a commitment to social change or a sense of powerlessness. As is the case for those in stigmatized statuses, in this stage those in privileged statuses also find themselves overwhelmed by all the forms of discrimination they see, often accompanied by a sense of personal guilt. In an attempt to affiliate and offer assistance, they are likely to seek alliances with those in stigmatized statuses. On college campuses this timing couldn't be worse, since many of those in stigmatized statuses are at their peak level of anger at those in privileged groups.

In stage three, those in privileged statuses focus less on trying to win the approval of those in stigmatized groups and instead explore the history of privileged and stigmatized statuses. Learning how privilege has affected one's own life is often a central question in this period.

The final stage involves integrating one's privileged statuses with all the other aspects of one's life, recognizing those in stigmatized categorizations as distinctive individuals rather than romanticizing them as a category ("just because oppressors are bad, doesn't mean that the oppressed are good" [Spivak, 1994]), and understanding that many with privilege have worked effectively against discrimination.

The research on cognitive development in higher education bears interestingly on the stages of race and ethnic identity development and on the diversity of the college population. For example,

> . . . Diversity experiences in the first year of college seem to be particularly important in developing critical thinking. Indeed, diversity experiences at the beginning of college may positively affect a student's cognitive growth throughout his or her entire college career. Finally . . . racially oriented diversity experiences may be particularly important for the critical-thinking growth of white students. Indeed, experiences like making friends with students from a different race and attending a racial or cultural awareness workshop had positive impacts on growth in critical thinking only for white men and women. (Pascarella, 2001:25)

It is interesting that perceptions about balkanization and self-segregation are shared by many [college] students, even when the evidence suggests that students are often part of diverse networks. In his dissertation on "The Impact of Friendship Groups in a Multicultural University," Anthony Antonio found that although the students he surveyed perceived the campus to be segregated, their friendship groups tended to be racially and ethnically mixed. It appears that students see ethnic clusters but do not see the increasingly diverse peer groups that are emerging of which they are a part. It may also be that students on our campuses are reflecting some disappointment with the campuses' inability to capitalize fully on the potential created by increasing diversity on campus. These findings underscore the fact that individuals, groups, and institutions thrive under campus conditions that acknowledge multiple affiliations and identities and facilitate their engagement. (Smith and Schonfeld, 2000:19)

Passage through the stages of ethnic or racial identity is positively related to self-esteem for all American race and ethnic groups, but the relationship is stronger for those who are Asian American, African American, and Latino than for those who are white (Hazen, 1994:55). Indeed, on various measures of self-esteem, African Americans score significantly higher than those in other race or ethnic groups (Hazen, 1992).

We once observed an African American student explain to his white classmates that he and his sister both self-identified as black, even though their mother was white. At that point a white student asked why he didn't call himself white since he looked white and that status would yield him more privilege. In response, he detailed all the qualities he prized in the black community and said he would never give up that status to be white. Much of what he said was new to the white students; many had never thought there was anything positive about being black in America.

The student's question reflected the common assumption that those who are stigmatized wish they belonged to the privileged group. Yet the woman who asked the question was clear that she never wanted to be a male, which was equally surprising to the men in the class. Thus, many men presume there is nothing positive about being female, many straights assume there is nothing positive about being gay, many able-bodied people assume that being disabled ensures misery and loneliness (French, 1996), and many in the middle and upper classes assume there is nothing positive in life for those who are poor. But most people value and appreciate the statuses they occupy. We may wish those statuses weren't stigmatized or overprivileged, but that does not mean we would want to be other than who we are.

THE READINGS IN THIS SECTION

Our goal in this essay was to provide you with a framework by which to make sense of people's experience of privilege and stigma. Because there is a great deal of material that illustrates privilege and stigma, for this section we tried to select readings with broad applicability.

KEY CONCEPTS

discredited and discreditable The discredited are those whose stigma is known or apparent to others. The discreditable are those whose stigma is unknown or invisible to others; they are not yet discredited. (pages **180–85**)

double consciousness A concept first offered by W. E. B. Du Bois to describe seeing oneself (or members of one's group) through the eyes of a critical, dominant group member. (pages **183–84**)

entitlement The belief that one has the right to respect, protection, reward, and other privileges. (page **174**)

flaming As used in this text, a flagrant display of one's stigmatized status; more often used to refer to gay men acting effeminately. (pages **182–86**)

looping or rereading Interpreting (and usually dismissing) someone's words or actions because of the status that the person occupies. (page **177**)

marked and unmarked statuses A marked status is one identified as "special" in some way, for example, a *blind* musician or a *woman* doctor. Unmarked statuses, such as musician or doctor, do not have such qualifiers. (page **174**)

passing Not revealing a stigmatized identity. (pages **180–82**)

privilege The advantages provided by some statuses. (pages **167–75**)

REFERENCES

Alba, Richard D. 1990. *Ethnic Identity: The Transformation of White America.* New Haven, CT: Yale University Press.

Amnesty International. 1997. *Amnesty International Death Penalty Developments in the U.S.A. in 1997.* www.amnesty-usa/abolish/race.html.

Ashe, Arthur. 1993. *Days of Grace.* New York: Ballantine.

Associated Press. 2003. Are Legacy College Admissions Racist? March 5.

Bartky, Sandra. 1990. *Femininity and Domination: Studies in the Phenomenology of Oppression.* New York: Routledge.

Berke, Richard. 1998. Chasing the Polls on Gay Rights. *New York Times,* August 2, 4:3.

Blauner, Bob. 1992. Talking Past Each Other: Black and White Languages of Race. *The American Prospect,* Summer.

Carter, Tom. 2002. Profiling Is "Flawed" Tool to Beat Terror. *The Washington Times,* January 14, 12.

Cary, Lorene. 1991. *Black Ice.* New York: Knopf.

Cross, H., G. Kenney, J. Mell, and W. Zimmerman. 1990. *Employer Practices: Differential Treatment of Hispanic and Anglo Job Seekers.* Washington, DC: The Urban Institute.

Cross, W. E., Jr. 1971. The Negro-to-Black Conversion Experience: Toward a Psychology of Black Liberation. *Black World,* 20 (9):13–17.

———. 1978. The Thomas and Cross Models of Psychological Nigresence: A Review. *The Journal of Black Psychology,* 5(1):13–31.

Davis, F. James. 1991. *Who Is Black? One Nation's Definition.* University Park, PA: Pennsylvania University Press.

Du Bois, W. E. B. 1982. *The Souls of Black Folk.* New York: Penguin. (Originally published in 1903.)

Ettinger, Maia. 1994. The Pocahontas Paradigm, or Will the Subaltern Please Shut Up? *Tilting the Tower,* edited by Linda Garber, 51–55. New York: Routledge.

Frankenberg, Ruth. 1993. *White Women, Race Matters: The Social Construction of Whiteness.* Minneapolis: University of Minnesota Press.

French, Sally. 1996. Simulation Exercises in Disability Awareness Training: A Critique. *Beyond Disability: Towards an Enabling Society,* edited by Gerald Hales, 114–23. London: Sage Publications.

Gallup Organization, Gallup Poll News Service. 2004. Homosexual Relations.

Goffman, Erving. 1961. *Asylums.* New York: Doubleday Anchor.

———. 1963. *Stigma: Notes on the Management of Spoiled Identity.* Englewood Cliffs, NJ: Prentice-Hall.

Hare, Nathan. 1982. W. E. Burghart Du Bois: An Appreciation, pp. xiii–xxvii in *The Souls of Black Folk.* New York: Penguin. (Originally published in 1969.)

Harris, David. 2002. Flying While Arab: Lessons from the Racial Profiling Controversy. *Civil Rights Journal,* 6(1):8–14.

———. 2003. The Reality of Racial Disparity in Criminal Justice: The Significance of Data Collection. *Law and Contemporary Problems,* 66(3):71–95.

Hazen, Sharlie Hogue. 1992. *The Relationship between Ethnic/Racial Identity Development and Ego Identity Development.* Ph.D. proposal, Department of Psychology, George Mason University.

———. 1994. *The Relationship between Ethnic/Racial Identity Development and Ego Identity Development.* Ph.D. dissertation, Department of Psychology, George Mason University.

Helms, J. E. 1990. An Overview of Black Racial Identity Theory. *Black and White Racial Identity: Theory, Research, and Practice,* edited by J. E. Helms, 9–33. New York: Greenwood Press.

Herek, Gregory M. 1992. The Social Context of Hate Crimes. *Hate Crimes: Confronting Violence against Lesbians and Gay Men,* edited by Gregory Herek and Kevin Berrill, 89–104. Newbury Park, CA: Sage.

———, and Eric K. Glunt. 1993. Heterosexuals Who Know Gays Personally Have More Favorable Attitudes. *The Journal of Sex Research,* 30:239–44.

Hocker, Cliff. 2004. Worst Labor Market for Black Professionals in 25 Years. *Black Enterprise,* May, 26.

hooks, bell. 1989. *Talking Back: Thinking Feminist, Thinking Black.* Boston: South End Press.

Institute of Medicine, Board on Health Sciences. 2003. *Unequal Treatment: Confronting Racial and Ethnic Disparities in Health Care.* Washington, DC: National Academy of Sciences.

Kahlenberg, Richard D. 2004. Toward Affirmative Action for Economic Diversity. *The Chronicle of Higher Education,* March 19, B11–B13.

Kanter, Rosabeth Moss. 1993. *Men and Women of the Corporation.* New York: Basic Books. (Originally published in 1976.)

———, with Barry A. Stein. 1980. *A Tale of 'O': On Being Different in an Organization.* New York: Harper and Row.

Kennedy, Florynce. 1976. *Color Me Flo: My Hard Life and Good Times.* Englewood Cliffs, NJ: Prentice-Hall.

Kimmel, Michael S., and Michael A. Messner, eds. 1989. *Men's Lives.* New York: Macmillan.

Kirp, David L. 2003. No-Brainer. *Nation,* November 10, 17–19.

Kocieniewski, David. 2002. New Jersey Troopers Avoid Jail in Case That Highlighted Profiling. *The New York Times,* January 15, A1.

Kornheiser, Tony. 1990. The Ordinary Face of Racism. *Washington Post,* May 16, F:1, 9.

Kroeger, Brooke. 2004. When a Dissertation Makes a Difference. *The New York Times,* March 20, B9.

Lester, Joan. 1994. *The Future of White Men and Other Diversity Dilemmas.* Berkeley, CA: Conari Press.

Massey, Douglas S. 2001. Residential Segregation and Neighborhood Conditions in U.S. Metropolitan Areas. *America Becoming: Racial Trends and Their Consequences,* edited by Neil J. Smelser, William Julius Wilson, and Faith Mitchell, 391–434. Washington, DC: National Academy Press.

McIntosh, Peggy. 1988. White Privilege and Male Privilege: A Personal Account of Coming to See Correspondences through Work in Women's Studies. Working Paper Number 189, Wellesley College, Center for Research on Women, Wellesley, MA.

Morton, G., and D. R. Atkinson. 1983. Minority Identity Development and Preference for Counselor Race. *Journal of Negro Education,* 52(2):156–61.

Omi, Michael. 1996. Racialization in the Post-Civil Rights Era. *Mapping Multiculturalism,* edited by Avery F. Gordon and Christopher Newfield, 178–86. Minneapolis: University of Minnesota Press.

Pager, Devah. 2003. Discrimination in Hiring. *Northwestern University Newsfeed,* November 12.

Pascarella, Ernest T. 2001. Cognitive Growth in College. *Change,* November–December, 21–27.

Rosenhan, D. L. 1973. On Being Sane in Insane Places. *Science,* 179:250–58.

Ross, Stephen, and John Yinger. 2002. *The Color of Credit: Mortgage Discrimination, Research Methodology, and Fair-Lending Enforcement.* Cambridge, MA: MIT Press.

Russell, Kathy, Midge Wilson, and Ronald Hall. 1992. *The Color Complex: The Politics of Skin Color among African Americans.* New York: Harcourt Brace Jovanovich.

Schur, Edwin. 1984. *Labeling Women Deviant: Gender, Stigma, and Social Control.* New York: Random House.

Sedgwick, Eve Kosofsky. 1990. *The Epistemology of the Closet.* Berkeley: University of California Press.

Smith, Daryl G., and Natalie B. Schonfeld. 2000. The Benefits of Diversity: What the Research Tells Us. *About Campus,* November–December, 16–23.

Smith, Tom W. 2001. *Intergroup Relations in a Diverse America: Data from the 2000 General Social Survey.* The American Jewish Committee. www.ajc.org.

Sniderman, Paul M., and Edward G. Carmines. 1997. *Reaching beyond Race.* Cambridge, MA: Harvard University Press.

Spelman, Elizabeth. 1988. *Inessential Woman.* Boston: Beacon Press.

Spivak, Gayatre. 1994. George Mason University Cultural Studies presentation.

Thomas, C. 1970. Different Strokes for Different Folks. *Psychology Today* 4(4):48–53, 78–80.

———, and S. Thomas. 1971. Something Borrowed, Something Black. In *Boys No More: A Black Psychologist's View of Community,* edited by C. Thomas. Beverly Hills, CA: Glencoe Press.

Tokarczyk, Michelle M. 2004. Promises to Keep: Working Class Students and Higher Education. *What's Class Got to Do with It? American Society in the Twenty-First Century,* edited by Michael Zweig, 161–167. Ithaca, NY: ILR Press.

Turner, Margery Austin, Michael Fix, and Raymond J. Struyk. 1991. *Opportunities Denied, Opportunities Diminished: Discrimination in Hiring.* Washington, DC: The Urban Institute.

U.S. Bureau of the Census. 1997. *Money Income in the United States.* Washington, DC: U.S. Government Printing Office.

————. 2003. *Money Income in the United States.* www.census.gov.

U.S. Department of Commerce. 1993. *Statistical Abstract of the United States, 1992.* Washington, DC: U.S. Government Printing Office.

U.S. Department of Labor, Bureau of Labor Statistics. 1993. *Employment and Earnings.* Washington, DC: U.S. Government Printing Office

Waters, Mary C. 1990. *Ethnic Options: Choosing Identities in America.* Berkeley: University of California Press.

White, C. L., and P. J. Burke. 1987. Ethnic Role Identity among Black and White College Students: An Interactionist Approach. *Sociological Perspectives,* 30(3):310–31.

Williams, Patricia J. 1991. Teleology on the Rocks. *The Alchemy of Race and Rights.* Cambridge, MA: Harvard University Press.

READING 21

Oppression

Marilyn Frye

It is a fundamental claim of feminism that women are oppressed. The word "oppression" is a strong word. It repels and attracts. It is dangerous and dangerously fashionable and endangered. It is much misused, and sometimes not innocently.

The statement that women are oppressed is frequently met with the claim that men are oppressed too. We hear that oppressing is oppressive to those who oppress as well as to those they oppress. Some men cite as evidence of their oppression their much-advertised inability to cry. It is tough, we are told, to be masculine. When the stresses and frustrations of being a man are cited as evidence that oppressors are oppressed by their oppressing, the word "oppression" is being stretched to meaninglessness; it is treated as though its scope includes any and all human experience of limitation or suffering, no matter the cause, degree or consequence. Once such usage has been put over on us, then if ever we deny that any person or group is oppressed, we seem to imply that we think they never suffer and have no feelings. We are accused of insensitiv-

ity; even of bigotry. For women, such accusation is particularly intimidating, since sensitivity is one of the few virtues that has been assigned to us. If we are found insensitive, we may fear we have no redeeming traits at all and perhaps are not real women. Thus are we silenced before we begin: the name of our situation drained of meaning and our guilt mechanisms tripped.

But this is nonsense. Human beings can be miserable without being oppressed, and it is perfectly consistent to deny that a person or group is oppressed without denying that they have feelings or that they suffer.

We need to think clearly about oppression, and there is much that mitigates against this. I do not want to undertake to prove that women are oppressed (or that men are not), but I want to make clear what is being said when we say it. We need this word, this concept, and we need it to be sharp and sure.

The root of the word "oppression" is the element "press." *The press of the crowd; pressed into military service; to press a pair of pants; printing press; press the button.* Presses are used to mold things or flatten them or reduce them in bulk, sometimes to reduce them by squeezing out the gasses or liquids in them. Something pressed is something caught between or among forces and barriers which are so related to each other that jointly they restrain, restrict or prevent the thing's motion or mobility. Mold. Immobilize. Reduce.

Marilyn Frye is a professor of philosophy at Michigan State University.

The mundane experience of the oppressed provides another clue. One of the most characteristic and ubiquitous features of the world as experienced by oppressed people is the double bind situations in which options are reduced to a very few and all of them expose one to penalty, censure or deprivation. For example, it is often a requirement upon oppressed people that we smile and be cheerful. If we comply, we signal our docility and our acquiescence in our situation. We need not, then, be taken note of. We acquiesce in being made invisible, in our occupying no space. We participate in our own erasure. On the other hand, anything but the sunniest countenance exposes us to being perceived as mean, bitter, angry or dangerous. This means, at the least, that we may be found "difficult" or unpleasant to work with, which is enough to cost one one's livelihood; at worst, being seen as mean, bitter, angry or dangerous has been known to result in rape, arrest, beating and murder. One can only choose to risk one's preferred form and rate of annihilation.

Another example: It is common in the United States that women, especially younger women, are in a bind where neither sexual activity nor sexual inactivity is all right. If she is heterosexually active, a woman is open to censure and punishment for being loose, unprincipled or a whore. The "punishment" comes in the form of criticism, snide and embarrassing remarks, being treated as an easy lay by men, scorn from her more restrained female friends. She may have to lie and hide her behavior from her parents. She must juggle the risks of unwanted pregnancy and dangerous contraceptives. On the other hand, if she refrains from heterosexual activity, she is fairly constantly harassed by men who try to persuade her into it and pressure her to "relax" and "let her hair down"; she is threatened with labels like "frigid," "uptight," "manhater," "bitch" and "cocktease." The same parents who would be disapproving of her sexual activity may be worried by her inactivity because it suggests she is not or will not be popular, or is not sexually normal. She may be charged with lesbianism. If a woman is raped, then if she has been heterosexually active she is subject to the presumption that she liked it (since her activity is presumed to show that she likes sex), and if she has not been heterosexually active, she is subject to the presumption that she liked it (since she is supposedly "repressed and frustrated"). Both heterosexual activity and heterosexual nonactivity are likely to be taken as proof that you wanted to be raped, and hence, of course, weren't *really* raped at all. You can't win. You are caught in a bind, caught between systematically related pressures.

Women are caught like this, too, by networks of forces and barriers that expose one to penalty, loss or contempt whether one works outside the home or not, is on welfare or not, bears children or not, raises children or not, marries or not, stays married or not, is heterosexual, lesbian, both or neither. Economic necessity; confinement to racial and/or sexual job ghettos; sexual harassment; sex discrimination; pressures of competing expectations and judgments about *women, wives* and *mothers* (in the society at large, in racial and ethnic subcultures and in one's own mind); dependence (full or partial) on husbands, parents or the state; commitment to political ideas; loyalties to racial or ethnic or other "minority" groups; the demands of self-respect and responsibilities to others. Each of these factors exists in complex tension with every other, penalizing or prohibiting all of the apparently available options. And nipping at one's heels, always, is the endless pack of little things. If one dresses one way, one is subject to the assumption that one is advertising one's sexual availability; if one dresses another way, one appears to "not care about oneself" or to be "unfeminine." If one uses "strong language," one invites categorization as a whore or slut; if one does not, one invites categorization as a "lady," one too delicately constituted to cope with robust speech or the realities to which it presumably refers.

The experience of oppressed people is that the living of one's life is confined and shaped by forces and barriers which are not accidental or occasional and hence avoidable, but are systematically related to each other in such a way as to catch one between and among them and restrict or penalize motion in any direction. It is the experience of being caged in:

all avenues, in every direction, are blocked or booby trapped.

Cages. Consider a birdcage. If you look very closely at just one wire in the cage, you cannot see the other wires. If your conception of what is before you is determined by this myopic focus, you could look at that one wire, up and down the length of it, and be unable to see why a bird would not just fly around the wire any time it wanted to go somewhere. Furthermore, even if, one day at a time, you myopically inspected each wire, you still could not see why a bird would have trouble going past the wires to get anywhere. There is no physical property of any one wire, *nothing* that the closest scrutiny could discover, that will reveal how a bird could be inhibited or harmed by it except in the most accidental way. It is only when you step back, stop looking at the wires one by one, microscopically, and take a macroscopic view of the whole cage, that you can see why the bird does not go anywhere; and then you will see it in a moment. It will require no great subtlety of mental powers. It is perfectly *obvious* that the bird is surrounded by a network of systematically related barriers, no one of which would be the least hindrance to its flight, but which, by their relations to each other, are as confining as the solid walls of a dungeon.

It is now possible to grasp one of the reasons why oppression can be hard to see and recognize: one can study the elements of an oppressive structure with great care and some good will without seeing the structure as a whole, and hence without seeing or being able to understand that one is looking at a cage and that there are people there who are caged, whose motion and mobility are restricted, whose lives are shaped and reduced.

The arresting of vision at a microscopic level yields such common confusion as that about the male door opening ritual. This ritual, which is remarkably widespread across classes and races, puzzles many people, some of whom do and some of whom do not find it offensive. Look at the scene of the two people approaching a door. The male steps slightly ahead and opens the door. The male holds the door open while the female glides through.

Then the male goes through. The door closes after them. "Now how," one innocently asks, "can those crazy womenslibbers say that is oppressive? The guy *removed* a barrier to the lady's smooth and unruffled progress." But each repetition of this ritual has a place in a pattern, in fact in several patterns. One has to shift the level of one's perception in order to see the whole picture.

The door-opening pretends to be a helpful service, but the helpfulness is false. This can be seen by noting that it will be done whether or not it makes any practical sense. Infirm men and men burdened with packages will open doors for able bodied women who are free of physical burdens. Men will impose themselves awkwardly and jostle everyone in order to get to the door first. The act is not determined by convenience or grace. Furthermore, these very numerous acts of unneeded or even noisome "help" occur in counterpoint to a pattern of men not being helpful in many practical ways in which women might welcome help. What *women* experience is a world in which gallant princes charming commonly make a fuss about being helpful and providing small services when help and services are of little or no use, but in which there are rarely ingenious and adroit princes at hand when substantial assistance is really wanted either in mundane affairs or in situations of threat, assault or terror. There is no help with the (his) laundry; no help typing a report at 4:00 a.m.; no help in mediating disputes among relatives or children. There is nothing but advice that women should stay indoors after dark, be chaperoned by a man, or when it comes down to it, "lie back and enjoy it."

The gallant gestures have no practical meaning. Their meaning is symbolic. The door-opening and similar services provided are services which really are needed by people who are for one reason or another incapacitated—unwell, burdened with parcels, etc. So the message is that women are incapable. The detachment of the acts from the concrete realities of what women need and do not need is a vehicle for the message that women's actual needs and interests are unimportant or irrelevant. Finally, these gestures imitate the behavior of servants toward masters and thus mock women, who are in most respects the servants and caretakers of men. The message of the false helpfulness of male gallantry is female dependence, the invisibility or insignificance of women, and contempt for women.

One cannot see the meanings of these rituals if one's focus is riveted upon the individual event in all its particularity, including the particularity of the individual man's present conscious intentions and motives and the individual woman's conscious perception of the event in the moment. It seems sometimes that people take a deliberately myopic view and fill their eyes with things seen microscopically in order not to see macroscopically. At any rate, whether it is deliberate or not, people can and do fail to see the oppression of women because they fail to see macroscopically and hence fail to see the various elements of the situation as systematically related in larger schemes.

As the cageness of the birdcage is a macroscopic phenomenon, the oppressiveness of the situations in which women live our various and different lives is a macroscopic phenomenon. Neither can be *seen* from a microscopic perspective. But when you look macroscopically you can see it a network of forces and barriers which are systematically related and which conspire to the immobilization, reduction and molding of women and the lives we live. . . .

It seems to be the human condition that in one degree or another we all suffer frustration and limitation, all encounter unwelcome barriers, and all are damaged and hurt in various ways. Since we are a social species, almost all of our behavior and activities are structured by more than individual inclination and the conditions of the planet and its atmosphere. No human is free of social structures, nor (perhaps) would happiness consist in such freedom. Structure consists of boundaries, limits and barriers; in a structured whole, some motions and changes are possible, and others are not. If one is looking for an excuse to dilute the word "oppression," one can use the fact of social structure as an excuse and say that everyone is oppressed. But if one would rather get clear about what oppression is

and is not, one needs to sort out the sufferings, harms and limitations and figure out which are elements of oppression and which are not.

From what I have already said here, it is clear that if one wants to determine whether a particular suffering, harm or limitation is part of someone's being oppressed, one has to look at it *in context* in order to tell whether it is an element in an oppressive structure: one has to see if it is part of an enclosing structure of forces and barriers which tends to the immobilization and reduction of a group or category of people. One has to look at how the barrier or force fits with others and to whose benefit or detriment it works. As soon as one looks at examples, it becomes obvious that not everything which frustrates or limits a person is oppressive, and not every harm or damage is due to or contributes to oppression.

If a rich white playboy who lives off income from his investments in South African diamond mines should break a leg in a skiing accident at Aspen and wait in pain in a blizzard for hours before he is rescued, we may assume that in that period he suffers. But the suffering comes to an end; his leg is repaired by the best surgeon money can buy and he is soon recuperating in a lavish suite, sipping Chivas Regal. Nothing in this picture suggests a structure of barriers and forces. He is a member of several oppressor groups and does not suddenly become oppressed because he is injured and in pain. Even if the accident was caused by someone's malicious negligence, and hence someone can be blamed for it and morally faulted, that person still has not been an agent of oppression.

Consider also the restriction of having to drive one's vehicle on a certain side of the road. There is no doubt that this restriction is almost unbearably frustrating at times, when one's lane is not moving and the other lane is clear. There are surely times, even, when abiding by this regulation would have harmful consequences. But the restriction is obviously wholesome for most of us most of the time. The restraint is imposed for our benefit, and does benefit us; its operation tends to encourage our *continued* motion, not to immobilize us. The limits imposed by traffic regulations are limits most of us would cheerfully impose on ourselves given that we knew others would follow them too. They are part of a structure which shapes our behavior, not to our reduction and immobilization, but rather to the protection of our continued ability to move and act as we will.

Another example: The boundaries of a racial ghetto in an American city serve to some extent to keep white people from going in, as well as to keep ghetto dwellers from going out. A particular white citizen may be frustrated or feel deprived because s/he cannot stroll around there and enjoy the "exotic" aura of a "foreign" culture, or shop for bargains in the ghetto swap shops. In fact, the existence of the ghetto, of racial segregation, does deprive the white person of knowledge and harm her/his character by nurturing unwarranted feelings of superiority. But this does not make the white person in this situation a member of an oppressed race or a person oppressed because of her/his race. One must look at the barrier. It limits the activities and the access of those on both sides of it (though to different degrees). But it is a product of the intention, planning and action of whites for the benefit of whites, to secure and maintain privileges that are available to whites generally, as members of the dominant and privileged group. Though the existence of the barrier has some bad consequences for whites, the barrier does not exist in systematic relationship with other barriers and forces forming a structure oppressive to whites; quite the contrary. It is part of a structure which oppresses the ghetto dwellers and thereby (and by white intention) protects and furthers white interests as dominant white culture understands them. This barrier is not oppressive to whites, even though it is a barrier to whites.

Barriers have different meanings to those on opposite sides of them, even though they are barriers to both. The physical walls of a prison no more dissolve to let an outsider in than to let an insider out, but for the insider they are confining and limiting while to the outsider they may mean protection from what s/he takes to be threats posed by insiders—freedom from harm or anxiety. A set of social and economic barriers and forces separating two groups may be felt, even painfully, by members of both groups and yet may mean confinement to one and liberty and enlargement of opportunity to the other.

The service sector of the wives/mommas/assistants/girls is almost exclusively a woman-only sector; its boundaries not only enclose women but to a very great extent keep men out. Some men sometimes encounter this barrier and experience it as a restriction on their movements, their activities, their control or their choices of "lifestyle." Thinking they might like the simple nurturant life (which they may imagine to be quite free of stress, alienation and hard work), and feeling deprived since it seems closed to them, they thereupon announce the discovery that they are oppressed, too, by "sex roles." But that barrier is erected and maintained by men, for the benefit of men. It consists of cultural and economic forces and pressures in a culture and economy controlled by men in which, at every economic level and in all racial and ethnic subcultures, economy, tradition—and even ideologies of liberation—work to keep at least local culture and economy in male control.*

DISCUSSION QUESTIONS

1. What are the central elements of Marilyn Frye's definition of oppression and an oppressed group?
2. Frye argues that the concept of "oppression" needs to be clearly defined. Why? Do you agree with her?
3. Do you find Frye's birdcage metaphor convincing?

---

*Of course this is complicated by race and class. Machismo and "Black manhood" politics seem to help keep Latin or Black men in control of more cash than Latin or Black women control; but these politics seem to me also to ultimately help keep the larger economy in *white* male control.

RACE AND ETHNICITY

What Are You?

Joanne Nobuko Miyamoto

when I was young
kids used to ask me
what are you?
I'd tell them what my mom told me
I'm an American
chin, chin, Chinaman
you're a Jap!
flashing hot inside
I'd go home
my mom would say
don't worry
he who walks alone
walks faster
people kept asking me
what are you?
and I would always answer
I'm an American
they'd say
no, what nationality
I'm an American!
that's where I was born
flashing hot inside
and when I'd tell them what they wanted to know
Japanese
. . . Oh, I've been to Japan
I'd get it over with
me they could catalogue and file me
pigeon hole me
so they'd know just how
to think of me
priding themselves
they could guess the difference
between Japanese and Chinese
they had me wishing
I was American
just like them
they had me wishing I was what I'd

been seeing in movies and on TV
on bill boards and in magazines
and I tried
while they were making laws in California
against us owning land
we were trying to be american
and laws against us intermarrying with white
people
we were trying to be american
our people volunteered to fight against
their own country
trying to be american
when they dropped the atom bomb
Hiroshima and Nagasaki
we were still trying
finally we made it
most of our parents
fiercely dedicated to give us
a good education
to give us everything they never had
we made it
now they use us as an example
to the blacks and browns
how we made it
how we overcame
but there was always
someone asking me
what are you?
Now I answer
I'm an Asian
and they say
why do you want to separate yourselves
now I say
I'm Japanese
and they say
don't you know this is the greatest country
in the world
Now I say in america
I'm part of the third world people
and they say
if you don't like it here
why don't you go back.

DISCUSSION QUESTIONS

1. Why are people asked what are you?
2. What should you do to be an American?

Joanne Nobuko Miyamoto is artistic director of Great Leap, Inc., a nonprofit arts organization that uses the arts to promote deeper understanding between the diverse cultures of America. Her works include musicals such as *Chop Suey, Talk Story,* and *Joanne Is My Middle Name;* the short film *Gaman;* and a video, *A Gathering of Joy.* She also produces *A Slice of Rice, Frijoles and Greens,* a touring multicultural theater production.

READING 23

Everybody's Ethnic Enigma

Jelita McLeod

The forty-something black man I was sharing an elevator with looked at me for a while before he asked the question I had been expecting. He wanted to know my ethnicity.

"I'm mixed," I told him. "Half-Caucasian, half-Asian."

"Oh," he said, disappointed. "I thought you were one of us."

I knew what the question would be because people have been asking me the same thing as long as I can remember. I've found that curiosity easily overrides courtesy. I am asked in stores, on the bus, on the street, in line at McDonald's, even in public bathrooms. Almost always the inquirers are total strangers, as if not knowing me allows them to abandon social graces they might otherwise feel the need to display. Sometimes they will ask me

---

Jelita McLeod is a writer-editor at Prince George's Community College in Largo, Maryland. Her work has appeared in *The Washington Post, The Sun,* and *International Educator.* She has also provided commentary for National Public Radio.

straight out, but very often they use coded language, as in "What's your background?" Then there's "Where are you from?" which is really a two-part question, to be followed by "Where are you *really* from?"

Why is it that people feel they can approach me for this personal information? Would they ask total strangers their age or marital status? What do they need the information for? Are they census takers? Once, in a truly surreal episode, a casino dealer stopped in the middle of a hand of poker to ask me, as if he couldn't stand to wait a second longer. After I offered my usual answer, he shook his finger in my face and said he wasn't convinced, that I didn't look white enough. He was Asian.

I wonder why, after having been subjected to this treatment for years, I still respond. I can't remember a time when doing so has resulted in a pleasant encounter or a meaningful conversation. Yet I've never quite found the strength to meet such inquiries with "It's none of your business" or, better yet, silence. What's quite strange is that people often feel the need to comment, as if what I've told them is an opinion they can't quite agree with. Comedian Margaret Cho tells a story about a TV producer who asked her to act "a little more Chinese," to which she replied, "But I'm Korean." "Whatever," the producer said. I had a similar experience with a man in a bookstore, who crept out from behind a shelf of cookbooks to ask me where I was from. Before I had a chance to say anything, he guessed: "Japan?" I could have said Oregon, where my father is from, but I knew he wouldn't go for that, so I said, "Indonesia." "Ah," he said. "Close." It's not close. Not really. Not unless you consider London close to Djibouti. The distances are similar.

In the game of "Name that Ethnicity," I am the trick question. I have been mistaken for almost every Asian nationality, but also as Hispanic, Native American, Arab and, of course, African American. There's something in being a chameleon. It's human nature to look for unifying bonds. When people think that they have something in common with you, particularly something so personal as identity, they feel they know you and they imagine that you have an innate understanding of them, too. They will speak to you in a certain unguarded way. The idea that any person can be truly "color-blind" is a fallacy. As long as the human eye can detect differences in skin tone, eye shape, hair texture, these differences will play a role in how we interact with one another. Because of my ambiguous appearance, I have experienced from people the kind of familiarity they would normally reserve for one of their "own."

The unfortunate consequence of this ambiguity is the misunderstanding I frequently encounter from those who haven't gotten the full story. The Mexican immigration official who looks disgusted when I can't understand Spanish, as I surely should. The kindly Vietnamese waiter who helps me "remember" how to pronounce the names of dishes. This puts me in the slightly ridiculous position of being apologetic for not being what people expect me to be, however unreasonable.

When I think back to the man in the elevator, I feel disappointed, too. The way he said "I thought you were one of us" made me feel as if we might have bonded but now couldn't, as if I'd been refused entry into a club because I didn't have the right password. My immediate reaction was that I was missing out on something. But I see the artificiality of this classification mentality. If the opportunity for bonding existed before he knew my ethnic makeup, wasn't it still there after he found out? After all, I was still the same person.

When my parents were married, my grandfather was against the union. His objection was that the children of mixed marriages had no foothold in any one community but instead were doomed to a lifetime of identity crises and disorientation.

If my grandfather were still alive, I'd tell him that the crisis comes not from within, but from without.

I know who I am. It's everyone else that's having trouble.

DISCUSSION QUESTIONS

1. Does an ambiguous appearance lead to stereotypic assumptions?

2. If you don't identify with the questioner, what are the likely consequences?

Ethnic Identity and Racial Formations

RACE AND RACISM AMERICAN-STYLE AND *a lo Latino*

Marta Cruz-Janzen

I am a Latinegra. Racism has been with me all my life. Born and raised a U.S. citizen in the U.S. Commonwealth of Puerto Rico, I completed most of my schooling on the island. In high school I moved back and forth between the island and the mainland. On the island, I became aware of Latina/o racism at an early age. On the mainland, U.S. racism was added to my consciousness and understanding. Today my life is affected not only by U.S. racism but also by Latina/o racism and the intersection of the two. Latina/o and U.S. racial ideologies seem to represent fundamentally divergent systems of social order. U.S. racism enforces the black-versus-white dichotomy; Latina/o racism appeases it. U.S. racism is sharp and clear; Latina/o racism is stratified and nebulous. The intersection of these doctrines unleashes a dilemma for Latinas/os in the United States: What to do with a racial heritage shrouded in secrecy? What to do with a long history of blurred racial lines and deeply hidden family secrets in a world controlled by a rigid color line? I am rejected by both U.S. and Latina/o forms of racism. Latinas/os in Latin America accept me marginally; Latinas/os in the United States openly spurn me. The repudiation by Latinas/os has intensified over the years, and I know why. Through me Latinas/os see the blackness in themselves; I am a living re-

Marta Cruz-Janzen is a professor of multicultural education at Florida Atlantic University.

minder of the ancestors they thought they had left behind. Oppressors rely on their victims' shame and silence. Breaking the shackles of oppression requires telling what is really happening and addressing all the sources of racism. With this chapter I break my own psychological shackles of oppression. I explore the forces impacting racism in Latinas/os today, among them: (1) racism in Latin America, especially Mexico, Puerto Rico, and Cuba, (2) Spanish racism before colonization, (3) U.S. racism, and (4) the intersection of U.S. and Latina/o racial doctrines.

Mucho que poco, todos tenemos la mancha de platano (Much or little, we all have the plantain stain). Latina/o cultures are rich in oral traditions. Popular expressions bear witness to a long and complex history. Oral histories tell more and are often closer to the truth than what is written in books or discussed in polite society. This popular adage states what is known but not acknowledged in most Latina/o cultures—that everyone has some non-European blood. A green vegetable resembling a banana, the plantain is white inside but, when touched, quickly produces a stain that darkens to black and sets permanently. *La mancha de platano*—black and Indian heritage—may or may not be apparent but is present in all Latinas/os and cannot be washed away. When I was growing up, my father's [black] family called me *trigueña* (wheat-colored), whereas the favorite term of my mother's [white] family was *morena* (black), considered a step down. Sometimes, they both called me *negra,* or some variation of the term. When my black grandma called me *negrita* (little black) it was usually with pride and accompanied by a loving hug. When my white grandma called me *negra,* it signaled anger and impending punishment. Outside of the family the labels varied, but when *negra* was used it was as a derisive reminder of my race and lower status. In the latter instances, *negra* tended to be followed by *sucia* (immoral, but literally "dirty") or *parejera* (arrogant). *Parejero/a* is not used for whites, only for blacks and Indians. It denotes people who do not accept *su lugar* (their place) beneath whites and do

not remain quiet like children or humbly obey (Zenon Cruz, 1975). An equivalent term, used in Mexico and many other parts of Latin America, is *igualada/o.* Both terms signify a false sense of equality and belonging among superiors.

It has always intrigued me that my father's birth certificate defines him as *mestizo.* The explanation for this was that because his parents, both black, were educated and middle-class they were *mejorando la raza* (improving the race). They had moved out of Barrio San Antón, the black quarters of the coastal town of Ponce, and lived in a predominantly white neighborhood. They maintained an impeccable home with a beautiful front garden and, aware of their neighbors' scrutiny, never ventured out unless well groomed. When I visited, though, I recall always playing alone, never having friends in the neighborhood. A white girl next door and I sometimes played together through the iron fence but never at each other's home. As I played in the front yard I saw children from across the street watching but knew that we could not get together. My black grandparents had five children. While concerned for all of them, they worried most about their two daughters; one attended the university, became a teacher, and taught in a remote rural school, while the other was considered fortunate for marrying a white man. San Antón was known as an *arrabal,* an impoverished slum beyond the city limits. Grandma was admired and respected there and often took me with her while distributing food and clothes. The differences in living conditions between my grandparents' neighborhood and San Antón were staggering: streets were narrow and unpaved, buildings were in disrepair and lacked indoor plumbing, most houses were makeshifts built of discarded wood and cardboard with zinc roofs. Distinctively, most residents were dark-skinned *puros prietos* (pure blacks).

My two sets of grandparents lived in what appeared to be two separate worlds. I do not recall a single time when they or their families visited each other. My siblings and I were shuttled between them on weekends and holidays. On one side we were *mejorando la raza*, on the other *una pena* (disgrace, sorrow, shame). On one side we were *trigueños finos* (wheat-colored and refined), on the other *morenos y prietos* (black and dark). My paternal black grandma reminded me to pinch my nose between my fingers each day to sharpen its roundness; my maternal white grandma wanted my *greñas* and *ceretas* (curly, wild hair) restrained at all times. Uninhibitedly, my mother's family voiced concerns for me and my siblings as black persons, and especially for me and my sisters as Latinegras in a white, male-dominated Latina/o society. Whereas my father "elevated" his family and himself by marrying a white, my mother was openly chastised for marrying *ese negro feo* (that ugly black), lowering herself and her entire family. Repeatedly, she was told, *Cada oveja con su pareja* (Each sheep with its pair), a reminder that interracial marriages were frowned upon even by the Catholic Church, which preached that we were all *ovejas de Dios* (God's sheep). . . .

RACISM IN MEXICO, PUERTO RICO, AND CUBA

Aqui, el que no tiene dinga tiene mandinga. El que no tiene congo tiene carabali. Y pa' los que no saben na', ¿y tu abuela a'onde esta? (Here, those who don't have Dinga have Mandinga. Those who don't have Congo have Carabali. And for those who don't know anything, where's your grandma?). Carabalis, Congos, and Mandingas were African nations; Dingas and Ingas were Indians. This aphorism makes clear the preponderance of interracial bloodlines within the Latino world. At the same time, *Hoy dia los negros quieren ser blancos y los mulatos caballeros* (Nowadays blacks want to be whites and mulattoes knights) reveals the rancor of white Latinas/os over the social advances of Latinas/os of color.

Mexicans have a long history of interracial unions between Africans, Indians, and Spaniards. The contributions of Africans have influenced every aspect of Mexican culture, history, and life. Esteban el Negro explored northern Mexico; the hit song "La Bamba" comes from the Bamba or Mbamba people

of Veracruz, and the national *corrido* song style is partially African in origin; the muralist and painter Diego Rivera was of African descent. The African presence is apparent, but it is denied in Mexico and by Mexicans in the United States. In spite of their impressive contributions, Afro-Mexicans remain a marginalized group, not yet even recognized as full citizens (Muhammad, 1995). Mexican historians and academicians endorse the claim that the "discovery" of Mexico represented an encounter of two worlds, the Indian and the Spanish, with little if any mention of the Africans brought there (Muhammad, 1995). By the middle of the eighteenth century, Mexico's second-largest population group was largely of African extraction. In 1810 blacks represented 10.2 percent of the Mexican population (Muhammad, 1995). It is estimated that about two hundred thousand Spaniards and two hundred and fifty thousand Africans had migrated to Mexico up to 1810 (Forbes, 1992), and the African population was largely assimilated by the rapidly emerging interracial population. Although Mexico identifies itself as a nation of mestizos, the term "mestizo" is normally not used for identifiable Afro-Mexicans, who are instead referred to as *morenos*. The 1921 census was the last in which racial categories were used in Mexico. Today it is estimated that mestizos make up approximately 85–90 percent of the Mexican population and indigenous persons only 8–10 percent (Fernandez, 1992). There are no current data, demographic or otherwise, for Afro-Mexicans, but Miriam Jiménez Romón of New York's Schomburg Center for Research in Black Culture estimates that 75 percent of the population of Mexico has some African admixture (Muhammad, 1995). Mexicans will boast about their Spanish relatives and may even admit to Indian ones but will rarely admit to a black forebear. Whereas indigenous groups have gained national and international visibility and support, Afro-Mexicans remain suppressed and unheard. Contemporary social research in Mexico tends to exclude Afro-Mexican communities, and no major study on Mexican race relations has ever been done (Muhammad, 1995). Within the past decade anthropologists and others have visited Afro-Mexican communities and reported their deplorable living conditions and rampant illiteracy, their inadequate schools and medical facilities, and their lack of electricity, potable water, plumbing, sewerage, drainage, and paved streets. Visiting Mexico in 1988, I searched for and found Afro-Mexicans living in a clearly segregated shanty town outside of Guadalajara. The squalor of their homes and community was appalling. They openly talked about blatant racism and their financial and legal inability to migrate to the United States. These Afro-Mexicans have been ignored and neglected by government agencies; they receive little or no assistance (Muhammad, 1995).

Puerto Rico, after four centuries of Spanish colonial rule, had developed into a multiracial society. French people and multiracial Creoles went to Puerto Rico after the U.S. Louisiana Purchase from France and migrated from Haiti when the slaves revolted (U.S. Commission on Civil Rights, 1976). Labor shortages throughout the island in the 1840s brought Chinese, Italians, Corsicans, Lebanese, Germans, Scots, Irish, and many others. As the twentieth century approached, the racial composition of Puerto Rico covered the spectrum from whites to blacks with a large in-between interracial group known as *trigueños* (U.S. Commission on Civil Rights, 1976). Racially speaking, most Puerto Ricans are of interracial black, Taino, and white origin. It is believed that racial mixing has touched at least 70 percent of Puerto Rico's population. With U.S. invasion of the island and installation of military rule in 1898, citizenship in 1917, and the establishment of the Commonwealth in 1952, U.S. whites became first-class citizens. Elite Puerto Rican whites were quick to ingratiate themselves with the new upper class by impressing them with their whiteness (Toplin, 1976). The advent of U.S. racism brought the exclusion of social whites who declared themselves white in official U.S. demographic surveys. Whereas the 1846 census reported 51.24 percent of the Puerto Rican population as African or Negro, in 1959 the count dropped to only 23 percent (Toplin, 1976). Members of Congress were not discreet in expressing their low opinion of Puerto Ricans and wondering how there could be so many whites in a "black man's country." Several were openly angered by the degree of racial mixture, stating that the "horror" of racial mixing had gone too far and prevented them from establishing clear racial categorization. They concluded that it was the "duty" of the United States to impose a strict color code on Puerto Rican society in order to ensure propagation of the white race, that is, the newly established elite (Toplin, 1976).

Racial prejudice increased with U.S. occupation of the island (Toplin, 1976; Zenon Cruz, 1974) and became prevalent in public places during the 1950s and 1960s. It persists in social clubs, public and private universities, businesses, banks, tourist facilities, public and private schools, and housing today. Although the local government stopped using racial classifications in 1950, the legal and penal systems, which remain predominantly white, continue to use them against black and dark-skinned poor urban youth (Santiago-Valles, 1995). Little if anything is done to correct the open racism, and many areas remain "hermetically closed" to the darker-skinned Puerto Rican (Toplin, 1976). The Puerto Rican elite, comprised mostly of the descendants of Spaniards with increasing numbers of U.S. whites and European immigrants, treat darker Puerto Ricans with visible contempt. Few Puerto Ricans of African descent explicitly identify as such because of a long history of discrimination and a present fear of police brutality and persecution (Santiago-Valles, 1995). Elite Puerto Ricans still claim that the Spanish white race prevailed in the island, making it the "whitest of all the Antilles," and seek closer ties with Spain (Santiago-Valles, 1995). The 1992 Columbus Quincentennial was celebrated with much emphasis on the Spanish roots of the island. Subsequent annual "Nuestra Hispanidad" (Our Hispanicism) celebrations have focused on Spain and white Puerto Ricans. There is a dearth of information about black and dark-skinned Puerto Ricans but a strong association between black and poor. Black and dark-skinned Puerto Ricans live disproportionately in slums under extremely deprived conditions. U.S. citizenship granted all Puerto Ricans, including those of black heritage, an open door to the continental United States. The enormous loss of jobs between 1940 and 1970 created a massive exodus of Puerto Ricans to the U.S. mainland (U.S. Commission on Civil Rights, 1976). This immense socioeconomic dislocation brought increased visibility to the predominantly black and interracial Puerto Ricans on the mainland.

The Cuban population has historically been African and Spanish (Fernandez, 1992). Almost all Cuban-born Latinas/os came to the United States as refugees from the Revolution of 1959 and the Mariel boatlift in 1980. Although the vast majority of Cubans today are black, most Cuban-Americans are white (McGarrity and Cardenas, 1995). Revolution refugees were mostly educated middle- and upper-class white Cubans with backgrounds in the professions, businesses, and government who soon became integrated into the U.S. middle class. The "less congenial" Marielos were mainly uneducated and poor lower-class black Cubans (Rivera, 1991). The long-standing racism of white Cubans against black Cubans is well known. In Cuba, blacks were excluded from certain schools, especially private Catholic schools, public beaches, hotels, restaurants, and parks. They could not rent homes in some areas (McGarrity and Cardenas, 1995). Before the Marielos, Cubans were welcomed in the United States and given preferential treatment with much transitional support. These elite Cubans were "proudly and adamantly white," uncontaminated, as they emphasized (McGarrity and Cardenas, 1995). Social and elite white Cuban Americans did not welcome the visibility brought on by the Marielos, the black compatriots they thought they had left behind in Cuba (Rivera, 1991). White Cubans are the most successful of the three major U.S. Latina/o groups; Mexicans follow, and Puerto Ricans, with more apparent African bloodlines, are the least (Forbes, 1992). . . .

THE INTERSECTION OF LATINA/O AND U.S. RACISM

Individuals in the United States may believe that times have changed—that conditions for Latinegros have improved. After all, many U.S. educational institutions advocate multicultural education, the af-firmation of diversity, and the teaching of tolerance. The sad reality is that racism continues to be part of everyday life among Latinas/os in the United States and is today confounded by U.S. racism. Latina/o racial antagonism has been transported to U.S. soil. Elite white Latinas/os, seeking acceptance by U.S. whites, quickly disown compatriots of known African lineage even when they appear white and are socially accepted as white in their home countries. In the United States these social white Latinas/os become *negros mal agradecidos* (ungrateful), *changos* (insolent), and *alzaos* (uppity) for wanting the privileges that elite white Latinas/os take for granted. Essentially, social white Latinas/os seek a closeness to elite white Latinas/os that remains simply unacceptable within the U.S. racial and social structure. In this struggle for acceptance, many social white Latinas/os fear focusing attention on themselves and their African legacy. When I moved to the mainland United States, I was told by some Latinas/os that since I would be perceived and treated as black I should identify with African Americans. Others advised me to accentuate my Latina attributes and deemphasize the black ones. Gone were most of the polite, if superficial, niceties—it no longer surprises me when I encounter Latinas/os whom I know in public places and they pretend not to see me. When U.S. Latinas/os emphasize their Hispanicism, they also tend to make sure that I understand my lack of it and the social abyss that separates us. Just three years ago, a "Hispanic" educator in Colorado told me that I was not one of them: "Hispanics are from Spain. You are not Hispanic. Everyone knows you are black." At a Latina/o educators' meeting where I raised concerns about the educational needs of African American students I was addressed scornfully: "You ought to know; you are black like 'them.'" A Latino friend explained, "Some Hispanics here don't want you to be one of them because you represent everything they don't want to be. 'How dare this black woman speak Spanish and claim to be one of us?' They see you as black, and they don't want to be black." In 1993 a "Hispanic" reader from New Mexico wrote to *Hispanic* magazine, in response to its earlier coverage of Latino major-league baseball players, including black Latinos: "I would appreciate knowing how the writer arrived at the classification of apparent Blacks as Hispanics. Does the fact that men come from Spanish-speaking countries such as Puerto Rico or Cuba automatically give them the Hispanic title designation? History shows that Africans were transported to the Americas as slaves and took the names of their slave masters.". . .

One of the most insidious and pervasive forms of racism, one that appears to be escalating through globalized technology, is the promotion of images that exalt whiteness (Forbes, 1992). Historically, people of African background in Latin America have been stereotyped and vilified in popular culture in a number of ways. Media programs from Latin America and particularly Mexico are very popular among Latinas/os worldwide, especially in the United States, and are rapidly gaining other international audiences. *Telenovelas* (soap operas) and television programming are Mexico's largest export, sold throughout Latin America, the United States, and 125 other countries (Quinones, 1997). In these programs dark-skinned persons, particularly Latinegros, are presented as beggars, criminals, and servants. Latinegras are cooks, maids, nannies, and prostitutes. A term broadly used for dark-skinned Latinos in these programs is "Ladino," which also means a "liar" and a "thief." The upper class usually reflects the Nordic ideal, with light-colored eyes and hair and black and/ or Indian servants. Latinegros are also promoted as either athletes or singers but are mostly depicted in a distorted way and made the object of ridicule.

CONCLUSION

Clearly, Latinas/os present a dilemma for the United States—what to do with a rapidly increasing population of mixed racial ancestry that defies categorization, resists homogenization, and cannot be readily assimilated. Today some Latinas/os mock the term as "His Panic," to signify the perceived fear of the white male-dominated U.S. government of non-white Latina/o population growth. Through its racial policies and the "His-

panic" category the United States has chosen to advance Spanishness or put bluntly, whiteness, among Latinas/os (Forbes, 1992). It has established a system whereby Latinas/os are deluded into believing that they are all members of this new Hispanic group. While being reminded of my lack of "Hispanicness," I am reminded that politically my self-identification as a "Hispanic" is needed. What is concealed is that Latinas/os with uninterrupted descent from white Spaniards are glorified and established as the group's leaders. Most Latinas/os in the United States migrated in search of opportunities denied and/or made unavailable to them by the white elites of their homelands. They do not realize that the United States is re-creating this power structure among them. Perhaps "His Panic" is Latinas/os' own panic—their own, even greater dilemma. The U.S. color line makes no allowance for middle groups; it is designed to disperse the middle cloud in opposite directions. Individuals are either white or "something else" (Cruz-Janzen, 1997). That "something else" may be African American, Asian American, Native American, or Hispanic, but only white Europeans—more specifically, white Europeans with the exception of Spaniards—can be white. As Hispanics, Latinas/os are spuriously classified as Europeans and white Latinas/os are deluded into believing that they are accepted as White Europeans. Latinos fail to recognize that ultimately, U.S. rejection is directed at all of them. Although their predecessors were present in this hemisphere before the arrival of the Pilgrims, U.S. Latinas/os are relegated to foreign status, forever designated as immigrants from Spain, whereas other Europeans are integrated as "Americans." Latinas/os of color are rendered invisible as only white Latinas/os are recognized.

Issues of race and racism are not talked about openly in Latina/o cultures in the United States because many Latinas/os argue that they are discriminated against as an ethnic group and discussions of internal racism divide the group and prevent coalescence against White/European-American oppression. But Latinegras/os in the United States as elsewhere resent their oppression. They are aware of the *tapujos*—the secrets, contradictions, and hypocrisy—among Latinas/os that provide fertile ground for U.S. racial policies. They express their anger and frustration over a situation that has been with them all their lives and is getting worse. Many realize that the stringent black-versus-white dichotomy is widening the racial divide that has existed among Latinas/os.

DISCUSSION QUESTIONS

1. Does education whiten one's color?
2. Does having a higher income whiten?
3. Does racism operate on the same principles across cultures?

REFERENCES

Cruz-Janzen, Marta I. 1997. *Curriculum and the Self-Concept of Biethnic and Biracial Persons.* Ann Arbor, MI: UMI Dissertation Services.

Fernandez, Carlos A. 1992. "*La raza* and the Melting Pot: A Comparative Look at Multiethnicity/Multiraciality," pp. 126–43 in Maria P. Root (ed.), *Racially Mixed People in America.* Newbury Park, CA: Sage.

Forbes, Jack D. 1992. "The Hispanic Spin: Party Politics and Governmental Manipulation of Ethnic Identity." *Latin American Perspectives* 19 (Fall): 59–78.

McGarrity, Gayle and Osvaldo Cardenas. 1995. "Cuba," pp. 77–108 in Minority Rights Group (ed.), *No Longer Invisible: Afro-Latin Americans Today.* London: Minority Rights Publications.

Muhammad, Jameelah S. 1995. "Mexico and Central America," pp. 163–80 in Minority Rights Group (ed.), *No Longer Invisible: Afro-Latin Americans Today.* London: Minority Rights Publications.

Quinones, Sam. 1997. "Hooked on *Telenovelas.*" *Hemispheres* (November): 125–29.

Rivera, Mario A. 1991. *Decision and Structure: U.S. Refugee Policy in the Mariel Crisis.* Lanham, MD: University Press of America.

Santiago-Valles, Kelvin A. 1995. "Puerto Rico," pp. 139–62 in Minority Rights Group (ed.), *No Longer Invisible: Afro-Latin Americans Today.* London: Minority Rights Publications.

Toplin, Robert B. 1976. *Slavery and Slave Relations in Latin America.* Westport, CT: Greenwood Press.

U.S. Commission on Civil Rights. 1976. *Puerto Ricans in the Continental United States: An Uncertain Future.*

Zenon Cruz, Isabelo. 1975. *Narciso descrube su trasero: El negro en la cultura puertorriqueña.* Vol. 2. Humacao, PR: Editorial Furidi.

The Cost of Whiteness

Thandeka

Most white Americans believe they were born white. Yet their own stories of early racial experiences describe persons who were bred white. Which is it—nature or nurture? Neither. The social process that creates whites produces persons who must think of their whiteness as a biological fact.

The process begins with a rebuke. A parent or authority figure reprimands the child because it's not yet white. The language used by the adult is racial, but the content of the message pertains to the child's own feelings and what the child must do with feelings the adult doesn't like. Stifle them. Philosopher Martha Nussbaum, in her book *Cultivating Humanity: A Classical Defense of Reform in Liberal Education,* tells how she learned to do this as a child being taught to be white.

Nussbaum's reflections begin with a description of the incident that provoked her father's racial rebuke: "In Bryn Mawr, Pennsylvania, in the early 1960s, I encountered black people only as domestic servants. There was a black girl my age named Hattie, daughter of the live-in help of an especially wealthy neighbor. One day, when I was about ten, we had been playing in the street and I asked her to come in for some lemonade. My father, who grew up in Georgia, exploded, telling me that I must never invite a black person into the house again." Nussbaum's first lessons ended at school where the only African Americans present were "kitchen help." Here, she and her classmates learned how to "efface them from our minds when we studied." The target of Nussbaum's first lessons in whiteness was her own sentient awareness of the surrounding environment. She had to learn how

Thandeka, associate professor of theology and culture, Meadville/Lombard Theological School, is author of *Learning to Be White: Money, Race, and God in America* (Continuum 1999). Her name, "lovable" in Xhosa, was given to her by Archbishop Desmond Tutu.

to disengage her own feelings, how to dissociate herself from them.

Most discussions of the creation of whites overlook this stage in the development of a white racial consciousness and thus assume that whites are insensitive to blacks by nature. White supremacist and anti-racist groups seem to hold this belief in common—that whites are born racist with a biologically predetermined disposition to hate blacks. To begin elsewhere, we have to pay attention to the feelings the child learns to squelch. I was able to listen in on these feelings when I conducted interviews for my book, *Learning to Be White.* An adult I call "Jay," for example, described the rationale for his parents' decision to take him on a car tour of the "black ghetto" when he was four. His parents knew he had never seen black people before and did not want him to embarrass the family by staring at "them" when the family went to New York on vacation the following month. The adult motivation for this mini tour of black America was to pre-empt a parental rebuke that would have occurred if Jay had indeed stared at "them" while on vacation. Jay thus learned something about what to do with his own natural curiosity. Suppress it. The protocol associated with this new knowledge was self-evident: Don't stare at them. The deeper implications of the message Jay received would develop over time: Don't even notice that they are there. Such behavior, of course, is described by Ralph Ellison's protagonist in *Invisible Man:* "I am invisible, understand, simply because people refuse to see me." Jay had begun to learn not to see what he saw.

Another example. "Sally's" parents, strong civil rights supporters, preached racial equality both at home and in the streets. She was thus flabbergasted when her parents prevented her from going out with a high school friend who came to pick her up for a Friday night date. He was black. The parents sent him away and forbade her to date him. "What will our neighbors say if they see you on the arms of a black man?" Sally was furious with them and thought them hypocrites. But she submitted to their dictates. "What was I going to do?" she asked rhetorically. "Rebel? Not in my household. They

would have disowned me." So she suppressed her feelings.

Then there's "Dan." In college during the late 1950s, Dan joined a fraternity. With his prompting, his chapter pledged a black student. When the chapter's national headquarters learned of this first step toward the integration of its ranks, headquarters threatened to rescind the local chapter's charter unless the black student was expelled. The local chapter caved in to the pressure and Dan was elected to tell the black student member he would have to leave. Dan did it. "I felt so ashamed of what I did," he told me. "I have carried this burden for forty years," he said. "I will carry it to my grave." And he began to cry. Why? Because as psychoanalytic theorist Judith Lewis Herman reminds us in the opening pages of her book, *Trauma and Recovery,* the unspeakable will out.

"Sarah." At age sixteen, Sarah brought her best friend home with her from high school. After the friend left, Sarah's mother told her not to invite her friend home again. "Why?" Sarah asked, astonished and confused. "Because she's colored," her mother responded. That was not an answer, Sarah thought to herself. It was obvious that her friend was colored, but what kind of reason was that for not inviting her? So Sarah persisted, insisting that her mother tell her the real reason. None was forthcoming. The indignant look on her mother's face, however, made Sarah realize that if she persisted, she would jeopardize her mother's affection toward her. Horrified by what she had just glimpsed, Sarah severed her friendship with the girl. Sarah told me she had not thought of this incident in twenty years. She also said that until now, she had never consciously said to herself that for her the deepest tragedy in this incident was her loss of trust in her mother's love. Sarah, like Dan, began to cry.

Every European American I interviewed could tell me a tale about how they learned as youth to blunt positive feelings toward persons beyond the pale. These aren't the kinds of tales I had expected when I asked them to recount stories of their earliest racial incidents. To my astonishment, instead of describing interracial incidents, they described intra-racial conflicts. The message they learned was repress, deny, and split off from consciousness feelings that, if expressed, would provoke racial attacks from the adults in their own community. From these stories, I learned that becoming white is the product of a child's siege mentality. It's a defense mechanism to stop racial rebukes from one's own kith and kin.

Few accounts reveal this white siege mentality better than a story by writer Don Wallace in his *New York Times*, October 11, 1995, op-ed piece, "How I Learned to Fear the Cops." Wallace, in this essay, describes several incidents in which he was accosted by cops. The first altercation occurred when Wallace was ten. Wallace uses the third-person singular to tell this tale in the opening paragraphs of his essay:

> The 10-year-old boy skipped down the sidewalk a few steps ahead of his parents in the warmth of a Los Angeles night in 1962. Behind him glowed Olvera Street, a slice of the old California's Mexican heritage. . . . He heard the screech of brakes but paid no mind until a police officer seized him by the shoulder and pushed him against a wall. Another officer shoved his 12-year old brother. Then the boy saw something even more terrifying: the gun in the cop's hand.

Wallace's father spoke up, berating the cop and demanding an apology for pointing a gun at his sons, who were church-goers, Boy and Cub Scout members, and good students. The cops stood their ground, demanding that he get out of the way or face arrest. Wallace, who until this point has not told the reader the "race" of the family, now teases the reader, asking: "What do you think happened next? You've read the papers. You followed the Rodney King case. If the family in this true story were black, what odds would you give on the father staying out of jail? Or staying alive?" But he and his family are white, Wallace tells us, and they "got to go home to [their] all-white suburb."

As a teenager, Wallace continued to play on the wrong side of town. He attended a large inner-city high school in Long Beach and would often visit his first girlfriend, "a biology whiz" who had a Spanish surname and lived on the west side. To visit her, Wallace had to go through a Checkpoint Charlie consisting of a concrete levee, oil fields, and two eight-lane boulevards marking a racial change from all-white to brown, black, and yellow. The few streets which led in or out of the area created choke points and were usually "guarded by a squad car at each one, day and night." In his sophomore year, almost every night as he drove from his girlfriend's house, a squad car would swing behind him and tail him. "I got used to it," Wallace says with the determination of a teenage Rambo. He treated "each drive home as if it were a mission through hostile territory: my signals perfect, my turns crisp, my speed steady and always five miles per hour below the limit." Nevertheless, in spite of his white, "preppie look," he was stopped eleven times "with nary a ticket to show for it." The policemen's message was clear: Whites were not allowed to socialize in a non-white zone. Recounting an incident in which he and two friends were caught in the wrong zone, Wallace writes: "The police marched three of us into a field behind a screen of oil wells and then separated and handcuffed us. For an hour, we were threatened with a beating and arrest, yet no infraction was mentioned. The police were delivering their message of intimidation, insuring the crackle of fear, the walking-on-eggshells feeling, everytime we entered the nonwhite zone." Similarly, when Wallace, who was president of the student body and a football letterman, chose to sit with black friends during a basketball game, two police officers "waded into the bleachers and hauled me out to the floor to be searched, in full view of my teachers and friends."

Such incidents made it clear not only that race mixing was prohibited by these cops, but that neither whites nor non-whites are safe from police brutality when they enter a racial zone off limits to their kind. There is, however, another story being told. Wallace, in the process of recounting his youthful escapades with the police, also sings a different tune. He tells us how "this white boy [who] got the message long ago" grew up to "fear the cops." Wallace recounts this adult tale of submission to authority in another key.

Wallace's journalistic eye focuses our attention on the fact that as a youth, in spite of his ostensibly rebellious nature, he did not rebel. The boy did not protest his harassment but adjusted. Writes Wallace: "I am astonished how we adjusted to this state of constant siege." This adult astonishment forces us to set aside his teenage bravado and focus on a fact that neither the teenager nor the adult could state directly: Both the white youth and white adult civilians in Wallace's recollections submitted to the policemen's harassment. That he submitted to authority is clear. We simply must pay attention to the unsaid. Absent from Wallace's account is a description of complaints to his parents or schoolteachers. Nor does he report having gone to either the local police station or to the District Attorney's office to file a complaint. Such acts would have been made less likely by the fact that both his parents and the adults at his school were models of submission to police abuse rather than rebellion. Even Wallace's father, after an initial dismayed protest against the officer who had pulled a gun on white boys who were good (Scouts, Christian, and smart), relented and took his family home to their "all-white suburb." This, of course, was what the cops had wanted in the first place.

Wallace is recounting the antics of a teenager who grandstanded rather than rebelled. He is describing more than members of a police force out of control. He is also exposing a pervasive white adult submission to the threatening presence of its own police force, which is dead set on preventing so-called race mixing. The adult submission to this threat, in the boy's eyes, was the same as consent. Police harassment, together with the massive submission of adults to this brute force, taught the boy and the adult he grew up to be what he must do to act like a white person: Submit to the unwritten race laws of his policed state. This demand for submission to white race laws created a zone of fear and timidity within Wallace, the adult. As he writes: "Layer upon layer of incidents like these build a foundation of mistrust. It's why I'm a very cautious driver today." Wallace, in effect, has described the origins of his present siege mentality.

He had learned through experience that in a *de jure* and/or *de facto* system of racial apartheid, every member of the community is under siege. Instead of inspiring his rebellious rage, however, this siege mentality actually prevents Wallace from expressing his rage toward the police force. Even in his essay, instead of calling for more civilian oversight of an out-of-control police force, Wallace muffles his impulse to protest by cloaking it in blackness and concludes his essay with the moral tepidity of an interracial truism: "I firmly believe there will be no peace until black people can walk the same streets as white people without fearing the sound of the squad car's brakes, as I learned to do that night on Olvera Street." By referring to the risk African Americans run when they enter white zones, Wallace expresses in blackface his own fears as a European American caught in the wrong racial zone. Albeit unwittingly, this gesture towards tolerance ends up confirming the system Wallace criticizes.

After the siege mentality is in place, race talk by the newly created white usually follows. Such talk, however, often distracts attention from what produced it: white adult abuse against their own kids. The story of Dorothy, a middle-aged woman I met at a dinner party in an Upper West Side Manhattan apartment, shows how race talk about racism begins as a distraction from the emotional pain entailed in becoming white.

Dorothy and I were introduced by the host of the dinner party. Dorothy was a "poet," whose most recent volume of poetry was prominently displayed on the coffee table in front of the couch on which we were seated. I was a "writer" working on white identity issues. After our host departed, Dorothy wanted to know what a "white identity" was. She did not have one, she assured me. She was simply an American. I could help her find hers, I responded, if she wanted to know what it looked like. Her interest piqued, she accepted the offer. True to form, I asked her to recollect her earliest memory of knowing what it means to be white.

After a little excavation, she finally found the memory: When Dorothy was five, she and her family lived in Mexico for a year. Although her family's housekeeper brought her daughter, who was also five, to work, Dorothy's parents forbade her to play with the little girl. Dorothy, in fact, was never allowed to play with any Mexican children, and she and her two brothers were forbidden to venture beyond the gates of their backyard. Dorothy remembered her feelings of sadness and regret. The Mexican children and their parents seemed so much more at ease with themselves and each other. They seemed warm and tactile, unlike her own family, whose manners and expressions were cold and constrained.

Dorothy told me she had not thought of these feelings in years. She confessed that she now recalled how often, during that year, she wished to be brown. I suggested that the term "white" might not mean anything consciously to her today because it had too much negative meaning for her when she was five. She agreed and now expressed surprise that she had not written about these feelings, memories, or experiences in her work. She said much of her life had been devoted to freeing herself from the emotional strictures imposed on her by her parents. Most of her poetry was about them and the way they had drained life out of her. She reiterated her astonishment that this set of memories had not surfaced in her work. As she blushed, the resurrected feelings of the child seemed to disappear.

I now watched Dorothy transfer her own disease to me and I braced myself for an attack. She was no longer the object of her painful racial memories. Now, I was. "You know," Dorothy now said pointedly, "you are the first black I've ever felt comfortable with talking about racism." To which I responded, "Why is it so easy for you to think of me as a 'black,' and yet until a few minutes ago you could not make any sense out of thinking about yourself as a 'white'?" Further—"Were we really talking about racism? And if so, whose? Your parents'? Yours? That of the five-year-old girl who wanted to be brown?"

Dorothy was silent for a long moment. "I now understand what I've just done, and I'm horrified," she finally confessed. She realized that if I were a

black, she, too, must have a race: the one that had enraged her as a child. Not surprisingly, Dorothy now confessed that she was afraid to say anything else—not because I might condemn her, but much more tellingly because, as she put it, "I might not like what I hear myself saying." If she'd been forced to listen to herself continue to talk, she would have had to listen to a white woman speak in ways that the five-year-old child would have despised. She did not want to listen to such talk. Nor did I. Our conversation very quickly came to an end.

Dorothy had recalled the feelings of the child whose parents wanted to love a *white* child. The parts of her that were not "white"—her positive feelings toward Mexicans—had to be set aside as unloved and therefore unlovable. This sense of being unlovable is the core content of shame, psychoanalyst Léon Wurmser reminds us in his book, *The Mask of Shame.* Shame, Wurmser suggests, "forces one to hide, to seek cover and to veil or mask oneself." Such feelings, self psychologist Heinz Kohut notes in *The Search for the Self,* actually result from the failure of the parents or caretakers to adequately love the child, but the child blames itself rather than its parent or caretaking environment. Guilt, by contrast with shame, Helen Merrell Lynd notes in her book, *On Shame and the Search for Identity,* results from a wrongful deed, a self-condemnation for what one has done. A penalty can be exacted for this wrongful act. Recompense can be made and restitution paid. Not so with shame. Nothing can be done because shame results not from something one did wrong but rather from something wrong with oneself. Split-off feelings can create this feeling of personal shame. . . .

What can we conclude from these various examples of the processes entailed in becoming white in America? Two things. Whites like to think of themselves as biologically white in order to hide what they'd like to forget: Once upon a time they were attacked by whites in their own community because they weren't yet white. To stop the attack, they learned to disdain their own feelings. Who wants to remember such attacks? Who wants to know that they were once racial outsiders to their own racial group? Who wants to unearth denied feelings? Better to blame the blacks (and other so-called "colored groups"—"so-called" because I've never met anyone who didn't have a color!) than face the truth: whites are race victims of their own community's racial codes of conduct.

Most whites suffer from a survivor complex. They are products of a race war that rages within white America. The fact that there's a racial pecking order among ethnic groups in white America exacerbates this problem. As social psychologist Gordon Allport notes in his classic 1954 study *The Nature of Prejudice,* this race rating-scheme is widespread and remarkably uniform in judgments "concerning the relative acceptability [that is, whiteness] of various ethnic stocks: Germans, Italians, Armenians, and the like. Each of these can in sequence look down upon all groups lower in the series." Such racial abuse meted out to the "ethnics" who are too far away from the Anglo-Saxon Protestant ethnic ideal can have devastating effects not only on one's personality but also on one's paycheck.

This economic penalty is difficult to grasp because Americans have been taught to think only of the benefits—the "privileges"—of whiteness accorded to Europeans who immigrated to America and became white. W. E. B. Du Bois called the race privileges given to these workers and their progeny "the wages of whiteness." Whiteness, as Du Bois notes in his book *Black Reconstruction in America: 1860–1880,* meant "public deference and titles of courtesy"; access to "public functions, public parks and the best schools"; jobs as policemen; the right to sit on juries; voting rights; flattery from newspapers while Negro news was "almost utterly ignored except in crime and ridicule." These privileges also included the right, based on legal indifference and social approval, to taunt, police, humiliate, mob, rape, lynch, jibe, rob, jail, mutilate, and burn Negroes, which became a sporting game, "a sort of permissible Roman holiday for the entertainment of vicious whites." During the late 1800s, for example, "practically all white southern men went armed and the South reached the extraordinary distinction of being the only modern civilized country where human beings were publicly burned alive."

The price exacted for these privileges, however, was also considerable. Du Bois summarizes the main cost in the nineteenth century antebellum South: no major labor movement to protect the region's five million poor whites, who owned no slaves, from the 8,000 largest slave-holders who, in effect, ruled the South. Hatred of the Negro, slave and free, blocked furtive attempts by the lower classes to fight their own race's class exploiters. By playing the labor costs of both whites and Negroes against each other, contractors kept the earnings of both groups low. Both before and after the civil war, white privileges functioned as a kind of "public and psychological wage," supplementing the low-paying jobs that whites could easily lose to a lower-paid black worker.

I am not denying "white privilege." "All whites," as legal scholar Cheryl J. Harris notes in her essay "Whiteness as Property"—regardless of class position—"benefit from their wage of whiteness." Such talk of privilege, however, is incomplete unless we also speak of its penalty. For poorer wage earners "without power, money or influence," their wage of whiteness functions as a kind of workers' "compensation." It is a "consolation prize" to persons who, although not wealthy, do not have to consider themselves losers because they are, at least, white.

The irony, of course, is that neither in the past nor today are low-paid wage earners held in high esteem by their own white bosses who exploit their labor. These workers are, in effect, exploited twice: first as workers and then as "whites." Their "race" is used to distract them from their diminishing value as wage earners. Diminished as workers, they feel shame. Inflated as whites, they feel white supremacist pride. This is the double jeopardy of whiteness Martin Luther King, Jr., pointed to in his 1967 book *Where Do We Go from Here: Chaos or Community?* when noting that racial prejudice put poorer whites in the ironic position of fighting not only against the Negro, but also against themselves. White supremacy, King wryly noted, can feed the egos of poor whites but not their stomachs.

Play Some Rolling Stones

I left my favorite tavern late on a Friday night. On my way home I stopped to listen to the acoustic reggae of a black street musician. I threw a few dollars into a jar, and he asked me what I would like to hear. He spoke with a heavy Jamaican accent and said he could only play reggae. As he began to play my request, several other white males gathered around. As my song ended, a member of the group told the street musician to stop playing that "nigger music" and play some Rolling Stones. The musician replied that he only knew the words to reggae songs. With that, the white male kicked the musician's money jar from his stool, shattering it on the sidewalk. When I objected, the white guy turned on me. Luckily he had spent several hours in the tavern, because his first punch missed its mark. Unfortunately, the other five punches were on target.

At night in the hospital and twenty-two sutures later, I wondered if it was worth it. But when I went back down to the same area the following weekend, the musician thanked me graciously. Then he began to play a classic Rolling Stones song.

Mark Donald Stockenberg

Today's "poor whites" are the working poor, the "over-spent Americans" be they lower- or middle-class—all the white Americans who are living from paycheck to paycheck. Whiteness functions as a distraction from the pervasive class problem of the white American worker. Talk of white privilege from this class perspective is really talk about the privileges entailed in being and remaining poor and exploited in America. Such talk is cheap. Too cheap.

We can do better than this—but only if we attend to the way in which most "whites" are broken by the persons who ostensibly made them white "for their own good": their parents, caretakers, and bosses.

In his September/October 1996 essay "Can the Left Learn to Take Yes for an Answer?" TIKKUN editorial board member Michael Bader describes a repeated pattern among white American progressives: "an unconscious belief that they're somehow not supposed to have a happier and healthier life than their loved ones, past and present." To explain this syndrome, Bader talks about "survivor guilt." We must begin to talk about survivor shame in Americans who are forced to become white. Without such discourse, the fact that European Americans racially abuse their own children, suffer from class exploitation under the guise of "white-skin privilege," mask their own racialized feelings of shame, and then download their self-contempt on the rest of us will remain America's invisible race problem.

DISCUSSION QUESTIONS

1. Do you learn to be white or are you born white?
2. What is your first recollection of a racial identity?
3. What are some of the privileges or benefits of whiteness?

"Why Are All the Black Kids Sitting Together in the Cafeteria?"

Beverly Daniel Tatum

Walk into any racially mixed high school cafeteria at lunch time and you will instantly notice that in the sea of adolescent faces, there is an identifiable group of Black students sitting together. Conversely, it could be pointed out that there are many groups of White students sitting together as well, though people rarely comment about that. The question on the tip of everyone's tongue is "Why are the Black kids sitting together?" Principals want to know, teachers want to know, White students want to know, the Black students who aren't sitting at the table want to know.

Beverly Daniel Tatum is president of Spelman College. Prior to her appointment to the Spelman presidency in 2002, she spent 13 years at Mount Holyoke College as professor of psychology, department chair, dean of the college, and acting president.

How does it happen that so many Black teenagers end up at the same cafeteria table? They don't start out there. If you walk into racially mixed elementary schools, you will often see young children of diverse racial backgrounds playing with one another, sitting at the snack table together, crossing racial boundaries with an ease uncommon in adolescence. Moving from elementary school to middle school (often at sixth or seventh grade) means interacting with new children from different neighborhoods than before, and a certain degree of clustering by race might therefore be expected, presuming that children who are familiar with one another would form groups. But even in schools where the same children stay together from kindergarten through eighth grade, racial grouping begins by the sixth or seventh grade. What happens?

One thing that happens is puberty. As children enter adolescence, they begin to explore the question of identity, asking "Who am I? Who can I be?" in ways they have not done before. For Black youth, asking "Who am I?" includes thinking about "Who am I ethnically and/or racially? What does it mean to be Black?"

As I write this, I can hear the voice of a White woman who asked me, "Well, all adolescents struggle with questions of identity. They all become more self-conscious about their appearance and more concerned about what their peers think. So what is so different for Black kids?" Of course, she is right that all adolescents look at themselves in new ways, but not all adolescents think about themselves in racial terms.

The search for personal identity that intensifies in adolescence can involve several dimensions of an adolescent's life: vocational plans, religious beliefs, values and preferences, political affiliations and beliefs, gender roles, and ethnic identities. The process of exploration may vary across these identity domains. James Marcia described four identity "statuses" to characterize the variation in the identity search process: (1) *diffuse,* a state in which there has been little exploration or active consideration of a particular domain, and no psychological commitment; (2) *foreclosed,* a state in which a commitment has been made to particular roles or belief systems, often those selected by parents, without actively considering alternatives; (3) *moratorium,* a state of active exploration of roles and beliefs in which no commitment has yet been made; and (4) *achieved,* a state of strong personal commitment to a particular dimension of identity following a period of high exploration.[1]

An individual is not likely to explore all identity domains at once, therefore it is not unusual for an adolescent to be actively exploring one dimension while another remains relatively unexamined. Given the impact of dominant and subordinate status, it is not surprising that researchers have found that adolescents of color are more likely to be actively engaged in an exploration of their racial or ethnic identity than are White adolescents.[2]

Why do Black youths, in particular, think about themselves in terms of race? Because that is how the rest of the world thinks of them. Our self-perceptions are shaped by the messages that we receive from those around us, and when young Black men and women enter adolescence, the racial content of those messages intensifies. A case in point: If you were to ask my ten-year-old son, David, to describe himself, he would tell you many things: that he is smart, that he likes to play computer games, that he has an older brother. Near the top of his list, he would likely mention that he is tall for his age. He would probably not mention that he is Black, though he certainly knows that he is. Why would he mention his height and not his racial group membership? When David meets new adults, one of the first questions they ask is "How old are you?" When David states his age, the inevitable reply is "Gee, you're tall for your age!" It happens so frequently that I once overheard David say to someone, "Don't say it, I know. I'm tall for my age." Height is salient for David because it is salient for others.

When David meets new adults, they don't say, "Gee, you're Black for your age!" If you are saying to yourself, of course they don't, think again. Imagine David at fifteen, six-foot-two, wearing the adolescent attire of the day, passing adults he doesn't know on the sidewalk. Do the women hold their purses a little tighter, maybe even cross the street to avoid him? Does he hear the sound of the automatic door locks on cars as he passes by? Is he being followed around by the security guards at the local mall? As he stops in town with his new bicycle, does a police officer hassle him, asking where he got it, implying that it might be stolen? Do strangers assume he plays basketball? Each of these experiences conveys a racial message. At ten, race is not yet salient for David, because it is not yet salient for society. But it will be.

UNDERSTANDING RACIAL IDENTITY DEVELOPMENT

Psychologist William Cross, author of *Shades of Black: Diversity in African American Identity,* has offered a theory of racial identity development that I have found to be a very useful framework for understanding what is happening not only with David, but with those Black students in the cafeteria.[3] According to Cross's model, referred to as the psychology of nigrescence, or the psychology of becoming Black, the five stages of racial identity development are *pre-encounter, encounter, immersion/emersion, internalization,* and *internalization-commitment.* For the moment, we will consider the first two stages as those are the most relevant for adolescents.

In the first stage, the Black child absorbs many of the beliefs and values of the dominant White culture, including the idea that it is better to be White. The stereotypes, omissions, and distortions that reinforce notions of White superiority are breathed in by Black children as well as White. Simply as a function of being socialized in a Eurocentric culture, some Black children may begin to value the role models, lifestyles, and images of beauty represented by the dominant group more highly than those of their own cultural group. On the other hand, if Black parents are what I call race-conscious—that is, actively seeking to encourage positive racial identity by providing their children with positive cultural images and messages about what it means to be Black—the impact of the dominant society's messages are reduced.[4] In either case, in the pre-encounter stage, the personal and social significance of one's racial group member-

ship has not yet been realized, and racial identity is not yet under examination. At age ten, David and other children like him would seem to be in the pre-encounter stage. When the environmental cues change and the world begins to reflect his Blackness back to him more clearly, he will probably enter the encounter stage.

Transition to the encounter stage is typically precipitated by an event or series of events that force the young person to acknowledge the personal impact of racism. As the result of a new and heightened awareness of the significance of race, the individual begins to grapple with what it means to be a member of a group targeted by racism. Though Cross describes this process as one that unfolds in late adolescence and early adulthood, research suggests that an examination of one's racial or ethnic identity may begin as early as junior high school.

In a study of Black and White eighth graders from an integrated urban junior high school, Jean Phinney and Steve Tarver found clear evidence for the beginning of the search process in this dimension of identity. Among the forty-eight participants, more than a third had thought about the effects of ethnicity on their future, had discussed the issues with family and friends, and were attempting to learn more about their group. While White students in this integrated school were also beginning to think about ethnic identity, there was evidence to suggest a more active search among Black students, especially Black females.[5] Phinney and Tarver's research is consistent with my own study of Black youth in predominantly White communities, where the environmental cues that trigger an examination of racial identity often become evident in middle school or junior high school.[6]

Some of the environmental cues are institutionalized. Though many elementary schools have self-contained classrooms where children of varying performance levels learn together, many middle and secondary schools use "ability grouping," or tracking. Though school administrators often defend their tracking practices as fair and objective, there usually is a recognizable racial pattern to how children are assigned, which often represents the system of advantage operating in the schools.[7] In racially mixed schools, Black children are much more likely to be in the lower track than in the honors track. Such apparent sorting along racial lines sends a message about what it means to be Black. One young honors student I interviewed described the irony of this resegregation in what was an otherwise integrated environment, and hinted at the identity issues it raised for him.

> It was really a very paradoxical existence, here I am in a school that's 35 percent Black, you know, and I'm the only Black in my classes. . . . That always struck me as odd. I guess I felt that I was different from the other Blacks because of that.

In addition to the changes taking place within school, there are changes in the social dynamics outside school. For many parents, puberty raises anxiety about interracial dating. In racially mixed communities, you begin to see what I call the birthday party effect. Young children's birthday parties in multiracial communities are often a reflection of the community's diversity. The parties of elementary school children may be segregated by gender but not by race. At puberty, when the parties become sleepovers or boy-girl events, they become less and less racially diverse.

Black girls, especially in predominantly White communities, may gradually become aware that something has changed. When their White friends start to date, they do not. The issues of emerging sexuality and the societal messages about who is sexually desirable leave young Black women in a very devalued position. One young woman from a Philadelphia suburb described herself as "pursuing White guys throughout high school" to no avail. Since there were no Black boys in her class, she had little choice. She would feel "really pissed off" that those same White boys would date her White friends. For her, "that prom thing was like out of the question."[8]

Though Black girls living in the context of a larger Black community may have more social choices, they too have to contend with devaluing messages about who they are and who they will become, especially if they are poor or working-class. As social scientists Bonnie Ross Leadbeater and Niobe Way point out,

The school drop-out, the teenage welfare mother, the drug addict, and the victim of domestic violence or of AIDS are among the most prevalent public images of poor and working-class urban adolescent girls. . . . Yet, despite the risks inherent in economic disadvantage, the majority of poor urban adolescent girls do not fit the stereotypes that are made about them.[9]

Resisting the stereotypes and affirming other definitions of themselves is part of the task facing young Black women in both White and Black communities.

As was illustrated in the example of David, Black boys also face a devalued status in the wider world. The all too familiar media image of a young Black man with his hands cuffed behind his back, arrested for a violent crime, has primed many to view young Black men with suspicion and fear. In the context of predominantly White schools, however, Black boys may enjoy a degree of social success, particularly if they are athletically talented. The culture has embraced the Black athlete, and the young man who can fulfill that role is often pursued by Black girls and White girls alike. But even these young men will encounter experiences that may trigger an examination of their racial identity.

Sometimes the experience is quite dramatic. *The Autobiography of Malcolm X* is a classic tale of racial identity development, and I assign it to my psychology of racism students for just that reason. As a junior high school student, Malcolm was a star. Despite the fact that he was separated from his family and living in a foster home, he was an A student and was elected president of his class. One day he had a conversation with his English teacher, whom he liked and respected, about his future career goals. Malcolm said he wanted to be a lawyer. His teacher responded, "That's no realistic goal for a nigger," and advised him to consider carpentry instead.[10] The message was clear: You are a Black male, your racial group membership matters, plan accordingly. Malcolm's emotional response was typical—anger, confusion, and alienation. He withdrew from his White classmates, stopped participating in class, and eventually left his predominately white Michigan home to live with his sister in Roxbury, a Black community in Boston.

No teacher would say such a thing now, you may be thinking, but don't be so sure. It is certainly less likely that a teacher would use the word *nigger,* but consider these contemporary examples shared by high school students. A young ninth-grade student was sitting in his homeroom. A substitute teacher was in charge of the class. Because the majority of students from this school go on to college, she used the free time to ask the students about their college plans. As a substitute she had very limited information about their academic performance, but she offered some suggestions. When she turned to this young man, one of few Black males in the class, she suggested that he consider a community college. She had recommended four-year colleges to the other students. Like Malcolm, this student got the message.

In another example, a young Black woman attending a desegregated school to which she was bussed was encouraged by a teacher to attend the upcoming school dance. Most of the Black students did not live in the neighborhood and seldom attended the extracurricular activities. The young woman indicated that she wasn't planning to come. The well-intentioned teacher was persistent. Finally the teacher said, "Oh come on, I know you people love to dance." This young woman got the message, too.

COPING WITH ENCOUNTERS: DEVELOPING AN OPPOSITIONAL IDENTITY

What do these encounters have to do with the cafeteria? Do experiences with racism inevitably result in so-called self-segregation? While certainly a desire to protect oneself from further offense is understandable, it is not the only factor at work. Imagine the young eighth-grade girl who experienced the teacher's use of "you people" and the dancing stereotype as a racial affront. Upset and struggling with adolescent embarrassment, she bumps into a White friend who can see that something is wrong. She explains. Her White friend responds, in an effort to make her feel better perhaps, and says, "Oh, Mr. Smith is such a nice guy, I'm sure he didn't mean it like that. Don't be so sensi-

tive." Perhaps the White friend is right, and Mr. Smith didn't mean it, but imagine your own response when you are upset, perhaps with a spouse or partner. He or she asks what's wrong and you explain why you are offended. Your partner brushes off your complaint, attributing it to your being oversensitive. What happens to your emotional thermostat? It escalates. When feelings, rational or irrational, are invalidated, most people disengage. They not only choose to discontinue the conversation but are more likely to turn to someone who will understand their perspective.

In much the same way, the eighth-grade girl's White friend doesn't get it. She doesn't see the significance of this racial message, but the girls at the "Black table" do. When she tells her story there, one of them is likely to say, "You know what, Mr. Smith said the same thing to me yesterday!" Not only are Black adolescents encountering racism and reflecting on their identity, but their White peers, even when they are not the perpetrators (and sometimes they are), are unprepared to respond in supportive ways. The Black students turn to each other for the much needed support they are not likely to find anywhere else.

In adolescence, as race becomes personally salient for Black youth, finding the answer to questions such as, "What does it mean to be a young Black person? How should I act? What should I do?" is particularly important. And although Black fathers, mothers, aunts, and uncles may hold the answers by offering themselves as role models, they hold little appeal for most adolescents. The last thing many fourteen-year-olds want to do is to grow up to be like their parents. It is the peer group, the kids in the cafeteria, who hold the answers to these questions. They know how to be Black. They have absorbed the stereotypical images of Black youth in the popular culture and are reflecting those images in their self-presentation.

Based on their fieldwork in U.S. high schools, Signithia Fordham and John Ogbu identified a common psychological pattern found among African American high school students at this stage of identity development.[11] They observed that the anger and resentment that adolescents feel in response to their growing awareness of the systematic exclusion of Black people from full participation in U.S. society leads to the development of an oppositional social identity. This oppositional stance both protects one's identity from the psychological assault of racism and keeps the dominant group at a distance. Fordham and Ogbu write:

> Subordinate minorities regard certain forms of behavior and certain activities or events, symbols, and meanings as *not appropriate* for them because those behaviors, events, symbols, and meanings are characteristic of white Americans. At the same time they emphasize other forms of behavior as more appropriate for them because these are *not* a part of white Americans' way of life. To behave in the manner defined as falling within a white cultural frame of reference is to "act white" and is negatively sanctioned.[12]

Certain styles of speech, dress, and music, for example, may be embraced as "authentically Black" and become highly valued, while attitudes and behaviors associated with Whites are viewed with disdain. The peer groups's evaluation of what is Black and what is not can have a powerful impact on adolescent behavior.

Reflecting on her high school years, one Black woman from a White neighborhood described both the pain of being rejected by her Black classmates and her attempts to conform to her peer's definition of Blackness:

> "Oh you sound White, you think you're White," they said. And the idea of sounding White was just so absurd to me. . . . So ninth grade was sort of traumatic in that I started listening to rap music, which I really just don't like. [I said] I'm gonna be Black, and it was just that stupid. But it's more than just how one acts, you know. [The other Black women there] were not into me for the longest time. My first year there was hell.

Sometimes the emergence of an oppositional identity can be quite dramatic, as the young person tries on a new persona almost overnight. At the end of one school year, race may not have appeared to be significant, but often some encounter takes place over the summer and the young person returns to school much more aware of his or her Blackness and ready to make sure that the rest of the world is

aware of it, too. There is a certain "in your face" quality that these adolescents can take on, which their teachers often experience as threatening. When a group of Black teens are sitting together in the cafeteria, collectively embodying an oppositional stance, school administrators want to know not only why they are sitting together, but what can be done to prevent it.

We need to understand that in racially mixed settings, racial grouping is a developmental process in response to an environmental stressor, racism. Joining with one's peers for support in the face of stress is a positive coping strategy. What is problematic is that the young people are operating with a very limited definition of what it means to be Black, based largely on cultural stereotypes.

OPPOSITIONAL IDENTITY DEVELOPMENT AND ACADEMIC ACHIEVEMENT

Unfortunately for Black teenagers, those cultural stereotypes do not usually include academic achievement. Academic success is more often associated with being White. During the encounter phase of racial identity development, when the search for identity leads toward cultural stereotypes and away from anything that might be associated with Whiteness, academic performance often declines. Doing well in school becomes identified as trying to be White. Being smart becomes the opposite of being cool.

While this frame of reference is not universally found among adolescents of African descent, it is commonly observed in Black peer groups. Among the Black college students I have interviewed, many described some conflict or alienation from other African American teens because of their academic success in high school. For example, a twenty-year-old female from a Washington, D.C., suburb explained:

> It was weird, even in high school a lot of the Black students were, like, "Well, you're not really Black." Whether it was because I became president of the sixth-grade class or whatever it was, it started pretty

much back then. Junior high, it got worse. I was then labeled certain things, whether it was "the oreo" or I wasn't really Black.

Others described avoiding situations that would set them apart from their Black peers. For example, one young woman declined to participate in a gifted program in her school because she knew it would separate her from the other Black students in the school.

In a study of thirty-three eleventh-graders in a Washington, D.C., school, Fordham and Ogbu found that although some of the students had once been academically successful, few of them remained so. These students also knew that to be identified as a "brainiac" would result in peer rejection. The few students who had maintained strong academic records found ways to play down their academic success enough to maintain some level of acceptance among their Black peers.[13]

Academically successful Black students also need a strategy to find acceptance among their White classmates. Fordham describes one such strategy as *racelessness*, wherein individuals assimilate into the dominant group by de-emphasizing characteristics that might identify them as members of the subordinate group.[14] Jon, a young man I interviewed, offered a classic example of this strategy as he described his approach to dealing with his discomfort at being the only Black person in his advanced classes. He said, "At no point did I ever think I was White or did I ever want to be White. . . . I guess it was one of those things where I tried to de-emphasize the fact that I was Black." This strategy led him to avoid activities that were associated with Blackness. He recalled, "I didn't want to do anything that was traditionally Black, like I never played basketball. I ran cross-country. . . . I went for distance running instead of sprints." He felt he had to show his White classmates that there were "exceptions to all these stereotypes." However, this strategy was of limited usefulness. When he traveled outside his home community with his White teammates, he sometimes encountered overt racism. "I quickly realized that I'm Black, and that's the thing that they're going to see first, no matter how much I try to de-emphasize my Blackness."

A Black student can play down Black identity in order to succeed in school and mainstream institutions without rejecting his Black identity and culture.[15] Instead of becoming raceless, an achieving Black student can become an *emissary,* someone who sees his or her own achievements as advancing the cause of the racial group. For example, social scientists Richard Zweigenhaft and G. William Domhoff describe how a successful Black student, in response to the accusation of acting White, connected his achievement to that of other Black men by saying, "Martin Luther King must not have been Black, then, since he had a doctoral degree, and Malcolm X must not have been Black since he educated himself while in prison." In addition, he demonstrated his loyalty to the Black community by taking an openly political stance against the racial discrimination he observed in his school.[16]

It is clear that an oppositional identity can interfere with academic achievement, and it may be tempting for educators to blame the adolescents themselves for their academic decline. However, the questions that educators and other concerned adults must ask are, How did academic achievement become defined as exclusively White behavior? What is it about the curriculum and the wider culture that reinforces the notion that academic excellence is an exclusively White domain? What curricular interventions might we use to encourage the development of an empowered emissary identity?

An oppositional identity that disdains academic achievement has not always been a characteristic of Black adolescent peer groups. It seems to be a post-desegregation phenomenon. Historically, the oppositional identity found among African Americans in the segregated South included a positive attitude toward education. While Black people may have publicly deferred to Whites, they actively encouraged their children to pursue education as a ticket to greater freedom.[17] While Black parents still see education as the key to upward mobility, in today's desegregated schools the models of success—the teachers, administrators, and curricular heroes—are almost always White.

Black Southern schools, though stigmatized by legally sanctioned segregation, were often staffed by

African American educators, themselves visible models of academic achievement. These Black educators may have presented a curriculum that included references to the intellectual legacy of other African Americans. As well, in the context of a segregated school, it was a given that the high achieving students would all be Black. Academic achievement did not have to mean separation from one's Black peers.

THE SEARCH FOR ALTERNATIVE IMAGES

This historical example reminds us that an oppositional identity discouraging academic achievement is not inevitable even in a racist society. If young people are exposed to images of African American academic achievement in their early years, they won't have to define school achievement as something for Whites only. They will know that there is a long history of Black intellectual achievement.

This point was made quite eloquently by Jon, the young man I quoted earlier. Though he made the choice to excel in school, he labored under the false assumption that he was "inventing the wheel." It wasn't until he reached college and had the opportunity to take African American studies courses that he learned about other African Americans besides Martin Luther King, Malcolm X, and Frederick Douglass—the same three men he had heard about year after year, from kindergarten to high school graduation. As he reflected on his identity struggle in high school, he said:

> It's like I went through three phases. . . . My first phase was being cool, doing whatever was particularly cool for Black people at the time, and that was like in junior high. Then in high school, you know, I thought being Black was basically all stereotypes, so I tried to avoid all of those things. Now in college, you know, I realize that being Black means a variety of things.

Learning his history in college was of great psychological importance to Jon, providing him with role models he had been missing in high school. He was particularly inspired by learning of the intellectual legacy of Black men at his own college:

> When you look at those guys who were here in the Twenties, they couldn't live on campus. They couldn't eat on campus. They couldn't get their hair cut in town. And yet they were all Phi Beta Kappa. . . . That's what being Black really is, you know, knowing who you are, your history, your accomplishments. . . . When I was in junior high, I had White role models. And then when I got into high school, you know, I wasn't sure but I just didn't think having White role models was a good thing. So I got rid of those. And I basically just, you know, only had my parents for role models. I kind of grew up thinking that we were on the cutting edge. We were doing something radically different than everybody else. And not realizing that there are all kinds of Black people doing the very things that I thought we were the only ones doing. . . . You've got to do the very best you can so that you can continue the great traditions that have already been established.

This young man was not alone in his frustration over having learned little about his own cultural history in grade school. Time and again in the research interviews I conducted, Black students lamented the absence of courses in African American history or literature at the high school level and indicated how significant this new learning was to them in college, how excited and affirmed they felt by this newfound knowledge. Sadly, many Black students never get to college, alienated from the process of education long before high school graduation. They may never get access to the information that might have helped them expand their definition of what it means to be Black and, in the process, might have helped them stay in school. Young people are developmentally ready for this information in adolescence. We ought to provide it.

NOT AT THE TABLE

As we have seen, Jon felt he had to distance himself from his Black peers in order to be successful in high school. He was one of the kids *not* sitting at the Black table. Continued encounters with racism and access to new culturally relevant information empowered him to give up his racelessness and become an emissary. In college, not only did he sit at the Black table, but he emerged as a campus leader, confident in the support of his Black peers. His example illustrates that one's presence at the Black table is often an expression of one's identity development, which evolves over time.

Some Black students may not be developmentally ready for the Black table in junior or senior high school. They may not yet have had their own encounters with racism, and race may not be very salient for them. Just as we don't all reach puberty and begin developing sexual interest at the same time, racial identity development unfolds in idiosyncratic ways. Though my research suggests that adolescence is a common time, one's own life experiences are also important determinants of the timing. The young person whose racial identity development is out of synch with his or her peers often feels in an awkward position. Adolescents are notoriously egocentric and assume that their experience is the same as everyone else's. Just as girls who have become interested in boys become disdainful of their friends still interested in dolls, the Black teens who are at the table can be quite judgmental toward those who are not. "If I think it is a sign of authentic Blackness to sit at this table, then you should too."

The young Black men and women who still hang around with the White classmates they may have known since early childhood will often be snubbed by their Black peers. This dynamic is particularly apparent in regional schools where children from a variety of neighborhoods are brought together. When Black children from predominantly White neighborhoods go to school with Black children from predominantly Black neighborhoods, the former group is often viewed as trying to be White by the latter group. We all speak the language of the streets we live on. Black children living in White neighborhoods often sound White to their Black peers from across town, and may be teased because of it. This can be a very painful experience, particularly when the young person is not fully accepted as part of the White peer group either.

One young Black woman from a predominantly White community described exactly this situation in an interview. In a school with a lot of racial tension, Terri felt that "the worst thing that happened" was the rejection she experienced from the other Black children who were being bussed to her school. Though she wanted to be friends with them, they teased her, calling her an "oreo cookie" and sometimes beating her up. The only close Black friend Terri had was a biracial girl from her neighborhood.

Racial tensions also affected her relationships with White students. One White friend's parents commented, "I can't believe you're Black. You don't seem like all the Black children. You're nice." Though other parents made similar comments, Terri reported that her White friends didn't start making them until junior high school, when Terri's Blackness became something to be explained. One friend introduced Terri to another White girl by saying, "She's not really Black, she just went to Florida and got a really dark tan." A White sixth-grade "boyfriend" became embarrassed when his friends discovered he had a crush on a Black girl. He stopped telling Terri how pretty she was, and instead called her "nigger" and said, "Your lips are too big. I don't want to see you. I won't be your friend anymore."

Despite supportive parents who expressed concern about her situation, Terri said she was a "very depressed child." Her father would have conversations with her "about being Black and beautiful" and about "the union of people of color that had always existed that I needed to find. And the pride." However, her parents did not have a network of Black friends to help support her.

It was the intervention of a Black junior high school teacher that Terri feels helped her the most. Mrs. Campbell "really exposed me to the good Black community because I was so down on it" by getting Terri involved in singing gospel music and introducing her to other Black students who would accept her. "That's when I started having other Black friends. And I thank her a lot for that."

The significant role that Mrs. Campbell played in helping Terri open up illustrates the constructive potential that informed adults can have in the identity development process. She recognized Terri's need for a same-race peer group and helped her find one. Talking to groups of Black students about the variety of living situations Black people come from and the unique situation facing Black adolescents in White communities helps to expand the definition of what it means to be Black and increases intragroup acceptance at a time when that is quite important.

For children in Terri's situation, it is also helpful for Black parents to provide ongoing opportunities for their children to connect with other Black peers even if that means traveling outside the community they live in. Race-conscious parents often do this by attending a Black church or maintaining ties to Black social organizations such as Jack and Jill. Parents who make this effort often find that their children become bicultural, able to move comfortably between Black and White communities, and able to sit at the Black table when they are ready.

Implied in this discussion is the assumption that connecting with one's Black peers in the process of identity development is important and should be encouraged. For young Black people living in predominantly Black communities, such connections occur spontaneously with neighbors and classmates and usually do not require special encouragement. However, for young people in predominantly White communities they may only occur with active parental intervention. One might wonder if this social connection is really necessary. If a young person has found a niche among a circle of White friends, is it really necessary to establish a Black peer group as a reference point? Eventually it is.

As one's awareness of the daily challenges of living in a racist society increase, it is immensely helpful to be able to share one's experiences with others who have lived it. Even when White friends are willing and able to listen and bear witness to one's struggles, they cannot really share the experience. One young woman came to this realization in her senior year of high school:

> [The isolation] never really bothered me until about senior year when I was the only one in the class.... That little burden, that constant burden of you always having to strive to do your best and show that you can do just as much as everybody else. Your White friends can't understand that, and it's really hard to communicate to them. Only someone else of the same racial, same ethnic background would understand something like that.

When one is faced with what Chester Pierce calls the "mundane extreme environmental stress" of racism, in adolescence or in adulthood, the ability to see oneself as part of a larger group from which one can draw support is an important coping strategy.[18] Individuals who do not have such a strategy available to them because they do not experience a shared identity with at least some subset of their racial group are at risk for considerable social isolation.

DISCUSSION QUESTIONS

1. Could the stages of identity development that Tatum describes for African American adolescents apply to gay adolescents? Latino adolescents? Young women?

2. What are the positive and negative consequences of the adolescent choice to "sit at the table" with other African Americans?

3. When you were in high school, did the popular kids, the athletes, or other cliques eat lunch together? How does that compare to what Tatum describes?

NOTES

1. J. Marcia, "Development and validation of ego identity status," *Journal of Personality and Social Psychology* 3 (1966): 551–58.

2. For a review of the research on ethnic identity in adolescents, see J. Phinney, "Ethnic identity in adolescents and adults: Review of research," *Psychological Bulletin* 108, no. 3 (1990): 499–514. See also "Part I: Identity development" in B. J. R. Leadbeater and N. Way (Eds.), *Urban girls: Resisting stereotypes, creating identities* (New York: New York University Press, 1996).

3. W. E. Cross, Jr., *Shades of Black: Diversity in African-American identity* (Philadelphia: Temple University Press, 1991).

4. For an expanded discussion of "race-conscious" parenting, see B. D. Tatum, *Assimilation blues,* ch. 6.

5. J. S. Phinney and S. Tarver, "Ethnic identity search and commitment in Black and White eighth graders," *Journal of Early Adolescence* 8, no. 3 (1988): 265–77.

6. See B. D. Tatum, "African-American identity, academic achievement, and missing history," *Social Education* 56, no. 6 (1992): 331–34; B. D. Tatum, "Racial identity and relational theory: The case of Black women in White communities," in *Work in progress, no. 63* (Wellesley, MA: Stone Center Working Papers, 1992); B. D. Tatum, "Out there stranded? Black youth in White communities," pp. 214–33 in H. McAdoo (Ed.), *Black families,* 3d ed. (Thousand Oaks, CA: Sage, 1996).

7. For an in-depth discussion of the negative effects of tracking in schools, see J. Oakes, *Keeping track: How*

schools structure inequality (New Haven: Yale University Press, 1985).

8. For further discussion of the social dynamics for Black youth in White communities, see Tatum, "Out there stranded?"

9. Leadbeater and Way, *Urban girls*, p. 5.

10. A. Haley and Malcolm X, *The autobiography of Malcolm X* (New York: Grove Press, 1965), p. 36.

11. S. Fordham and J. Ogbu, "Black students' school success: Coping with the burden of 'acting White,'" *Urban Review* 18 (1986): 176–206.

12. Ibid., p. 181.

13. For an expanded discussion of the "trying to be White" phenomenon, see Fordham and Ogbu, "Black students' school success," and S. Fordham, "Racelessness as a factor in Black students' school success: Pragmatic strategy or Pyrrhic victory?" *Harvard Educational Review* 58, no. 1 (1988): 54–84.

14. Fordham, "Racelessness as a factor in Black students' school success." See also S. Fordham, *Blacked out: Dilemmas of race, identity, and success at Capital High* (Chicago: University of Chicago Press, 1996).

15. For further discussion of this point, see R. Zweigenhaft and G. W. Domhoff, *Blacks in the White establishment? A study of race and class in America* (New Haven: Yale University Press, 1991), p. 155.

16. Ibid.

17. Ibid., p. 156.

18. C. Pierce, "Mundane extreme environment and its effects on learning," in S. G. Brainard (Ed.), *Learning disabilities: Issues and recommendations for research* (Washington, DC: National Institute of Education, 1975).

READING 27

The Minority Quarterback

Ira Berkow

BATON ROUGE, LOUISIANA

A late summer morning and the sun was already harsh on the dusty high school football field. The shirtless blond nineteen-year-old in shorts stained with sweat kept dropping back to pass, his hands at times so wet it was hard to grip the ball. He was throwing to a friend, working "up the ladder," as it is called, starting with short passes and ending long.

Ira Berkow writes for *The New York Times*. Sections of this story about the Morgan family, Jabari Morgan, and life at Southern University were contributed by Kirk Johnson.

But his mind wasn't totally on his receiver. He could feel the eyes of the man in the dark glasses who sat in a car on the other side of a chain-link fence, a hundred yards away.

The boy knew the man was watching. It had been subtly arranged. The National Collegiate Athletic Association does not allow tryouts, but if a college coach happens by a field where kids regularly throw the ball around, well, a coach may argue, where's the harm?

At that time, in July of 1996, Southern University, a football powerhouse among black colleges, desperately needed a quarterback, and the boy, Marcus Jacoby, badly needed a place to play quarterback.

After half an hour, the man in dark glasses, Mark Orlando, Southern's offensive coordinator, had seen enough and drove off.

It had gone well. The boy was invited to the coach's apartment, where after a short visit he was offered a full football scholarship.

The coach explained that the boy had a shot at the starting job, that the intended starter's poor grades had lost him his place on the team and that the two backups did not have the coaches' confidence.

"Sounds good," Jacoby, who had been a star at Catholic High, one of Baton Rouge's schoolboy powers, recalled saying. "But I have to think about it—talk with my parents."

"Practice starts in four days," the coach responded. "We're going to need an answer soon."

Marcus Jacoby was unaware that if he accepted the scholarship, he would be the first white to play quarterback for Southern University. And he would be the first white to start at quarterback in the seventy-six-year history of the black Southwestern Athletic Conference.

Jacoby had grown up in Baton Rouge, and yet he knew practically nothing about Southern, had never even been to the other side of town to see the campus. Until that July day he had spent his life surrounded by whites.

The Business of How to Succeed

Southern's head coach, Pete Richardson, worked out of a modest wood-paneled office lined with trophies. In his three years there, he had turned a laughingstock into a national force. Southern won eleven of twelve games his first year, 1993, and two years later it was the No. 1 black college in the nation.

It is not easy for a black man to become a head coach. Despite his record, Richardson, fifty-four, has never had an offer from one of the 114 Division I-A colleges; only three of them have black head football coaches.

In college he played at the University of Dayton, hardly a football school, and though he had limited natural talent, he reached the professional level, playing three years for the Buffalo Bills. He coached high school ball for a few years, then took the head coach job at Winston-Salem State in North Carolina. Finally, in 1993, he got his big break at Southern, which with its combined campuses is the largest historically black college in the nation.

"I can't get caught up with the thought that, 'Hey, why shouldn't I be at Notre Dame?'" he said in an interview. "I can't get sidetracked or go around with a chip on my shoulder." He is a stoical man and expected stoicism from his players.

That day in his office, the Jacobys said, they were impressed by his quiet intellect, the way he measured his words, his determination. Indeed, the president of Southern, Dr. Dorothy Spikes, often said that she had hired Richardson over better-known candidates not just because his teams had been winners but because of his reputation for integrity, for running a clean program.

Coach Richardson and the Jacobys discussed everything from Southern's rich athletic tradition to the engineering courses that interested Marcus, but for a long while they didn't mention the thing that worried the parents most. The quarterback is team leader. Would a black team accept a white leader? Would the black campus? The night before, at the Jacobys' home in the upper-middle-class white Tara section of Baton Rouge, talk had become heated. "What if they don't like Marcus?" Marian Jacoby had said, tears in her eyes. "What if there's some kind of . . . action?" Marcus had not been able to sleep he was so upset.

Now his father, Glen, an environmental engineer, asked the coach, "How are you going to protect my son?"

The room went silent, Glen Jacoby said later. "I realize that you're concerned," Richardson began, "but I just don't think it will be that big a deal. Sure, there will be some adjustments from all sides. But Marcus will have the backing of the administration as well as the coaching staff."

Coach Richardson pointed out that there were other minorities on campus. He meant that of the 10,500 students, 5 percent were not black, but Marian Jacoby kept thinking about how it would feel to be in a stadium with her husband and 30,000 black fans.

The coach didn't say it to the Jacobys, but no one knew better than he about the strain Marcus would feel being in the minority. As a successful black man Richardson was used to the stares of surprise.

"Walking into a place with a suit and tie on, you're always going to get that second look because you're not supposed to be there." When he coached at Winston-Salem, he had a state government car. "Whites look at you and ask you what you're doing driving the state's car," he said. "You pull over to get some gas and people will address you the wrong way or policemen will look at you funny."

There was something else Richardson didn't say that morning: He was well aware how hostile Southern's fans could be to any newcomer, regardless of creed or color. Many had not wanted him hired. They felt he had come from too small a college; they had wanted a big name in black college football. They had even used race on *him*. Shortly after he arrived, a rumor started that Richardson's wife, who is light-skinned, was white, and that his white offensive coordinator was his wife's brother. None of it was true, but Richardson didn't let it get to him. He knew the best answer was to win, and since he had done so, he was—as Southern's registrar, Marvin Allen, liked to point out—a campus god.

The coach thought he could make this Jacoby thing work. He wasn't sitting there fretting about whether Marcus could learn to be part of the minority. The first game was only six weeks away. As he would say later, he didn't have "ample time to find another black quarterback." Marcus would have to do what all good players did, what the coach himself had done: suck it up.

To reassure the Jacobys, the coach told them about his staff. Of six assistants he had hired when he started in 1993, two were white, one Asian. He was told Southern fans would never stand for that. But after his 11–1 debut season—the year before they had been 6–5—a popular T-shirt on campus featured a photo of the integrated staff, with the phrase "In Living Color."

The parents wanted to think about it overnight, but Marcus did not. He climbed into his Jeep, he said later, and went riding. He was getting his shot, finally. There was nothing he loved like football. As a boy, when he couldn't find a friend, he tossed footballs into garbage-can lids in his yard. His parents held him back in ninth grade, so he would have time to grow, and a better chance to play high school ball. After starring at Catholic, he went to Louisiana Tech, but there, prospects for playing were dim.

Now he envisioned a game night at Southern with a crowd cheering as he threw yet another touchdown pass. When he stopped at a red light, he lifted his head and at the top of his lungs screamed, "Praise God!"

Hard Work, or Privilege?

From the Jacobys' home, Southern was a twenty-minute car trip, literally to the other side of the tracks. On the ride to the first practice, as he drove over the Hump—the small hill that is one of the barriers between Southern and white Baton Rouge—the momentousness of what he had done started sinking in. As he looked around, he began imagining himself playing a game, he recalled. "Would I see a white face?"

Southern's decision to sign a white quarterback made headlines, first locally, then nationally, and the reaction of some whites he knew startled him. When Jacoby called his girlfriend to talk about it, her mother answered. "The niggers over there will kill you," he recalled her saying. "There are bullets flying all over the place. It's a war zone." When his girlfriend got on the phone, she said, "Marcus, I don't want you to call me again." To many on the white side of town, who had never visited this campus bustling with middle-class black students on the bluffs of the Mississippi, it was as if Jacoby had voluntarily moved to the ghetto.

Like many white Americans, he knew there was still prejudice—though, he says, not at home. He had been raised to believe that, after generations of injustice, the country was now a fair place when it came to race, and he had made a few black friends while playing high school ball.

The Jacobys were considered a little eccentric for Baton Rouge, having moved here from California when Marcus was three. His paternal grandfather was Jewish. His mother had attended Berkeley in the 1960s and still had some of the flower child in her. She was a fitness buff, and had even tried putting her family on a vegetarian diet, stocking the refrigerator with so many oat products that Marcus's buddies asked whether they owned a horse. Marcus and his sister at first attended a private school, but their mother felt too many children there were spoiled by wealth. So she taught them at home for five years, until Marcus was a sophomore.

Friends and teachers at Catholic High remember him as hard-working, smart and moralistic, with a strong Christian bent. "We'd make fun of his being so innocent," said John Eric Sullivan, one of his best friends. "By that I mean, he didn't do anything that most normal high school kids are doing. He'd be, 'Watch out, watch yourself,' when guys would be drinking. We'd say, like, 'Marc, relax, man.'" He told them he was waiting until he was twenty-one to drink.

The Southern coaches were impressed with his arm and had never seen a quarterback learn Coach Richardson's complex offense so fast. Jacoby stayed to do extra throwing and often studied game films well past midnight. Southern at times uses a no-huddle offense, meaning the quarterback has to call plays rapidly right at the line, and Coach Richardson felt that of the three candidates, only Marcus Jacoby knew the system well enough to do that. Within days of arriving, he was first string.

That sparked anger among many of his new black teammates. For over a year they had been friendly with the two quarterbacks now relegated to backup, and they resented the newcomer, complaining that he had not earned his stripes. "He was *given* his stripes," said Virgil Smothers, a lineman. "There was a lingering bitterness."

Several felt the decision was racial. "It just became the fact that we were going to have this white quarterback," said Sam George, a quarterback prospect who was academically ineligible that year. "It wasn't about ability no more." Teammates picked at Jacoby's weaknesses—he didn't have "fast feet" and rarely scrambled—and joked that he was the typical bland white athlete, which angered Richardson. "A lot of minorities, they want the flash," the coach said. "We felt we needed a system in order to be successful and a quarterback to operate within the confines of that system."

Except for the coaches, he was isolated. In the locker room, Jacoby recalled, "I would walk around the corner and people would just stop talking."

Even in the huddles there was dissension. Scott Cloman, a Southern receiver, recalled: "The minute Marcus was like, 'Everybody calm down, just shut up,' they were like: 'Who are you talking to? You're not talking to me.' You know, stuff like that. If it was a black person it wouldn't be a problem. They all felt that 'I'm not going to let a white person talk to me like that.'"

His entire time at Southern, Jacoby kept his feelings about all this inside, "sucking it up," repeatedly telling the inquiring reporters what a *great* experience it was being exposed to a new culture. "As soon as I signed and walked onto the campus," he told one interviewer, "I felt like part of the family. I definitely feel at home here."

School and Students in Step

On September 7, 1996, Southern opened at Northwestern State, with Marcus Jacoby at quarterback. Of the 25,000 spectators, half had made the three-hour trip from Southern, not unusual for this football-crazy place. "Fans plan their lives around games," Richardson said. "They fight to get schedules, to see where we're going to play so they can take holidays and go to games."

Southern University families like the Morgans will take more than twenty people to an away game, filling several hotel rooms. Mo Morgan, a supervisor at the local Exxon plant who attended Southern in the 1960s, went so far as to buy a motor home just for Southern football, which made him the object of good-natured ribbing. Friends insisted that "black people don't drive Winnebagos." His wife, Wanda, and about twenty-five of their relatives are Southern graduates, and his youngest son, Jabari, a freshman drummer and cymbals player, was on the field for that same opening game.

For the youngest Morgan, the band was only partly about music. More famous than Southern's football team—having performed at five Super Bowls and three presidential inaugurations—it had real power and importance on campus. The 180-piece Southern band thrived on intimidating lesser rivals on the black college circuit. With its hard-brass sound and its assertive style, the group had a militant edge that old-timers on campus attributed to the influence of the civil rights era, when the band's show was honed.

Robert Gray, who played cymbals with Morgan, said: "When people think about Southern band, they think about a bunch of big, tough-looking, tight-looking dudes with psychotic looks on their faces, ready to go to war. I just think—Southern band—black, all male, just rowdy, loud."

Families like the Morgans were fiercely proud of *their* school and its role in helping generations of blacks into the middle and professional classes—even if the state had long treated it as second-rate. In the early 1900s, legislators planning to create a new campus for Southern considered several locations around Louisiana. But in city after city, white residents rose in protest, and finally the state settled on a site that no one else then coveted. In the 1950s, blacks like Audrey Nabor-Jackson, Wanda Morgan's aunt, were prohibited from attending the big white public campus across town, Louisiana State University. Southern was their only alternative.

Even as late as the 1970s, Louisiana's public higher education system was capable of inflicting deep racial wounds. Wanda Morgan was required to take several courses at LSU as part of a master's program at Southern. In one class, she was one of four blacks, and for every exam, she said, the four were removed by the professor and put in an empty classroom across the hall, one in each corner, while the white students took the exam in their regular seats. The message was missed by no one: black students would cheat.

By the mid-1990s, change was brewing. The year before Marcus Jacoby arrived, Southern and LSU settled a twenty-year-old federal desegregation lawsuit. Both institutions pledged sharp minority increases on their campuses, with 10 percent of enrollment set aside for other races—more whites to Southern, more blacks to LSU.

Alumni like the Morgans were worried. Would Southern soon become just another satellite campus of LSU? Was the white quarterback the beginning of the end?

Mo Morgan and Audrey Nabor-Jackson agreed with an editorial in Southern's student paper saying that a white quarterback did not belong. "There are plenty of young black athletes," it said, "who could benefit from Jacoby's scholarship."

Mo Morgan said, "I didn't like the fact that he was there." About the only Morgan not upset was Jabari. Mo Morgan worried that his eighteen-year-old son was not race-conscious enough. "I came through the movement, I was confronted with things," said the father. "That's one of the things that concerns me—that he hasn't." But Jabari Morgan couldn't have cared less, he was so consumed with the band. Long before starting college, he had begun assembling on his bedroom wall what he called his shrine, a montage about the Southern band that included a picture of the first white band member, in the early 1990s.

Now, in his freshman year, his long-nurtured fantasy was coming true. Standing there that day with cymbals weighing nine pounds each, ready to march into Northwestern State's stadium, he was at the front of the band. The director, Dr. Isaac Greggs, always positioned his tallest and most imposing players—his "towers of terror"—at the front, and Jabari Morgan, at six foot one, was one of them. Football, he said, was about the last thing on his mind.

"It was like winning the lottery."

He wouldn't have cared if Marcus Jacoby were purple, as long as Southern won and people stayed in their seats for the halftime show.

A Mutinous Beginning

Southern lost its first two games. The team was young—ten of eleven offensive starters were new—but what people remembered was the 11–1 record the year before.

For fans, the quarterback, more than any other player, *is* the team—hero or goat. During the second loss, Jacoby recalled, "I heard the entire stadium booing me."

Jean Harrison, the mother of the quarterback prospect Sam George, remembered, "One lady had a megaphone and she was screaming, 'Get that white honky out of there!'"

Chris Williams, an offensive lineman, believed that the other team hit Jacoby harder because he was white: "Teams took cheap shots at him. I really believe that. I mean they hit him sometimes blatantly late after the whistle." Scott Cloman recalled that after one Southern loss, opposing players said, "That's what you all get for bringing white boys on the field."

Jacoby was hit so hard and so often during the first game that he was hospitalized with a concussion. Glen Jacoby, Marcus's father, was sure the blockers were sandbagging their white quarterback, but in interviews at the time, the young man denied it. He still says he believes that it was just the mistakes of an inexperienced line.

After Southern's second loss, an angry fan threatened Jacoby. A coach had to jump between them. For the rest of his career, Jacoby would have a police escort at games. There was a disturbance outside the stadium at another game. Gunshots were fired. Jacoby recalls thinking the shots were aimed at him.

The Tuesday after the second loss, Jacoby rose at 5 A.M., worked out in the weight room, then walked to the cafeteria for the team breakfast. No one was there. He checked his watch. Shortly after he sat down, Coach Orlando came in, took him by the arm and led him through a nearby door.

As Jacoby remembered it, the entire team and coaching staff sat squeezed into a small room. All chairs were taken, so he stood alone against a wall. No one looked at him. Coach Richardson stood. "I think Marcus should know what's going on," he said, adding, "Who wants to say something?"

Smothers, the senior defensive end, rose. The night before, he had talked about staging a strike.

Now he mentioned some minor gripes, then added: "We're losing and we feel changes ought to be made. Some guys aren't getting a fair chance."

Someone else said, "Guys are playing who shouldn't."

Orlando walked to the front. As offensive coordinator, he naturally worked closely with the quarterback. But several players felt he favored Jacoby because they were both white. "Let's get this in the open," Orlando said, adding, "This is mostly about Jacoby, isn't it?" Insisting that the quarterback had been chosen fairly, he said: "You have to accept Marcus, he's one of us. We're 0 and 2, but we have to put this behind us."

Lionel Hayes, who had lost the quarterback job to Jacoby, interrupted Orlando. "You're just saying that," Hayes said, "because you're Jacoby's dad." It got a laugh, though his tone was angry. Jacoby said later: "There was a lot of hate in that room. I felt like I was falling into a hole, and I couldn't grab the sides."

Richardson spoke again: "We win as a team, we lose as a team. Jacoby's doing what he's supposed to be doing, and he'll get better. We all will." He said practice would be at three. "If anyone doesn't want to be on the team with Jacoby as the starting quarterback, don't come."

Richardson remembered: "What I saw was a frustration by some players—mostly seniors—who weren't playing. They weren't playing because they didn't deserve to. And so they needed a scapegoat."

Jacoby remembers feeling like the invisible man. "It was almost as though I weren't there, and they were talking about me," he said. "I wasn't sure where to turn. I felt they didn't want me there—not me personally, but any white quarterback—that I was just another problem."

Three or four players didn't show up for practice, and Richardson cut them. Not long afterward, Virgil Smothers and one of the coaches argued, and Smothers was told, "Clear out your locker."

When the players gathered the next day at practice, before the coaches arrived, Jacoby said, he stood to talk. A few tried to shout him down, but John Williams, a star senior cornerback and devout Christian who would go on to play for the Baltimore Ravens, rose and said, "Man, let the man talk."

"I don't care if you like me or hate me," Jacoby recalled saying. "All I ask is that we can go out and play football together. This is not a popularity contest. I'm trying to win. I'm just trying to be your quarterback."

Winning Works Wonders

Things improved dramatically. Southern won six of its next seven games, beating the two top-ranked black colleges, and was invited to the Heritage Bowl in Atlanta, the black college championship.

"I wasn't getting booed nearly as much," Jacoby said. Some teammates began warming to him. More than anything, they were impressed by his work ethic. During a practice break, players drank from a garden hose. "Sorry, Marcus," one teased, "this is the black water fountain." They called him "Tyrone," and "Rasheed."

"I appreciated it," he recalled. "Things had changed to the extent that some of the players were calling me 'the man.'"

Before games, he and John Williams prayed together. One Sunday the two went to the black church where Williams was a minister.

Occasionally strangers would wish Jacoby well. One day the band's legendary director, Dr. Greggs, greeted him warmly and urged him to persevere.

He felt he was developing real friendships with teammates and Southern students. When Scott Cloman needed a place to stay for a month, Jacoby had him to his parents' home and the two grew close. "Marcus was the first white person I ever really got to know," Cloman said. "I always felt a lot of tension around whites. I'd go into a store and I could just feel the tension. Sometimes you just feel like, 'I can't stand white people.' I didn't understand them. I really didn't want to be near them."

"His parents treated me like a son," added Cloman. Some players now joked when they saw him, "Where's your brother?"

"And some," he said, "called me 'white lover.' Didn't bother me. I had come to understand the Jacobys. A lot of times people fear what they can't understand. Because of being around the Jacobys my attitude toward whites in general changed."

Failure Is Not an Option

At the Heritage Bowl that first year, on national television, Southern took a 24–10 halftime lead against Howard University, then fell behind, 27–24. In the closing minute, Southern drove to Howard's 15-yard line. On third down, with 42 seconds left, Marcus Jacoby dropped back and, under pressure, threw off the wrong foot, floating a pass into the end zone.

"I heard the crowd gasp," he said. "I couldn't believe this was happening." He'd been intercepted. "Their fans must have cheered, but I remember everything being silent." A camera captured Coach Richardson on his knees, hands over his head.

"I dragged myself off the field and sat on a bench and buried my head in my arms," Jacoby said. "A few people, like John Williams, came by and patted me on the back, to be encouraging. But I heard, 'You screwed up real bad this time, whitey,' and, 'You're as dumb as they come.' It was the lowest point of my life."

After the game, Coach Orlando received an anonymous call: "If Jacoby ever plays for Southern again, we'll kill him—and you." The coach said he averaged a threat a week that season. Later, as Orlando and Jacoby headed to their cars, the coach pointed to several trees. In the light of the streetlamps, Jacoby could see a yellow rope hung from each tree. The ropes were tied in nooses.

Eyes of Southern Are upon Him

On campus, Jacoby struggled with all the daily irritations that go with being in the minority. As a white who grew up among whites, he was used to being inconspicuous. Here, he always felt on display. "I hated that," he said, "because it was like I had become just a novelty act."

He found that things he had done unconsciously all his life were suddenly brought to his attention and analyzed. One was the way he dressed. He liked to wear a T-shirt, shorts and flip-flops to class; most students at Southern dressed up for class in slacks.

Another was that the way he spoke, his slang, was different from the black majority's. "Many times I would say something at Southern and they would repeat it and I wouldn't get my point across," he said. "It would get lost in the mocking of how I said it instead of what I said. I might walk into a room and I'd say, 'Hey, how y'all doin'?'" Instead of answering, someone would do an imitation of a white person talking, enunciating slowly. "They'd say 'Hi, guy, how are you doing?' So I just learned to say, 'Hey.'" He believed the classmates were only needling him, but being constantly reminded was exhausting.

"People's eyes were on him," said Chris Williams, a teammate. "He just didn't blend in. I mean, like me, I just blended in wherever I went."

A white with a different personality might have fared better. There was one other white on the seventy-man squad, Matt Bushart. And though as a punter he was at the periphery of the team and little noticed by fans, Bushart had the personality and experience to cope better as a minority. While Marcus had seemed protected and naive even to the middle-class white students at Catholic High, Matt's years at a local public high school where most of his football teammates were black had taught him how to live comfortably among them. While Marcus was more introspective, a loner, a little too sensitive for some of his coaches' tastes, Matt was noisy, funny, sometimes crude—so outgoing, his girlfriend said, that he could talk to a wall.

When Bushart's teammates made fun of the country music he liked, he gave it right back to them about their rap, and kept listening to his music. "I get kidded about it," he said, "but there's been a song that's been playing and one of the black guys will come by and say, 'Play that again, that's actually not too bad.'"

Jacoby loved music, too; playing guitar was an important outlet for relieving the pressure, but he would not play on campus. As he put it: "At times the rap just blared from the dorms; I longed for something that was my own. I couldn't play it on campus because for most of the time, I was apologizing for who I was. I didn't want to cause any more turmoil than there was. I didn't want to make myself look like I was any more separate than I was."

Interracial dating is complicated at Southern. Ryan Lewis, Jacoby's roommate, says most black men would not openly date a white woman on campus. "They would keep it low so nobody knew about it but them," Lewis said. "I've never seen it."

As quarterback, Jacoby often had female students flirting with him. He felt uneasy, caught between the white and black sides of town. Among whites, he said, "everybody just assumed the worst, that I was dating a black girl now because I was at Southern." But even though there were some "gorgeous light-skinned black girls over there," he said, and a couple of women from his classes became good friends, he wasn't attracted. He thinks it was "a cultural thing."

Though college students are confronted with new ideas—sometimes only partially understood—and encouraged to speak out about them, Jacoby felt that when he did, he was criticized. At first, in his African-American history class, when they discussed slavery, he said he tried to be conciliatory in an oral report. "I would say something like, 'I can't imagine how terrible it must have been, that people could do those kinds of things to other people.' And others in the class made some kind of jokes, but it was like bitter jokes: 'What are you talking about, Marcus? You're one of those whites.' It was like they were saying to me, 'Quit Uncle Tomming.'"

Then he worried he wasn't being true to his white roots. "I felt that I had lost my pride and the respect of friends that I had grown up with," he said. For his next oral report, he decided to speak his mind and said that it was unhealthy for blacks to dwell too much on past racial violence. "There have been tragedies like slavery throughout time," he said. "I don't think one is more important than any other." When he finished, he recalled, "there was an eerie silence and I saw at least three or four people glaring at me."

Increasingly, being in the minority alienated him, made him feel alone. "I learned early on that I was a pioneer in all this and no one else had gone through it and often the best advice I could get was from myself. Because I was the only one who knew the whole situation."

It didn't help that his preoccupied parents were going through a divorce. At one point when he was upset about not fitting in, his mother gave him a copy of *Black Like Me*, the story of a white man in the 1960s who dyes his skin and travels the South to experience being black during segregation. At the time, Jacoby said, "I resented my mother giving me the book. I felt she was almost taking the other side."

One Fits, the Other Doesn't

Blacks, of course, are much better at being in the minority, since they have far more practice and, usually, no choice. When Jabari Morgan was considering colleges, his father told him he was free to pick Southern or a "white" college, but if he picked white, he had better be prepared. Then he gave him the talk about being in the minority that so many black American men give their sons. "You are going to face being called a nigger," Mo Morgan told Jabari. "Now, are you ready to deal with it? If you're not ready to deal with it, don't go."

The Morgans have a family council of elders that meets regularly to guide their young, and one message emphasized is this: "A black person in America has to be smarter and sharper and work harder to achieve the same things as a white person of the same abilities." Mo Morgan says, as a minority, he understands that "the majority is white, and *you* have control and *you* want to keep control."

But Jabari Morgan did not think like his father.

He had always dreamed of attending Southern, but for him its great appeal was not as a racial sanctuary. He considered race simply part of the rough and tumble of life, the cost of doing business in a mostly white world. Southern was the place where he might be able to play in the best marching band in America, as his father had before him.

He determined very early that the best high school marching bands, like the best college bands, were black, and so he fudged his address in order to attend a nearly all-black Baton Rouge school where the band rocked. He figured that that would give him an edge when he tried out at Southern.

As a marketing major who graduated in 2000, Morgan fully expects that he will one day work for a big white-controlled corporation. But as a marching band member at Southern for four years, he was in many ways the ultimate insider in the self-contained black-majority culture of the Yard, as Southern's campus is known.

All the things that Marcus Jacoby found so irritating were second nature to Jabari Morgan—the music, the dress, the vernacular of put-downs and nicknames that is the campus currency. He loved African-American literature class because the poetry and stories reinforced what his family had taught him about black history.

Like all new band members, Morgan went through hazing. But as part of the majority, he never worried that it was about race. Jacoby, on the other hand, felt so unsettled as part of the minority that he often had trouble sleeping.

Morgan eventually joined a fraternity—a support in its own way as strong as the band's.

And, where Marcus Jacoby the minority had no steady girlfriend during his years at Southern, Jabari Morgan the majority began, in his second semester, dating Monique Molizone, an economics major from New Orleans. She had also come to Southern partly for the band—to join the Dancing Dolls, who perform at the band's side.

Comeback and Competition

As much as anything, what got Jacoby through his second year at Southern was a determination to avenge that Heritage Bowl interception, to show everyone he could be a champion. He moved through the 1997 season with a passion, working so hard in the weight room that he could now bench-press 350 pounds; running endless drills to improve his foot speed; and doing so much extra throwing that by day's end it took an hour to ice and treat his arm.

Again, he was first string, but he had competition. Sam George had returned from academic probation. George was a popular figure on campus, known for his hard-partying ways. Though he was only five foot seven, he had a strong arm and terrific speed. His teammates, responding to his take-charge style in huddles, nicknamed him the Little General. "And," Scott Cloman said, "he was black."

Although Jacoby started, Coach Richardson liked bringing in George when the team seemed flat. Both quarterbacks saw race as the true reason behind the coach's substitutions. Jacoby was convinced that Richardson was giving the black quarterback playing time to pander to the black fans; George was convinced that Richardson—influenced by Coach Orlando—was starting the white quarterback because of favoritism.

George wound up playing in five of twelve games. By Southern's third game, against Arkansas-Pine Bluff, both quarterbacks were bitter. After winning its first two games, Southern was losing to Pine Bluff 7–6 at the half. Richardson decided to replace the white quarterback with the black. Jacoby was devastated; he felt he was a proven winner and should not be yanked for one bad half.

Given his chance, George threw a last-ditch thirty-seven-yard pass that tied the game, and threw another touchdown in triple overtime for a 36–33 Southern win.

And yet, come Monday practice, Jacoby was the starter again. Now George was frustrated.

Southern had a 9–1 record going into its two final games. A victory in the next game—the Bayou Classic, against Grambling, its archrival—would assure a return to the Heritage Bowl and a chance for Jacoby to redeem himself. His parents and teammates had never seen him so obsessed. He had trouble sleeping and little appetite. His father called Coach Orlando, worried that Marcus's weight was down.

In a journal account of that period, Marcus Jacoby wrote: "I sat down and wrote out a detailed plan of how I was going to get through these last two games, including my political and motivational moves. My survival as a person depended on these last two games. Nobody, including Coach Orlando, knew the amount of outside forces that were pressing on these last two games. I was at a point where I felt that I was crawling on my knees."

He added, "I dreamed of a time when I could just say that I had accomplished something, instead of fighting for respect, fighting in a classroom full of people who disagreed with everything I stood for, and could have a day of true rest."

Before the big game against Grambling, he pleaded with Coach Orlando. "If you don't pull me," Jacoby said, "I guarantee we'll win our next two games."

"You can't guarantee that," the coach said.

"I just did," Jacoby said. Orlando suggested that if Marcus Jacoby played a little more like Sam George, sometimes scrambling out of the pocket, he might be more effective. Jacoby felt that he was being told to become something he was not, but he was so desperate, so nervous about being yanked, that he followed the advice. He ran, and it worked. In a 30–7 win against Grambling, Jacoby threw three touchdown passes and played the entire game. He was named the Bayou Classic's most valuable player.

A month later he achieved his redemption, throwing the winning pass in a 34–28 Heritage Bowl victory over South Carolina State, capping an 11–1 season that earned Southern the black national championship. "I was happier than I had ever been at Southern," he recalled. On the trip back from that game he slept soundly for the first time in months.

The Going Gets Too Tough

The more you achieve, the more is expected. After that 11–1 season, the talk on campus was that Southern would go undefeated in 1998. But in the opener, with the team trailing 7–0 at the half, Jacoby was pulled for George. Southern lost anyway, 28–7.

In practice on Tuesday, Jacoby overthrew a pass to one of his ends, John Forman, who yelled at him in front of everybody.

Forman would say later that it was just the frustration of having lost the opener, but to Jacoby it was so much more—the final straw. He was sure that Forman was trying to subvert his control of the team to help George, his roommate. "If you have a choice, you choose black first," Jacoby would later say. "I felt that I was all alone again, on an island by myself. It was like I was right back where I had started two years before, with a lot of the same attitudes against me."

He quit football and Southern.

Coach Richardson was surprised and asked Jacoby to stay. But more recently, he said he understood the decision. Because of "the type person he is," the coach said, "it was the best thing for Marcus because it would have killed him." The coach meant that Marcus Jacoby was not emotionally equipped to continue being the solitary white.

When Branch Rickey of the Brooklyn Dodgers wanted to break major league baseball's color line in 1947, he chose Jackie Robinson, not simply because he was a great black ballplayer—there were greater black stars—but because he had experience inside white institutions. Jackie Robinson was twenty-eight that first year in the majors, a mature man who had attended UCLA and served in the Army. He knew what it was like to be in the minority.

When Coach Richardson went after Jacoby, he was just looking for a quarterback.

Reporters hounded Jacoby to find why he had left, but he never spoke openly about it. He never mentioned race. In brief interviews, he told them he was burned out, and in a sense this was true. He had burned out on being in the minority. And as a white, he didn't have to be. In those last months at Southern, he often thought about returning to a white life. "You kind of look over your shoulder and see your old life and you say, 'I could go back.'"

There had been such anguish over the Jacoby-George quarterback battle, and all its racial nuances, but at least on the field, in the end, it didn't seem to make much difference. That year Southern, with Sam George at the helm, finished 9–3, once again winning the Heritage Bowl.

A white quarterback at Southern did make people think. Mo Morgan had been against it, but not after watching Jacoby at practices. "I looked at the three quarterbacks that were there and he was the best at the time. I'm just telling you straight out. It wasn't his ability and I'm not saying he was brighter than the other kids. He just put in the work."

Morgan's son Jabari said he, too, was sorry to see Jacoby go; he liked the idea of a white guy being open to attending a black college.

As a senior, Jabari Morgan reached out to a white freshman tuba player, Grant Milliken, who tried out for the band. He helped him through the hazing. One of Jabari Morgan's friends said he had done it because Milliken was white, but Morgan said no, he had done it because Milliken was really good on tuba.

Morgan even helped Milliken create a dance solo full of shakes and shivers and fancy steps, which was performed at halftimes to wild applause. What the crowd loved, said Morgan, was not just that a white guy could dance.

"The whole point of letting the white guy dance is that we were saying to the world, 'Hey, you can learn our culture just like we can learn yours.'"

Morgan's father continues to be both fearful of his son's more relaxed attitude about race, and a little in awe of it.

"He doesn't think it's something he can't overcome," said Mo Morgan, "and you know, I think he's right. You can get caught up in this, and it will screw up your thinking."

No More Apologies

One weekend in the fall of 1999, at the request of a reporter, Jacoby went to a Southern game for the first time since quitting. This was Homecoming Day, and from his seat in the stands he watched Southern seniors and their families being introduced to the crowd at midfield. It could have been his moment. Ryan Lewis, his old roommate, was there, and so was Matt Bushart, the white punter.

Bushart's name was called, to applause. Jacoby had read in the newspaper Bushart's saying how much he had enjoyed Southern.

The team had won seven straight games at that point, and so Jacoby was surprised during the first quarter when Southern's starting quarterback was replaced after throwing an interception. Jacoby had always been so sure he'd been replaced with Sam George to pander to fans; now Coach Richardson was using the exact same strategy with two black quarterbacks. In the paper the next day, Richardson said he had just been trying to light a spark under the offense.

After the game, outside the stadium, a large black man spotted Jacoby and, extending his hand, said, "Hi, Marcus, how ya doin'?"

"OK, Virgil," Jacoby said. "How you doin'?" The two chatted for a moment outside the stadium—the man said he had left school and was working as an account executive for a drug company—then they went their separate ways.

"That was Virgil Smothers," Jacoby said afterward. It was Smothers who had led the aborted strike against Jacoby. "I guess he figures it's all in the past."

It was not all in Jacoby's past. Though he had moved on—he was now majoring in finance at LSU—his Southern experience still unsettled him. "Just last night I had a dream about it," he said. "Weird dreams. Like some of these people are coming back to haunt me in some way. By these people I mean some of those who I considered friends and who I felt kind of turned on me."

At times he talks about being lucky to have experienced another culture; at others he describes it as "a personal hell." His sister Dana says, "There are some scars that haven't gone away, from the bad things."

After leaving Southern, Jacoby took a while to realize how much pressure he had felt. "I remember one time a few months after I quit—and this was part of the healing process—I said something about country music, that I liked it. And I remember standing around with four white people and thinking, 'Oh, my God, I can't believe I just said that.' And then I caught myself right before I got through that whole thing in my mind and I looked at the people's faces and they were agreeing with me. I went 'Whoa,' I didn't have to apologize for that anymore."

These days, he appreciates walking around anonymously on the mostly white LSU campus. "I got burned out as far as being somebody," he said. "At LSU I've just enjoyed being a part of the crowd."

Marcus Jacoby graduated from Louisiana State in December 2000, and was hoping to find a job in marketing. He still kept in touch with two teammates from his playing days at Southern, Scott Cloman and Ryan Lewis. As for football, he did not play competitively, but occasionally he would head over to a field near his home, send a receiver deep and loft hard, tight spirals into the sky.

After graduating from Southern in May 2000, Jabari Morgan returned as an unpaid "consultant" to the marching band, working with the drum section and helping create new dance routines. He also worked at a local car dealership, and was planning to go to business school. The question was where. His father felt that Louisiana State was the place to go, but the son thought he would probably stay where he felt at home—Southern.

DISCUSSION QUESTIONS

1. What characteristics might make someone able to cope as a minority? If Jabari Morgan had gone to a white school, do you think he would have had an easier time than Marcus Jacoby did at Southern? Why or why not?
2. Being a minority in some settings is often exhausting. Why?
3. What do you see as the hopeful and the discouraging aspects of this story?

A Day in the Life of Two Americas

Leonard Steinhorn

Barbara Diggs-Brown

Some people simply call it "the box." It's usually a large cardboard box found hidden away in a walk-in closet or down in the basement next to the washing machine. It contains diplomas, artwork, books, music, and especially all the family photos—anything that can identify the family as black. If a black family living in a predominantly white neighborhood wants to sell their house, they are often advised by friends or their real estate agent to put everything identifiably black—any vestige of who they are—in the box. Otherwise, white people may not buy the house.

For understandable reasons, real estate agents are often unwilling to acknowledge this practice.

Leonard Steinhorn is a professor at the American University School of Communication. Barbara Diggs-Brown is a professor at the American University School of Communication.

Nor are black homeowners very effusive about something so tinged with shame and regret. But walk into an open house any Saturday or Sunday, and if there are no family photos or mementos around, rest assured they're in the box. It happened once to the man who would become the highest-ranking civil rights official in America, former Assistant Attorney General Deval Patrick: "Yes. Actually, one time in one city, and I'll leave it at that. The realtor asked my wife and me to put all of our family photos away." It happened to a *Wall Street Journal* editor, who, after his house was appraised significantly below market value, decided not only to replace all the family photos with those of his white secretary but asked her and her blond son to be in the house when a new appraiser came by. The strategy worked. Black families are also advised to clear out when prospective white buyers want to see the house. Too many times a white family will drive up to a house, see the black homeowner working in the garden or garage, and quickly drive away.[1]

The box is a very small part of the daily commerce between blacks and whites, and its use is by nature limited to the relatively rare black family living in an overwhelmingly white community. But as a metaphor for race relations it looms very large, because it shows the lengths to which many whites will go to avoid intimate contact with anything black, and the degree to which blacks accept and grudgingly accommodate this reality. For blacks to succeed in the predominantly white world, they must—figuratively—carry this box around with them every day.

On a typical day in America, the lives of blacks and whites may intersect. but rarely do they integrate. In the matters most intimate and important to our lives—our neighborhoods, schools, work, faith, entertainment, and social life—we either go separate ways or, when forced together, follow what seems like a shadow dance of polite interaction. This by no means denies the real and meaningful contacts between some blacks and whites, but these instances are infrequent enough to be the conspicuous exceptions that prove the rule. Black and white Americans wake up in separate neighborhoods, send their kids off to separate schools, listen to different radio stations during the morning commute, briefly interact on the job but rarely as equals, return to their own communities after work, socialize in separate environments, and watch different television shows before going to sleep and starting the same process all over again. This is a day in the life of two Americas.

SEPARATE NEIGHBORHOODS

Most days begin the same for everyone, with the fresh morning air and the hustle to get out for work. But for black and white Americans, our lives begin to diverge after that. Chances are that a black family leaving home in the morning will see other black faces leaving their homes, and that a white family will see almost exclusively whites. Where we live defines so much of our lives—how we get to work, where our kids go to school, where we shop, whom we chat with, and who our friends will be. And where we live is more often than not determined by race.

About a third of all black Americans live in neighborhoods that are 90 percent or more black, and most other blacks live in neighborhoods disproportionately or predominantly black. Scholars Douglas Massey and Nancy Denton write in their book *American Apartheid* that "blacks remain the most spatially isolated population in U.S. history."[2] The isolation of blacks in central cities is as well documented as it is tragic. As Massey and Denton have pointed out, many blacks in these areas would have to go clear across town simply to find a white family. In cities like Chicago, Detroit, New York, Cleveland, St. Louis and Birmingham, blacks and whites are as divided and in some cases more divided than they were 40 years ago. Most whites lead parallel lives, living in virtually all-white neighborhoods, though often with a smattering of Hispanics and Asians. We may live in a nominally multiracial society, but millions upon millions of white Americans have no regular contact in their neighborhoods with blacks.

Years ago the suburbs were seen as the integration panacea, fresh fields for color-blind Americans to live together. More Americans now live in suburbs than anywhere else. But with the rise of black suburban migration over the last generation—close to a third of all blacks now live in the suburbs—the same pattern of separation has taken hold there as well. Most typical is the white suburb that stays virtually all white, the established black suburb that becomes more black, or the previously white suburb that in due time becomes all black once the color line has been broken. Very few suburbs boast a stable racial balance similar to the mix of middle-class blacks and whites in the metropolitan area, and even in these communities, residents still tend to cluster by race.

Consider the case of Bloomfield, Connecticut, which in 1971 was honored as an All-American City by *Look* magazine and the National Municipal League for its commitment to racial harmony and integrated schools. A small town with barely two thousand inhabitants, Bloomfield sits outside Hartford in pristine New England splendor, complete with a town green, church steeples, and well-appointed single-family homes. But with each passing year, Bloomfield has slowly become less and less white, and more and more black, first five percent black, then 10, then 20, and now nearing 50. First to change were the public schools, which by 1996 were nearly 85 percent black, despite a lingering white majority in town. It won't be long before the actual population follows suit. While many communities in the 1960s turned from all white to all black in a matter of months and years, today the transformation is more gradual. But it is a transformation nonetheless. Bloomfield is indeed an all-American city.

Bloomfield may be different from most communities because it tries to maintain a certain degree of integration, but it is no different in the inexorable residential process taking place there. It is a process that occurs in almost any region of the country where there is a substantial enough black population for whites to feel potentially threatened. The first harbinger of change in a community is the public school—much like the proverbial canary in the coal mine. As black students begin to populate the schools in more than token amounts, white flight from the schools begins to accelerate. White families either send their children to private schools or move out altogether—usually to an established white community or to a new development they call "a nice place to raise kids." In this beginning stage, the number of blacks in public schools is always higher than the number of blacks in the community. Usually the black and white neighbors are cordial and will stop each other to talk and say hello. As years go by and white families move out, few white families will move in. In some communities not a single white person will move in after the first black person calls the area home. Blocks and neighborhoods soon become racially identifiable. Eventually the only whites in the community are those who can't afford to move out, those with no children in school—empty-nesters—or those who can afford private school. Ultimately the remaining whites move out and the community turns predominantly black. This process is not always evident from the beginning, as the presence of one or two black families is often celebrated by most white neighbors as evidence of tolerance and diversity rather than feared as a sign of change. But once the welcome mat is put out for blacks, all it takes is a few white families to worry and move away and a few black families to take their place, and the domino effect begins.

Call it black humor if you wish, but the joke among blacks living in neighborhoods like these is to ask each other what the most popular vehicle is among the remaining white residents. The answer is a U-Haul. Humor is certainly a defense against disappointment, as it is indeed dispiriting to see neighbors move simply because of the color of one's skin. Study after study has shown that blacks would prefer to live in well-integrated neighborhoods between one-third and two-thirds black. All-black and especially all-white neighborhoods are the least desirable locations.[3] The reason is simple: A well-integrated neighborhood would be black enough to buffer against prejudice and isolation, but diverse enough to expose their children to people of all backgrounds. The problem for blacks is that a neighbor-

hood that appears integrated will attract more blacks, which then accelerates white flight and the changeover to a predominantly black neighborhood. And so what many hail as racially mixed neighborhoods are actually neighborhoods undergoing racial transition. Seeing this, a number of blacks have simply stopped trying to integrate and are increasingly opting for identifiably black communities.

Whites see it very differently. Although public opinion surveys show considerable white support for residential integration, what actually happens in the neighborhoods is quite the opposite. If whites could be guaranteed that the number of blacks in their neighborhood would not rise above, say, five or six percent, few would move. But there are no such guarantees, so the white discomfort level begins to rise with each new black face on the block, and the neighborhood begins to tip. With the image of black crime and urban blight so formidable and pervasive, middle-class whites don't want to take what they perceive as a risk. It doesn't seem to matter if the new black residents have equal-status jobs or higher incomes. Whites still move away. It doesn't matter if the schools remain good, if crime doesn't increase, or if home values continue to rise. Whites still say the neighborhood will eventually go bad. Nor does it matter that homes in all-white areas tend to cost more than homes in racially diverse neighborhoods. Whites will pay the extra. For most whites, integration really means managed tokenism, and anything beyond that evokes anxiety and fear. . . .

Three fairly recent phenomena reinforce the residential separation of the races. First is the rapid growth of the gated community, where an estimated four million Americans—mostly white—currently live. With private security guards, visitor passes, locked entry gates, and tightly run residential associations, these communities have become, according to a 1995 article in the *Yale Law Journal*, "homogeneous enclaves undisturbed by the undesirably different." For many of these communities, the residential association serves as community gatekeeper and is often "a powerful tool for segregation," according to the *Yale Law Journal* article. One gated community described itself in marketing materials as a place that makes you "secure within the boundaries of your own neighborhood." It's unclear how much irony was intended when the gated communities on South Carolina's Hilton Head Island were officially called "plantations," but the message of most gated communities is clear to blacks: These are walled-off, peaceful oases for whites, and no matter how much you've accomplished in life, you are not welcome as a purchaser or guest.[4]

Whereas gated communities enable white Americans to live in isolation close to the city, the second phenomenon sees whites exiting the city to more distant suburbs and outlying communities relatively far from the urban core—so-called exurbs—that are attracting high-tech industries and an increasing number of residents. States especially popular for this white exodus are Nevada, Idaho, Utah, Colorado, and Washington. Between 1990 and 1994, more than one million Americans left the suburbs for these exurbs, and the trend is growing rapidly. The search for a more basic, pastoral life is nothing new in American history, so it is perfectly possible to ascribe this phenomenon to a desire for innocence, peace, and simplicity. But it would be naïve not to acknowledge that part of what whites want to escape is proximity to blacks. As one Utah executive candidly explained: "One thing people don't want to worry about is race relations. Companies think if they go to a neighborhood where everyone is like me, it makes it easier. It takes away from stress. People want to remove some of the variables of their lives."[5]

The third phenomenon reinforcing separation is the stabilization and growth of identifiably black middle-class communities, which are increasingly becoming the neighborhoods of choice for upwardly mobile blacks who want a secure place to raise families and are tired of rejection by whites. These are often urban enclaves or inner-ring suburbs just outside the city that years ago housed the first wave of white suburban migrants but have long since turned predominantly black. In Chicago, for example, nearly nine in ten black middle-class households with incomes above $35,000 live in predominantly black neighborhoods in just two parts of town, a pattern also found in other cities with a substantial black middle-class population.[6] Many blacks are also setting down roots deeper into the suburbs and moving to predominantly black communities such as Mitchellville outside Washington, D.C., Brook Glen outside Atlanta, and Rolling Oaks outside Miami. Builders in these areas understand what's going on and market these communities specifically to blacks. As *Los Angeles Times* reporter Sam Fulwood III writes in his compelling autobiography: "Without fully comprehending why, I was smitten by the model home with its subtle, subliminal persuasions aimed at racial pride and feelings of estrangement from white neighborhoods. . . . Indeed, I had never before seen a model home that featured decorations aimed at middle-income black buyers. The book with Dr. King's image on the cover was one item . . . on the bookshelf along with storybooks and a black-faced rag doll."[7]

Marketing isn't the only reason this is happening. It's a matter of living with dignity and respect. "We're flocking to mostly black suburbs partly because we still can't readily integrate with white society," said an editor of the black-oriented magazine *Emerge*. "We work in these corporations, law firms, hospitals, what have you, but we see what the limitations are. You also want to make sure your children can function without the stings of racism penetrating them all the time. . . . If I locked myself out of my house one night in a mostly white neighborhood, my neighbor might hesitate to open his door because of the color of my skin. That happened to me recently. But in an all-black area, I'd merely be inconveniencing my neighbors. They'd let me in."[8] . . .

DISCUSSION QUESTIONS

1. Is your school or neighborhood integrated?
2. Have we become two Americas?

NOTES

1. Personal interview with Assistant Attorney General Deval Patrick, December 13, 1996; the appraisal experience is

described in Joseph Boyce, "L.A. Riots and the 'Black Tax,'" *Wall Street Journal*, May 12, 1992, p. A24. See also Jean Bryant, "For Blacks and Whites in the Region, It's Still a House Divided," *Pittsburgh Post-Gazette*, April 14, 1996, p. A1, and NBC's *Dateline*, "Why Can't We Live Together," June 27, 1997, and Kevin Helliker, "To Sell to Whites, Blacks Hide Telltale Ethnic Touches," *Wall Street Journal*, March 26, 1998, pp. B1–2.

2. Douglas S. Massey and Nancy A. Denton, *American Apartheid* (Cambridge, MA: Harvard University Press, 1993), p. 114.

3. The best and most comprehensive study of racial housing preferences is the University of Michigan's Detroit Area Study. See also the *Detroit Free Press*, October 10, 1992.

4. David J. Kennedy, "Residential Associations as State Actors: Regulating the Impact of Gated Communities on Nonmembers," *Yale Law Journal*, December 1995, pp. 761–793. See also Dale Maharidge, "Walled Off," *Mother Jones*, November–December 1994, pp. 26–33.

5. On the exurbs, see Joel Kotkin, "White Flight to the Fringes," *Washington Post*, March 10, 1996, pp. C1–2. The Utah executive is quoted in Kotkin's article.

6. For the Chicago information, see an analysis by Ron Grossman and Byron P. White, "Poverty Surrounds Black Middle Class," *Chicago Tribune*, February 2, 1997, p. 1.

7. Sam Fulwood III, *Waking from the Dream* (New York: Anchor, 1996), p. 189.

8. Susan McHenry, executive editor of *Emerge* magazine, interviewed in *Fortune*, November 2, 1992, p. 128.

READING 29

At a Slaughterhouse, Some Things Never Die

Charlie LeDuff

Tar Heel, N.C.—It must have been 1 o'clock. That's when the white man usually comes out of his glass office and stands on the scaffolding above the factory floor. He stood with his palms on the rails, his elbows out. He looked like a tower guard up there or a border patrol agent. He stood with his head cocked.

One o'clock means it is getting near the end of the workday. Quota has to be met and the workload doubles. The conveyor belt always overflows with meat

---

Charlie LeDuff is a reporter for *The New York Times*.

around 1 o'clock. So the workers double their pace, hacking pork from shoulder bones with a driven single-mindedness. They stare blankly, like mules in wooden blinders, as the butchered slabs pass by.

It is called the picnic line: 18 workers lined up on both sides of a belt, carving meat from bone. Up to 16 million shoulders a year come down that line here at the Smithfield Packing Co., the largest pork production plant in the world. That works out to about 32,000 a shift, 63 a minute, one every 17 seconds for each worker for eight and a half hours a day. The first time you stare down at that belt you know your body is going to give in way before the machine ever will.

On this day the boss saw something he didn't like. He climbed down and approached the picnic line from behind. He leaned into the ear of a broad-shouldered black man. He had been riding him all day, and the day before. The boss bawled him out good this time, but no one heard what was said. The roar of the machinery was too ferocious for that. Still, everyone knew what was expected. They worked harder.

The white man stood and watched for the next two hours as the blacks worked in their groups and the Mexicans in theirs. He stood there with his head cocked.

At shift change the black man walked away, hosed himself down and turned in his knives. Then he let go. He threatened to murder the boss. He promised to quit. He said he was losing his mind, which made for good comedy since he was standing near a conveyor chain of severed hogs' heads, their mouths yoked open.

"Who that cracker think he is?" the black man wanted to know. There were enough hogs, he said, "not to worry about no fleck of meat being left on the bone. Keep treating me like a Mexican and I'll beat him."

The boss walked by just then and the black man lowered his head.

WHO GETS THE DIRTY JOBS

The first thing you learn in the hog plant is the value of a sharp knife. The second thing you learn is that you don't want to work with a knife. Finally you learn that not everyone has to work with a knife. Whites, blacks, American Indians and Mexicans, they all have their separate stations.

The few whites on the payroll tend to be mechanics or supervisors. As for the Indians, a handful are supervisors; others tend to get clean menial jobs like warehouse work. With few exceptions, that leaves the blacks and Mexicans with the dirty jobs at the factory, one of the only places within a 50-mile radius in this muddy corner of North Carolina where a person might make more than $8 an hour.

While Smithfield's profits nearly doubled in the past year, wages have remained flat. So a lot of Americans here have quit and a lot of Mexicans have been hired to take their places. But more than management, the workers see one another as the problem, and they see the competition in skin tones.

The locker rooms are self-segregated and so is the cafeteria. The enmity spills out into the towns. The races generally keep to themselves. Along Interstate 95 there are four tumbledown bars, one for each color: white, black, red and brown.

Language is also a divider. There are English and Spanish lines at the Social Security office and in the waiting rooms of the county health clinics. This means different groups don't really understand one another and tend to be suspicious of what they do know.

You begin to understand these things the minute you apply for the job.

BLOOD AND BURNOUT

"Treat the meat like you going to eat it yourself," the hiring manager told the 30 applicants, most of them down on their luck and hungry for work. The Smithfield plant will take just about any man or woman with a pulse and a sparkling urine sample, with few questions asked. This reporter was hired using his own name and acknowledged that he was currently employed, but was not asked where and did not say.

Slaughtering swine is repetitive, brutish work, so grueling that three weeks on the factory floor leave

no doubt in your mind about why the turnover is 100 percent. Five thousand quit and five thousand are hired every year. You hear people say, "They don't kill pigs in the plant, they kill people." So desperate is the company for workers, its recruiters comb the streets of New York's immigrant communities, personnel staff members say, and word of mouth has reached Mexico and beyond.

The company even procures criminals. Several at the morning orientation were inmates on work release in green uniforms, bused in from the county prison.

The new workers were given a safety speech and tax papers, shown a promotional video and informed that there was enough methane, ammonia and chlorine at the plant to kill every living thing here in Bladen County. Of the 30 new employees, the black women were assigned to the chitterlings room, where they would scrape feces and worms from intestines. The black men were sent to the butchering floor. Two free white men and the Indian were given jobs making boxes. This reporter declined a box job and ended up with most of the Mexicans, doing knife work, cutting sides of pork into smaller and smaller products.

Standing in the hiring hall that morning, two women chatted in Spanish about their pregnancies. A young black man had heard enough. His small town the next county over was crowded with Mexicans. They just started showing up three years ago—drawn to rural Robeson County by the plant—and never left. They stood in groups on the street corners, and the young black man never knew what they were saying. They took the jobs and did them for less. Some had houses in Mexico, while he lived in a trailer with his mother.

Now here he was, trying for the only job around, and he had to listen to Spanish, had to compete with peasants. The world was going to hell.

"This is America and I want to start hearing some English, now!" he screamed.

One of the women told him where to stick his head and listen for the echo. "Then you'll hear some English," she said.

An old white man with a face as pinched and lined as a pot roast complained, "The tacos are worse than the niggers," and the Indian leaned against the wall and laughed. In the doorway, the prisoners shifted from foot to foot, watching the spectacle unfold from behind a cloud of cigarette smoke.

The hiring manager came out of his office and broke it up just before things degenerated into a brawl. Then he handed out the employment stubs. "I don't want no problems," he warned. He told them to report to the plant on Monday morning to collect their carving knives.

$7.70 AN HOUR, PAIN ALL DAY

Monday. The mist rose from the swamps and by 4:45 a.m. thousands of headlamps snaked along the old country roads. Cars carried people from the backwoods, from the single and doublewide trailers, from the cinder-block houses and wooden shacks: whites from Lumberton and Elizabethtown; blacks from Fairmont and Fayetteville; Indians from Pembroke; the Mexicans from Red Springs and St. Pauls.

They converge at the Smithfield plant, a 973,000-square-foot leviathan of pipe and steel near the Cape Fear River. The factory towers over the tobacco and cotton fields, surrounded by pine trees and a few of the old whitewashed plantation houses. Built seven years ago, it is by far the biggest employer in this region, 75 miles west of the Atlantic and 90 miles south of the booming Research Triangle around Chapel Hill.

The workers filed in, their faces stiffened by sleep and the cold, like saucers of milk gone hard. They punched the clock at 5 a.m., waiting for the knives to be handed out, the chlorine freshly applied by the cleaning crew burning their eyes and throats. Nobody spoke.

The hallway was a river of brown-skinned Mexicans. The six prisoners who were starting that day looked confused.

"What the hell's going on?" the only white inmate, Billy Harwood, asked an older black worker named Wade Baker.

"Oh," Mr. Baker said, seeing that the prisoner was talking about the Mexicans. "I see you been away for a while."

Billy Harwood had been away—nearly seven years, for writing phony payroll checks from the family pizza business to buy crack. He was Rip Van Winkle standing there. Everywhere he looked there were Mexicans. What he didn't know was that one out of three newborns at the nearby Robeson County health clinic was a Latino; that the county's Roman Catholic church had a special Sunday Mass for Mexicans said by a Honduran priest; that the schools needed Spanish speakers to teach English.

With less than a month to go on his sentence, Mr. Harwood took the pork job to save a few dollars. The word in jail was that the job was a cakewalk for a white man.

But this wasn't looking like any cakewalk. He wasn't going to get a boxing job like a lot of other whites. Apparently inmates were on the bottom rung, just like Mexicans.

Billy Harwood and the other prisoners were put on the picnic line. Knife work pays $7.70 an hour to start. It is money unimaginable in Mexico, where the average wage is $4 a day. But the American money comes at a price. The work burns your muscles and dulls your mind. Staring down into the meat for hours strains your neck. After thousands of cuts a day your fingers no longer open freely. Standing in the damp 42-degree air causes your knees to lock, your nose to run, your teeth to throb.

The whistle blows at 3, you get home by 4, pour peroxide on your nicks by 5. You take pills for your pains and stand in a hot shower trying to wash it all away. You hurt. And by 8 o'clock you're in bed, exhausted, thinking of work.

The convict said he felt cheated. He wasn't supposed to be doing Mexican work. After his second day he was already talking of quitting. "Man, this can't be for real," he said, rubbing his wrists as if they'd been in handcuffs. "This job's for an ass. They treat you like an animal."

He just might have quit after the third day had it not been for Mercedes Fernández, a Mexican. He took a place next to her by the conveyor belt. She smiled at him, showed him how to make incisions. That was the extent of his on-the-job training. He was peep-eyed, missing a tooth and squat from the starchy prison food, but he acted as if this tiny woman had taken a fancy to him. In truth, she was more fascinated than infatuated, she later confided. In her year at the plant, he was the first white person she had ever worked with.

The other workers noticed her helping the white man, so unusual was it for a Mexican and a white to work shoulder to shoulder, to try to talk or even to make eye contact.

As for blacks, she avoided them. She was scared of them. "Blacks don't want to work," Mrs. Fernández said when the new batch of prisoners came to work on the line. "They're lazy."

Everything about the factory cuts people off from one another. If it's not the language barrier, it's the noise—the hammering of compressors, the screeching of pulleys, the grinding of the lines. You can hardly make your voice heard. To get another's attention on the cut line, you bang the butt of your knife on the steel railings, or you lob a chunk of meat. Mrs. Fernández would sometimes throw a piece of shoulder at a friend across the conveyor and wave good morning.

THE KILL FLOOR

The kill floor sets the pace of the work, and for those jobs they pick strong men and pay a top wage, as high as $12 an hour. If the men fail to make quota, plenty of others are willing to try. It is mostly the blacks who work the kill floor, the stone-hearted jobs that pay more and appear out of bounds for all but a few Mexicans.

Plant workers gave various reasons for this: The Mexicans are too small; they don't like blood; they don't like heavy lifting; or just plain "We built this country and we ain't going to hand them everything," as one black man put it.

Kill-floor work is hot, quick and bloody. The hog is herded in from the stockyard, then stunned with an electric gun. It is lifted onto a conveyor belt, dazed but not dead, and passed to a waiting group of men wearing bloodstained smocks and blank faces. They slit the neck, shackle the hind legs and watch a machine lift the carcass into the air, letting its life flow out in a purple gush, into a steaming collection trough.

The carcass is run through a scalding bath, trolleyed over the factory floor and then dumped onto a table with all the force of a quarter-ton water balloon. In the misty-red room, men slit along its hind tendons and skewer the beast with hooks. It is again lifted and shot across the room on a pulley and bar, where it hangs with hundreds of others as if in some kind of horrific dry-cleaning shop. It is then pulled through a wall of flames and met on the other side by more black men who, stripped to the waist beneath their smocks, scrape away any straggling bristles.

The place reeks of sweat and scared animal, steam and blood. Nothing is wasted from these beasts, not the plasma, not the glands, not the bones. Everything is used, and the kill men, repeating slaughterhouse lore, say that even the squeal is sold.

The carcasses sit in the freezer overnight and are then rolled out to the cut floor. The cut floor is opposite to the kill floor in nearly every way. The workers are mostly brown—Mexicans—not black; the lighting yellow, not red. The vapor comes from cold breath, not hot water. It is here that the hog is quartered. The pieces are parceled out and sent along the disassembly lines to be cut into ribs, hams, bellies, loins and chops.

People on the cut lines work with a mindless fury. There is tremendous pressure to keep the conveyor belts moving, to pack orders, to put bacon and ham and sausage on the public's breakfast table. There is no clock, no window, no fragment of the world outside. Everything is pork. If the line fails to keep pace, the kill men must slow down, backing up the slaughter. The boxing line will have little to do, costing the company payroll hours. The blacks who kill will become angry with the Mexicans who cut, who in turn will become angry with the white superintendents who push them.

10,000 UNWELCOME MEXICANS

The Mexicans never push back. They cannot. Some have legitimate work papers, but more, like Mercedes Fernández, do not.

Even worse, Mrs. Fernández was several thousand dollars in debt to the smugglers who had sneaked her and her family into the United States and owed a thousand more for the authentic-looking birth certificate and Social Security card that are needed to get hired. She and her husband, Armando, expected to be in debt for years. They had mouths to feed back home.

The Mexicans are so frightened about being singled out that they do not even tell one another their real names. They have their given names, their work-paper names and "Hey you," as their American supervisors call them. In the telling of their stories, Mercedes and Armando Fernández insisted that their real names be used, to protect their identities. It was their work names they did not want used, names bought in a back alley in Barstow, Texas.

Rarely are the newcomers welcomed with open arms. Long before the Mexicans arrived, Robeson County, one of the poorest in North Carolina, was an uneasy racial mix. In the 1990 census, of the 100,000 people living in Robeson, nearly 40 percent were Lumbee Indian, 35 percent white and 25 percent black. Until a dozen years ago the county schools were de facto segregated, and no person of color held any meaningful county job from sheriff to court clerk to judge.

At one point in 1988, two armed Indian men occupied the local newspaper office, taking hostages and demanding that the sheriff's department be investigated for corruption and its treatment of minorities. A prominent Indian lawyer, Julian Pierce, was killed that same year, and the suspect turned up dead in a broom closet before he could be charged. The hierarchy of power was summed up on a plaque that hangs in the courthouse commemorating the dead of World War I. It lists the veterans by color: "white" on top, "Indian" in the middle and "colored" on the bottom.

That hierarchy mirrors the pecking order at the hog plant. The Lumbees—who have fought their way up in the county apparatus and have built their own construction businesses—are fond of saying they are too smart to work in the factory. And the few who do work there seem to end up with the cleaner jobs.

But as reds and blacks began to make progress in the 1990s—for the first time an Indian sheriff was elected, and a black man is now the public defender—the Latinos began arriving. The United States Census Bureau estimated that 1,000 Latinos were living in Robeson County last year. People only laugh at that number.

"A thousand? Hell, there's more than that in the Wal-Mart on a Saturday afternoon," said Bill Smith, director of county health services. He and other officials guess that there are at least 10,000 Latinos in Robeson, most having arrived in the past three years.

"When they built that factory in Bladen, they promised a trickledown effect," Mr. Smith said. "But the money ain't trickling down this way. Bladen got the money and Robeson got the social problems."

In Robeson there is the strain on public resources. There is the substandard housing. There is the violence. Last year 27 killings were committed in Robeson, mostly in the countryside, giving it a higher murder rate than Detroit or Newark. Three Mexicans were robbed and killed last fall. Latinos have also been the victims of highway stickups.

In the yellow-walled break room at the plant, Mexicans talked among themselves about their three slain men, about the midnight visitors with obscured faces and guns, men who knew that the illegal workers used mattresses rather than banks. Mercedes Fernández, like many Mexicans, would not venture out at night. "Blacks have a problem," she said. "They live in the past. They are angry about slavery, so instead of working, they steal from us."

She and her husband never lingered in the parking lot at shift change. That is when the anger of a long day comes seeping out. Cars get kicked and faces slapped over parking spots or fender benders. The traffic is a serpent. Cars jockey for a spot in line to make the quarter-mile crawl along the plant's one-lane exit road to the highway. Usually no one will let you in. A lot of the scuffling is between black and Mexican.

BLACK AND BLEAK

The meat was backing up on the conveyor and spilling onto the floor. The supervisor climbed down off the scaffolding and chewed out a group of black women. Something about skin being left on the meat. There was a new skinner on the job, and the cutting line was expected to take up his slack. The whole line groaned. First looks flew, then people began hurling slurs at one another in Spanish and English, words they could hardly hear over the factory's roar. The black women started waving their knives at the Mexicans. The Mexicans waved theirs back. The blades got close. One Mexican spit at the blacks and was fired.

After watching the knife scene, Wade Baker went home and sagged in his recliner. CNN played. Good news on Wall Street, the television said. Wages remained stable. "Since when is the fact that a man doesn't get paid good news?" he asked the TV. The TV told him that money was everywhere—everywhere but here.

Still lean at 51, Mr. Baker has seen life improve since his youth in the Jim Crow South. You can say things. You can ride in a car with a white woman. You can stay in the motels, eat in the restaurants. The black man got off the white man's field.

"Socially, things are much better," Mr. Baker said wearily over the droning television. "But we're going backwards as black people economically. For every one of us doing better, there's two of us doing worse."

His town, Chad Bourne, is a dreary strip of peeling paint and warped porches and houses as rundown as rotting teeth. Young men drift from the cinder-block pool hall to the empty streets and back. In the center of town is a bank, a gas station, a chicken shack and a motel. As you drive out, the lights get dimmer and the homes older until eventually you're in a flat void of tobacco fields.

Mr. Baker was standing on the main street with his grandson Monte watching the Christmas parade march by when a scruffy man approached. It was Mr. Baker's cousin, and he smelled of kerosene and had dust in his hair as if he lived in a vacant building and warmed himself with a portable heater. He asked for $2.

"It's ironic isn't it?" Mr. Baker said as his cousin walked away only eight bits richer. "He was asking me the same thing 10 years ago."

A group of Mexicans stood across the street hanging around the gas station watching them.

"People around here always want to blame the system," he said. "And it is true that the system is antiblack and antipoor. It's true that things are run by the whites. But being angry only means you failed in life. Instead of complaining, you got to work twice as hard and make do."

He stood quietly with his hands in his pockets watching the parade go by. He watched the Mexicans across the street, laughing in their new clothes. Then he said, almost as an afterthought, "There's a day coming soon where the Mexicans are going to catch hell from the blacks, the way the blacks caught it from the whites."

Wade Baker used to work in the post office, until he lost his job over drugs. When he came out of his haze a few years ago, there wasn't much else for him but the plant. He took the job, he said, "because I don't have a 401K." He took it because he had learned from his mother that you don't stand around with your head down and your hand out waiting for another man to drop you a dime.

Evelyn Baker, bent and gray now, grew up a sharecropper, the granddaughter of slaves. She was raised up in a tarpaper shack, picked cotton and hoed tobacco for a white family. She supported her three boys alone by cleaning white people's homes.

In the late 60s something good started happening. There was a labor shortage, just as there is now. The managers at the textile plants started giving machine jobs to black people.

Mrs. Baker was 40 then. "I started at a dollar and 60 cents an hour, and honey, that was a lot of money then," she said.

The work was plentiful through the 70s and 80s, and she was able to save money and add on to her home. By the early 90s the textile factories started moving away, to Mexico. Robeson County has lost about a quarter of its jobs since that time.

Unemployment in Robeson hovers around 8 percent, twice the national average. In neighboring Columbus County it is 10.8 percent. In Bladen County it is 5 percent, and Bladen has the pork factory.

Still, Mr. Baker believes that people who want to work can find work. As far as he's concerned, there are too many shiftless young men who ought to be working, even if it's in the pork plant. His son-in-law once worked there, quit and now hangs around the gas station where other young men sell dope.

The son-in-law came over one day last fall and threatened to cause trouble if the Bakers didn't let him borrow the car. This could have turned messy; the 71-year-old Mrs. Baker keeps a .38 tucked in her bosom.

When Wade Baker got home from the plant and heard from his mother what had happened, he took up his pistol and went down to the corner, looking for his son-in-law. He chased a couple of the young men around the dark dusty lot, waving the gun. "Hold still so I can shoot one of you!" he recalled having bellowed. "That would make the world a better place!"

He scattered the men without firing. Later, sitting in his car with his pistol on the seat and his hands between his knees, he said, staring into the night: "There's got to be more than this. White people drive by and look at this and laugh."

LIVING IT, HATING IT

Billy Harwood had been working at the plant 10 days when he was released from the Robeson County Correctional Facility. He stood at the prison gates in his work clothes with his belongings in a plastic bag, waiting. A friend dropped him at the Salvation Army shelter, but he decided it was too much like prison. Full of black people. No leaving after 10 p.m. No smoking indoors. "What you doing here, white boy?" they asked him.

He fumbled with a cigarette outside the shelter. He wanted to quit the plant. The work stinks, he said, "but at least I ain't a nigger. I'll find other work soon. I'm a white man." He had hopes of landing a roofing job through a friend. The way he saw it, white society looks out for itself.

On the cut line he worked slowly and allowed Mercedes Fernández and the others to pick up his slack. He would cut only the left shoulders; it was easier on his hands. Sometimes it would be three minutes before a left shoulder came down the line.

When he did cut, he didn't clean the bone; he left chunks of meat on it.

Mrs. Fernández was disappointed by her first experience with a white person. After a week she tried to avoid standing by Billy Harwood. She decided it wasn't just the blacks who were lazy, she said.

Even so, the supervisor came by one morning, took a look at one of Mr. Harwood's badly cut shoulders and threw it at Mrs. Fernández, blaming her. He said obscene things about her family. She didn't understand exactly what he said, but it scared her. She couldn't wipe the tears from her eyes because her gloves were covered with greasy shreds of swine. The other cutters kept their heads down, embarrassed.

Her life was falling apart. She and her husband both worked the cut floor. They never saw their daughter. They were 26 but rarely made love anymore. All they wanted was to save enough money to put plumbing in their house in Mexico and start a business there. They come from the town of Tehuacán, in a rural area about 150 miles southeast of Mexico City. His mother owns a bar there and a home but gives nothing to them. Mother must look out for her old age.

"We came here to work so we have a chance to grow old in Mexico," Mrs. Fernández said one evening while cooking pork and potatoes. Now they were into a smuggler for thousands. Her hands swelled into claws in the evenings and stung while she worked. She felt trapped. But she kept at it for the money, for the $9.60 an hour. The smuggler still had to be paid.

They explained their story this way: The coyote drove her and her family from Barstow a year ago and left them in Robeson. They knew no one. They did not even know they were in the state of North Carolina. They found shelter in a trailer park that had once been exclusively black but was rapidly filling with Mexicans. There was a lot of drug dealing there and a lot of tension. One evening, Mr. Fernández said, he asked a black neighbor to move his business inside and the man pulled a pistol on him.

"I hate the blacks," Mr. Fernández said in Spanish, sitting in the break room not 10 feet from Mr.

Baker and his black friends. Mr. Harwood was sitting two tables away with the whites and Indians.

After the gun incident, Mr. Fernández packed up his family and moved out into the country, to a prefabricated number sitting on a brick foundation off in the woods alone. Their only contact with people is through the satellite dish. Except for the coyote. The coyote knows where they live and comes for his money every other month.

Their 5-year-old daughter has no playmates in the back country and few at school. That is the way her parents want it. "We don't want her to be American," her mother said.

"WE NEED A UNION"

The steel bars holding a row of hogs gave way as a woman stood below them. Hog after hog fell around her with a sickening thud, knocking her senseless, the connecting bars barely missing her face. As co-workers rushed to help the woman, the supervisor spun his hands in the air, a signal to keep working. Wade Baker saw this and shook his head in disgust. Nothing stops the disassembly lines.

"We need a union," he said later in the break room. It was payday and he stared at his check: $288. He spoke softly to the black workers sitting near him. Everyone is convinced that talk of a union will get you fired. After two years at the factory, Mr. Baker makes slightly more than $9 an hour toting meat away from the cut line, slightly less than $20,000 a year, 45 cents an hour less than Mrs. Fernández.

"I don't want to get racial about the Mexicans," he whispered to the black workers. "But they're dragging down the pay. It's pure economics. They say Americans don't want to do the job. That ain't exactly true. We don't want to do it for $8. Pay $15 and we'll do it."

These men knew that in the late 70s when the meatpacking industry was centered in northern cities like Chicago and Omaha, people had a union getting them $18 an hour. But by the mid-80s, to cut costs, many of the packing houses had moved to small towns where they could pay a lower, nonunion wage.

The black men sitting around the table also felt sure that the Mexicans pay almost nothing in income tax, claiming 8, 9, even 10 exemptions. The men believed that the illegal workers should be rooted out of the factory. "It's all about money," Mr. Baker said.

His co-workers shook their heads. "A plantation with a roof on it," one said.

For their part, many of the Mexicans in Tar Heel fear that a union would place their illegal status under scrutiny and force them out. The United Food and Commercial Workers Union last tried organizing the plant in 1997, but the idea was voted down nearly two to one.

One reason Americans refused to vote for the union was because it refuses to take a stand on illegal laborers. Another reason was the intimidation. When workers arrived at the plant the morning of the vote, they were met by Bladen County deputy sheriffs in riot gear. "Nigger Lover" had been scrawled on the union trailer.

Five years ago the work force at the plant was 50 percent black, 20 percent white and Indian, and 30 percent Latino, according to union statistics. Company officials say those numbers are about the same today. But from inside the plant, the breakdown appears to be more like 60 percent Latino, 30 percent black, 10 percent white and red.

Sherri Buffkin, a white woman and the former director of purchasing who testified before the National Labor Relations Board in an unfair-labor-practice suit brought by the union in 1998, said in an interview that the company assigns workers by race. She also said that management had kept lists of union sympathizers during the '97 election, firing blacks and replacing them with Latinos. "I know because I fired at least 15 of them myself," she said.

The company denies those accusations. Michael H. Cole, a lawyer for Smithfield who would respond to questions about the company's labor practices only in writing, said that jobs at the Tar Heel plant were awarded through a bidding process and not assigned by race. The company also denies ever having kept lists of union sympathizers or singled out blacks to be fired.

The hog business is important to North Carolina. It is a multibillion-dollar-a-year industry in the state, with nearly two pigs for every one of its 7.5 million people. And Smithfield Foods, a publicly traded company based in Smithfield, Va., has become the No. 1 producer and processor of pork in the world. It slaughters more than 20 percent of the nation's swine, more than 19 million animals a year.

The company, which has acquired a network of factory farms and slaughterhouses, worries federal agriculture officials and legislators, who see it siphoning business from smaller farmers. And environmentalists contend that Smithfield's operations contaminate local water supplies. (The Environmental Protection Agency fined the company $12.6 million in 1996 after its processing plants in Virginia discharged pollutants into the Pagan River.) The chairman and chief executive, Joseph W. Luter III, declined to be interviewed.

Smithfield's employment practices have not been so closely scrutinized. And so every year, more Mexicans get hired. "An illegal alien isn't going to complain all that much," said Ed Tomlinson, acting supervisor of the Immigration and Naturalization Service bureau in Charlotte.

But the company says it does not knowingly hire illegal aliens. Smithfield's lawyer, Mr. Cole, said all new employees must present papers showing that they can legally work in the United States. "If any employee's documentation appears to be genuine and to belong to the person presenting it," he said in his written response, "Smithfield is required by law to take it at face value."

The naturalization service—which has only 18 agents in North Carolina—has not investigated Smithfield because no one has filed a complaint, Mr. Tomlinson said. "There are more jobs than people," he said, "and a lot of Americans will do the dirty work for a while and then return to their couches and eat bonbons and watch Oprah."

NOT FIT FOR A CONVICT

When Billy Harwood was in solitary confinement, he liked a book to get him through. A guard would come around with a cartful. But when the prisoner asked for a new book, the guard, before handing it to him, liked to tear out the last 50 pages. The guard was a real funny guy.

"I got good at making up my own endings," Billy Harwood said during a break. "And *my* book don't end standing here. I ought to be on that roof any day now."

But a few days later, he found out that the white contractor he was counting on already had a full roofing crew. They were Mexicans who were working for less than he was making at the plant.

During his third week cutting hogs, he got a new supervisor—a black woman. Right away she didn't like his work ethic. He went too slow. He cut out to the bathroom too much.

"Got a bladder infection?" she asked, standing in his spot when he returned. She forbade him to use the toilet.

He boiled. Mercedes Fernández kept her head down. She was certain of it, she said: he was the laziest man she had ever met. She stood next to a black man now, a prisoner from the north. They called him K. T. and he was nice to her. He tried Spanish, and he worked hard.

When the paychecks were brought around at lunch time on Friday, Billy Harwood got paid for five hours less than everyone else, even though everyone punched out on the same clock. The supervisor had docked him.

The prisoners mocked him. "You might be white," K. T. said, "but you came in wearing prison greens and that makes you good as a nigger."

The ending wasn't turning out the way Billy Harwood had written it: no place to live and a job not fit for a donkey. He quit and took the Greyhound back to his parents' trailer in the hills.

When Mrs. Fernández came to work the next day, a Mexican guy going by the name of Alfredo was standing in Billy Harwood's spot.

DISCUSSION QUESTIONS

1. Can you give examples of job segregation by race/ethnicity in other lines of work?
2. What are some of the ways to keep wages low?

Diversity and Its Discontents

Arturo Madrid

My name is Arturo Madrid. I am a citizen of the United States, as are my parents and as were my grandparents and my great-grandparents. My ancestors' presence in what is now the United States antedates Plymouth Rock, even without taking into account any American Indian heritage I might have.

I do not, however, fit those mental sets that define America and Americans. My physical appearance, my speech patterns, my name, my profession (a professor of Spanish) create a text that confuses the reader. My normal experience is to be asked, "And where are *you* from?" My response depends on my mood. Passive-aggressive, I answer, "From here." Aggressive-passive, I ask, "Do you mean where am I originally from?" But ultimately my answer to those follow-up questions that ask about origins will be that we have always been from here.

Overcoming my resentment I try to educate, knowing that nine times out of ten my words fall on inattentive ears. I have spent most of my adult life explaining who I am not. I am exotic, but—as Richard Rodriguez of *Hunger of Memory* fame so painfully found out—not exotic enough . . . not Peruvian, or Pakistani, or whatever. I am, however, very clearly the *other,* if only your everyday, garden-variety, domestic *other.* I will share with you another phenomenon that I have been a part of, that of being a missing person, and how I came late to that awareness. But I've always known that I was the *other,* even before I knew the vocabulary or understood the significance of otherness.

I grew up in an isolated and historically marginal part of the United States, a small mountain village in the state of New Mexico, the eldest child of parents native to that region, whose ancestors had always lived there. In those vast and empty spaces, people who look like me, speak as I do, and

have names like mine predominate. But the *americanos* lived among us: the descendants of those nineteenth-century immigrants who dispossessed us of our lands; missionaries who came to convert us and stayed to live among us; artists who became enchanted with our land and humanscape and went native; refugees from unhealthy climes, crowded spaces, unpleasant circumstances; and, of course, the inhabitants of Los Alamos, whose socio-cultural distance from us was accentuated by the fact that they occupied a space removed from and proscribed to us. More importantly, however, they—*los americanos*—were omnipresent (and almost exclusively so) in newspapers, newsmagazines, books, on radio, in movies and, ultimately, on television.

Despite the operating myth of the day, school did not erase my otherness. It did try to deny it, and in doing so only accentuated it. To this day what takes place in schools is more socialization than education, but when I was in elementary school—and given where I was—socialization was everything. School was where one became an American, because there was a pervasive and systematic denial by the society that surrounded us that we were Americans. That denial was both explicit and implicit.

Quite beyond saluting the flag and pledging allegiance to it (a very intense and meaningful action, given that the United States was involved in a war and our brothers, cousins, uncles, and fathers were on the frontlines), becoming American was learning English, and its corollary: not speaking Spanish. Until very recently ours was a proscribed language, either *de jure*—by rule, by policy, by law—or *de facto*—by practice, implicitly if not explicitly, through social and political and economic pressure. I do not argue that learning English was not appropriate. On the contrary. Like it or not, and we had no basis to make any judgments on that matter, we were Americans by virtue of having been born Americans, and English was the common language of Americans. And there was a myth, a pervasive myth, to the effect that if we only learned to speak English well—and particularly without an accent—we would be welcomed into the American fellowship.

Sam Hayakawa and the official English movement folks notwithstanding, the true text was not

---

Arturo Madrid is the Murchison Distinguished Professor of the Humanities at Trinity University in San Antonio, Texas.

our speech, but rather our names and our appearance, for we would always have an accent, however perfect our pronunciation, however excellent our enunciation, however divine our diction. That accent would be heard in our pigmentation, our physiognomy, our names. We were, in short, the *other*.

Being the *other* involves a contradictory phenomenon. On the one hand being the *other* frequently means being invisible. Ralph Ellison wrote eloquently about that experience in his magisterial novel *Invisible Man*. On the other hand, being the *other* sometimes involves sticking out like a sore thumb. What is she/he doing here?

For some of us being the *other* is only annoying; for others it is debilitating; for still others it is damning. Many try to flee otherness by taking on protective colorations that provide invisibility, whether of dress or speech or manner or name. Only a fortunate few succeed. For the majority of us otherness is permanently sealed by physical appearance. For the rest, otherness is betrayed by ways of being, speaking, or doing.

The first half of my life I spent downplaying the significance and consequences of otherness. The second half has seen me wrestling to understand its complex and deeply ingrained realities; striving to fathom why otherness denies us a voice or visibility or validity in American society and its institutions; struggling to make otherness familiar, reasonable, even normal to my fellow Americans.

I spoke earlier of another phenomenon that I am part of: that of being a missing person. Growing up in northern New Mexico I had only a slight sense of us being missing persons. *Hispanos,* as we called (and call) ourselves in New Mexico, were very much a part of the fabric of the society and there were *hispano* professionals everywhere about me: doctors, lawyers, schoolteachers, and administrators. My people owned businesses, ran organizations, and were both appointed and elected public officials.

My awareness of our absence from the larger institutional life of society became sharper when I went off to college, but even then it was attenuated by the circumstances of history and geography. The demography of Albuquerque still strongly reflected its historical and cultural origins, despite the influx of Midwesterners and Easterners. Moreover, many of my classmates at the University of New Mexico were *hispanos,* and even some of my professors. I thought that would obtain at UCLA, where I began graduate studies in 1960. Los Angeles had a very large Mexican population and that population was visible even in and around Westwood and on the campus. Many of the groundskeepers and food-service personnel at UCLA were Mexican. But Mexican-American students were few and mostly invisible, and I do not recall seeing or knowing a single Mexican-American (or, for that matter, black, Asian, or American Indian) professional on the staff or faculty of that institution during the five years I was there. Needless to say, persons like me were not present in any capacity at Dartmouth College, the site of my first teaching appointment, and of course were not even part of the institutional or individual mind-set. I knew then that we—a we that had come to encompass American Indians, Asian-Americans, African-Americans, Puerto Ricans, and women—were truly missing persons in American institutional life.

Over the past three decades, the *de jure* and *de facto* types of segregation that have ironically characterized American institutions have been under assault. As a consequence, minorities and women have become part of American institutional life. Although there are still many areas where we are not to be found, the missing persons phenomenon is not as pervasive as it once was. However, the presence of the *other,* particularly minorities, in institutions and institutional life resembles what we call in Spanish a *flor de tierra* (a surface phenomenon): we are spare plants whose roots do not go deep, vulnerable to inclemencies of an economic, or political, or social nature.

Our entrance into and our status in institutional life are not unlike a scenario set forth by my grandmother's pastor when she informed him that she and her family were leaving their mountain village to relocate to the Rio Grande Valley. When he asked her to promise that she would remain true to the faith and continue to involve herself in it, she asked why he thought she would do otherwise. "Doña

Trinidad," he told her, "in the Valley there is no Spanish church. There is only an American church." "But," she protested, "I read and speak English and would be able to worship there." The pastor responded, "It is possible that they will not admit you, and even if they do, they might not accept you. And that is why I want you to promise me that you are going to go to church. Because if they don't let you in through the front door, I want you to go in through the back door. And if you can't get in through the back door, go in the side door. And if you are unable to enter through the side door I want you to go in through the window. What is important is that you enter and stay."

Some of us entered institutional life through the front door; others through the back door; and still others through side doors. Many, if not most of us, came in through windows, and continue to come in through windows. Of those who entered through the front door, some never made it past the lobby; others were ushered into corners and niches. Those who entered through back and side doors inevitably have remained in back and side rooms. And those who entered through windows found enclosures built around them. For, despite the lip service given to the goal of the integration of minorities into institutional life, what has frequently occurred instead is ghettoization, marginalization, isolation.

Not only have the entry points been limited, but in addition the dynamics have been singularly conflictive. Gaining entry and its corollary, gaining space, have frequently come as a consequence of demands made on institutions and institutional officers. Rather than entering institutions more or less passively, minorities have of necessity entered them actively, even aggressively. Rather than waiting to receive, they have demanded. Institutional relations have thus been adversarial, infused with specific and generalized tensions.

The nature of the entrance and the nature of the space occupied have greatly influenced the view and attitude of the majority population within those institutions. All of us are put into the same box; that is, no matter what the individual reality, the assessment of the individual is inevitably conditioned by a perception that is held of the class. Whatever our

history, whatever our record, whatever our validations, whatever our accomplishments, by and large we are perceived unidimensionally and dealt with accordingly. I remember an experience I had in this regard, atypical only in its explicitness. A few years ago I allowed myself to be persuaded to seek the presidency of a well-known state university. I was invited for an interview and presented myself before the selection committee, which included members of the board of trustees. The opening question of that brief but memorable interview was directed at me by a member of that august body. "Dr. Madrid," he asked, "why does a one-dimensional person like you think he can be the president of a multi-dimensional institution like ours?"

Over the past four decades America's demography has undergone significant changes. Since 1965 the principal demographic growth we have experienced in the United States has been of peoples whose national origins are non-European. This population growth has occurred both through birth and through immigration. A few years ago discussion of the national birthrate had a scare dimension: the high—"inordinately high"—birthrate of the Hispanic population. The popular discourse was informed by words such as "breeding." Several years later, as a consequence of careful tracking by government agencies, we now know that what has happened is that the birthrate of the majority population has decreased. When viewed historically and comparatively, the minority populations (for the most part) have also had a decline in birthrate, but not one as great as that of the majority.

There are additional demographic changes that should give us something to think about. African-Americans are now to be found in significant numbers in every major urban center in the nation. Hispanic-Americans now number over 15 million people, and although they are a regionally concentrated (and highly urbanized) population, there is a Hispanic community in almost every major urban center of the United States. American Indians, heretofore a small and rural population, are increasingly more numerous and urban. The Asian-American population, which has historically consisted of small and concentrated communities of Chinese-, Filipino-, and Japanese-Americans, has doubled over the past decade, its complexion changed by the addition of Cambodians, Koreans, Hmongs, Vietnamese, et al.

Prior to the Immigration Act of 1965, 69 percent of immigration was from Europe. By far the largest number of immigrants to the United States since 1965 have been from the Americas and from Asia: 34 percent are from Asia; another 34 percent are from Central and South America; 16 percent are from Europe; 10 percent are from the Caribbean; the remaining 6 percent are from other continents and Canada. As was the case with previous immigration waves, the current one consists principally of young people: 60 percent are between the ages of 16 and 44. Thus, for the next few decades, we will continue to see a growth in the percentage of non-European-origin Americans as compared to European-Americans.

To sum up, we now live in one of the most demographically diverse nations in the world, and one that is increasingly more so.

During the same period social and economic change seems to have accelerated. Who would have imagined at mid-century that the prototypical middle-class family (working husband, wife as homemaker, two children) would for all intents and purposes disappear? Who could have anticipated the rise in teenage pregnancies, children in poverty, drug use? Who among us understood the implications of an aging population?

We live in an age of continuous and intense change, a world in which what held true yesterday does not today, and certainly will not tomorrow. What change does, moreover, is bring about even more change. The only constant we have at this point in our national development is change. And change is threatening. The older we get the more likely we are to be anxious about change, and the greater our desire to maintain the status quo.

Evident in our public life is a fear of change, whether economic or moral. Some who fear change are responsive to the call of economic protectionism, others to the message of moral protectionism. Parenthetically, I have referred to the movement to require more of students without in turn giving

them more as academic protectionism. And the pronouncements of E. D. Hirsch and Allan Bloom are, I believe, informed by intellectual protectionism. Much more serious, however, is the dark side of the populism which underlies this evergoing protectionism—the resentment of the *other*. An excellent and fascinating example of that aspect of populism is the cry for linguistic protectionism—for making English the official language of the United States. And who among us is unaware of the tensions that underlie immigration reform, of the underside of demographic protectionism?

A matter of increasing concern is whether this new protectionism, and the mistrust of the *other* which accompanies it, is not making more significant inroads than we have supposed in higher education. Specifically, I wish to discuss the question of whether a goal (quality) and a reality (demographic diversity) have been erroneously placed in conflict, and, if so, what problems this perception of conflict might present.

As part of my scholarship I turn to dictionaries for both origins and meanings of words. Quality, according to the *Oxford English Dictionary,* has multiple meanings. One set defines quality as being an essential character, a distinctive and inherent feature. A second describes it as a degree of excellence, of conformity to standards, as superiority in kind. A third makes reference to social status, particularly to persons of high social status. A fourth talks about quality as being a special or distinguishing attribute, as being a desirable trait. Quality is highly desirable in both principle and practice. We all aspire to it in our own person, in our experiences, in our acquisitions and products, and of course we all want to be associated with people and operations of quality.

But let us move away from the various dictionary meanings of the word and to our own sense of what it represents and of how we feel about it. First of all we consider quality to be finite; that is, it is limited with respect to quantity; it has very few manifestations; it is not widely distributed. I have it and you have it, but they don't. We associate quality with homogeneity, with uniformity, with standardization, with order, regularity, neatness. All too often we equate it with smoothness, glibness, slickness, elegance. Certainly it is always expensive. We tend to identify it with those who lead, with the rich and famous. And, when you come right down to it, it's inherent. Either you've got it or you ain't.

Diversity, from the Latin *divertere,* meaning to turn aside, to go different ways, to differ, is the condition of being different or having differences, is an instance of being different. Its companion word, diverse, means differing, unlike, distinct; having or capable of having various forms; composed of unlike or distinct elements. Diversity is lack of standardization, of regularity, of orderliness, homogeneity, conformity, uniformity. Diversity introduces complications, is difficult to organize, is troublesome to manage, is problematical. Diversity is irregular, disorderly, uneven, rough. The way we use the word diversity gives us away. Something is too diverse, is extremely diverse. We want a little diversity.

When we talk about diversity, we are talking about the *other,* whatever that other might be: someone of a different gender, race, class, national origin; somebody at a greater or lesser distance from the norm; someone outside the set; someone who possesses a different set of characteristics, features, or attributes; someone who does not fall within the taxonomies we use daily and with which we are comfortable; someone who does not fit into the mental configurations that give our lives order and meaning.

In short, diversity is desirable only in principle, not in practice. Long live diversity . . . as long as it conforms to my standards, my mind set, my view of life, my sense of order. We desire, we like, we admire diversity, not unlike the way the French (and others) appreciate women; that is, *Vive la différence!*— as long as it stays in its place.

What I find paradoxical about and lacking in this debate is that diversity is the natural order of things. Evolution produces diversity. Margaret Visser, writing about food in her latest book, *Much Depends on Dinner,* makes an eloquent statement in this regard:

Machines like, demand, and produce uniformity. But nature loathes it: her strength lies in multiplicity and

in differences. Sameness in biology means fewer possibilities and therefore weakness.

The United States, by its very nature, by its very development, is the essence of diversity. It is diverse in its geography, population, institutions, technology; its social, cultural, and intellectual modes. It is a society that at its best does not consider quality to be monolithic in form or finite in quantity, or to be inherent in class. Quality in our society proceeds in large measure out of the stimulus of diverse modes of thinking and acting; out of the creativity made possible by the different ways in which we approach things; out of diversion from paths or modes hallowed by tradition.

One of the principal strengths of our society is its ability to address, on a continuing and substantive basis, the real economic, political, and social problems that have faced and continue to face us. What makes the United States so attractive to immigrants is the protections and opportunities it offers; what keeps our society together is tolerance for cultural, religious, social, political, and even linguistic difference; what makes us a unique, dynamic, and extraordinary nation is the power and creativity of our diversity.

The true history of the United States is one of struggle against intolerance, against oppression, against xenophobia, against those forces that have prohibited persons from participating in the larger life of the society on the basis of their race, their gender, their religion, their national origin, their linguistic and cultural background. These phenomena are not consigned to the past. They remain with us and frequently take on virulent dimensions.

If you believe, as I do, that the well-being of a society is directly related to the degree and extent to which all of its citizens participate in its institutions, then you will have to agree that we have a challenge before us. In view of the extraordinary changes that are taking place in our society, we need to take up the struggle again, irritating, grating, troublesome, unfashionable, unpleasant as it is. As educated and educator members of this society we have a special responsibility for ensuring that all American institutions, not just our elementary and secondary schools, our juvenile halls, or our jails, reflect the diversity of our society. Not to do so is to risk greater alienation on the part of a growing segment of our society; is to risk increased social tension in an already conflictive world; and, ultimately, is to risk the survival of a range of institutions that, for all their defects and deficiencies, provide us the opportunity and the freedom to improve our individual and collective lot.

Let me urge you to reflect on these two words—quality and diversity—and on the mental sets and behaviors that flow out of them. And let me urge you further to struggle against the notion that quality is finite in quantity, limited in its manifestations, or is restricted by considerations of class, gender, race, or national origin; or that quality manifests itself only in leaders and not in followers, in managers and not in workers, in breeders and not in drones; or that it has to be associated with verbal agility or elegance of personal style; or that it cannot be seeded, nurtured, or developed.

Because diversity—the *other*—is among us, will define and determine our lives in ways that we still do not fully appreciate, whether that other is women (no longer bound by tradition, house, and family); or Asians, African-Americans, Indians, and Hispanics (no longer invisible, regional, or marginal); or our newest immigrants (no longer distant, exotic, alien). Given the changing profile of America, will we come to terms with diversity in our personal and professional lives? Will we begin to recognize the diverse forms that quality can take? If so, we will thus initiate the process of making quality limitless in its manifestations, infinite in quantity, unrestricted with respect to its origins, and more importantly, virulently contagious.

I hope we will. And that we will further join together to expand—not to close—the circle.

DISCUSSION QUESTIONS

1. Why do non-European immigrants have to demonstrate that diversity does not lower quality?
2. How would you describe an "American"?

SEX AND GENDER

READING 31

Fast Girls

TEENAGE TRIBES AND THE MYTH OF THE SLUT

Emily White

"They say the devil is whispering in your ear."
"I cannot help it if they do say it."

Transcript of the trial of Dorcas Hoar,
convicted of witchcraft in 1871

———

Emily White is a freelance writer who has written for *The New York Times Magazine* and was the editor of *The Stranger*, an alternative weekly newspaper in Seattle. Her work has appeared in *Spin* magazine, *The New York Times Book Review*, the *Village Voice*, *Nest*, and *L.A. Weekly*.

It's the day of the big pep assembly at Calhoun High. Teachers corral the kids into the gym, admonishing, "Hustle, people, hustle. No playing around!" Bleachers unfold to the rafters; kids take the steps two at a time. Slowly the shining metal skeleton of bleachers is covered with shifting bodies. The bleachers are tree branches, the kids are gathering birds. The gym's light is flat and much too bright. Sneakers screech on varnished wood. Twittery, sugar-high cheerleaders practice their routines.

On the far wall of the gym the school fight song is posted:

Victory, victory for Calhoun High!
Our pride and honor reach the sky!
Win, win, win and never rest!
Calhoun High is the best!

The school-spirit banner looks like it was just pulled out of a dusty closet—faded red-and-white felt, a crust of dirt forming around the edges. Its a meaningless and forgotten bit of encouragement, like the cheerful *Hang In There!* posters on the wall of the counseling center. These sunny truisms and cadences fade into the background of the school's life like elevator music.

The idea behind school spirit goes something like this: if you feel the school is something you are proud of, something you're "true" to, then you will feel like a winner all around. The banner at Calhoun High advertises the hollow and hegemonic peppiness that many remember long after high school as a fantastic example of disingenuousness. In the late 1990s a series of horror movies, most notably *The Faculty,* played on the idea of school spirit as an evil, alien language and attitude. In this particular movie, the football team, the cheerleaders, all the be-true-to-your-school fanatics, were actually invaders from a hostile planet.

School-spirit language rings false mostly because high school is such a clear spectacle of cruelty. Clearly the school has no one truth, no abiding or benevolent spirit. The evidence is all around me as I sit in the bleachers at the pep assembly. I'm next to a clutch of girls who keep straining their necks trying to flirt with the jocks in the row behind us, muscular boys buff from sports practice, wearing team jerseys with their names on the back. These boys are always moving, slapping one another, pulling one another's hat off, flicking spitballs. The girls next to me are hyperaware of them and desperate to get a look, a glance, a moment in their radar.

The assembly features the candidates for various student government positions. The kids campaigning to win have postered the school: VOTE FOR NORM FOR REFORM. ANNE BEST IS THE BEST. Today's the day they make their campaign speeches. "Vote for me, I'm Paul D.," a geeky white boy chants, rapping against the backdrop of a drum machine. He promises longer lunches and more money for dances. He's unfazed by the huge crowd and by the deep-voiced boy in the back row yelling repeatedly: "You are a fag!"

Just as Paul D. finishes his campaign pitch, in the short dead space between candidates, a rumor begins, a rumor about a girl I'll call Heather Adams.

The rumor goes like this: *Heather Adams masturbates. Pass it on!*

The rumor begins among the jocks behind me. Soon it has been heard by a dozen kids or more. *Pass it on, pass it on.* Over and over the phrase is repeated, cupped hands touching ears, the whisper as loud as a stage whisper: "*Heather Adams masturbates. Pass it on!*"

"Gross!" says the female recipient of this news, a redfaced beanpole. She hesitates for a moment, then whispers the news into the ear of the girl sitting in front of her. "Are you kidding?" the girl shouts. "She is sooo sick!"

The rumor moves west through the crowd. The point of the rumor, its defining quality, is that it moves. The rumor can't stop. Its a hot rock that must be passed quickly before it begins to burn.

While down below, in the middle of the basketball court, the student council candidates make a variety of optimistic campaign promises about dances and athletic budgets and the great history of Calhoun High, up here in the bleachers, sitting side by side and influenced by one another's skin and smell and possibility, the kids stop hearing the messages and promises of school-spirit language. They do not care about the future or about the school's phony history. They care about the present. They care about what it feels like to be sitting so near to one another. The nearness is almost unbearable. They are dying for a reaction, and they have found a phrase sure to create one: *Heather Adams masturbates.*

A 1963 book called *Improvised News: A Sociological Study of Rumor* attempted a quasi-scientific exploration of how rumors work. Writer Tamotsu Shibutani explained that a rumor "is a message transmitted by word of mouth from person to person. Indeed, oral interchange is frequently regarded as *the* identifying characteristic rumor. Whereas news in print is fixed, in oral transmission some transformation is inevitable, for only a few can remember a complicated message verbatim."

Through documents and stories from various historical periods when rumors seemed to flourish—during the McCarthy era, among civilian populations during wartime, soldiers in the midst of battle—Shibutani attempted to find out why some stories flourish, flowering into rumors, while others don't travel far out of the circle where they've originated. He wanted to get to the bottom of this strange, hysterical tendency of human societies.

Shibutani's book is not widely printed or read anymore; it's a dated volume, earnest in its objectivity, that does not incorporate postmodern theories, which always admit to some subjectivity on the part of the author. Nevertheless, *Improvised News* is illuminating on the subject of the rumor's context. Although it's a book that never addresses teenagers, the contexts Shibutani describes as ideal for rumor from his studies of various populations sound a lot like descriptions of high school. "Rumors thrive among populations desperately trying to comprehend their environment," Shibutani writes. Rumors "flourish in periods of sudden crises, sustained tension, impending decisions, boredom from monotony."

All Shibutani's elements are overwhelmingly present in high school. The author could have been writing from the interior of a cafeteria. Like the populations *Improvised News* analyzed, high school kids spread rumors to alleviate the sense of crisis and the atmosphere of monotony. Clustered together on the bleachers or crammed onto the cafeteria benches, kids are perched in an in-between state, neither here nor there, and all they can do is succumb to deep compulsions of exaggerated storytelling. The stories are vessels that rescue them from the sea of confusion.

As the pep assembly drags on, the "Heather Adams masturbates" rumor drifts from kid to kid. The story they are telling about Heather Adams is perhaps the most private story possible. It's a story that hinges on the idea that a girl pleasuring herself is scandalous. The way the kids react, full of gusto and outrage, indicates that even thirty years after the sexual revolution, the idea of women masturbating is still taboo. Even in the post-Madonna American high school, the notion of Heather Adams and her gross pleasures shocks the kids who hear the rumor.

The word itself, "masturbate," qualifies as a dirty word. Watching the rumor and its effect, I remember my mother asking me and my sisters, "Are you talking dirty?" (Inevitably, she always knew when we were.) Other warnings: Don't be dirty minded. Get your mind out of the gutter. Yet the dirty mind keeps reemerging, and in high school the dirty mind—the desire to gross one another out, to talk about the extremes of the body—is arguably the mind that rules the school. It's the one great constant, the true school spirit.

In the theater of the dirty mind, Heather Adams is the temporary star. I don't know if Heather Adams is the slut of Calhoun High. But I know the way the kids are talking about her resembles the way kids talked about the girls I interviewed; they are simultaneously aroused and disgusted by her sexuality. The reaction to her is visceral, physical. She gets all the way under the skin.

Like a landscape transformed by fire, a girl's life can be swiftly transformed by rumor. The whole attitude of the hallway can change in an instant. "All of a sudden people are looking at you and you wonder, is there toilet paper on my shoe?" explains Sasha, a twenty-eight-year-old who attended a small East Coast boarding school. Her reputation began forming over a three-day weekend, and by Tuesday she was the focus of an unfamiliar energy. "In a small school it's not like you can lose yourself," she says. "So I just stayed there, on the receiving end of all this bizarre stuff." Another girl, who was called Missile Tits because of her large breasts, remembers how she felt caught in a "bizarre web of repression," unable to move or change, unable to progress. Throughout my interviews I heard stories of how the rumors would build around a girl, getting thicker and thicker, like a chrysalis. The girls would try to disassociate themselves from the stories but they would find they could not move out from under the rumor's influence.

Generally the girls I interviewed were most impressed by the rumor's swiftness, its strange efficiency. One day they were part of the crowd; the next day they were the crowd's target. This transformation happens quickly and it happens outside the realm of adult supervision. Like my mother warning my sisters and me against talking dirty, the conventional role of the adult is to tell kids, "Don't talk that way," and then close the door. Once teenagers' talk becomes graphic, adults reflexively pull away from the posture of listening and close themselves off. Outside the radar of supervision, set adrift with a series of last-minute warnings, the kids talk trash amongst themselves. The rumors spread effortlessly. The girl becomes more and more a figment of the imagination. In the clouded atmosphere of the collective dirty mind, the slut takes on a sheen of unreality. She's not really a girl, she's more like a hallucination.

Madeline is a twenty-five-year-old Calhoun High graduate. She's the reason I chose this school to infiltrate. Even though she attended classes in the old school building that was later demolished, the way she says the name Calhoun High—the bitter sarcasm in her voice, the apparent volume of her rage—eventually makes me want to go out and see it for myself. When Madeline talks about her years there, I realize how much power one small building can have, how it houses certain experiences that brand themselves in the memory, so that even after the structure of the building is demolished, the structure of its experiences still exists.

Madeline is a voluptuous, dark-eyed girl with a theatrical persona—the kind of person who looks like she could make a big pronouncement at any time, or ruin a dinner party. She exudes a complex and troubled energy, seems all wound up by grief, believes the world owes her something. She says of being the slut of Calhoun, "It really pisses me off when I start to wonder, why did this happen to me?"

The rumors about Madeline were various: She had crabs, AIDS, herpes. She liked to suck dick. She was a lesbian. She moonlighted as a prostitute. "I had books thrown at me. People wrote WHORE on my locker in lipstick. They left a bottle of RID in front of my locker. One time I was at the mall and a bunch of girls came up to me and started shoving me. This girl I had never seen in my life was shoving me and calling me a slut." Once a group of girls beat her up in the driveway of a party, grinding the side of her face into the pavement.

Madeline identified a period before she was branded the slut, when the world seemed to open out before her, when she felt at home and at peace. "As a kid I was really happy. I rode horses," Madeline said. "Then I somehow got completely screwed up."

Once, she and her mother took a trip to Ireland to meet their relatives. Her Irish grandmother warned her, "Don't write in red pen or you will become a whore." The fear of becoming a whore was prevalent among the women in her family; it was a destiny they often commented on and warned Madeline about.

By the time she entered high school, Madeline's mother had married a "major asshole," and Madeline's body had started to betray her. The period when she was happy and rode horses darkened, narrowed to the size of a scene watched through a keyhole. She was fourteen but her breasts belonged to the body of a woman: size 36D. The kids in the hallway stared, talked loudly about her "big tits." At twenty-five, looking back, she realizes she must have looked like "a goddess, only a hundred and twenty-five pounds." But to the kids she wasn't a goddess; she was a monster.

The kids weren't the only ones who gossiped about her; the faculty thought Madeline was trouble, too. She dressed provocatively and strutted into class late. She hung out with smokers. Once a teacher stopped her in front of everyone and said, "Go home and put some clothes on, young woman." Faculty, other students, girlfriends—everyone agreed Madeline was asking for it.

At home her stepdad tried to rape her. They were alone in the house and she fought him off. When she told her brother about it he simply said, "What do you expect, walking around the house in your nightgown?" Like the teacher in school, her brother equated Madeline's visual presence with all the abuse she'd been getting; he talked as if she should be punished for the way she looked. If she dressed a certain way, these things were going to happen to her, her life was going to take a certain course. It was only a matter of time.

All the contradictions and injustices started to revolve in her brain much too fast. She smoked pot, and pot slowed things down a little, but not enough. She was part of the stoner culture, which at Calhoun High meant "fishnet stockings, cutoffs, heavy metal concert T-shirts." Yet although on the surface she was part of a group of friends, girls within the group started to look at her warily, checking out her breasts, her eyes, her hair. They perceived something slutty about her, some bad energy.

"All of us girls, the clothes we wore were provocative. So I presented this image, but every single one of my girlfriends dressed the same way. I had a hard time figuring out why I was singled out when all of my friends had been sleeping with other people and I was the one that wasn't."

Guarding their men against her nefarious influence, the other stoner girls would call Madeline at home, two or three girls on the line at once, whispering, "You stay away from our boyfriends or we're gonna kick your ass." These whispery threats on the other end of the phone, and Madeline's stepdad in the next room, full of beer, it all added up to "a bad scene. I couldn't go anywhere or do anything," she says. "There was nothing I could do to stop any of it."

Madeline had been chosen as a type by the kids around her, a type that was part of the American sexual imagination, part of the world they were born into. In 1967, *The Seventeen Guide to Knowing Yourself* succinctly described the fast girl as "someone who is using sex to work out problems that have little to do with sex; and her solution only creates deeper problems. . . . It is a fact that most boys lose respect for an 'easy mark' and after a torrid affair are quite likely to decide that the young woman is 'not the kind of girl I want to be the mother of my children.'"

The idea expressed in this passage is an age-old cliché about a promiscuous woman's sexual cheapness, an idea integral to the high school slut experience. Just as married women often describe themselves as "off the market," so too the metaphors of the marketplace attach themselves to the slut girl's sense of herself. The girls I interviewed often

felt that by being the slut they had been devalued; they would no longer have currency in the love-story economy and consequently they would never be allowed the redemption of romantic love.

Now in her twenties, Madeline has carried into adulthood the feeling of cheapness, evoked by the slut story. She described the way she never felt like she belonged in "classy places"; for example, when she was in a nice restaurant one night and saw someone from high school, "all those worthless feelings came back." Other girls talked around this notion of worthlessness, of a decline in value brought on by being the center of the rumor mill.

Women confessed that they were not sure if a guy would want to spend much time with them once he knew the whole story of the slut years. For these women the sordid past does not have to do with sexual partners or sexual acts committed so much as it has to do with the bizarre experience of being the focus of the rumor mill—the unforgettable experience of being constantly talked about in sexually explicit terms. Being a slut is not about the body so much as all the things that have been spoken about the body. In my interviews I talked to some girls who had actually been promiscuous, some girls who hadn't. Some girls were virgins; one girl had slept with seventy men in the space of her high school years. But in the mind of the crowd, all of these girls had slept with "everyone."

When Madeline talked about her fourteen-year-old, 36D body and the way kids reacted to it, as if her body meant something about the things she would do, she was echoing the stories of many of the girls I interviewed. Girls who experienced bad reputations tended to be under the spell of what physicians call precocious puberty, a state of development when the body is moving ahead of time, hasty and accelerated.

"I had hips and underwire bras when I was twelve," says Andrea, who grew up in Orange County "My boobs were huge," says Jenny, an East Coast tattoo artist. "The kids just called me Big." Other breast-related nicknames I heard included the aforementioned Missile Tits, Dolly Parton,

Stacks, Big Rack. These names might be shouted out of car windows, blurted out in prank calls, or chanted by a group of boys in the middle of the cafeteria.

Twenty-two-year-old Tricia tells the story of how her overdeveloped breasts brought on all forms of crisis. At ten years old she had the body of a woman, and the boys thought this meant she *was* one, somehow, and that she was a woman meant for them. "My brother had a lot of friends, and they would come over to our house, and whenever they would see me they would chase after me. When I was ten, that was the first time I experienced washing cum out of my hair," she says. One night, her brother's friends became so hot and bothered they chased her out into the street and up into a huge oak tree that bordered the family's property. She climbed up there like a cat. "I can't believe I've been trapped in trees before. And I almost got raped two or three times. We'd be playing games at night and they'd trap me in corners."

Trapped in a corner with her erupting body, Tricia could not fathom why these boys wanted to touch her so desperately. Her experience is an example of the way the girl who is experiencing precocious puberty endures a split at adolescence far more intense than the conventional split of moody teenage alienation, the split between childhood and adulthood For these girls, the split is literal: Her body begins to demolish and erase her interior life. Her body becomes the focus of a kind of visceral attention, a fiery need.

In this way, the girl who develops ahead of time feels like she is being pulled forward, suddenly thrust into the harsh light of the world's gaze. To awaken into the body of a woman when you are still a girl, to be wearing Playtex eighteen-hour underwires when the girls around you are wearing training bras, is to be a true alien. The big-breasted girl looks like a girl in a pornographic movie, "eye candy" in a school of boys who are just discovering their dad's basement stash of magazines. The boys look at her as if she is some sort of demented actress. The girls look at her as if she is an interloper, as if the extra amount of space she takes up is space

she is stealing from them. The self-consciousness such attention can cause fostered an alienation so pronounced and deep among the girls I interviewed that I found myself understanding Madeline when she described this strange logic: she *suffered* for her breasts. "My girlfriends have had boob jobs, girls I see out in the clubs. And to me this isn't fair. These girls have these huge breasts overnight and I suffered, I suffered for years. They don't deserve those breasts."

Breasts and their associations of fertility become warped in the rumor mill; for the kids making quick, panicky associations, fertility is equated with the sex act, and so the girls whose bodies look like the bodies of mothers, of grown women, are assumed to be doing the things women do. Because their bodies have moved from childhood to adulthood so fast, these girls are assumed to be fast girls. The quickness of the body is extrapolated into a general quickness, a belief that she will go to bed with anyone in no time. The assumption is that the acts of the body create the body. "Big boobs meant you were having sex, I guess," says Margaret. Although she's still a virgin at twenty-six, Margaret's larger-than-life breasts made the kids think she'd been screwing around for years when she was only fourteen.

So the flesh and the shapes it takes are held as evidence of a girl's bad acts. This kind of logic prevails in the slut story: kids feel certain just by looking at her that they *know* what she's up to; they can just *tell.* Faced with this unflinching and irrational certainty, a girl might begin to wonder if the kids are right, if they know something she herself does not know. Listen to the rumors long enough and you will start to believe they are a sign of something. You will start to believe they're basically true.

DISCUSSION QUESTIONS

1. From your experience of high school or middle school, is White's description accurate?
2. Why is early physical development negative for females?
3. What are the defining characteristics of a slut?

PERSONAL ACCOUNT

Just Something You Did as a Man

In a class we had discussed the ways men stratify themselves in terms of masculinity. I decided I would put that discussion to the test at work.

As I sat at a table, one of my coworkers approached me with a copy of a popular men's magazine, which portrays nude women. He said, "Frank, there is this bitch in here with the most beautiful big tits I have ever seen in my life." I told him that I wasn't interested in looking at the magazine because I had decided I did not agree with the objectification of women. His reply was, "What's the matter, are you getting soft on us?" I joked that it was not a matter of getting soft, it was simply a decision I had made due to a "new and improved consciousness."

At my job, talk about homosexuals, the women who walk by, and graphic (verbal) depictions of sexual aggression toward women abound, but on this occasion I either rejected the conversation or said nothing at all. By the end of the day I was being called, sometimes jokingly and sometimes not, every derogatory homosexual slur in the English language. I was no longer "one of the boys."

I did not engage in the "manly" discourse of the day so therefore I was labeled (at best) a "sissy."

My coworkers assumed that I had had or was about to have a change of sexual orientation simply because I did not engage in their conversations about women and homosexuals. Since men decide how masculine another man is by how much he is willing to put down women and gays, I was no longer considered masculine.

This experience affected me as much as it did because it opened my eyes to a system of stratification in which I have been immersed but still had no idea existed. Demeaning women and homosexuals, to me, was just something you did as a man. But to tell you the truth, I don't think I could go back to talking like that. I am sure that my coworkers will get used to my new thinking, but even if they don't I believe that it is worth being rejected for a cause such as this. I had not thought about it, but I would not want men talking about my sisters and mother in such a demeaning way.

Francisco Hernandez

READING 32

How Do We Know What Manhood Really *Is?*

John Stoltenberg

Often we're at a loss to know what manhood is all about, so we grope for answers wherever we suppose we can find them—in myths, in holy writ, in rude jokes, on toilet stalls. Many tales have been told to inspire us to manhood, to reveal its true nature, to allay our doubts about its existence, to help us remember where we lost it, to help us remember next time to put it back where it belongs. Many yarns have been spun about exemplars of man-

hood, heroic and stoic, cocksure and strong. Understandably, such gonzo bombast may underwhelm. Regrettably, not all such educative epics may be to your taste. So here's one that's certifiably tongue-in-cheek.

THE WONDROUS FABLE OF A YOUNG MAN'S SEARCH FOR MANHOOD

This is the story of a child named Tom.

All the time that Tom was growing up, he noticed something that made him feel terribly uneasy and queasy inside: He noticed he always felt *compared* to other boys and to older men. And he noticed he always felt that some of them had *more* of something that he was supposed to have. And he didn't have *enough* of it, whatever it was.

It wasn't exactly strength, and it wasn't exactly size, and it wasn't exactly money, and it wasn't exactly age, and it wasn't exactly toughness, and it wasn't exactly anger—although certainly everyone who seemed to have *enough* of this something (*whatever* it was)

John Stoltenberg is the radical feminist author of *Refusing to Be a Man: Essays on Sex and Justice; The End of Manhood: Parables on Sex and Selfhood;* and *What Makes Pornography "Sexy"?* He is cofounder of men against Pornography.

seemed to Tom to be stronger, bigger, richer, older, tougher, and angrier.

Tom was never sure what this mysterious something was. Was it some *stuff?* Did it come installed in your *body* somewhere? *Where?*

Or was it in *what you did?* or *how you did things?*

Or was it in how everyone acted toward you when you acted that way?

Or was it in how you treated people?

Or was it in how everyone else treated you?

Tom could not be certain. Tom's questions only led to more questions.

"What *is* it with this stuff?" Tom wondered thoughtfully. "And how do you get enough of it, anyway?"

So Tom kept on the lookout for clues. Tom checked out everyone he met who seemed to have it—to see who really had it, to see who seemed to have more of it (and who seemed to have less), to see who seemed to have really a lot (maybe more than enough—maybe enough to share?), to see how they got it, and to see how Tom could get enough too.

Tom turned into a very smart sleuth.

As years went by, and as Tom grew older, he kept doing his detective thing—which had started out as a hobby but now took up more and more of his time. He paid close attention to whoever seemed to have this stuff and he began asking clever questions of everyone he met who seemed to have it. Two of the cleverer questions Tom asked always got very surprising answers. One was:

"Do you ever feel compared to someone else who has more of this stuff?"

And the other was:

"Do you ever feel someone out there has more of it than you will ever possibly have?"

What was surprising about the answers to those two questions was that all the answers were "yes." Always. Without exception. No matter what different answers Tom got to the other clever questions he asked, he always got "yes" to those two.

Over a period of many, many years, Tom met and talked to many, many people who seemed to have this ineffable stuff—and every one of them told Tom they felt compared to someone else who had more of the stuff, and every one of them said they felt there was someone out there who had more than they themselves could ever possibly hope to have.

Tom—who had now taken to wearing a trench coat—became a full-time dick. He pursued his ques-

tioning, and his quest, through many lands, through many generations, and always he got the same answer, in words more or less the same: "Someone else has more of this stuff than I do. I'm afraid I will always have less stuff than they do. Try as I might, my stuff will always be compared to theirs unfavorably."

So Tom had an idea. He tried asking, "*Who* has more stuff than you do? *Who exactly?* Could you please tell me their *names?*"

To Tom's surprise, everyone he asked had at least one name to provide. And some people had quite a few. Some people gave Tom the names of their fathers, big brothers, uncles, stepfathers. Some people gave Tom the names of playmates from childhood—and popularly merchandised action figures. Some people gave Tom names of neighborhood bullies, gang leaders, coaches, high school sports stars, fraternity brothers. Some people gave Tom names of bosses, higher-ranking military officers, higher-ranking fellow prisoners, professional athletes, movie stars, CEOs.

Tom also found he got a lot of names that fell into a big category he first called "miscellaneous" because he couldn't make any sense of it. Then he realized what it was about and called the category "wished-for chums." It was for those who you once wanted very much to befriend you but they wouldn't have anything to do with you because you had insufficient stuff.

Tom persevered. "Who has more stuff than you?" he asked insouciantly. "Who exactly?"

As Tom logged the answers, he swiftly accumulated lists and lists of names. The lists became long and complex, so Tom got himself a computer to keep track. He got himself one of those superpowerful supercomputers. He got himself a gigantic grant to hire interviewers. His worldwide field-research staff was soon enormous.

"Who has more stuff than you? Who exactly?" And Tom's supercomputer crunched all the data and traced all the contacts and cross-tabulated all the referrals and cross-indexed all the nicknames and finally plotted and printed out the results.

The printout was a maze, a diagram actually, approximately in the shape of a pyramid, showing the names of everyone alive who had grown up to be a man, whom they felt unfavorably compared with, who they felt had more stuff, and who *those people* felt had more stuff, and so on and so on all the way to the pinnacle.

At the peak of the pyramid was a single name: The one man more men felt unfavorably compared with than absolutely any other, statistically speaking. The one man whose name had never shown up when interviewers asked, "Who has *less* stuff than you?" The one man whose name only showed up in answer to the question "Who has *more* stuff than you?"

Tom stared at that name for a long, long time. For a trembling moment, Tom felt a cosmic feeling sweep through him, a premonition that he might be close to the end of his quest—for the man whose name appeared at the apex of the pyramid had not yet been interviewed. Somehow he had been overlooked.

So Tom went back to the supercomputer and keyboarded in a query:

DOSSIER?

And here's what the supercomputer screen shot back:

NAME: Deep Bob
ADDRESS: A bosky bog

AGE: Ancient
SEX: What, are you kidding?

"So this is the ultimate man's man," thought Tom marvelingly. "A man among men—a man among *all* men! The fullest flowering of manhood known to man!

"He's got so much stuff he never has to prove it and it's never *ever* in doubt!

"He's the all-time greatest. The big enchilada."

Needless to say, Tom rushed off to that bosky bog forthwith.

There were hanging vines overhead, rank and scummy ponds all around, fungi and tree rot underfoot. It looked like the set from a Hollywood science-fiction film. It was.

"Deep Bob?" Tom called out imploringly. "Deep Bob?"

A nearby pond burbled.

"Deep Bob? Where *are* you? It's *me*—Tom!"

The murky surface of the swamp seemed to swell.

"I have some questions to ask you, if you don't mind? Clever questions? I won't be but a minute?" Tom felt a shiver. Tom also felt himself asking statements of fact.

Tom cringed—and had a momentary flashback to his mother. He recalled her musical voice, inflected just this way: she would voice statements as questions,

no matter what their factual basis. Tom had always hated that. Tom swore he'd never do that, ever, himself. He vowed he'd never talk like his mother that way, he'd never let deference show that way, he'd always *ask* his questions and *state* his statements, and that was that. He had a right to say what he meant, dammit. And now here he was in the bosky bog about to meet Deep Bob—and sounding just like his mother! Intimidated, deferential, insubstantial, seeming to be nobody. The shame of it all! The humiliation!

Just then a massive hairy creature rose up out of the goo, slime sheeting down its matted fur. Tom felt a dank wind blow, and he wrapped himself inside his trench coat for warmth, shuddering with awe and angst.

The massive hairy creature loomed larger and larger. Its eyes glared, its tongue lolled, its throat cleared, and it roared.

Tom could not believe his eyes.

"I *know* you—" stammered Tom, clearing his own throat, lowering his voice somewhat, making a statement on his own authority. "I *know* you from somewhere—!"

The hairy swampthing roared some more.

"Aren't you—?" Tom sputtered, for now he really did have a to ask. "Aren't you—?"

The Bob Beast growled at Tom even louder.

"Aren't you—*the tooth fairy?*"

"Yes," admitted the swampthing, suddenly sniveling from the cold and sheepish. "I only do this part-time."

That story has a punch line, which goes as follows: "Either Deep Bob exists, or else manhood doesn't." So it's probably not the sort of story that would clear up anyone's confusion on the subject. And it's certainly not the sort of story that gets tucked away in the collective unconscious of all seekers after deep manhood.

Actually, out of our confusion, we often compose manhood stories of our own, out of our own lives, writing little legends now and then about our gender to remind us "who we are." These stories are sometimes modeled after other stories that we've been told or that were acted out before our eyes. But each has an original, personal touch. And because it seems our lot in life to make up our manhood as we go alone, when we make up such distinctive stories, they stay with us remarkably well—even when we have completely forgotten what really originally happened.

This is one such personal episode, first acted out many years ago and only recently recollected.

THE TRUE STORY OF A YOUNG BOY'S SEARCH FOR MANHOOD

This is the story of a child named John.

If John had been interviewed by Tom (see above), his name would have been entered in Tom's imaginary computer, and on the pyramidic printout, John's name would be nearer to the base than to the apex—especially when he was young, when he was called Johnny, but also into puberty, his teens, and his twenties.

John grew up experiencing a great gulf between who he felt he was and the masculinity he perceived in other men. John grew up feeling that there were always other boys who had more masculinity than he did, even at the earliest age he could remember. There were older boys, bigger boys, meaner boys; there were stronger boys, more athletic boys, more muscular boys, tougher boys. Everywhere John looked, there were boys who were more "all boy." And that's not counting the adult men in John's family, especially his gruff, pipesmoking paternal grandfather, a man whom Johnny loved dearly, except when he embarrassed Johnny by remarking on what broad shoulders he thought young Johnny had grown, and what a tough football player he thought Johnny would become someday—and except now and then when he frightened Johnny by goading him into fistfights with an older, far more street-tough boy cousin, a prospect Johnny dreaded and dodged however he could.

Early on, Johnny got the idea that there was such a thing as rock-hard, fail-safe masculinity—the real stuff, the right stuff—perhaps whatever it was that Johnny's paternal grandfather expected him to have. And it was Johnny's job in life to have it—to have as much as he could muster.

But he never felt he had enough.

Inside, he felt he was just passing. Even if he was convincing to those around him—playmates, family members, schoolmates, teachers—he wasn't completely convincing to himself. He wasn't constantly certain he had enough. He was always afraid he'd be

found out, discovered in his ruse. And then he'd be rejected by the boyfriends he wanted most to be liked by.

There were some older, meaner boys in the neighborhood who used to threaten Johnny and his boyfriends. Johnny especially seemed to be picked on and teased by those older boys. They would throw rocks at him and call him names. Once, they got him alone and they beat him up and stuffed him into a dirt tunnel they'd dug in a vacant lot and trapped him there and he cried his heart out with terror and pain.

But the boyfriends Johnny hung out with weren't mean like that. There were three of them, all about Johnny's age, and they often played together. Johnny enjoyed and valued their companionship.

Throughout his early years, Johnny did a lot of things to act convincingly like a real boy with his boyfriends, because he wanted them to like him and accept him and because he was scared of seeming a girl. None of those things Johnny did stands out as vividly today as the things he did to his sister.

Johnny had a sister two years younger. Johnny's boyfriends liked her. Johnny's boyfriends liked to play with her too. None of Johnny's boyfriends had a sister their age, so she was special to them, and they accepted her as one of the kids in the neighborhood they sometimes played with.

But by the age of five, Johnny had begun to tease and taunt his sister cruelly. Johnny began to make fun of her in private and also in front of his boyfriends. Johnny made crayon drawings of her face and nailed them to trees in neighborhood backyards, cartoons of her with her name scrawled on them, caricatures that reduced her to tears and sent her wailing to their mother for comfort. "Don't let Johnny get your goat," was generally the extent of their mother's counsel. But Johnny had discovered that he *could,* and he could get away with it, and so for the next several years, he habitually tormented his little sister—beating up on her repeatedly in private—so Johnny could believe he was a real boy, so Johnny would not feel like a girl, so his boyfriends would believe he was one of them, so his boyfriends would like and accept him, and so Johnny could like and accept himself.

Johnny had figured out this strategy of sibling battery by the time he was six.

I know this story is true, because Johnny's behavior was mine. Although the behavior ended many years ago (and violence is now abhorrent to me), I have no

He Hit Her

I was raised in Charleston, South Carolina, a city where racial and class lines are both evident and defined by street address. I had been taught all my life that black people were different than "us" and were to be feared, particularly in groups.

One summer afternoon when I was eighteen or nineteen, I was sitting in my car at a traffic light at the corner of Cannon and King streets, an area on the edge of the white part of the peninsular city, but progressively being inhabited by more and more blacks. It was hot, had been for weeks, and the sticky heat of South Carolina can be enraging by itself.

As I waited at the light, a young black couple turned the corner on the sidewalk and began to walk towards where I was sitting. The man was yelling and screaming and waving his arms about his head. The woman, a girl really, looked scared and was walking and trying to ignore his tirade. Perhaps it was her seeming indifference that finally did it, perhaps the heat, I don't know. As they drew right up next to my car though, he hit her. He hit her on the side of her head, open palmed, and her head bounced off the brick wall of the house on the corner and she sprawled to the ground, dazed and crying. The man stood over her, shaking his fist and yelling.

I looked around at the other people in cars around me, mostly whites, and at the other people on the sidewalks, mostly blacks, and I realized as everyone gaped that no one was going to do anything, no one was going to help, and neither was I. I don't think it was fear of the man involved that stopped me; rather, I think it was fear generated by what I had been told about the man that stopped me. Physically I was bigger than he was and I knew how to handle myself in a fight: I worked as a bouncer in a nightclub. What I was afraid of was what I had been told about blacks: that *en masse,* they hated whites, and that given the opportunity they would harm me. I was afraid getting out of the car in that neighborhood would make me the focus of the fight and in a matter of time I would be pummeled by an angry black crowd. Also in my mind were thoughts of things I had heard voiced as a child: "They are different. Violence is a part of life for them. They beat, stab, and shoot each other all the time, and the women are just as bad as the men." So I sat and did nothing. The light changed and I pulled away.

The incident has haunted me over the last almost fifteen years. I have often thought about it and felt angry when I did. I believe that as I examined it over time the woman who had been hit, the victim, became less and less prominent, and the black man and myself more prominent. Then I had an epiphany about it.

What bothered me about the incident was not that a man had hit a woman and I had done nothing to intervene, not even to blow my horn, but that a man had hit a woman and I had done nothing to intervene and that this reflected on me as a man. "Men don't hit women, and other men don't let men hit women," was also part of my masculinity training as a boy. There was a whole list of things that "real" men did and things that "real" men didn't do, and somewhere on there was this idea that men didn't let other men hit women. I realized that the incident haunted me not because a man had hit a woman, but because my lack of response was an indictment of *my* masculinity. The horror had become that I was somehow less of a man because of my inaction. Part of the dichotomy that this set up was the notion that the black man had done something to *me,* not to the woman he hit, and it was here that my anger lay. I wonder how this influenced my perception of black men I encountered in the future.

Tim Norton

doubt today that in some significant sense my behavior then *gendered* me—and probably my sister too.

I remembered this story with some difficulty, with some assistance from my sister. At first my story had significant gaps. I recalled my behavior toward her during our childhoods generally, but my sister brought crucial details of it to my attention in a conversation about a year and a half ago. When I recently showed her a version I had written, she alerted me to the fact that my telling of the story was still less than truthful. Understanding more fully the effects of what I did to her those many years ago, I revised it, trying to narrate more accurately the part about my violence, which she continues to recall far more clearly than I, but which I do not doubt I did.

The one who is making up the manhood has to forget a lot that goes into the legend of one's gender. The people whom one hurt along the way—the people one paid less attention to because one was paying more attention to one's quest for manhood—may eventually become but distant voices or may never be heard from again. That way the legend continues.

To make up one's own story of manhood is easy. The key is in what to leave out. What you especially need to forget is your violation of someone's self-hood. Then what you get to remember is the validation of your manhood.

DISCUSSION QUESTIONS

1. Is masculinity about "passing"?
2. Why is it important (to be or feel) really masculine?
3. To be a real boy or man must you make fun of someone?

Chappals and Gym Shorts

AN INDIAN-MUSLIM WOMAN IN THE LAND OF OZ

Almas Sayeed

It was finals week during the spring semester of my sophomore year at the University of Kansas, and I was buried under mounds of papers and exams. The stress was exacerbated by long nights, too much coffee and a chronic, building pain in my permanently splintered shins (left over from an old sports

---

Almas Sayeed graduated in 2002 from Kansas University with degrees in philosophy, women's studies, and international studies.

injury). Between attempting to understand the nuances of Kant's *Critique of Pure Reason* and applying the latest game-theory models to the 1979 Iranian revolution, I was regretting my decision to pursue majors in philosophy, women's studies *and* international studies.

My schedule was not exactly permitting much down time. With a full-time school schedule, a part-time job at Lawrence's domestic violence shelter and preparations to leave the country in three weeks, I was grasping to hold onto what little sanity I had left. Wasn't living in Kansas supposed to be more laid-back than this? After all, Kansas was the portal to the magical land of Oz, where wicked people melt when doused with mop water and bright red, sparkly shoes could substitute for the services of American Airlines, providing a quick getaway. Storybook tales aside, the physical reality of this period was that my deadlines were inescapable. Moreover, the most pressing of these deadlines was completely non-school related: my dad, on his way home to Wichita, was coming for a brief visit. This would be his first stay by himself, without Mom to accompany him or act as a buffer.

Dad visited me the night before my most difficult exam. Having just returned from spending time with his family—a group of people with whom he historically had an antagonistic relationship—Dad seemed particularly relaxed in his stocky six-foot-four frame. Wearing one of the more subtle of his nineteen cowboy hats, he arrived at my door, hungry, greeting me in Urdu, our mother tongue, and laden with gifts from Estée Lauder for his only daughter. Never mind that I rarely wore makeup and would have preferred to see the money spent on my electric bill or a stack of feminist theory books from my favorite used bookstore. If Dad's visit was going to include a conversation about how little I use beauty products, I was not going to be particularly receptive.

"Almas," began my father from across the dinner table, speaking in his British-Indian accent infused with his love of Midwestern colloquialisms, "You know that you won't be a spring chicken forever. While I was in Philadelphia, I realized how important it is for you to begin thinking about our culture, religion and your future marriage plans. I think it is time we began a two-year marriage plan so you can find a husband and start a family. I think twenty-two will be a good age for you. You should be married by twenty-two."

I needed to begin thinking about the "importance of tradition" and be married by twenty-two? This, from the only Indian man I knew who had Alabama's first album on vinyl and loved to spend long weekends in his rickety, old camper near Cheney Lake, bass fishing and listening to traditional Islamic Quavali music? My father, in fact, was in his youth crowned "Mr. Madras," weightlifting champion of 1965, and had left India to practice medicine and be an American cowboy in his spare time. But he wanted *me* to aspire to be a "spring chicken," maintaining some unseen hearth and home to reflect my commitment to tradition and culture.

Dad continued, "I have met a boy that I like for you very much. Masoud's son, Mahmood. He is a good Muslim boy, tells great jokes in Urdu and is a promising engineer. We should be able to arrange something. I think you will be very happy with him!" Dad concluded with a satisfied grin.

Masoud, Dad's cousin? This would make me and Mahmood distant relatives of some sort. And Dad wants to "arrange something"? I had brief visions of being paraded around a room, serving tea to strangers in a sari or a shalwar kameez (a traditional South Asian outfit for women) wearing a long braid and chappals (flat Indian slippers), while Dad boasted of my domestic capabilities to increase my attractiveness to potential suitors, I quickly flipped through my mental Rolodex of rhetorical devices acquired during years of women's studies classes and found the card blank. No doubt, even feminist scholar Catherine MacKinnon would have been rendered speechless sitting across the table in a Chinese restaurant speaking to my overzealous father.

It is not that I hadn't already dealt with the issue. In fact, we had been here before, ever since the marriage proposals began (the first one came when I

was fourteen). Of course, when they first began, it was a family joke, as my parents understood that I was to continue my education. The jokes, however, were always at my expense: "You received a proposal from a nice boy living in our mosque. He is studying medicine," my father would come and tell me with a huge, playful grin. "I told him that you weren't interested because you are too busy with school. And anyway you can't cook or clean." My father found these jokes particularly funny, given my dislike of household chores. In this way, the eventuality of figuring out how to deal with these difficult issues was postponed with humor.

Dad's marriage propositions also resembled conversations that we had already had about my relationship to Islamic practices specific to women, some negotiated in my favor and others simply shelved for the time being. Just a year ago, Dad had come to me while I was home for the winter holidays, asking me to begin wearing *hijab*, the traditional headscarf worn by Muslim women. I categorically refused, maintaining respect for those women who chose to do so. I understood that for numerous women, as well as for Dad, hijab symbolized something much more than covering a woman's body or hair; it symbolized a way to adhere to religious and cultural traditions in order to prevent complete Western immersion. But even my sympathy for this concern didn't change my feeling that hijab constructed me as a woman first and a human being second. Veiling seemed to reinforce the fact that inequality between the sexes was a natural, inexplicable phenomenon that is impossible to overcome, and that women should cover themselves, accommodating an unequal hierarchy, for the purposes of modesty and self-protection. I couldn't reconcile these issues and refused my father's request to don the veil. Although there was tension—Dad claimed I had yet to have my religious awakening—he chose to respect my decision.

Negotiating certain issues had always been part of the dynamic between my parents and me. It wasn't that I disagreed with them about everything. In fact, I had internalized much of the Islamic perspective of the female body while simultaneously admitting to its problematic nature (To this day, I would rather wear a wool sweater than a bathing suit in public, no matter how sweltering the weather). Moreover, Islam became an important part of differentiating myself from other American kids who did not have to find a balance between two opposing cultures. Perhaps Mom and Dad recognized the need to concede certain aspects of traditional Islamic norms, because for all intents and purposes, I had been raised in the breadbasket of America.

By the time I hit adolescence, I had already established myself outside of the social norm of the women in my community. I was an athletic teenager, a competitive tennis player and a budding weightlifter. After a lot of reasoning with my parents, I was permitted to wear shorts to compete in tennis tournaments, but I was not allowed to show my legs or arms (no tank tops) outside of sports. It was a big deal for my parents to have agreed to allow me to wear shorts in the first place. The small community of South Asian Muslim girls my age, growing up in Wichita, became symbols of the future of our community in the United States. Our bodies became the sites to play out cultural and religious debates. Much in the same way that Lady Liberty had come to symbolize idealized stability in the *terra patria* of America, young South Asian girls in my community were expected to embody the values of a preexisting social structure. We were scrutinized for what we said, what we wore, being seen with boys in public and for lacking grace and piety. Needless to say, because of disproportionate muscle mass, crooked teeth, huge Lucy glasses, and a disposition to walk pigeon-toed, I was not among the favored.

To add insult to injury, Mom nicknamed me "Amazon Woman," lamenting the fact that she—a beautiful, petite lady—had produced such a graceless, unfeminine creature. She was horrified by how freely I got into physical fights with my younger brother and armwrestled boys at school. She was particularly frustrated by the fact that I could not wear her beautiful Indian jewelry, especially her bangles and bracelets, because my wrists were too

big. Special occasions, when I had to slather my wrists with tons of lotion in order to squeeze my hands into her tiny bangles, often bending the soft gold out of shape, caused us both infinite amounts of grief. I was the snot-nosed, younger sibling of the Bollywood (India's Hollywood) princess that my mother had in mind as a more appropriate representation of an Indian daughter. Rather, I loved sports, sports figures and books. I hated painful makeup rituals and tight jewelry.

It wasn't that I had a feminist awakening at an early age. I was just an obnoxious kid who did not understand the politics raging around my body. I did not possess the tools to analyze or understand my reaction to this process of social conditioning and normalization until many years later, well after I had left my parents' house and the Muslim community in Wichita. By positioning me as a subject of both humiliation and negotiation, Mom and Dad had inadvertently laid the foundations for me to understand and scrutinize the process of conditioning women to fulfill particular social obligations.

What was different about my dinner conversation with Dad that night was a sense of immediacy and detail. Somehow discussion about a "two-year marriage plan" seemed to encroach on my personal space much more than had previous jokes about my inability to complete my household chores or pressure to begin wearing hijab. I was meant to understand that that when it came to marriage, I was up against an invisible clock (read: social norms) that would dictate how much time I had left: how much time I had left to remain desirable, attractive and marriageable. Dad was convinced that it was his duty to ensure my long-term security in a manner that reaffirmed traditional Muslim culture in the face of an often hostile foreign community. I recognized that the threat was not as extreme as being shipped off to India in order to marry someone I had never met. The challenge was more far more subtle than this. I was being asked to choose my community; capitulation through arranged marriage would show my commitment to being Indian, to being a good Muslim woman and to my parents by proving that they had raised me with a sense of duty and the willingness to sacrifice for my culture, religion and family.

There was no way to tell Dad about my complicated reality. Certain characteristics of my current life already indicated failure by such standards. I was involved in a long-term relationship with a white man, whose father was a prison guard on death row, an occupation that would have mortified my upper-middle-class, status-conscious parents. I was also struggling with an insurmountable crush on an *actress* in the Theater and Film Department. I was debating my sexuality in terms of cultural compatibility as well as gender. Moreover, there was no way to tell Dad that my social circle was supportive of these nontraditional romantic explorations. My friends in college had radically altered my perceptions of marriage and family. Many of my closest friends, including my roommates, were coming to terms with their own life-choices, having recently come out of the closet but unable to tell their families about their decisions. I felt inextricably linked to this group of women, who, like me, often had to lead double lives. The immediacy of fighting for issues such as queer rights, given the strength and beauty of my friends' romantic relationships, held far more appeal for me than the topics of marriage and security that my father broached over our Chinese dinner. There was no way to explain to my loving, charismatic, steadfastly religious father, who was inclined to the occasional violent outburst, that a traditional arranged marriage not only conflicted with the feminist ideology I had come to embrace, but it seemed almost petty in the face of larger, more pressing issues.

Although I had no tools to answer my father that night at dinner, feminist theory had provided me with the tools to understand *why* my father and I were engaged in the conversation in the first place.

I understood that in his mind, Dad was fulfilling his social obligation as father and protector. He worried about my economic stability and, in a roundabout way, my happiness. Feminism and community activism had enabled me to understand these things as part of a proscribed role for women. At the same time, growing up in Kansas and coming to feminism here meant that I had to reconcile a number of different issues. I am a Muslim, first-generation Indian, feminist woman studying in a largely homogeneous white, Christian community in Midwestern America. What sacrifices are necessary for me to retain my familial relationships as well as a sense of personal autonomy informed by Western feminism?

There are few guidebooks for women like me who are trying to negotiate the paradigm of feminism in two different worlds. There is a delicate dance here that I must master—a dance of negotiating identity within interlinking cultural spheres. When faced with the movement's expectations of my commitment to local issues, it becomes important for me to emphasize that differences in culture and religion are also "local issues." This has forced me to change my frame of reference, developing from a rebellious tomboy who resisted parental imposition to a budding social critic, learning how to be a committed feminist and still keep my cultural, religious and community ties. As for family, we still negotiate despite the fact that Dad's two-year marriage plan has yet to come to fruition in this, my twenty-second year.

DISCUSSION QUESTIONS

1. Do you have your own example of "politics raging around my body"?
2. What are the symbols of a traditional lifestyle in your parent's cultural heritage?

SEXUAL ORIENTATION

Anti-gay Slurs Common at School

A LESSON IN CRUELTY

Laura Sessions Stepp

Emmett English, a cheerful, easygoing boy, started third grade last year at a new school, Chevy Chase Elementary in Bethesda, Maryland. On his first day he proudly wore a new red Gap sweatshirt and almost immediately wished he had chosen something else.

"A girl called me 'gay,'" he remembered. "I didn't know what that meant but I knew it was something bad." His mother, Christina Files, confirmed this. "He came home quite upset," she said.

"That's soooo gay." "Faggot." Or "lesbo." For all the outcry over harassment of gays following the murder of college student Matthew Shepard two years ago, anti-gay insults are still the slang of choice among children and teenagers, according to teachers, counselors and youths themselves. Some say the insults are increasing in school classrooms and hallways—among children as young as 8 or 9— partly because gay youths and their supporters have become more visible and more active.

"Schools are seen as a safe place to say things and get away with it," said Jerry Newberry, director of health information for the National Education Association, a teachers' union. A recent survey of students in seven states backs up his impression. Human Rights Watch, an international research and advocacy group, reported last month that 2 million U.S. teenagers were having serious problems in school because they were taunted with anti-gay slurs.

Young people use these slurs in two different ways, one generally derogatory and one referring insultingly to sexual orientation. Schools have a hard time policing either use.

Laura Sessions Stepp is a staff writer for the *Washington Post.*

Taunts and slurs, particularly the words "fag" and "faggot," were cited in more than half of the publicized schoolyard shootings of the last three years, according to Newberry. Columbine shooters Eric Harris and Dylan Klebold were called fags. So was Andy Williams, who sprayed a San Diego high school with gunfire [in 2001], killing two people.

Anti-gay language first appears on elementary school playgrounds. "Kids at our school say, 'That kid is sooo gay,'" said Julia Pernick, a classmate of Emmett's in fourth grade at Chevy Chase Elementary. "They think it means stupid or unusual or strange."

The insults multiply in the emotionally precarious years of early adolescence. "If you're too short, too tall, too fat, too skinny, you get targeted in middle school," said David Mumaugh, now a junior at Walter Johnson High School in Bethesda. "Kids sign their yearbooks, 'See you next year, fag.'"

Sarah Rothe, an eighth-grader at Lake Braddock Middle School in Burke, [Virginia,] said such words "are as common as the word 'like'" at her school. Classmate Christina Jagodnick said "there's a big difference" between anti-gay slurs and other derogatory terms. "If we were to say other words which we all know are wrong," she said, "someone would stop us."

At Lake Braddock this year, according to students, a boy was targeted by classmates who glued his locker shut, writing the word "gay" on the outside. No one knew the boy's sexual orientation, but the bullies called him names until, recently, he transferred to another school. The school would not comment on the situation.

Gay teens are reluctant to discuss personal harassment on the record for fear of attracting more. But when they're offered anonymity, they won't stop talking.

A junior at Magruder High School in Rockville, [Maryland,] said: "I have a lot of friends who say, 'Oh, that's so gay.' They don't associate it with homosexuality. You could plant that word in the dictionary for 'stupid.' Do I face a whole life of this?"

At Herndon High School in Herndon, [Virginia,] a junior said, "I was walking with a friend down the hall and this kid yells, 'Faggot.' How am I supposed to defend who I am?"

When straight students are bullied, they usually can count on an adult coming to their aid, counselors say. Gays don't have that assurance. According to several surveys, four out of five gay and lesbian students say they don't know one supportive adult at school.

"Teachers are aware they may offend someone if they speak about homosexuality in anything other than negative terms," said Deborah Roffman, who teaches sex education in the Baltimore and Washington areas. "They don't know how to cross that street safely, so they don't even step off the curb."

A LONELY CAMPAIGN

Jerry Newberry and other educators suggest that anti-gay insults are increasing partly because gay youths and their supporters have become more assertive in trying to stop them. Justen Deal, 16, has fought such a campaign alone.

A cherubic-looking blond kid from south of Charleston, W.Va., Justen heard anti-gay words from the time he could talk, even used them himself on occasion. But by the age of 12, when he first suspected he was gay, "they made my skin crawl," he said.

Unlike children in other minority groups, he had no natural support group to comfort him. His parents had relinquished custody of him to his paternal grandmother, Patty Deal, when he was born, and her only knowledge of homosexuals was what she had seen on the TV comedy "Ellen."

She did her best once she found out in his eighth-grade year that he was gay. He had written a letter to his school counselor that Patty Deal read. She immediately sought psychiatric help for him, took him to a hospital on the night he overdosed on antidepressants, [and] enrolled him in a new middle school in Boone County.

Neither she nor Justen knows how, but rumors started flying at Sherman Junior High. "I was asked eight times a day if I was gay," Justen remembered. "I'd say no, or not say anything. That year is when I learned for sure that the things you hear about words not hurting is a fairy tale."

Justen thought he'd be safe from gay-bashing once he reached Sherman Senior High. He knew principal Theresa Lonker, a tough-looking administrator who sends students to detention for cursing. When she told Justen, "We'll look out for you," she seemed to mean it.

But she couldn't be everywhere. Name-calling started slowly in his freshman year and picked up this year, according to Justen's friend Lindsey Light. Fed up this past spring, Justen tried to do something about language in a very visible way.

He drafted a new harassment policy for Sherman High to include sexual orientation and left it on Lonker's desk. He lobbied the county school superintendent, Steve Pauley, to rewrite the county's harassment policy.

He visited West Virginia Gov. Robert Wise's office asking the governor to convene a task force to investigate harassment. He testified before the legislature on an amendment to the state's hate crime bill that would have included protection based on sexual orientation. His comments made both Charleston newspapers, including the front page of the *Daily Mail*.

Some of his classmates were not exactly thrilled with the attention. They threw coins and paper wads at him on a school bus during a field trip and also one afternoon in a science class. "Everyone [in the class] heard me tell them to stop, but the teacher was in his own little world," Justen said.

The science teacher, Robert Britton, said he didn't realize at the time there was any harassment going on. "I heard [Justen] say something about stuff being thrown at him but I thought he was just talking about words," Britton said.

Justen's one-person language crusade was rebuffed at every turn. Principal Lonker said she never saw the recommendation for changing the school's harassment policy. Superintendent Pauley said he was reluctant to single out gay students for special mention. Gov. Wise's office de-

PERSONAL ACCOUNT

An Opportunity to Get Even

When I was a freshman in high school, my parents sent me to a private school. I got harassed a lot by a few of the sophomore guys there because I wore pants with the uniform (instead of the pleated mini-skirts), I didn't wear makeup, and probably most important, I would not date any of them (and couldn't give a reason for that). Most of this harassment was anti-gay slurs with specific references to me on the bathroom walls. One of the guys often yelled comments such as "Hey Dyke, I got what you need right here" while grabbing his crotch. My name was written on many of the bathroom stalls (both male and female), with my sexual orientation, and a rhyme about a gang bang.

After about six weeks of this, I confided in my soccer coach. I told her about the harassment and came out to her. I don't know what I expected, but I did not expect any positive reaction. She told me she was glad I came out to her, and she promised to keep my confidentiality. She also offered me an opportunity to get back at the three guys who were harassing me the most. She told me that this was my battle and that I was going to have to learn how to fight.

She knew that the three guys were part of the boys' soccer team, and made arrangements so that, as part of the homecoming festivities, our soccer team would play theirs. By doing this she gave me the opportunity to "show them up" and make them look bad in front of the school. I did my best to accomplish that. For example, every time any of them came near me, I would run into them or trip them. My goal was to embarrass them in front of the school. It did not look good for the guys because a "dyke" challenged and defeated the "jocks."

What my soccer coach did for me meant a lot. First, she was literally the only person I was out to at that time, so she was a source of support. Further, she went out of her way to help me get even with the harassers. Because of what she did for me, the harassment stopped.

Gillian Carroll

---

clined to appoint a task force on the needs of gay students. The legislature voted against adding sexual orientation to its anti-harassment statute. By mid-April, Justen, feeling defeated, decided to change what he could: his school.

He transferred to Huntington High, about 90 miles north. The school has a sizable population of openly gay students, and friends found a gay couple with whom he could live.

On his last day at Sherman High, his grandmother waited for him in her blue Chevy Impala. She appeared both nervous and sad.

"I've always taught Justen to tell the truth," she said. "I reckon he just listened too good. I knew he'd leave one day—I just didn't know it would be so soon."

Justen didn't want to leave his grandma. But despite Lonker's efforts to keep him safe at school, he said, he didn't *feel* safe and thus had a hard time keeping his mind on equations and Civil War battles. His pals had told him to shrug off the verbal digs, but he could not.

"My friends don't understand that every time I hear the word 'fag' it really hurts," he said. "It reminds me that I'm so far away from what kids see as normal."

Walking out of Sherman on that soggy Tuesday, buoyed by the hugs of several students and his principal, he said, "It was a good day. I only heard the word 'faggot' four times."

DISCUSSION QUESTIONS

1. Were antigay insults common among students in the secondary schools you attended? Were racist insults also present? If so, what was the response of parents, teachers, and administrators to the behavior?

2. What would you recommend school administrators do to eliminate antigay insults in the schools?

For Children of Gays, Marriage Brings Joy

Patricia Leigh Brown

San Francisco, March 18—On a recent rainy Sunday morning, Gabriel Damast had planned to laze around the house, watching cartoons and eating French toast. Instead, he snapped his favorite chain-mail key chain to his belt loop, grabbed his MP3 player and headed to City Hall to watch his two moms, Fredda Damast and Birch Early, marry.

"It was so cool," said Gabriel, 13, who served as the ringbearer, after standing in line overnight with his parents. "I always accepted that 'Yeah, they're my moms,' but they were actually getting married. I felt thick inside with happiness. Just thick."

The explosion of same-sex wedding ceremonies here and around the country has catalyzed a national debate over gay marriage. As the legal and rhetorical battles rage, . . . one group is watching with more than casual interest: the children of same-sex couples. . . .

But even if gay marriage goes away, gay parents will go on living de facto married lives, rearing children from past heterosexual marriages or forming families through adoption, foster care or sperm or egg donation. For the children of these families, who know their parents as car-poolers, class mother, soccer coaches and Scout leaders, the recent marriages have been at once historic and deeply personal. Some use the Word "we" to describe marrying.

"Before it was, 'Oh, your parents are just partners,' " said Max Blachman, the 13-year-old son of lesbian parents in Berkeley. "Now, they're spouses. So it's a bigger way of thinking about them."

The 2000 census reported that 594,000 households in the United States were headed by same-sex partners, a figure considered by some experts to be conservative. Of those, about 33 percent of lesbian couples reported having children 18 years old or under, while 22 percent of male couples did.

There are no reliable comparisons to the 1990 census, but "it's very clear that gay fatherhood has risen significantly over the past 10 years," said Judith Stacey, a sociology professor at the Center for the Study of Gender and Sexuality at New York University.

In a sense, Alex Morris, a precocious 11-year-old who has dreams of becoming president, has an embarrassment of riches—two sets of doting parents. His biological mother, Paula Morris, 43, just married her partner of 16 years, Cory Pohley, 44. The pregnancy was planned cooperatively with their friend Tony Humber, 45, Alex's father, who lives with Harvey Yaw, 47, his partner of 23 years. They all share responsibilities for Alex, who travels between the houses every few days. They sometimes vacation together.

Speaking of his mothers' marriage, Alex said: "It is something I always wanted. I've always been around people saying, 'Oh, my parents' anniversary is this week.' It's always been the sight of two parents, married, with rings. And knowing I'd probably never experience it ever."

That changed in the City Hall rotunda as his mothers exchanged vow. "The atmosphere was just springing with life," Alex recalled. "I just couldn't hold myself in. It was oh my god oh my god oh my god. I felt so happy I wanted to scream."

The perception of the legitimacy of their relationship, Ms. Morris said, will be important to their son, who switched schools recently, in part because he had trouble making friends. Alex chalks up some of his difficulties to the fear of being teased about his family situation.

"I shut up like a clam," he said. "If I told someone about it they'd laugh me out of the next dimension."

He has felt less alone, he said, since being put in touch with Colage (Children of Lesbians and Gays Everywhere), a national support and advocacy group for children of lesbian, gay, bisexual and transgender parents, in San Francisco. The wedding was an even more important milestone.

Patricia Leigh Brown writes for *The New York Times.*

"Politically and officially, everybody now knows it's true—they're together," Alex said of his moms. "It's something I felt I needed to experience. I think people who think it's terrible have no heart whatsoever."

Recently, Jaclyn Mullins, 13, an eighth grader in suburban Dublin, east of San Francisco, had dreaded going to current-events class. She is one of three children adopted by Dianna Gewing-Mullins, 39, and Rudi Gewing-Mullins, 38, who recently married. They also have a biological daughter.

When the subject of same-sex marriage comes up in class, "I hear a lot of rude comments like, 'Eew, that's disgusting,' Jaclyn said "A lot of kids say, 'That's really gross.'" She says that she has never confided in classmates about her family and that she sits there silently.

"I wish they'd stop," she said, her eyes looking at the floor.

Studies show that children of gay and lesbian parents are developmentally similar to those with heterosexual parents, said Charlotte J. Patterson, a professor of psychology at the University of Virginia who has studied gay and lesbian families. In general, Professor Patterson noted, parenthood for gay and lesbian couples is a conscious choice, but there are as yet no adequate studies measuring stress levels in their children.

Like members of other minorities, children of gay and lesbian parents have to negotiate social and economic differences, which can be "big emotional freight," Professor Patterson said, adding, "Knowing your parents have made a commitment to stay together and take care of you forever makes children feel more secure."

Parke Humphrey-Keever, 21, a junior at Portland State University in Oregon, has witnessed two recent weddings of his mothers—the first, in Canada, the second in San Francisco. When Mr. Humphrey-Keever was 10, his mothers had a commitment ceremony in which they gave him an earring that matched their rings. They have been together 19 years.

In elementary school, Mr. Humphrey-Keever recalled, only slightly in jest, "they had Diversity Day pretty much because of my family."

In middle school, "I didn't really make it known I had two moms," he said. "The other kids preached acceptance, but you could hear in the halls it wasn't happening. I just kind of skirted it with white lies."

Now that he is older, he has had time to reflect.

"I'm not gay," Mr. Humphrey-Keever said. "I'm a fiscally conservative Democrat. I've had a really stable household. I've had two excellent role models with a strong work ethic. I've seen two people who have loved each other."

Along with other children of same-sex couples, he is aware that their parents' marriages are built on tenuous legal ground.

"I don't think they can take it away," said Alex Morris, mulling over a possible constitutional amendment while sitting in his empty sixth-grade classroom with his parents. "Maybe they can go into the Hall of Marriages and rip up the papers. But emotionally, they can never take away the feeling that my parents are married."

DISCUSSION QUESTIONS

1. Do you think that marriage affects the children of lesbian or gay couples differently than it affects the children of heterosexuals?
2. If your parents were gay or lesbian, how do you think that would have affected your behavior in middle school? In high school?

SOCIAL CLASS

All Souls' Night

Michael Patrick MacDonald

I was back in Southie, "the best place in the world," as Ma used to say before the kids died. That's what we call them now, "the kids." Even when we want to say their names, we sometimes get confused about who's dead and who's alive in my family. After so many deaths, Ma just started to call my four brothers "the kids" when we talked about going to see them at the cemetery. But I don't go anymore. They're not at the cemetery; I never could find them there. When I accepted the fact that I couldn't feel them at the graves, I figured it must be because they were in heaven, or the spirit world, or whatever you want to call it. The only things I kept from the funerals were the mass cards that said, "Do not stand at my grave and weep, I am not there, I do not sleep. I am the stars that shine through the night," and so on. I figured that was the best way to look at it. There are seven of us kids still alive, and sometimes I'm not even sure if that's true.

I came back to Southie in the summer of 1994, after everyone in my family had either died or moved to the mountains of Colorado. I'd moved to downtown Boston after Ma left in 1990, and was pulled one night to wander through Southie. I walked from Columbia Point Project, where I was born, to the Old Colony Project where I grew up, in the "Lower End," as we called it. On that August night, after four years of staying away, I walked the streets of my old neighborhood, and finally found the kids. In my memory of that night I can see them clear as day. *They're right here,* I thought, and it was an ecstatic feeling. I cried, and felt alive again myself. I passed by the outskirts of Old Colony, and it

all came back to me—the kids were joined in my mind by so many others I'd last seen in caskets at Jackie O'Brien's Funeral Parlor. They were all here now, all of my neighbors and friends who had died young from violence, drugs, and from the other deadly things we'd been taught didn't happen in Southie.

We thought we were in the best place in the world in this neighborhood, in the all-Irish housing projects where everyone claimed to be Irish even if his name was Spinnoli. We were proud to be from here, as proud as we were to be Irish. We didn't want to own the problems that took the lives of my brothers and of so many others like them: poverty, crime, drugs—those were black things that happen in the ghettos of Roxbury. Southie was Boston's proud Irish neighborhood.

On this night in Southie, the kids were all here once again—I could feel them. The only problem was no one else in the neighborhood could. My old neighbors were going on with their nightly business—wheeling and dealing on the corners, drinking on the stoops, yelling up to windows, looking for a way to get by, or something to fight for. Just like the old days in this small world within a world. It was like a family reunion to me. That's what we considered each other in Southie—family. There was always this feeling that we were protected, as if the whole neighborhood was watching our backs for threats, watching for all the enemies we could never really define. No "outsiders" could mess with us. So we had no reason to leave, and nothing ever to leave for. It was a good feeling to be back in Southie that night, surrounded by my family and neighbors; and I remember hating having to cross over the Broadway Bridge again, having to leave the peninsula neighborhood and go back to my apartment in downtown Boston.

Not long after, I got a call at Citizens for Safety, where I'd been working on antiviolence efforts across Boston since 1990. It was a reporter from *U.S. News & World Report* who was working on an article about what they were calling "the white un-

---

Michael Patrick MacDonald helped launch Boston's successful gun-buyback program; he is the founder of the South Boston Vigil Group and works with survivor families and young people in the antiviolence movement.

derclass." The reporter had found through demographic studies that Southie showed three census tracts with the highest concentration of poor whites in America. The part of Southie he was referring to was the Lower End, my own neighborhood at the bottom of the steep hills of City Point, which was the more middle-class section with nicer views of the harbor. The magazine's findings were based on rates of joblessness and single-parent female-headed households. Nearly three-fourths of the families in the Lower End had no fathers. Eighty-five percent of Old Colony collected welfare. The reporter wasn't telling me anything new—I was just stunned that someone was taking notice. No one had ever seemed to believe me or to care when I told them about the amount of poverty and social problems where I grew up. Liberals were usually the ones working on social problems, and they never seemed to be able to fit urban poor whites into their world view, which tended to see blacks as the persistent dependent and their own white selves as provider. Whatever race guilt they were holding onto, Southie's poor couldn't do a thing for their consciences. After our violent response to court-ordered busing in the 1970s, Southie was labeled as the white racist oppressor. I saw how that label worked to take the blame away from those able to leave the city and drive back to all-white suburban towns at the end of the day.

Outsiders were also used to the image, put out by our own politicians, that we were a working-class and middle-class community with the lowest rates of social problems anywhere, and that we wanted to keep it that way by not letting blacks in with all their problems. Growing up, I felt alone in thinking this attitude was an injustice to all the Southie people I knew who'd been murdered. Then there were all the suicides that no one wanted to talk about. And all the bank robberies and truck hijackings, and the number of addicts walking down Broadway, and the people limping around or in wheelchairs, victims of violence.

The reporter asked me if I knew anyone in Southie he could talk to. He wanted to see if the socioeconomic conditions in the neighborhood had some of the same results evident in the highly concentrated black ghettos of America. I called some people, but most of them didn't want to talk. We were all used to the media writing about us only when something racial happened, ever since the neighborhood had erupted in antibusing riots during the seventies. Senator Billy Bulger, president of the Massachusetts Senate, had always reminded us of how unfair the media was with its attacks on South Boston. He told us never to trust them again. No news was good news. And his brother, neighborhood drug lord James "Whitey" Bulger, had liked it better that way. Whitey probably figured that all the shootings in the nearby black neighborhood of Roxbury, and all the activists willing to talk over there, would keep the media busy. They wouldn't meddle in Southie as long as we weren't as stupid and disorganized as Roxbury's drug dealers. And by the late eighties, murders in Southie had started to be less visible even to us in the community. Word around town was that Whitey didn't allow bodies to be left on the streets anymore; instead, people went missing, and sometimes were found hog-tied out in the suburbs, or washed up on the shores of Dorchester Bay. The ability of our clean-cut gangsters to keep up appearances complemented our own need to deny the truth. Bad guy stuff seemed to happen less often within the protected turf of South Boston. Maybe a few suicides here and there, or maybe an addict "scumbag," but that was the victim's own problem. Must have come from a bad family—nothing to do with "Our Beautiful World," as the *South Boston Tribune* was used to calling it, above pictures of church bazaars, bake sales, christenings, and weddings.

I agreed to take the reporter on a tour through Southie. We stayed in the car, because I was too nervous to walk around with an "outsider" in a suit. It was bad enough that I was driving his rented sports car. People in Southie usually drove big Chevys, or when they were in with "the boys," as we called our revered gangsters, they'd upgrade to an even bigger Caddy or Lincoln Continental. I wore sunglasses and a scally cap, the traditional local cap once favored by hard-working Irish immigrants and longshoremen, and more recently made popular by tough guys and wannabes. I disguised myself so I wouldn't be identified collaborating with an outsider. Everyone knew I was an activist working to reduce violence and crime. But when they saw me on the news, I was usually organizing things over in Roxbury or Dorchester, the black places that my neighbors thanked God they didn't live in. "That stuff would never happen in Southie," a mother in Old Colony once told me. Her own son had been run over by gangsters for selling cocaine on their turf without paying up.

When I rode around the Lower End with the reporter, I pointed to the landmarks of my childhood: St. Augustine's grammar school, where Ma struggled to keep up with tuition payments so we wouldn't be bused to black neighborhoods; the Boys and Girls Club, where I was on the swim team with my brother Kevin; Darius Court, where I played and watched the busing riots; the liquor store with a giant green shamrock painted on it, where Whitey Bulger ran the Southie drug trade; the sidewalk where my sister had crashed from a project rooftop after a fight over drugs; and St. Augustine's Church, down whose front steps I'd helped carry my brothers' heavy caskets. "I miss this place," I said to him. He looked horrified but kept scribbling notes as I went on about this being the best place in the world. "I always had a sense of security here, a sense of belonging that I've never felt anywhere else," I explained. "There was always a feeling that someone would watch your back. Sure, bad things happened to my family, and to so many of my neighbors and friends, but there was never a sense that we were victims. This place was ours, it was all we ever knew, and it was all ours."

Talking to this stranger, driving through the streets of Southie, and saying these things confused me. I thought about how much I'd hated this place when I'd learned that everything I'd just heard myself say about Southie loyalty and pride was a big myth, one that fit well into the schemes of career politicians and their gangster relatives. I thought about how I'd felt betrayed when my brothers ended up among all the other ghosts in our town who were looked up to when they were alive, and shrugged off when they were dead, as punks only asking for trouble.

I didn't know if I loved or hated this place. All those beautiful dreams and nightmares of my life were competing in the narrow littered streets of Old Colony Project. Over there, on my old front stoop at 8 Patterson Way, were the eccentric mothers, throwing their arms around and telling wild stories. Standing on the corners were the natural-born comedians making everyone laugh. Then there were the teenagers wearing their flashy clothes, "pimp" gear, as we called it. And little kids running in packs, having the time of their lives in a world that was all theirs. But I also saw the junkies, the depressed and lonely mothers of people who'd died, the wounded, the drug dealers, and a known murderer accepted by everyone as warmly as they accepted anything else in the familiar landscape. "I'm thinking of moving back," I told the reporter.

I moved back to Southie after four years of working with activists and victims of violence, mostly in Roxbury, Dorchester, and Mattapan, Boston's largely black and Latino neighborhoods. In those neighborhoods I made some of the closest friends of my life, among people who too often knew the pain of losing their loved ones to the injustices of the streets. Families that had experienced the same things as many of my Southie neighbors. The only difference was in the black and Latino neighborhoods, people were saying the words: *poverty, drugs, guns, crime, race, class, corruption.*

Two weeks after I moved back home, every newsstand in town had copies of *U.S. News & World Report* with a picture of me, poster boy for the white underclass, leading the article, and demographic evidence telling just a few of Southie's dirty little secrets. South Boston's Lower End was called the white underclass capital of America, with a report showing all the obvious social problems that usually attend concentrated poverty in urban areas. The two daily papers in Boston wrote stories about the article's findings, with their own interviews of housing project residents, politicians, and a local priest, mostly refuting the findings. A group of women sitting on a stoop in the housing development laughed at the article. "We're not poor," one said. "We shop at Filene's and Jordan Marsh." I remember how I spent my teenage years, on welfare, making sure that I too had the best clothes from those department stores, whether stolen or bought with an entire check from the summer jobs program. I thought I looked rich, until I saw that all the rich kids in the suburbs were wearing tattered rags.

A local politician said that the article in *U.S. News* was a lie, that it was all about the liberal media attacking South Boston's tight-knit traditional community. A local right-wing community activist called the magazine a "liberal rag." And a *Boston Herald* columnist who'd grown up in one of the census tracts wrote that he was better off not knowing he was poor. But he grew up long before the gangsters started opening up shop in liquor stores on the edge of the housing projects, marketing a lucrative cocaine trade to the children of single women with few extended family support structures or men around.

Our priest said that it was terrible to stigmatize Southie children with such findings, labeling them "underclass." I didn't like the term either, but I thought at least now some of the liberal foundations might begin to offer real support for social service agencies struggling to keep up with the needs of Southie families in crisis. People from Southie nonprofits had told me that they were constantly denied funding because their population was not diverse, and probably also because the name "Southie" automatically brings "racists" to mind—the same kind of generalizing that makes all black children "gang bangers" in the minds of bigots. One thing growing up in Southie taught me is that the right wing has no monopoly on bigotry. Eventually, I saw, the priest and other local social service agencies started to refer to the article when they looked for funding or other support.

When I first moved back to Southie, I was always looking over my shoulder. I wasn't sure if anyone minded all the stuff I'd been saying to the press. Instead, people I didn't even know started coming up to me, telling me their own stories. It was as if they felt it was safe to come out, and they wanted to take the tape off their mouths. Before this, I would walk through the main streets of Southie and see so many people who had experienced drug- and crime-related catastrophes, but who didn't connect with others who'd suffered in similar ways, the way I'd been doing with people in Roxbury. It seemed that people wanted to talk after years of silence.

I knew we could do it in Southie once I'd seen how a group of families from Charlestown had banded together when their children were murdered, to break that neighborhood's own infamous code of silence. When I was organizing a citywide gun buyback, getting people in Boston to turn in their working firearms to be destroyed, I met Sandy King and Pam Enos. They had founded the Charlestown After Murder Program. Sandy's son Chris had been murdered in 1986 in front of a hundred people who remained silent. Then in 1991, her son Jay was murdered. Pam's son Adam was murdered in 1992 by the same person who'd murdered Jay. The women organized other mothers of the tight-knit one-square-mile Irish American neighborhood, which had experienced up to six public executions a year, to speak out against the gangsters who controlled the town. They assisted in their neighborhood's gun buyback, which brought in the most guns citywide in 1994 and 1995, and they built close bonds with mothers of murdered children in neighborhoods of color. They pressured law enforcement to pay attention to murder in Charlestown, put a media spotlight on "the town," exposed corruption, and organized an annual vigil to bring neighbors out of isolation and fear. When I went to Charlestown's vigil, I saw mothers' faces that looked so much like Southie faces, pictures of murdered children who looked so much like Southie kids, and I looked around at the symbols of a community so much like our own: shamrocks and claddaghs, symbolizing "friendship, loyalty, and love." Their vigil took place at St. Catherine's Church, just outside Charlestown's mostly Irish housing projects. By the time I moved back to Southie, I knew what we could do with all the people who at last seemed ready to tell their painful stories. . . .

DISCUSSION QUESTIONS

1. How are the Southies MacDonald describes both stigmatized and privileged?
2. How are their lives affected by race and racism?
3. Why would these South Boston residents have been so convinced that they "lived in the best place in the world"?

Stupid Rich Bastards

Laurel Johnson Black

Sunday morning, six o'clock. Dad knocks on my door and in a stage whisper tells me to get up and get going. Trying not to wake up my sister, I crawl out of bed into the chilly Massachusetts air and pull on jeans, a T-shirt, a sweatshirt, and sneakers. Nothing that can't get dirty. This isn't church, but it might as well be, an education full of rituals, its own language, its mystery and rewards, its punishments for falling away.

Every Sunday, each child in turn went with Dad to the flea markets, the yard sales, the junk yards, the little stores with names like "Bob's Salvage," "Junk n Stuff," or "The Treasure House." Even in winter, when the outdoor flea markets closed down and leaves spun with litter in circles in the yards, the salvage stores stood waiting for us, bleak and weathered, paint hanging in little flaps from the concrete-block walls, and our breath hanging in the still, frigid air surrounding the old desks and radio tubes, the file cabinets and chandeliers. In each place the man behind the counter would grab the lapels of his old wool coat and pull them tighter around him, saying how one day he'd like to heat the joint. Dad would tell him about the great buy we just saw at the last place but had to pass up this time and then ask him what was new. And each time the answer was, "In heayah? Nothin's evah new! But I got some stuff I didn't have befoah!" They'd laugh with one another, and I would trace my initials next to someone else's in the dust on the display cabinet.

In summer, we passed by the vendors who hawked T-shirts, socks, perfume, or cheap jewelry and walked to the tables covered with stuff from home, tables full of things that someone had wanted

Laurel Johnson Black is an associate professor of English at Indiana University of Pennsylvania.

and needed for a long time until they needed money more, to pay their rent, fix their car, or feed the next child. Wall hangings, little plaques, beverage glasses with superheroes on them, ashtrays, bedspreads, tricycles, lawn mowers, table lamps, kitchen pots and pans, picture frames, shoes, a spice rack. Always behind one of these tables stood an older man, deeply tanned and showing muscles from long years of hard work, gray-haired and with a cigarette and a hopeful smile, always willing to come down a little on an item, even though it meant a lot to him. Sometimes his wife would also be there, heavy, quiet, holding a styrofoam cup coffee, sitting in a webbed lawn chair set back a little from the table, judging those who would judge the things she had loved and used for so long.

We touched these items carefully, with respect, because we were that child who needed to be fed, because we knew what it felt like to have your things laid on such a table, touched by many hands and turned over and over while the dew burned off and the pavement heated up and people began to move as though through water, their legs lost in the shimmering heat that slipped sticky arms around buyers, sellers, lookers, and dreamers. And the *language* of these people behind the tables, and those who respected them and understood why they were there, filled the air like the smell of French fries from the dirty little restaurant next door and hung in my mind and sifted down into my heart. . . .

Language for me has always been inseparable from what I am, from what and who people are. My house was filled with the language I associate with the working class and the poor, people who haven't the means to keep all the "dirty" parts of life at bay and who see no reason to do so with words. Shouting to each other across the yards in the old mill town where I grew up, my mother and her friends Pat and Barbara kept up their friendship and shared gossip and complaints about their lives. They wove their voices into the fabric of words and life I knew. As we played after school in the stand of woods along the river down behind the factory, we heard our names called for supper. The more time we took to get home to the table, the sharper the tone became and the longer the wonderful string of curses stretched out, echoing off the brick walls.

We talked about whatever had touched us as we sat down to eat—who had stopped up the upstairs toilet, who had fought in the hallway at school, the girl who was stabbed in the head with a fork in the lunchroom, name calling on the bus, whether the home economics teacher was having an affair with the phys. ed. teacher, what my father saw in the house he'd just put a tub in, who we knew who'd been arrested. Bodily functions, secretions, garbage, crimes and delinquency, who got away with what were as much a part of our language as they were of our lives. They were part of the humor that filled my home. My father rising up from his chair to fart, shouting out in mock seriousness, "'Repoaht from the reah!' the sahgent replied," set us off in hysterics, imitations, and stories of passed gas and the contexts that made them so funny. Swearing was also a pan of our lives—among adults, among kids away from their parents, and in the bad kids' homes, everyone swore fluently before they were eighteen or out of school. "Damn" and "shit" were every other word and so became like "and" and "well" to us as we talked with each other.

I lived in a web of narrative, something I've missed in graduate school. My father was a storyteller and a traveler, would go away for a week or two at a time on "business" of an undetermined nature. When he came back, he didn't bring presents but stories. Only a few years ago did I realize why the tale of Odysseus had seemed so familiar to me in the eighth grade and again as an undergraduate. In the tales told by my father and the men he bartered with, the "stupid rich bastards" almost always "got it" in the end, outwitted by the poor little guy. I learned that the stupid rich bastards always underestimated us, always thought we were as dumb as we were poor, always mistook our silence for ignorance, our shabby clothes and rusted cars for lack of ambition or enterprise. And so they got taken, and sharing stories about winning these small battles made us feel better about losing the war.

My father knew all the regular merchants at the flea markets. As we wandered along the aisles he'd yell over to Tony, a heavy man with thinning black hair patted into an ugly, oily arc across his head, "Hey! Ya fat Guinea! Ya still sellin' the same old junk? Huh? I've seen stuff move fasta in the toilets I unplug!" Tony would wave him off, turning a little away from him and throwing back over his shoulder, "What would you know about merchandise, ya stupid Swede? Huh? Shit for brains!" He'd touch his forehead with his middle finger, grin maliciously, and so would my father. As we worked our way closer to Tony, past the booth with old tools, past the book booth, Dad would ask, "So why haven't the cops bustid ya yet for alla this, Tony? What, you got a captain on ya payroll? This stuff is hot enough to burn ya hands off!" He'd blow on his fingers and wave them in the air, grinning. Tony grinned back at the compliment. "Naah, I buy this legit." He'd widen his eyes and look cherubic. "Really." They'd both laugh.

During the week, my father was a sometimes plumber, sometimes car salesman, sometimes junkman. My mother worked as a cook, a school crossing guard, a McDonald's clerk. It was never enough. I remember one Saturday afternoon in August, my father was melting down old lead pipes. All afternoon he cut the soft pipes into small pieces and fed them into the heat of the kettle, then poured the liquid metal out into the little cupcake-shaped molds he'd set in the dirt of the driveway. Late in the afternoon, the heavy clouds broke and rain began spattering down on his back and shoulders. While I watched from the kitchen he kept working, the rain hissing and turning into steam as it struck the melting lead. Over and over, he reached forward to drop chunks of pipe in to melt, and his arms, then shoulders, then head disappeared in the fog of metal and mist. He became that man to me, the half-man in steam. He was the back I saw sometimes wearily climbing the stairs to sleep for a few hours. He was the chains rattling in the truck as it bounced down the pitted driveway and whined back up late at night as he came home. It wasn't enough. A stack of dunnings and notices littered the end of the old stereo.

I remember when the man from the bank came to repossess our car. I had just broken my foot, and

I hung onto the car door handle while my mother stood next to me talking to the man who wanted to take the car. Her voice was high, and with one hand she opened and dosed the metal clasp on her purse. Finally she opened the car door, pushing me in and sliding in next to me. The man from the bank stepped back as she started the engine, and she rolled up the window as he leaned over to say something to us. She gunned it, careening wildly backward across the yard out into the street, crying. "So this is what we've got," she said. "This is it."

Working poor, we were alternately afraid and ashamed and bold and angry. We prayed to nothing in particular that no one would notice our clothes or that the police wouldn't notice the car didn't have a valid inspection sticker. My mother had to decide between a tank of gas and an insurance payment. She had to decide whether or not we really needed a doctor. We shopped as a group so that if my new dress for the year cost two dollars less than we had thought it would, my sister could get one that cost two dollars more. We didn't say such things out loud, though we thought them all the time. If I ate seconds, maybe I was eating my sister's dress. If Susan was really sick, then maybe I couldn't get new shoes. But if anyone ever said those things, it would all come crashing in. All of it—the idea that working hard would get you some place better, that we were just as good as anyone else—would crash to the floor like some heirloom dish that would never be the same again, even if we could find all the shards.

At some point in my life, when I was very young, it had been decided that I would be the one who went on to college, who earned a lot of money, who pulled my family away from the edge of the pit, and who gave the stupid rich bastards what they had coming to them. I would speak like them but wouldn't be one of them. I would move among them, would spy on them, learn their ways, and explain them to my own people—a guerrilla fighter for the poor. My father had visions of litigation dancing in his head, his daughter in a suit, verbally slapping the hell out of some rich asshole in a courtroom.

As I was growing up, the most important people I knew, the ones I most respected, were my teachers. I wanted to be like them. They had made the supreme sacrifice, had gone away and succeeded, but had chosen to come back to help us. They drove cars I could imagine appearing occasionally in my father's lot. They wore scuffed shoes and shopped at K-Mart. They didn't belong to a country club, didn't refuse to teach us because we were poor, didn't treat us with pity or condescension. They often worked year round, teaching summer school or even, as with my history teacher, driving a beer truck from June through August.

They were the only people I knew and trusted who might be able to teach me to speak like and understand the stupid rich bastards who held our lives in their hands and squeezed us until we couldn't breathe: doctors who refused to treat us without money up front; lawyers who wrote short, thick, nasty letters for credit companies; insurance agents who talked in circles and held up payment; loan officers who disappeared into the backs of banks and didn't look at us when they told us we were too much of a risk; police and town selectmen who told us to get rid of our cars and clean up our disgraceful yards and lives—all the people who seemed always to be angry that they had to deal with us in any way. My teachers moved, I thought, with ease between my world and this other world. I hoped they would help me do the same.

My teachers tried to bridge the gap with speech. "In other words," they said, looking from the text to us, "what they're saying is . . ." They tried to bridge the gap with their bodies, one hand pointing to the board, the other hand stretched out palm up, fingers trying to tug words from mouths contorted with the effort to find the right speech. We were their college-bound students, the ones who might leave, might be them again, might even do better. They were like our parents in their desire to have us succeed, but they had skills and knowledge that counted to the white-shirted men who sat behind the glass windows at the savings and loan, to the woman who handled forms for free butter, cheese, and rice.

I wanted to be like my teachers, but I was afraid of standing up before a classroom filled with students like the ones who laughed in the back of the classroom. The only writing these students did was carving names and sexual slurs or boasts on their desks, and their dreams, I imagined, were of lives like they already knew. I was afraid, too, that when I had become like these teachers I admired so much, I would still drive down the main street of a rotting industrial town and go into the 7-Eleven and somehow I would be no different than I was now. The very ones I admired most I also most suspected: if my teachers were such successes, why were they back here? Why did they make so little money? Drive those cars? I was afraid I would have nothing to say or show to the students who sat in the back, afraid that if they actually asked what I only thought—"So what?"—would have no answer. . . .

I decided on three colleges, all small, private ones because I was afraid of the throngs of students in the brochures for the state schools. Some of the schools had said they were "teaching institutions"; I avoided those too, believing that I would have to become a teacher if I went there. I was going to be a lawyer, was going to fulfill my father's vision. I was going to go where the kids of lawyers went. I filled out forms largely on my own, knowing that my parents didn't understand the questions and would be embarrassed at not being able to help. I took all the standardized tests and did only okay, confused by analogies of bulls and bears (I thought they referred to constellations, not the stock market) and questions about kinds of sailing boats.

When my first-choice college sent me a letter telling me I was on their waiting list, my mother hugged me and told me how proud she was. My father asked me how long I'd have to wait and if I'd work in the meantime. My mother thought that merely making the waiting list was an achievement, something she could brag about to Pat and Barbara and the mailman, while my father thought that there was only a limited number of spaces in colleges all over the country and each student waited in turn to get in. I went upstairs and cried for hours.

When I came back down for supper, my mother had fixed a cake in celebration.

I was in my first English class at my second-choice school, never having made it off the waiting list at the first one. I'd never visited this college and knew little about it. I hadn't gone to orientation, begging off because of work. Actually, I had begun to look at those smiling catalogue faces and bodies and then to look at myself. I had crooked teeth. I wore makeup. I wasn't tanned and lithe from summers of tennis and sailing. I wore old jeans patched at the thighs and ragged around the cuffs. I wore T-shirts and work boots, not clothing from L. L. Bean's. I read statements from the happy students, moving my lips and trying to make the words sound like they could be mine, but I realized that it was wrong, that I was wrong. What could I say to all these people? What could they say to me? And what people did I belong to? . . .

Now I was here, dropped off by my sister and brother, who had turned the car around and headed for home after dumping off my box and bag. My roommate was crying because she couldn't fit all her Pendleton wools in her closet and drawers and had taken over some of mine. Her father, a successful lawyer, sized up the situation, watching me sit in silence in my flannel shirt and unfashionable jeans. "What should we call you?" he asked politely. I thought for a moment. "Johnson." He laughed delightedly. "Johnson? That's great! Sue, this'll be good for you," he chortled as he led his sniffling daughter and perfectly coiffed wife out to get lunch.

Now I was being asked to write editorials, but I didn't know what one was. My family had always bought the newspaper with the big photos in it, and the little local weekly had columns about who'd been arrested and what stores had gone out of business. I didn't understand the articles I had to read in order to write my editorials. I summarized what I'd read in two major paragraphs and turned it in, over and over, week after week. I got a B each time, no comments.

In French government class, students talked excitedly about their travels abroad. I felt the chip on my shoulder getting heavier and heavier. I'd been through all of New England; they'd been to France. Big fucking deal. Lions, Lee-ons, Lyons, it's all the same. Unless someone laughs at you for not knowing how to say what everyone else can not only say but describe from personal experience. Poetry class. I describe in a long narrative poem what things I see around my neighborhood. The teacher gushes over it. It reminds him of T. S. Eliot, he says, and when I say, "Who's that?" he is astounded. He decides he has a diamond in the rough; he calls me a lump of coal with lots of potential. (Later, he asks me if I want to sleep with him.)

I understand my students where I now teach. I understand their fear of poverty, of sliding backwards, of not being as successful as their very successful parents. They recoil in disgust and loathing from the poor, from the working class, and that, too, is familiar to me. They insist that if we all just try hard enough, everyone can succeed. But until then, they don't want to live with those who haven't really made it, who haven't tried. I understand how deep and visceral that fear of failure is. It keeps them in college. . . .

In the dormitories at night the girls gathered into groups in the lounges or on the hallway floors and told stories about their lives. I was silent, stricken dumb with fear. What would I tell them when my turn came? The truth? A lie? But I needn't have worried. My turn never came. I don't know whether it was out of compassion or snobbishness, but no one ever asked me about my family, my home, my friends, even my major or my hoped-for career. And as much as I hated myself for being ashamed of my life, I hated the girls more for knowing it. In my conferences with teachers I sat mute, nodding weakly when it seemed called for, when their voices rose as if in a question. Whatever they suggested was right. In lectures, I took notes furiously, narrative notes, full sentences, trying to get the exact words spoken by the teacher. I knew if I took down just a word here and there I would have to fill in the gaps with my own words, and those words were horribly wrong. I was horribly wrong.

Maybe my mother knew. She's dead now and I never asked her. But she wrote me letters every now and then, and not once did she say she'd like me back. Not once did she explicitly give me the option of returning. After one letter in which I came close to admitting my despair, she wrote back, "We love you and we're proud of you. Don't show your face in the door until you're supposed to."

I had gotten an F+ on an English paper. On the bottom of the last page, Dr. B. had written, "Come and see me about this." I was now a second-semester sophomore and still had not gotten an A in my major, English; in fact, I had barely survived the drinking and class cutting of my first year. My parents had never seen my grade report, only knew that I was allowed to come back a second year, more reason for pride. I had learned to buy my classmates' thrown-away clothes at the local thrift store, and if I kept my mouth shut I could pass as one of them in most of my classes. I stopped wearing makeup, even stopped sitting in the groups in the dorms. Instead, I worked in the library on Friday nights and Saturday mornings, which gave me an excuse (I imagined one day I would need one) for never going out and spending money with anyone on weekends. Now, though, I had to hide from teachers, the people I had once wanted so much to be like.

I went to Dr. B.'s office about one minute before his office hours were over. I made sure the secretary saw me and that I had a piece of paper to write a note like: "Stopped by to talk about my paper. I'll catch you some other time." I inched my way down the hall toward his door, reading the numbers so I could pretend I had missed him because I had gotten lost.

Dr. B. was still in his office. He welcomed me in, appearing surprised. He pulled his chair over next to mine, took my paper, and began to go over it, line by line, word by word. He peered over his little glasses, sometimes giving his head a violent nod so they would drop down on his chest and he could sit back and watch my reactions to his statements. I couldn't breathe. My chest felt like it was full, but I had no air. I didn't dare blink because my eyes were full of tears. I kept my head bent, my chin in my hand, and stared at my paper.

He sighed. Finally, he said something like, "Look. See this paragraph? This is a good one. There's a good idea in here. That's your idea. But it's not phrased well. Listen to it phrased this way." And he reread my idea in words that sounded like all my professors. Words that could have kept a stupid rich bastard listening. My idea. His words. But they were connected then. For the first rime, I felt like I might make it through. I choked out a thank you, and he looked up, surprised. The conference wasn't over, but I was standing up. I thanked him again, stuffing the paper into my bookbag, and left before the tears came pouring down my face. I didn't know why I was crying, whether it was because I was so stupid that I got an F+ and had to sit there and make a nice man frustrated or because I felt that I could take that one paragraph and begin again, begin learning how to speak about what I thought and felt to people who weren't like me. Stupidity and relief. They've dogged me ever since. . . .

My parents (and in some ways, my whole family) never got over my defection from law. I tried to soften the blow by going into archeology; while it paid little, it was at least exotic and held out the hope of discovering some kind of lost treasure—imagine, money without working! But it was reconstructing lives and words, not ancient cultures but my own culture, that I kept being drawn to. I have come through poetry, sales, admissions, and finally composition, where first-year students begin to learn how their words hurt and heal, probe and hide, reshape, connect, embrace, and gag. It is a field that feels like work, where the texts are of a home and life so close to the world that the arguments mean something. They are like "sista," not "college."

No one in my family has ever read what I write. No one has visited my office or my classroom. I tell my students about my family, though; I talk to them in my language to show them there are many ways to say things. When we share our writing, I share a letter to home, full of swear words, little jokes, scatological humor, assertions that will be accepted without evidence solely because my sister and I "know" what stupid rich bastards are like and what they will say and do. And then we look at an essay

I've written and then a poem, all dealing with my life, with words. They begin to feel their own words working in different ways, different contexts, begin to value the phrases and words that make them one thing and understand that these same words make it hard to be another thing. For most of my students, these exercises are often just an interesting diversion from reading literature. Some of them write in their journals of their relief. They, too, are first-generation college students, working class, afraid and silent. They appear at my door, ready to talk, knowing that I have been there and do not entirely want to leave.

When I work with my colleagues, with "real" faculty, I say little. I rehearse what I will say if I can predict the course of a meeting, and I miss some of what is going on while I hold my speech in my head, waiting for the opening in which I will speak like them long enough to fool them into thinking I *am* one of them. I am and I am not. My father's dream of how I would live and move between two worlds, two ways of speaking and knowing, haunts me. I used to sit on the school bus on the way home from high school and look around at my classmates and wonder who would still be in my town in twenty years, who would go on, get out, succeed in ways that no one dreamed of. I used to think I would be one of those. Now I sometimes sit in meetings and classrooms and wonder who else would like to cut the shit and say what they feel. I feel suspended, dangling. If I put my toe down at any point, I might root there. I cannot move among the rich, the condescending, the ones who can turn me into an object of study with a glance or word, cannot speak like them, live in a house like them, learn their ways, and share them with my family without being disloyal to someone. I thought learning would make it easier for me to protect and defend my family, myself, but the more I learn the harder it is to passionately defend anything.

I am seeking a way to keep the language of the working class in academia, not just in my office with my working-class office mate, to nurture its own kind of vitality and rawness and directness, its

That Moment of Visibility

I never realized how much my working-class background and beliefs played a role in my education. My family, friends, and neighbors never placed much importance on college. Instead, we were strongly encouraged to find work immediately after high school so we could support ourselves financially. My sisters and I were encouraged to do secretarial work until we married. There was no particular positive status attached to obtaining a degree except maybe the chance of making a lot of money. In fact, friends who went to college were looked at somewhat suspiciously. Among my reference group, college was often seen as a way to get out of having to work.

No one in my family had ever gone to college. It was not financially feasible and a college environment was equal to the unknown. It really was scary terrain. When I decided to go to a local community college after having worked for five years in a secretarial position, family and friends could not understand my decision. Why would I choose college when I already had a job? I could pay bills, buy what I needed, and I had a savings account. So I started by taking a course a semester—and I barely got through the first course. Although I received a good grade, I felt incredibly isolated, like I was an impostor who did not belong in a classroom. I had no idea how someone in college was supposed to act. I stayed silent, scared, and consciously invisible most of the time. I was not even close to making a commitment to a college education when I signed up for a second course—but because my job payed for it (one of the benefits), I felt I had nothing to lose. I signed up for Introduction to Juvenile Delinquency and midway through, our class received an assignment to do a fifteen-page self-analysis applying some of the theories we were learning. The thought of

consciously revealing myself when I was trying so hard not to look, act, or be different was not something I was willing (or, I think, able at the time) to do. When I discussed the assignment with the people close to me, they agreed that the assignment was too personal and revealing. I decided not to do it and I also decided that college was probably not for me.

I went to see my professor (who was the only woman in her department) to let her know that I was refusing to do the assignment and would not complete the course. We had spoken two or three times outside of class and she knew a little about me. I knew that she was also from a working-class background and had returned to school after working some years. I felt the least I could do was tell her I was quitting the class. When I said that I was unwilling to do the assignment, she stared at me for some time, and then asked me what I would prefer to write about. I was stunned that I was noticed and was being asked what I would like to do. When I had no reply, she asked if I would write a paper on the importance of dissent. All I could think to say was yes. I completed the course successfully and found an ally in my department. I can't overstate the importance of that moment of acknowledgment. It was the first time I felt listened to. It was the moment when you feel safe enough to reveal who you are, the deep breath you can finally take when you figure out that the person you're talking to understands, appreciates, and may even share your identity.

I think of this experience as a turning point for me— when I realized that despite all my conscious efforts to be invisible and to "pass," it was that moment of visibility and acknowledgment that kept me in school.

Rose B. Pascarell

---

tendency to ask "Why?" even as it says "Ah, what the fuck." I would like my colleagues to listen for the narratives embedded in their own writing, to feel the power of that movement forward just as they feel the power of the turning concept, the academic idea. And I would like my colleagues to turn my language over in their mouths with the same respect that my father and I turned over the items on those flea market tables.

DISCUSSION QUESTIONS

1. How does language differ by class status?
2. What forces do you think kept Laurel Johnson Black from giving up her university studies?
3. Even though she is now a professor, Black still feels like an outsider. Why do you think that is the case?

Why Are Droves of Unqualified, Unprepared Kids Getting into Our Top Colleges? Because Their Dads Are Alumni

John Larew

Growing up, she heard a hundred Harvard stories. In high school, she put the college squarely in her sights. But when judgment day came in the winter of 1988, the Harvard admissions guys were frankly unimpressed. Her academic record was solid—not special. Extracurriculars, interview, recommendations? Above average, but not by much. "Nothing really stands out" one admissions officer scribbled on her application folder. Wrote another, "Harvard not really the right place."

At the hyperselective Harvard, where high school valedictorians, National Merit Scholar-finalists, musical prodigies—11,000 ambitious kids in all—are rejected annually, this young woman didn't seem to have much of a chance. Thanks to Harvard's largest affirmative action program, she got in anyway. No, she wasn't poor, black, disabled, Hispanic, native American, or even Aleutian. She got in because her mom went to Harvard.

Folk wisdom at Harvard holds that "Mother Harvard does not coddle her young." She sure treats her grandkids right, though. For more than 40 years, an astounding one-fifth of Harvard's students have received admissions preference because parents attended the school. Today, these overwhelming affluent, white children of alumni—"legacies"—are three times more likely to be accepted to Harvard than high school kids who lack that handsome lineage.

Yalies, don't feel smug: Offspring of the Old Blue are two-and-a-half times more likely to be accepted

than their unconnected peers. Dartmouth this year admitted 57 percent of its legacy applicants, compared to 27 percent of nonlegacies. At the University of Pennsylvania, 66 percent of legacies were admitted last year—thanks in part to an autonomous "office of alumni admissions" that actively lobbies for alumni children before the admissions committee. "One can argue that it's an accident, but it sure doesn't look like an accident," admits Yale Dean of Admissions Worth David.

If the legacies' big edge seems unfair to the tens of thousands who get turned away every year, Ivy League administrators have long defended the innocence of the legacy stat. Children of alumni are just smarter; they come from privileged backgrounds and tend to grow up in homes where parents encourage learning. That's what Harvard Dean of Admissions William Fitzsimmons told the campus newspaper, the *Harvard Crimson,* when it first reported on the legacy preference last year. Departing Harvard President Derek Bok patiently explained that the legacy preference worked only as a "tie-breaking factor" between otherwise equally qualified candidates.

Since Ivy League admissions data is a notoriously classified commodity, when Harvard officials said in previous years that alumni kids were just better, you had to take them at their word. But then federal investigators came along and pried open those top-secret files. The Harvard guys were lying.

This past fall, after two years of study, the U.S. Department of Education's Office for Civil Rights (OCR) found that, far from being more qualified or even equally qualified, the average admitted legacy at Harvard between 1981 and 1988 was significantly *less* qualified than the average admitted nonlegacy. Examining admissions office ratings on academics, extracurriculars, personal qualities, recommendations, and other categories, the OCR concluded that "with the exception of the athletic rating, [admitted] nonlegacies scored better than legacies in *all* areas of comparison."

Exceptionally high admit rates, lowered academic standards, preferential treatment . . . hmmm. These sound like the cries heard in the growing fury over

---

John Larew wrote this article when he was Editor of Harvard's student newspaper, *The Harvard Crimson.*

affirmative action for racial minorities in America's elite universities. Only no one is outraged about legacies.

- In his recent book, *Preferential Policies,* Thomas Sowell argues that doling out special treatment encourages lackluster performance by the favored and resentment from the spurned. His far-ranging study flits from Malaysia to South Africa to American college campuses. Legacies don't merit a word.
- Dinesh D'Souza, in his celebrated jeremiad *Illiberal Education,* blames affirmative action in college admissions for declining academic standards and increasing racial tensions. Lowered standards for minority applicants, he hints, may soon destroy the university as we know it. Lowered standards for legacies? The subject doesn't come up.
- For all his polysyllabic complaints against preferential admissions, William F. Buckley Jr. (Yale '50) has never bothered to note that son Chris (Yale '75) got the benefit of a policy that more than doubled his chance of admission.

With so much silence on the subject, you'd be excused for thinking that in these enlightened times hereditary preferences are few and far between. But you'd be wrong. At most elite universities during the eighties, the legacy was by far the biggest piece of the preferential pie. At Harvard, a legacy is about twice as likely to be admitted as a black or Hispanic student. As sociologists Jerome Karabel and David Karen point out, if alumni children were admitted to Harvard at the same rate as other applicants, their numbers in the class of 1992 would have been reduced by about 200. Instead, those 200 marginally qualified legacies outnumbered all black, Mexican-American, native American, and Puerto Rican enrollees put together. If a few marginally qualified minorities are undermining Harvard's academic standards as much as conservatives charge, think about the damage all those legacies must be doing.

Mind you, colleges have the right to give the occasional preference—to bend the rules for the brilliant oboist or the world-class curler or the guy whose remarkable decency can't be measured by the SAT. (I happened to benefit from a geographical edge: It's easier to get into Harvard from West Virginia than from New England.) And until standardized tests and grade point average perfectly reflect the character, judgment, and drive of a student, tips like these aren't just nice, they're fair. Unfortunately, the extent of the legacy privilege in elite American colleges suggests something more than the occasional tie-breaking tip. Forget meritocracy. When 20 percent of Harvard's student body gets a legacy preference, aristocracy is the word that comes to mind.

A CASTE OF THOUSANDS

If complaining about minority preferences is fashionable in the world of competitive colleges, bitching about legacies is just plain gauche, suggesting an unhealthy resentment of the privileged. But the effects of the legacy trickle down. For every legacy that wins, someone—usually someone less privileged—loses. And higher education is a high-stakes game.

High school graduates earn 59 percent of the income of four-year college graduates. Between high school graduates and alumni of prestigious colleges, the disparity is far greater. A *Fortune* study of American CEOs shows the usual suspects—graduates of Yale, Princeton, and Harvard—leading the list. A recent survey of the Harvard Class of 1940 found that 43 percent were worth more than $1 million. With some understatement, the report concludes, "A picture of highly advantageous circumstances emerges here, does it not, compared with American society as a whole?"

An Ivy League diploma doesn't necessarily mean a fine education. Nor does it guarantee future success. What it *does* represent is a big head start in the rat race—a fact Harvard will be the first to tell you. When I was a freshman, a counselor at the Office of Career Services instructed a group of us to make the Harvard name stand out on our résumés: "Underline it, boldface it, put it in capital letters."

Of course, the existence of the legacy preference in this fierce career competition isn't exactly news. According to historians, it was a direct result of the influx of Jews into the Ivy League during the twenties. Until then, Harvard, Princeton, and Yale had admitted anyone who could pass their entrance exams, but suddenly Jewish kids were outscoring the WASPs. So the schools began to use nonacademic criteria—"character," "solidity," and, eventually, lineage—to justify accepting low-scoring blue bloods over their peers. Yale implemented its legacy preference first, in 1925—spelling it out in a memo four years later: The school would admit "Yale sons of good character and reasonably good record . . . regardless of the number of applicants and the superiority of outside competitors." Harvard and Princeton followed shortly thereafter.

Despite its ignoble origins, the legacy preference has only sporadically come under fire, most notably in 1978's affirmative action decision, *University of California Board of Regents v. Bakke.* In his concurrence, Justice Harris Blackmun observed, "It is somewhat ironic to have us so deeply disturbed over a program where race is an element of consciousness, and yet to be aware of the fact, as we are, that institutions of higher learning . . . have given conceded preferences to the children of alumni."

If people are, in fact, aware of the legacy preference, why has it been spared the scrutiny given other preferential policies? One reason is public ignorance of the scope and scale of those preferences—an ignorance carefully cultivated by America's elite institutions. It's easy to maintain the fiction that your legacies get in strictly on merit as long as your admissions bureaucracy controls all access to student data. Information on Harvard's legacies became publicly available not because of any fit of disclosure by the university, but because a few civil rights types noted that the school had a suspiciously low rate of admission for Asian-Americans, who are statistically stronger than other racial groups in academics.

While the ensuing OCR inquiry found no evidence of illegal racial discrimination by Harvard, it did turn up some embarrassing information about how much weight the "legacy" label gives an otherwise flimsy file. Take these comments scrawled by admissions officers on applicant folders:

- "Double lineage who chose the right parents."
- "Dad's [deleted] connections signify lineage of more than usual weight. That counted into the equation makes this a case which (assuming positive TRs [teacher recommendations] and Alum IV [alumnus interview]) is well worth doing."
- "Lineage is main thing."
- "Not quite strong enough to get the clean tip."
- "Classical case that would be hard to explain to dad."
- "Double lineage but lots of problems."
- "Not a great profile, but just strong enough #'s and grades to get the tip from lineage."
- "Without lineage, there would be little case. With it, we'll keep looking."

In every one of these cases, the applicant was admitted.

Of course, Harvard's not doing anything other schools aren't. The practice of playing favorites with alumni children is nearly universal among private colleges and isn't unheard of at public institutions, either. The rate of admission for Stanford's alumni children is "almost twice the general population," according to a spokesman for the admissions office. Notre Dame reserves 25 percent of each freshman class for legacies. At the University of Virginia, where native Virginians make up two-thirds of each class, alumni children are automatically treated as Virginians even if they live out of state—giving them a whopping competitive edge. The same is true of the University of California at Berkeley. At many schools, Harvard included, all legacy applications are guaranteed a read by the dean of admissions himself—a privilege nonlegacies don't get.

LITTLE WHITE ELIS

Like the Harvard deans, officials at other universities dismiss the statistical disparities by pointing to the superior environmental influences found in the homes of their alums. "I bet that, statistically, [legacy qualifications are] a little above average, but not by much," says Paul Killebrew, associate director of admissions at Dartmouth. "The admitted group [of legacies] would look exactly like the profile of the class."

James Wickenden, a former dean of admissions at Princeton who now runs a college consulting firm, suspects otherwise. Wickenden wrote of "one Ivy League university" where the average combined SAT score of the freshman class was 1,350 out of a possible 1,600, compared to 1,280 for legacies. "At most selective schools, [legacy status] doubles, even trebles the chances of admission," he says. Many colleges even place admitted legacies in a special "Not in Profile" file (along with recruited athletes and some minority students), so that when the school's SAT scores are published, alumni kids won't pull down the average.

How do those kids fare once they're enrolled? No one's telling. Harvard, for one, refuses to keep any records of how alumni children stack up academically against their nonlegacy classmates—perhaps because the last such study, in 1956, showed Harvard sons hogging the bottom of the grade curve.

If the test scores of admitted legacies are a mystery, the reason colleges accept so many is not. They're afraid the alumni parents of rejected children will stop giving to the colleges' unending fundraising campaigns. "Our survival as an institution depends on having support form alumni," says Richard Steele, director of undergraduate admissions at Duke University, "so according advantages to alumni kids is just a given."

In fact, the OCR exonerated Harvard's legacy preference precisely because legacies bring in money. (OCR cited a federal district court ruling that a state university could favor the children of out-of-state alumni because "defendants showed that the alumni provide monetary support for the university.") And there's no question that alumni provide significant support to Harvard: Last year, they raised $20 million for the scholarship fund alone.

In a letter to OCR defending his legacies, Harvard's Fitzsimmons painted a grim picture of a school where the preference did not exist—a place peeved alumni turned their backs on when their kids failed to make the cut. "Without the fundrais-

ing activities of alumni," Fitzsimmons warned darkly, "Harvard could not maintain many of its programs, including needs-blind admissions."

Ignoring, for the moment, the question of how "needs-blind" a system is that admits one-fifth of each class on the assumption that, hey, their parents might give us money, Fitzsimmons's defense doesn't quite ring true. The "Save the Scholarship Fund" line is a variation on the principle of "Firemen First," whereby bureaucrats threatened with a budget cut insist that essential programs rather than executive perks and junkets will be the first to be slashed. Truth be told, there is just about nothing that Harvard, the richest university in the world, could do to jeopardize needs-blind admissions, provided that it placed a high enough priority on them.

But even more unclear is how closely alumni giving is related to the acceptance of alumni kids. "People whose children are denied admission are initially upset," says Wickenden, "and maybe for a year or two their interest in the university wanes. But typically they come back around when they see that what happened was best for the kids." Wickenden has put his money where his mouth is: He rejected two sons of a Princeton trustee involved in a $420 million fundraising project, not to mention the child of a board member who managed the school's $2 billion endowment, all with no apparent ill effect.

Most university administrators would be loath to take such a chance, despite a surprising lack of evidence of the legacy/largess connection. Fitzsimmons admits Harvard knows of no empirical research to support the claim that diminishing legacies would decrease alumni contributions, relying instead on "hundreds, perhaps thousands of conversations with alumni whose sons and daughters applied."

No doubt some of Fitzsimmons's anxiety is founded: It's only natural for alumni to want their kids to have the same privileges they did. But the historical record suggests that alumni are far more tolerant than administrators realize. Admit women and blacks? *Well, we would*, said administrators earlier this century—*but the alumni just won't have it.* Fortunately for American universities, the bulk of those alumni turned out to be less craven than administrators thought they'd be. As more blacks and women enrolled over the past two decades, the funds kept pouring in, reaching an all-time high in the eighties.

Another significant historical lesson can be drawn from the late fifties, when Harvard's selectiveness increased dramatically. As the number of applications soared, the rate of admission for legacies began declining from about 90 percent to its current 43 percent. Administration anxiety rose inversely, but Harvard's fundraising machine has somehow survived. That doesn't mean there's *no* correlation between alumni giving and the legacy preference, obviously; rather, it means that the people who would withhold their money at the loss of the legacy privilege were far outnumbered by other givers. "It takes time to get the message out," explains Fitzsimmons, "but eventually people start responding. We've had to make the case [for democratization] to alumni, and I think that they generally feel good about that."

HEIR CUT

When justice dictates that ordinary kids should have as fair a shot as the children of America's elite, couldn't Harvard and its sister institutions trouble themselves to "get the message out" again? Of course they could. But virtually no one—liberal or conservative—is pushing them to do so.

"There must be no goals or quotas for any special group or category of applicants," reads an advertisement in the right-wing *Dartmouth Review.* "Equal opportunity must be the guiding policy. Males, females, blacks, whites, Native Americans, Hispanics . . . can all be given equal chance to matriculate, survive, and prosper based solely on individual performance."

Noble sentiments from the Ernest Martin Hopkins Institute, an organization of conservative Dartmouth alumni. Reading on, though, we find these "concerned alumni" aren't sacrificing *their* young

to the cause. "Alumni sons and daughters," notes the ad further down, "should receive some special consideration."

Similarly, Harvard's conservative *Salient* has twice in recent years decried the treatment of Asian-Americans in admissions, but it attributes their misfortune to favoritism for blacks and Hispanics. What about legacy university favoritism—a much bigger factor? *Salient* writers have twice endorsed it.

What's most surprising is the indifference of minority activists. With the notable exception of a few vocal Asian-Americans, most have made peace with the preference for well-off whites.

Mecca Nelson, the president of Harvard's Black Students Association, leads rallies for the hiring of more minority faculty. She participated in an illegal sit-in at an administration building in support of Afro-American studies. But when it comes to the policy that Asian-American activist Arthur Hu calls "a 20-percent-white quota," Nelson says, "I don't have any really strong opinions about it. I'm not very clear on the whole legacy issue at all."

Joshua Li, former co-chair of Harvard's Asian-American Association, explains his complacency differently: "We understand that in the future Asian-American students will receive these tips as well."

At America's elite universities, you'd expect a somewhat higher standard of fairness than that—especially when money is the driving force behind the concept. And many Ivy League types *do* advocate for more just and lofty ideals. One of them, as it happens, is Derek Bok. In one of Harvard's annual reports, he warned that the modern university is slowly turning from a truth-seeking enterprise into a money-grubbing corporation—at the expense of the loyalty of its alums. "Such an institution may still evoke pride and respect because of its intellectual achievements," he said rightly. "But the feelings it engenders will not be quite the same as those produced by an institution that is prepared to forgo income, if need be, to preserve values of a nobler kind."

Forgo income to preserve values of a nobler kind—it's an excellent idea. Embrace the preferences for the poor and disadvantaged. Wean alumni from the idea of the legacy edge. And above all, stop the hypocrisy that begrudges the great unwashed a place at Harvard while happily making room for the less qualified sons and daughters of alums.

After 70 years, it won't be easy to wrest the legacy preference away from the alums. But the long-term payoff is as much a matter of message as money. When the sons and daughters of today's college kids fill out *their* applications, the legacy preference should seem not a birthright, but a long-gone relic from the Ivy League's inequitable past.

DISCUSSION QUESTIONS

1. Do you think legacy preferences are unfair? Why or why not? How do you think they compare to minority preferences?
2. John Larew, then editor of the *Harvard Crimson*, was the first to bring the subject of legacy preference to national attention. Since then, these preferences have received a good deal of media attention. Do you think that legacy admissions are now stigmatized admissions like affirmative action admissions?

DISABILITY

READING 39

Public Transit

John Hockenberry

New York was not like Iran.

It was a shock to return to the United States in 1990, where it routinely took an act of God to hail a taxi. There was nothing religious about New York City, even on Christmas Eve. I had taken a cab from midtown to Riverside Church on the west side of Manhattan only to find that my information about a Christmas Eve service there was mistaken. The church was padlocked, which I only discovered after getting out of the cab into the forty-mile-an-hour wind and the twenty-degree weather. I tried all of the doors of the church and found myself alone at close to midnight, without a taxi, on December 24 at 122d Street and Riverside Drive.

I was wearing a wool sports jacket and a heavy scarf, but no outer jacket. There were no cars on the street. Being wrong about the service and having come all the way uptown was more than a little frustrating. I suspected that I was not in the best psychological condition to watch the usual half-

dozen or so New York cabs pass me by and pretend not to see me hailing them. I knew the most important thing was to try and not look like a panhandler. This was always hard. Many times in New York I had hailed a cab only to have the driver hand me a dollar. Once I was so shocked that I looked at the cabbie and said, as though I were correcting his spelling, "No, I give you the money."

"You want a ride?" he said. "Really?"

The worst were the taxis that stopped but had some idea that the wheelchair was going to put itself into the trunk. After you hopped into the backseat, these drivers would look at you as though you were trying to pull a fast one, tricking them into having to get out of their cabs and load something in the trunk that you had been cleverly hiding. Some cabbies would say that I should have brought someone with me to put the chair in, or that it was too heavy for them to lift. My favorite excuse was also the most frequent, "Look, buddy, I can't lift that chair. I have a bad back."

"I never heard of anyone who became paralyzed from lifting wheelchairs," I'd say. My favorite reply never helped. If the drivers would actually load the chair, you could hear them grumbling, throwing it around to get it to fit, and smashing the trunk lid down on it. When we would arrive at our destination, the driver would throw the chair at me like it was a chunk of nuclear waste and hop back behind the wheel. The only thing to do in these situations was to smile, try not to get into a fight, and hope the anger would subside quickly so

---

John Hockenberry is a correspondent for *Dateline NBC*. He has been a broadcast journalist for National Public Radio and *ABC News*, and is the author of *Moving Violations: War Zones, Wheelchairs, and Declarations of Independence*.

you could make it wherever you were going without having a meltdown.

There were some drivers who wouldn't load the chair at all. For these people, at one time, I carried a Swiss army knife. The rule was, if I had to get back out of a cab because a driver wouldn't load my chair, then I would give the driver a reason to get out of his cab shortly after I was gone. I would use the small blade of the knife to puncture a rear tire before the cab drove away, then hail another one. A few blocks ahead, when the first driver had discovered his difficulties, he was generally looking in his trunk for the tire jack when I passed by, waving.

The trouble with this idea was that other people often did not have the same righteous attitude that I did about tire puncturing in Manhattan traffic, and using knives to get freelance revenge in New York City under any circumstances. Most of my friends put me in the same league with subway vigilante Bernhard Goetz, and concluded that I needed serious help. So I had stopped using the Swiss army knife and was without it that Christmas Eve on 122d and Riverside Drive.

The first cab drove toward me and slowed down; the driver stared, then quickly drove by. A second cab approached. I motioned emphatically. I smiled and tried to look as credible as I could. Out in this December wind, I was just another invisible particle of New York misery. The driver of the second cab shook his head as he passed with the lame, catch-all apologetic look New York cabbies use to say, "No way, Mac. Sorry, no way I can take you."

I had one advantage. At least I was white. Black males in New York City have to watch at least as many cabs go by as someone in a wheelchair does before getting a ride. Black male friends of mine say they consciously have to rely on their ritzy trench coats or conservative "Real Job" suits to counter skin color in catching a cab. If I could look more white than crippled, I might not freeze to death on Christmas Eve. I was a psychotic, twentieth-century hit man named Tiny Tim, imagining all sorts of gory ways to knock off a cabbie named Scrooge. The wind was blowing furiously off the Hudson, right up over Riverside Drive.

A third cab drove by. I wondered if I could force a cab to stop by blocking the road. I wished I had a baseball bat. For a period of a few minutes, there was no traffic. I turned and began to roll down Riverside. After a block, I turned around, and there was one more empty cab in the right lane coming toward me. I raised my hand. I was sitting directly under a streetlight. The cabbie clearly saw me, abruptly veered left into the turn lane, and sat there, signaling at the red light.

I rolled over to his cab and knocked on the window. "Can you take a fare?" The driver was pretending I had just landed there from space, but I was freezing and needed a ride, so I tried not to look disgusted. He nodded with all of the enthusiasm of someone with an abscessed tooth, I opened the door and hopped onto the backseat. I folded the chair and asked him to open the trunk of his cab.

"Why you want me to do that?" he said.

"Put the chair in the trunk, please." I was half-sitting in the cab, my legs still outside. The door was open and the wheelchair was folded next to the cab. "No way, man," he said. "I'm not going to do that. It's too damn cold." I was supposed to understand that I would now simply thank him for his trouble, get back in my wheelchair, and wait for another cab.   "Just put the chair in the trunk right now. It's Christmas Eve, pal. Why don't you just pretend to be Santa for five fucking minutes?" His smile vanished. I had crossed a line by being angry. But he also looked relieved, as though now he could refuse me in good conscience. It was all written clearly on his face. "You're crazy, man. I don't have to do nothing for you." I looked at him once more and said, "If you make me get back into this chair, you are going to be very sorry." It was a moment of visceral anger. There was no turning back now. "Go away, man. It's too cold."

I got back into the chair. I placed my backpack with my wallet in it on the back of my chair for safekeeping. I grabbed his door and, with all of my strength, pushed it back on its hinges until I heard a loud snap. It was now jammed open. I rolled over to his passenger window, and two insane jabs of my right fist shattered it. I rolled around to the front of the cab, and with my fist in my white handball glove took out first one, then the other headlight. The light I was bathed in from the front of the cab vanished. The face of the driver could now be seen clearly, illuminated by the dashboard's glow.

I could hear myself screaming at him in a voice that sounded far away. I knew the voice, but the person it belonged to was an intruder in this place. He had nothing to do with this particular cabbie and his stupid, callous insensitivity; rather, he was the overlord to all such incidents that had come before. Whenever the gauntlet was dropped, it was this interior soul, with that screaming voice and those hands, who felt no pain and who surfed down a wave of hatred to settle the score. This soul had done the arithmetic and chosen the weapons. I would have to live with the consequences.

I rolled over to the driver's seat and grabbed the window next to his face. I could see that he was absolutely terrified. It made me want to torture him. I hungered for his fear; I wanted to feel his presumptions of power and physical superiority in my hands as he sank up to his neck in my rage, my fists closed around his throat. I attacked his half-open window. It cracked, and as I hauled my arm back to finish it, I saw large drops of blood on the driver's face. I looked at him closely. He was paralyzed with fear and spattered with blood. There was blood on his window, as well. A voice inside me screamed, "I didn't touch you, motherfucker. You're not bleeding. Don't say that I made you bleed. You fucking bastard. Don't you dare bleed!"

I rolled back from the cab. It was my own blood shooting from my thumb. It gushed over the white leather of my glove: I had busted an artery at the base of my thumb, but I couldn't see it because it was inside the glove. Whatever had sliced my thumb had gone neatly through the leather first, and as I rolled down the street I could hear the cabbie saying behind me, "You're crazy, man, you're fucking crazy." I rolled underneath a street lamp to get a closer look. It was my left hand, and it had several lacerations in addition to the one at the base of my thumb. It must have been the headlight glass. The blood continued to gush. Wind blew it off my fingers in festive red droplets, which landed stiffly on the frozen pavement under the street lamp. Merry Christmas.

Up the street, a police squad car had stopped next to the cab, which still had its right rear door jammed open. I coasted farther down the street to see if I could roll the rest of the way home. With each push of my hand on the wheel rim of my chair, blood squirted out of my glove. I could feel it filled with blood inside. The cops pulled up behind me. "Would you like us to arrest that cabbie? Did he attack you?" All I could think of was the indignity of being attacked by him. I thought about screaming, "That piece of human garbage attacked me? No way. Maybe it was me who attacked him as a public service. Did you donut eaters ever think of that? I could have killed the bastard. I *was* trying to kill him, in fact. I insist that you arrest me for attempted murder right now, or I will sue the NYPD under the Americans with Disabilities Act." I thought better of this speech. Intense pain had returned my mind to practical matters. Spending the night in jail for assaulting a cabbie after bragging about it while bleeding to death seemed like a poor way to cap off an already less than stellar Christmas Eve.

"Everything's fine, officer. I'll just get another taxi." I continued to roll one-handed and dripping down Riverside Drive. The cops went back to talk to the cabbie, who was screaming now. I began to worry that he was going to have me arrested, but the cops drove back again. Once more, the officer asked if I wanted to file a complaint against the cabbie. As more blood dripped off my formerly white glove, the officers suggested that I go to the hospital. They had figured out what had happened. As I started to explain, they told me to get in the squad car. "Let's just say it was an unfortunate accident," one officer said. "I don't think he'll ever stop for someone in a wheelchair again. If we can get you to the emergency room in time, maybe you won't lose your thumb."

I got in the backseat while the cops put the chair in the trunk. Seven blocks away was the emergency room of St. Luke's Hospital. Christmas Eve services at St. Luke's included treatment of a young woman's mild overdose. An elderly man and his worried-looking wife were in a corner of the treatment room. His scared face looked out from beneath a green plastic oxygen mask. A number of men stood around watching CNN on the waiting-room television. A woman had been brought in with fairly suspicious-looking bruises on her face and arms. One arm was broken and being set in a cast. She sat quietly while two men talked about football in loud voices. The forlorn Christmas decorations added to the hopelessness of this little band of unfortunates in the emergency room.

When I arrived, everything stopped. Police officers are always an object of curiosity, signaling the arrival of a shooting victim or something more spectacular. For a Christmas Eve, the gushing artery at the base of my thumb was spectacular enough. The men sitting around the emergency room shook their heads. The overdose patient with the sunken cocaine eyes staggered over to inspect the evening's best carnage. "Where did you get that wheelchair?" She looked around as though she was familiar with all of the wheelchairs in this emergency room from previous visits. "It's my own," I replied. "That's a good idea," she said. "Why didn't I think of that?"

I got nine stitches from a doctor who suggested politely that whatever my complaint with the taxi driver, I was one person on the planet who could ill afford to lose a thumb. The deep laceration was just a few millimeters from the nerve and was just as close to the tendon. Severing either one would have added my thumb to an already ample chorus of numbness and paralysis. The thought of losing the use of my thumb was one thing, but what was really disturbing was the thought of its isolation on my hand, numb in the wrong zone. Trapped on a functional hand, a numb and paralyzed thumb would have no way of communicating with my numb and paralyzed feet. It would be not only paralyzed, it would be in exile: an invader behind enemy lines, stuck across the checkpoint on my chest.

Today, there is a one-inch scar that traces a half circle just to the left of my knuckle. The gloves were a total loss, but they no doubt saved my thumb. Nothing could save my pride, but pride is not always salvageable in New York City. I have taken thousands of cabs, and in each case the business of

loading and unloading delivers some small verdict on human nature. Often it is a verdict I am in no mood to hear, as was the case on that Christmas Eve. At other times, the experience is eerie and sublime. At the very least, there is the possibility that I will make a connection with a person, not just stare at the back of an anonymous head.

In my life, cabbies distinguish themselves by being either very rude and unhelpful or sympathetic and righteous. Mahmoud Abu Holima was one of the latter. It was his freckles I remembered, along with his schoolboy nose and reddish-blond hair, which made his Islamic tirades more memorable. He was not swarthy like other Middle Eastern cabbies. He had a squeaky, raspy voice. He drove like a power tool carving Styrofoam. He used his horn a lot. He made constant references to the idiots he said were all around him.

He was like a lot of other New York cabbies. But out of a sea of midtown yellow, Mahmoud Abu Holima was the one who stopped one afternoon in 1990, and by stopping for me he wanted to make it clear to everyone that he was not stopping for anyone else, especially the people in expensive-looking suits waiting on the same street corner I was. His decision to pick me up was part of some protest Mahmoud delivered to America every day he drove the streets of Manhattan.

His cab seemed to have little to do with transporting people from place to place. It was more like an Islamic institute on wheels. A voice in Arabic blared from his cassette player. His front seat was piled with books in Arabic and more cassettes. Some of the books were dog-eared Korans. There were many uniformly bound blue and green books open, marked, and stacked in cross-referenced chaos, the arcane and passionate academic studies of a Muslim cabbie studying hard to get ahead and lose his day job, interrupting his studies in mid-sentence to pick up a man in a wheelchair.

I took two rides with him. The first time I was going somewhere uptown on Third Avenue. Four cabs had passed me by. He stopped. He put the chair in the trunk and, to make more space there, brought stacks of Arabic books from the trunk into the front seat. He wore a large, knit, dirty-white skullcap and was in constant motion. He seemed lost in the ideas he had been reading about before I got in. At traffic lights, he would read. As he drove, he continually turned away from the windshield to make eye contact with me. His voice careened from conversation to lecture, like his driving. He ignored what was going on around him on the street. He told me he thought my wheelchair was unusually light. He said he knew many boys with no legs who could use such a chair. There were no good wheelchairs in Afghanistan.

"Afghanistan, you know about the war in Afghanistan?" he asked.

I said I knew about it. He said he wasn't talking about the Soviet invasion of Afghanistan and the American efforts to see that the Soviets were defeated. He said that the war was really a religious war. "It is the war for Islam." On a lark, in my broken, rudimentary Arabic, I asked him where he was from. He turned around abruptly and asked, "Where did you learn Arabic?" I told him that I had learned it from living in the Middle East. I apologized for speaking so poorly. He laughed and said that my accent was good, but that non-Muslims in America don't speak Arabic unless they are spies. "Only the Zionists really know how to speak," he said, his voice spitting with hatred.

I thanked him for picking me up. He removed my chair from his trunk, and as I hopped back into it I explained to him that it was difficult sometimes to get a cab in New York. He said that being in America was like being in a war where there are only weapons, no people. "In Islam," he said, "the people are the weapons."

"Why are you here?" I asked him.

"I have kids, family." He smiled once, and the freckles wrinkled on his nose and face, making him look like Tom Sawyer in a Muslim prayer cap. The scowl returned as he drove away. He turned up the cassette. The Arabic voice was still audible a block away.

The second time I saw him, I remembered him and he remembered me. He had no cassettes this time. There were no books in the car, and there was plenty of room in the trunk for my chair this time. Where were all of the books? He said he had finished studying. I asked him about peace in Afghanistan and the fact that Iran and Iraq were no longer at war. He said something about Saddam Hussein I didn't catch, and then he laughed. He seemed less nervous but still had the good-natured intensity I remembered from before. "Are you from Iran?" I asked him, and this time he answered. He told me he was from Egypt. He asked me if I knew about the war in Egypt, and I told him I didn't.

Before he dropped me off, he said that he wanted me to know when we would lose the war against Islam. He said that we won't know when we have lost. "Americans never say anything that's important." He looked out the window. His face did not express hatred as much as disappointment. He shook his head. "It is quiet now."

He ran a red light and parked squarely in the middle of an intersection, stopping traffic to let me out. Cars honked and people yelled as I got into the wheelchair. He scowled at them and laughed. I laughed too. I think I said to him, "*Salaam,*" the Arabic word for peace and good-bye. He said something that sounded like "*Mish Salaam fi Amerika,*" no peace in America. Then he said, "*Sa'at.*" In Arabic, it means difficult. He got into his cab, smiled, and drove away. On February 26, 1993, cabbie, student of Islam, and family man Mahmoud Abu Holima, along with several others, planted a bomb that blew up in the World Trade Center. Today, he is serving a life sentence in a New York prison. . . .

When I returned to New York City from the Middle East in 1990, I lived in Brooklyn, just two blocks from the Carroll Street subway stop on the F train. It was not accessible, and as there appeared to be no plans to make it so, I didn't think much about the station. When I wanted to go into Manhattan, I would take a taxi, or I would roll up Court Street to the walkway entrance to the Brooklyn Bridge and fly into the city on a ribbon of oak planks suspended from the bridge's webs of cable that appeared from my wheelchair to be woven into the sky itself. Looking down, I could see the East River through my wheelchair's spokes. Looking up, I saw the clouds through the spokes of the bridge. It was always an uncommon moment of physical integrity with the city, which ended when I came to rest at the traffic light on Chambers Street, next to city hall.

It was while rolling across the bridge one day that I remembered my promise to Donna, my physical therapist, about how I would one day ride the rapid transit trains in Chicago. Pumping my arms up the incline of the bridge toward Manhattan and then coasting down the other side in 1990, I imagined that I would be able physically to accomplish everything I had theorized about the subway in Chicago in those first days of being a paraplegic back in 1976. In the Middle East, I had climbed many stairways and hauled myself and the chair across many filthy floors on my way to interviews, apartments, and news conferences. I had also lost my fear of humiliation from living and working there. I was even intrigued with the idea of taking the train during the peak of rush hour when the greatest number of people of all kinds would be underground with me.

I would do it just the way I had told Donna back in the rehab hospital. But this time, I would wire myself with a microphone and a miniature cassette machine to record everything that happened along the way. Testing my own theory might make a good commentary for an upcoming National Public Radio program about inaccessibility. Between the Carroll Street station and city hall, there were stairs leading in and out of the stations as well as to transfer from one line to another inside the larger stations. To get to Brooklyn Bridge/City Hall, I had to make two transfers, from the F to the A, then from the A to the 5, a total of nearly 150 stairs.

I rolled up to the Brooklyn Carroll Street stop on the F train carrying a rope and a backpack and wired for sound. Like most of the other people on the train that morning I was on my way to work. Taking the subway was how most people crossed the East River, but it would have been hard to come up with a less practical way, short of swimming, for a paraplegic to cover the same distance. Fortunately, I had the entire morning to kill. I was confident that

I had the strength for it, and unless I ended up on the tracks, I felt sure that I could get out of any predicament I found myself in, but I was prepared for things to be more complicated. As usual, trouble would make the story more interesting.

The Carroll Street subway station has two staircases. One leads to the token booth, where the fare is paid by the turnstiles at the track entrance, the other one goes directly down to the tracks. Near the entrance is a newsstand. As I rolled to the top of the stairs, the man behind the counter watched me closely and the people standing around the newsstand stopped talking. I quickly climbed out of my chair and down onto the top step.

I folded my chair and tied the length of rope around it, attaching the end to my wrist. I moved down to the second step and began to lower the folded chair down the steps to the bottom. It took just a moment. Then, one at a time, I descended the first flight of stairs with my backpack and seat cushion in my lap until I reached a foul-smelling landing below street level. I was on my way. I looked up. The people at the newsstand who had been peering sheepishly down at me looked away. All around me, crowds of commuters with briefcases and headphones walked by, stepping around me without breaking stride. If I had worried about anything associated with this venture, it was that I would just be in the way. I was invisible.

I slid across the floor to the next flight of stairs, and the commuters arriving at the station now came upon me suddenly from around a corner. Still, they expressed no surprise and neatly moved over to form an orderly lane on the side of the landing opposite me as I lowered my chair once again to the bottom of the stairs where the token booth was.

With an elastic cord around my legs to keep them together and more easily moved (an innovation I hadn't thought of back in rehab), I continued down the stairs, two steps at a time, and finally reached the chair at the bottom of the steps. I stood it up, unfolded it, and did a two-armed, from-the-floor lift back onto the seat. My head rose out of the sea of commuter legs, and I took my place in the subway token line.

"You know, you get half price," the tinny voice through the bulletproof glass told me, as though this were compensation for the slight inconvenience of having no ramp or elevator. There, next to his piles of tokens, the operator had a stack of official half-price certificates for disabled users. He seemed thrilled to have a chance to use them. "No, thanks, the tokens are fine." I bought two and rolled through the rickety gate next to the turnstiles and to the head of the next set of stairs. I could hear the trains rumbling below.

I got down on the floor again, and began lowering the chair. I realized that getting the chair back up again was not going to be as simple as this lowering maneuver. Most of my old theory about riding the trains in Chicago had pertained to getting up to the tracks, because the Chicago trains are elevated. Down was going well, as I expected, but up might be more difficult.

Around me walked the stream of oblivious commuters. Underneath their feet, the paper cups and straws and various other bits of refuse they dropped were too soiled by black subway filth to be recognizable as having any connection at all to their world above. Down on the subway floor, they seemed evil, straws that could only have hung from diseased lips, plastic spoons that could never have carried anything edible. Horrid puddles of liquid were swirled with chemical colors, sinister black mirrors in which the bottoms of briefcases sailed safely overhead like rectangular airships. I was freshly showered, with clean white gloves and black jeans, but in the reflection of one of these puddles, I too looked as foul and discarded as the soda straws and crack vials. I looked up at the people walking by, stepping around me, or watching me with their peripheral vision. By virtue of the fact that my body and clothes were in contact with places they feared to touch, they saw and feared me much as they might fear sudden assault by a mugger. I was just like the refuse, irretrievable, present only as a creature dwelling on the rusty edge of a dark drain. By stepping around me as I slid, two steps at a time, down toward the tracks, they created a quarantine space, just for me, where even the air seemed depraved.

I rolled to the platform to wait for the train with the other commuters. I could make eye contact again. Some of the faces betrayed that they had seen me on the stairs by showing relief that I had not been stuck there, or worse, living there. The details they were too afraid to glean back there by pausing to investigate, they were happy to take as a happy ending which got them off the hook. They were curious as long as they didn't have to act on what they had learned. As long as they didn't have to act, they could stare.

I had a speech all prepared for the moment anyone asked if I needed help. I felt a twinge of satisfaction over having made it to the tracks without having to give it. My old theory, concocted while on painkillers in an intensive care unit in Pennsylvania, had predicted that I would make it. I was happy to do it all by myself. Yet I hadn't counted on being completely ignored. New York is such a far cry from the streets of Jerusalem, where Israelis would come right up to ask how much you wanted for your wheelchair, and Arabs would insist on carrying you up a flight of stairs whether you wanted to go or not. . . .

I rolled to the stairs and descended into a corridor crowded with people coming and going. "Are you all right?" A black woman stopped next to my chair. She was pushing a stroller with two seats, one occupied by a little girl, the other empty, presumably for the little boy with her, who was standing next to a larger boy. They all beamed at me, waiting for further orders from Mom.

"I'm going down to the A train," I said. "I think I'll be all right, if I don't get lost."

"You sure you want to go down there?" She sounded as if she was warning me about something. "I know all the elevators from having these kids," she said. "They ain't no elevator on the A train, young man." Her kids looked down at me as if to say, *What can you say to that?* I told her that I knew there was no elevator and that I was just seeing how many stairs there were between Carroll Street and city hall. "I can tell you, they's lots of stairs." As she said good-bye, her oldest boy looked down at me as if he understood exactly what I was doing, and why. "Elevators smell nasty," he said.

I Am Legally Blind

Like approximately 1.1 million people in the United States, I am legally blind, which means that I have some remaining vision. Therefore, I have the option to "come out" as a blind person or "pass" as someone who is fully sighted.

When I am passing, I avoid using my magnifier or my reading glasses, which have an obviously protruded lens and require me to hold items close to my face. By not asking for assistance, I avoid having to tell anyone I am blind. In restaurants, I order without consulting the menu. If I go out walking, I leave my white cane at home. I get on buses and subway trains without asking anyone to identify which line I'm boarding. I purchase items in stores without using my pocket magnifier to read labels or prices. On elevators that have not been adapted to meet ADA (Americans with Disabilities Act of 1990) guidelines of "reasonable accommodation," I take my best shot at hitting the right button. Therefore, I am never quite sure if I am exiting on the floor that I want. I wander through unfamiliar neighborhoods and buildings that are invariably marked with small print signs that are placed above doorways.

There is a price I pay for passing as a sighted person. I give away ten-dollar bills when I mean to pay one dollar. I come home from grocery stores with brands or flavors of items that I don't like or that cost too much. But, the highest cost is freedom: I relinquish my rights to life, liberty and the pursuit of happiness. Here's what happens when I don't ask for help.

When I don't solicit information about buses, trains, and elevators, I waste a lot of time trying to find specific destinations and end up feeling frustrated, angry, and exhausted. When I leave my white cane at home, I give up my right to travel freely because I can't navigate in unfamiliar places or go anywhere at all after dark: I jeopardize my own safety because I trip and fall on curbs, stairs, bumps, and potholes. I surrender my freedom of choice when, in fast food restaurants where the menus are inaccessible to me, I order the same food time and time again. I limit my choice of products when I don't use my visual aids because I have to choose by label color rather than to read the print, and I don't learn about new products, either. If I hadn't identified myself as a blind person at the university, I would have relinquished my right to pursue an education because I would have had no adaptive equipment nor would I have made use of the university's Disability Support Services. I would have failed in school, which is exactly what I did, both in high school and the first time I attended college.

So, why in the world would I ever choose to pass? Because sometimes, I get sick of people's stares, whispers, ignorant comments, and nosy questions. When I ask for directions or for someone to read something to me, I am often responded to as if I am stupid or a child. People often answer my questions in irritated or condescending tones. More times than not, they don't answer verbally, but point at the object instead, which forces me to have to ask again or to explain why I am asking. This happens a lot at checkout stands.

I have had people grab my arm and try to pull me where I don't want to go. Recently, at a concert, my companion and I, with my white cane in hand, were easing our way through the aisle to our seats when a woman jumped up, grabbed my arm, knocking me off balance, then pushed me toward my seat. She didn't even ask if I wanted help. It really was an assault. Indeed, to a mugger or rapist, my white cane identifies me as a potential victim.

When I go shopping, I behave differently than fully sighted people do. I must juggle my list, purse, magnifier, reading glasses as well as the product and shopping basket or cart. I hold items very close to my face to read product labels, tags, and prices. A surprising number of people have asked "What are you looking for?" Sometimes, I reply, "Why do you ask?" I don't like having to explain my methods of adaptation. I have been followed by security guards and even stopped once in a drug store. The guard said that I was "acting suspiciously." He felt pretty bad when I told him that I was trying to see the prices. After that, whenever I went into that store, he was right there asking me if I needed any help finding things. Even though he meant well, the end result was that he still was following me. Ever since that experience, I stay alert to the possibility that I might look suspicious and I stand in open areas when I go into my purse for my glasses. I don't like having to be concerned about this, but I like the idea of being nabbed for shoplifting even less.

These are the paradoxical consequences of passing or coming out. Both cause me trouble, although I have learned the hard way that the more I use adaptive techniques and aids, and the more often I ask for help, the more efficient and independent I become. Thus, when I am "out," I am true to my own needs and desires.

Beth Omansky

Once on the A train, I discovered at the next stop that I had chosen the wrong side of the platform and was going away from Manhattan. If my physical therapist, Donna, could look in on me at this point in my trip, she might be more doubtful about my theory than I was. By taking the wrong train, I had probably doubled the number of stairs I would have to climb.

I wondered if I could find a station not too far out where the platform was between the tracks, so that all I had to do was roll to the other side and catch the inbound train. The subway maps gave no indication of this, and the commuters I attempted to query on the subject simply ignored me or seemed not to understand what I was asking. Another black woman with a large shopping bag and a brown polka-dotted dress was sitting in a seat across the car and volunteered that Franklin Avenue was the station I wanted. "No stairs there," she said.

At this point, every white person I had encountered had ignored me or pretended that I didn't exist, while every black person who had come upon me had offered to help without being asked. I looked at the tape recorder in my jacket to see if it was running. It was awfully noisy in the subway, but if any voices at all were recorded, this radio program was going to be more about race than it was going to be about wheelchair accessibility. It was the first moment that I suspected the two were deeply related in ways I have had many occasions to think about since.

At Franklin Avenue I crossed the tracks and changed direction, feeling for the first time that I was a part of the vast wave of migration in and out of the Manhattan that produced the subway, all the famous bridges, and a major broadcast industry in traffic reporting complete with network rivals and local personalities, who have added words like *rubbernecking* to the language. I rolled across the platform like any other citizen and onto the train with ease. As we pulled away from the station, I thought how much it would truly change my life if there were a way around the stairs, if I could actually board the subway anywhere without having to be Sir Edmund Hillary.

DISCUSSION QUESTIONS

1. As Hockenberry notes, black men and disabled people share the inability to get cabs to pick them up. Why does that experience make them so angry?
2. Is this story limited to New York City?
3. Why do people shun interaction with the disabled?

"Can You See the Rainbow?" The Roots of Denial

Sally French

CHILDHOOD

Some of my earliest memories are of anxious relatives trying to get me to see things. I did not understand why it was so important that I should do so, but was acutely aware of their intense anxiety if I could not. It was aesthetic things like rainbows that bothered them most. They would position me with great precision, tilting my head to precisely the right angle, and then point to the sky saying "Look, there it is; look, there, there . . . THERE!" As far as I was concerned there was nothing there, but if I said as much their anxiety grew even more intense; they would rearrange my position and the whole scenario would be repeated.

In the end, despite a near total lack of color vision and a complete indifference to the rainbow's whereabouts, I would say I could see it. In that way I was able to release the mounting tension and escape to pursue more interesting tasks. It did not take long to learn that in order to avert episodes such as these and to protect the feelings of the people around me, I had to deny my disability.

Sally French is a lecturer in health and social welfare at the Open University in England.

The adults would also get very perturbed if ever I looked "abnormal." Being told to open my eyes and straighten my face, when all I was doing was trying to see, made me feel ugly and separate. Having adults pretend that I could see more than I could, and having to acquiesce in the pretence, was a theme throughout my childhood.

Adults who were not emotionally involved with the issue of whether or not I could see also led me along the path of denial. This was achieved by their tendency to disbelieve me and interpret my behavior as "playing up" when I told them I could not see. Basically they were confused and unable to cope with the ambiguities of partial sight and were not prepared to take instruction on the matter from a mere child. One example of this occurred in the tiny country primary school that I attended. On warm, sunny days we had our lessons outdoors where, because of the strong sunlight, I could not see to read, write or draw. It was only when the two teachers realized I was having similar difficulties eating my dinner that they began to doubt their interpretation that I was a malingerer. On several occasions I was told off by opticians when I failed to discriminate between the different lenses they placed before my eyes. I am not sure whether they really disbelieved me or whether their professional pride was hurt when nothing they could offer seemed to help; whatever it was I rapidly learned to say "better" or "worse," even though all the lenses looked the same.

It was also very difficult to tell the adults, when they had scraped together the money and found the time to take me to the pantomime or wherever, that it was a frustrating and boring experience. I had a strong sense of spoiling other people's fun, just as a sober person among a group of drunken friends may have. As a child, explaining my situation without appearing disagreeable, sullen and rude was so problematic that I usually denied my disability and suffered in silence. All of this taught me from a very early age that, while the adults were working themselves up about whether or not I could see rainbows, my own anxieties must never be shared.

These anxieties were numerous and centered on getting lost, being slow, not managing and, above all, looking stupid and displaying fear. I tried very hard to be "normal," to be anonymous and to merge with the crowd. Beaches were a nightmare; finding my way back from the sea to specific people in the absence of landmarks was almost impossible, yet giving in to panic was too shameful to contemplate. Anticipation of difficulties could cause even greater anguish than the difficulties themselves and was sufficient to ruin whole days. The prospect of outings with lots of sighted children to unfamiliar places was enough to make me physically ill, and with a bewildering mix of remorse and relief, I would stay at home.

Brownie meetings were worrying if any degree of independent movement was allowed; in the summer when we left the confines and safety of our hut to play on the nearby common, the other children would immediately disperse, leaving me alone among the trees, feeling stupid and frightened and wondering what to do next. The adults were always adamant that I should join in, that I should not miss out on the fun, but how much they or the other children noticed my difficulties I do not know; I was never teased or blamed for them, they were simply never discussed, at least not with me. This lack of communication gave me a powerful unspoken message that my disability must be denied.

By denying the reality of my disability I protected myself from the anxiety, disapproval, frustration and disappointment of the adults in my life. Like most children I wanted their acceptance, approval and warmth, and quickly learned that this could best be gained by colluding with their perceptions of my situation. I denied my disability in response to their denial, which was often motivated by a benign attempt to integrate me in a world which they perceived as fixed. My denial of disability was thus not a psychopathological reaction, but a sensible and rational response to the peculiar situation I was in.

Special School

Attending special school at the age of nine was, in many ways, a great relief. Despite the crocodile walks,[1] the bells, the long separations from home, the regimentation and the physical punishment, it was an enormous joy to be with other partially sighted children and to be in an environment where limited sight was simply not an issue. I discovered that many other children shared my world and, despite the harshness of institutional life, I felt relaxed, made lots of friends, became more confident and thrived socially. For the first time in my life I was a standard product and it felt very good. The sighted adults who looked after us were few in number with purely custodial roles, and although they seemed to be in a permanent state of anger, provided we stayed out of trouble we were basically ignored. We lived peer-orientated, confined and unchallenging lives where lack of sight rarely as much as entered our heads.

Although the reality of our disabilities was not openly denied in this situation, the only thing guaranteed to really enthuse the staff was the slightest glimmer of hope that our sight could be improved. Contact lenses were an innovation at this time, and children who had previously been virtually ignored were nurtured, encouraged and congratulated, as they learned to cope with them, and were told how good they looked without their glasses on. After I had been at the school for about a year, I was selected as one of the guinea pigs for the experimental "telescopic lenses" which were designed, at least in part, to preserve our postures (with which there was obsessive concern) by enabling us to read and write from a greater distance. For most of us they did not work.

I remember being photographed wearing the lenses by an American man whom I perceived to be very important. First of all he made me knit while wearing them, with the knitting held right down on my lap. This was easy as I could in any case knit without looking. He was unduly excited and enthusiastic and told me how much the lenses were helping. I knew he was wrong. Then he asked me to read, but this changed his mood completely; he became tense, and before taking the photograph he pushed the book, which was a couple of inches from my face, quite roughly to my knees. Although I knew he had cheated and that what he had done

was wrong, I still felt culpable for his displeasure and aware that I had failed an important test.

We were forced to use equipment like the telescopic lenses even though it did not help, and sometimes actually made things worse; the behavior of the adults clearly conveyed the message, "You are not acceptable as you are." If we dared to reject the equipment we were reminded of the cost, and asked to reflect on the clever and dedicated people who were tirelessly working for the benefit of ungrateful creatures like ourselves. No heed was ever taken of our own suggestions; my requests to try tinted lenses were always ignored and it was not until I left school that I discovered how helpful they would be.

The only other times that lack of sight became an issue for us at the school were during the rare and clumsy attempts to integrate us with able-bodied children. The worst possible activity, netball,[2] was usually chosen for this. These occasions were invariably embarrassing and humiliating for all concerned and could lead to desperate maneuvers on the part of the adults to deny the reality of our situation— namely that we had insufficient sight to compete. I am reminded of one netball match, with the score around 20/nil, during which we overheard the games mistress[3] of the opposing team anxiously insisting that they let us get some goals. It was a mortifying experience to see the ball fall through the net while they stood idly by. Very occasionally local Brownies would join us for activities in our extensive grounds. We would be paired off with them for a treasure hunt through the woods, searching for milk-bottle tops—the speed at which they found them was really quite amazing. They seemed to know about us, though, and would be very kind and point the "treasure" out, and even let us pick it up ourselves sometimes, but relying on their bounty spoiled the fun and we wished we could just talk to them or play a different game.

Whether the choice of these highly visual activities was a deliberate denial of our disabilities or simply a lack of imagination on the part of the adults, I do not know. Certainly we played such games successfully among ourselves, and as we were never seen in any other context, perhaps it was the latter. It was only on rare occasions such as these that our lack of sight (which had all but been forgotten) and the artificiality of our world became apparent.

As well as denying the reality of their disabilities, disabled children are frequently forced to deny painful feelings associated with their experiences because their parents and other adults simply cannot cope with them. I am reminded of a friend who, at the age of six or seven, was repeatedly promised expensive toys and new dresses provided she did not cry when taken back to school; we knew exactly how we must behave. Protecting the feelings of the adults we cared about became an arduous responsibility which we exercised with care.

Bravery and stoicism were demanded by the institution too; any outward expression of sadness was not merely ridiculed and scorned, it was simply not allowed. Any hint of dejection led to stern reminders that, unlike most children, we were highly privileged to be living in such a splendid house with such fantastic grounds—an honor which was clearly not our due. There was no one to turn to for comfort or support, and any tears which were shed were, of necessity, silent and private. In contrast to this, the institution, normally so indifferent to life outside its gates, was peculiarly concerned about our parents' states of mind. Our letters were meticulously censored to remove any trace of despondency and the initial letter of each term had a compulsory first sentence: "I have settled down at school and am well and happy." Not only were we compelled to deny our disabilities, but also the painful feelings associated with the lifestyles forced upon us because we were disabled.

Such was our isolation at this school that issues of how to behave in the "normal" world were rarely addressed, but at the next special school I attended, which offered a grammar school education and had an entirely different ethos, much attention was paid to this. The headmaster, a strong, resolute pioneer in the education of partially sighted children, appeared to have a genuine belief not only that we were as good as everyone else, but that we were almost certainly better, and he spent his life tirelessly battling with people who did not share his view.

He liked us to regard ourselves as sighted and steered us away from any connection with blindness; for example, although we were free to go out by ourselves to the nearby town and beyond, the use of white canes was never suggested although many of us use them now. He delighted in people who broke new, visually challenging ground, like acceptance at art school or reading degrees in mathematics, and "blind" occupations, like physiotherapy, were rarely encouraged. In many ways his attitudes and behavior were refreshing, yet he placed the onus to achieve and succeed entirely on ourselves; there was never any suggestion that the world could adapt, or that our needs could or should be accommodated. The underlying message was always the same: "Be superhuman and deny your disability."

ADULTHOOD

In adulthood, most of these pressures to deny disability persist, though they become more subtle and harder to perceive. If disabled adults manage to gain control of their lives, which for many is very difficult, these pressures may be easier to resist. This is because situations which pose difficulties, create anxieties or cause boredom can be avoided, or alternatively adequate assistance can be sought; many of the situations I was placed in as a child I now avoid. As adults we are less vulnerable and less dependent on other people, we can more easily comprehend our situation, and our adult status makes the open expression of other people's disapproval, frustration and disbelief less likely. In addition, disabled adults arouse less emotion and misplaced optimism than disabled children, which serves to dilute the insatiable drive of many professionals to cure or "improve" us. Having said this, many of the problems experienced by disabled adults are similar to those experienced by disabled children.

Disabled adults frequently provoke anxiety and embarrassment in others simply by their presence. Although they become very skillful at dealing with this, it is often achieved at great cost to themselves by denying their disabilities and needs. It is not unusual for disabled people to endure boredom or distress to safeguard the feelings of others. They may, for example, sit through lectures without hearing or seeing rather than embarrass the lecturer, or endure being carried rather than demanding an accessible venue. In situations such as these reassuring phrases such as "I'm all right" or "Don't worry about me" become almost automatic.

One of the reasons we react in this way, rather than being assertive about our disabilities, is to avoid the disapproval, rejection and adverse labeling of others, just as we did when we were children. Our reactions are viewed as resulting from our impairments rather than from the ways we have been treated. Thus being "up front" about disability and the needs which emanate from it can easily lead us to be labeled "awkward," "selfish" or "warped." Such labeling is very difficult to endure without becoming guilty, anxious and depressed; it eats away at our confidence, undermining our courage and leading us to deny our disabilities.

Disbelief remains a common response of able-bodied people when we attempt to convey the reality of our disabilities. If, for example, I try to explain my difficulty in coping with new environments, the usual response is, "Don't worry we all get lost" or "It looks as if you're doing fine to me." Or when I try to convey the feelings of isolation associated with not recognizing people or not knowing what is going on around me, the usual response is "You will in time" or "It took me ages too." This type of response renders disabled people "just like everyone else." For those of us disabled from birth or early childhood, where there is no experience of "normality" with which to compare our situation, knowing how different we really are is problematic and it is easy to become confused and to have our confidence undermined when others insist we are just the same.

An example of denial through disbelief occurred when I was studying a statistics component as part of a course in psychology. I could see absolutely nothing of what was going on in the lectures and yet my frequent and articulate requests for help were met with the response that all students panic about statistics and that everything would work out fine in the end. As it happens it did, but only after spending many hours with a private tutor. As people are generally not too concerned about how we "got there," our successes serve to reinforce the erroneous assumption that we really are "just like everyone else." When I finally passed the examination, the lecturer concerned informed me, in a jocular and patronizing way, that my worries had clearly been unfounded! When people deny our disabilities they deny who we really are.

This tendency to disbelieve is exacerbated by the ambiguous nature of impairments such as partial sight. It is very hard for people to grasp that although I appear to manage "normally" in many situations, I need considerable help in others. The knowledge of other people's perceptions of me is sufficiently powerful to alter my behavior in ways which are detrimental to myself; for example, the knowledge that fellow passengers have seen me use a white cane to cross the road, can be enough to deter me from reading a book on the train. A more common strategy among people with limited sight is to manage roads unaided, thereby risking life and limb to avoid being labeled as frauds.

A further reaction, often associated with the belief that we are really no different, is that because our problems are no greater than anyone else's we do not deserve any special treatment or consideration. People who react in this way view us as whining and ungrateful complainers whenever we assert ourselves, explain our disabilities, ask that our needs be met or demand our rights. My most recent and overt experience of this reaction occurred during a visit to Whitehall to discuss the lack of transport for disabled people. Every time I mentioned a problem which disabled people encounter, such as not being able to use the underground system or the buses, I was told in no uncertain terms that many other people have transport problems too; what about old people, poor people, people who live in remote areas? What was so special about disabled people, and was not a lot being done for them anyway? I was the only disabled person present in this meeting and my confidence was undermined sufficiently to affect the quality of my argument. Reactions such as this can easily give rise to feelings of insecurity and doubt; it is, of course, the case that many people do have problems, but disabled people are among them and cannot afford to remain passive or to be passed by.

College

At the age of 19, after working for two years, I started my physiotherapy training at a special segregated college for blind and partially sighted students. For the first time in my life my disability was, at least in part, defined as blindness. Although about half the students were partially sighted, one of the criteria for entry to the college was the ability to read and write braille (which I had never used before) and to type proficiently, as, regardless of the clarity of their handwriting, the partially sighted students were not permitted to write their essays or examinations by hand, and the blind students were not permitted to write theirs in braille. No visual teaching methods were used in the college and, for those of us with sight, it was no easy matter learning subjects like anatomy, physiology and biomechanics without the use of diagrams.

The institution seemed unable to accept or respond to the fact that our impairments varied in severity and gave rise to different types of disability. We were taught to use special equipment which we did not need and were encouraged to "feel" rather than "peer" because feeling, it was thought, was aesthetically more pleasing, especially when dealing with the poor, unsuspecting public. There was great concern about the way we looked in our professional roles; white canes were not allowed inside the hospitals where we practiced clinically, even by totally blind students, and guide dogs were completely banned. It appeared that the blind students were expected to be superhuman whereas the partially sighted students were expected to be blind. Any attempt to defy or challenge these rules was very firmly quashed so, in the interests of "getting through," we outwardly denied the reality of our disabilities and complied.

Employment

Deciding whether or not to deny disability probably comes most clearly to the fore in adult life when we attempt to gain employment. Until very recently it was not uncommon to be told very bluntly that, in order to be accepted, the job must be done in exactly the same way as everyone else. In many ways this was easier to deal with than the situation now, where "equal opportunity" policies have simultaneously raised expectations and pushed negative attitudes underground, and where, in reality, little has changed. Although I have no way of proving it, I am convinced that the denial of my disability has been absolutely fundamental to my success in gaining the type of employment I have had. I have never completely denied it (it is not hidden enough for that) but rather, in response to the interviewers' skeptical and probing questions, I have minimized the difficulties I face and portrayed myself in a way which would swell my headmaster's pride.

Curiously, once in the job, people have sometimes decided that certain tasks, which I can perform quite adequately, are beyond me, while at the same time refusing to relieve me of those I cannot do. At one college where I worked it was considered impossible for me to cope with taking the minutes of meetings, but my request to be relieved of invigilating large numbers of students, on the grounds that I could not see them, was not acceded to; once again the nature of my disability was being defined by other people. On the rare occasions I have been given "special" equipment or consideration at work it has been regarded as a charitable act or donation for which I should be grateful and beholden. This behavior signals two distinct messages: first that I have failed to be "normal" (and have therefore failed), and second that I must ask for nothing more.

In these more enlightened days of "equal opportunities," we are frequently asked and expected to educate others at work about our disabilities. "We know nothing about it, you must teach us" is the frequent cry. In some ways this is a positive development but, on the other hand, it puts great pressure on us because few formal structures have been developed in which this educative process can take place. In the absence of proactive equal opportunity policies, we are rarely taken seriously and what we say is usually forgotten or ignored. Educating others in this way can also mean that we talk of little else but disability, which, as well as becoming boring to ourselves, can lead us to be labeled adversely or viewed solely in terms of problems. Challenging disabling attitudes and structures, especially as a lone disabled person, can become frustrating and exhausting, and in reality it is often easier and (dare I say) more functional, in the short term at least, to cope with inadequate conditions rather than fight to improve them. We must beware of tokenistic gestures which do little but put pressure on us.

CONCLUSION

The reasons I have denied the reality of my disability can be summarized as follows:

1. To avoid other people's anxiety and distress.
2. To avoid other people's disappointment and frustration.
3. To avoid other people's disbelief.
4. To avoid other people's disapproval.
5. To live up to other people's ideas of "normality."
6. To avoid spoiling other people's fun.
7. To collude with other people's pretences.

I believe that from earliest childhood denial of disability is totally rational given the situations we find ourselves in, and that to regard it as a psychopathological reaction is a serious mistake. We deny our disabilities for social, economic and emotional survival and we do so at considerable cost to our sense of self and our identities; it is not some-thing we do because of flaws in our individual psyches. For those of us disabled from birth or early childhood, denial of disability has deeply penetrating and entangled roots; we need support and encouragement to make our needs known, but this will only be achieved within the context of genuine structural and attitudinal change.

In this paper I have drawn upon my life experiences and personal reactions to elucidate the pressures placed upon disabled people to deny the reality of their experience of disability. This approach is limited inasmuch as personal experiences and responses can never be divorced from the personality and biography of the person they concern. In addition these pressures will vary according to the individual's impairment. But with these limitations in mind, I am confident that most disabled people will identify with what I have described and that only the examples are, strictly speaking, mine.

DISCUSSION QUESTIONS

1. What are all the ways that French and those around her conspire to deny that she is disabled?
2. Would those in other stigmatized statuses have experiences similar to French's?

NOTES

1. Walking two-by-two in a long file.
2. Girls' basketball.
3. Physical education teacher.

THE MEANING OF DIFFERENCE

FRAMEWORK ESSAY

The first framework essay in this book considered how contemporary American master statuses are named, dichotomized, and stigmatized. The second essay focused on the experience of privilege and stigma that accompanies those master statuses. In this section, we will look at the *meaning* that is attributed to difference. What significance are differences of race, sex, class, disability, and sexual orientation presumed to have? What difference does difference make? The concept of ideology is critical to understanding the specific meanings that are attributed to differences, and so we will focus on ideology in this essay.

Ideology

The concept of *ideology* was first elaborated by Marx and Engels, particularly in *The German Ideology* (1846). It is now a concept used throughout the social sciences and humanities. In general, an ideology can be defined as a widely shared belief or idea that has been constructed and disseminated by the powerful, primarily reflects their experiences, and functions for their benefit.

Ideologies are anchored in the experiences of their creators; thus, they offer only a partial view of the world. "Ideologies are not simply false, they can be 'partly true,' and yet also incomplete [or] distorted. . . . [They are not] consciously crafted by the ruling class and then injected into the minds of the majority; [they are] instead *produced* by specifiable, complex, social conditions" (Brantlinger, 1990:80). Because those who control the means of disseminating ideas have a better chance of having *their* ideas become the ones that prevail, Marx and Engels concluded that "the ideas of the ruling class are in every epoch the ruling ideas." Ideologies have the power to supplant, distort, or silence the experiences of those outside their production.

The idea that people are rewarded on the basis of their merit is an example of an ideology. It is an idea promoted by those with power—for example, teachers and supervisors—and many opportunities are created for the expression of the belief. Report cards, award banquets, and merit raises are all occasions for the expression of the belief that people are rewarded on the basis of their merit.

But certainly, most know this idea is not really true: People are not rewarded only, or even primarily, on the basis of their merit. The idea that merit is rewarded is only partly true and reflects only *some* people's experiences. The frequent repetition of the idea, however, has the potential to overwhelm contrary experience. Even those whose experience has not generally been that people are rewarded based on merit are likely to subscribe to this philosophy, because they hear it so often. In any event, there are few safe opportunities to describe beliefs to the contrary or have those beliefs widely disseminated.

Thus, the idea that people are rewarded on the basis of merit is an ideology. It is a belief that reflects primarily the experiences of those with power, but it is presented as universally valid. The idea overwhelms and silences the voices of those who are outside its production. In effect, ideologies ask us to discount our own experience.

This conflict between one's own experience and the ideas conveyed by an ideology is implied in W. E. B. Du Bois's description of the "double consciousness" experienced by African Americans discussed in Framework Essay II (page 166). It is also what many feminists refer to as the double or fractured consciousness experienced by women. In both cases, the dominant ideas fail to reflect the real-life experiences of people in these categories. For example, the *actual* experience of poverty, discrimination, motherhood, disability, sexual assault, life in a black neighborhood, or in a gay relationship rarely coincides with the public discussion on these topics. Because those in stigmatized categories do not control the production or distribution of the prevailing ideas, *their* experience is not likely to be reflected in them. The ideology not only silences their experience; it may invalidate it even in their own minds: "I must be the one who's crazy!" In this way, the dominant discourse can invade and overwhelm our own experience, since what we know doesn't fit with it (Kasper, 1986; Smith, 1978, 1990).

An ideology that so dominates a culture as to become the prevailing and unquestioned belief was described in the 1920s by Italian political theorist Antonio Gramsci as the *hegemonic,* or ruling, ideology. Gramsci argued that social control was primarily accomplished by the control of ideas, and that whatever was considered to be "common sense" was especially effective as a mechanism of social control (Omi and Winant, 1994:67). Common sense beliefs are likely to embody widely shared ideas primarily reflecting the interests and experience of those who are powerful. We are all encouraged to adhere to common sense even when that requires discounting our own experience. The discussion of natural-law language that follows especially shows how this operates.

Conveying Ideologies: Natural-Law Language and Stereotypes

Hegemonic, or ruling, ideologies often take the form of commonsense beliefs and are especially embodied in stereotypes and what is called *natural-law language.*

Natural-Law Language   When people use the word *natural,* they usually mean that something is inevitable, predetermined, or outside human control (Pierce, 1971). *Human nature* and *instinct* are often used in the same way. For example, "It's only natural to care about what others think," "It's human nature to want to get ahead," or "It's just instinctive to be afraid of someone different" all convey the sense that something is inevitable, automatic, and independent of one's will.

Thus, it is not surprising when, in discussions about discrimination, someone says, "It's only natural for people to be prejudiced" or "It's human nature to want to be with your own kind." Each of these commonsense ideas conveys a belief in the inevitability of discrimination and prejudice, as if such processes emerged independently of anyone's will.

Even for issues of which we disapprove, the word *natural* can convey this sense of inevitability. For example, "I am against racism, but it's only natural" puts nature on the side of prejudice. Arguing that something is natural because it happens frequently has the same consequence. "All societies have discriminated against women," implies that something that happens frequently is therefore inevitable. But in truth, something that happens frequently could just as likely mean there is an extensive set of social controls ensuring the outcome.

At least three consequences follow from using natural-law language. First, it ends discussion, as if having described something as natural makes any further exploration of the topic unnecessary. This makes sense given that the word *natural* is equated with inevitability: If something is inevitable, there is little sense in questioning it.

Second, because natural-law language treats behavior as predetermined, it overlooks the actual cultural and historical variation of human societies. If something is natural, it should always happen. Yet virtually no human behavior emerges everywhere and always; all social life is susceptible to change. Thus, natural-law language ignores the variability of social life.

Third, natural-law language treats individuals as passive, lacking an interest in or control over social life. If it is "natural" to dislike those who are different, then there is really nothing we can do about that feeling. It is no one's responsibility; it is just natural. If there is nothing I can do about my own behavior, there is little I could expect to do about the behavior of others. Human nature thus is depicted as a limitation beyond which people cannot expect to move (Gould, 1981). Describing certain behavior as "only natural" implies that personal and social change are impossible.

In all these ways—by closing off discussion, masking variation and change, and treating humans as passive—natural-law language tells us not to question the world that surrounds us. Natural-law language has this effect no matter what context it emerges in: "It's only natural to discriminate," "It's only natural to want to have children," "It's only natural to marry and settle down," "Inequality is only natural; the poor will always be with us," "Aggression and war are just human nature," "Greed is instinctive." In each case, natural-law language not only discourages questions, it carries a covert recommendation about what you *ought* to do. If something is "just natural," you cannot prevent others from doing it, and you are well advised to do it yourself. Thus, natural-law language serves as a forceful mechanism of social control (Pierce, 1971).

Natural-law language is used to convey hegemonic ideologies. It reduces the complexity and historic variability of the social world to a claim for universal processes, offering a partial and distorted truth that silences those with contrary experience. Natural-law language can make discrimination appear to be natural, normal, and inevitable. Thus, natural-law language itself creates and maintains ideas about difference.

Stereotypes A *stereotype* is a prediction that "members of a group will behave in certain ways" (Andre, 1988:259)—that black men will have athletic ability or that Asian American students will excel in the sciences. As Frank Wu wrote in Reading 51, "Before I can talk about Asian American experiences at all, I have to kill off the model minority myth because the stereotype obscures many realities."

Stereotypes assume that all the individuals in a category possess the same characteristics. Stereotypes persist despite evidence to the contrary because they are not formulated in a way that is testable or falsifiable (Andre, 1988). In this way stereotypes differ from descriptions. Descriptions offer no prediction; they can be tested for accuracy and rejected when they are wrong; they encourage explanation and a consideration of historical variability.

For example, "Most great American athletes are African American" is a description. First, there is no prediction that a particular African American can be expected to be a good athlete, or that someone who is white will be a poor one. Second, the claim is falsifiable; that is, it can be tested for accuracy and proven wrong (e.g., by asking what proportion of the last two decades' American Olympic medal winners were African American). Third, the statement turns our attention to explanation and historical variation: Why might this be the case? Has this always been the case?

In contrast, "African Americans are good athletes" is a stereotype. It attempts to characterize a whole population, thus denying the inevitable differences among the people in the category. It predicts that members of a group will behave in a particular way. It cannot be falsified since there is no direct way to test the claim. Further, the stereotype denies the reality of historical and cultural variation by suggesting that this has always been the case. Thus, stereotypes essentialize: they assume that if you know something about the physical package someone comes in, you can predict that person's behavior.

Both stereotypes and natural-law language offer broad-based predictions about behavior. Stereotypes predict that members of a particular category will possess particular attributes; natural-law language predicts that certain behavior is inevitable. Neither stereotypes nor natural-law language is anchored in any social or historical context, and, for that reason, both are frequently wrong. Basketball great Bill Russell's reaction when asked if he thought African Americans were "natural" athletes makes clear the similarity of natural-law language and stereotyping. As Russell said, this was a stereotypic image of African American athletes that deprecated the skill and effort he brought to his craft—as if he were great because he was black rather than because of the talent he cultivated in hours of work.

Stereotyping and Asian Americans   As we have said, stereotypes explain life outcomes by attributing some essential, shared quality to all those in a particular category. The current depiction of Asian Americans as a "model minority" is a good example of this. This stereotype masks the considerable economic, educational, and occupational heterogeneity among Asian Americans. For example, the college degree attainment rate of Vietnamese Americans is only one-quarter the rate for Asian Americans overall. The model-minority stereotype is itself a fairly recent invention. Among those now called "model minority" are categories of people who have been categorized as "undesirable" immigrants, denied citizenship through naturalization, and placed in internment camps as potential traitors.

In American culture, stereotypes are often driven by the necessity to explain why some categories of people succeed more than others (Steinberg, 1989). Thus, the model-minority stereotype is often used to claim that if racism has not hurt Asian Americans' success, it could not have hurt African Americans'.

The myth of the Asian-American "model minority" has been challenged, yet it continues to be widely believed. One reason for this is its instructional value. For whom are Asian Americans supposed to be a "model"? Shortly after the Civil War, southern planters recruited Chinese immigrants in order to pit them against the newly freed blacks as "examples" of laborers willing to work hard for low wages. Today, Asian Americans are again being used to discipline blacks. . . . Our society needs an Asian-American "model minority" in an era anxious about a growing black underclass. (Takaki, 1993:416)

A brief review of American immigration policy explains the misguided nature of the comparison between African and Asian Americans. From 1921 until 1965, U.S. immigration was restricted by quotas that set limits on the number of immigrants from each nation based on the percentage of people from that country residing in the United States at the time of the 1920 census. This had the obvious and intended effect of severely restricting immigration from Asia, as well as that from Southern and Eastern Europe and Africa. The civil rights movement of the 1960s raised such national embarrassment about this quota system that in 1965 Congress replaced national-origin quotas with an annual 20,000-person limit for every nation regardless of its size. Within that quota, preference went first to those who were relatives of U. S. citizens and then to those with occupational skills needed in America.

The result was a total increase in immigration and a change in its composition. Because few individuals from non-European countries could immigrate on the grounds of having family in America—previous restrictions would have made that almost impossible—the quotas were filled with people meeting designated *occupational* needs. Thus, those immigrating to the United States since 1965 have had high educational and occupational profiles. The middle- and upper-class professionals and entrepreneurs who have immigrated to the United States did not suddenly become successful here; rather, they continued their home-country success here. These high occupational and educational profiles have characterized immigrants from African as well as Asian countries.

The high Asian American educational and occupational profile has yielded the country's highest median *household* income, but not its highest *individual* income. The chart below compares family and individual income by race and shows the degree to which family size affects household income.

FAMILY, HOUSEHOLD, AND PER CAPITA INCOME BY RACE AND ETHNICITY

Race/ethnicity	Median family income	Median household size	Median per capita Income
White (non-Hispanic)	$45,904	2.45	$25,278
Black	$30,439	2.67	$15,159
Latino	$33,447	3.49	$12,306
Asian American	$55,521	3.10	$22,352

Source: U.S. Census Bureau, 2001.
Note: Between 2000 and 2001, "median household money income did not change for households with a non-Hispanic White householder, or for those with a householder who reported a single race of Asian. However, income fell for Blacks by 2.5 to 3.0 percent, for Asians who reported more than one race by 4.0 to 4.5 percent, and for Hispanics by 2.9 percent" (Weinberg, 2003).

Despite a higher educational profile, Asian Americans' per capita income lags behind that of non-Hispanic whites. The following 1999 data compare college graduation with unemployment and poverty rates.

EDUCATION, UNEMPLOYMENT, AND POVERTY RATES BY RACE AND ETHNICITY

Race/ethnicity	Percent with college degree	Unemployment rate	Percent of families in poverty
Whites	25.9	3.7	8.0
Blacks	15.4	8.0	23.4
Latinos	10.9	6.4	22.7
Asian Americans	42.4	4.2	11.0

Source: U.S. Census Bureau, 2000; in Le, 2001.

A more telling statistic is how much more money a person earns with each additional year of schooling completed, or what sociologists call "returns on education." Using this measure, research consistently shows that for each additional year of education attained, Whites earn another $522 [a year.] That is, beyond a high school degree, a White [worker] with four more years of education (equivalent to a college degree) can expect to earn $2,088 [more] per year in salary.

In contrast, return on each additional year of education for a Japanese American is only $438 [a year]. For a Chinese American, it's $320. For Blacks, it's even worse at only $284. What this means is that, basically, a typical Asian American has to get more years of education just to make the same amount of money that a typical White [worker] makes with less education. (Le, 2001)

While selective immigration goes a long way toward explaining the success of some recent immigrants from Asian countries, it's important to distinguish between people who are immigrants and those who are refugees. The circumstances of arrival and resettlement for those who have fled their home countries make the refugee population exceedingly heterogeneous and quite different from those who have immigrated to the United States (Haines, 1989). Thus, Vietnamese, Laotian, Cambodian, and Hmong refugees are unlikely to have the high occupational or educational profiles of other Asian immigrants.

The misguided contemporary formulation—if Asian Americans can make it, why can't African Americans?—echoes an earlier question: If European immigrants can make it, why can't African Americans? The answer to that question is summarized as follows:

Conditions within the cities to which they had migrated [beginning in the 1920s], not slavery, strained blacks' ability to retain two-parent families. Within those cities, blacks faced circumstances that differed fundamentally from those found earlier by European immigrants. They entered cities in large numbers as unskilled and semiskilled manufacturing jobs were leaving, not growing. The discrimination they encountered kept them out of the manufacturing jobs into which earlier immigrants had been recruited. One important goal of public schools had been the assimilation and "Americanization" of immigrant children; by contrast, they excluded and segregated blacks. Racism enforced housing segregation, and residential concentration among blacks increased at the same time it lessened among immigrants and their children. Political machines had embraced earlier immigrants and incorporated them into the system of "city trenches" by which American cities were governed; they excluded blacks from effective political power until cities had been so abandoned by industry and deserted by whites that resistance to black political participation no longer mattered. All the processes that had opened opportunities for immigrants and their children broke down for blacks. (Katz, 1989:51)

Stereotyping and African Americans   While Asian Americans suffer the effects of what may be called a positive stereotype, African Americans experience just the opposite. The trajectory, nature, and impact of racial stereotypes have been examined extensively in terms of whites' attitudes toward blacks. The picture is a complicated one.

Certainly, in terms of belief in the principles of racial equality and integration, the research has shown a significant and sustained improvement in whites' attitudes across the board—but the *degree* of that improvement has varied by the topic. About public transportation and jobs, virtually all whites endorsed the ideas of equal access and integration by the mid-1970s. But it wasn't until the mid-1990s that a 95 percent level of white support was reached on the question of school integration, and white support of unconstrained access to housing is still only about 60 percent (Bobo, 2001). The acceptance of interracial marriage has reached 70 percent among whites (and 80 percent among blacks), with 66 percent saying they would approve their child or grandchild marrying outside their race (Ludwig, 2004). Less than 1 percent of U.S. marriages include a white and black spouse, which is twice what it was in the early 1980s.

Alongside this increased commitment to equality and integration, research also shows a persistence of negative stereotypes about blacks among whites.

> Bobo and Kluegel (1997:100–101) show that 31 percent of Whites gave Blacks a low absolute rating in terms of intelligence, 47 percent did so in terms of laziness, 54 percent did so concerning proclivity to violence, and 59 percent did so concerning preference to live off welfare. . . . These negative stereotypes often also apply in terms of Whites' views of Hispanics (Smith, 1990). Although Whites' views of Asians and Pacific Islanders are seldom as negative as those regarding Blacks and Hispanics, Asians and Pacific Islanders typically receive unfavorable relative ratings. The 1990 General Social Survey reported that considerably more than 50 percent of Whites rated Blacks and Hispanics as less intelligent. A similar percentage rated Blacks and Hispanics as prone to violence. Considerably more than two-thirds of Whites rated Blacks and Hispanics as actually preferring to live off welfare. (Bobo, 2001: 277–278)

Not surprisingly, these stereotypes affect everthing from support of social policies to interpersonal interactions.

> Research indicating Whites' fearfulness of a Black stranger is indicative [of interpersonal interactions]. Based on a survey that involved the use of sophisticated experimental vignettes, St. John and Heald-Moore (1995) found that Whites were more fearful of a Black stranger than of a White stranger. This was true irrespective of other situational factors such as time of day or neighborhood characteristics. The degree of fear was strongly

conditioned by only two factors: age and gender of the Black person (young Black males were feared more than others) and age of the White person (feelings of fear and vulnerability were greatest among older Whites). . . .

This work implies that the interaction between Blacks and Whites in many public settings is rife with the potential for missteps, misunderstanding, and insult. Precisely this sort of dynamic is suggested by events and experiences recounted in qualitative interviews with middle-class Blacks (Feagin, 1991; Cose, 1993; Feagin and Sikes, 1994). (Bobo, 2001:278–279)

When considering the ultimate affect of stereotypes—that is, discriminatory behavior—whites and blacks disagree about the extent of discrimination. Response to the annual Gallop poll about how different groups are treated in American society is typical: In a 2003 survey, 73 percent of whites, but only 39 percent of blacks felt that blacks and whites were treated the same in their local community. When the question is about the treatment of blacks and whites in the country as a whole, 39 percent of whites but only 11 percent of blacks feel that treatment is the same (Ludwig, 2003). (These gaps in the perception of discrimination also appear between whites and Asians and Latinos, although they are somewhat smaller.)

Finally, African Americans (and other people of color) are likely to understand discrimination as institutionally based, while whites attribute it to isolated events or individuals.

In short, to Whites, the [New York City police] officers who tortured Abner Louima constitute a few bad apples. To Blacks, these officers represent only the tip of the iceberg. [Hatian immigrant Abner Louima was beaten and sexually assaulted by police after he was arrested outside a Brooklyn nightclub in 1997.]

To Whites, the Texaco tapes are shocking. To Blacks, the tapes merely reflect that in this one instance the guilty were caught. [In 1996, a Texaco executive turned over audiotapes of Texaco executives making racist remarks and plotting to purge the documents in a discrimination case. Ultimately, Texaco paid more than $115 million for having failed to hire, promote, and treat its black staff with general decency.]

But differences in perception cut deeper than this. . . . Although many Whites recognize that discrimination plays some part in higher rates of unemployment, poverty, and a range of hardships in life that minorities often face, the central cause is usually understood to be the level of effort and cultural patterns of the minority group members themselves (Schuman, 1971; Apostle et al., 1983; Kluegel and Smith, 1986; Schuman, et al., 1997). For minorities, especially Blacks, it is understood that the persistence of race problems has something to do with how our institutions operate. For many Whites, larger patterns of inequality are understood as mainly something about minorities themselves. . . . [T]he most popular view holds that blacks should "try harder," should get ahead "without special favors," and fall behind because they "lack motivation." (Bobo, 2001:281–282)

Social Institutions and the Support of Ideologies

The specific messages carried by natural-law language and stereotypes are often echoed by social institutions. The term *social institution* refers to the established mechanisms by which societies meet their predictable needs. For example, the need to socialize new members of the society is met by the institutions of the family and education. In addition to these, social institutions include science, law, religion, politics, the economy, military, medicine, and mass media or popular culture. Ideologies—in our case ideologies about the meaning of difference—naturally play a significant role in the operation of social institutions. Thus, the readings in this section are organized around the social institutions of law, politics, economy, science, and popular culture. We have also included a section on language, but that is not generally considered a social institution *per se*.

In the discussion that follows, we will consider how late-19th- and early-20th-century science and popular culture constructed the meaning of race, class, sex, and sexual orientation differences. Throughout, there is a striking congruence among scientific pronouncements, popular culture messages, and the prejudices of the day.

Science The need to explain the meaning of human difference forcefully emerged when 15th-century Europeans encountered previously unknown regions and peoples. "Three centuries of exploration brought home as never before the tremendous diversity of human behavior and life patterns within environments and under circumstances dramatically different from those of Europe. . . . Out of that large laboratory of human experience was born the [idea of the] conflict between nature and nurture" (Degler, 1991:4–5).

The "nature-nurture" conflict offered two ways to explain human variation. Explanations from the nature side stressed that the diversity of human societies—and the ability of some to conquer and dominate others—reflected significant biological differences among populations. Explanations from the nurture side argued that human diversity resulted from historical, environmental, and cultural difference. From the nature side, humans were understood to act out behaviors that are biologically driven. From the nurture side, humans were something of a *tabula rasa,* a blank slate, on which particular cultural expectations were inscribed.

Whether nature or nurture was understood to dominate, however, the discussion of the meaning of human difference always assumed that people could be ranked as to their worth (Gould, 1981). Thus, the real question was whether the rankings reflected in social hierarchies were the result of nature, and thus inevitable and fixed, or whether they could be affected by human action and were thus subject to change.

The question was not merely theoretical. The 1800s in America witnessed appropriation of Native American territories and the forced relocation of vast numbers of people under the Indian Removal Act of 1830; the 1848 signing of the Treaty of Guadalupe Hidalgo ending the Mexican-American War and ceding what is now Texas, New Mexico, California, Utah, Nevada, Colorado, and Arizona to the United States with the 75,000 Mexican nationals residing in those territories becoming U.S. citizens; passage of the Chinese Exclusion Act; a prolonged national debate about slavery and women's suffrage; and the unprecedented number of poor and working-class immigrants from Southern and Eastern Europe. The century closed with the internationally publicized trial of English playwright Oscar Wilde, who was sentenced to two years' hard labor for his homosexuality.

Thus, whether social hierarchy reflected natural, permanent, and inherent differences in capability (the nature side) or was the product of specific social and historical circumstances and therefore susceptible to change (the nurture side) raised a profound question. Because Africans were held by whites in slavery, did that mean Africans were by their nature inferior to whites? Were Native Americans literally "savages" occupying some middle ground between animals and civilized humans, and did they therefore benefit from domination by those who supposedly were more advanced? Did the dissimilarity of Chinese immigrants from American whites mean they were not "human" in the way whites were? If homosexuality was congenital, did that mean homosexuals were profoundly different from heterosexuals? Were women closer to plants and animals than to civilized men? Were the poor and working classes composed of those who not only lacked the talents by which to rise in society but also passed their defects on to their children? In all, were individuals and categories of people located in the statuses for which they were best suited? This was the question driving public debate (Degler, 1991). If one believed that the social order simply reflected immutable biological differences, the answer to the question would probably be yes. That would not have been the case, however, for those who believed these differences were the outcome of specific social and historical processes overlaying a shared humanity. In all, the question behind the nature-nurture debate was about the *meaning* of what appeared to be *natural* difference. The answer to that question was shaped by the hegemonic ideologies of the time—especially those informed by science.

Charles Darwin's publication of *The Origin of the Species* (1859) and *The Descent of Man* (1871) shifted the weight of popular and scholarly opinion toward the nature side of the equation (Degler, 1991). In its broadest terms, Darwin's conclusions challenged the two central beliefs of the time. (Darwin himself was quite distressed to have arrived at these conclusions [Shipman, 1994].) First, the idea of evolutionary change challenged "traditional, Christian belief in a single episode of creation of a static, perfect, and unchanging world." The significance of evolutionary change was clear: "If the world were not created perfect, then there was no implicit justification for the way things were . . ." (Shipman, 1994:18).

Second, Darwin's work implied that all humans share a common ancestry. If differences among birds were the result of their adaptation to distinctive environments, then *their differences existed within an overall framework of similarity and common ancestry.* By analogy, the distinctiveness of human populations might also be understood as "variability within overall similarity" (Shipman, 1994:22)—a shocking possibility at the time. "It was the age of imperialism and most non-Europeans were regarded, even by Darwin, as 'barbarians'; he was astonished and taken aback by their wildness and animality. The differences among humans seemed so extreme that the humanity . . . of some living groups was scarcely credible" (Shipman, 1994:19).

The idea that change in the physical environment resulted in the success of some species and demise of others (the idea of natural selection) bolstered the pre-existent concept of "survival of the fittest." This phrase had been authored by English sociologist Herbert Spencer, who had been considering the evolutionary principles of human societies several years before Darwin published *The Origin of the Species.*

Spencer's position, eventually called *social Darwinism,* was extremely popular in America. Spencer strongly believed that modern societies are inevitably improvements over earlier forms of social organization and that progress would necessarily follow from unimpeded competition for social resources. In all, social Darwinism argued that those who are more advanced naturally rise to the top of any stratification ladder.

Through social Darwinism, the prevailing hierarchies—slave owner over people held in slavery, white over Mexican and Native American, native born over immigrant, upper class over poor, male over female—could be attributed to natural processes and justified as a reflection of inherent differences among categories of people. As one sociologist at the turn of the century framed it, "under the tutelage of Darwinism the world returns again to the idea that *might* as evidence of fitness has something to do with *right*" (Degler, 1991:13). Social Darwinism lacked a socially or historically grounded explanation for social stratification. Instead, it treated those hierarchies as a reflection of the biological merit of categories of people. Thus, the ideology of social Darwinism was used to justify slavery, colonialism, immigration quotas, the criminalization of homosexuality, the forced relocation of Native Americans, and the legal subordination of women.

Spencer argued that the specialization of tasks, also called the *division of labor,* was the outcome of a biologically mandated evolution. The sexual division of labor "was a product of the organic law of progress," thus making equal treatment of men and women impossible and even potentially dangerous.

The social Darwinist position was used by those opposed to providing equal education for women. Just when American institutions of higher education were opening to women—Vassar College was founded in 1865, Smith and Wellesley 10 years later, and by 1870 many state universities had become coeducational—biologist Edward Clarke published a book (1873) that argued that the physical energy education required would endanger women's reproductive abilities (an idea first put forward by Spencer). Clarke's case was based on meager and questionable empirical evidence: seven clinical cases, only one of which actually supported his position (Sayers, 1982:14). His work was a response to *social* rather than scientific developments, since it was prompted by no new discoveries in biology. Nonetheless, the book was an immediate and enduring success. For the next 30 years it was used in the argument against equal education despite the accumulation of evidence refuting its claims. While Clarke's research should have been suspect, it instead became influential in policymaking. In part, "the reason why Clarke's argument seemed so serviceable to those opposed to women's higher education was that it was couched in biological terms and thus appeared to offer a legitimate scientific basis for conservative opposition to equal education" (Sayers, 1982:11).

In a similar fashion, science shaped ideas about the meaning of same-sex relationships. By the turn of the century in Europe, a gay rights movement had arisen in Germany and gay themes had emerged in French literature (Adam, 1987). At the same time, however, an international move to criminalize sexual relations between men gathered momentum: a revision of the German criminal code increased the penalties for male homosexuality, the British imprisoned Oscar Wilde, and Europe and the United States experienced a social reform movement directed against prostitution and male homosexuality. (The possibility of sexual relations between women was not considered until later.)

The move to criminalize homosexuality was countered by physicians arguing, from a social Darwinist position, that homosexuality is the product of "hereditary weakness" and is thus beyond individual control. Though their hope was for increased tolerance, scientists who took this position offered the idea of "homosexuality as a medical entity and the homosexual as a distinctive kind of person" (Conrad and Schneider, 1980:184). Thus, they contributed to the idea that heterosexual and homosexual people were profoundly different from each other.

Science also supported the argument that people of different skin colors are different in significant, immutable ways. Certainly Spencer's idea of the survival of the fittest was understood to support the ideology that whites are superior to all people of color: "The most prevalent form of social Darwinism at the turn of the century was actually racism, that is, the idea that one people might be superior to another because of differences in their biological nature" (Degler, 1991:15).

The scientific defense of American slavery first emerged with the work of two eminent scientists, Swiss naturalist Louis Agassiz and Philadelphia physician Samuel Morton. Agassiz immigrated to America in 1840 and became a professor at Harvard. There he garnered immense popularity by countering the biblically based theory of the unity of all people (which attributed racial differences to "degeneration" from a shared origin) with a "scientific" theory that different races had descended from different moments of creation—"different Adams" as it was called (Gould, 1981:39).

Samuel Morton tested Agassiz's theories by assessing the skull capacity of people of different races. His idea was that the size of the skull would correlate with the intelligence of the race. His results "matched every good Yankee's prejudices—whites on top, Indians in the middle, and blacks on the bottom; and among whites, Teutons and Anglo-Saxons on top, Jews in the middle, and Hindus on the bottom" (Gould, 1981:53).

As we now know, Morton's findings were simply wrong. Others who replicated his measurements did not arrive at the same conclusions about skull capacity: There were "*no* significant differences among races for Morton's own data" (Gould, 1981:67). Morton's research was inadequate even by the scientific standards of his time. There is no evidence that Morton intended to deceive. Rather, his assumptions of white superiority were so firm that he was oblivious to his own errors and illogic, errors that yielded the conclusion of white superiority only because of his miscalculations.

The use of questionable research to support prevailing beliefs (Gould, 1981) was also evident in the development of intelligence testing. In 1904, Alfred Binet, director of the psychology lab at the Sorbonne, was commissioned by the French minister of public education to develop a test to identify children whose poor performance in school might indicate a need for special education. Binet developed a test with a series of tasks that children of "normal" intelligence were expected to have mastered. Binet's own claims for the test were fairly limited. He did not equate intelligence with the score produced by his test, arguing that intelligence was too complex a factor to be reduced to a simple number. Nor did he construe his test as measuring inborn, permanent, or inherited limitations (Gould, 1981).

Binet's hesitations regarding the significance of the test, however, were ignored by the emerging field of American psychology, which used intelligence as a way to explain social hierarchies. "The people who are doing the drudgery are, as a rule, in their proper places," wrote H. H. Goddard, who introduced the Binet test to America. Stanford psychologist Lewis M. Termin (author of the Stanford-Binet IQ test) argued that "the children of successful and cultured parents test higher than children from wretched and ignorant homes for the simple reason that their heredity is better" (Degler, 1991:50). Indeed, "Terman believed that class boundaries had been set by innate intelligence" (Gould, 1981:183).

Such conclusions were used to shape decisions about the distribution of social resources. For example, intelligence was described as a capacity like the capacity of a jug to hold a certain amount of milk. A pint jug could not be expected to hold a quart of milk; similarly, it was pointless to waste "too much" education on someone whose capacity was supposedly limited. The findings of intelligence testers were thus used to advocate particular social policies such as restrictions on immigration. While it is not clear that the work of intelligence testers directly affected the Immigration Restriction Act of 1924 (Degler, 1991), the ultimate shape of the legislation limited immigration from Southern and Eastern Europe, which was consistent with intelligence testers' claims about the relative intelligence of the "races" in Europe. These quotas barred the admission of European Jews fleeing the impending holocaust (Gould, 1981).

Still, by about 1930 a considerable body of research showed that social environment more than biology accounts for differing IQ scores and that the tests themselves measured not innate intelligence but familiarity with the culture of those who wrote the tests. In the end, the psychologists who had promoted intelligence testing were forced to repudiate the idea that intelligence is inherited or that it can be separated from cultural knowledge.[1]

Whether measuring cranial capacity, developing paper-and-pencil intelligence tests, positing the effect of education on women, or arguing for hereditary weakness as an explanation of homosexuality, the work of these scientists supported the prevailing ideologies about the merit and appropriate social position of people of different sexes, races, ethnic groups, sexual orientations, and social classes. Most of these scientists do not appear to have been ideologically motivated; indeed they were sometimes troubled by their own findings. Still, their research was riddled with technical errors and questionable findings. Their research proved "the surprising mal-

---

[1] ". . . There is also a lot of evidence for the whole American population, for American ethnic groups, and for populations wherever tests are given that IQ is changing in ways that can't possibly be genetic because they happen too fast. It is widely recognized that average IQs are increasing fairly rapidly. These changes in IQ clearly must have more to say about relationships between testing and real performance, or about social patterns of learning, than about biologically rooted 'intelligence.' The genes of a large population don't change that fast unless there is a very dramatic episode of natural selection such as an epidemic. It is also widely recognized that African Americans are slowly but steadily gaining on white Americans in IQ" (Cohen, 1998:210).

leability of 'objective,' quantitative data in the interest of a preconceived idea" (Gould, 1981:147). Precisely because their research confirmed prevailing beliefs, it was more likely to be celebrated than scrutinized.

Why were these findings eventually repudiated? Since they offered a defense of the status quo and confirmed the prevailing ideology, who would have criticized them?

First, the scientific defense of immutable hierarchy was eroded by the steady accumulation of evidence about the "intellectual equality and therefore the equal cultural capacity of all peoples" (Degler, 1991:61). A good deal of the research that made that point was produced by the many "prominent or soon to be prominent" scholars of African American, Chinese, and European immigrant ancestry who, after finally being admitted to institutions of higher education, were pursuing scientific research. Black scholars such as W. E. B. Du Bois and E. Franklin Frazier, and scholars of recent European immigrant ancestry such as anthropologists Franz Boas, Alfred Kroeber, and Edward Sapir, trenchantly criticized the social science of the day and by their very presence challenged the prevailing expectations about the "inherent inferiority" of people like themselves (Degler, 1991).

The presumptions about the meaning of race were also challenged by increased interracial contact. The 1920s began the Great Migration, in which hundreds of thousands of African Americans from the rural South moved to northern cities. This movement continued through two world wars as black, Latino, Asian, and Native American men joined the armed forces and women followed wartime employment opportunities. The 1920s also brought the Harlem Renaissance, an outpouring of creativity from black writers, scholars, and artists in celebration of African and African American culture. Overall, white social scientists "gained an unprecedented opportunity to observe blacks in a fresh and often transforming way" (Degler, 1991:197). Their attitudes and expectations changed as a result of this increased contact.

In sum, the scientific argument for the inherent inferiority of some groups of people was advanced by upper-class, native-born, white male faculty members of prestigious universities. Few others would have had the means with which to disseminate their ideas or the prestige to make those ideas influential. These theories of essential difference were not written by Native Americans, Mexicans, women, gays, African Americans, or immigrants from Asia or Southern and Eastern Europe. Most of these people lacked access to the public forums to present their experiences until the rise of the antislavery, suffrage, labor, and gay rights movements. Insofar as the people in these categories could be silenced, it was easier to depict them as essentially and profoundly different.

Popular Culture   Like the sciences, popular culture (the forms of entertainment available for mass consumption such as popular music, theater, film, literature, and television) may convey ideologies about difference and social stratification. At virtually the same time that social Darwinism gained popularity in America—indeed within two years of Louis Agassiz's arrival in the United States in 1840—America's first minstrel show was organized. Like social Darwinism, minstrel shows offered a defense of slavery.

Minstrel shows, which became an enormously popular form of entertainment, were musical variety shows in which white males in "blackface" ridiculed blacks, abolitionism, and women's suffrage. Their impact can be seen in the movies and cartoons of the 1930s and 1940s and in current American stereotypes. As the shows traveled the country, their images were impressed on whites who often had no direct contact with blacks and thus no information to contradict the minstrel images.

The three primary characters of the minstrel show were the happy slave, Zip Coon, and the mammy (Riggs, 1987). The image of the happy slave—singing and dancing, naive and childlike, taken care of through old age by the master, a virtual member of the family—asserted that blacks held in slavery were both content and cared for. Zip Coon was a northern, free black man characterized by a ridiculous use of language and laughable attempts to emulate whites; the caricature was used to show that blacks lacked the intelligence to handle freedom. The mammy was depicted as a large and presumably unattractive black woman fully devoted to the white family she served. Like the happy slave, the mammy was unthreatening and content—no sexual competition to the white mistress of the house, no children of her own needing attention, committed to and fulfilled by her work with her white family. Thus, the characters of the minstrel show hid the reality of slavery. The happy slave and mammy denied the brutality of the slave system. Zip Coon denied the reality of blacks' organization of the underground railroad, their production of slave narratives in books and lectures, and their undertaking of slave rebellions and escapes.

In all, minstrel shows offered an ideology about slavery constructed by and in the interests of those with power. They ridiculed antislavery activists and legitimatized the status quo. Minstrel shows asserted that blacks did not mind being held as slaves and that they did not suffer loss and pain in the same way whites did. The minstrel show was not the only source of this ideology, but as a form of popular entertainment it was a very effective means of disseminating such beliefs. The shows traveled to all parts of the country, with a racial message masked as mere entertainment.

But within popular culture, an effective counter to the ideology of the minstrel show emerged through the speakers of the antislavery lecture circuit and the publication of numerous slave narratives. Appearing as early as 1760, these narratives achieved an enormous and enduring popularity among northern white readers. Frederick Douglass, former slave and the renowned antislavery activist, was the most famous public lecturer in the history of the movement and wrote its best-selling slave narrative. Whether as book or lecture, slave narratives provided an image of blacks as human beings. Access to these life histories provided the first opportunity for most whites to see a shared humanity between themselves and those held in slavery (Bodziock, 1990). Thus, slave narratives directly countered the images of the minstrel show. While popular culture may offer a variety of messages, all parties do not meet equally on its terrain. Those with power have better access and more legitimacy, but popular culture cannot be so tightly controlled as to entirely exclude the voice of the less powerful.

Conclusion

As Karl Marx considered it, ideology was "the mechanism whereby there can occur a difference between how things really are in the economy and the wider society and how people think they are" (Marshall, 1994:234). In this framework essay, we have examined how science and popular culture have contributed to ideologies about the meanings of color, class, sexual orientation, and sex. The readings that follow focus on law and politics, the economy, science, and popular culture as social institutions that construct what difference is understood to mean. For example, in Reading 53, Michael Oliver describes how scientific research structures the meaning that is attributed to differences in human abilities, and in Reading 43, Cheryl Zarlenga Kerchis and Iris Marion Young explore whether, in the context of social change movements, difference between groups is understood to be something valued or something to transcend. Indeed, each of the Supreme Court decisions described in Reading 42 is ultimately about the *meaning* of difference—for example, in the determination of citizenship or access to higher education, what meaning are we going to attribute to race differences, or to sex differences? At the level of social institutions, the meaning that is made of difference has the potential for far-reaching impact.

KEY CONCEPTS

hegemonic Dominating or ruling. A **hegemonic ideology** is a belief that is pervasive in a culture. (page **305**)

ideology A widely shared belief that primarily reflects the experiences of those with power, but is presented as universally valid. (pages **304–05**)

natural-law language Language that treats human behavior as bound by natural law. (pages **305–06**)

social Darwinism The belief that those who dominate a society are necessarily the fittest. (page **314**)

social institution Established system for meeting societal needs; for example, the family. (page **311–12**)

stereotype A characterization of a category of people as all alike, as possessing the same set of characteristics and likely to behave in the same ways. (pages **306–11**)

REFERENCES

Adam, Barry D. 1987. *The Rise of a Gay and Lesbian Movement.* Boston: G. K. Hall & Co.

Andre, Judith. 1988. Stereotypes: Conceptual and Normative Considerations. *Racism and Sexism: An Integrated Study,* edited by Paula S. Rothenberg, 257–62. New York: St. Martin's Press.

Apostle, Richard, Charles Glock, Thom Piazza, and Marijean Suelzle. 1983. *The Anatomy of Racial Attitudes.* Berkeley, CA: University of California Press.

Bobo, Lawrence D. 2001. Racial Attitudes and Relations at the Close of the Twentieth Century. *America Becoming: Racial Trends and Their Consequences,* edited by Neil J. Smelser, William Julius Wilson, and Faith Mitchell, 264–301. Washington, DC: National Academy Press.

———, and James Kluegel. 1997. Status, Ideology, and Dimensions of Whites' Racial Beliefs and Attitudes: Progress and Stagnation. *Racial Attitudes in the 1990s: Continuity and Change,* edited by S. Tuch and J. Martin, 93–120. Westport, Conn.: Praeger.

Bodziock, Joseph. 1990. The Weight of Sambo's Woes. *Perspectives on Black Popular Culture,* edited by Harry B. Shaw, 166–79. Bowling Green, OH: Bowling Green State University Popular Press.

Brantlinger, Patrick. 1990. *Crusoe's Footprints: Cultural Studies in Britain and America.* New York: Routledge.

Cherry, Robert. 1989. *Discrimination: Its Economic Impact on Blacks, Women, and Jews.* Lexington, MA: Lexington Books.

Cohen, Mark Nathan. 1998. *Culture of Intolerance: Chauvinism, Class, and Race in the United States.* New Haven, CT: Yale University Press.

Conrad, Peter, and Joseph W. Schneider. 1980. *Deviance and Medicalization.* Philadelphia: Temple University Press.

Cose, Eliott. 1993. *The Rage of a Privileged Class.* New York: HarperCollins.

Degler, Carl N. 1991. *In Search of Human Nature: The Decline and Revival of Darwinism in American Social Thought.* New York: Oxford University Press.

Feagin, Joe. 1991. The Continuing Significance of Race: Anti-black Discrimination in Public Places. *American Sociological Review,* 56:101–116.

———, and Melvin Sikes. 1994. *Living with Racism: The Black Middle Class Experience.* Boston: Beacon.

Garber, Marjorie. 1992. *Vested Interests: Cross Dressing and Cultural Anxiety.* New York: Harper.

Gould, Stephen Jay. 1981. *The Mismeasure of Man.* New York: W. W. Norton.

Haines, David W. 1989. *Refugees as Immigrants.* Totowa, NJ: Rowman and Littlefield.

Kasper, Anne. 1986. Consciousness Re-evaluated: Interpretive Theory and Feminist Scholarship. *Sociological Inquiry* 56(1).

Katz, Michael B. 1989. *The Undeserving Poor.* New York: Pantheon Books.

Kluegel, James, and Eliot Smith. 1986. *Beliefs about Inequality: Americans' Views of What Is and What Ought to Be.* New York: Aldine de Gruyter.

Le, C. N. 2001. The Model Minority Image. *Asian-Nation.* www.asian-nation.org/issues2.html.

Ludwig, Jack. 2003. Blacks and Whites Still Perceive Local Treatment of Blacks Differently. Gallup Organization, Gallup Poll News Service. May 27.

——— 2004. Acceptance of Interracial Marriage at Record High. Gallup Organization, Gallup Poll News Service. June 1.

Marshall, Gordon. 1994. *The Concise Oxford Dictionary of Sociology.* Oxford, UK: Oxford University Press.

Omi, Michael, and Howard Winant. 1994. *Racial Formation in the United States.* New York: Routledge.

Pierce, Christine. 1971. Natural Law Language and Women. *Woman in Sexist Society,* edited by Vivian Gornick and Barbara K. Moran, 242–58. New York: New American Library.

Riggs, Marlon. 1987. *Ethnic Notions.* California Newsreel (video).

St. John, C., and T. Heald-Moore. 1995. Fear of Black Strangers. *Social Science Research,* 24:262–280.

Sayers, Janet. 1982. *Biological Politics: Feminist and Anti-feminist Perspectives.* London: Tavistock Publications.

Schuman, Howard. 1971. Free Will and Determinism in Beliefs about Race. *Majority and Minority: The Dynamics of Racial and Ethnic Relations,* edited by N. Yetman and C. Steeh, 375–380. Boston: Allyn & Bacon.

———, Charlotte Steeh, Lawrence Bobo, and Maria Krysan. 1997. *Racial Attitudes in America: Trends and Interpretations.* Rev. ed. Cambridge: Harvard University Press.

Shipman, Pat. 1994. *The Evolution of Racism: Human Differences and the Use and Abuse of Science.* New York: Simon and Schuster.

Smith, Dorothy. 1978. A Peculiar Eclipsing: Women's Exclusion from Men's Culture. *Women's Studies International Quarterly* 1:281–95.

———. 1990. *The Conceptual Practices of Power: A Feminist Sociology of Knowledge.* Boston: Northeastern University Press.

Smith, Tom. 1990. Ethnic Images. General Social Survey Technical Report, No. 19, National Opinion Research Center. University of Chicago.

Steinberg, Steven. 1989. *The Ethnic Myth: Race, Ethnicity, and Class in America.* Boston: Beacon Press.

Takaki, Ronald. 1993. *A Different Mirror: A History of Multicultural America.* Boston: Little, Brown.

U.S. Census Bureau. 2000. *Statistical Abstract of the United States: 2000* (120th ed.). Washington DC: United States Department of Commerce.

U.S. Census Bureau. 2001. *Money Income in the United States: 2000.* Current Population Reports. P60-213. September.

Weinberg, Daniel H. 2003. Press Briefing on 2002 Income and Poverty Estimates. U.S. Census Bureau. September 26.

LAW, POLITICS, AND POLICY

Thirteen Key Supreme Court Cases and the Civil War Amendments

Individuals' lives are affected not only by social practices but also by law as interpreted in the courts. Under U.S. federalism Congress makes laws, the president swears to uphold the law, and the Supreme Court interprets the law. When state laws appear to be in conflict with the United States Constitution or when the terminology of the Constitution is vague, the Supreme Court interprets such laws. We will focus here on Supreme Court rulings that have defined the roles individuals are allowed to assume in American society.

As the supreme law above laws enacted by Congress, the U.S. Constitution determines individual and group status. A brief document, the Constitution describes the division of power between the federal and state governments, as well as the rights of individuals. Only 16 amendments to the Constitution have been added since the ratification of the Bill of Rights (the first 10 amendments). Although the Constitution appears to be sweeping in scope—relying on the principle that all men are created equal—in reality the Constitution is an exclusionary document. It omitted women, Native Americans, and African Americans except for the purpose of determining a population count. In instances where the Constitution was vague on the rights of each of these groups, clarification was later sought through court cases.

Federalism provides four primary methods by which citizens may influence the political process. First, the Constitution grants citizens the right to petition the government, that is, the right to lobby. Second, as a civic duty, citizens are expected to vote and seek office. Once in office citizens can change conditions by writing new legislation, known as *statutory law*. Third, changes can be achieved through the lengthy procedure of passing constitu-

tional amendments, which affect all citizens. Controversial amendments have often become law after social movement activists advocated passage for several years or after a major national upheaval, such as the Civil War.

Last, the Constitution provides that citizens can sue to settle disputes. Through this method, sweeping social changes can take place when Supreme Court decisions affect all the individuals in a class. Thus, the assertion of individual rights has become a key tool of those who were not privileged by the Constitution to clarify their status in American society.

An examination of landmark cases reveals the continuous difficulties some groups have had in securing their rights through legal remedy. The Court has often taken a narrow perspective on what classes of people were to receive equal protection of the law, or were covered under the privileges and immunities clause.[1] Each group had to bring suit in every area where barriers existed. For example, white women who were citizens had to sue to establish that they had the right to inherit property, to serve on juries, to enter various professions, and in general to be treated as a class apart from their husband and family. Blacks sued to attend southern state universities and law schools, to participate in the all-white Democratic Party primary election,[2] to attend public schools which had been ordered to desegregate by the Supreme Court, and to vote without having to pay a poll tax. When these landmark cases were decided, they were perceived to herald sweeping changes in policy. Yet they proved to be only a guide to determining the rights of individuals.

I. *DRED SCOTT V. SANFORD* (1857)

Prior to the Civil War the Constitution was not precise on whether one was simultaneously a citizen of a given state and of the entire United States. Slavery further complicated the matter because the status of slaves and free persons of color was not specified in the Constitution, nor were members of either group considered citizens. Each state had the option of determining the status and rights of these nonwhites.

A federal form of government permitted flexibility by allowing states to differ on matters such as rights for its citizens. Yet as a newly invented form of government, a number of issues that were clear under British law were not settled until the Thirteenth, Fourteenth, and Fifteenth Amendments were added to the United States Constitution. Federalism raised questions about rights and privileges because a citizen was simultaneously living under the laws of a state and of the United States. Who had rights and privileges guaranteed by the Constitution? Did all citizens have all rights and privileges?

For example, what was the status of women? The Constitution provided for citizenship, but did not specify which rights and privileges were granted to female citizens. State laws considered white men and white women citizens, yet white women were often not allowed to own property, sue in court, or vote. Under federalism, each state enacted laws determining the rights and status of free blacks, slaves, white men, and white women so long as the laws did not conflict with the United States Constitution.

The *Dred Scott* case of 1846 considered the issues of slavery, property, citizenship, and the supremacy of the United States over individual states when a slave was taken to a free territory. The Court's holding primarily affected blacks, now called African Americans,[3] who sought the benefits of citizenship. Broadly, the case addressed American citizenship, a matter not clearly defined until passage of the Fourteenth Amendment in 1868.

Dred Scott was an enslaved man owned by Dr. John Emerson, a U.S. Army surgeon stationed in Missouri. When Emerson was transferred to Rock Island, Illinois, where slavery was forbidden, he took Dred Scott with him. Emerson was subsequently transferred to Fort Snelling, a territory (now Minnesota) where slavery was forbidden by the Missouri Compromise of 1820. In 1838, he returned to Missouri with Dred Scott.

In 1846 Scott brought suit in a Missouri circuit court to obtain his freedom on the grounds he had resided in free territory for periods of time. Scott won the case and his freedom. However, the judgment was reversed by the Missouri Supreme Court. Later, when John Sanford, a citizen of New York and the brother of Mrs. Emerson, arranged for the sale of Scott, the grounds were established for Scott to take his case to the federal circuit court in Missouri. The federal court ruled that Scott and his family were slaves and therefore the "lawful property" of Sanford. With the financial assistance of abolitionists, Scott appealed his case to the Supreme Court.

The Court's decision addressed these key questions:

1. Are blacks citizens?
2. Are blacks entitled to sue in court?
3. Can one have all the privileges and immunities of citizenship in a state, but not the United States?
4. Can one be a citizen of the United States and not be qualified to vote or hold office?

Excerpts from the Supreme Court Decision in *Dred Scott v. Sanford*[4]

Mr. Chief Justice Taney delivered the opinion of the Court:

> . . . The question is simply this: Can a Negro, whose ancestors were imported into this country and sold as slaves, become a member of the political community formed and brought into existence by the Constitution of the United States, and as such become entitled to all the rights, and privileges and immunities, guaranteed by that instrument to the citizen? One of which rights is the privilege of suing in a court of the United States. . . .
>
> The question before us is whether the class of persons described are constituent members of this sovereignty? We think they are not, and that they are not included, and were not intended to be included, under the word "citizens" in the Constitution, and can therefore claim none of the rights and privileges which that instrument provides for and secures to citizens of the United States.
>
> In discussing this question, we must not confound the rights of citizenship which a State may confer

within its own limits and the rights of citizenship as a member of the Union. It does not by any means follow, because he has all the rights and privileges of a citizen of a State, that he must be a citizen of the United States. He may have all of the rights and privileges of a citizen of a State, and yet not be entitled to the rights and privileges of a citizen in any other State. . . .

Undoubtedly a person may be a citizen . . . although he exercises no share of the political power, and is incapacitated from holding particular office. Those who have not the necessary qualifications cannot vote or hold the office, yet they are citizens.

The court is of the opinion, that . . . Dred Scott was not a citizen of Missouri within the meaning of the Constitution of the United States, and not entitled as such to sue in its courts: and, consequently, that the Circuit Court had no jurisdiction. . . .

II. THE CIVIL WAR AMENDMENTS

The Civil War (1861–1865) was fought over slavery, as well as the issue of supremacy of the national government over the individual states.

After the Civil War, members of Congress known as the Radical Republicans sought to protect the freedom of the former slaves by passing the Thirteenth, Fourteenth, and Fifteenth Amendments. These amendments, especially the Fourteenth, have provided the foundation for African Americans, as well as women, gays, Native Americans, immigrants, and those who are disabled to bring suit for equal treatment under the law.

Amendment XIII, 1865

(Slavery)

This amendment prohibited slavery and involuntary servitude in the United States. The entire amendment follows:

Section 1. Neither slavery nor involuntary servitude, except as a punishment whereof the party shall have been duly convicted, shall exist within the United States, or any place subject to their jurisdiction.

Section 2. Congress shall have power to enforce this article by appropriate legislation.

Amendment XIV, 1868

(Citizenship, Due Process, and Equal Protection of the Laws)

This amendment defined citizenship; prohibited the states from making or enforcing laws that abridged the privileges or immunities of citizenship; forbade states to deprive persons of life, liberty, or property without due process of law; and forbade states to deny equal protection of the law to any person. Over time the Fourteenth Amendment became the most important of the Reconstruction amendments. Key phrases such as "privileges and immunities," "deprive any person of life, liberty, or the pursuit of justice," and "deny to any person within its jurisdiction equal protection of the law" have caused this amendment to be the subject of more Supreme Court cases than any other provision of the Constitution. The entire amendment follows:

Section 1. All persons born or naturalized in the United States, and subject to the jurisdiction thereof, are citizens of the United States and of the State wherein they reside. No State shall make or enforce any law which shall abridge the privileges or immunities of citizens of the United States; nor shall any State deprive any person of life, liberty, or property, without due process of law; nor deny to any person within its jurisdiction the equal protection of the laws.

Section 2. Representatives shall be apportioned among the several States according to their respective numbers, counting the whole number of persons in each State, excluding Indians not taxed. But when the right to vote at any election for the choice of electors for President and Vice President of the United States, Representatives in Congress, the Executive and Judicial officers of a State, or the members of the Legislature thereof, is denied to any of the male inhabitants of such State, being twenty-one years of age, and citizens of the United States, or in any way abridged, except for participation in rebellion, or other crime, the basis of representation therein shall be reduced in proportion which the number of such male citizens shall bear to the whole number of male citizens twenty-one years of age in such State.

Section 3. No person shall be a Senator or Representative in Congress, or elector or President and Vice

President, or hold any office, civil or military, under the United States, or under any State, who, having previously taken an oath, as a member of Congress, or as an officer of the United States, or as a member of any State legislature, or as an executive or judicial officer of any State, to support the Constitution of the United States, shall have engaged in insurrection or rebellion against the same, or given aid or comfort to the enemies thereof. But Congress may by a vote of two-thirds of each House, remove such disability.

Section 4. The validity of the public debt of the United States, authorized by law, including debts incurred for payments of pensions and bounties for services in suppressing insurrection or rebellion, shall not be questioned. But neither the United States nor any State shall assume or pay any debt or obligation incurred in aid of insurrection or rebellion against the United States, or any claim for the loss or emancipation of any slave, but all such debts, obligations and claims shall be held illegal and void.

Section 5. The Congress shall have power to enforce, by appropriate legislation, the provisions of this article.

Amendment XV, 1870

(The Right to Vote)

The entire amendment follows:

Section 1. The right of citizens of the United States to vote shall not be denied or abridged by the United States or by any State on account of race, color, or previous condition of servitude.

Section 2. The Congress shall have power to enforce this article by appropriate legislation.

As we have seen, the Thirteenth, Fourteenth, and Fifteenth Amendments were added to the Constitution expressly with former slaves in mind. In Section 1 of the Fourteenth Amendment, the definition of *citizenship* was clarified and granted to blacks. In the Fifteenth Amendment black males, former slaves, were granted the right to vote. For women, however, the situation was different.

During the 19th century there was no doubt that white females were U.S. citizens, but their rights as citizens were unclear. For example, although they were citizens, women were not automatically enfranchised. Depending on state laws, they were barred from owning property, holding office, or voting. The 1872 case of *Bradwell v. The State of Illinois* specifically tested whether women as United States citizens had the right to become members of the bar. More generally, it addressed whether the rights of female citizens included the right to pursue any employment.

III. *MINOR V. HAPPERSETT* (1875)

The Fifteenth Amendment was not viewed as a triumph for women because it specifically denied them the vote. Section 2 of the Fourteenth Amendment for the first time made reference to males as citizens. Since black men were included but women of all races were omitted, women were left to continue to seek changes through the courts. This was a difficult route because in subsequent cases, judges often held a narrow view that the legislators wrote the amendment only with black males in mind. Thus, a pattern was soon established in which white women followed black men and women in asserting their rights as citizens as seen in the 1875 case of *Minor v. Happersett*. In *Dred Scott* the question was whether Scott was a citizen; in *Minor* the question was whether *Minor* as a citizen had the right to vote. In both cases the Supreme Court said no.

Virginia Minor, a native-born, free, white citizen of the United States and the state of Missouri, and over the age of 21 wished to vote for president, vice president, and members of Congress in the election of November 1872. She applied to the registrar of voters but was not allowed to vote because she was not a "male citizen of the United States." As a citizen of the United States, Minor sued under the privileges and immunities clause of the Fourteenth Amendment.

The Court's decision addressed these key questions:

1. Who is covered under the term *citizen?*
2. Is suffrage one of the privileges and immunities of citizenship?
3. Did the Constitution, as originally written, make all citizens voters?

4. Did the Fifteenth Amendment make all citizens voters?

5. Can a state confine voting to only male citizens without violating the Constitution?

While women were citizens of the United States and the state where they resided, they did not automatically possess all the privileges granted to male citizens, such as suffrage. This landmark case was not overturned until the passage of the Nineteenth Amendment, which enfranchised women, in 1920.[5]

Excerpts from the Supreme Court Decision in *Minor v. Happersett*[6]

Mr. Chief Justice Waite delivered the opinion of the Court:

. . . It is contended [by Minor's counsel] that the provisions of the Constitution and laws of the State of Missouri which confine the right of suffrage and registration therefore to men, are in violation of the Constitution of the United States, and therefore void. The argument is, that as a woman, born or naturalized in the United States is a citizen of the United States and of the State in which she resides, she has the right of suffrage as one of the privileges and immunities of her citizenship, which the State cannot by its laws or Constitution abridge.

There is no doubt that women may be citizens. . . .

. . . From this it is apparent that from the commencement of the legislation upon this subject alien women and alien minors could be made citizens by naturalization, and we think it will not be contended that native women and native minors were already citizens by birth.

. . . More cannot be necessary to establish the fact that sex has never been made one of the elements of citizenship in the United States. In this respect men have never had an advantage over women. The same laws precisely apply to both. The Fourteenth amendment did not affect the citizenship of women any more than it did of men . . . therefore, the rights of Mrs. Minor do not depend upon the amendment. She has always been a citizen from her birth, and entitled to all the privileges and immunities of citizenship. The amendment prohibited the State, of which she is a citizen, from abridging any of her privileges and immunities as a citizen of the United States.

. . . The direct question is, therefore, presented whether all citizens are necessarily voters.

The Constitution does not define the privileges and immunities of citizens. For that definition we must look elsewhere.

. . . The [Fourteenth] amendment did not add to the privileges and immunities of a citizen. It simply furnished an additional guarantee for the protection of such as he already had. No new voters were necessarily made by it.

. . . No new State has ever been admitted to the Union which has conferred the right of suffrage upon women, and this has never been considered a valid objection to her admission.

. . . Certainly, if the courts can consider any question settled, this is one. For nearly ninety years the people have acted upon the idea that the Constitution, when it conferred citizenship, did not necessarily confer the right of suffrage. . . . Our province is to decide what the law is, not to declare what it should be.

The *Dred Scott, Bradwell,* and *Minor* cases point to the similarity in the status of black men and women of all races in 19th-century America. As one judicial scholar noted, race and sex were comparable classes, distinct from all others. Historically, these "natural classes" were considered permanent and unchangeable.[7] Thus, both slavery and the subjugation of women have been described as a caste system where one's status is fixed from birth and not alterable based on wealth or talent.[8]

Indeed, the connection between the enslavement of black people and the legal and social standing of women was often traced to the Old Testament. Historically slavery was justified on the grounds that one should look to Abraham; the Bible refers to Abraham's wives, children, men servants, maid servants, camels, and cattle as his property. A man's wife and children were considered his slaves. By the logic of the 19th century, if women were slaves, why shouldn't blacks be also?

Thus, the concepts of race and sex have been historically linked. Since "the doctrines were developed by the same people for the same purpose it is not surprising to find anti-feminism to be an echo of racism, and vice versa."[9]

Additional constitutional amendments were necessary for women and African Americans to exercise the privileges of citizenship that were automatically granted to white males. Nonetheless, even after amendments were enacted, African Americans still had to fight for enforcement of the law.

IV. *PLESSY V. FERGUSON* (1896)

After the Civil War the northern victors imposed military rule on the South.[10] White landowners and former slaveholders often found themselves with unproductive farmland and no free laborers. Aside from the economic loss of power, white males were in a totally new political environment: Black men had been elevated to citizens; former slaves were now eligible to vote, run for office, and hold seats in the state or national legislature. To ensure the rights of former slaves, the U.S. Congress passed the Civil War Amendments and provided federal troops to oversee federal elections.

However, when federal troops were withdrawn from the southern states in 1877, enfranchised black men became vulnerable to former masters who immediately seized political control of the state legislatures. In order to solidify political power, whites rewrote state constitutions to disenfranchise black men. To ensure that all blacks were restricted to a subordinate status, southern states systematically enacted "Jim Crow" laws, rigidly segregating society into black and white communities. These laws barred blacks from using the same public facilities as whites, including schools, hospitals, restaurants, hotels, and recreation areas. With the cooperation of southern elected officials, the Ku Klux Klan, a white supremacist, terrorist organization, grew in membership. The return of political power to whites without any federal presence to protect the black community set the stage for "separate but equal" legislation to become a constitutionally valid racial doctrine.

Under slavery, interracial sexual contact was forbidden but white masters nonetheless had the power to sexually exploit the black women who worked for them. The children of these relationships, especially if they looked white, posed potential inheritance problems because whites feared that such children might seek to exercise the privileges accorded to their white fathers. In order to keep all children of such relationships subordinate in the two-tiered racial system, descent was based on the race of the mother. Consequently, regardless of color, all the children of black women were defined as black.

This resulted in a rigid biracial structure where all persons with "one drop" of black blood were labeled black. Consequently, the "black" community consisted of a wide range of skin color based on this one-drop rule. Therefore, at times individuals with known black ancestry might look phenotypically white. This situation created a group of African Americans who had one-eighth or less African ancestry.

Louisiana was one of the few states to modify the one-drop rule of racial categorization because it considered mulattoes a valid racial category. A term derived from Spanish, *mulatto* refers to the offspring of a "pure African Negro" and a "pure white." Over time, *mulatto* came to encompass children of whites and "mixed Negroes."

These were the social conditions in 1896, when Homer Adolph Plessy, a mulatto, sought to test Louisiana laws that imposed racial segregation. Plessy and other mulattoes decided to test the applicability of the law requiring racial separation on railroad cars traveling in interstate transportation.

In 1890, Louisiana had followed other southern states in enacting Jim Crow laws that were written in compliance with the Equal Protection Clause of Section 1 of the Fourteenth Amendment. These laws required separate accommodations for white and black railroad passengers. In this case, Plessy, a U.S. citizen and a resident of Louisiana who was one-eighth black, paid for a first-class ticket on the East Louisiana Railway traveling from New Orleans to Covington, Louisiana. When he entered the passenger train, Plessy took a vacant seat in a coach designated for white passengers. He claimed that he was entitled to every "recognition, right, privilege, and immunity" granted to white citizens of the

United States by the Constitution. Under Louisiana law, the conductor, who knew Plessy, was required to ask him to sit in a coach specifically assigned to nonwhite persons. By law, passengers who sat in the inappropriate coach were fined or imprisoned. When Plessy refused to comply with the order, he was removed from the train and imprisoned.

Plessy v. Ferguson is the one case that solidified the power of whites over blacks in southern states. Through state laws, and with the additional federal weight in the *Plessy* decision, whites began to enforce rigid separation of the races in every aspect of life.

In *Plessy,* Justice John Marshall Harlan wrote the only dissenting opinion. Usually in Supreme Court cases, attention is focused on the majority, rather than the dissenting opinion. However, in this case Justice Harlan's dissent is noteworthy because his views on race and citizenship pointed out a line of reasoning that eventually broke down segregation and second-class citizenship for blacks.

Justice Harlan's background as a Kentucky slaveholder who later joined the Union side during the Civil War is cited as an explanation of his views. Some scholars speculate that his shift from slaveholder to a defender of the rights of blacks was caused by his observation of beatings, lynchings, and the use of intimidation tactics against blacks in Kentucky after the Civil War. In a quirk of history, when *Plessy v. Ferguson* was overturned in 1954 by a unanimous opinion in *Brown v. Board of Education,* Justice Harlan's grandson was a member of the Supreme Court.

The Court's decision addressed these key questions:

1. How is a black person defined?
2. Who determines when an individual is black or white?
3. Does providing separate but equal facilities violate the Thirteenth Amendment?
4. Does providing separate but equal facilities violate the Fourteenth Amendment?
5. Does a separate but equal doctrine imply inferiority of either race?
6. Can state laws require the separation of the two races in schools, theaters, and railway cars?
7. Does the separation of the races when applied to commerce within the state of Louisiana abridge the privileges and immunities of the "colored man,"[11] deprive him of equal protection of the law, or deprive him of his property without due process of law under the Fourteenth Amendment?

Excerpts from the Supreme Court Decision in *Plessy v. Ferguson*[12]

Mr. Justice Brown delivered the opinion of the Court:

... An [1890] act of the General Assembly of the State of Louisiana, provid[ed] for separate railway carriages for the white and colored races.

... No person or persons, shall be admitted to occupy seats in coaches, other than the ones assigned to them on account of the race they belong to.

... The constitutionality of this act is attacked upon the ground that it conflicts both with the Thirteenth Amendment of the Constitution, abolishing slavery, and the Fourteenth Amendment, which prohibits certain restrictive legislation.

... A statute which implied merely a legal distinction between the white and colored races ... has no tendency to destroy the legal equality of the two races, or reestablish a state of servitude.

... The object of the amendment [the Fourteenth Amendment] was undoubtedly to enforce the absolute equality of the two races before the law, but in the nature of things it could not have been intended to abolish distinctions based upon color, or a commingling of the two races upon terms unsatisfactory to either.

Laws permitting and even requiring their separation in places where they are liable to be brought into contact do not necessarily imply the inferiority of either race to the other, and have been generally, if not universally recognized as within the competency of the state legislatures in the exercise of their police power. The most common instance of this is connected with the establishment of separate schools for white and colored children, which has been held to be a valid exercise of the legislative power even by courts of States where the political rights of the colored race have been longest and most earnestly enforced. One of the earliest of these cases is that of *Roberts v. City of Boston,* 5 Cush. 198, in which the Supreme Judicial Court of Massachusetts held that the general school committee of Boston had power to make provision for the instruction of colored children in separate schools established exclusively for them, and to prohibit their attendance upon the other schools.

. . . We are not prepared to say that the conductor, in assigning passengers to the coaches according to their race, does not act at his peril. . . . The power to assign to a particular coach obviously implies the power to determine to which race the passenger belongs, as well as the power to determine who, under the laws of the particular State, is to be deemed a white, and who is a colored person.

. . . We consider the underlying fallacy of the plaintiff's argument to consist in the assumption that the enforced separation of the two races stamps the colored race with a badge of inferiority. If this be so, it is not by reason of anything found in the act, but solely because the colored race chooses to put that construction upon it. . . . The argument also assumes that social prejudices may be overcome by legislation, and that equal rights cannot be secured to the negro except by an enforced commingling of the two races. We cannot accept this proposition. If the two races are to meet upon terms of social equality, it must be the result of natural affinities, a mutual appreciation of each other's merits and a voluntary consent of individuals.

. . . If the civil and political rights of both races be equal one cannot be inferior to the other civilly or politically. If one race be inferior to the other socially, the Constitution of the United States cannot put them upon the same plane.

It is true that the question for the proportion of colored blood necessary to constitute a colored person, as distinguished from a white person, is one upon which there is a difference of opinion in the different States, some holding that any visible admixture of black blood stamps the persons as belonging to the colored races, others that it depends upon the preponderance of blood . . . still others that the predominance of white blood must only be in the proportion of three fourths. . . . But these are questions to be determined under the laws of each State. . . .

Mr. Justice Harlan in the dissenting opinion:

. . . It was said in argument that the statute of Louisiana does not discriminate against either race, but prescribes a rule applicable alike to white and colored citizens. . . . [But] everyone knows that the statute in question had its origin in the purpose, not so much to exclude white persons from railroad cars occupied by blacks, as to exclude colored people from coaches occupied by or assigned to white persons.

. . . It is one thing for railroad carriers to furnish, or to be required by law to furnish, equal accommodations for all whom they are under a legal duty to carry. It is quite another thing for government to forbid citizens of the white and black races from traveling in the same public conveyance, and to punish officers of railroad companies for permitting persons of the two races to occupy the same passenger coach. If a State can prescribe, as a rule of civil conduct, that whites and blacks shall not travel as passengers in the same railroad coach, why may it not so regulate the use of the streets of its cities and towns as to compel white citizens to keep on one side of a street and black citizens to keep on the other? Why may it not, upon like grounds, punish whites and blacks who ride together in street cars or in open vehicles on a public road or street? Why may it not require sheriffs to assign whites to one side of a court-room and blacks to the other? And why may it not also prohibit the commingling of the two races in the galleries of legislative halls or in public assemblages convened for the consideration of the political questions of the day? Further, if this statute of Louisiana is consistent with the personal liberty of citizens, why may not the State require the separation in railroad coaches of native and naturalized citizens of the United States, or of Protestants and Roman Catholics?

. . . In my opinion, the judgment this day rendered will, in time, prove to be quite pernicious as the decision made by this tribunal in the Dred Scott case.

. . . The thin disguise of "equal" accommodations for passengers in railroad coaches will not mislead anyone, nor atone for the wrong this day done.

Thus, the *Plessy v. Ferguson* decision firmly established the separate but equal doctrine in the South until the National Association for the Advancement of Colored Persons (NAACP) began to systematically attack Jim Crow laws. It is ironic that in *Plessy* the systematic social, political, and economic suppression of blacks in the South through Jim Crow laws was justified in terms of a case decided in the northern city of Boston, where the segregation of schools occurred in practice (*de facto*), but not by force of law (*de jure*). In that 1849 case (*Roberts v. City of Boston,* 5 Cush. 198), a parent had unsuccessfully sued on behalf of his daughter to attend a public school. Thus, educational access became both the first and last chapter—in the 1954 case of *Brown v. Board of Education*—of the doctrine of separate but equal.

V. *BROWN V. BOARD OF EDUCATION* (1954)

Unlike many of the earlier cases brought by individual women, blacks, or Native Americans, *Brown v. Board of Education* was the result of a concerted campaign against racial segregation led by Howard University School of Law graduates and the NAACP. In the 1930s, the NAACP Legal Defense Fund began to systematically fight for fair employment, fair housing, and desegregation of public education. Key lawyers in the campaign against segregation were Charles Houston, Thurgood Marshall, James Nabrit, and William Hastie. Marshall later became a Supreme Court justice, Nabrit became president of Howard University, and Hastie became a federal judge.

By using the Fourteenth Amendment, *Brown* became the key case in an attempt to topple the 1896 separate but equal doctrine. Legal strategists knew that educational opportunity and better housing conditions were essential if black Americans were to achieve upward mobility. While one group of lawyers focused on restrictive covenant cases,[13] which prevented blacks from buying housing in white neighborhoods, another spearheaded the drive for blacks to enter state-run professional schools.

In 1954, suits were brought in Kansas, South Carolina, Virginia, and Delaware on behalf of black Americans seeking to attend nonsegregated public schools. However, the case is commonly referred to as *Brown v. Board of Education*. The plaintiffs in the suit contended that segregation in the public schools denied them equal protection of the laws under the Fourteenth Amendment. The contention

was that since segregated public schools were not and could not be made equal, black American children were deprived of equal protection of the laws.

The Court's unanimous decision addressed these key questions:

1. Are public schools segregated by race detrimental to black children?
2. Does segregation result in an inferior education for black children?
3. Does the maintenance of segregated public schools violate the Equal Protection Clause of the Fourteenth Amendment?
4. Is the maintenance of segregated public school facilities *inherently* unequal?
5. What was the intent of the framers of the Fourteenth Amendment regarding distinctions between whites and blacks?
6. Is the holding in *Plessy v. Ferguson* applicable to public education?
7. Does segregation of children in public schools *solely on the basis of race,* even though the physical facilities and other "tangible" factors may be equal, deprive the children of the minority group of equal educational opportunities?

Excerpts from the Supreme Court Decision in *Brown v. Board of Education*[14]

Mr. Chief Justice Warren delivered the opinion of the Court:

> . . . In each of these cases [NAACP suits in Kansas, South Carolina, Virginia, and Delaware] minors of the Negro race, through their legal representatives, seek the aid of the courts in obtaining admission to the public schools of their community on a nonsegregated basis. . . . This segregation was alleged to deprive the plaintiffs of the equal protection of the laws under the Fourteenth Amendment. In each of the cases other than the Delaware case, a three-judge federal district court denied relief to the plaintiffs on the so-called "separate but equal" doctrine announced by this Court in *Plessy v. Ferguson,* 163 U.S. 537. Under that doctrine, equality of treatment is accorded when the races are provided substantially equal facilities, even though these facilities be separated. . . .

The plaintiffs contend that segregated schools are not "equal" and cannot be made "equal," and that hence they are deprived of the equal protection of the laws.

. . . The most avid proponents of the post–[Civil] War amendments undoubtedly intended them to remove all legal distinctions among "all persons born or naturalized in the United States."

In the first cases in this Court construing the Fourteenth Amendment, decided shortly after its adoption, the Court interpreted it as prescribing all state imposed discriminations against the Negro race. The doctrine of "separate but equal" did not make its appearance in this Court until 1896 in the *Plessy v. Ferguson, supra,* involving not education but transportation.

In these days, it is doubtful that any child may reasonably be expected to succeed in life if he is denied the opportunity of an education. Such an opportunity where the state has undertaken to provide it, is a right which must be made available to all on equal terms.

We come then to the question presented: Does segregation of children in public schools solely on the basis of race, even though the physical facilities and other "tangible" factors may be equal, deprive the children of the minority group of equal educational opportunities? We believe that it does.

To separate them [the children] from others of similar age and qualifications solely because of their race generates a feeling of inferiority as to their status in the community that may affect their hearts and minds in a way unlikely ever to be undone.

We conclude that in the field of public education the doctrine of "separate but equal" has no place. Separate educational facilities are inherently unequal. Therefore, we hold that the plaintiffs and others similarly situated for whom the actions have been brought are, by reason of the segregation complained of, deprived of the equal protection of the laws guaranteed by the Fourteenth Amendment.

. . . We have now announced that such segregation is a denial of the equal protection of the laws.

VI. *YICK WO V. HOPKINS* (1886)

In the 1880s, the questions of citizenship and the rights of citizens were raised again by Native Americans and Asian immigrants. While the status of citizenship for African Americans was settled by the Thirteenth and Fourteenth Amendments, the extent of the privileges and immunities clause still needed clarification. Yick Wo, a Chinese immigrant living in San Francisco, brought suit under the Fourteenth Amendment to see if it covered all persons in the territorial United States regardless of race, color, or nationality.

The Chinese were different from European immigrants because they came to the United States under contract to work as laborers building the transcontinental railroad. When Chinese workers remained, primarily in California, after the completion of the railroad in 1869, Congress became anxious about this "foreign element" that was non-Christian and non-European. Chinese immigrants were seen as an economic threat because they would work for less than white males. To address the issue of economic competition, the Chinese Exclusion Act was passed in 1882 to prohibit further immigration to the United States. This gave the Chinese the unique status among immigrants of being the only group barred from entry into the United States and barred from becoming naturalized U.S. citizens.

Yick Wo, a subject of the Emperor of China, went to San Francisco in 1861, where he operated a laundry at the same premise for 22 years with consent from the Board of Fire Wardens. When the consent decree expired on October 1, 1885, Yick Wo routinely reapplied to continue to operate a laundry. He was, however, denied a license. Of the over 300 laundries in the city and county of San Francisco, about 240 were owned by Chinese immigrants. Most of these laundries were wooden, the most common construction material used at that time, although it posed a fire hazard. Yick Wo and more than 150 of his countrymen were arrested and charged with carrying on business without having special consent, while those who were not subjects of China and were operating some 80 laundries under similar conditions, were allowed to conduct business.

Yick Wo stated that he and 200 of his countrymen with similar situations petitioned the Board of Supervisors for permission to continue to conduct business in the same buildings they had occupied for more than 20 years. The petitions of all the Chinese were denied, while all petitions of those who were not Chinese were granted (with one exception).

Did this prohibition of the occupation and destruction of the business and property of the Chinese laundrymen in San Francisco constitute the proper regulation of business, or was it discrimination and a violation of important rights secured by the Fourteenth Amendment?

The Court's decision addressed these key questions:

1. Does this municipal ordinance regulating public laundries within the municipality of San Francisco violate the United States Constitution?
2. Does carrying out this municipal ordinance violate the Fourteenth Amendment?
3. Does the guarantee of protection of the Fourteenth Amendment extend to all persons within the territorial jurisdiction of the United States regardless of race, color, or nationality?
4. Are the subjects of the Emperor of China who, temporarily or permanently, reside in the United States entitled to enjoy the protection guaranteed by the Fourteenth Amendment?

Excerpts from the Supreme Court Decision in *Yick Wo v. Hopkins*[15]

Mr. Justice Matthews delivered the opinion of the Court:

> ... In both of these cases [*Yick Wo v. Hopkins* and *Wo Lee v. Hopkins*] the ordinance involved was simply a prohibition to carry on the washing and ironing of clothes in public laundries and washhouses, within the city and county of San Francisco, from ten o'clock p.m. until six o'clock a.m. of the following day. This provision was held to be purely a police regulation, within the competency of any municipality.
>
> ... The rights of the petitioners are not less because they are aliens and subjects of the Emperor of China.
>
> The Fourteenth amendment to the Constitution is not confined to the protection of citizens. It says: "Nor shall any State deprive any person of life, liberty, or property without due process of law; nor deny to any person within its jurisdiction the equal protection of the laws." These provisions are universal in their application, to all persons within the territorial jurisdiction, without regard to any differences of race, or color, or of nationality; and the equal protection from the laws is a pledge of the protection of equal laws. ...
>
> Though the law itself be fair on its face and impartial in appearance, yet, it is applied and administered by public authority with an evil eye and unequal hand, so as practically to make unjust and illegal discriminations between persons in similar circumstances. ...
>
> ... No reason whatever, except the will of the supervisors, is assigned why they should not be permitted to carry on, in the accustomed manner, their harmless and useful occupation, on which they depend for a livelihood. And while this consent of the supervisors is withheld from them and from two hundred others who have also petitioned, all of whom happened to be Chinese subjects, eighty others, not Chinese subjects, are permitted to carry on similar business under similar conditions. The fact of this discrimination is admitted. No reason for it is shown, ... no reason for it exists except hostility to the race and nationality to which the petitioners belong, and which in the eye of the law is not justified. The discrimination is, therefore, illegal, and the public administration which enforces it is a denial of the equal protection of the laws and a violation of the Fourteenth amendment of the Constitution. The imprisonment of the petitioners is, therefore illegal, and they must be discharged.

The decision in *Yick Wo* demonstrated the Court's perspective that the Fourteenth Amendment applied to all persons, citizens and noncitizens.

VII. *ELK V. WILKINS* (1884)

In the late 19th century, Native Americans constituted a problematic class when the Supreme Court considered citizenship. Although Native Americans were the original inhabitants of the territory that became the United States, they were considered outside the concept of citizenship. They were viewed as a separate nation, and described as uncivilized, alien people who were not worthy of citizenship in the political community. As Native Americans were driven from their homeland and pushed farther west, the United States government developed a policy of containment by establishing reservations. Native Americans who lived with their tribes on such reservations were presumed to be members of "not strictly speaking, foreign states, but alien nations." The Constitution made no provisions for naturalizing Native Americans or defining the status of those who chose to live in the territorial United States rather than be assigned to reservations. It was presumed that Native Americans would remain on the reservations. The framers of the Constitution had not given any thought as to when or how a Native American might become a U.S. citizen. When the Naturalization Law of 1790 was written, only Europeans were anticipated as future citizens. The citizenship of Native Americans was not settled until 1924, when a statutory law, not a constitutional amendment, granted citizenship.

Elk v. Wilkins raised the question of citizenship and voting behavior as a privilege of citizenship. In 1857, the Court had easily dismissed Dred Scott's suit on the grounds that he was not a citizen. Since he did not hold citizenship, he could not sue. *Minor v. Happersett* in 1872 considered the citizenship and voting issue with a female plaintiff. In that case, citizenship was not in doubt but the court stated that citizenship did not automatically confer the right to suffrage. In *Elk,* a Native American claimed citizenship and the right to vote. Before considering the right to vote, the Court first examined whether Elk was a citizen and the process by which one becomes a citizen.

As midwestern cities emerged from westward expansion in the 1880s, a few Native Americans left their reservations to live and work in those cities. John Elk left his tribe and moved to Omaha, Nebraska, under the jurisdiction of the United States. In April 1880, he attempted to vote for members of the city council. Elk met the residency requirements in Nebraska and Douglas County for voting. Claiming that he complied with all of the statutory provisions, Elk asserted that under the Fourteenth and Fifteenth Amendments, he was a citizen of the United States who was entitled to exercise the franchise, regardless of race or color. He further

claimed that Wilkins, the voter registrar, "designedly, corruptly, willfully, and maliciously" refused to register him for the sole reason that he was a Native American.

The Court's decision addressed these key questions:

1. Is a Native American still a member of an Indian tribe when he voluntarily separates himself from his tribe and seeks residence among the white citizens of the state?
2. What was the intent of the Fourteenth Amendment regarding who could become a citizen?
3. Can Native Americans become naturalized citizens?
4. Can Native Americans become citizens of the United States without the consent of the U.S. government?
5. Must Native Americans adopt the habits of a "civilized" life before they become U.S. citizens?
6. Is a Native American who is taxed a citizen?

Excerpts from the Supreme Court Decision in *Elk v. Wilkins*[16]

Mr. Justice Gray delivered the opinion of the Court.

... The plaintiff ... relies on the first clause of the first section of the Fourteenth amendment of the Constitution of the United States, by which "all persons born or naturalized in the United States, and subject to the jurisdiction thereof, are citizens of the United States and of the State wherein they reside"; and on the Fifteenth amendment, which provides that "the right of citizens of the United States to vote shall not be denied or abridged by the United States or by any State on account of race, color, or previous condition of servitude."

... The question then is, whether an Indian, born a member of the Indian tribes within the United States, is, merely by reason of his birth within the United States, and of his afterwards voluntarily separating himself from his tribe and taking up his residence among white citizens, a citizen of the United States, within the meaning of the first section of the Fourteenth amendment of the Constitution.

... The Indian tribes, being within the territorial limits of the United States, were not, strictly speaking, foreign States; but they were alien nations, distinct political communities, with whom the United States might and habitually did deal, as they thought fit, either through treaties made by the President and Senate, or through acts of Congress in the ordinary forms of legislation. The members of those tribes owed immediate allegiance to their several tribes, and were not a part of the United States. They were in a dependent condition, a state of pupilage, resembling that of a ward to his guardian.

. . . They were never deemed citizens of the United States, except under explicit provisions of treaty or statute to that effect, either declaring a certain tribe, or such members of it as chose to remain behind on the removal of the tribe westward, to be citizens, or authorizing individuals of particular tribes to become citizens. . . .

This [opening] section of the Fourteenth amendment contemplates two sources of citizenship, and two sources only: birth and naturalization.

. . . Slavery having been abolished, and the persons formerly held as slaves made citizens. . . . But Indians not taxed are still excluded from the count [U.S. Census count for apportioning seats in the U.S. House of Representatives],[17] for the reason that they are not citizens. Their absolute exclusion from the basis of representation, in which all other persons are now included, is wholly inconsistent with their being considered citizens.

. . . Such Indians, then, not being citizens by birth, can only become so in the second way mentioned in the Fourteenth amendment, by being "naturalized in the United States," by or under some treaty or statute.

. . . The treaty of 1867 with the Kansas Indians strikingly illustrates the principle that no one can become a citizen of a nation without its consent, and directly contradicts the supposition that a member of an Indian tribe can at will be alternately a citizen of the United States and a member of the tribe.

. . . But the question whether any Indian tribes, or any members thereof, have become so far advanced in civilization, that they should be let out of the state of pupilage, and admitted to the privileges and responsibilities of citizenship, is a question to be decided by the nation whose wards they are and whose citizens they seek to become, and not by each Indian for himself.

. . . And in a later case [Judge Deady in the District Court of the United States for the District of Oregon]

said: "But an Indian cannot make himself a citizen of the United States without the consent and cooperation of the government. The fact that he has abandoned his nomadic life or tribal relations, and adopted the habits and manners of civilized people, may be a good reason why he should be made a citizen of the United States, but does not of itself make him one. To be a citizen of the United States is a political privilege which no one, not born to, can assume without its consent in some form.

Mr. Justice Harlan in the dissenting opinion:

. . . We submit that the petition does sufficiently show that the plaintiff is taxed, that is, belongs to the class which, by the laws of Nebraska, are subject to taxation.

. . . The plaintiff is a citizen and *bona fide* resident of Nebraska. . . . He is subject to taxation, and is taxed, in that State. Further: The plaintiff has become so far incorporated with the mass of the people of Nebraska that . . . he constitutes a part of her militia.

By the act of April 9, 1866, entitled "An Act to protect all persons in the United States in their civil rights, and furnish means for their vindication" (14 Stat. 27), it is provided that "all persons born in the United States and not subject to any foreign power, excluding Indians not taxed, are hereby declared to be citizens of the United States." . . . Beyond question, by that act, national citizenship was conferred directly upon all persons in this country, of whatever race (excluding only "Indians not taxed"), who were born within the territorial limits of the United States, and were not subject to any foreign power. Surely every one must admit that an Indian, residing in one of the States, and subject to taxation there, became by force alone of the act of 1866, a citizen of the United States, although he may have been, when born, a member of a tribe.

. . . If he did not acquire national citizenship on abandoning his tribe [moving from the reservation] and . . . by residence in one of the States, subject to the complete jurisdiction of the United States, then the Fourteenth amendment has wholly failed to accomplish, in respect of the Indian race, what, we think, was intended by it, and there is still in this country a despised and rejected class of persons, with no nationality; who born in our territory, owing no allegiance to foreign power, and subject, as residents of the States, to all the burdens of government, are yet not members of any political community nor entitled to any of the rights, privileges, or immunities of citizens of the United States.

In all, the Court never addressed Elk's right to vote because the primary question involved Elk's citizenship. By excluding him from citizenship because he had not been naturalized and because there was no provision for naturalization, John Elk was left outside of the political community as was Dred Scott.

VIII. *LAU V. NICHOLS* (1974)

In the 19th century, Native Americans and Asian immigrants sought to exercise rights under the Fourteenth Amendment although it had been designed explicitly to protect blacks. In the 20th century, issues first raised by African Americans, such as equality in public education, again presented other minority groups with an opportunity to test their rights under the Constitution.

Brown v. Board of Education forced the Court to consider the narrow question of the distribution of resources between black and white school systems. The *Brown* decision addressed only education. It did not extend to the other areas of segregation in American society, such as the segregation of public transportation (e.g., buses) or public accommodations (e.g., restaurants and hotels). Indeed, *Brown* had not even specified how the integration of the school system was to take place. All of these questions were taken up by the Civil Rights movement that followed the *Brown* decision.

Once the separate but equal doctrine was nullified in education, immigrants raised other issues of equality. In the 1970s, suits were brought on behalf of the children of illegal immigrants, non-English-speaking children of Chinese ancestry, and children of low-income parents.

In *Lau v. Nichols,* a non-English-speaking minority group questioned equality in public education. The case was similar to *Brown* because it concerned public education, the Equal Protection Clause of the Fourteenth Amendment, and the suit was brought on behalf of minors; but the two cases also differed in many respects. The 1954 decision in

Brown was part of a series of court cases attacking segregated facilities primarily in southern states. It addressed only the issues of black-white interaction.

In *Lau v. Nichols,* a suit was brought on behalf of children of Chinese ancestry who attended public schools in San Francisco. Although the children did not speak English, their classes in school were taught entirely in that language. (Some of the children received special instruction in the English language; others did not.) The suit did not specifically ask for bilingual education, nor did the Court require it, but *Lau* led to the development of such programs. In bilingual education, the curriculum is taught in children's native language, but they are also given separate instruction in the English language, and over time they are moved into English throughout their courses.

The *Lau* decision hinged in part on Department of Health, Education, and Welfare guidelines that prohibited discrimination in federally assisted programs. The decision was narrow because it instructed only the lower court to provide appropriate relief. The Court's ruling did not guarantee minority language rights, nor did it require bilingual education.

The Court's decision addressed these key questions:

1. Does a public school system that provides for instruction only in English violate the equal protection clause of the Fourteenth Amendment?
2. Does a public school system that provides for instruction only in English violate section 601 of the Civil Rights Act of 1964?
3. Do Chinese-speaking students who are in the minority receive fewer benefits from the school system than the English-speaking majority?
4. Must a school system that has a minority of students who do not speak English provide bilingual instruction?

Excerpts from the Supreme Court Decision in *Lau v. Nichols*[18]

Mr. Justice Douglas delivered the opinion of the Court:

The San Francisco, California, school system was integrated in 1971 as a result of a federal court decree. The District Court found that there are 2,856 students of Chinese ancestry in the school system who do not speak English. Of those who have that language deficiency, about 1,000 are given supplemental courses in the English language. About 1,800 however, do not receive that instruction.

This class suit brought by non-English-speaking Chinese students against officials responsible for the operation of the San Francisco Unified School District seeks relief against the unequal educational opportunities, which are alleged to violate, *inter alia,* the Fourteenth Amendment. No specific remedy is urged upon us. . . .

The Court of Appeals [holding that there was no violation of the Equal Protection Clause of the Fourteenth Amendment or of section 601 of the Civil Rights Act of 1964] reasoned that "[e]very student brings to the starting line of his educational career different advantages and disadvantages caused in part by social, economic and cultural background, created and continued completely apart from any contribution by the school system." . . . Section 71 of the California Education Code states that "English shall be the basic language of instruction in all schools." That section permits a school district to determine "when and under what circumstances instruction may be given bilingually." . . .

Under these state-imposed standards there is no equality of treatment merely by providing students with the same facilities, textbooks, teachers, and curriculum; for students who do not understand English are effectively foreclosed from any meaningful education.

. . . We know that those who do not understand English are certain to find their classroom experiences wholly incomprehensible and in no way meaningful.

We do not reach the Equal Protection Clause argument which has been advanced but rely solely on section 601 of the Civil Rights Act of 1964, 42 U.S.C. section 2000d. to reverse the Court of Appeals.

That section bans discrimination based "on the ground of race, color, or national origin, in any program or activity receiving Federal financial assistance." The school district involved in this litigation receives large amounts of federal financial assistance. The Department of Health, Education, and Welfare (HEW), which has authority to promulgate regulations pro-

hibiting discrimination in federally assisted school systems, in 1968 issued one guideline that "[s]chool systems are responsible for assuring that students of a particular race, color, or national origin are not denied the opportunity to obtain the education generally obtained by other students in the system." In 1970 HEW made the guidelines more specific, requiring school districts that were federally funded "to rectify the language deficiency in order to open" the instruction to students who had "linguistic deficiencies." . . .

It seems obvious that the Chinese-speaking minority receive fewer benefits than the English-speaking majority from respondents' school system which denies them a meaningful opportunity to participate in the educational program—all earmarks of the discrimination banned by the regulations. . . .

Lau differed from *Brown* because it was decided not on the basis of the Fourteenth Amendment but on the Civil Rights Act of 1964. In reference to *Brown,* the justices noted that equality of treatment was not achieved by providing students with the same facilities, textbooks, teachers, or curriculum. *Lau* underscores the idea that equality may not be achieved by treating different categories of people in the same way.

IX. *SAN ANTONIO SCHOOL DISTRICT V. RODRIGUEZ* (1973)

The 1973 case of *San Antonio School District v. Rodriguez* raised the question of equality in public education from another perspective. As was the case in *Brown* and *Lau,* the Fourteenth Amendment required interpretation. However, unlike the earlier cases, the issue was the financing of local public schools.

Education is not a right specified in the Constitution. Under a federal system, education is a local matter in each state. This allows for the possibility of vast differences among states and even within states on the quality of instruction, methods of financing, and treatment of nonwhite students. Whereas the *Brown* decision examined inequality between races, *San Antonio* considered inequality based on financial resources through local property taxes. *San Antonio* raised the question of the consequence of the unequal distribution of wealth among Texas school districts. As with *Brown* and *Lau,* minors were involved; however, the issue was not race or language instruction but social class. Did the Texas school system discriminate against the poor?

Traditionally, the states have financed schools based on property tax assessments. Since wealth is not evenly distributed, some communities are able to spend more on education and provide greater resources to children. This is the basis of the *San Antonio* case, where the charge was that children in less affluent communities necessarily received an inferior education because those communities had fewer resources to draw on. The Rodriguez family contended that the Texas school system of financing public schools through local property taxes denied them equal protection of the laws in violation of the Fourteenth Amendment.

Financing public schools in Texas entailed state and local contributions. About half of the revenues were derived from a state-funded program that provided a minimal educational base; each district then supplemented state aid with a property tax. The Rodriguez family brought a class action suit on behalf of school children who claimed to be members of poor families who resided in school districts with a low property tax base. The contention was that the Texas system's reliance on local property taxation favored the more affluent and violated equal protection requirements because of disparities between districts in per-pupil expenditures.

The Court's decision addressed these key questions:

1. Does Texas's system of financing public school education by use of a property tax violate the Equal Protection Clause (Section 1) of the Fourteenth Amendment?
2. Does the Equal Protection Clause apply to wealth?
3. Is education a fundamental right?
4. Does this state law impinge on a fundamental right?
5. Is a state system for financing public education by a property tax that results in interdistrict dis-

parities in per-pupil expenditures unconstitutionally arbitrary under the Equal Protection Clause?

Excerpts from the Supreme Court Decision in *San Antonio School District v. Rodriguez*[19]

Mr. Justice Powell delivered the opinion of the Court:

. . . The District Court held that the Texas system [of financing public education] discriminates on the basis of wealth in the manner in which education is provided for its people. Finding that wealth is a "suspect" classification and that education is a "fundamental" interest, the District Court held that the Texas system could be sustained only if the State could show that it was premised upon some compelling state interest.

. . . We must decide, first, whether the Texas system of financing public education operates to the disadvantage of some suspect class or impinges upon a fundamental right explicitly or implicitly protected by the Constitution, thereby requiring strict judicial scrutiny. If so, the Texas scheme must still be examined to determine whether it rationally furthers some legitimate, articulated state purpose and therefore does not constitute an invidious discrimination in violation of the Equal Protection Clause of the Fourteenth Amendment.

. . . In concluding that strict judicial scrutiny was required, the [District] court relied on decisions dealing with the rights of indigents to equal treatment in the criminal trial and appellate processes, and on cases disapproving wealth restrictions on the right to vote. Those cases, the District Court concluded, established wealth as a suspect classification. Finding that a local property tax system discriminated on the basis of wealth, it regarded those precedents as controlling. It then reasoned, based on decisions of this Court affirming the undeniable importance of education, that there is a fundamental right to education and that, absent some compelling state justification, the Texas system could not stand.

We are unable to agree that this case, which in significant aspects is *sui generis,* may be so neatly fitted under the Equal Protection Clause. Indeed, we find neither the suspect-classification nor the fundamental-interest analysis persuasive.

The wealth discrimination discovered by the District Court in this case, and by several other courts that have recently struck down school financing in other States, is quite unlike any of the forms of wealth discrimination heretofore reviewed by this Court.

. . . First, in support of their charge that the system discriminates against the "poor," appellees have made no effort to demonstrate that it operates to the peculiar disadvantage of any class fairly definable as indigent, or as composed of persons whose incomes are beneath any designated poverty level. Indeed, there is reason to believe that the poorest families are not necessarily clustered in the poorest property districts. . . .

Second, neither appellees nor the District Court addressed the fact that . . . lack of personal resources has not occasioned an absolute deprivation of the desired benefit. The argument here is not that the children in districts having relatively low assessable property values are receiving no public education; rather, it is that they are receiving a poorer quality education than that available to children in districts having more assessable wealth. Apart from the unsettled and disputed question whether the quality of education may be determined by the amount of money expended for it, a sufficient answer to appellee's argument is that, at least where wealth is involved, the Equal Protection Clause does not require absolute equality or precisely equal advantages. . . .

For these two reasons . . . the disadvantaged class is not susceptible of identification in traditional terms. . . .

. . . [I]t is clear that appellee's suit asks this Court to extend its most exacting scrutiny to review a system that allegedly discriminates against a large, diverse, and amorphous class, unified only by the common factor of residence in districts that happen to have less taxable wealth than other districts. The system of alleged discrimination and the class it defines have none of the traditional indicia of suspectness: the class is not saddled with such disabilities, or subjected to such a history of purposeful unequal treatment, or relegated to such a position of political powerlessness as to command extraordinary protection from the majoritarian political process.

We thus conclude that the Texas system does not operate to the peculiar disadvantage of any suspect class. . . .

Education, of course, is not among the rights afforded explicit protection under our Federal Constitution. Nor do we find any basis for saying it is implicitly so protected. . . .

In sum, to the extent that the Texas system of school financing results in unequal expenditures between children who happen to reside in different districts, we cannot say that such disparities are the product of a system that is so irrational as to be invidiously discriminatory. . . .

Mr. Justice White, with whom Mr. Justice Douglas and Mr. Justice Brennan join, dissenting:

. . . In my view, the parents and children in Edgewood, and in like districts, suffer from an invidious discrimination violative of the Equal Protection Clause. . . .

There is no difficulty in identifying the class that is subject to the alleged discrimination and that is entitled to the benefits of the Equal Protection Clause. I need go no further than the parents and children in the Edgewood district, who are plaintiffs here and who assert that they are entitled to the same choice as Alamo Heights to augment local expenditures for schools but are denied that choice by state law. This group constitutes a class sufficiently definite to invoke the protection of the Constitution. . . .

In *San Antonio v. Rodriguez,* the Court did not find that the differences between school districts constituted invidious discrimination. A majority of the justices felt that Texas satisfied constitutional standards under the Equal Protection Clause. On the other hand, four justices in dissenting opinions saw a class (the poor) that was subject to discrimination and that lacked the protection of the Constitution.

X. *BOWERS V. HARDWICK* (1986)

In most of the cases we have considered, plaintiffs have sued on the basis that their rights under the Fourteenth Amendment were violated. However, cases can reach the Supreme Court by several routes, one of which is a *writ of certiorari,* which is directed at an inferior court to bring the record of a case into a superior court for re-examination and review. This was the case in *Bowers v. Hardwick,* in which the constitutionality of a Georgia sodomy statute was challenged. This became a key case in the battle for constitutional rights for gay women and men.

The case of *Bowers v. Hardwick* began on the issue of privacy because the behavior in question took place in Michael Hardwick's home. In deciding the case, however, the justices shifted from the issue of privacy to question whether gays have a fundamental right to engage in consensual sex.

Michael Hardwick's suit was based on the following facts. On August 3, 1982, a police officer went to Hardwick's home to serve Hardwick a warrant for failure to pay a fine. Hardwick's roommate answered the door, but was not sure if Hardwick was at home. The roommate allowed the officer to enter and approach Hardwick's bedroom. The officer found the bedroom door partly open and observed Hardwick engaged in oral sex with another man. The officer arrested both men, charged them with sodomy, and held them in the local jail for 10 hours.

The Georgia sodomy statute under which the men were charged made "any sexual act involving the sex organs of one person and the mouth or anus of another" a felony punishable by imprisonment for up to 20 years. When the district attorney decided not to submit the case to a grand jury, Hardwick brought suit attacking the constitutionality of the Georgia statute. Later, a divided court of appeals held that the Georgia statute violated Hardwick's fundamental rights. The attorney general of Georgia appealed that judgment to the Supreme Court.

The Court's decision on the case was split. Five justices ruled that the constitutional right of privacy did not apply to Hardwick's case; four argued that it did. While the Georgia statute did not specify that only homosexual sodomy was prohibited, the Court's majority opinion was framed in those terms. (Most legal prohibitions are directed at non-procreative acts irrespective of the sex of the participants.) The majority opinion also equated consensual sex within the home to criminal conduct within the home, an equation criticized by both gay rights activists and the dissenting justices.

[The majority opinion] emphasized that the home does not confer immunity for criminal conduct, com-

paring gay sex first to drugs, firearms, and stolen goods and then to adultery, incest, and bigamy. In so doing, the Court evoked images of dissolution, fear, seizure, and instability. . . . [and] the stereotypical fear of gay men as predators and child molesters. . . . The majority [opinion] advances, mostly by implication, its view of gay sexuality as unrelated to recognized forms of sexual activity or intimate relationships, and as exploitative, predatory, threatening to personal and social stability. [Writing for the dissent] Justice Blackmun excoriates the majority's choice of analogies and its failure to explain why it did not use nonthreatening analogies such as private, consensual heterosexual activity or even sodomy within marriage for comparison.[20]

While the majority argued that the past criminalization of sodomy argued for its continued criminalization, critics responded that "Whereas the task of the Court was to decide whether the criminalization of sodomy is consistent with the Constitution, the majority treated the fact of past criminalization as determinative. . . . It had no answer to Justice Blackmun's contention 'that by such lights, the Court should have no authority to invalidate miscegenation laws.'"[21]

The Court's decision addressed these key questions:

1. Does Georgia's sodomy law violate the fundamental rights of gays?
2. Does the Constitution confer the fundamental right to engage in homosexual sodomy?
3. Is Georgia's sodomy law selectively being enforced against gays?

Excerpts from the Supreme Court Decision in *Bowers v. Hardwick*[22]

Mr. Justice White delivered the opinion of the Court:

This case does not require a judgment on whether laws against sodomy between consenting adults in general, or between homosexuals in particular, are wise or desirable. . . . The issue presented is whether the Federal Constitution confers a fundamental right upon homosexuals to engage in sodomy and hence invalidates the laws of the many States that still makes such contact illegal and have done so for a very long time.

We first register our disagreement with the Court of Appeals and with respondent that the Court's prior cases have construed the Constitution to confer a right of privacy that extends to homosexual sodomy. . . .

Precedent aside, however, respondent would have us announce, as the Court of Appeals did, a fundamental right to engage in homosexual sodomy. This we are quite unwilling to do. . . .

It is obvious to us that neither of these formulations [*Palko v. Connecticut,* 302 U.S. 319 (1937) and *Moore v. East Cleveland,* 431 U.S. 494 (1977)] would extend a fundamental right to homosexuals to engage in acts of consensual sodomy. Proscriptions against that conduct have ancient roots. . . . Sodomy was a criminal offense at common law and was forbidden by the laws of the original thirteen States when they ratified the Bill of Rights. In 1868, when the Fourteenth Amendment was ratified, all but 5 of the 37 States in the Union had criminal sodomy laws. In fact, until 1961, all 50 States outlawed sodomy, and today 24 States and the District of Columbia continue to provide criminal penalties for sodomy performed in private and between consenting adults. . . . Against this background, to claim that a right to engage in such conduct is "deeply rooted in this Nation's history and tradition" or "implicit in the concept of ordered liberty" is, at best, facetious. . . .

Respondent . . . asserts that the result should be different where the homosexual conduct occurs in the privacy of the home. He relies on *Stanley v. Georgia,* 394 U.S. 557, (1969) . . . where the Court held that the First Amendment prevents conviction for possessing and reading obscene material in the privacy of one's home: "If the First Amendment means anything, it means that a State has no business telling a man, sitting alone in his house, what books he may read or what films he may watch . . .".

Stanley did protect conduct that would not have been protected outside the home, and it partially prevented the enforcement of state obscenity laws; but the decision was firmly grounded in the First Amendment. The right pressed upon us here has no similar support in the text of the Constitution, and it does not qualify for recognition under the prevailing principles for construing the Fourteenth Amendment. Its limits are also difficult to discern. Plainly enough, otherwise illegal conduct is not always immunized whenever it occurs in the home. Victimless crimes, such as the possession and use of illegal drugs, do not escape the law where

they are committed at home. *Stanley* itself recognized that its holding offered no protection for the possession in the home of drugs, firearms, or stolen goods. . . . And if respondent's submission is limited to the voluntary sexual conduct between consenting adults, it would be difficult, except by fiat, to limit the claimed right to homosexual conduct while leaving exposed to prosecution adultery, incest, and other sexual crimes even though they are committed in the home. We are unwilling to start down that road. . . .

Justice Blackmun, with whom Justice Brennan, Justice Marshall, and Justice Stevens join, dissenting:

This case is no more about "a fundamental right to engage in homosexual sodomy," as the Court purports to declare, . . . than *Stanley v. Georgia,* 394 U.S. 557 (1969), . . . was about a fundamental right to watch obscene movies. . . . Rather, this case is about "the most comprehensive of rights and the right most valued by civilized men," namely, "the right to be let alone." *Olmstead v. United States,* 277 U.S. 438, (1928) (Brandeis, J., dissenting).

The statute at issue, Ga. Code Ann. section 16-6-2 (1984), denies individuals the right to decide for themselves whether to engage in particular forms of private, consensual sexual activity. The Court concludes that section 16-6-2 is valid essentially because "the laws of . . . many States . . . still make such conduct illegal and have done so for a very long time . . ." (Holmes, J., dissenting). Like Justice Holmes [dissenting in *Lochner v. New York,* 198 U.S. 45 (1905)], I believe that "[i]t is revolting to have no better reason for a rule of law than that it was laid down in the time of Henry IV. It is still more revolting if the grounds upon which it was laid down have vanished long since, and the rule simply persists from blind imitation of the past." Holmes, The Path of Law, 10 *Harvard Law Review* 457, 469 (1897). I believe we must analyze Hardwick's claim in the light of the values that underlie the constitutional right to privacy. If that right means anything, it means that, before Georgia can prosecute its citizens for making choices about the most intimate aspects of their lives, it must do more than assert that the choice they have made is an "'abominable crime not fit to be named among Christians.'"

Like the statute that is challenged in this case, the rationale of the Court's opinion applies equally to the prohibited conduct regardless of whether the parties who engage in it are married or unmarried, or are of the same or different sexes. Sodomy was condemned as an odious and sinful type of behavior during the formative period of the common law. That condemnation was equally damning for heterosexual and homosexual sodomy. Moreover, it provided no special exemption for married couples. The license to cohabit and to produce legitimate offspring simply did not include any permission to engage in sexual conduct that was considered a "crime against nature."

The Court's decision did not uphold Michael Hardwick's contention that his sexual conduct in the privacy of his own home was constitutionally protected. While the decision was seen as a blow to the assertion of gay rights, the majority's narrow one-vote margin also indicated the Court's shifting opinion on this issue.

XI. REGENTS OF THE UNIVERSITY OF CALIFORNIA V. BAKKE (1978)

The Supreme Court has reviewed several cases concerning equitable treatment in public education. Key cases include racially separate public schools (*Brown v. Board of Education,* 1954); the practice of English-only instruction for Chinese students in public schools (*Lau v. Nichols,* 1974); and the practice of operating public schools based solely on revenue from local property taxes (*San Antonio School District v. Rodriguez,* 1973).

African Americans not only had to fight for equity in public schools but also had to sue to gain admission to law and medical schools in state universities. See *Sipuel v. Oklahoma,* 1948; *Missouri ex rel Gaines,* 1938; and *Sweatt v. Painter,* 1950.

In 1978, race-based admissions became an issue again when a *white* person sued for admission to the medical school at the University of California at Davis. The case of *The Regents of the University of California v. Bakke,* however, must be seen in light of the policy of affirmative action, which sought to redress historic injustices against racial minorities and other specified groups by providing educational and employment opportunities to members of these groups.

In 1968, the University of California at Davis opened a medical school with a track admission policy for a 100-seat class. In 1974, applicants who identified themselves as economically and/or educationally disadvantaged or a member of a minority group (blacks, Chicanos, Asians, American Indians) were reviewed by a special committee. They could also compete for the remaining 84 seats. However, no disadvantaged white was ever admitted to the school through the special admissions program, although some applied. Bakke, a white male, applied to the medical school in 1973 and 1974 under the general admissions program. He was rejected both times because he did not meet the requisite cutoff score. In both years, special applicants with significantly lower scores than Bakke were admitted. After his second rejection Bakke sued for admission to the medical school, alleging that the special admissions program excluded him on the basis of his race in violation of the Equal Protection Clause of the Fourteenth Amendment, a provision of the California Constitution, and section 601 of Title VI of the Civil Rights Act of 1964, which provides that no person shall, on the ground of race or color, be excluded from participating in any program receiving federal financial assistance. The California Supreme Court applied a strict-scrutiny standard. It concluded that the special admissions program was not the least intrusive means of achieving the goals of the admittedly compelling state interests of integrating the medical profession and increasing the number of doctors willing to serve minority patients. The California court held that Davis's special admissions program violated the Equal Protection Clause of the U.S. Constitution. The Davis Medical School was ordered to admit Bakke.

The Court's divided opinion addressed these key questions:

1. Does the University of California, Davis Medical School's admission policy violate the Fourteenth Amendment?
2. Does giving preference to a group of nonwhite applicants constitute discrimination?

3. Does the University of California, Davis Medical School use a racial classification that is suspect?
4. Was Bakke denied admission to the University of California, Davis Medical School on the basis of race?
5. Can race be used as a criterion for admission to a university?

Excerpts from the Supreme Court Decision in *The Regents of the University of California v. Bakke*[23]

Mr. Justice Powell delivered the opinion of the Court:

The guarantees of the Fourteenth Amendment extend to all persons. Its language is explicit: "No State shall . . . deny to any person within its jurisdiction the equal protection of the laws." . . . The guarantee of equal protection cannot mean one thing when applied to one individual and something else when applied to a person of another color. . . .

. . . the [Fourteenth] Amendment itself was framed in universal terms, without reference to color, ethnic origin, or condition of prior servitude.

Petitioner [University of California, Davis] urges us to adopt for the first time a more restrictive view of the Equal Protection Clause and hold that discrimination against members of the white "majority" cannot be suspect if its purpose can be characterized as "benign."

. . . Moreover, there are serious problems of justice connected with the idea of preference itself. First, it may not always be clear that a so-called preference is in fact benign. . . . Second, preferential programs may only reinforce common stereotypes holding that certain groups are unable to achieve success without special protection based on a factor having no relationship to individual worth. Third, there is a measure of inequity in forcing innocent persons in respondent's position to bear the burdens of redressing grievances not of their making.

. . . When a classification denies an individual opportunities or benefits enjoyed by others solely because of his race or ethnic background, it must be regarded as suspect.

If petitioner's purpose is to assure within its student body some specified percentage of a particular group merely because of its race or ethnic origin, such

a preferential purpose must be rejected. . . . Preferring members of any one group for no reason other than race or ethnic origin is discrimination for its own sake. This the Constitution forbids.

. . . [A] goal asserted by petitioner is the attainment of a diverse student body. This clearly is a constitutionally permissible goal for an institution of higher education. Academic freedom, though not a specifically enumerated constitutional right, long has been viewed as a special concern of the First Amendment. . . .

Ethnic diversity, however, is only one element in a range of factors a university properly may consider in attaining the goal of a heterogeneous student body.

It may be assumed that the reservation of a specified number of seats in each class for individuals from the preferred ethnic groups would contribute to the attainment of considerable ethnic diversity in the student body. But petitioner's argument that this is the only effective means of serving the interest of diversity is seriously flawed. . . . Petitioner's special admissions program, focused solely on ethnic diversity, would hinder rather than further attainment of genuine diversity.

. . . In summary, it is evident that the Davis special admissions program involves the use of an explicit racial classification never before countenanced by this Court. It tells applicants who are not Negro, Asian, or Chicano that they are totally excluded from a specific percentage of the seats in the class.

The fatal flaw in petitioner's preferential program is its disregard of individual rights as guaranteed by the Fourteenth Amendment. Such rights are not absolute.

Mr. Justice Brennan, Mr. Justice White, Mr. Justice Marshall, and Mr. Justice Blackmun, concurring in part and dissenting in part:

We conclude . . . that racial classifications are not *per se* invalid under the Fourteenth Amendment.

Unquestionably we have held that a government practice or statute which restricts "fundamental rights" or which contains "suspect classifications" is to be subjected to "strict scrutiny" and can be justified only if it furthers a compelling government purpose. . . . But no fundamental right is involved here. Nor do whites as a class have any of the "traditional indicia of suspectness; the class is not saddled with such disabilities, or subjected to such a history of purposeful unequal treatment, or relegated to such a history of purposeful unequal treatment, or relegated to such position of political powerlessness as to command extraordinary protection from the majoritarian political process." ...

Certainly ... Davis had a sound basis for believing that the problem of under-representation of minorities was substantial and chronic. ... Until at least 1973, the practice of medicine in this country was, in fact, if not in law, largely the prerogative of whites. In 1950, for example, while Negroes constituted 10% of the total population, Negro physicians constituted only 2.2% of the total number of physicians. The overwhelming majority of these ... were educated in two predominantly Negro medical schools, Howard and Meharry. By 1970, the gap between the proportion of Negroes in medicine and their proportion in the population had widened: The number of Negroes employed in medicine remained frozen at 2.2% while the Negro population had increased to 11.1%. The number of Negro admittees to predominantly white medical schools, moreover, had declined in absolute numbers during the years 1955 to 1964.

Moreover, Davis had very good reason to believe that the national pattern of under-representation of minorities in medicine would be perpetuated if it retained a single admissions standard. ...

Davis clearly could conclude that the serious and persistent under-representation of minorities in medicine depicted by these statistics is the result of handicaps under which minority applicants labor as a consequence of ... deliberate, purposeful discrimination against minorities in education and in society generally, as well as in the medical profession. ...

It is not even claimed that Davis' program in any way operates to stigmatize or single out any discrete ... or even any identifiable, nonminority group. Nor will harm comparable to that imposed upon racial minorities by exclusion or separation on grounds of race be the likely result of the program. ...

Nor was Bakke in any sense stamped as inferior by the Medical School's rejection of him. Indeed, it is conceded by all that he satisfied those criteria regarded by the school as generally relevant to academic performance better than most of the minority members who were admitted. Moreover, there is absolutely no basis for concluding that Bakke's rejection that was a result of Davis' use of racial preference will affect him throughout his life in the same way as the segregation of the Negro schoolchildren in *Brown I* would have affected them. Unlike discrimination against racial minorities, the use of racial preferences for remedial purposes does not inflict a pervasive injury upon individual whites in the sense that wherever they go or whatever they do there is a significant likelihood that they will be treated as second-class citizens because of their color. ...

In addition, there is simply no evidence that the Davis program discriminated intentionally or unintentionally against any minority group which it purports to benefit. The program does not establish a quota in the invidious sense of a ceiling on the number of minority applicants to be admitted. ...

Finally, Davis' special admissions program cannot be said to violate the Constitution. ...

... we would reverse the judgment of the Supreme Court of California holding the Medical School's special admissions program unconstitutional and directing respondent's admission.

Justices Stevens and Stewart, along with Chief Justice Rehnquist, concurred and dissented in part. They found that the university's special admissions program violated Title VI of the Civil Rights Act of 1964, which prohibits discrimination under any program or activity receiving federal funding assistance. This dissent found that Bakke was not admitted to the Davis Medical School because of his race.

Race-based admissions were again considered in *Hopwood v. Texas,* a 1994 case in the Western District of Texas. The suit, brought by four white Texas residents, claimed that the affirmative action admissions program of the University of Texas School of Law violated the Equal Protection Clause of the Fourteenth Amendment and Title VI of the Civil Rights Act of 1964. The district court agreed that the plaintiffs' equal protection rights had been violated, but refused to direct the school to cease making admission decisions based on race. The case was subsequently appealed in the Court of Appeals for the Fifth Circuit, which held that the University of Texas School of Law could not use race as an admissions factor in order to achieve a diverse student body. The holding of the circuit court stands because the Supreme Court refused to hear the case.

This decision in effect overruled Justice Powell's opinion in *Bakke,* which held that universities can take account of an applicant's race in some circumstances. He asserted that the goal of achieving a diverse student body was permissible under the Constitution.

XII. *TENNESSEE V. LANE* (2004)

Historically, disabled people have been thought of as possessed or wicked. Often they were scorned and shut off from society in mental institutions. Today, however, the medical model is the dominant perspective that "those with disabilities have some kind of physical, mental, or emotional defect that not surprisingly limits their performance." Essentially, we don't expect those who are "flawed" to function as well as other people.[24]

Disabled people constantly face discrimination resulting in exclusion from housing, public buildings, and public transportation. This has prevented them from attending school, visiting museums, shopping, or living without assistance.

The 1990 Americans with Disabilities Act forbids discrimination against persons with disabilities in three key areas of public life. Title I covers employment; Title II encompasses public services, programs, and activities; and Title III covers public accommodations. In 2001 Casey Martin sued the PGA Tour,[25] under the public accommodations provisions of Title III to allow him to play golf on the tour while riding a golf cart because he suffers from Klippel-Trenaunay-Weber syndrome, a degenerative circulatory disorder that causes severe pain in his lower leg. Martin won his case when the Court held that the PGA walking rule was not compromised by allowing him to use a cart.

The provisions of Title II, which include access to the services, programs, or activities of a public entity such as a courthouse are questioned in *Tennessee v. Lane*. In this case, residents of the state who are paraplegics sued Tennessee because they were denied access to a courthouse under Title II of the Americans with Disabilities Act (ADA). Because this case involves a suit by an individual against a state, the Supreme Court has to consider the provisions of the Eleventh Amendment,[26] which provides state immunity against suits by citizens seeking equity and the enforcement clause, Section 5 of the Fourteenth Amendment.[27] After Tennessee was unsuccessful in getting the case dismissed because the plaintiffs sought damages, the case went to the Supreme Court. This issue then became an interpretation of Congress's power to enforce by appropriate legislation (Section 5) the guarantee that "no State shall make or enforce any law which shall abridge the privileges or immunities of citizens of the United States; nor shall any State deprive any person of life, liberty, or property, without due process of law; nor deny to any person within its jurisdiction the equal protection of the laws."

In 1998 George Lane and Beverly Jones, both paraplegics who use wheelchairs, filed suit against the state of Tennessee and a number of counties under Title II of the ADA, which states that no qualified individual with a disability shall, because of the disability be excluded from participation or denied the benefits of the services, programs, or activities of a public entity. Both parties claimed that they were denied access to the state court system because of their disability. Lane alleged that he was forced to appear to answer criminal charges on the second floor of a county courthouse. The courthouse had no elevator. In his first court appearance Lane crawled up two flights to reach the courtroom. When Lane had to return for a second time, he refused to crawl or to be carried to the courtroom. He was arrested and sent to jail for failure to appear for his hearing. Jones, a certified court reporter, claimed that she had not been able to obtain work because she could not gain access to several county courthouses.

The court's decision addressed these key questions:

1. Is Title II a valid exercise of Congress's Section 5 enforcement powers under the Fourteenth Amendment?
2. Does Title II enforce a variety of basic constitutional guarantees such as the right of access to the courts?
3. Does Title II validly enforce these constitutional rights?

4. Is Title II an appropriate response to this history of discrimination and pattern of unequal treatment?

Excerpts from the Supreme Court Decision in *Tennessee v. George Lane et al.*[28]

Mr. Justice Stevens delivered the opinion of the Court:

> The ADA was passed by large majorities in both Houses of Congress after decades of deliberation and investigation into the need for comprehensive legislation to address discrimination against persons with disabilities.
>
> . . . Title II, sections 12131–12134, prohibits any public entity from discrimination against "qualified" persons with disabilities in the provision or operation of public services, programs, or activities. The Act defines the term "public entity" to include state and local governments. . . .
>
> Title II, like Title I, seeks to enforce this prohibition on irrational disability discrimination. But it also seeks to enforce a variety of other basic constitutional guarantees, infringements of which are subject to more searching judicial review. . . . These rights include some, like the right of access to the courts at issue in this case, that are protected by the Due Process Clause of the Fourteenth Amendment. The Due Process Clause [as] applied to the states via the Fourteenth Amendment both guarantee to a criminal defendant such as respondent Lane the "right to be present at all stages of the trial where his absence might frustrate the fairness of the proceedings." . . . The Due Process Clause also requires the States to afford certain civil litigants a "meaningful opportunity to be heard" by removing obstacles to their full participation in judicial proceedings. . . . And, finally, we have recognized that members of the public have a right of access to criminal proceedings secured by the First Amendment.
>
> . . . It is not difficult to perceive the harm that Title II is designed to address. Congress enacted Title II against a backdrop of pervasive unequal treatment in the administration of state services and programs, including systematic deprivations of fundamental rights.
>
> . . . With respect to the particular services at issue in this case, Congress learned that many individuals, in many States across the country, were being excluded from courthouses and court proceedings by reason of their disabilities. A report before Congress showed that some 76% of public services and programs housed in state-owned buildings were inaccessible to and unusable by persons with disabilities. . . .
>
> The conclusion that Congress drew from this body of evidence is set forth in the text of the ADA itself: "Discrimination against individuals with disabilities persists in such critical areas as . . . education, transportation, communication, recreation, institutionalization, health services, voting, and access to public services. . . . This finding, together with the extensive record of disability discrimination that underlies it, makes clear beyond peradventure that inadequate provision of public services and access to public facilities was an appropriate subject for prophylactic legislation.
>
> . . . Whatever might be said about Title II's other applications, the question presented in this case is not whether Congress can validly subject the States to private suits for money damages for failing to provide reasonable access to hockey rinks, or even to voting booths, but whether Congress had the power under Section 5 to enforce the constitutional right of access to the courts. Because we find that Title II unquestionably is valid Section 5 legislation as it applies to the class of cases implicating the accessibility of judicial services, we need go no further.
>
> . . . Title II's affirmative obligation to accommodate persons with disabilities in the administration of justice cannot be said to be "so out of proportion to a supposed remedial or preventive object that it cannot be understood as responsive to, or designed to prevent, unconstitutional behavior. . . . It is, rather, a reasonable prophylactic measure, reasonably targeted to a legitimate end.
>
> For these reasons, we conclude that Title III, as it applies to the class of cases implicating the fundamental right of access to the courts, constitutes a valid exercise of Congress's Section 5 authority to enforce the guarantees of the Fourteenth Amendment.

XIII. THE MICHIGAN CASES

Gratz v. Bollinger et al. (2003) and *Grutter v. Bollinger et al.* (2003) considered admission standards for the University of Michigan's undergraduate program and its Law School. This marked the first time in the 25 years since the *Bakke* decision that the Supreme Court had considered the legal status of race-conscious admissions. In *Bakke*, Justice Powell held that race could be taken into consideration if it served a compelling government interest. He then held that the goal of achieving a diverse student body was a circumstance where race could be considered. However, the *Bakke* decision generated six separate opinions, but no majority opinion.[29]

The University of Michigan cases question whether Justice Powell's opinion set a precedent for considering diversity a constitutional justification for race-conscious admissions.

Gratz v. Bollinger et al. (2003)

Jennifer Gratz and Patrick Hamacher were both white residents of Michigan who applied for admission to the University of Michigan's College of Literature, Science, and the Arts (LSA). Both were considered qualified for admission. However, both were denied early admission, and upon further review neither was admitted to the university. The university's Undergraduate Admissions Office uses a written guideline system which includes such factors as high school grades, standardized test scores, the quality of the high school, curriculum strength, geography, alumni relationships, leadership, and race. Although the guidelines have changed since 1995, the university consistently considered African Americans, Hispanics, and Native Americans as "underrepresented minorities." The guidelines provided that all applicants from an underrepresented racial or ethnic minority group were automatically given 20 points out of the 100 needed for admission. The university never disputed the claim that practically every qualified applicant from these groups was admitted.

In 1997 Gratz and Hamacher filed a class-action suit alleging violation of their rights under the Fourteenth Amendment and the Civil Rights Act of 1964. The Equal Protection Clause of the Fourteenth Amendment provides that a state cannot act unfairly or arbitrarily toward or discriminate against a person within its jurisdiction because the individual has "the equal protection of the laws." Title VI of the Civil Rights Act prohibits discrimination on the grounds of race, color, or national origin against anyone participating in a program or activity which receives federal financial assistance.

The Court's decision addressed these key questions:

1. Under strict scrutiny does the university's use of race in its current admission policy constitute narrowly tailored measures that further compelling government interests?
2. Does the undergraduate admission policy violate the Equal Protection Clause of the Fourteenth Amendment?
3. Does the undergraduate admission policy violate Title VI of the Civil Rights Act of 1964?

Excerpts from the Supreme Court Decision in Gratz v. Bollinger et al. (2003)[30]

Chief Justice Rehnquist delivered the opinion of the Court:

. . . Because the University's use of race in its current freshman admission policy is not narrowly tailored to achieve respondents' asserted interest in diversity, the policy violates the Equal Protection Clause. For the reasons set forth in *Grutter v. Bollinger* . . . the Court has today rejected petitioners' argument that diversity cannot constitute a compelling state interest. However, the Court finds that the University's current policy, which automatically distributes 20 points, or one-fifth of the points needed to guarantee admission, to every single "underrepresented minority" applicant solely because of race, is not narrowly tailored to achieve educational diversity. In *Bakke,* Justice Powell explained his view that it would be permissible for a university to employ an admissions program in which "race or ethnic background may be deemed a 'plus' in a particular applicant's file" . . . he emphasized, however, the importance of considering each particular applicant as an individual, assessing all of the qualities that individual possesses, and in turn, evaluating that individual's ability to contribute to the unique setting of higher education. The admissions program Justice Powell described did not contemplate that any single characteristic automatically ensured a specific and identifiable contribution to a university's diversity. . . . The current LSA policy does not provide the individualized consideration Justice Powell contemplated. The only consideration that accompanies the 20-point automatic distribution to all applicants from underrepresented minorities is a factual review to determine whether an individual is a member of one of these minority groups. Moreover, unlike Justice Powell's example, where the race of a "particular black applicant" could be "considered without being decisive" . . . the LSA's 20-point distribution has the effect of making "the factor of race . . . decisive" for virtually every minimally qualified underrepresented minority applicant. The fact that the LSA has created the possibility of an applicant's file being flagged for individualized consideration only emphasizes the flaws of the University's system as a whole when compared to that described by Justice Powell. The record does not reveal precisely how many applications are flagged, but it is undisputed that consideration is the exception and not the rule in the LSA's program. Also, this individualized review is only provided *after* admissions counselors automatically distribute the University's version of a "plus" that makes race a decisive factor for virtually every minimally qualified underrepresented minority applicant. . . . Nothing in Justice Powell's *Bakke* opinion signaled that a university may employ whatever means it desires to achieve diversity without regard to the limits imposed by strict scrutiny. Because the University's use of race in its current freshman admission policy violates the Equal Protection Clause, it also violates Title VI.

Grutter v. Bollinger et al. (2003)

Barbara Grutter, a white Michigan resident, applied to the University of Michigan Law School in 1996. She was originally placed on a waiting list but was ultimately not admitted. She alleged that her application was rejected because the Law School used race as a "predominant" factor, which gave applicants from certain minority groups "a significantly greater chance of admission than students with similar credentials from disfavored racial groups." The Law School asserted that it had a compelling interest in obtaining the educational benefits derived from a diverse student body. Law School officials contended that the admissions staff was not

directed to admit a specific percentage or number of minority students, but rather to consider race among several factors. The goal was to obtain a "critical mass" of underrepresented minority students in order to realize the educational benefits of a diverse student body. The critical mass concept was never stated in terms of a fixed number, or percentage, or even a range of numbers or percentages. Admission officers acknowledged that minority group membership was a strong factor in the acceptance decisions and that applicants from minority groups were given large allowance for admission compared to applicants from nonfavored groups. However, it was asserted that race was not considered the predominant factor in the Law School's admission formula.

The Court's decision addressed these key questions:

1. Was race a predominant or a plus factor when reviewing the files of Law School applicants?
2. Did the Law School have a compelling interest in creating a diverse study body?
3. Does seeking a critical mass of minority students equal a quota?
4. Does the Law School admissions policy violate the Fourteenth Amendment and Title VI of the Civil Rights Act of 1964?

Excerpts from the Supreme Court Decision in *Grutter v. Bollinger et al.*[31]

Justice O'Connor delivered the opinion of the Court:

We last addressed the use of race in public higher education over 25 years ago. In the landmark *Bakke* case, we reviewed a racial set-aside program that reserved 16 out of 100 seats in a medical school class for members of certain minority groups. . . . The decision produced six separate opinions, none of which commanded a majority of the Court. . . . The only holding for the court in *Bakke* was that a "State has a substantial interest that legitimately may be served by a properly devised admissions program involving the competitive consideration of race and ethnic origin."

. . . Public and private universities across the nation have modeled their own admissions programs on

Justice Powell's views on permissible race-conscious policies.

. . . Justice Powell approved the university's use of race to further only one interest: "the attainment of a diverse student body" . . . Justice Powell grounded his analysis in the academic freedom emphasized that nothing less than the "'nation's future depends upon leaders trained through wide exposure' to the ideas and mores of students as diverse as the nation of many peoples." . . . Both "tradition and experience lend support to the view that the contribution of diversity is substantial."

Justice Powell was, however, careful to emphasize that in his view race "is only one element in a range of factors a university properly may consider in attaining the goal of a heterogeneous student body." . . . For Justice Powell "[i]t is not an interest in simple ethnic diversity, in which a specified percentage of the student body is in effect guaranteed to be members of selected ethnic groups," that can justify the use of race. . . . Rather, "[t]he diversity that furthers a compelling state interest encompasses a far broader array of qualifications and characteristics of which racial or ethnic origin is but a single though important element."

. . . We have held that all racial classifications imposed by government "must be analyzed by a reviewing court under strict scrutiny." . . . This means that such classifications are constitutional only if they are narrowly tailored to further compelling governmental interests.

. . . The Law School asks us to recognize, in the context of higher education, a compelling state interest in student body diversity.

. . . Today, we hold that the Law School has a compelling interest in attaining a diverse student body.

. . . Our conclusion that the Law School has a compelling interest in a diverse student body is informed by our view that attaining a diverse student body is at the heart of the Law School's proper institutional mission, and that "good faith" on the part of a university is "presumed" absent "a showing to the contrary."

. . . The Law School's concept of critical mass is defined by reference to the educational benefits that diversity is designed to produce.

These benefits are substantial. As the District Court emphasized, the Law School's admissions policy promotes "cross-racial understanding," helps to break down racial stereotypes, and "enables [students] to better understand persons of different races."

. . . The Law School has determined, based on its experience and expertise, that a "critical mass" of underrepresented minorities is necessary to further its compelling interest in securing the educational benefits of a diverse student body.

. . . To be narrowly tailored, a race-conscious admissions program cannot use a quota system—it cannot "insulat[e] each category of applicants with certain desired qualifications from competition with all other applicants" (opinion of Justice Powell). Instead, a university may consider race or ethnicity only as a "'plus' in a particular applicant's file," without "insulat[ing] the individual from comparison with all other candidates for the available seats."

. . . We find that the Law School's admissions program bears the hallmarks of a narrowly tailored plan. As Justice Powell made clear in *Bakke,* truly individualized consideration demands that race be used in a flexible, nonmechanical way.

. . . We are satisfied that the Law School's admissions program . . . does not operate as a quota. Properly understood, a "quota" is a program in which a certain fixed number or proportion of opportunities are "reserved exclusively for certain minority groups."

. . . The Law School's goal of attaining a critical mass of underrepresented minority students does not transform its program into a quota. . . . "[S]ome attention to numbers," without more, does not transform a flexible admissions system into a rigid quota.

. . . The Law School affords this individualized consideration to applicants of all races. There is no policy, either *de jure* or *de facto,* of automatic acceptance or rejection based on any single "soft" variable. Unlike the program at issue in *Gratz v. Bollinger* the Law School awards no mechanical, predetermined diversity "bonuses" based on race or ethnicity.

. . . What is more, the Law School actually gives substantial weight to diversity factors besides race. The Law School frequently accepts nonminority applicants with grades and test scores lower than underrepresented minority applicants (and other nonminority applicants) who are rejected.

. . . We agree that, in the context of its individualized inquiry into the possible diversity contributions of all applicants, the Law School's race-conscious admissions program does not unduly harm nonminority applicants.

. . . the Equal Protection Clause does not prohibit the Law School's narrowly tailored use of race in admissions decisions to further a compelling interest in obtaining the educational benefits that flow from a diverse student body.

NOTES

1. *Privileges and immunities* refer to the ability of one state to discriminate against the citizens of another state. A resident of one state cannot be denied legal protection, access to the courts, or property rights in another state.

2. In *Smith v. Allwright,* 321 U.S. 649 (1944), the Supreme Court held that a 1927 Texas law that authorized political parties to establish criteria for membership in the state Democratic party violated the Fifteenth Amendment. In effect, the criteria excluded nonwhites from the Democratic party. Since only party members could vote in the primary election, the result was a whites-only primary. The Democratic party so dominated politics in the southern states after the Civil War that winning the primary was equivalent to winning the general election.

3. Americans of African descent have been called *blacks, Negroes, colored,* or *African Americans,* depending on the historical period.

4. 19 Howard 393 (1857).

5. The Nineteenth Amendment that was ratified on August 18, 1920, stated, "The right of citizens of the United States to vote shall not be denied or abridged by the United States or by any state on account of sex. Congress shall have the power to enforce this article by appropriate legislation."

6. 21 Wallace 162 (1875).

7. Crozier, "Constitutionality of Discrimination Based on Sex," 15 *B.U.L. Review,* 723, 727–28 (1935) as quoted in William Hodes, "Women and the Constitution: Some Legal History and a New Approach to the Nineteenth Amendment" *Rutgers Law Review,* Vol. 25, 1970, p. 27.

8. Hodes, p. 45.

9. Gunnar Myrdal, *An American Dilemma: The Negro Problem and Modern Democracy.* New York: Harper and Row (2d ed. 1962 [1944]), pp. 1073–74, as quoted in Hodes, p. 29. This same biblical ground has yielded the idea that a woman is an extension of her husband and his status.

10. The states under military rule were Virginia, North Carolina, South Carolina, Georgia, Florida, Tennessee, Alabama, Mississippi, Texas, Louisiana, and Arkansas.

11. The term *colored* was used in Louisiana to describe persons of mixed race who had some African ancestry.

12. 163 U.S. 537 (1896).

13. Restrictive covenants were written in deeds restricting the use of the land. Covenants could prohibit the sale of land to nonwhites or non-Christians.

14. 347 U.S. 483 (1954).

15. 118 U.S. 356 (1886).

16. 112 U.S. 94 (1884).

17. Native Americans and slaves posed a problem when taking the census count, which was the basis for apportioning seats in the U.S. House of Representatives. Some states stood to lose representation if some of their slave or Native American population was not counted. Blacks were counted as three-fifths of a white man, and only those Native Americans who were taxed were counted.

18. 414 U.S. 563 (1974).

19. 411 U.S. 1 (1973).

20. Rhonda Copelon, "A Crime Not Fit to Be Named: Sex, Lies, and the Constitution," p. 182. In David Kairys (ed.), *The Politics of Law,* pp. 177–94, New York: Pantheon.

21. Copelon, p. 184.

22. 478 U.S. 186 (1986).

23. 438 U.S. 265 (1978).

24. Paul C. Higgins, *Making Disability.* Springfield, IL: Charles C. Thomas (1992), pp. 26–27.

25. *PGA Tour, Inc. v. Casey Martin,* 532 U.S. 661.

26. The Eleventh Amendment pertains to suits against the states. The interpretation is that a state cannot be sued by U.S. citizens of that state or another state nor by a foreign country.

27. Section 5 of the Fourteenth Amendment grants Congress the power to enforce the provisions of this amendment by appropriate legislation.

28. 124 S. Ct. 1978 (2004).

29. Four justices supported the University of California's admissions program against all objections on the ground that the government could use race "to remedy disadvantages cast on minorities by past racial prejudice." Four other justices did not interpret *Bakke* on constitutional grounds, but instead struck down the program on statutory grounds. Justice Powell's position was against the set-aside admissions policy, but was also for "reversing the state court's injunction against any use of race whatsoever." The holding in *Bakke* was that a "State has a substantial interest that legitimately may be served by a properly devised admissions program involving the competitive consideration of race and ethnic origin."

30. 539 U.S. 244 (2003).

31. 539 U.S. 982 (2003).

Social Movements and the Politics of Difference

Cheryl Zarlenga Kerchis

Iris Marion Young

There was once a time of caste and class when tradition held that each group had its place in the social hierarchy—that some were born to rule and others to be ruled. In this time of darkness, rights, privileges, and obligations were different for people of different sexes, races, religions, classes, and occupations. Inequality between groups was justified by both the state and the church on the grounds that some kinds of people were better than others.

Then one day, a period in the history of ideas known as the Enlightenment dawned, and revolutionary ideas about the equality of people emerged. During the Enlightenment, which reached its zenith in Europe in the eighteenth century, philosophers called into question traditional ideas and values that justified political inequality between groups. They declared that all people are created equal because all people are able to reason and to think about morality. They also argued that because all people are created equal, all people should have equal political and civil rights.

The ideas of Enlightenment thinkers have marked the battle lines of political struggle in the United States for the past two hundred years. The Revolutionary War was fought on Enlightenment principles, and our Constitution was based on the principles of liberty and equality. In the beginning, however, the vision of liberty and equality of our founders (as well as most Enlightenment philosophers) excluded certain groups. Women did not have equal political and civil rights, and African

Americans were enslaved. Inspired by the ideals of liberty and equality, women and African Americans engaged in a long and bitter struggle for political equality. By the 1960s, the battle for legal equal political and civil rights was won, though the struggle for equality in all walks of life continues.

Today in our society, prejudice and discrimination remain, but in many respects we have realized the vision that the Enlightenment thinkers set out. Our laws express rights in universal terms, that is, applied equally to everyone. We strive for a society in which differences of race, sex, religion, and ethnicity do not affect people's opportunities to participate in all aspects of social life. We believe that people should be treated as individuals, not as members of groups, and that their rewards in life should be based on their individual achievement—not on their race, sex, or any other purely accidental characteristic.

Though there is much to admire in this vision of a society that eliminates group differences, it has its own limitations, which contemporary social movements have called into question. Just as Enlightenment social movements challenged widely held traditional ideas and values that justified oppression in their time, today's social movements are challenging widely held ideas about justice that justify oppression in our time. These social movements criticize the idea that a just society is one that eliminates group differences under the law and guarantees equal treatment for all individuals. The central question they wish to ask is this: is it possible that the ideal of equal treatment of all persons under the law and the attempt to eliminate group differences under the law in fact perpetuates oppression of certain groups?

. . . We will argue that the answer to this question is yes. In our argument we will first discuss the ideal of justice that defines liberation as the transcendence of group difference. We call this the *ideal of assimilation*. This ideal usually promotes the equal treatment of all groups as the primary way to achieve justice. In this discussion, we will show how recent social movements of oppressed groups in the United States have challenged this ideal of assimilation. These movements believe that by organizing

Cheryl Zarlenga Kerchis is a teaching fellow and graduate student in public and international affairs at the University of Pittsburgh. Iris Marion Young is a professor of political science at the University of Chicago.

themselves and defining their own positive group cultural identity they will be more likely to achieve power and increase their participation in public institutions. We call this positive recognition of difference the politics of difference, and explain how it is more likely to aid in the liberation of oppressed groups.

. . . We will [also] discuss the need to change the way we think about group differences in order to have a politics of difference that leads to the liberation of oppressed groups. We will explore the risks associated with a politics of difference, in particular, the risk of recreating the harmful stigma that group difference has had in the past. To avoid this restigmatizing of groups, we will argue for a new and positive understanding of difference that rejects past exclusionary understandings of difference.

. . . [Finally,] we will consider practical issues of policy and representation in relation to a politics of difference. First, we will discuss the issue of group-neutral versus group-conscious policies. By this we mean policies that treat all groups in the same way (group-neutral) versus policies that treat different groups differently (group-conscious). We will discuss two specific cases in which group-conscious policies are needed to ensure fairness to disadvantaged groups. Lastly, we will argue for group representation in American social institutions including governmental and non-governmental institutions. We will explain how group representation promotes justice, suggest the kinds of groups that should be represented, and give some examples of group representation within some already-existing organizations and movements in the United States.

LIBERATION FOR OPPRESSED GROUPS THROUGH THE IDEAL OF ASSIMILATION

The Ideal of Assimilation and Equal Treatment of Social Groups

What strategy of reform is most effective for achieving the liberation of oppressed groups? If we desire a non-racist, non-sexist society, how can we get there? One strategy for achieving this society is to pursue what we call an ideal of assimilation. The ideal of assimilation as a strategy for the liberation of oppressed groups involves the elimination of group-based differences under the law. Thus, in a truly non-racist, non-sexist society, a person's race or sex would be no more significant in the eyes of the law than eye color or any other accidental characteristic. People would have different physical characteristics (such as skin color), but these would play no part in determining how people treated each other or how they were treated under the law. Over time, people would see no reason to consider race or sex in policies or in everyday activities, and group-based differences by and large would no longer matter.

Many contemporary thinkers argue for this ideal of assimilation and against the ideal of diversity that we will argue for later in this chapter. And there are many convincing reasons to support such an ideal. Perhaps the most convincing reason is that the principle of equal treatment of groups provides a clear and easily applied standard of equality and justice for use by courts and government institutions that deal with issues of race and sex discrimination. Under a standard of equal treatment, any discrimination whatsoever on the basis of group differences is considered illegal. Any law, regulation, employment practice, or government policy that treats persons differently on the basis of the race or sex is labeled unjust. The simplicity of this principle of equal treatment makes it a very attractive standard of justice.

There are two other convincing reasons to support the ideal of assimilation and the principle of justice as equal treatment. First, the ideal of assimilation may help to change the way people think about group differences. It treats classifications of people according to accidental characteristics like skin color or gender as arbitrary, not natural or necessary. Some people happen to be Black. Some are female or Hispanic or Jewish or Italian. But these differences do not mean that these people have different moral worth or that they necessarily aspire to anything different than anyone else in political life, in the workplace, or in the family. By suggesting that these categories are not important, the ideal of assimilation helps us realize how often we limit people's opportunities in society (because they are Black, female, and so on) for arbitrary reasons. Second, the ideal of assimilation gives individuals a great deal of choice in their lives. When group differences have no social importance, people are free to develop themselves as individuals, without feeling the pressures of group expectations. If I am a woman, I can aspire to anything I wish to and not feel any special pressure to pursue or settle for, for instance, one occupation versus another.

The ideal of assimilation, which calls for equal treatment of groups and the elimination of group difference in social life, has been extremely important in the history of oppressed groups. Its assertion of the equal moral worth of all persons (regardless of their group characteristics) and the right of all to participate in the institutions of society inspired many movements against discrimination. There is no question that it continues to have considerable value in our nation today, where many forms of discrimination against groups persist.

Contemporary Challenges to the Ideal of Assimilation

Since the 1960s, a number of groups have questioned the value of this ideal of assimilation and equal treatment. Is it possible, they have asked, that this ideal is not truly liberating for some oppressed groups? Instead of seeking to eliminate group difference, they wonder, would it not be more liberating for groups to organize themselves and assert their own positive group cultural identity? These groups see a politics of difference as opposed to a politics without difference as a better strategy for achieving power and participation in the institutions of social and political life. In the next section, we will discuss the efforts of four contemporary social movements to redefine the importance of group difference and cultural identity in social and political life in a way that they find more liberating.

The African American Movement   In the 1960s, with the enactment of the Civil Rights Act of 1964, the Voting Rights Act of 1965, and numerous law-

suits spawned by these new laws, African Americans won major victories that declared racial discrimination in politics and the workplace illegal. Despite these successes, however, criticisms of the civil rights strategy emerged from within the African American community in the form of the Black Power movement. Black Power leaders criticized the civil rights movement for three reasons: they were unhappy with the civil rights movement's goal of integration of African Americans into a society dominated by whites; they criticized the movement's alliance with white liberals and instead called upon African Americans to confidently affirm their cultural identity; and they criticized the movement for not encouraging African Americans to organize themselves on their own terms and to determine their political goals within their own organizations.

Instead of supporting integration with whites, Black Power leaders called on African Americans to strengthen their own separate and culturally distinct neighborhoods as a better means of obtaining economic and political power. In sum, they rejected the ideal of assimilation and the suppression of group difference in political and economic life. In its place, they advocated self-organization and a strengthening of cultural identity as a better strategy for achieving power and participation in dominant institutions.

In recent years, many of the ideas of the Black Power movement have resurfaced among African Americans. Despite the legal protections won during the civil rights era, African American economic and political oppression persists. In economic life today, African Americans experience unemployment rates more than twice those of whites and poverty rates more than three times those of whites. And they still face substantial discrimination in educational opportunities, business opportunities, and the housing market.

What has happened since the 1960s? Why the persistence of inequalities almost forty years after *Brown v. Board of Education,* and almost thirty years after the Civil Rights and Voting Rights acts? Many African Americans argue that the push toward integration by the civil rights movement had unintended negative effects on the African American community. While civil rights protections opened the doors of opportunity for some African Americans, those left behind were made worse off. Many African Americans have been assimilated into the middle class and no longer associate as closely with poor and working class African Americans. As a consequence, African American solidarity has been weakened, and in many neighborhoods African American businesses, schools, and churches have been hurt by the exodus of middle-class African American families. Hence, once again, many African American leaders are calling for a rejection of the goal of integration and assimilation and are calling upon African Americans to organize themselves and seek economic and political empowerment within their own neighborhoods.

Another legacy of the Black Power movement that lives on today is the assertion of a positive Black cultural identity. The "Black is beautiful" movement that emerged in the 1960s celebrated a distinct African American culture and struggled against the assimilation of that culture into the dominant culture of American society. In their clothing and hairstyles, members confidently asserted their own cultural styles and rejected the narrow definition of style and beauty of the predominantly white culture. Since that time, African American historians and educators have sought to recover the rich history of African America and have retold the stories of African American writers, artists, musicians, inventors, and political figures, who received little attention in the history textbooks of white America. And they have subsequently fought with school boards across the nation to ensure that respect for African American history and culture is integral to the history curricula under which every student in this country is educated.

All of these examples reflect a rejection of the idea that assimilation of African Americans into the dominant culture of America is a desirable goal. They instead reflect a desire for an alternative politics of difference through which African Americans can gain their fair share of power and increase their participation in social, political, and economic life in America without shedding their own self-determined group cultural identity.

The American Indian Movement   Not long after the Black Power movement emerged in the 1960s, a movement with similar ideals arose among Native Americans. American Indian Movement leaders called for Red Power, which, like Black Power, rejected the assimilation of Native American peoples that had been the goal of government policies toward Indians throughout the nineteenth and twentieth centuries. In many ways, their rejection of the dominant culture and its values was even stronger than that of Black Power.

The American Indian Movement claimed a right to self-government on Indian lands and struggled to gain a powerful Indian voice in the federal government branch responsible for policy making toward Native American peoples—the Bureau of Indian Affairs. They went to the courts to fight for land taken away from them. They also used the court system to fight for Indian control of natural resources on reservations that were being exploited by mining companies and other corporations.

Like Black Power, Red Power also extended its struggle beyond political and economic issues. Red Power advocates wanted to restore and strengthen cultural pride among Native Americans. In the last twenty years, Native Americans have struggled to recover and preserve elements of their traditional culture such as religious rituals, crafts, and languages that have been ravaged by the government's policy of Indian assimilation.

The Gay and Lesbian Movement   The gay and lesbian movement that emerged in the 1960s began, much like the African American movement of that period, as a struggle for equality and civil rights. Gay-rights advocates wanted to protect gay men and lesbians from discrimination in government institutions and in employment. The movement strived for the ideal of assimilation and equal treatment that we have talked about throughout this [article]. They asked society to recognize that gay people are no different from anyone else in their aspirations or moral worth, and that they too deserve the same protections under the law extended to all other U.S. citizens.

Over time, however, many members of the gay and lesbian movement came to believe that the achievement of civil rights alone would not liberate gay men and lesbians from the discrimination they faced in society. Though they had achieved some legal victories, gay men and lesbians were still often harassed, beaten up, and intimidated by heterosexuals who disapproved of their gay "lifestyle." It seemed the dominant culture could tolerate gays and even extend limited legal protection to gay people as long as they kept their sexuality a *private* matter. But *public* displays of gay lifestyles were (and still are) often met with hostility and violence. For many gay men and lesbians, concealing their sexuality and lifestyles in a private world is just as oppressive as the public and explicit discrimination they often face in institutions.

Today, most gay and lesbian liberation groups seek not only equal protection under the law but also group solidarity and a positive affirmation of gay men and lesbians as social groups with shared experiences and cultures. They reject the ideal of assimilation that suppresses group differences in political and social life and makes these differences a purely private matter. They refuse to accept the dominant heterosexual culture's definition of healthy sexuality and respectable family life, and instead have insisted on the right to proudly display their gay or lesbian identity. Like the other groups mentioned above, they have engaged in a politics of difference that they find more liberating than the politics of assimilation.

The Women's Movement Until the late 1970s, the aims of the contemporary women's movement were for the most part those of the ideal of assimilation. Women's movement members fought for women's civil rights and the equal treatment of and equal opportunity for women in political institutions and the workplace. The movement strived to eliminate the significance of gender differences in social life.

Women and men were to be measured by the same standards and treated in the same way in social institutions. Women's rights advocates saw any attempt to define men and women as fundamentally different in their aspirations for successful careers outside the home as just another means of oppressing women and limiting their opportunity to participate in the male-dominated spheres of government and business. This strategy of assimilation was extremely successful in undermining traditional ways of thinking about sex differences and women's roles. The idea that women naturally aspired to less in terms of participation in politics and the workplace was finally overturned.

Despite these successes, however, many in the women's movement grew uncomfortable with this strategy of assimilation, which defined equality as the elimination of sex differences in social life. Since the late seventies, a politics of difference has emerged from within the women's movement that rejects the goals of gender assimilation. The first signs of this rejection were seen among women who advocated feminist separatism.

Feminist separatists believed that women should aspire to more than formal equality in a male-dominated world. They argued that entering the male-dominated world meant playing according to rules and standards that men had set up and had used against women for centuries and across cultures. Instead of trying to measure up to male-defined standards, they called for the empowerment of women through self-organization and the creation of separate and safe places where women could share their experiences and devise their own rules of the game. In such separate and safe places, women could decide for themselves what was socially valuable activity instead of uncritically accepting the values and activities of a male-dominated society. One of the outcomes of this separatism was the creation of women's organizations and services to address the needs of women that have historically received little attention from male-dominated society. The organizations formed in this period include women's health clinics, battered women's shelters, and rape crisis centers, all of which today continue to improve the lives of many women.

Some of the ideas of this separatist movement are reflected in the recent work of feminist philosophers and political thinkers. Unlike earlier feminist thinkers, these women question the idea that women's liberation means equal participation of women in male-dominated political institutions and workplaces. While they do not suggest that women withdraw from such institutions, they suggest that society ought to rethink the value of femininity and women's ways of approaching human relations. These theorists suggest that women tend to be socialized in a way that, in comparison with men, makes them more sensitive to others' feelings, more empathetic, more nurturing of others and the world, and better at smoothing over tensions between people.

They argue that this more caring, nurturing, and cooperative approach to relations with other people should not be rejected out of hand by feminists as limiting women's human potential or their ability to contribute to the world. They suggest that women's attitudes toward others and toward nature constitute a healthier way to think about the world than the competitive and individualistic attitudes that characterize male-dominated culture in the Western world. By holding on to these values, women can help to transform institutions, human relations, and the interaction of people with nature in ways that may better promote people's self-development within institutions and better protect the environment.

Thus, a political strategy that asks women to give up the values of caring or nurturing in order to succeed in the workplace or in politics not only undervalues what women have to contribute to those spheres, but undermines the possibility of transforming male-dominated institutions in a way that will result in a healthier society as a whole. To resolve this dilemma, then, the politics of assimilation needs to be replaced by a politics of difference that makes it possible for women to participate fully in social and political institutions without suppressing or undervaluing gender differences.

WHY IS THE POLITICS OF DIFFERENCE LIBERATING?

The Importance of Group Difference in Social Life

All of the social movements discussed above have offered an alternative view of liberation that rejects the ideal of assimilation. In their assertion of a positive sense of group difference, these social movements have put forth an ideal of liberation that we will call the politics of difference. In their view, a just society does not try to eliminate or ignore the importance of group differences. Rather, society seeks equality among social groups, requiring each to recognize and respect the value of the experiences and perspectives of all other groups. No group asks another to give up or hide its distinct experiences and perspectives as a condition of participation in social institutions.

Is a politics of difference really necessary? Are group differences really that important? Many political philosophers deny the importance of social groups. To them, the notion of group difference was created and kept alive by people who sought to justify their own privilege and the oppression of specific groups. Some theorists agree that there are important differences among groups that affect the way people see themselves and others, but they see these differences as undesirable. The ideal of assimilation either denies the importance of social groups or sees them as undesirable.

In contrast, we doubt that a society without social groups is possible *or* desirable. Today, whether we like it or not, our society is structured by social groups that have important consequences for people's lives. Social groups do affect the way people see themselves and others in both positive and negative ways. People form their identities—their sense of who they are—in part through their membership in social or cultural groups. There is nothing inherently bad about people identifying with certain groups. Attachment to an ethnic tradition, language, culture, or set of common experiences has always been a feature of social life. The problem for a democratic nation occurs when group membership affects people's capacities to participate fully in our social institutions. In the United States today, some groups are privileged while others are oppressed. The politics of difference offers a way of retaining the positive, identity-affirming aspect of group difference while eliminating the negative aspect—the privileging of some groups over others.

The Oppressive Consequences of Ignoring Group Difference

None of the social movements that we have discussed deny the claim that the strategy of eliminating group difference and treating all groups the same has helped improve the situation of oppressed social groups. On the contrary, each of these social movements at one time pursued such a strategy. But why did they eventually begin to question its effectiveness in eliminating group oppression? Why was assimilation called into question?

Many of these social movements of oppressed groups found that the achievement of formal equality under the law did not put an end to their disadvantaged position. Even though in many respects the law is now blind to group differences like sex and race, certain groups continue to be oppressed while other groups are privileged. Many forms of oppression, such as racial slurs, are more subtle, yet they are just as corrosive than the more easily identifiable forms of overt and intentional discrimination. They persist in the structure of institutions that make it difficult for members of disadvantaged groups to develop their capacities. Oppression also exists in forms of everyday interaction and decision making in which people make assumptions about the aspirations and needs of women, African Americans, Hispanics, gay men and lesbians, and other groups that continue to be oppressed. The idea that equality and liberation can only be achieved by ignoring group differences has three oppressive consequences for disadvantaged social groups.

First, ignoring group difference disadvantages groups whose experience and culture differ from those of privileged groups. The strategy of assimilation aims to bring excluded groups into the mainstream of social life. But assimilation always implies coming into the game after it has already begun, after the rules and standards have already been set. Therefore, disadvantaged groups play no part in making up the rules and standards that they must prove themselves by—those rules and standards are defined by privileged groups. The rules and standards may appear to be neutral since they are applied equally to all groups. In actuality though, their formation was based only upon the experiences of privileged groups—oppressed groups being excluded from the rule-making process.

If such standards are applied equally to all groups, why do they then place some groups at a disadvantage? The real differences between oppressed groups and dominant groups often make it difficult for oppressed groups to measure up to the standards of the privileged. These real differences may have to do with cultural styles and values or with certain distinct capacities (for example, women's capacity to bear children). But quite often these differences are themselves the result of group oppression. For example, the long history of exclusion and marginalization of African American people from the economic and educational systems of this country has made it very difficult for many of them to gain the levels of educational attainment and technical skills that whites have. Yet, despite this history of oppression, they must compete for jobs on the basis of qualifications that are the same for all groups, including historically privileged groups.

The second oppressive consequence of ignoring group difference is that it allows privileged groups in society to see their own culture, values, norms, and experiences as universal (shared by all groups) rather than group specific. In other words, ignoring group differences allows the norms and values that express the point of view and experience of privileged groups to appear neutral and uncontroversial. When the norms and values of particular privileged groups are held as normal, neutral, and universal, those groups that do not adhere to those norms and values are viewed by society as deviant or abnormal. . . .

When groups that do not share the supposedly neutral values and norms of privileged groups are viewed as deviant or abnormal, a third oppressive consequence of ignoring difference is produced. Members of those groups that are viewed as deviant often internalize society's view of them as abnormal or deviant. The internalization of the negative attitudes of others by members of oppressed groups often produces feelings of self-hatred and ambivalence toward their own culture. The ideal of assimilation asks members of oppressed groups to fit in and be like everyone else, yet society continues to see them as different, making it impossible for them to fit in comfortably. Thus, members of groups marked as different or deviant in comparison to privileged groups are caught in a dilemma they cannot resolve. On one hand, participating in mainstream society means accepting and adopting an identity that is not their own. And on the other, when they do try to participate, they are reminded by society and by themselves that they do not fit in.

The Liberating Consequences of the Politics of Difference

We have given three reasons why a strategy of assimilation that attempts to ignore, transcend, or devalue group differences is oppressive. We would now like to turn to the politics of difference and to explain the ways in which it is liberating and empowering for members of oppressed groups. The key difference between the politics of difference and the politics of assimilation lies in the definition of group difference itself. The politics of assimilation defines group difference in a negative way, as a liability or disadvantage to be overcome in the process of assimilating into mainstream society. In contrast, the politics of difference defines group difference in a positive way, as a social and cultural condition that can be liberating and empowering for oppressed groups. There are four ways in which this positive view of difference is liberating for oppressed groups.

First, a politics of difference that defines group difference in a positive way makes it easier for members of oppressed groups to celebrate and be proud of their identity, which the dominant culture has taught them to despise. In a politics of difference, members of oppressed groups are not asked to

assimilate, to try to be something they are not. They are not asked to reject or hide their own culture as a condition of full participation in the social life of the nation. Instead, the politics of difference recognizes that oppressed groups have their own cultures, experiences, and points of view that have positive value for themselves *and* society as a whole. Some of their values and norms may even be superior to those of more privileged groups in society.

Second, by recognizing the value of the cultures and experiences of oppressed groups, the politics of difference exposes the values and norms of privileged groups as group specific, not neutral or universal. The politics of difference recognizes that the values and norms of privileged groups are expressions of their own experience and may conflict with those of other groups. In the politics of difference, oppressed groups insist on the positive value of their own cultures and experiences. When they insist on this, it becomes more and more difficult for dominant groups to parade their norms and values as neutral, universal, or uncontroversial. It also becomes more difficult for dominant groups to point to oppressed groups as deviant, abnormal, or inferior.

Thus, for example, when feminists assert the positive value of a caring and nurturing approach to the world, they call into question the competitive and individualistic norms of white male society. When African Americans proudly affirm the culture and history of Afro-America, they expose the culture and history of white society as expressing a particular experience—only *one* part of America's story. When Native Americans assert the value of a culture tied to and respectful of the land, they call into question the dominant culture's materialism, which promotes pollution and environmental destruction. All of these questions posed by oppressed groups suggest that the values and norms of dominant groups comprise one perspective, one way of looking at the world, that is neither neutral, shared, nor necessarily superior to the ways of oppressed groups.

When we realize that the norms and values of privileged groups are not universal, it becomes possible to think about the relation between groups in a more liberating way. Oppressed groups are not deviant with respect to privileged groups. They simply differ from privileged groups in their values, norms, and experiences, just as privileged groups are different from them. Difference is a two-way street; each group differs from the other; each earns the label "different." When the relations among groups are defined this way, we eliminate the assumption of the inferiority of oppressed groups and the superiority of privileged groups and replace it with a recognition and respect for the value of the particular experiences and perspectives of all groups.

Third, by asserting the positive value of different groups' experiences, the politics of difference makes it possible to look critically at dominant institutions and values from the perspective of oppressed groups. In other words, the experiences and perspectives of oppressed groups provide critical insights into mainstream social institutions and values that can serve as a starting point for reform of those institutions and values. For example, by referring to their members as "brother" or "sister," African Americans engender in their traditional neighborhoods a sense of community and solidarity not found in the highly individualistic mainstream society. As mentioned earlier, feminists find in the human values of nurturing and caring a more superior way of approaching social and ecological relations than the competitive, militarist, and environmentally destructive approach of male-dominated society. The politics of difference takes these critiques by oppressed groups seriously, as a basis for reform of dominant institutions. Such critiques shed light on the ways that dominant institutions should be changed so that they no longer reinforce patterns of privilege and oppression.

Fourth, the politics of difference promotes the value of group solidarity amidst the pervasive individualism of contemporary social life and the politics of assimilation. Assimilationist politics treats each person as an individual, ignoring differences of race, sex, religion, and ethnicity; everyone should be treated equally and evaluated according to his or her individual effort and achievement. It is true that under this politics of assimilation many members of oppressed groups have achieved individual success, even by the standards of privileged groups. However, as we have already learned, many groups continue to be oppressed despite the individual success of some group members. For example, over the last thirty years, Blacks have increased their representation in well-paying occupations such as law, medicine, and engineering. Yet they are still very much underrepresented in these fields and overrepresented in less well-paying occupations like orderlies, taxicab drivers, and janitors. That is why oppressed groups refuse to see these individual successes as evidence that group oppression has been eliminated. Instead of celebrating the success of some of their members, they insist that the celebration wait until their whole group is liberated. In the politics of difference, oppressed groups, in solidarity, struggle for the fundamental institutional changes that will make this liberation possible.

By now, the distinctions between the politics of assimilation and the politics of difference should be clear. Some people might object to the way we have made these distinctions. We anticipate that the strongest objection will be that we have not presented fairly the advantages of a politics of assimilation that strives to transcend or get beyond group differences. Many who support the politics of assimilation do recognize the value of a pluralistic society in which a variety of lifestyles, cultures, and associations can flourish. We do not, however, take issue with this vision of a pluralistic society. What we emphasize is that this vision does not deal with fundamental issues that suggest the need for the politics of difference.

As we have repeated throughout this [article], we think it is counterproductive and dishonest to try to eliminate the public and political significance of group difference in a society in which some groups are more privileged than others. The danger in this approach is that group differences get pushed out of the sphere of public discussion and action and come to be seen as a purely private or non-political matter. When this happens, the problem of oppression of some groups tends to go unaddressed in our public institutions, and patterns of privilege and oppression among groups are reinforced. The politics of difference that we advocate recognizes and takes seriously the public and political importance of group differences, and takes the experiences of oppressed groups as a starting point for reform of our public institutions. The goal of this politics of difference is to change our institutions so that no group is disadvantaged or advantaged due to its distinct culture or capacities, thus ensuring that all groups have the opportunity to participate fully in the nation's social and political institutions.

REDEFINING THE MEANING OF DIFFERENCE IN CONTEMPORARY LIFE

The Risk of Restigmatizing Oppressed Groups

Many people inside and outside the liberation movements we have discussed in this chapter are fearful of the politics of difference and its rejection of the politics of assimilation. The fear of many is that any public admission of the fact that groups are different will be used to justify once again the exclusion and separation of certain kinds of people from mainstream society. Feminists fear that the affirmation of values of caring and nurturing that are associated with motherhood will lead to a call for women to return to the kitchen and the home, places where it is claimed those values can best be utilized.

African Americans fear that an affirmation of their different values and experiences will lead again to a call for separate schools and communities, "where they can be with their own kind." Many in these groups are willing to accept the fact that formal equality (treating everyone the same under the law) reinforces current patterns of advantage. This, they say, is preferable to a politics of difference that risks the restigmatization of certain groups and the reestablishment of separate and unequal spheres for such groups.

We are sympathetic to these fears. It certainly is not unusual in political life for one's ideas, actions, or policies to have unintended negative effects because others have used them to justify ends different from those intended. Nevertheless, we believe that

this risk is warranted since the strategy of ignoring group differences in public policy has failed to eliminate the problem of group oppression; the same patterns of privilege and oppression continue to be reproduced. All of which begs the question, Is there a way to avoid this risk of restigmatizing groups and rejustifying their exclusion? We believe there is a solution and it depends on redefining the meaning of difference itself.

Rejecting the Oppressive Meaning of Difference

In order to avoid the risk of recreating the stigma that oppressed groups have faced in the past, the meaning of difference itself must be redefined. In other words, we must change the way people think about differences among groups. In the politics of difference, the meaning of difference itself becomes an issue for political struggle.

There is an oppressive way of understanding difference that has dominated Western thinking about social groups for many centuries. This meaning of difference, which we will call the essentialist meaning, defines social groups in opposition to a normative group—typically the dominant social group. The culture, values, and standards of one social group provide the standards against which all other groups are measured.

The attempt to measure all groups against some universal standard or norm generates a meaning of difference as dichotomy, a relation of two opposites. Thus we have paired categories of groups—men/women, white/Black, healthy/disabled, rich/poor, young/old, civilized/uncivilized, to name a few. Very often, the second term in the pair is defined negatively in relation to the first. Those in the second category are defined as lacking valued qualities of those in the first. There are rational men, and there are irrational women. There are productive, active young people, and there are feeble old people. There is a superior standard of humanity, and there is an inferior one.

This way of thinking about difference as a good/bad opposition in which groups are defined in relation to a supposedly universal norm has oppressive consequences. Some groups are marked out as having different natures, which leads quickly to the assumption that they therefore must have different aspirations and dispositions that fit them for some activities and not others. It also leads to the argument that because nature is static, change is impossible. Women are defined as lacking men's rationality, which justifies their exclusion from high-ranking positions in business and government. People with disabilities are seen as unhealthy or helpless, which justifies isolating them in institutions.

The essentialist meaning of difference just described lies at the heart of racism, sexism, anti-Semitism, homophobia, and other negative attitudes toward specific groups. In these ideologies only the oppressed groups are defined as different. When oppressed groups are thought of as having fundamentally different natures from the "normal" group, it becomes easier for the "normal" group to justify excluding those groups from mainstream institutions and communities. On the other hand, once it is admitted that all groups have some things in common and that no group represents a universal or "normal" standard, it becomes more difficult to justify any group's exclusion from political and social life.

Redefining Difference as Variation

The politics of difference rejects the essentialist definition of difference, which defines it as deviance from a neutral norm and holds that some groups have essentially different natures and aspirations. In the politics of difference, however, group difference is seen as ambiguous and shifting, without clear categories of opposites that narrowly define people. Difference represents variation among groups that have similarities and dissimilarities. Groups are neither completely the same nor complete opposites. In the politics of difference, the meaning of group difference encompasses six key principles:

1. *Group difference is relational.* We can only understand groups in relation to each other. Group differences can be identified when we compare different groups, but no group can be held up as the standard of comparison. Thus, whites are just as specific a group as African Americans or Hispanics, men just as specific as women, able-

bodied people just as specific as people with disabilities. Difference does not mean a clear and specific set of attributes that a group shares, but means variation and heterogeneity. It appears as a relationship between groups and the interaction of groups with social institutions.

2. *Group difference is contextual.* That difference is contextual simply means that group differences may be more or less relevant depending on the context or situation in which they come up. In any context, the importance of group difference will depend on the groups being compared and the reasons for the comparison. For example, in the context of athletics, health care, or social service support, wheel chair–bound people are different from others in terms of the special needs they might have. But in many other contexts, these differences would be unimportant. In the past, people with disabilities were often excluded and segregated in institutions because their physical difference was seen as extending to all their capacities and all facets of their lives. Understanding difference as contextual eliminates this oppressive way of thinking about difference as all-encompassing.

3. *Group difference does not mean exclusion.* An understanding of difference as relational and contextual rejects the possibility of exclusion. No two groups lie exclusively outside each other in their experiences, perspectives, or goals. All groups have overlapping experiences and therefore are always similar in some respects.

4. *Members within a group share affinity for each other, not a fixed set of attributes.* Groups are not defined by a fixed set of characteristics or attributes that all group members share. What makes a group a group is the fact that they have a particular affinity for each other. The people I have an affinity for are simply those who are familiar to me and with whom I feel the most comfortable. Feelings of affinity develop through a social process of interaction and shared experience. People in an affinity group often share common values, norms, and meanings that express their shared experience. No person's affinities are fixed: a person's affinities may shift with changes

in his or her life. Likewise, group identities may shift over time with changes in social realities. . . .

5. *Groups define themselves.* Once we reject the idea that groups are defined by a set of common, essential attributes, groups are left to define for themselves what makes their particular group a group. This process of *self*-definition is emancipating in that it allows groups to reclaim a positive meaning for their difference and to decide collectively what they wish to affirm as their culture. Thus, the culture of oppressed groups is no longer defined by dominant groups in negative relation to mainstream culture. Many social movements of oppressed groups have begun this process of redefining their group identity for themselves. Both African American and Native American social movements have sought to redefine and reaffirm their cultural distinctiveness, often reclaiming from the past traditional values and norms that have meaning for them today. Some gays and lesbians are reappropriating the term "queer" and redefining it themselves.

6. *All groups have differences within them.* Our society is highly complex and differentiated, and no group is free of intragroup difference. For instance, a woman who is African American and a lesbian might identify with a variety of social groups—women, African Americans, lesbians. A woman who is Hispanic and heterosexual might have different affinities. Within the context of a social movement such as the women's movement, these differences between women are potential sources of wisdom and enrichment as well as conflict and misunderstanding. Because there is a potential for conflict within groups among persons who identify with more than one group, groups, like society as a whole, must also be attentive to difference. . . .

CONCLUSION

This [article] relies on a handful of clear principles, which we will summarize here. Social justice requires democracy. People should be involved in collective discussion and decision making in all the settings that ask for their obedience to rules—workplaces, schools, neighborhoods, and so on. Unfortunately, these social and political institutions privilege some groups over others. When some groups are more disadvantaged than others, ensuring democracy requires group representation for the disadvantaged. Group representation gives oppressed groups a voice in setting the public agenda and discussing matters on it. It also helps to ensure just outcomes of the democratic process by making sure that the needs and interests of all groups are expressed.

. . . We have asserted that the ideal of a society that eliminates, transcends, or ignores group difference is both unrealistic and undesirable. Justice in a society with groups requires the social equality of all groups, and mutual and explicit recognition and affirmation of the value of group differences. The politics of difference promotes social equality and undermines group oppression by affirming the value of group difference, attending to group-specific needs, and providing for group representation in social institutions.

The challenges faced by such a politics are formidable. While many public and private institutions have begun to recognize the value of diversity, demands for a real voice for oppressed groups in decision-making processes are often met with fear and hostility. Still, we are hopeful that a politics of difference may be on the horizon. The United States is becoming more diverse, not less. Women and minorities comprise increasing proportions of the labor force and their needs are more and more difficult for employers and public officials to ignore.

However, demographic changes alone are unlikely to induce substantive policy change. Politics matters. While oppressed groups are increasing their representation in political institutions, social movements of oppressed groups will continue to play a critical role in shaping attitudes and dialogues about change and mobilizing the public to act. It is our hope that the ideas [presented here] provide a source of inspiration to social movements. The politics of difference is an alternative vision of politics that challenges the assumption that the present system is the only or best system. It is not meant as a blueprint for change, but as a starting point for dialogue. It provides a standpoint from which we can identify forms of injustice in our current institutions and explore different strategies to remedy them.

DISCUSSION QUESTIONS

1. According to Kerchis and Young, why hasn't a politics of equal treatment eliminated group oppression?
2. Why might a society based on a politics of difference be more successful in the reduction of oppression?

READING 43

After *Brown*

THE RISE AND RETREAT OF SCHOOL DESEGREGATION

Charles T. Clotfelter

INTERRACIAL CONTACT INCREASED DRAMATICALLY

The overriding fact that emerges about post-1954 developments is the radical change in school environments [following the Supreme Court's 1954 *Brown v. Board of Education* decision]. For the 40 percent of the nation's public school students who lived in states under de jure segregation at the time of the *Brown* decision, this transformation was the most dramatic. Measured segregation in the South and Border regions [the border states were Delaware, Kentucky, Maryland, Missouri, Okla-

Charles T. Clotfelter is Z. Smith Reynolds Professor of Public Policy and professor of economics and law at Duke University. He is also a research associate of the National Bureau of Economics.

homa, and West Virginia] declined from its maximum value to rates that by 1972 made schools in those regions the least segregated in the country. In many communities across the South, where school districts often covered large geographic areas and court-ordered desegregation plans required a complete overhaul of student assignments, public schools reached nearly perfect racial balance. This kind of racial balance was easily achieved—logistically, at least—in metropolitan counties with only a few schools. In large urban districts such as Charlotte and Louisville, however, racially balancing the schools required elaborate reassignment plans and extensive use of school buses to transport students to schools sometimes many miles from their homes. But the results were dramatic. As a result of court-ordered desegregation, the percentage of black students attending schools that were 90–100 percent minority fell in Charlotte from 58 percent immediately before its plan was put into effect to 2 percent immediately after, and in Louisville, from 66 percent to 2 percent. For the South as a whole, the comparable percentage declined from 78 percent in 1968, the highest of any region in that year, to 25 percent in 1972, the lowest.

Less precipitous but significant all the same were the declines in segregation experienced in other regions. Next to the South, the Border region experienced the next largest change. These six states plus the District of Columbia, where slavery had been practiced up to the Civil War but which had remained in the Union, had practiced de jure segregation in their elementary and secondary schools until 1954. All of them ended this policy shortly after the *Brown* decision, but actual segregation failed to decrease as rapidly or completely as it did in the South. Perhaps surprisingly, average segregation also declined in districts across the Midwest and West. Public school districts in the Midwest were in fact fairly well segregated at the time of the *Brown* decision and stayed that way for another decade and a half, after which segregation there gradually declined until about 1990. In the West, estimates based on unpublished data from a sample of districts suggest that segregation increased during the

1960s but then fell markedly thereafter, leaving districts in that region, along with those in the South, as the least segregated in the country at the turn of the century. Only in the Northeast did segregation not clearly decline. In that region, measures of racial isolation based on all districts showed no decrease in segregation, but measures based on metropolitan area data suggest that segregation within districts did decline between 1970 and 2000.

In addition to public schools, interracial contact also increased in private schools and in colleges and universities. Based on the sparse data available, the exposure of whites to blacks increased in the Catholic schools of most regions between 1970 and 2000. The average change was not large, however, leaving interracial exposure rates generally quite low. Similarly, the ranks of non-Catholic private schools became racially more diverse, though again by degrees quite modest in comparison to the changes occurring in public schools. By 2000, counting public and private schools, the average white student attended a school that was 74 percent white, the average black student attended a school that was 31 percent black, and the average Hispanic student attended a school that was 25 percent Hispanic.[1] Although schools were far from being racially integrated, these figures show that, on average, students were in schools with significant shares of those of other races or ethnic groups. In short, by the end of the twentieth century, interracial contact in schools was common.

In the nation's colleges, the five decades after *Brown* brought profound change in interracial contact. Aside from the historically black colleges and universities, college in 1954 was an almost all-white experience. By the turn of the century, the racial composition of these predominantly white institutions had changed quite significantly. In four-year institutions, both public and private, in all regions of the country, white college students encountered student bodies of increasing racial diversity. For example, a sample of eleven private universities, whose black enrollments averaged just 0.3 percent of all undergraduates in 1951, by 1998 had increased that share to 7.0 percent. The overall non-

white percentage over that period rose from 1.0 percent to 32.2 percent.

This evidence based on school enrollments is an outward manifestation of a radical transformation of the educational experience of young Americans in the fifty years following the *Brown* decision. While the change has differed by region and community, for the nation as a whole, the opportunities for students of various races and ethnic groups to interact with each other in comfortable, often cooperative settings have multiplied enormously compared to the years before 1954 or, indeed, 1968. This is true at every level of education, including—perhaps, especially—higher education. One indicator of the extent of this change is suggested by results gleaned from an annual survey of high school seniors, summarized in Figure 1. When asked how often they did things—such as having a conversation, eating together, or playing sports—with people of other races, the percentage of white students who said they did this "a lot" increased over time between 1976 and 2000, approximately doubling. For black students, the percentages were higher but increased only a little. For white students, at least, the world changed during the second half of the post-*Brown* era, and it seems reasonable to believe that it had begun to change before that. Schools represented the most important source of contact for these young people. Two-thirds of blacks and more than one-third of whites said they had gotten to know people of other races a lot in school. Next most important as venues for this contact were employment, sports teams, and clubs, in that order.[2]

CONTRARY FORCES RESTRAINED THE INCREASE IN INTERRACIAL CONTACT

As great as the increases were in interracial contact that accompanied school desegregation, they were smaller than they might otherwise have been. Four forces served to retard the increase in interracial contact in schools. First, and most important, was a tendency for whites to avoid racially mixed schools and the things that were associated with those schools. This tendency was especially pronounced

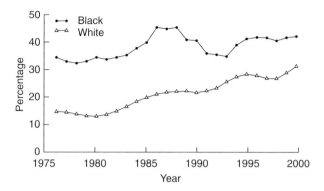

FIGURE 1
Percentage of High School Seniors Who Report Doing "a Lot"
with People of Other Races, 1976–2000
Sources: Monitoring the Future survey of high school seniors,
Tuch, Sigelman, and MacDonald (1999, appendix); Johnston,
Bachman, and O'Malley (various years); author's calculations.
Note: Figures are three-year moving averages. Question was:
"How often do you do things (like having a conversation, eating
together, playing sports) with people of other races?"

where the actual or potential percentage of non-whites was large.

Second, whites often had at their disposal multiple options for minimizing the impact of desegregation. Not only were private schools an option that usually promised smaller shares of nonwhites than public schools, so were suburban schools. Most of the white parents living in central cities could feasibly reduce the nonwhite share in their children's school by moving to a nearby suburban school district. Wherever that suburban option did not exist or was inconvenient, entrepreneurial and civic initiative being what it is, the private school option tended to spring up. Another commonly available option for white parents who sought to cushion the effects of desegregation was the possibility of enrolling their children in classes that offered larger shares of white students, made available due to academic tracking. Beyond the choice of school, whites also had ways of blunting the effect of desegregation on the extracurricular life of students by way of segregation in school activities. The social world of the public school, especially the public high school,

could have been turned on its head by desegregation. Through various means, whites, the more powerful group in most schools, were able to preserve some of the elements of the previous social order, thus moderating the extent of change in social relations. An interesting by-product created by this multiplicity of avenues of escape was that it provided something like moral cover for white avoidance. It allowed whites to favor racial integration in principle while avoiding it in practice. Reflecting on the growing support for academic tracking in 1958, the psychologist Bruno Bettelheim noted:

> Large numbers of the intelligentsia can advocate desegregation of the public schools all the more freely as their own children (the "gifted" children) are already segregated, either by placement in special classes for the gifted, or in the suburbs. It is not that these groups who fight *against* segregation and *for* special facilities for the gifted wish to establish a new color line. On the contrary, they want to do away with the old-fashioned color line, to replace the "white color" elite by a more up-to-date "white collar" elite, composed of all highly educated persons of all colors.[3]

A third factor retarding interracial contact was that this white avoidance imperative was accommodated and in many cases actively supported by state and local governments, in particular by local school officials. Before the active intervention of federal courts, many districts, North and South, gerrymandered school attendance zones, allowed pupil transfers, and strategically expanded schools or located new ones so as to minimize the extent of racial mixing. These techniques gave way to more subtle approaches, including academic tracking. If track assignments were based on objective criteria such as achievement test scores, such an approach could lead to racially identifiable tracks. If, in addition, parental pressure or outright discrimination came to influence assignments to tracks and special classes, the classrooms could become even more racially demarcated. Outside of the classroom, some school officials looked the other way or endorsed segregated school activities, although this was by no means a predominant stance.

Fourth, desegregation's impact was blunted because its initial sponsors gradually lost their resolve to press the case. No doubt influenced by the intensity of white opposition to urban busing orders—opposition that was no means confined to the South—as well as the success of Republican presidents in appointing conservative jurists, the Supreme Court began to back away from aggressive desegregation measures after just two decades. Beginning with the *Milliken* decision in 1974, which limited desegregation efforts in Detroit to its central city district, the court increasingly limited the scope of allowable remedies and turned away from racial balance as a measure of compliance. As the new century began, federal courts in much of the South had not only begun to release local school districts from continuing scrutiny of racial balance but had forbidden the use of race in making student assignments.[4] Meanwhile, the support that black leaders had traditionally given to school desegregation steadily weakened. Frustrated by white resistance to desegregation and disappointed by the perception that blacks had borne the bulk of desegregation's costs—including longer bus rides, inferior teaching

assignments, and the closing of black schools—leaders increasingly stressed school quality over desegregation.[5] . . .

Another factor also restrained the increase in interracial contact: segregation within schools. Although contemporary nationwide data on within-school segregation has not been collected, evidence for the state of North Carolina shows its extent at four grade levels. As a percentage of total segregation in North Carolina's districts (measured here at the classroom level), within-school racial disparities are much more important in the upper grades than in elementary schools. Whereas the within-school portion accounted for only one-fifth of total segregation in the first grade, it was almost two-thirds of total segregation in the tenth grade, where the latter is based on English classes. This large share results from grouping tenth-grade students into English classes according to various academic levels.

Racial disparities are evident as well in extracurricular activities, ranging from school newspapers to sports teams. Based on data obtained from almost two hundred high school yearbooks, disparities between the racial compositions of organizations and student bodies arose because of lower participation by nonwhites and the uneven distribution of those who did participate. Even in quite racially mixed schools, all-white groups occasionally appeared, as did groups with no whites. White students were rarely in groups where they were greatly outnumbered by non-whites. It is worth noting the possibility that within-school segregation in classrooms or student activities could have had a secondary effect favoring interracial contact. It may have had the effect of holding some whites in desegregated schools who would otherwise have left for suburban or private schools.

At the college level, the phenomenon that stands in starkest contrast to the marked increase in interracial contact is the continued existence of historically black institutions. A vestige of the Jim Crow era seemingly oblivious to the desegregation occurring all around them, they enrolled a steady number, but a declining percentage, of black college students through the first fifty years of the post-*Brown* era. . . .

PATTERNS OF CLASSROOM SEGREGATION

That racial segregation has existed within many schools is hardly novel. Numerous studies have uncovered it, ranging from blatant racial separation to otherwise nondiscriminatory class assignment policies that produce racial disparities across classrooms. An example of blatant separation was schools in south Texas, which, in the years immediately before *Brown,* commonly placed Mexican American children in separate classrooms.[6] In 1963 Milwaukee was found to be doing the same thing to its black students, by placing them in entirely separate classrooms within otherwise predominantly white schools. Rapid growth in black enrollment had caused overcrowding in the district's black schools, leading school authorities to take this step.[7] Similar practices were employed by some Southern districts in the immediate aftermath of thoroughgoing desegregation in the late 1960s. In the fall of 1970 a group of six nonprofit organizations sent monitors to more than four hundred districts in the South to assess local school policies regarding interracial contact. Some districts in predominantly black counties, in an attempt to keep whites from being vastly outnumbered in any class, established minimum numbers or percentages of whites in assigning students to classrooms. In at least a few districts schools established classes that were completely segregated by race. Where classrooms contained both whites and blacks, they found some instances of strict segregation within those classrooms. In a few of these an actual physical barrier—a row of empty seats or movable chalkboards—enforced the separation; elsewhere it was imposed or self-imposed.[8]

But blatant tactics such as these were neither widespread nor longlasting. In the South, the combination of desegregation and tracking produced immediate racial differentiation across classrooms. When track assignments were based on standard-ized tests, tracks ranging from college preparatory to vocational quickly became racially distinctive, with the lower tracks being completely or predominantly black, often with black teachers assigned to them.[9] An example of this phenomenon is Louisiana's Washington Parish, a district that began using standardized tests to group its white elementary students in 1953 but included blacks in this testing only after the black and white schools were combined in 1969. In the resulting assignments, whites predominated in the upper tracks, leaving the bottom tracks nearly all-black.[10] To be sure, not all districts practiced tracking. One urban district in the South, for example, explicitly discouraged tracking and forbade racially unrepresentative classrooms for periods of seventy-five minutes per day. This was, however, a majority-black district led by a majority-black school board.[11]

Tracking was by no means confined to the South. One study of tracking reports that its use increased in the urban North during the late 1950s, in the wake of Sputnik and the influx of blacks from the South and Hispanics from Puerto Rico and Mexico.[12] Another study, based on interviews with a sample of school officials, found that the use of tracking increased after court-ordered desegregation.[13] Other research found that tracking was used heavily in the Southwest in districts where Hispanics were numerous.[14] The example of Rockford, Illinois, noted above, is a particularly well documented case, since the federal court's findings of fact are part of the judicial record. In an attempt to comply with state desegregation mandates during the 1970s, that district "desegregated" some of its schools with high nonwhite percentages by establishing predominantly white gifted programs within them. One of these programs was established at Wilson Middle School in the fall of 1975. Whereas nonwhites had comprised 48 percent of enrolled students in the previous school year, they made up only 8 percent of the new gifted program in 1975.[15] Because the program used entirely separate classes, the federal court concluded that the district had effectively created "a school within a school" for white students.[16] About the same time, the U.S. Office for

Civil Rights (OCR) undertook a detailed investigation of the New York City public schools, looking in part for evidence of within-school segregation. The resulting report found segregation in classroom assignments in about one-fifth of the thousand schools in the system.[17]

Indeed, routine policies of academic tracking tend to segregate students within schools by producing classrooms with different racial compositions. These differences arise not only because the percentage of students eligible by objective placement criteria may differ among racial groups, but also because of the effect of discriminatory placements and parental pressure. In its study of New York City cited above, the OCR reported that it could find no rationale for classroom assignments in one-quarter of the approximately two hundred New York City schools cited for segregated classroom assignments. In the remainder, the report said, "criteria to place minority students in low-ability groups are often both vague and subjective."[18] Another study of placements into ninth-grade honors English classes revealed that, holding constant achievement test scores and previous placements, students in higher socioeconomic groups were more likely to be placed in honors classes. As evidence of racial bias, black and Hispanic students were less likely to be so placed, controlling for these other factors.[19] One force acting on classroom and track assignments was parental pressure: schools might yield to pressure exerted by middle-class parents to give their children favorable placement.[20] Even where students of different abilities shared the same classrooms, interracial contact could be affected by ability grouping within classrooms. A detailed study of teaching methods and classroom dynamics in one desegregated middle school showed, for example, that the use of homogeneous ability grouping as a classroom instructional method reduced opportunities for interracial contact.[21] . . .

EXPLAINING CLASSROOM SEGREGATION

. . . Evidence of [more recent] racial discrimination in track assignments appears in various social science studies. I will cite three. In 1992 Adam Gamoran analyzed the placement of ninth graders into honors English classes in five Midwestern communities. He found that, holding both achievement scores and social class constant, minority students were less likely than whites to be assigned to the honors classes.[22] In a 1993 study, Jeannie Oakes showed that, controlling for achievement test scores, whites were more likely than Hispanics to be placed in an accelerated course. She obtained similar results for placement of students in a college preparatory course in ninth grade.[23] And, in a 2001 study of English placements in three Charlotte high schools, Roslyn Mickelson identified a pattern of preferences toward whites in advanced placement, International Baccalaureate, and academically gifted twelfth-grade English classes. Black students were consistently more likely to be placed in regular English classes, holding constant scores on a standardized language test.[24] These practices can result in starkly segregated classrooms. One middle school teacher in Johnson County, Georgia, described tracking in her school this way: "We track throughout. The upper social classes are found in the upper group. We have two influential black families, and both of their kids are in the upper group. You might have thirty kids and two will be black in the top group, and at the bottom you might have twenty-five kids and two of them white."[25]

To explain such assignment practices, one might naturally think of racial prejudice on the part of teachers and school administrators as a driving force. Indeed, there is some indirect evidence to support this view. One study of fifth-grade teachers in ninety-four schools across the country showed that ability grouping within classes was more often used in the South, by teachers who had negative views of the educational benefits of integration, and in classrooms with more blacks. However, ability grouping was also used more often by black teachers, controlling for other variables, making it impossible to make easy inferences about racial prejudice.[26] And such patterns are commonly observed outside the South, as a 1993 federal court decision regarding Yonkers, New York, illustrates.[27]

Another likely explanation for biased classroom and track assignments arises in interactions between parents and principals. Parents who want their children to be in advanced classes contact the school and lobby for their children to be so placed. Consistent with the middle school teacher's statement quoted above, sociological studies reveal that middle-class parents are more likely than parents with lower incomes not only to make such requests but to be successful in obtaining the desired placements.[28] Since many districts do not restrict their advanced classes on the basis of scores alone, such requests can often be granted without breaking any rules; yet the resulting assignment pattern can show the kind of bias revealed in the studies referred to above. The reasons that motivate parents to make such requests may be purely academic, or may have to do with keeping a child with her friends. Whatever the proximate reasons in the particular cases, however, the aggregate effect is to give higher socioeconomic-status parents—usually white or Asian American—disproportionate influence in determining assignments to tracks.[29] For their part, school administrators may see advantages in accommodating the wishes of high-status parents, since doing so enhances the chance of keeping them in the district, or, at the very least, reduces complaints and solidifies political support.[30] An illustration of this reason for tracking is the south Georgia school district of Calhoun County, which had a 70 percent black enrollment in 1995, but whose high school academic tracks were racially distinct. A federal investigation sought to determine whether discrimination contributed to this racial difference, causing several dozen white families to withdraw their children. One school board member remarked, "They're just abandoning the school. Before it's all over, we're probably going to lose some more. When you lose white kids, when you lose their families' support, it's going to hurt the school system."[31] Similarly, tracking in suburban high schools in St. Louis was found to minimize the potential opposition from white parents and students to a desegregation program that buses black students from the central city.[32] One study critical of academic tracking summarizes the calculus of

school administrators this way: "School districts have been willing to trade off black access to equal education opportunities for continued white enrollments in the school system."[33] . . .

POLICY CHOICES

The first half-century following *Brown v. Board of Education* is now prologue. The evil of officially sanctioned public schools is a thing of the past. Indeed, the America of 2004 is in many important ways radically different from that which received the *Brown* proclamation in 1954. Thanks to a massive and sustained civil rights movement and a thoroughgoing transformation of laws regarding access and opportunity, the legal status of racial and ethnic minorities in most realms of social and political life has been profoundly changed. Yet in some respects the America of 2004 bears a striking resemblance to that previous time. Racial segregation remains an ever-present fact, demarcating neighborhoods, urban jurisdictions, and thus many public schools. Middle schools and high schools that are desegregated often include classrooms and school activities that reveal obvious racial disparities. Although official segregation has ended, therefore, actual segregation still exists in various forms.

Public policy surrounding interracial contact in public schools is shaped first and foremost by the Supreme Court, through its evolving interpretation of the Constitution and federal law. Consequently, public policy discussions about segregation are inevitably constrained by the court's decisions. Just as *Brown* started the engine and *Green* and *Swann* stepped on the accelerator, *Milliken* and *Dowell* applied the brakes. By virtue of these decisions, the policy setting of 2004 is manifestly different from that which existed in 1964, or even 1984. Viewing the growing judicial reluctance to push desegregation further, some commentators have written with alarm about the "dismantling" of desegregation, one concluding that Republican appointees to the Supreme Court "undermined desegregation."[34] As it led the process of ending judicial supervision over numerous school districts by declaring them "unitary," the Supreme Court returned control over interracial contact in the schools to local authorities.[35] Once a school district was deemed to be unitary, almost any race-neutral and otherwise nondiscriminatory method of assigning students appeared acceptable, including traditional neighborhood schools. The 2003 *Grutter* decision may leave the door open to assignment plans designed to foster racial diversity, but at this writing the practical implications of that decision are anything but obvious. What does seem clear is that the era of federally mandated plans based on achieving racially balanced schools is over.

Despite the atrophy of judicial activism in pursuing school desegregation, state and local policy makers, including local school boards, nevertheless still have some policy options at their disposal. Indeed, in the post-unitary era to come, the degree to which public schools will be racially mixed will be largely a local policy decision, constrained of course by each district's demographic makeup. Options exist in at least three areas. The first and most important realm of choice lies in the assignment of public school students to schools. As the preceding discussion makes clear, the federal courts have left it up to local school districts to decide how to assign students. Given the preference of most whites for predominantly white schools, and the continuing reality of neighborhood segregation, the use of neighborhood attendance zones will produce at least moderate levels of school segregation. For most districts, the only way not to end up with many racially identifiable schools will be through proactive pupil assignment policies. One such proactive policy is to modify the kind of assignment plans previously used for racial balance by substituting other assignment criteria, such as free-lunch eligibility or test scores, in place of race. This approach is likely to achieve some degree of racial balance, but not as much as under a race-sensitive plan.

Other approaches appear less likely to increase interracial contact beyond what neighborhood schools would produce. For example, magnet schools, again stripped of explicit reference to race, may be used to offer programs likely to appeal to white families in schools located in neighborhoods with higher nonwhite proportions. An alternative to the magnet school approach is "controlled choice," which allows or requires all parents to choose specific schools for their children, subject perhaps to geographical limitations on the set of schools available to each family or to some overall balance constraint. Bolstered by the notion that they will foster competition among schools, such choice plans are similar to voucher proposals, only restricted to public schools within a single district.[36] . . .

Other policy options related to school assignment may affect interracial contact as well. One is the option of permitting voluntary transfers between school districts, as has been done, for example, in Boston, Hartford, and St. Louis, where minority students in central cities can volunteer to be bused to suburban schools.[37] Though likely to be small in scale, such programs can bring a degree of interracial contact into the school experience of students from both suburban and central city neighborhoods. Another policy option with a less obvious racial aspect is year-round schools. Their adoption can lead to unintended racial segregation, if the various schedules that divide the school's year-round enrollment receive disparate proportions of various racial and ethnic groups.[38] Where such self-segregation is likely, local school officials who wish to minimize it can design the rules for placement into the various schedule tracks to make them more racially balanced.

The second set of policy options open to state and local officials applies to organization and practice at the school level. Of greatest importance is probably the set of policies regarding academic grouping and academic tracks. In any elementary classroom, the teacher chooses from among a variety of approaches to organize her classroom and carry out instruction. Pupils can be grouped by ability or not; assignments can include cooperative group work or not. In middle schools, students can be organized to emphasize teamwork rather than individual assignments. In high schools, classes in English, math, and other academic subjects can be differentiated by level, and this differentiation can be modest or highly developed. School officials also decide what criteria they will use to assign students to special education classes or to suspend students for disciplinary problems or how students will be selected for sports teams and student organizations. With regard to all these choices, school principals and other local school officials have considerable influence. And, not incidentally, principals usually have substantial control over classroom assignments, especially in elementary schools. In high schools, they and other local officials make decisions affecting how much interaction there will be among students in different grades. The research on intergroup relations suggests strongly that these aspects of school organization affect the likelihood that students of different races will become acquainted and whether these acquaintances will affect attitudes.

DISCUSSION QUESTIONS

1. Which aspects of your high school experience were racially segregated? Which aspects were not segregated?
2. What can parents and students do to foster interracial contact?
3. Why does academic grouping minimize interracial contact?

NOTES

1. Author's calculations, U.S. Department of Education, National Center for Education Statistics (2001a and 2001b).
2. Johnston, Bachman, and O'Malley (1999, appendix, p. 190, question A07). The series of questions began with: "The next questions are about race relations. How much have you gotten to know people of other races?"
3. Bettelheim (1958, p. 337).
4. See Boger (2000).
5. See, for example, Allen and Jewell (1995), Bell (1980), Minow (1990) and Glenn C. Loury, "Integration Has Had Its Day," *New York Times,* April 23, 1997, p. A23.
6. See San Miguel (1987, p. 121).
7. Barndt, Janka, and Rose (1981, p. 243). Milwaukee's schools were highly segregated, with 72 percent of its black elementary students attending schools that were 90–100 percent black in 1965–1966 (U.S. Commission on Civil Rights 1967, appendix table A.3, p. 18).
8. American Friends Service Committee et al. (1970, pp. 31–38).

9. American Friends Service Committee et al. (1970, p. 35); Deever (1994, p. 284).
10. *Moses v. Washington Parish School Board,* 330 F. Supp. 1340 (E.D. La. 1971).
11. The district and its policies are described in Clement, Eisenhart, and Harding (1979, pp. 20–21).
12. "Thus the prevalence of a major form of differentiation, the practice of tracking, seems to be correlated with the ethnic composition of urban schools." Persell (1977, p. 85).
13. Meier, Stewart, and England (1989, p. 25).
14. Persell (1977, p. 87).
15. 851 F. Supp. 905, 1011 (1994).
16. 851 F. Supp. 905, 1012, 1026 (1994).
17. Rebell and Block (1985, pp. 67–68, 114–115).
18. Ibid. (p. 115).
19. Gamoran (1992, tables 4 and 6, pp. 197 and 200).
20. Hollingshead's (1949) case study offers evidence of the influence that middle-class parents have over the operation of a public high school. Rosenbaum (1976, pp. 9, 154–155) elaborates on the point. Sieber (1982) offers an ethnographic study of a New York City elementary school where gentrifying middle-class parents succeeded in placing all their children in the top classroom regardless of the usual meritocratic criteria. Gamoran (1992) found that the influence of parental pressure differed among the five school systems he analyzed but had a quantitatively significant effect for students with average achievement levels.
21. Ability grouping also heightened status differences by drawing attention to the black-white achievement gap. See Schofield (1982, pp. 79–84).
22. Gamoran (1992, tables 4 and 6, pp. 197, 200).
23. Oakes (1993, tables 11 and 12).
24. Mickelson (2001, table 3, p. 237).
25. See Deever (1994, p. 282).
26. Epstein (1985, pp. 28–29).
27. *United States v. City of Yonkers,* 833 F. Supp. 214, 218 (1993).
28. See Rosenbaum (1976, pp. 154–155), citing Hollingshead.
29. See Oakes and Guiton (1995, pp. 14, 30). The authors note that, once placed in a track or ability level, students tended to be placed similarly in succeeding years, or lower.
30. Meier, Stewart, and England (1989) present an analysis of several techniques to discriminate against and segregate blacks in desegregated schools. For tracking, see especially pp. 82, 98–99. Placing blacks in gifted classes is a function of percentage of black teachers, white poverty, black education, black-white income ratio, and district size (all with positive coefficients) and Southern region (negative). The techniques used are designed to act as a substitute for segregation and serve to limit white flight. The authors also emphasize the importance of black teachers and administrators.

31. "Georgia Superintendent Battles a Subtle Racism," *New York Times,* February 14, 1995, p. A6.
32. Wells and Crain (1997, p. 327).
33. Meier, Stewart, and England (1989, p. 131).
34. See Orfield and Eaton (1996) and Chemerinsky (2003, quotation from p. 1601).
35. Boger (2003, pp. 1394–1395) argues that the courts gradually shifted the burden of proof away from the defendant school districts and onto minority plaintiffs, lessening the prospect for judicial interventions to increase racial balance in schools. See chapter 1 for the definition of *unitary.*
36. For a thorough discussion of the rationale underlying choice plans, see Chubb and Moe (1990).
37. For descriptions, see Eaton (2001), McDermott, Bruno, and Varghese (2002) and Wells and Crain (1997, chapter 2).
38. For a study of the effect of year-round schooling on racial segregation, see Mitchell and Mitchell (2003).

REFERENCES

Allen, Walter R., and Joseph O. Jewell. 1995. "African American Education since *The American Dilemma.*" *Daedalus* 125, no. 1: 77–100.

American Friends Service Committee et al. 1970. *The Status of School Desegregation in the South, 1970.* Pamphlet.

Barndt, Michael, Rick Janka, and Harold Rose. 1981. "Milwaukee, Wisconsin: Mobilization for School and Community Cooperation." In *Community Politics and Educational Change: Ten School Systems under Court Order,* ed. Charles V. Willie and Susan L. Greenblatt, pp. 237–259. New York: Longman.

Bell, Derrick. 1980. "*Brown v. Board of Education* and the Interest-Convergence Dilemma." *Harvard Law Review* 93 (January): 518–533.

Bettelheim, Bruno. 1958. "Sputnik and Segregation: Should the Gifted Be Educated Separately?" *Commentary* 26: 332–339.

Boger, John Charles. 2000. "Willful Colorblindness: The New Racial Piety and the Resegregation of Public Schools." *North Carolina Law Review* 78 (September): 1719–1796.

———. 2003. "Education's 'Perfect Storm'? Racial Resegregation, High Stakes Testing, and School Resource Inequities: The Case of North Carolina." *North Carolina Law Review* 81 (May): 1375–1462.

Chemerinsky, Erwin. 2003. "The Segregation and Resegregation of American Public Education: The Court's Role." *North Carolina Law Review* 81 (May): 1597–1622.

Chubb, John E., and Terry M. Moe. 1990. *Politics, Markets, and America's Schools.* Washington, DC: Brookings Institution Press.

Clement, D. C, M. A. Eisenhart, and J. R. Harding. 1979. "The Veneer of Harmony: Social-Race Relations in a Southern Desegregated School." In *Desegregated Schools: Appraisals of an American Experiment,* ed. R. C. Rist, pp. 15–64. New York: Academic Press.

Deever, Bryan. 1994. "Living *Plessy* in the Context of *Brown:* Cultural Politics and the Rituals of Separation." *Urban Review* 26, no. 4: 273–288.

Eaton, Susan E. 2001. *The Other Boston Busing Story: What's Won and Lost across the Boundary Line.* New Haven, CT: Yale University Press.

Epstein, Joyce L. 1985. "After the Bus Arrives; Resegregation in Desegregated Schools." *Journal of Social Issues* 41, no. 3: 23–43.

Gamoran, Adam. 1992. "Access to Excellence: Assignment to Honors English Classes in the Transition from Middle to High School." *Educational Evaluation and Policy Analysis* 14 (Fall): 185–204.

Hollingshead, August B. 1949. *Elmtown's Youth: The Impact of Social Classes on Adolescents.* New York: John Wiley and Sons.

Johnston, Lloyd D., Jerald G. Bachman, and Patrick M. O'Malley. Various years. *Monitoring the Future: Questionnaire Responses from the Nation's High School Seniors.* Ann Arbor: Survey Research Center, Institute for Social Research, University of Michigan.

Loury, Glenn C. 2002. *The Anatomy of Racial Inequality.* Cambridge, MA; Harvard University Press.

McDermott, Kathryn A., Gordon Bruno, and Anna Varghese. 2002. "Have Connecticut's Desegregation Policies Produced Desegregation?" *Equity and Excellence in Education* 35, no. 1: 18–27.

Meier, Kenneth J., Joseph Stewart, and Robert E. England. 1989. *Race, Class, and Education: The Politics of Second-Generation Discrimination.* Madison: University of Wisconsin Press.

Mickelson, Roslyn Arlin. 2001. "Subverting *Swann:* First- and Second-Generation Segregation in the Charlotte-Mecklenburg Schools." *American Education Research Journal* 38 (Summer): 215–252.

Minow, Martha. 1990. *Making All the Difference: Inclusion, Exclusion, and the American Law.* Ithaca, NY: Cornell University Press.

Mitchell, Ross E., and Douglas E. Mitchell. 2003. "Student Segregation and Achievement Tracking in Year-Round Schools." Paper submitted for publication; originally presented at the Ninety-fourth Annual Meeting of the American Sociological Association under the title "Organizational Segregation of Student Achievement in Elementary Schools: The Influence of Multi-Track Year-Round Schools" (1999).

Moses v. Washington Parish School Board, 330 F. Supp. 1340 (E.D. La. 1971).

Oakes, Jeannie. 1993. "Ability Grouping, Tracking and Within-School Segregation in the San Jose Unified School District." Unpublished paper, University of California, Los Angeles, Graduate School of Education (October).

Oakes, Jeannie, and Gretchen Guiton. 1995. "Matchmaking: The Dynamics of High School Tracking Decisions." *American Educational Research Journal* 32, no. 1: 3–33.

Orfield, Gary, and Susan E. Eaton. 1996. *Dismantling Desegregation: The Quiet Reversal of* Brown v. Board of Education. New York: New Press.

Persell, Caroline H. 1977. *Education and Inequality: A Theoretical and Empirical Synthesis.* New York: Free Press.

Rebell, Michael A., and Arthur R. Block. 1985. *Equality and Education: Federal Civil Rights Enforcement in the New York City School System.* Princeton, NJ: Princeton University Press.

Rosenbaum, James E. 1976. *Making Inequality: The Hidden Curriculum of High School Tracking.* New York: John Wiley and Sons.

San Miguel, Guadalupe. 1987. *"Let All of Them Take Heed": Mexican Americans and the Campaign for Educational Equity in Texas, 1910–81.* Austin: University of Texas Press.

Schofield, Janet Ward. 1982. *Black and White in School: Trust, Tension, or Tolerance.* New York: Praeger.

Sieber, Timothy R. 1982. "The Politics of Middle-Class Success in an Inner-City Public School." *Boston University Journal of Education* 164: 30–47.

Tuch, Steven A., Lee Sigelman, and Jason A. MacDonald. 1999. "Race Relations and American Youth, 1976–1995." *Public Opinion Quarterly* 63: 109–148.

U.S. Commission on Civil Rights. 1967. *Racial Isolation in the Public Schools.* Washington, DC: Government Printing Office.

United States v. City of Yonkers, 833 F. Supp. 214, 218 (1993).

Wells, Amy Stuart, and Robert L. Crain. 1997. *Stepping over the Color Line: African-American Students in White Suburban Schools.* New Haven, CT: Yale University Press.

READING 44

The Minority Rights Revolution

John D. Skrentny

On January 6, 1969, Senator Barry Goldwater, Republican of Arizona, sent a letter to the new presidential administration of Richard M. Nixon. Goldwater personified the right wing of the Republican Party, argued passionately for limited government, and had previously written a book entitled

John D. Skrentny is a professor of sociology at the University of California, San Diego.

The Conscience of a Conservative.[1] He had also famously stuck to his principles and voted against the Civil Rights Act of 1964, the landmark law that ended racial segregation. On this day, however, Goldwater offered a lesson in political savvy for dealing with a disadvantaged group. The senator reminded the new administration that Nixon had promised a White House conference on Mexican American issues during his campaign, and that Nixon wanted to have "Mexicans" serve in his administration. Goldwater explained that this group preferred to be called "Mexican-Americans" and that the administration should avoid referring to them as Latin American—save that term for South America, coached Goldwater. The White House conference should occur "at the earliest possible time because these people are watching us to see if we will treat them the way the Democrats have." He reminded them that New York was the largest Spanish-speaking city in the United States and that nationwide there were 6 million in this category. "You will hear a lot on this subject from me," the strident, states' rights conservative warned, "so the faster you move, the less bother I will be."[2]

A few years later, Robert H. Bork, who would become a famously right-leaning federal judge and author of the 1996 book *Slouching towards Gomorrah: Modern Liberalism and American Decline,* also promoted the cause of federal recognition of disadvantaged groups. In 1974, Bork was Nixon's solicitor general, and in that year co-authored a brief to the Supreme Court arguing that the failure to provide special language education for immigrant children was racial discrimination, according to both the Constitution and the Civil Rights Act of 1964. The Supreme Court agreed with the statutory argument, though it did not wish to go as far as Bork and create constitutional language rights in schools.[3]

Goldwater and Bork were not alone in promoting rights for minorities. The 1965–75 period was a minority rights revolution. After the mass mobilization and watershed events of the black civil rights movement, this later revolution was led by the Establishment. It was a bipartisan project, including from both parties liberals and conservatives—though it was hard to tell the difference. Presidents, the Congress, bureaucracies, and the courts all played important roles. In the signature minority rights policy, affirmative action, the federal government went beyond African Americans and declared that certain groups were indeed "minorities"—an undefined term embraced by policymakers, advocates, and activists alike—and needed new rights and programs for equal opportunity and full citizenship. In the parlance of the period, minorities were groups seen as "disadvantaged" but not defined by income or education. African Americans were the paradigmatic minority, but there were three other ethnoracial minorities: Latinos, Asian Americans, and American Indians. Immigrants, women, and the disabled of all ethnic groups were also included and won new rights during this revolutionary period.

Bipartisanship was not the only notable aspect of the minority rights revolution. Consider also the *speed* of the development of its laws and regulations. While they appeared to have global momentum on their side, it still took two decades from the first proposition in 1941 that blacks be ensured nondiscrimination in employment to the law (Title VII of the Civil Rights Act of 1964) guaranteeing that right. Similarly, it took about twenty years between the first efforts to allow expanded immigration from outside northern and western Europe and the Immigration Act of 1965, ending all national origin discrimination in immigration. Following these landmarks, however, the government passed other laws and regulations almost immediately after first proposal. In most cases, it took only a few years to have a new law passed and there was little lobbying pressure. Bilingual education for Latinos, equal rights for women in education, and equal rights for the disabled all became law within two years of first proposal. Affirmative action expanded beyond blacks almost immediately. Such rapid success in American politics is rare. It is especially rare when achieved by groups that were defined precisely by their powerlessness and disadvantage in American society.

The rapidity and ease of the minority rights revolution brings up another puzzle. If minority rights were so easy to establish, why were not more groups included? For example, government officials perceived eastern and southern European Americans (Italians, Poles, Jews, Greeks, etc.) to be discriminated against, economically disadvantaged, or both. These "white ethnics" also had strong advocates. Yet they were never made the subjects of special policies for aid, protection, or preference. Despite widespread perceptions of their oppression, gays and lesbians similarly failed to gain a federal foothold in the minority rights revolution. Some members of Congress first submitted a bill to protect Americans from discrimination on the basis of sexual orientation in 1974. There still is no law ensuring this protection.

Another curious aspect of this minority rights revolution is that the 1960s recognition of the right to be free from discrimination was not just an American phenomenon. Nondiscrimation was quite suddenly a *world* right, a *human* right. That is, the United States was anything but alone in its recognition of minority rights.[4] Consider the dates of major American minority-rights developments and United Nations conventions and covenants guaranteeing human-rights protections (see Table 1). Though usually (and notoriously) unperturbed by world trends, Americans were guaranteeing nondiscrimination and other rights at the same time that much of the world was coming to a formal consensus on these same issues. Was it just a coincidence that America and many other nations traveled on parallel paths? Moreover, was it happenstance that Africans and Asians simultaneously threw off the yoke of colonialism and their new nations joined the UN while American citizens of third-world ancestry also gained more control of their destinies? The minority rights revolution is not only an intellectual puzzle. It was an event of enormous significance. It shaped our current understanding of American citizenship, which is more inclusive than ever before, while also drawing lines of difference between Americans. It was a major part of the development of the American regulatory

TABLE 1	
WORLD AND AMERICAN RIGHTS DEVELOPMENTS	
World developments	**U.S. developments**
1941 "Four Freedoms"	1941 Executive Order 8802
1945 UN Charter	
	1947 President's Committee on Civil Rights
1948 UN Universal Declaration of Human Rights	
1950s–60s Emerging nations in Africa and Asia	1954 *Brown v. Board of Education*
	1964 Civil Rights Act
1965 International Convention on the Elimination of All Forms of Racial Discrimination	1965 Voting Rights Act; Immigration Reform Act
1966 International Covenant on Economic, Social and Cultural Rights; International Covenant on Civil and Political Rights	
	1968 Bilingual Education Act, developing Affirmative Action policies

state, later decried by those same conservatives who joined with liberals in building it up. And it offers a unique look at American democracy. When the stars and planets line up in just the right way, politicians, bureaucrats, and judges can offer a range of efforts to help disadvantaged Americans—even if those Americans did not ask for them.

WHAT DO WE KNOW ABOUT THE MINORITY RIGHTS REVOLUTION?

The minority rights revolution was a sudden growth of federal legislation, presidential executive orders, bureaucratic rulings, and court decisions that established nondiscrimination rights. It targeted groups of Americans understood as disadvantaged but not defined by socioeconomic class. Many of these laws and regulations, especially affirmative action, were novel in that they created the new category of "minority" Americans and sought to guarantee nondiscrimination by giving positive recognition of group differences.

There is much research debating the fairness or efficacy of human rights laws. But how did we get them in the first place? . . .

The image that comes to most Americans' minds when they think of the period is angry protest—radical blacks, feminists, and Latinos shouting slogans, a white ethnic "backlash," newly assertive disabled and gay people, all joining Vietnam War protesters in creating a climate of upheaval. These images exist because there was, of course, a very large amount of social-movement activity. One account of the minority rights revolution might therefore emphasize the role of grassroots mobilizing. . . .

[But this discussion] fundamentally challenges the social-movement approach to understanding the late 1960s and early 1970s. One theme [here] is that while white men dominated government, by no means were social movements and minority advocates excluded. Scholars almost always assume social movements are discrete entities that exist *outside of* government.[5] There are "challenges from outside the polity" confronting "elites within it." In the late 1960s and early 1970s, however, formal members of social-movement organizations held positions of power in Congress and the bureaucracy, and strong advocates also worked out of the White House. They played crucial roles in formulating and pushing new rights. The images conjured up [here] are therefore mostly not of angry minority protests, raised fists, picket lines, and placards. The images of the minority rights revolution are mostly of mainstream Euro-American males and minority advocates, wearing suits, sitting at desks, firing off memos, and meeting in government buildings to discuss new policy directions. While these are not romantic images, they are the images of power. . . .

DYNAMICS OF CHANGE: UNDERSTANDING THE MINORITY RIGHTS REVOLUTION

To explain the minority rights revolution, this [discussion] emphasizes the importance of two factors: the perceived needs of national security and the various legacies of the black civil rights movement. . . . Significant themes throughout are the ways that prior policy developments and cultural meanings matter. Initial policymaking can make later policy development possible, easy, and quick. But understanding rapid policy development requires seeing the political importance of meanings—perceptions of what a thing, person, policy, or action *is*.

The Sequence of History and the Legacies of National Policy

An important concept used to study historical sequences in politics is the policy legacy (sometimes called "policy feedback").[6] The basic idea is simple: new policies remake politics. Government leaders, interest groups, and the public adjust their interests to take into account the existence of the new policy. This sometimes requires greatly changing their preferences. Policies may even call into being entirely new political organizations. This all means that the sequence of historical events matters greatly. For the present case, World War II and the Cold War helped make the minority rights (especially black) revolution possible, and the black civil rights movement helped make the rest of the revolution possible—and rapid.

National Security and Equal Rights   The minority rights revolution could not have occurred without the prior world battle against the Nazis and Japanese and the Cold War struggle with the Soviet Union.[7] World War II and especially the Cold War's broadly defined "national security" policy had important legacies in domestic politics. In some ways

this was direct and obvious: the perceived need for national security led to great investment in the means of warfare, driving a large part of the economy and building up firms that created weapons and other equipment. But there were other, more far-reaching effects.

During this dynamic period, war threats were staggering and horrifying, and national security prompted policies that included everything from education to highways to racial and ethnic equality. The latter became part of national security because American strategy in World War II set in motion the creation of global human-rights norms that gave a cause for the Allies and a structure to the later Cold War struggle with the Soviet Union. World War II marked the beginning of an unprecedented global cultural integration and the establishment of a global public sphere, held together by the UN and a few basic premises. The sanctity of human rights was one. At the top of the rights list was nondiscrimination. Race or ethnic discrimination, especially when practiced by those of European ancestry, was wrong. In short, geopolitical developments set into motion a dynamic where policies defined as furthering the goal of national security by fighting Nazism or global communism—including equal rights policies—found bipartisan support and rapid change in political fortunes.

Legacies of Black Civil Rights   The legacies of black civil rights policy were complex and varied. One important legacy was the creation of new "institutional homes" (to borrow Chris Bonastia's term) for rights advocates to have positions of real policy-making power.[8] Most important here were the Equal Employment Opportunity Commission (EEOC), the Department of Health, Education and Welfare's Office for Civil Rights, and the Department of Labor's Office of Federal Contract Compliance. All were created to enforce rights laws for blacks, and all attracted employees who supported equal-opportunity rights. Though they usually kept black rights as their priority, this was not uniformly true. The EEOC played a crucial role by implicitly designating four ethnoracial groups, plus women, as America's official minorities to be given special attention and included in affirmative action. These new sites of rights advocacy allowed the designated groups to concentrate their lobbying efforts to a sometimes very receptive audience, usually out of the public view.

Other policy legacies of the black civil rights movement were more cultural in character, though equally important. The Civil Rights Act of 1964, as well as other efforts to help blacks, created a tool kit or repertoire of policy models that could be extended again and again and adapted to deal with the problems of groups other than black Americans.[9] Through their own initiative, or when pressured by nonblack minority advocates, civil-rights bureaucrats responded with affirmative action—regardless of the specific demands of the minority advocates. Policymakers sometimes simply anticipated what minority constituents wanted. They created an "anticipatory politics" based on these policy tools and the new legitimacy of minority targeting.[10] Activist members of Congress used the Civil Rights Act's Title VI, barring federal funds for any program that discriminated on the basis of race, national origin, or religion, as part of a policy repertoire when seeking votes or social movement goals. Congress thus created Title IX of the Education Amendments of 1972, barring sex discrimination on the part of educational institutions receiving federal funds, and Section 504 of the Rehabilitation Act of 1973, which addressed discrimination on the basis of disability also by using the Civil Rights Act model.

. . . There are limits to the use of a policy as a model. The constellation of strategic interests that political actors have in particular contexts are based on the *meanings* they perceive in certain things. Meanings are constitutive—they tell us the identity of a person or thing. . . . Meanings may make a policy acceptable for one goal or group, but not for others. . . . Cultural meanings help us understand the speed of the revolution as well as its limits. . . .

Meaning and the Minority Rights Revolution

. . . To attract support for the Allied side during World War II, President Franklin Delano Roosevelt strongly promoted the United States as a symbol of human rights and race equality. These efforts then invited first the Axis and then the Soviet Union's propaganda strategies highlighting American racism and ethnic inequality. Especially with the parts of government aware of this propaganda and engaged with foreign audiences, specifically presidents and State Department officials, there was a rapid recategorization of domestic nondiscrimination as part of foreign policy and national security. This is apparent in both Democratic and Republican administrations. Comprehensive policy change, however, required convincing Congress and the American public, and both government leaders and rights groups actively promoted the meaning of nondiscrimination as national security. Change was incremental and needed mass mobilization for black civil rights and lobbying campaigns for immigration reform before breakthrough victories finally came in the mid-1960s.

Other rights could not be categorized as easily as national security. Women, for example, made few gains because gender was not a dividing principle in geopolitics as was race. Gender equality was not a part of Nazi, Japanese, or Communist propaganda and therefore served no national security interest. Social rights and welfare state development similarly did not become part of national security policy, even during the Cold War when America confronted an ideology based on economic egalitarianism. This was in part because many business and professional interest groups and Republican party leaders could quite plausibly argue that excessive interference with the market economy and market-based wealth distributions would push America *toward* socialism, rather than save it from this threat.

Recognition of the role of meanings is necessary to understand aspects of the minority rights revolution besides national security linkages and categorizations. If meanings are the foundations of the logics of appropriate action, then politicians will consciously or unreflectively use similar or different policies to appeal to different groups depending on their deservingness or some other meaning.[11] A key theme . . . is that different categories of Americans varied in their analogical similarity to African Americans, creating boundaries of appropriate or legitimate policies relating to them.

This was not only a matter of simple voting power, lobbying, or protest strength. Success and the speed at which it was achieved in the minority rights revolution depended greatly on the meaning of the group in question. After advocates for black Americans helped break the taboo on targeting policy at disadvantaged groups, government officials quickly categorized some groups as "minorities"—a never-defined term that basically meant "analogous to blacks." These classifications were *not* based on study, but on simple, unexamined prototypes of groups.[12] Most obviously, government officials saw the complex category of Latinos (then usually called "Spanish-surnamed" or "Spanish-speaking") in terms of a simple racial prototype, obscuring the fact that many Latinos consider themselves white. Racialized in this way, Latinos needed little lobbying to win minority rights. Women, who faced ridicule like no other group, needed significant meaning entrepreneurship. Their advocates pushed hard to make the black analogy. Though Asian Americans presumably possessed a clearer group racial definition than did Latinos, the analogy between Asians and blacks was weaker than that between Latinos and blacks. Policymakers sometimes dropped Asian Americans from their lists. This was apparently just a cognitive forgetting—it required only small reminders for them to be included in minority policy, at least formally. While rights for the disabled were included easily and without debate, gay rights were a political nonstarter. Government officials saw white ethnics in a multifaceted way that shifted policy away from the minority-rights paradigm, despite the efforts of ethnic advocates. Moreover, though seen as disadvantaged, policymakers saw white ethnics as insufficiently disadvantaged to be categorized as minorities. In fact, federal government officials never spelled out what were the necessary and sufficient conditions or qualities for minorityhood. They classified groups just the same, and had little trouble doing so.

Meanings of groups also greatly affected the types of justice each group received.[13] Being analogous to blacks served as an initial classification, but groups retained distinctiveness. Equal opportunity meant different things depending on the group in question. In the late 1960s, equal opportunity in education for blacks meant a rejection of the "separate-but-equal" policy of the Jim Crow south. It meant zealous integration of schools, the bussing of students around cities so that blacks and whites could learn together. For Latinos, it meant *rejection* of the zealous integration practiced in some southwestern schools which included forced English-language usage. Instead, Latino children were to receive special bilingual education. For women, it meant a combination of different approaches, including integration in classrooms while segregated dormitories, sororities, and sports teams flourished. Readers may protest that these differences in policies were based on "real" differences between groups, yet this claim neglects the fact that lawmakers see some differences as real and relevant and others as not.[14] For example, the one-drop rule (which until recently was broadly taken for granted) defines anyone with any black ancestry as black and the European ancestry in an estimated 75–90 percent of African Americans as unreal.[15] The whiteness of Latinos is similarly denied reality. Despite the footnotes that may appear at the bottom of census tables, federal policy and national debates do not acknowledge that many Latinos are physically indistinguishable from Euro-Americans and consider themselves white. Orlando Patterson was thus able to point out the absurdity of ubiquitous news media predictions of a decline in the percentage of US citizens who are white due to the 2000 census's reports of the growing Latino presence.[16] . . .

Meanings for Whom?

. . . While I stress the importance of policy legacies and meanings, creative, willful people are at the center of [the] story, though their identities and power may be constituted by institutions and meanings. Policy elites make decisions and those decisions matter. . . . After the meanings of certain groups shifted, and the groups became "minorities" and legitimate targets of policy, presidents, bureaucrats and members of Congress [followed] a "logic of consequences," they pursued support from and justice for these groups with public recognition and targeted policies. But these policymakers were always basing their appeals in the universe of social meanings, especially the black analogy, and using policy and discourses originating in black civil rights. This is clear because, once started, the expansion of minority rights policies could have gone further than it did. Instead, creativity and risk raking reached limits.

DISCUSSION QUESTIONS

1. Was Skrentny's review of the bipartisan global agenda behind affirmative action a surprise to you? Why might you have been unaware of this background?
2. How did the minority rights revolution for blacks help later groups?
3. How do blacks differ from other minority groups?

NOTES

1. Barry M. Goldwater, *The Conscience of a Conservative* (New York: McFadden Books, 1964 [1960]).
2. Letter from Barry Goldwater to Ray Price, January 6, 1969, in Hugh Davis Graham, ed., *Civil Rights during the Nixon Administration, 1969–74* (Bethesda: University Publications of America, 1989), Part I, Reel 1, frame 21. Also see the letter from John Rhodes to Peter M. Flanigan, June 17, 1969, in Graham, *Civil Rights during Nixon,* Part I, Reel 2, frame 2.
3. The brief was for *Lau v. Nichols,* 94 U.S. 786 (1974). . . . In his 1996 book, Bork writes, "Part of our national lore, and glory, is the fact that youngsters speaking not a word of English were placed in public schools where only English was used and very shortly were proficient in the language. That was crucial to the formation of American identity." Bork goes on to criticize bilingual education without mentioning his own role in the establishment of federal language rights. See Robert H. Bork, *Slouching towards Gomorrah: Modern Liberalism and American Decline* (New York: Regan Books, 1996), pp. 300–3.
4. Work by the sociologist John Meyer and his colleagues has examined the world development of rights protec-

tions as a part of the modern state, but has not clearly traced the processes through which this has occurred in the United States. The most recent statement is John Boli and George M. Thomas, eds., *Constructing World Culture* (Stanford: Stanford University Press, 1999). Philip Epp's work has examined processes of change in a comparative perspective, but concentrates solely on developments in courts. Philip Epp, *The Rights Revolution* (Chicago: University of Chicago Press, 1997).
5. For a rare dissenting view, see Mayor N. Zald and Michael A. Berger, "Social Movements in Organizations: Coup d'Etat, Insurgency, and Mass Movements," *American Journal of Sociology* 83 (1978): 823–61; and Meyer N. Zald, "Social Movements as Ideologically Structured Action: An Enlarged Agenda," *Mobilization* 5 (2000): 1–16.
6. Skocpol, *Protecting Soldiers and Mothers: The Political Origins of Social Policy in the U.S.* (Cambridge, Harvard University Press, 1992). Paul Pierson, *Dismantling the Welfare State?* (New York: Cambridge University Press, 1994); Margaret Weir, *Politics and Jobs: The Boundaries of Employment Policy in the United States* (Princeton: Princeton University Press, 1992).
7. Scholars have long linked war with state building and policymaking. In social science, the importance of national security, or war, in state building was recognized since Max Weber's writing, but has been most developed in the work of Charles Tilly. Charles Tilly, ed., *The Formation of National States in Western Europe* (Princeton: Princeton University Press, 1975); Tilly, "War Making and State Making as Organized Crime," in Peter B. Evans, Dietrich Rueschemeyer, and Theda Skocpol, eds., *Bringing the State Back In* (New York: Cambridge University Press, 1985), pp. 169–91. A more recent statement is Miguel Centeno, *Blood and Debt: War and the Nation-State in Latin America* (University Park: Pennsylvania State University Press, 2002). Michael Sherry's work surveys the relationship of national security to domestic politics. Michael Sherry, *In the Shadow of War* (New Haven: Yale University Press, 1994).
8. Chris Bonastia, "Why Did Affirmative Action in Housing Fail during the Nixon Era? Exploring the 'Institutional Homes' of Social Policies," *Social Problems* 47 (2000): 523–42.
9. The classic statement is Ann Swidler, "Culture in Action: Symbols and Strategies," *American Sociological Review* 51 (1986): 273–86. Elisabeth S. Clemens, *The People's Lobby* (Chicago: University of Chicago Press, 1997), Chapter 2, discusses repertoires as tool kits of organizational models. It is a simple adaptation to use the concept for models of policy. See Rogers Brubaker, *Citizenship and Nationhood in France and Germany* (Cambridge, Mass.: Harvard University Press, 1992), pp. 16–17, on the related concept of cultural "idioms." On "policy paradigms," a more cognitively oriented

concept, see Frank Dobbin, *Forging Industrial Policy* (New York: Cambridge University Press, 1994).

10. I thank Steve Teles for this concept. He traces it to Daniel Patrick Moynihan, "The Professionalization of Reform," *Public Interest* 1 (1965): 6–16.

11. As the economist Glenn Loury has written about racial groups, these meanings "bear on the identity, the status, and even the humanity of those who carry them" and "once established, these meanings may come to be taken for granted, enduring essentially unchallenged for millennia." Glenn Loury, *The Anatomy of Racial Inequality: Stereotypes, Stigma, and the Elusive Quest for Racial Justice* (Cambridge, Mass.: Harvard University Press, 2001).

12. See Lakoff and Johnson, *Metaphors We Live By,* p. 165, for a discussion of prototypes and how this process works on a cognitive level. On race and cognition, see

Rogers Brubaker, Mara Loveman, and Peter Stamatov, "Reviving Constructivism: The Case for a Cognitive Approach to Race, Ethnicity and Nationalism," unpublished manuscript.

13. Other scholars have identified plural justices but have not linked them to specific meanings, instead identifying them with "spheres." Michael Walzer, *Spheres of Justice* (New York: Basic Books, 1983) ("spheres"); Jennifer Hoschschild, *What's Fair? American Beliefs about Distributive Justice* (Cambridge, Mass.: Harvard University Press, 1981) ("domains").

14. Lakoff and Johnson, *Metaphors We Live By,* pp. 141–46.

15. F. James Davis, *Who Is Black?* (University Park: Pennsylvania State University Press, 1991), p. 21.

16. Orlando Patterson, "Race by the Numbers," *New York Times,* May 8, 2001.

THE ECONOMY

READING 45

The Possessive Investment in Whiteness

HOW WHITE PEOPLE PROFIT FROM IDENTITY POLITICS

George Lipsitz

Whiteness is everywhere in U.S. culture, but it is very hard to see. As Richard Dyer suggests, "[W]hite power secures its dominance by seeming not to be anything in particular."[1] As the unmarked category against which difference is constructed, whiteness never has to speak its name, never has to acknowledge its role as an organizing principle in social and cultural relations.[2] To identify, analyze, and oppose the destructive consequences of whiteness, we need what Walter Benjamin called "presence of mind." Benjamin wrote that people visit fortune-tellers less out of a desire to know the future than out of a fear of not noticing some important aspect of the present. "Presence of mind," he suggested, "is an abstract of the future, and precise awareness of the present

moment more decisive than foreknowledge of the most distant events."[3] In U.S. society at this time, precise awareness of the present moment requires an understanding of the existence and the destructive consequences of the possessive investment in whiteness that surreptitiously shapes so much of our public and private lives....

... The possessive investment is not simply the residue of conquest and colonialism, of slavery and segregation, of immigrant exclusion and "Indian" extermination. Contemporary whiteness and its rewards have been created and re-created by policies adopted long after the emancipation of slaves in the 1860s and even after the outlawing of *de jure* segregation in the 1960s. There has always been racism in the United States, but it has not always been the same racism....

Contemporary racism has been created anew in many ways over the past five decades, but most dramatically by the putatively race-neutral, liberal, social democratic reforms of the New Deal Era and by the more overtly race-conscious neoconservative reactions against liberalism since the Nixon years. It is a mistake to posit a gradual and inevitable trajectory of evolutionary progress in race relations; on the contrary, our history shows that battles won at one moment can later be lost. Despite hard-fought battles for change that secured important concessions during the 1960s in the form of civil rights

George Lipsitz is a professor of American studies at the University of California, Santa Cruz.

legislation, the racialized nature of social policy in the United States since the Great Depression has actually increased the possessive investment in whiteness among European Americans over the past half century.

During the New Deal Era of the 1930s and 1940s, both the Wagner Act and the Social Security Act excluded farm workers and domestics from coverage, effectively denying those disproportionately minority sectors of the work force protections and benefits routinely afforded whites. The Federal Housing Act of 1934 brought home ownership within reach of millions of citizens by placing the credit of the federal government behind private lending to home buyers, but overtly racist categories in the Federal Housing Agency's (FHA) "confidential" city surveys and appraisers' manuals channeled almost all of the loan money toward whites and away from communities of color.[4] In the post–World War II era, trade unions negotiated contract provisions giving private medical insurance, pensions, and job security largely to the white workers who formed the overwhelming majority of the unionized work force in mass production industries, rather than fighting for full employment, medical care, and old-age pensions for all, or even for an end to discriminatory hiring and promotion practices by employers in those industries.[5]

Each of these policies widened the gap between the resources available to whites and those available to aggrieved racial communities. Federal housing policy offers an important illustration of the broader principles at work in the possessive investment in whiteness. By channeling loans away from older inner-city neighborhoods and toward white home buyers moving into segregated suburbs, the FHA and private lenders after World War II aided and abetted segregation in U.S. residential neighborhoods. FHA appraisers denied federally supported loans to prospective home buyers in the racially mixed Boyle Heights neighborhood of Los Angeles in 1939, for example, because the area struck them as a "'melting pot' area literally honeycombed with diverse and subversive racial elements."[6] Similarly, mostly white St. Louis County

secured five times as many FHA mortgages as the more racially mixed city of St. Louis between 1943 and 1960. Home buyers in the county received six times as much loan money and enjoyed per capita mortgage spending 6.3 times greater than those in the city.[7]

The federal government has played a major role in augmenting the possessive investment in whiteness. For years, the General Services Administration routinely channeled the government's own rental and leasing business to realtors who engaged in racial discrimination, while federally subsidized urban renewal plans reduced the already limited supply of housing for communities of color through "slum clearance" programs. In concert with FHA support for segregation in the suburbs, federal and state tax monies routinely funded the construction of water supplies and sewage facilities for racially exclusive suburban communities in the 1940s and 1950s. By the 1960s, these areas often incorporated themselves as independent municipalities in order to gain greater access to federal funds allocated for "urban aid."[8]

At the same time that FHA loans and federal highway building projects subsidized the growth of segregated suburbs, urban renewal programs in cities throughout the country devastated minority neighborhoods. During the 1950s and 1960s, federally assisted urban renewal projects destroyed 20 percent of the central-city housing units occupied by blacks, as opposed to only 10 percent of those inhabited by whites.[9] More than 60 percent of those displaced by urban renewal were African Americans, Puerto Ricans, Mexican Americans, or members of other minority racial groups.[10] The Federal Housing Administration and the Veterans Administration financed more than $120 billion worth of new housing between 1934 and 1962, but less than 2 percent of this real estate was available to nonwhite families—and most of that small amount was located in segregated areas.[11]

Even in the 1970s, after most major urban renewal programs had been completed, black central-city residents continued to lose housing units at a rate equal to 80 percent of what had been lost in the

1960s. Yet white displacement declined to the relatively low levels of the 1950s.[12] In addition, the refusal first to pass, then to enforce, fair housing laws has enabled realtors, buyers, and sellers to profit from racist collusion against minorities largely without fear of legal retribution. During the decades following World War II, urban renewal helped construct a new "white" identity in the suburbs by helping to destroy ethnically specific European American urban inner-city neighborhoods. Wrecking balls and bulldozers eliminated some of these sites, while others were transformed by an influx of minority residents desperately competing for a declining supply of affordable housing units. As increasing numbers of racial minorities moved into cities, increasing numbers of European American ethnics moved out. Consequently, ethnic differences among whites became a less important dividing line in U.S. culture, while race became more important. The suburbs helped turn Euro-Americans into "whites" who could live near each other and intermarry with relatively little difficulty. But this "white" unity rested on residential segregation, on shared access to housing and life chances largely unavailable to communities of color.[13]

During the 1950s and 1960s, local "pro-growth" coalitions led by liberal mayors often justified urban renewal as a program designed to build more housing for poor people, but it actually destroyed more housing than it created. Ninety percent of the low-income units removed for urban renewal during the entire history of the program were never replaced. Commercial, industrial, and municipal projects occupied more than 80 percent of the land cleared for these projects, with less than 20 percent allocated for replacement housing. In addition, the loss of taxable properties and the tax abatements granted to new enterprises in urban renewal zones often meant serious tax increases for poor, working-class, and middle-class home owners and renters.[14] Although the percentage of black suburban dwellers also increased during this period, no significant desegregation of the suburbs took place. . . . By 1993, 86 percent of suburban whites still lived in places with a black population below 1 percent. At the

same time, cities with large numbers of minority residents found themselves cut off from loans by the FHA. For example, because of their growing black and Puerto Rican populations, neither Camden nor Paterson, New Jersey, in 1966 received one FHA-sponsored mortgage.[15] . . .

Federally funded highways designed to connect suburban commuters with downtown places of employment also destroyed already scarce housing in minority communities and often disrupted neighborhood life as well. Construction of the Harbor Freeway in Los Angeles, the Gulf Freeway in Houston, and the Mark Twain Freeway in St. Louis displaced thousands of residents and bisected neighborhoods, shopping districts, and political precincts. The processes of urban renewal and highway construction set in motion a vicious cycle: population loss led to decreased political power, which made minority neighborhoods more vulnerable to further urban renewal and freeway construction, not to mention more susceptible to the placement of prisons, incinerators, toxic waste dumps, and other projects that further depopulated these areas. . . .

Minority disadvantages craft advantages for others. Urban renewal failed to provide new housing for the poor, but it played an important role in transforming the U.S. urban economy from one that relied on factory production to one driven by producer services. Urban renewal projects subsidized the development of downtown office centers on previously residential land, and they frequently created buffer zones of empty blocks dividing poor neighborhoods from new shopping centers designed for affluent commuters. To help cities compete for corporate investment by making them appealing to high-level executives, federal urban aid favored construction of luxury housing units and cultural centers like symphony halls and art museums over affordable housing for workers. Tax abatements granted to these producer services centers further aggravated the fiscal crisis that cities faced, leading to tax increases on existing industries, businesses, and residences. . . .

When housing prices increased dramatically during the 1970s, white home owners who had been able to take advantage of discriminatory FHA financing policies in the past realized increased equity in their homes, while those excluded from the housing market by earlier policies found themselves facing even higher costs of entry into the market in addition to the traditional obstacles presented by the discriminatory practices of sellers, realtors, and lenders. The contrast between European Americans and African Americans is instructive in this regard. Because whites have access to broader housing choices than blacks, whites pay 15 percent less than blacks for similar housing in the same neighborhood. White neighborhoods typically experience housing costs 25 percent lower than would be the case if the residents were black.[16]

A recent Federal Reserve Bank of Boston study revealed that Boston bankers made 2.9 times as many mortgage loans per 1,000 housing units in neighborhoods inhabited by low-income whites than in neighborhoods populated by low-income blacks.[17] In addition, loan officers were far more likely to overlook flaws in the credit records of white applicants or to arrange creative financing for them than they were with black applicants.[18] A Los Angeles study found that loan officers more frequently used dividend income and underlying assets as criteria for judging black applicants than for whites.[19] In Houston, the NCNB Bank of Texas disqualified 13 percent of middle-income white loan applicants but 36 percent of middle-income black applicants.[20] Atlanta's home loan institutions gave five times as many home loans to whites as to blacks in the late 1980s. An analysis of sixteen Atlanta neighborhoods found that home buyers in white neighborhoods received conventional financing four times as often as those in black sections of the city.[21] Nationwide, financial institutions receive more money in deposits from black neighborhoods than they invest in them in the form of home mortgage loans, making home lending a vehicle for the transfer of capital away from black savers toward white investors.[22] In many locations high-income blacks were denied loans more often than low-income whites.[23]

When confronted with evidence of systematic racial bias in home lending, defenders of the posses-

sive investment in whiteness argue that the disproportionate share of loan denials to members of minority groups stems not from discrimination, but from the low net worth of minority applicants, even those who have high incomes. This might seem a reasonable position, but net worth is almost totally determined by past opportunities for asset accumulation, and therefore is the one figure most likely to reflect the history of discrimination. Minorities are told, in essence, "We can't give you a loan today because we've discriminated against members of your race so effectively in the past that you have not been able to accumulate any equity from housing and to pass it down through the generations."

Most white families have acquired their net worth from the appreciation of property that they secured under conditions of special privilege in a discriminatory housing market. In their prize-winning book *Black Wealth/White Wealth*, Melvin Oliver and Thomas Shapiro demonstrate how the history of housing discrimination makes white parents more able to borrow funds for their children's college education or to loan money to their children to enter the housing market. In addition, much discrimination in home lending is not based on considerations of net worth; it stems from decisions made by white banking officials based on their stereotypes about minority communities. The Federal Reserve Bank of Boston study showed that black and Latino mortgage applicants are 60 percent more likely to be turned down for loans than whites, even after controlling for employment, financial, and neighborhood characteristics.[24] Ellis Cose reports on a white bank official confronted with evidence at a board of directors' meeting that his bank denied loans to blacks who had credit histories and earnings equal to those of white applicants who received loans. The banker replied that the information indicated that the bank needed to do a better job of "affirmative action," but one of his colleagues pointed out that the problem had nothing to do with affirmative action—the bank was simply letting prejudice stand in the way of its own best interests by rejecting loans that should be approved.[25]

Yet bankers also make money from the ways in which discrimination creates artificial scarcities in the market. Minorities have to pay more for housing because much of the market is off limits to them. Blockbusters profit from exploiting white fears and provoking them into panic selling. Minority home owners denied loans in mainstream banks often turn to exploitative lenders who make "low end" loans at enormously high interest rates. If they fail to pay back these loans, regular banks can acquire the property cheaply and charge someone else exorbitant interest for a loan on the same property.

Federal home loan policies have put the power of the federal government at the service of private discrimination. Urban renewal and highway construction programs have enhanced the possessive investment in whiteness directly through government initiatives. In addition, decisions about where to locate federal jobs have also systematically subsidized whiteness. Federal civilian employment dropped by 41,419 in central cities between 1966 and 1973, but total federal employment in metropolitan areas grew by 26,558.[26] While one might naturally expect the location of government buildings that serve the public to follow population trends, the federal government's policy of locating offices and records centers in suburbs aggravated the flight of jobs to suburban locations less accessible to inner-city residents. Because racial discrimination in the private sector forces minority workers to seek government positions disproportionate to their numbers, these moves exact particular hardships on them. In addition, minorities who follow their jobs to the suburbs must generally allocate more for commuter costs, because housing discrimination makes it harder and more expensive for them than for whites to relocate. . . .

Group interests are not monolithic, and aggregate figures can obscure serious differences within racial groups. All whites do not benefit from the possessive investment in whiteness in precisely the same ways; the experiences of members of minority groups are not interchangeable. But the possessive investment in whiteness always affects individual and group life chances and opportunities. Even in cases where minority groups secure political and economic power through collective mobilization, the terms and conditions of their collectivity and the logic of group solidarity are always influenced and intensified by the absolute value of whiteness in U.S. politics, economics, and culture.[27] . . .

Walter Benjamin's praise for "presence of mind" came from his understanding of how difficult it may be to see the present. But more important, he called for presence of mind as the means for implementing what he named "the only true telepathic miracle"—turning the forbidding future into the fulfilled present.[28] Failure to acknowledge our society's possessive investment in whiteness prevents us from facing the present openly and honestly. It hides from us the devastating costs of disinvestment in America's infrastructure over the past two decades and keeps us from facing our responsibility to reinvest in human resources by channeling resources toward education, health, and housing—and away from subsidies for speculation and luxury. After two decades of disinvestment, the only further disinvestment we need is from the ruinous pathology of whiteness, which has always undermined our own best instincts and interests. In a society suffering so badly from an absence of mutuality, an absence of responsibility and an absence of justice, presence of mind might be just what we need.

DISCUSSION QUESTIONS

1. In this selection, Lipsitz doesn't define the "possessive investment in whiteness" (he does that elsewhere in his book), but what do you think he means by that phrase?
2. What are some of the costs of being black?
3. Why is home ownership a key to economic well-being?

NOTES

1. Richard Dyer, "White," *Screen* 29, 4 (Fall 1998): 44.
2. I thank Michael Schudson for pointing out to me that since the passage of civil rights legislation in the 1960s whiteness dares not speak its name, cannot speak in its own behalf, but rather advances through a color-blind language radically at odds with the distinctly racialized distribution of resources and life chances in U.S. society.

3. Walter Benjamin, "Madame Ariane: Second Courtyard on the Left," in *One-Way Street* (London: New Left Books, 1969), 98–99.

4. See Kenneth Jackson, *Crabgrass Frontier: The Suburbanization of the United States* (New York: Oxford University Press, 1985), and Douglas S. Massey and Nancy A. Denton, *American Apartheid: Segregation and the Making of the Underclass* (Cambridge, MA: Harvard University Press, 1993).

5. I thank Phil Ethington for pointing out to me that these aspects of New Deal policies emerged out of political negotiations between the segregationist Dixiecrats and liberals from the North and West. My perspective is that white supremacy was not a gnawing aberration within the New Deal coalition but rather an essential point of unity between southern whites and northern white ethnics.

6. Records of the Federal Home Loan Bank Board of the Home Owners Loan Corporation, City Survey File, Los Angeles, 1939, Neighborhood D-53, National Archives, Box 74, RG 195.

7. Massey and Denton, *American Apartheid,* 54.

8. John R. Logan and Harvey Molotch, *Urban Fortunes: The Political Economy of Place* (Berkeley and Los Angeles: University of California Press, 1987), 182.

9. Ibid., 114.

10. Arlene Zarembka, *The Urban Housing Crisis: Social, Economic, and Legal Issues and Proposals* (Westport, CT: Greenwood, 1990), 104.

11. Jill Quadagno, *The Color of Welfare: How Racism Undermined the War on Poverty* (New York: Oxford University Press, 1994), 92, 91.

12. Logan and Molotch, *Urban Fortunes,* 130.

13. See Gary Gerstle, "Working-Class Racism: Broaden the Focus," *International Labor and Working Class History* 44 (Fall 1993): 36.

14. Logan and Molotch, *Urban Fortunes,* 168–69.

15. Massey and Denton, *American Apartheid,* 55.

16. Logan and Molotch, *Urban Fortunes,* 116.

17. Jim Campen, "Lending Insights: Hard Proof that Banks Discriminate," *Dollars and Sense,* January–February 1991, 17.

18. Mitchell Zuckoff, "Study Shows Racial Bias in Lending," *Boston Globe,* October 9, 1992.

19. Paul Ong and J. Eugene Grigsby III, "Race and Life-Cycle Effects on Home Ownership in Los Angeles, 1970 to 1980," *Urban Affairs Quarterly* 23, 4 (June 1988): 605.

20. Massey and Denton, *American Apartheid,* 108.

21. Gary Orfield and Carol Ashkinaze, *The Closing Door: Conservative Policy and Black Opportunity* (Chicago: University of Chicago Press, 1991), 58, 78.

22. Logan and Molotch, *Urban Fortunes,* 129.

23. Campen, "Lending Insights," 18.

24. Alicia H. Munnell, Lyn E. Browne, James McEneany, and Geoffrey M. B. Tootel, "Mortgage Lending in Boston: Interpreting HMDA Data" (Boston: Federal Reserve Bank of Boston, 1993); Kimberly Blanton, "Fed Blocks Shawmut's Bid to Gain N.H. Bank," *Boston Globe,* November 16, 1993.

25. Ellis Cose, *Rage of a Privileged Class* (New York: HarperCollins, 1993), 191.

26. Gregory Squires, "'Runaway Plants,' Capital Mobility, and Black Economic Rights," in *Community and Capital in Conflict: Plant Closings and Job Loss,* ed. John C. Raines, Lenora E. Berson, and David McI. Gracie (Philadelphia: Temple University Press, 1983), 70.

27. The rise of a black middle class and the setbacks suffered by white workers during deindustrialization may seem to subvert the analysis presented here. Yet the black middle class remains fragile, far less able than other middle-class groups to translate advances in income into advances in wealth and power. Similarly, the success of neoconservatism since the 1970s has rested on securing support from white workers for economic policies that do them objective harm by mobilizing countersubversive electoral coalitions against busing and affirmative action, while carrying out attacks on public institutions and resources by representing "public" space as black space. See Oliver and Shapiro, "Wealth of a Nation." See also Logan and Molotch, *Urban Fortunes.*

28. Benjamin, "Madame Ariane," 98, 99.

What's Good Enough?

Peter Schrag

By now the list of a half-century of half-tried and discarded educational remedies seeking to honor the promise of *Brown v. Board of Education* fills volumes: attendance-zone redistricting, busing, magnet schools, compensatory education, bilingual education, ebonics, military schools, year-round schools, single-sex schools, Head Start and multiculturalism, plus scores of other curricular reforms. While gaps between the academic achievement of white and minority children were reduced in the first decades after the end of legal segregation, they were never eliminated. By almost any educational measure, the average black or Latino child contin-

Peter Schrag is author of *The Final Test: The Battle for Adequacy in America's Schools* and *Paradise Lost: California's Experience, America's Future.*

ues to lag behind her white or Asian counterpart. In 1973, with its decision in *San Antonio v. Rodriguez* that public schooling was not a right guaranteed under the Constitution, the Supreme Court itself effectively gave up its cause.

That threw the issue back to the states, where it has remained ever since, but where, in an accumulation of crucial state Supreme Court decisions and associated legislative reforms, the drive for decent schools for poor and minority children has taken a new, unexpected—and perhaps encouraging—set of turns.

At the heart of those cases is the principle of adequacy, a legal idea, rooted in variously worded state constitutional provisions, that's as promising as it is awkward. Many state constitutions require the state to maintain "thorough and efficient" schools or (as in New York) "free common schools wherein all the children of this state may be educated," or (as in North Carolina) to establish the "right to the privilege of education."

Most such provisions have been in state constitutions for generations. But in the past fifteen years, as state after state has adopted tougher academic standards, tests and accountability measures, those standards have become both the drivers and the gauge for new demands from parents, school districts, civil rights groups and others for better resources, especially in schools serving the neediest kids: If students are required to meet higher standards for promotion, or to pass exit exams to get a diploma, or if teachers or principals face sanctions if their schools don't measure up, the state has a commensurate responsibility to provide the resources—in trained teachers, materials and facilities—to enable them to succeed. In this way, advocates of educational equity have attempted to turn the "standards" movement—which has been championed by conservatives—into a lever for progressive change.

The list of states where this is happening continues to grow: Arkansas, Kansas, Kentucky, Massachusetts, Montana, New Jersey, New York, North Carolina, Ohio and Wyoming, among others. The courts have ordered these states to establish systems that base school funding not on the customary political sausage machine that allocates money according to local wealth and the relative clout of competing legislative interest groups but on the closest possible determination of what it actually costs to educate each child. In some of them the judges have ordered even more specific remedies—preschool for at-risk children, for example, or wholesale curricular reforms.

In others, like California, major lawsuits are still pending. Former Governor Gray Davis, a Democrat, hired high-priced corporate lawyers to fight a California suit first brought by the American Civil Liberties Union along with other civil rights groups. The state argued, among other things, that lousy schools weren't its responsibility. After the state spent some $18 million on its lawyers, Davis's Republican successor, Arnold Schwarzenegger, is now trying to negotiate a settlement.

The most influential model for the adequacy cases has been Kentucky, which until the late 1980s had one of the most underfunded, inequitable and often corrupt school systems in the nation. In a sweeping 1989 decision (*Rose v. Council for Better Education*) the Kentucky Supreme Court struck down that whole system—"all its parts and parcels"—as a violation of the state Constitution and ordered the legislature to start over. Among the standards the court set was a requirement that Kentucky provide every child with seven "capacities"—oral and written communication skills, "sufficient knowledge of economic, social, and political systems to enable the student to make informed choices . . . sufficient training . . . in either academic or vocational fields so as to enable each child to choose and pursue life work intelligently," plus several others. Within a year, the state legislature, with the support of a business community that badly needed a better-educated labor force, enacted a major education reform law, complete with significant new funding, tougher academic standards, a new testing program and other measures.

The reforms hardly produced miracles, but they quickly improved teacher salaries and qualifications, improved facilities and produced substantially better scores on national tests, where Kentucky moved from near-bottom to roughly average. In the years since, and particularly because of tight budgets brought by the recession that began in 2000, Kentucky's school funding, like that of many other states, has eroded, and now new negotiations as well as another suit based on the state's alleged failure to maintain adequate resources are under way. Still, the *Rose* case testifies more to the success of the principle than its failure.

Defining adequacy is hardly a simple process: Resources that are adequate for middle-class kids may not be adequate for those coming to school speaking little English or those who are educationally handicapped. Nor is it clear what level of schooling the respective state constitutions require. In a New York State case last year, a lower appellate court decreed that an eighth-grade education was enough. But the Court of Appeals, New York State's highest court, rejected that crimped standard. It would require a great deal more, the court effectively held, for a person to become a fully functioning citizen and member of contemporary society.

With the enactment in 2002 of the No Child Left Behind Act . . . a number of states have considered rejecting a major chunk of federal funds in the belief that NCLB represents unfunded mandates, and thus costs them more than they were getting from the Feds. Districts in Nebraska, Missouri and North Dakota filed adequacy suits against their states, complaining that NCLB, in combination with state tests and proficiency standards, was asking them to achieve levels of proficiency beyond the resources provided. The threat of such suits has also added steam to the spreading political backlash against NCLB, even in legislatures dominated by Republicans.

Perhaps the most significant thing about the adequacy argument is that it goes beyond the simple equity principles—essentially, equal funding for every child—that have been a prime legacy of *Brown.* The remedy sought in *Rodriguez,* a remedy ordered by a number of state courts in the 1970s and '80s, was for states to provide enough money to low-property-value districts—districts that didn't have enough resources of their own—so that each child in the state had roughly the same funding behind her as all other children. But what seemed eq-

uitable in theory often wasn't equitable in practice. Many poor children went to school in the ghettos and barrios of property-wealthy districts, where their schools were still run-down, the roofs leaked, the rats played, the books were out of date and sometimes not available at all, and their teachers were disproportionately underqualified. Many of those teachers doubted that their students could ever achieve real academic proficiency.

In states like California, moreover, which had been a model for the equity-funding cases of the 1970s, the ultimate outcome of a pair of state Supreme Court decisions ordering the state to equalize per-pupil spending, combined with the tax-cutting mandated by Proposition 13 (1978), was to equalize school funding *down.* Which is to say that nominal equity brought not better schooling for children but worse. Given the structure of the American federal system, moreover, no court has the authority to equalize spending among states. New York and New Jersey, for example, now spend more than half again as much per child as California and twice as much as Utah.

Most important, the pro forma equity ordered by courts like California's did not in fact equalize resources—even between schools in the same district—much less provide resources that gave poor children a shot at a decent education. Studies in Seattle, Cincinnati and Houston conducted by a group of University of Washington researchers have shown that because the most capable and experienced (and thus the highest paid) teachers cluster in schools with better conditions, real per-pupil spending in different schools within the same district ranged between as little as $4,000 per child and as much as $10,000 per child, with the gap almost always disfavoring the schools serving poor and minority children.

Economists and educational experts disagree about how much sheer money matters. While Washington, DC, for example, spends more than almost any other large urban district, its student achievement levels are among the poorest in the nation. And, as many conservatives contend, some low-wealth districts that allocate resources effectively do better than high-wealth districts that don't. Nonetheless, in most places the strong correlation between the poverty levels of students, the paucity of decent resources they get in the classroom and their low achievement is reflected in almost every measure of school quality there is: student test scores and graduation rates, the test scores and college rankings of the teachers, the crowding and physical condition of the schools, the availability of books and materials, class size and all the rest. A study done in New York State by Hamilton Lankford, an economist at the State University of New York at Albany, showed an almost perfect correlation between the percentage of teachers who had failed certain standard state teachers' exams at least once and the concentration of poor children in the schools where they taught. The poorest kids, in other words, tend to get the least-experienced and least-qualified teachers.

For the most part, and despite concerns about local control and the limits of judicial authority under constitutional separation of powers, the courts have accepted the adequacy arguments, even inviting them in states where they rejected the equity cases. Writing the adequacy formulas—some based on what "successful" schools spend, some on the judgment of education professionals—is hardly an exact science. But it's almost certainly more precise than conventional interest-group politics and backroom deals (as in New York, where it was "three men in a room in a room," the governor and the leaders of the Assembly and Senate). And as Michael Rebell, who heads the Campaign for Fiscal Equity in New York, points out, it gets beyond the zero-sum (and often self-defeating) equity argument under which additional money for poor schools comes from schools attended by more affluent kids. This has happened not only in California but in Texas, where an equity-based court decision led to a state rule ordering wealthy districts to share funds with low-wealth districts.

The political response to the adequacy decisions has varied according to the politics of the respective states. In New Jersey a series of court decisions spanning more than twenty years (all designated *Abbott*

v. Burke) have slowly succeeded in getting the state to fund its biggest urban districts at the same level as the highest-funded suburban schools—though so far with unclear results in student achievement. While major reforms—preschools, curricular changes, smaller classes—have been instituted in Newark, Camden, Jersey City and the almost thirty other urban "Abbott" districts, many of which now spend some $15,000 per child, far more than the national average, test scores have yet to show commensurate results.

Conversely, in Ohio, legislators asserting their authority as a co-equal branch of government have largely ignored the state Supreme Court's orders. In Alabama, where a series of court decisions ordered the state to revise its blatantly inadequate school-funding formula, the Supreme Court, after a set of judicial elections that radically changed the balance of the court, made a 180-degree turn and, on its own motion, decreed that the courts had no authority to meddle in school finance—only the legislature could do that.

The future of those cases—indeed, of the whole adequacy principle—remains unsettled. What is adequacy anyway, and who determines it? Is it an eighth-grade education, as the one New York court ruled? Is it high school graduation? Is it admission to college? Can the courts ever accomplish real reform without public (and thus political) willingness to provide decent resources to all children? How much are affluent taxpayers willing to spend for poor, minority and immigrant kids? What difference does money make, and if it makes a major difference, how should it be spent?

Yet some things are clear. Even conservative economists like Eric Hanushek of Stanford's Hoover Institution agree that good teachers make a critical difference in enabling poor and minority children to overcome the economic and cultural disadvantages they come to school with. That means creating the conditions that will attract and keep good teachers in the classrooms that most need them. It also means writing "weighted student formulas" that provide the additional resources essential for English-language learners, children from poor homes and learning-disabled students. . . .

A few weeks ago, a researcher for a PBS program on the *Brown* anniversary called to ask where she could find latter-day examples of tracking—the practice of moving poor and minority kids into un-challenging, dead-end programs. Those practices may be less blatant today, but they are still with us. And as Harvard's Gary Orfield points out, U.S. schools are now as segregated as they were thirty years ago—in the case of Latinos, more segregated than ever. But all over America, the biggest form of tracking and segregation these days is not the old system, where some kids are automatically enrolled in relatively demanding college-prep programs while others are consigned to shop and business math, but the massive de facto tracking of black, Latino and other poor kids into schools that don't begin to have the qualified teachers, textbooks, counselors, lab equipment, clean and safe spaces, working toilets and vermin-free classrooms that honor their work and that of their teachers, and that make them want to succeed. Desegregating schools can't alleviate that problem, because hous-ing patterns, white flight and sheer politics make it difficult to find anyone with whom to integrate. The only remedy is to make the schools serving poor kids vastly better.

Although it's now almost a cliché, it's truer than ever that education is the biggest—and maybe the ultimate—frontier in the battle for civil rights. *Brown* (and, to a slightly lesser degree, the civil rights acts of the Johnson era) contributed mightily to the progress that's been made in that battle over the past half-century. But it is hardly finished. For all its flaws, adequacy may be the most promising legal strategy to move it to the next stage.

DISCUSSION QUESTIONS

1. Should the right to an education be included in the U.S. Constitution?
2. How would you define an adequate high school education?
3. Would you agree that education is the "biggest—and maybe the ultimate—frontier in the battle for civil rights"?

ECONOMY

READING 47

Gender Discrimination in the Workplace

Jeanette N. Cleveland

Margaret Stockdale

Kevin R. Murphy

FEATURES OF THE WORKPLACE THAT CONTRIBUTE TO GENDER DISCRIMINATION

Gender discrimination occurs in a number of set-tings. Men and women are perceived differently, are assigned different roles and are assumed to have dif-ferent characteristics in most settings (e.g., around the house, cooking, cleaning, and caring for children are usually the woman's role, whereas home repairs, mowing the lawn, and maintaining the car are the man's role). To some extent, gender discrimination in the workplace can be thought of as a simple ex-tension of beliefs most of us hold about the roles men and women should have in society (sex-role spillover). However, specific features of the work-place heighten the influence of gender on attitudes and actions, particularly the stereotypes assigned to men, women, and jobs, and the relative rarity of women in many work settings.

Jeanette Cleveland is a professor of psychology at Pennsylvania State University. Margaret Stockdale is a professor of psychology at Southern Illinois University, Carbondale. Kevin Murphy is a professor of psychology at Penn State University.

Sex-Role Spillover

The term *female worker* describes two roles (woman and worker) that involve different behaviors, different demands, and different assumptions. The traditional role of a woman involves caring for others, self-sacrifice, submissiveness, and social facilitation, whereas the worker role often involves technical accomplishment, competition, development and exercise of skills, and leadership. Barbara Gutek (1985, 1992) noted that beliefs about the appropriate roles for men and women are likely to "spill over" into a work setting. That is, our expectations regarding female workers will be determined in part by our expectations and beliefs regarding women in general. Even in situations where the work has little to do with stereotypically female roles, expectations about the typical roles of men and women will likely have some influence on the way we perceive and treat male and female workers. For example, in a meeting that involves several men and one woman, it is not unusual to find that both the men and the woman assume that it is the woman's job to serve coffee, take notes, and carry out other "feminine" tasks.

You can think of *sex-role spillover* as a specific instance of a much more general issue, which is that everyone carries out a number of roles that may or may not be fully compatible. A female faculty member might have the roles of teacher, advisor, parent, wife, and young woman, and her interactions with others in the workplace are likely to be affected by the way she is seen in relation to each of these roles. What, then, is so special about sex roles? Why should we be more concerned with sex-role spillover than with spillover between the roles of, for example, parent and worker?

One reason for paying attention to sex-role spillover is that sex roles are both powerfully ingrained and highly salient. Unlike many other roles (e.g., teacher, parent), sex roles are just about universally applicable, and gender is usually a highly salient feature of a person. For example, if you were describing a colleague to someone else, you might fail to mention many characteristics, but you would probably not forget to mention whether you were talking about a man or a woman.

Some environments may be especially conducive to sex-role spillover. For example, work environments can become sexualized in the sense that they feature relatively high levels of sexual behavior (e.g., sexual jokes, flirting). These work environments seem to encourage people to emphasize sex roles when thinking about coworkers (Gutek, 1985), which may lead to an undue generalization of general societal expectations about men and women in the specialized setting of the workplace. Environments might also highlight gender differences (e.g., with dress codes) in ways that lead people to think of each other in terms of their sex roles rather than in terms of their roles as workers. In general, the more cues in the environment that point to a worker's gender, the higher the likelihood that men and women will be treated differently.

Stereotypes of People and Jobs

Table 1 lists a number of traits that could be used to describe a person. Many of these seem to "fit" better when applied to men than to women (or vice versa). Decisiveness, confidence, ambition, and recklessness are traits we expect to find in men, whereas warmth, sensitivity, understanding, and dependence are stereotypically feminine traits. The stereotypes of some traits are so strongly sex-typed that traits viewed as positive in men (e.g., assertiveness) may be viewed as negative for women. Similarly, traits that are viewed as positive in women (e.g., sensitivity) may be viewed as negative in men.

These same words might be used to describe jobs or, more precisely, the sort of person we would expect to find in a job (e.g., decisive executive, sensitive nurse). The same adjective can be positive when applied to some jobs (e.g., aggressive sales manager) and negative when applied to others (e.g., aggressive kindergarten teacher). The same adjective can take on different connotations when paired with both a job and a person. For example, "assertive nurse" probably brings to mind a different image when the nurse is male than when the nurse is female.

Finally, these descriptors take on different meanings when used to describe men or women in the same job. For example, "ambitious executive" might

TABLE 1

TRAITS THAT MIGHT BE USED TO DESCRIBE MEN, WOMEN, OR TYPICAL JOB HOLDERS

Decisiveness	Warmth
Confidence	Sensitivity
Ambition	Understanding
Recklessness	Dependence

suggest different traits when used to describe men than when used to describe women. (Stereotypes of successful female executives are often negative, focusing on the sacrifices they have made and on the out-of-stereotype behavior needed to succeed in this man's world.) Similarly, "sensitive teacher" is probably more positive when applied to females than to males. For a man, this characteristic may violate typical sex-role stereotypes and is unlikely to be viewed as an asset, whereas for women, sensitivity will probably be seen as a strength.

That jobs can often be described in terms that are strongly sex-typed has fundamental implications for understanding gender discrimination in the workplace. If you believe that men are more likely than women to possess some attribute thought to be necessary for a job, you will probably discriminate against women (and in favor of men) when evaluating applicants or incumbents in that job. For example, a person who thinks that dominance is an important part of police work will probably favor men over women as police officers (dominance is strongly sex-typed). Stereotyping of men, women, and jobs is not inevitable; people are often able to look past stereotypes and evaluate individuals strictly on their individual merits. (For a review of factors that moderate stereotyping, see Fiske & Taylor, 1991; Martell, 1996). However, there is compelling evidence that stereotypes do influence evaluations of men and women at work. The role of gender stereotypes in the evaluation of male and female managers has been studied extensively and offers a case in point.

Research suggests that women and men do not differ in management ability or motivation (Dipboye, 1987), but women are generally seen as less attractive candidates for managerial positions. Even when they have similar backgrounds and credentials, women are perceived to have fewer of the attributes associated with managerial effectiveness (Brenner, Tomkiewicz, & Schein, 1989; Heilman et al., 1989). Our stereotype of managerial success includes traits like decisiveness, confidence, and ambition, and women are usually assumed to be less decisive, less confident, and less ambitious than men. It is not clear whether this is really true or whether these traits contribute much to success as a manager, but the fact that the stereotype of a man fits the stereotype of a manager, whereas the stereotype of a woman does not, spells trouble for women attempting to enter and succeed in the managerial ranks.

A Lack of Fit

Madeline Heilman (1983) developed a "*lack of fit*" model to identify the conditions under which gender discrimination might be more or less likely to occur. Consistent with the preceding discussion, this model suggests that perceptions of jobs may be a critical issue in determining the extent to which gender influences work outcomes. Heilman noted that some jobs are more strongly sex-stereotyped than others. One basis for such stereotypes may be simple workforce demographics. Jobs that are mainly held by men tend to have male stereotypes, whereas jobs that are mainly held by women tend to have female stereotypes, almost independent of the content of the job. A second basis for such stereotypes is the content of the job. Jobs that include activities that are stereotypically masculine (e.g., working outdoors, working with heavy equipment) are likely to be viewed as more masculine than jobs that include stereotypically feminine activities (e.g., working with children, caring for others). Finally, jobs might have sex stereotypes because of attributes that are thought to be critical for success. As noted previously, successful managers are often described as ambitious, competitive, analytical, and interested in power, all of which are stereotypically masculine traits. Women are thought to have a number of very different skills (e.g., interpersonal skills, interest in consensus) that are clearly work related, but few of which correspond to the stereotype of a manager. In terms of this model, there is a poor fit between the stereotype of the manager and popular stereotypes of women.

Heilman suggested that gender discrimination is most likely to occur when the characteristics of the person do not fit with the stereotype of the job. That is, women are most likely to encounter gender discrimination when the job is seen as masculine. Conversely, men are most likely to encounter gender discrimination when entering jobs or occupations that are stereotypically feminine. Sackett, DuBois, and Noe (1991) provided striking confirmation for some of the predictions of the lack of fit model. They found that when women made up less than 20% of a work group, their performance evaluations were substantially lower than those received by men. In groups that were 50% or more female, women received slightly higher performance ratings.

Although the lack of fit model suggests some symmetry in gender discrimination (i.e., women are at a disadvantage in masculine jobs and men are at a disadvantage in feminine jobs), wage surveys suggest that lack of fit is a more serious issue for women than for men. That is, men in stereotypically feminine jobs (e.g., nurse, librarian) may receive lower ratings, lower salaries, and fewer opportunities for advancement than they would in the absence of any gender discrimination, but the effects of lack of fit are consistently stronger for women than for men. As we note subsequently, one reason for this is that stereotypically feminine jobs tend to be lower in prestige, responsibility, and pay than stereotypically masculine jobs, meaning that there is less to lose or to gain in these jobs as the result of systematic gender discrimination. . . .

OCCUPATIONAL SEGREGATION AND GENDER DISCRIMINATION

The term *segregation* is often associated with discrimination on the basis of race or ethnicity, and in many contexts (e.g., analyses of housing patterns in urban areas) race still is the primary basis for segregation. In the workplace, however, gender may be a more potent force in the segregation of the workforce than race, ethnicity, age, or other factors.

It is possible to find men and women doing just about any job in the U.S. economy. Jobs that are completely sex-segregated (e.g., Roman Catholic priest, NFL player, combat infantryman) do exist, but they are clear exceptions. However, although there are relatively few formal barriers to the equal participation of men and women in most occupations, men and women do fundamentally different types of work. It is not completely clear whether this is due to gender discrimination or to other factors (e.g., differences in training and skills). Before we consider why jobs and occupations are segregated by gender, it is useful to consider both the data on sex-segregation in the workplace and models (primarily economic models) that attempt to explain these data in terms of factors other than gender discrimination.

Segregation by Occupation

Historically, women have been concentrated in a relatively small number of occupations, particularly in service sector work, clerical work, and retail sales. Jobs in these categories are so female-dominated that they are sometimes referred to as "pink-collar" work. A number of indices of gender segregation in the workplace exist, but they all tell essentially the same story. A woman entering the workforce is very likely to be found in an occupation where the majority of workers are women; about half of all working women are employed in occupations that are more than 75% female (Dunn, 1997b; Jacobs, 1993).

Jobs that are held primarily by women tend to involve lower levels of technical skill and responsibility than jobs held primarily by men and are generally not as highly valued by organizations (P. England, 1992). In fact, one of the best predictors of the status and pay level of a job is the proportion of women holding that job. The more women found in a particular job, the lower the average pay (Dunn, 1997a). As we note later, one explanation for this trend is that women, for whatever reason, are concentrated in jobs that are of less value to organizations. An alternative, suggested by feminist scholars, is that the work done by women is simply devalued by organizations (Acker, 1989).

Occupational segregation is increasingly obvious the higher in the organization one goes. Surveys show that 95 to 98% of executive-level positions are filled by men (U.S. Department of Labor, 1995). The Federal Glass Ceiling Commission (U.S. Department of Labor, 1991; U.S. Department of Labor, 1995) concluded that equally qualified women are being denied advancement to top levels in organizations on the basis of gender (see also Powell & Butterfield, 1994). Male stereotypes of women and male-dominated culture (i.e., sociocultural factors) often are cited by women as explanations for this glass ceiling (Bucholz, 1996; Dobrzynski, 1996) whereas men sometimes cite lack of motivation (Maupin, 1993) or preparation (Dobrzynski, 1996) (i.e., individual-level factors) as explanations for the small number of female executives.

Devaluing Women's Work Many of the jobs that are dominated by women appear to require relatively high levels of interpersonal or nurturant skills (Kilbourne & England, 1997). Female-dominated jobs often involve serving, helping, or supporting others, and these jobs require a number of special skills and abilities. Although interpersonal and nurturant skills are clearly relevant to successful performance in many jobs and roles, there is evidence that these skills are not valued in the same way as technical skills. Kilbourne and England (1997) noted that jobs involving high levels of interpersonal and nurturant skills tend, on average, to involve lower wages than jobs that demand lower levels of these skills. The negative relationship between the level of interpersonal skill required in a job and the average pay level for that job is a concrete indicator of just how little value is assigned to the skills that often characterize "women's work."

Well-run organizations are likely to use careful and systematic processes in making decisions about pay levels assigned to different jobs and career tracks, and it is sometimes difficult to understand how gender discrimination could affect these decisions. Decisions about compensation often start with a systematic *job analysis,* which is a study of the tasks, duties, responsibilities, and content of a job. On the basis of job analysis, jobs might be classified into families and levels, and by combining information about job content with a careful analysis of movement from job to job and the skills required and developed by different jobs in an organization, career tracks might be identified. The process of making decisions about the compensation levels assigned to different jobs and job families is referred to as *job evaluation,* and it often incorporates both information about the content of the job and information about market pay rates into the formulas that are used to determine pay levels. Pay levels for different jobs are often linked to the degree to which *compensable factors* (such as responsibility, autonomy, working in stressful environments, technical skills, etc.) are present in each job.

Job evaluation seems so objective and thorough that many people question whether stereotypes and biases could affect decisions about the worth of different jobs. However, gender discrimination can enter into the process in at least two places. First, the use of market data perpetuates any historical bias that exists in the system. Suppose, for example, that garbage truck drivers have historically received higher pay than elementary school teachers (they have). If you define *worth* in terms of what people are willing to pay for something, you might conclude that garbage truck drivers should be paid more than elementary school teachers (see Sidelight 1). The very fact that they are paid more will lead some people to argue that they are in fact worth more. An alternative point of view is that the market has historically discriminated against "women's work" and that the continued reliance on market data simply further entrenches this discrimination.

Second, questions can be raised about the values that drive compensation systems. Typically, jobs that involve more responsibility offer higher pay than jobs involving less responsibility. This reflects a value statement—that responsibility is something that should be rewarded. On the other hand, jobs that involve working with children typically offer lower pay than similar jobs that involve working with adults. This also reflects a value statement—that working with children is not a valued activity (again, see Sidelight 1). Whenever you see a statement of values, it is useful to ask whose values are being reflected. Some

ARE WE CLOSING THE WAGE GAP?

One of the most persistent concerns in discussions of gender and work is the long-standing wage gap between men and women. The U.S. Department of Labor has tracked the earnings of full-time male and female workers, as illustrated in the following figure:

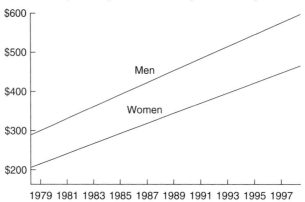

Median Weekly Earnings - Full-Time Wages and Salary Workers

In 1979, the average weekly earnings for men and women were $285 and $177, respectively. That is, at that time, women earned a bit under 62 cents for every dollar earned by men. In the first quarter of 1998, average weekly earnings for men and women were $596 and $455, respectively. That is, women earned a bit over 76 cents for every dollar earned by men. The trend over time is not quite as simple as depicted in the figure; there have been years when the gap was relatively larger or relatively smaller. However, there is still a large gap, and there is no sign that it is likely to close in the near future.

The size and nature of the wage gap depend substantially on another demographic characteristic—race. In 1983, White women earned 66.7% as much as White men, whereas in 1995, the gap had closed to 75.5%. For Black women, the gap hardly closed at all (59.7% in 1983 vs. 62.7% in 1995). For Hispanic women, there is no evidence that the wage gap is closing; in both 1983 and 1995, they earned 54% of that earned by White men.

scholars (e.g., Acker, 1989) suggest that assumptions about what aspects of work are or are not valuable themselves reflect broader societal biases. That is, the decision that level of responsibility is valued and rewarded whereas working with children is not may simply reflect dominant cultural assumptions that, on the whole, tend to assign more value to male-stereotyped activities than to female-stereotyped activities.

Suppose you accept the conclusion that at a broad societal level, the type of work done by women is not valued as much as the type of work done by men. It still might not be clear whether this reflects bias and discrimination or whether it reflects real differences in the work performed and the contribution of that work to organizations and society. If differences in the value assigned to work were based exclusively on the content of men's and women's jobs, it might be impossible to sort out competing explanations for differences in the perceived value of jobs. However, it is not only the activities done by women that tend to be devalued. There is also evidence that the very fact a job is done by women will lead to lower pay, lower status, and lower value. The clearest case for this phenomenon is the job of secretary.

Secretaries are almost always women, and given the skills required, the stress levels encountered, and the work expected from secretaries, it seems reasonable to argue that they are undervalued by organizations and by society. The job of secretary has relatively low pay and relatively low status, but this was not always the case. Prior to World War I, secretaries were almost always male, and the job of secretary had relatively high status. This job often brought young men into close proximity with the power elite, allowed them to work in comfortable surroundings, and provided good pay. As women entered the secretarial ranks, the status and pay of this job declined, even though the essential functions did not change much. This is a case where the feminization of a job seems to have directly reduced the pay, prestige, and status associated with the job.

Is Occupational Segregation Decreasing?   There have been substantial changes in gender segregation in recent years, at least for some high-status jobs. By 1990, approximately 50% of the bachelor's degrees and approximately 35% of the PhD degrees granted in the United States went to women. About 33% of the MD and 40% of the law degrees went to women. A number of professions have seen substantial growth in female representation, and as women take greater advantage of educational opportunities (e.g., college, professional school, and graduate school), the likelihood that they will inhabit the "pink-collar ghetto" has decreased. However, occupational segregation is still a fact of life for women with lower levels of education and training. The gender composition of fields like law and medicine is changing rapidly, but traditionally pink-collar jobs are still dominated by women. Despite the gains made by women with higher levels of education or socioeconomic status, it is still a good bet that receptionists, secretaries, dietitians, and day-care workers will be women.

Patterns of occupational segregation appear to differ as a function of socioeconomic variables, such as education and income. On the whole, women from relatively privileged backgrounds are less likely to find themselves in pink-collar jobs than women with less access to education and business contacts.

However, even when women enter the occupations that are not strongly dominated by men or women, they may still encounter a sex-segregated workplace.

Segregation by Job

Sex segregation in the workplace is most obvious when you compare broad occupations (e.g., clerical work vs. engineering). However, often there is also sex segregation in jobs and duties within the same occupation (Bielby & Baron, 1986). For example, female managers often lead less prestigious or less powerful departments, female bank managers tend to work in smaller, more remote branches, and female clerks have less prestige and less discretion than male clerks (Stover, 1997). Bielby and Baron's (1986) survey suggested that men and women performing similar duties in the same organization sometimes have different job titles (male-dominated jobs usually having more prestige) and different career tracks (female-dominated jobs having fewer promotion prospects).

In addition to holding jobs that are often less desirable than men's, women are increasingly likely to hold part-time jobs (Shockley, 1997). Even when job titles and career tracks are formally equivalent, women are more likely to hold jobs that have more tenuous status and prospects. Jobs held by women not only have lower pay than similar jobs held by men but are less likely to provide adequate benefits or job security. . . .

Is Discrimination to Blame for Occupational Segregation?

The only sensible answer to this question is "yes and no." The research evidence suggests that occupational segregation is not, for the most part, the result of individual employers' decisions not to hire women. . . . Stiff legal penalties can be imposed on employers who discriminate on the basis of gender in hiring, promotion, salary, and assignment to working conditions. If we define discrimination as a conscious and intentional decision on an individual level to treat similarly situated men and women differently when making hiring, job assignment, and promotion decisions, it is probably fair to say that gender discrimination is not the major cause of

SIDELIGHT 2

CLOSING THE GAP BY EXTERNAL MOVEMENT?

A basic assumption of many economic models is that competitive labor markets will sort out true differences, if any, in the value of what men and women do. In particular, if women are undervalued when they enter the job market, it is possible that they can recover lost value by moving from one job to another. Often, the most successful strategy for gaining a substantial raise is to move from your current organization to a competitor. Both men and women use this external market strategy, and it is possible that movement through the labor market might diminish the effects of initial differences in male and female salaries.

Brett and Stroh (1997) examined the use of external versus internal labor market strategies by men and women, and their analysis suggests that use of an external labor market strategy does not solve but rather magnifies the problem of male-female pay differences. Data from their study are shown in the following figure.

In this study, women were more likely than men to "jump ship" (i.e., leave the organization for a job elsewhere), but the effects of following an external labor market strategy were quite different for men than for women. Men who moved to other organizations gained substantially in salary, whereas women's salaries (which were in any case lower than men's) were not affected by their choice to move or stay.

These data suggest that an external labor market strategy will not address differences in the wages earned by men and women. On the contrary, movement in the labor market seems likely to increase rather than decrease the salary gap.

occupational segregation. Changes in the law and changes in society have removed many of the formal barriers to equal employment opportunities for men and women.

If we define discrimination as differences in the way men and women are treated when as they prepare for, aspire to, seeking training for, or perform in various jobs, it seems clear that gender discrimination defined in these terms is a critically important factor in occupational and job segregation. Differences in men's and women's vocational interests, work values, job preferences, and educational choices are rarely a matter of biology; whatever the causes of male-female differences in occupational choice, it is probably not the Y (or the second X) chromosome that explains occupational segregation.

Rather, male-female differences in a number of occupationally relevant skills, values, interests, and experiences seem to be a function of differences in the way society treats men and women. . . . Discrimination is sometimes defined as "prejudice in action." It seems reasonable to argue that discrimination (i.e., differences in the treatment of males and females) at a societal level is the most critical factor in determining the similarities and differences of the careers and career choices of men and women.

There is a useful distinction between individual and *structural discrimination.* Gender discrimination by a specific individual at a specific point in time is easier to recognize. . . . Structural discrimination on the basis of gender may be a much trickier issue. First, if men and women make different occupational choices because of the influence of their respective sex-role socialization experiences, it may be impossible to pinpoint the specific behaviors that constitute discrimination or the specific individuals who actively discriminate against women. If gender discrimination is part of the basic structure of society, it will be impossible to identify the responsible parties or the discriminatory acts. This does not mean that gender discrimination is not occurring. Rather, it is likely to mean that gender discrimination is such a part of the social fabric that the culprit is likely to be society and social systems in general rather than some individual.

Individual acts of discrimination in the workplace certainly do occur. However, the most potent form of gender discrimination is probably the form that occurs well before men and women enter the workplace—sex-role socialization. The idea that different patterns of behavior are appropriate for males and females is such a basic part of how boys and girls are raised that it is natural to believe they will have different attitudes toward, preferences for, interests in, and orientations toward the world of work. These differences are likely to become especially salient as the demands of work conflict with the demands of family, and men and women are socialized to deal with this conflict in different ways.

DISCUSSION QUESTIONS

1. Based on this article, what advice would you give a young woman just entering the job market who wants to maximize her earnings?
2. Identify cases of structural discrimination on the basis of gender.
3. Why is women's work devalued?

REFERENCES

Bielby, W. T,, & Baron, J. N. (1986). Men and women at work: Sex segregation and statistical discrimination. *American Journal of Sociology, 91,* 759–799.

Brenner, O. C., Tomkiewicz, J., & Schein, V. E. (1989). The relationship between sex role stereotypes and requisite management characteristics revisited. *Academy of Management Journal, 32,* 662–669.

Brett, J. B., & Stroh, L. K. (1997). Jumping ship: Who benefits from an external labor market strategy? *Journal of Applied Psychology, 82,* 331–341.

Bucholz, B. B. (1966, June 23). Slow gains for women who would be partners. *New York Times,* p. 10.

Dipboye, R. L. (1987). Problems and progress of women in management. In K. S. Koziara, M. S. Moskow, & L. D. Tanner (Eds.), *Working women: Past, present, and future* (pp. 118–153). Washington, DC: BNA Books.

Dobrzynski, J. H. (1996, February 28). Viewing barriers to women's careers. *Wall Street Journal,* p. d2.

Dunn, D. (1997a). Gender and earnings. In P. Dubeck & K. Borman (Eds.), *Women and work: A handbook* (pp. 61–64). New York: Garland.

Dunn, D. (1997b). Sex-segregated occupations. In P. Dubeck & K. Borman (Eds.), *Women and work: A handbook* (pp. 91–93). New York: Garland.

Fiske, S. T., & Taylor, S. E. (1991). *Social cognition* (2nd ed.). McGraw-Hill: New York.

Gutek, B. A. (1985). *Sex in the workplace: Impact of sexual behavior and harassment on women, men and organizations.* San Francisco: Josey-Bass.

Gutek, B. A. (1992). Understanding sexual harassment at work. *Notre Dame Journal of Law, Ethics and Public Policy, 6,* 335–358.

Heilman, M. E. (1983). Sex bias in work settings: The lack of fit model. In B. M. Slaw & L. L. Cummings (Eds.), *Research in organizational behavior* (Vol. 5, pp. 269–298). Greenwich, CT: JAI.

Heilman, M. E., Block, C. J., Martell, R. F., & Simon, M. C. (1989). Has anything changed? Current characterizations of men, women, and managers. *Journal of Applied Psychology.* 74(6), 935–942.

Kilbourne, B. S., & England, P. (1997). Occupational skill, gender and earnings. In P. Dubeck & K. Borman (Eds.), *Woman and work: A handbook* (pp. 68–70). Garland: New York.

Martell, R. F. (1996). Sex discrimination at work. In P. Dubeck & K. Borman (Eds.), *Women and work: A handbook* (pp. 329–331). New York: Garland.

Maupin, R. J. (1993). How can women's lack of upward mobility in accounting organizations be explained? *Group and Organization Management, 18,* 132–152.

Powell, G. N., & Butterfield, D. A. (1994). Investigating the "glass ceiling" phenomenon: An empirical study of actual promotions to top management. *Academy of Management Journal, 37,* 68–86.

Sackett, P. R., DuBois, C. L., & Noe, R. (1991). Tokenism in performance evaluation: The effects of work group representation on male-female and White-Black differences in performance ratings. *Journal of Applied Psychology, 76,* 263–267.

Shockey, M. L. (1997). Women and part-time work. In P. Dubeck & K. Borman (Eds.), *Women and work: A handbook* (pp. 7–9). New York: Garland.

Stover, D. L. (1997). The stratification of women within or-ganizations. In P. Dubeck & K. Borman (Eds.), *Women and work: A reader* (pp. 317–320). New Brunswick, NJ: Rutgers University Press.

U.S. Department of Labor. (1991). *A report on the glass ceil-ing initiative.* Washington, DC: Secretary's Office, U.S. Department of Labor.

U.S. Department of Labor. (1995). *The glass ceiling fact-finding report: Good for business—Making full use of the nation's human capital.* Washington DC: Author.

The Bankruptcy of Virtuous Markets

RACIAL INEQUALITY, POVERTY, AND "INDIVIDUAL FAILURE"

Michael K. Brown

Martin Carnoy

Elliott Currie

Troy Duster

David B. Oppenheimer

Marjorie M. Shultz

David Wellman

Almost forty years after the civil rights revolution ended, two questions bedevil most discussions of racial economic inequality: (1) Why has deep

Michael K. Brown is a professor and chair of the Department of Politics at the University of California, Santa Cruz. Martin Carnoy is a professor of education and economics at Stanford University. Elliott Currie is a lecturer in legal studies at the University of California, Berkeley, and a visiting professor in the School of Criminology and Criminal Justice, Florida State University. Troy Duster is a professor of sociology and a senior fellow at the Institute for the History of the Production of Knowledge at New York University. David B. Oppenheimer is a professor of law and associate dean for academic affairs at Golden Gate University. Marjorie M. Shultz is a professor of law at Boalt Hall School of Law, University of California, Berkeley. David Wellman is a professor of community studies at the University of California, Santa Cruz, and a research sociologist at the Institute for the Study of Social Change at the University of California, Berkeley.

poverty endured in the black community alongside a burgeoning black middle class? (2) Why do large gaps remain in family income, wages, and employ-ment between blacks and whites? For many people this is the paradox and the bane of the civil rights revolution. How is it, they ask, that civil rights laws ended racial discrimination and left behind an unruly black underclass and substantial racial in-equality? . . .

THE CHANGING STRUCTURE OF RACIAL INEQUALITY

In one respect, both black and white workers had similar experiences in the periods of economic growth and stagnation of the past sixty years: each group gained in real wages from 1940 to 1970, and each suffered from income stagnation and higher levels of unemployment after 1973. But in a racially stratified society, neither the gains nor the pains of economic change are distributed randomly. Because whites have historically controlled labor markets, black workers have been denied the economic benefits that white workers have received from in-creased education and they have been dispropor-tionately unemployed. Between 1940 and 1970, at the same time that wages of black workers rose rel-ative to those of whites, black employment *de-creased* relative to white employment. By 1953, the unemployment rate for black men in their prime working years, twenty-five to forty-four years of age, was three times the white unemployment rate. And since then the rate has been two to two and one-half times as high. All black men, not just the unskilled or poorly educated, routinely experience more unemployment than their white male coun-terparts. Black unemployment is substantially higher than white unemployment regardless of ed-ucation, age, occupation, or industry.[1] Even if one were to assume that black workers have the same education as white workers, black unemployment rates would still be 20 percent higher than the rates for whites.[2]

No doubt labor market discrimination has di-minished in the past sixty years, and whites are clearly less prejudiced today than they were in 1940.

But these developments tell us very little about contemporary patterns of racial discrimination and racial inequality. Why is it that twice as many blacks as whites are unemployed, regardless of the unemployment rate and long-run increases in black educational attainment? Reynolds Farley and Walter Allen pointed out some time ago that "if blacks had been incorporated into the economic mainstream and if racial discrimination declined, we would expect that their incomes would approach those of whites."[3] Why, then, did racial disparities in income and earnings widen over the 1980s, even though both black and white workers faced the same labor market environment: declining demand for unskilled labor, widening income and earnings inequality, and higher levels of unemployment? . . .

The Blue-Collar Breakthrough

. . . Contrary to the assumption that income always rises with increases in education, educated black workers [have been] more vulnerable to unemployment and wage discrimination than less educated blacks. Charles Killingsworth found that black-white unemployment ratios rose with education. In 1964 the unemployment rate for blacks with four years of college was more than three times the unemployment rate of college-educated white workers; but black workers with only four years or less of education had lower unemployment rates than comparable white workers. Baron and Hymer observe that wage gaps in the 1950s were not affected by education, noting that the "gap is greater at higher levels of education." In their study of the Chicago labor market, they discovered a stunning discrepancy. Black managers and sales workers earned just 57 percent and 54 percent of what whites in their respective occupations earned. But the wages of black operatives and laborers were 80 percent and 91 percent of whites in their occupations.[4] . . .

The White-Collar Breakthrough

Postwar occupational ceilings were undermined in the late 1960s and early 1970s by government policies and growing public sector employment. In this period, black workers made sharp income gains relative to white workers and significant occupational gains as they moved into professional, managerial, and technical positions. This white-collar breakthrough was due to the massive number of blacks moving into higher-ranking positions in the public sector and to the implementation of affirmative action policies that eliminated job ceilings and other exclusionary devices aimed at educated black workers. Federal policies also enabled blue-collar black workers to pull down the barriers erected by skilled white craftsmen. Segregated jobs in the South were abolished, and industries that had historically excluded black workers were opened up when antidiscrimination laws were enforced.[5]

This white-collar breakthrough indicates that one of the core conservative arguments against antidiscrimination legislation is misleading. Gains in education did not produce the growth of the African American middle class in the 1960s; rather, it was government policies—the very factor that conservatives consider irrelevant—that led to the white-collar breakthrough. Although historically blacks have been more likely to work in the public sector than whites, prior to the 1960s they were concentrated predominantly in low-level jobs in agencies like the U.S. Post Office. The growth of federal spending in the 1960s generated an enormous number of professional, managerial, and technical jobs in state and local government. As a result, until the 1970s most of the gains blacks made in high-ranking jobs were in publicly funded social welfare and education agencies.[6]

College-educated blacks were the main beneficiaries of the growth in public sector jobs. By 1970, half of all black male college graduates and three-fifths of black female college graduates worked for the government. Public employment was crucial to the wage and salary gains made by African Americans relative to white workers in the 1960s because the wage gap between black and white workers is far narrower in the public sector. There is also evidence that, unlike white workers, black public employees were paid a higher salary than their counterparts in the private sector.[7]

By the 1970s, blacks were also making job gains in the private sector. Among black male workers, the proportion working as professionals or managers

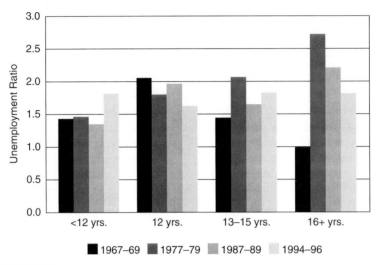

FIGURE 1

Black-White Male Unemployment Ratios by Years of Education, 1967–96.
Source: Chinhui Juhn, "Black-White Employment Differential in a Tight Labor
Market," in Robert Cherry and William Rodgers III, *Prosperity for All? The
Economic Boom and African Americans* (New York: Russell Sage Foundation,
2000), Table 3.2, p. 93.

rose from 6.8 percent in 1960 to 17.4 percent by
1980. These private sector gains were chiefly due to
affirmative action. . . . Enforcement of these policies
opened up employment in industries and occupations previously closed to blacks, raised the incomes
of college-educated blacks, and reduced wage discrimination for both black men and black women.[8]

Blacks were not the only group to benefit from
government policies in this period. The white middle class also gained, expanding after 1945 because
of a variety of public programs forged in the cru-
cibles of the depression and war. . . .

THE 1980S RACIAL BACKLASH

Blacks lost ground in the Reagan years, and some of
these reversals are quite startling. They also clearly
fly in the face of conservative assertions that education brings economic advancement. For example, in
this period young (twenty-five to thirty-four years
of age) college-educated black men's earnings

dropped to 72 percent of the white median income
from a high of more than 80 percent, a serious set-
back by any measure. Compared to white men and
women in the 1980s, black men made fewer occupational gains, and they were more likely to be
downwardly mobile.

Unemployment rose for all black men relative to
white workers, but especially for highly educated
black workers. By the end of the 1960s the ratio of
unemployed college-educated black workers to similarly unemployed white workers was even, a stunning
reversal of the pattern Charles Killingsworth found in
the 1950s and early 1960s. By 1980, as figure 1 shows,
college-educated black workers were once again at an
employment disadvantage relative to college-
educated whites. They were almost three times as
likely to be unemployed as college-educated white
workers were. While black high school dropouts also
experienced high unemployment rates during the
1980s, they were just one and one-half times as likely
to be unemployed as white high school dropouts.

These reversals are not explained by a failure of black workers to learn or acquire job skills. By the 1970s, the difference between the proportions of black and white youth attending secondary schools had all but disappeared. Despite this, some conservative writers insist that racial gaps in earnings and occupation result from deep differences in educational and job skills between educated blacks and whites. In other words, they assume that the attainments of college-educated blacks and whites are not comparable. Yet as Martin Carnoy points out, black Scholastic Aptitude Test (SAT) and Graduate Record Examination (GRE) scores *increased* relative to whites in the 1980s. Thus, the notion that college-educated blacks lost ground to whites because of an increase in the gap between so-called unmeasured educational skills is simply wrong.[9]

Nor can the widening pay gap between black and white workers be explained by the increase in wage inequality among all workers. Although both white and black workers lost jobs and income, it is usually assumed that black workers lost more ground in the shift to a service economy because they were concentrated in the high-wage manufacturing jobs that were eliminated in the 1970s and 1980s. The notion that blacks just happened to be in the wrong place at the wrong time oversimplifies matters and ignores persistent discrimination. As the President's Council of Economic Advisers (CEA) recently concluded, there is "indirect evidence that discrimination also contributed to widening pay gaps across racial groups" in the 1980s.[10]

The evidence that labor market discrimination persisted in the 1980s is even stronger than the CEA's measured statement suggests. In some cases labor market discrimination endures despite repeated efforts to regulate an industry. Certain sectors of the economy are impervious to antidiscrimination policies. For example, black workers have been consistently excluded from construction jobs that do not require high levels of education. As Roger Waldinger and Thomas Bailey conclude, "The low levels of black penetration into construction's skilled trades are prima facie evidence of continuing discrimination." They show that fla-

grant discrimination continues in the construction industry because white-controlled unions resist efforts to break down the color barrier.[11] Another more recent study confirms the persistence of labor market discrimination. Deirdre Royster systematically followed the experiences of an evenly divided group of fifty young black and white men searching for entry-level jobs. All of these men had graduated from a vocational high school and had similar grades, attendance records, motivation and character, and commitment to hard work. Royster found that white male students gained the inside track to jobs routinely thought to be available only because of standard interviews and institutionally certified qualifications. Skill deficits in human capital could not explain why young black men were denied blue-collar jobs.[12]

The major reason why black economic progress was reversed is that competition for jobs intensified between black and white workers in the 1980s. Like the immediate postwar years, the Reagan era was good for white upward mobility. In this period, deindustrialization and rising wage inequality reduced the middle-class jobs and incomes that were the backbone of economic progress after World War II. Although both black and white low-income workers saw their wages decline, the earnings gap between low-income, young (sixteen to twenty-four years of age) black and white male family heads widened in the 1980s. The earnings ratio of white high school dropouts to white college-educated males remained mostly stable from 1970 to 1988. In contrast, however, the earnings ratio of poorly educated young black male family heads to black college graduates sharply declined. The problem, as William Darity Jr. and Samuel Myers Jr. point out, is that if "the widening [income] gap between black and white families . . . is to be attributed to the higher representation of blacks among the less skilled and the uneducated, then why is there a widening gap between black and white family heads with the *same* low degree of educational preparation?"[13] The answer will not be found by examining who had the necessary job and educational skills. Rather one must look at how black and white workers fared in the scramble for jobs after deindustrialization. The evidence indicates that blacks lost out.

In the period after 1970 as blacks lost blue-collar jobs (mostly work as operatives because few made it into the ranks of skilled craftworkers), they found employment in white-collar sales jobs. But they also took a 13 percent pay cut. White workers who had also been pushed out of good manufacturing jobs, on the other hand, moved into well-paying sales jobs, which gave them a 36 percent pay increase. Thus, black-white income ratios in 1989 were lower for white-collar jobs (67 percent) than for blue-collar jobs (75 percent).[14] The important change during the 1980s was that black workers moved from good (high-paying) jobs to bad (low-paying) jobs. The employment rates of young black and white workers also differed depending on whether they worked in manufacturing or service industries. Employment rates for white and black youth in the manufacturing sector have been relatively equal over the past four decades. In the service industry, however, which is where nearly all the new jobs are found, whites enjoy an accumulated advantage of nearly three times the employment rate of blacks.

The problem black workers faced was that there were fewer good jobs to go around, and they lost out in the racially competitive and discriminatory labor markets of the 1980s. Convincing evidence indicates that retail establishments, one of the fastest growing sectors of the economy, are far more likely to discriminate against black youth than manufacturing firms. One group of researchers sent matched pairs of white and black high school graduates from the Newark, New Jersey, class of 1983 out in the world to seek employment. These job applicants were not faking an interest in employment. They had been screened to make sure they were actually seeking work and were matched for academic achievement. In the manufacturing sector, blacks and whites had about equal success in obtaining employment. In the service sector, however, whites were four times as likely as blacks to be fully employed.[15] In fact, in audit studies, whites or males are 5 to 20 percent more likely on the average to receive job offers than blacks or women.[16]

Although both black and white workers lost good jobs, persuasive evidence demonstrates that blacks lost a greater share of the good jobs and gained more of the bad jobs than whites. Darity and Myers report a 30 percent decline in the ratio of good jobs held by blacks compared to whites and a 1 percent increase in the ratio of bad jobs.[17] Carnoy discovered a similar pattern. He showed that the proportion of white males in low-paying jobs was mostly constant throughout the 1980s, about 31 percent, while the proportion of black and Latino males in these jobs increased sharply. The proportions of black, Latino, and white workers in midlevel jobs declined in the 1980s. Unlike white men and women, however, who made large gains in high-paying jobs, black and Latino workers were downwardly mobile.[18]

Competition between black and white workers for good jobs escalated during this period, a "classic case of protecting one's occupational turf from darker rivals," much like white workers did during the Great Depression. Declining wages and sluggish economic growth exacerbated competition over layoffs, reemployment, and job credentials. Downwardly mobile white workers in the 1980s acted just like unemployed white workers in the 1930s: they played the race card to keep or acquire good jobs.[19]

White workers were not the only culprits responsible for the exclusion of young blacks from high-paying jobs. Employers, as the matched-pairs studies of black and white youth seeking work demonstrate, are less likely to hire young blacks, particularly in service sector jobs. Indeed, some of the most powerful evidence for the persistence of labor market discrimination comes from recent studies of employers' attitudes and decisions. These studies show that many employers strongly prefer to hire white men and avoid hiring black men. Employers prefer white workers because they assume that black workers are less qualified and that there is a "lack of fit" between their own expectations and the cultural values of black employees. Faced with stiff competition, employers demand workers with more soft skills—motivation and the ability to interact with customers and other employees—to the detriment of black workers. Employers believe that black workers lack the soft skills necessary to stay competitive and frequently use negative stereotypes to characterize blacks' abilities.[20] Irate customers who complain about black workers reinforce employers' reluctance to hire them. One employer told researchers, "You do get customers coming in and they'll tell you, 'You need to hire more whites.'" Another study of employers' hiring decisions found that employers with mostly white customers were less likely to hire blacks.[21]

In their study of racial inequality in four cities, Philip Moss and Chris Tilly found that suburban employers were more likely to hire white women, Latinos, and black women than black men. The ratio of the percentage of black males hired in suburban firms to the percentage of black applicants was just .51. The ratio for whites was 1.22 and for Latinos, .87. Among central city employers the pattern was the same, though it was marginally better.[22] Other research shows that employers recruit applicants primarily in white neighborhoods to avoid potential black applicants, or advertise only in suburban or white ethnic newspapers.[23]

Many employers have cleverly taken advantage of these negative stereotypes of black workers. One study in New York City showed that as whites vacated desirable jobs, employers reclassified these well-paying jobs as low-skilled work. They did so partly for economic reasons—reclassification lowers labor costs. But they also assumed that black and Latino workers were incapable of anything but the most rudimentary of tasks. As a result, as "nonwhite New Yorkers get more jobs and have greater access to previously white occupations, [they] still find themselves locked into the [low-wage, dead-end jobs of the] secondary labor market."[24]

Blacks lost out in the 1980s for another reason. Republican policies hostile to affirmative action and labor intensified racial labor market competition. The enforcement of antidiscrimination laws was relaxed, and this was crucial in unleashing racial competition over jobs. Evaluations of affirmative action show that one of the traditional advantages whites have used to cope with economically tough times was restored when antidiscrimination laws were not strictly enforced in the 1980s. . . .

This is the context that set the stage for the recent political conflict over affirmative action. . . . White voters clearly understand the stakes in this controversy. A 1995 poll of likely voters on California's anti-affirmative action ballot proposition (Proposition 209) discovered that white voters were more concerned about losing jobs or promotions because of affirmative action policies (45 percent) than about the potential effects of racial discrimination for blacks and Latinos (25 percent). On the other hand, 80 percent of African Americans and 54 percent of Latinos were concerned that minorities would lose out because of discrimination.[25] Whatever the reality—and there is very little evidence that whites have lost jobs to affirmative action— white workers see themselves as an embattled group whose economic well-being is seriously threatened by affirmative action.

DISCUSSION QUESTIONS

1. Why do you think this article is titled "The Bankruptcy of Virtuous Markets"?
2. What most surprised you in this article?

NOTES

1. Reynolds Farley and Walter R. Allen, *The Color Line and the Quality of America* (New York: Oxford University Press, 1989), p. 225; Cordelia W. Reimers, "The Effect of Tighter Labor Markets on Unemployment of Hispanics and African Americans: The 1990s Experiences," in Robert Cherry and Williams Rodgers III, eds., *Prosperity for All? The Economic Boom and African Americans* (New York: Russell Sage Foundation, 2000), pp. 3–49.
2. William E. Spriggs and Rhonda M. Williams, "What Do We Need to Explain about African American Unemployment?" in Cherry and Rodgers, eds., *Prosperity for All?* pp. 195, 200.
3. Farley and Allen, *The Color Line and the Quality of Life in America,* p. 295.
4. Charles C. Killingsworth, "Negroes in a Changing Labor Market," in Arthur M. Ross and Herbert Hill, eds., *Employment, Race, and Poverty* (New York: Harcourt, Brace and World, 1967), p. 60; Harold Baron and Bennett Hymer, "The Negro Worker in the Chicago Labor Market," p. 255 in Julius Jacobson, ed., *The Negro and the Labor Movement.* New York: Anchor Books, 1968; Gerald David Jaynes and Robin M. Williams, eds., *A Common*

Destiny: Blacks and American Society (Washington, D.C.: National Academy Press, 1989), p. 301.

5. Herbert R. Northrup, *Negro Employment in Basic Industry: A Study of Racial Policies in Six Industries* (Philadelphia: University of Pennsylvania Press, 1970), p. 30; James J. Heckman, "The Central Role of the South in Accounting for the Economic Progress of Black Americans," *American Economic Review* 80 (May 1990): 245

6. Michael K. Brown and Steven P. Erie, "Blacks and the Legacy of the Great Society: The Economic and Political Impact of Federal Social Policy," *Public Policy* 29 (1981): 299–330.

7. Carnoy, *Faded Dreams*, pp. 162–65.

8. Ibid., p. 185; Jaynes and Williams, *A Common Destiny*, pp. 316–18.

9. Carnoy, *Faded Dreams*, pp. 82–83.

10. Council of Economic Advisers, *Economic Report of the President*, 1998 (Washington, D.C.: U.S. Government Printing Office, 1998), p. 150.

11. Roger Waldinger and Thomas Bailey, "The Continuing Significance of Race: Racial Conflict and Racial Discrimination in Construction," *Politics and Society* 19 (1991): 293. This is a classic example of opportunity hoarding; see introduction, "Group Hoarding and the Economic Theory of Discrimination."

12. Deirdre Royster, *Race and the "Invisible Hand"* (Berkeley and Los Angeles: University of California Press, 2003).

13. William Darity Jr. and Samuel L. Myers Jr., *Persistent Disparity: Race and Economic Inequality in the United States since 1945* (Northhampton, Mass.: Edward Elgar Publishing, 1998), pp. 9, 65–67, 69.

14. Darity and Myers, *Persistent Disparity*, pp. 47–48. The salaries of black workers moving from jobs as operatives to sales workers declined from $16,220 to $14,114; the salaries of white workers increased from $18,526 to $25,292.

15. Jerome Culp and Bruce H. Dunson, "Brothers of a Different Color: A Preliminary Look at Employer Treatment of White and Black Youth," in Richard B. Freeman and Harry J. Holzer, eds., *The Black Youth Unemployment Crisis* (Chicago: University of Chicago Press, 1986), p. 241.

16. Harry J. Holzer and David Neumark, "Assessing Affirmative Action," *Journal of Economic Literature* 38 (2000): 496. For a summary of recent research on discrimination, see Darity and Mason, "Evidence on Discrimination in Employment," pp. 79–81. Audit studies have been criticized on both conceptual and empirical grounds, but Deirdre Royster's study of employment discrimination takes the matched-pairs analysis common to audit studies to a new level of sophistication and overcomes the limits of previous studies. See Royster, *Race and the "Invisible Hand."*

17. Darity and Myers, *Persistent Disparity*, pp. 29–30.

18. Carnoy, *Faded Dreams*, pp. 95–99.

19. Darity and Myers, *Persistent Disparity*, p. 51. For a description of the experience of black workers during the depression, see Arthur M. Ross, "The Negro Worker in the Depression," *Social Forces* 18 (1940): 550–59.

20. Philip Moss and Chris Tilly, "'Soft' Skills and Race: An Investigation of Black Men's Employment Problems," *Work and Occupations* 23 (1996): 252–76; Philip Moss and Chris Tilly, "Why Opportunity Isn't Knocking: Racial Inequality and the Demand for Labor," in Alice O'Connor, Chris Tilly, and Lawrence D. Bobo, eds., *Urban Inequality: Evidence from Four Cities* (New York: Russell Sage Foundation, 2001), pp. 444–95.

21. Philip Moss and Chris Tilly, *Stories Employers Tell: Race, Skill, and Hiring in America* (New York: Russell Sage Foundation, 2001), p. 106; Harry J. Holzer, "Employer Hiring Decisions and Antidiscrimination Policy," in Richard B. Freeman, ed., *Generating Jobs: How to Increase Demand for Less-Skilled Workers* (New York: Russell Sage Foundation, 1998), p. 241.

22. Moss and Tilly, "Why Isn't Opportunity Knocking?" pp. 482–83.

23. Kathryn M. Neckerman and Joleen Kirschenman, "Hiring Strategies, Racial Bias, and Inner-City Workers," *Social Problems* 38 (1991): 433–47.

24. Gordon Lafer, "Minority Employment, Labor Market Segmentation, and the Failure of Job-Training Policy in New York City," *Urban Affairs Quarterly* 28 (1992): 224.

25. "Discrimination and Affirmative Action," *California Opinion Index,* (San Francisco: The Field Institute, May 1995), p. 2.

REFERENCES

Baron, Harold and Bennett Hymer. "The Negro Worker in the Chicago Labor Market," in Julius Jacobson, ed., *The Negro and the Labor Movement.* New York: Anchor Books, 1968.

Brown, Michael K., and Steven P. Erie. "Blacks and the Legacy of the Great Society: The Economic and Political Impact of Federal Social Policy." *Public Policy* 29 (1981): 299–330.

Carnoy, Martin. *Faded Dreams: The Politics and Economics of Race in America.* New York: Cambridge University Press, 1994.

Cherry, Robert, and William M. Rodgers III, eds. *Prosperity for All? The Economic Boom and African Americans.* New York: Russell Sage Foundation, 2001.

Council of Economic Advisers. *Economic Report of the President,* 1998. Washington, D.C.: U.S. Government Printing Office, 1998.

Culp, Jerome, and Bruce H. Dunson. "Brothers of a Different Color: A Preliminary Look at Employer Treatment of White and Black Youth." In Richard B. Freeman and Harry J. Holzer, eds., *The Black Youth Unemployment Crisis.* Chicago: University of Chicago Press, 1986.

PERSONAL ACCOUNT

Just Like My Mama Said

I remember when I was just a little boy, my mother used to tell me, "Anthony you have to work twice as hard in life as everyone else, because being black means that you already have one strike against you." When I was growing up in a predominately black area, I did not know what she meant by this. Then we moved to an area that was filled with white people. I found myself constantly lagging behind, and I couldn't figure out why.

When I was 19 years old, I hit rock bottom and had nothing. I then remembered what my mama had said, and I began to work twice as hard as everyone else. I managed to afford my own apartment and eventually get married.

My wife is white, but her parents dislike me because of my color. They told her all the stereotypes about "the black male" and swore to her that I would follow suit. Soon after we moved in together, I was laid off from my job. I began to worry that she would think her parents were correct, so I tried to teach her about the black experience. I began to worry that her parents would negatively influence her and I would lose her. I was ready to give in and let her parents win, when I remembered something that my mama had said: "Sometimes you can't teach people; they have to learn on their own." Little did I know an appropriate lesson would soon follow.

As I was going through the want ads, I saw an advertisement for a job delivering pianos. The job paid nine dollars an hour, more money than I had ever earned. I set up an interview for that evening. When my then-fiancée arrived home, I put on a shirt and a tie, grabbed my résumé, and headed for the interview. When I asked her if she thought I would get the job, she said, "I don't see why not. You work hard, you have good references, and you are enrolled in school." Needless to say I felt pretty good about my chances. I interviewed with a middle-aged white lady. The interview went very well. She nearly assured me that I had the job, but said that she just needed to run it by the storeowner. She left and returned with the owner minutes later. He was a middle-aged man of apparently white and Asian descent. He looked at me for a few seconds, and our eyes met. Then he shook his head and said, "No this is not who I want for the job" and walked out. The lady and I dejectedly looked at each other. She attempted to make an excuse for him, but I told her, "Don't worry, it's not your fault." I walked out and told my fiancée what had happened. We rode home in silence. She had just gotten her first taste of what it is like to be black in America.

Anthony McNeill

Darity, William A. Jr., and Patrick L. Mason. "Evidence on Discrimination in Employment: Codes of Color, Codes of Gender." *Journal of Economic Perspectives* 12 (1998): 63–90.

Darity, William Jr., and Samuel L. Myers Jr. *Persistent Disparity: Race and Economic Inequality in the United States since 1945.* Northhampton, Mass.: Edward Elgar Publishing, 1998.

Farley, Reynolds, and Walter Allen. *The Color Line and the Quality of Life in America.* New York: Oxford University Press, 1989.

Heckman, James J. "The Central Role of the South in Accounting for the Economic Progress of Black Americans." *American Economic Review* 80 (May 1990): 242–46.

Holzer, Harry J. "Employer Hiring Decisions and Antidiscrimination Policy." In Richard B. Freeman, ed., *Generating Jobs: How to Increase Demand for Less-Skilled Workers.* New York: Russell Sage Foundation, 1998.

Holzer, Harry J., and David Neumark. "Assessing Affirmative Action." *Journal of Economic Literature* 38 (2000): 483–568.

Jaynes, Gerald David and Robin M. Williams, eds., *A Common Destiny: Blacks and American Society.* Washington, D.C.: National Academy Press, 1989.

Killingsworth, Charles C. "Negroes in a Changing Labor Market," in Arthur M. Ross and Herbert Hill, eds., *Employment, Race, and Poverty.* New York: Harcourt, Brace and World, 1967.

Lafer, Gordon. "Minority Employment, Labor Market Segmentation, and the Failure of Job-Training Policy in New York City." *Urban Affairs Quarterly* 28 (1991): 206–35.

Moss, Philip, and Chris Tilly. "'Soft' Skills and Race: An Investigation of Black Men's Employment Problems." *Work and Occupations* 23 (1996): 252–76.

———. "Why Opportunity Isn't Knocking: Racial Inequality and the Demand for Labor." In Alice O'Connor, Chris Tilly, and Lawrence D. Bobo, eds., *Urban Inequality: Evidence from Four Cities.* New York: Russell Sage Foundation, 2001.

———. *Stories Employers Tell: Race, Skill, and Hiring in America.* New York: Russell Sage Foundation, 2001.

Neckerman, Kathryn M., and Joleen Kirschenman. "Hiring Strategies, Racial Bias, and Inner-City Workers." *Social Problems* 38 (1991): 433–47.

Northrup, Herbert R. *Negro Employment in Basic Industry: A Study of Racial Policies in Six Industries.* Philadelphia: University of Pennsylvania Press, 1970.

O'Connor, Alice, Chris Tilly, and Lawrence D. Bobo, eds., *Urban Inequality: Evidence from Four Cities,* New York: Russell Sage Foundation, 2001.

Oddone, Eugene, et al. "Race, Presenting Signs and Symptoms, Use of Carotid Artery Imaging, and Appropriateness of Carotid Endarterectomy." *Stroke* 30 (1999).

Reimers, Cordelia W. "The Effect of Tighter Labor Markets on Unemployment of Hispanics and African Americans: The 1990s Experiences." In Robert Cherry and Williams Rodgers III, eds., *Prosperity for All? The Economic Boom and African Americans.* New York: Russell Sage Foundation, 2000.

Ross, Arthur M. "The Negro Worker in the Depression." *Social Forces* 18 (1940): 550–59.

Royster, Deirdre. *Race and the "Invisible Hand."* Berkeley: University of California Press, 2003.

Spriggs, William E., and Rhonda M. Williams. "What Do We Need to Explain about African American Unemployment?" In Robert Cherry and Williams Rodgers III, eds., *Prosperity for All? The Economic Boom and African Americans.* New York: Russell Sage Foundation, 2000.

Waldinger, Roger, and Thomas Bailey. "The Continuing Significance of Race: Racial Conflict and Racial Discrimination in Construction." *Politics and Society* 19 (1991).

READING 49

The Model Minority: Asian American "Success" as a Race Relations Failure

Frank Wu

Student: "Asians are threatening our economic future. . . . We can see it right here in our own school. Who are getting into the best colleges, in disproportionate numbers? Asian kids! It's not fair."

Teacher: "Uh . . . That certainly was an unusual essay. . . . Unfortunately, it's racist."

Frank Wu is the dean of Wayne State University's Law school. He was the first Asian American to serve as a law professor at the Howard University School of Law, in Washington, D.C. He has written for a range of publications including *The Washington Post, The Los Angeles Times, The Chicago Tribune,* and *The Nation,* and he writes a regular column for *Asian Week.*

Student: "Um . . . are you sure? My parents helped me."

Garry Trudeau

Recycled Doonesbury: Second Thoughts on a Gilded Age

REVENGE OF THE NERDS

I am not the model minority. Before I can talk about Asian American experiences at all, I have to kill off the model minority myth because the stereotype obscures many realities. I am an Asian American, but I am not good with computers. I cannot balance my checkbook, much less perform calculus in my head. I would like to fail in school, for no reason other than to cast off my freakish alter ego of geek and nerd. I am tempted to be very rude, just to demonstrate once and for all that I will not be excessively polite, bowing, smiling, and deferring. I am lazy and a loner, who would rather reform the law than obey it and who has no business skills. I yearn to be an artist, an athlete, a rebel, and, above all, an ordinary person.

I am fascinated by the imperviousness of the model minority myth against all efforts at debunking it. I am often told by nice people who are bewildered by the fuss, "You Asians are all doing well. What could you have to complain about anyway? Why would you object to a positive image?" To my frustration, many people who say with the utmost conviction that they would like to be color blind revert to being color conscious as soon as they look at Asian Americans, but then shrug off the contradiction. They are nonchalant about the racial generalization, "You Asians are all doing well," dismissive in asking "What could you have to complain about anyway?," and indifferent to the negative consequences of "a positive image."

Even people who are sympathetic to civil rights in general, including other people of color, sometimes resist mentioning civil rights and Asian Americans together in the same sentence. It is as if Asian American civil rights concerns can be ruled out categorically without the need for serious consideration of the facts, because everyone knows that Asian Americans are prospering.

Consider the term "overachiever." I am reluctant to accept the title for myself, and not out of Asian modesty. To be called an "overachiever" begs the question: What, exactly, is it that individuals have achieved over—what others expected of them or what they deserve?

In either case, overachievers have surprised observers by surpassing the benchmark, and their exploits are not quite right. They will get their comeuppance sooner or later. Applied to an entire racial group, as "overachiever" is to Asian Americans, the implications are troubling. Asian Americans, often thought of as intellectuals, will be consigned to the same fate as intellectuals. As Columbia University historian Richard Hofstadter stated in the opening pages of his *Anti-intellectualism in American Life,* "The resentment from which the intellectual has suffered in our time is a manifestation not of a decline in his position but of his increasing prominence."[1]

And so it is with Asian Americans. "You Asians are all doing well anyway" summarizes the model minority myth. This is the dominant image of Asians in the United States. Ever since immigration reforms in 1965 led to a great influx of Asian peoples, we have enjoyed an excellent reputation. As a group, we are said to be intelligent, gifted in math and science, polite, hard working, family oriented, law abiding, and successfully entrepreneurial. We revere our elders and show fidelity to tradition. The nation has become familiar with the turn-of-the-century Horatio Alger tales of "pulling yourself up by your own bootstraps" updated for the new millennium with an "Oriental" face and imbued with Asian values.

This miracle is the standard depiction of Asian Americans in fact and fiction, from the news media to scholarly books to Hollywood movies. From the 1960s to the 1990s, profiles of whiz kid Asian Americans became so common as to be cliches. In 1971, *Newsweek* magazine observed that we were "out-whiting the whites."[2] *People* magazine one year made celebrities of the five Asian American

teenagers who swept the highest prizes in the annual Westinghouse science talent search in an article headlined "Brain Drain Boon for the U.S.," and it followed up the next year by profiling an entire family of Asian American winners.[3] Brown University history professor Stephen Graubard wrote an op-ed for *The New York Times* asking "Why Do Asian Pupils Win Those Prizes?"[4] The Asian refugee who was a finalist in a spelling bee, but who lost on the word "enchilada," has become legendary.[5] *Time, Newsweek, Sixty Minutes,* and other media outlets have awarded Asian Americans the title "model minority."[6] *Fortune* magazine dubbed us the "superminority."[7] The *New Republic* heralded, "the triumph of Asian Americans" as "America's greatest success story" and *Commentary* magazine referred to Asian Americans as "a trophy population."[8] The *New York Times* announced that we are "going to the head of the class."[9] The *Washington Post* said in a headline, "Asian Americans Outperform Others at School and Work."[10] Smith College sociologist Peter Rose has described Asian Americans as making a transition "from pariahs to paragons."[11] Memoirist Richard Rodriguez and Washington Post columnist William Raspberry have wondered whether Hispanics and blacks, respectively, might be able to emulate Asian immigrants.[12] A minority group could become the equivalent of a white real estate developer: *Advertising Age* quoted a consultant who opined that Asian Americans were "the Donald Trumps of the 1990s."[13]

Conservative politicians especially like to celebrate Asian Americans. President Ronald Reagan called Asian Americans "our exemplars of hope."[14] President George [H.] Bush, California Governor Pete Wilson, House Speaker Newt Gingrich—all have been unduly awed by the model minority myth. In a brief for the *Heritage Foundation Policy Review,* California politician Ron Unz said that Asian Americans come from an "anti-liberal Confucian tradition" that "leaves them a natural constituency for conservatives."[15] In the *National Review,* author William McGurn made the model minority myth a partisan parable: "Precisely because Asian Americans are making it in their adoptive land, they hold the potential not only to add to Republican rolls but to define a bona-fide American language of civil rights."[16]

According to the model minority myth, Asian immigrants have followed the beacon of economic opportunity from their homes in China, Japan, Korea, the Philippines, India, Vietnam, and all the other countries on the Asian continent and within the Pacific Rim. They might be fleeing despotism or Communism, backwardness or the deprivations of war and famine, but whatever the conditions of their past they know that the legend of Golden Mountain, to use the Cantonese phrase, guides their future.

They arrive in America virtually penniless. They bring barely more than the clothes on their backs. Their meager physical possessions are less important than their mental capacity and work ethic. Thanks to their selfless dedication to a small business or an advanced degree in electrical engineering— or both—they are soon achieving the American Dream.

They run a corner grocery in Manhattan, offering the freshest fruits and vegetables and serving up a take-out luncheon buffet priced by the pound. They buy a dry cleaning establishment in Los Angeles, featuring one-hour turnaround times and giving discounts to police officers. They start a motel franchise, which spreads throughout the Midwest, boasting such low rates with amenities like free cable television that other proprietors have no choice but to post signs identifying their accommodations inaccurately as "Native American Owned." They begin a computer chip manufacturing plant in the Silicon Valley, inventing the hottest miniaturized gadgets before selling their shareholdings and retiring at thirty-five. Or they open a boutique in Washington, D.C., with a display case of real-hair wigs on the wall above a bevy of manicurists chatting among themselves in another language while painting their customers' nails. . . .

They come to dominate their trades after less than a decade, reducing their competition to the verge of bankruptcy and then buying up their warehouse stocks. Their associations become monopolies, lending money cooperatively among their own members to preserve their collective advantage. In some cities, they hold more than half the commercial licenses and operate a majority of the downtown "mom and pop" retail outlets. Hospitals and universities have departments wholly staffed by Asian immigrants. Private industries ranging from automobile manufacturers to software developers to government agencies, such as the Defense Department, depend on them for research and development.

In turn, their American-born progeny continue the tradition with their staggering academic prowess. They start off speaking pidgin, some of them even being held back a grade to adjust. They are willing to do as they are told, changing their given names to Anglicized Christian names chosen with the help of their teachers and their friends and told matter of factly to their parents. Above all, they study, study, study.

They are brought up under the strict tutelage of parents who have sacrificed everything in the hopes that their children will garner more than what they themselves have lost. The parents defer everything for themselves and invest it in their young, giving them the mission of redeeming the family. They maintain that anything less than a straight-A report card will shame the ancestors, and they beat their children for receiving a single B-plus. The elders have faith in the school system. They instill respect for educators. They take their children to weekend language lessons instead of allowing them to watch Saturday morning cartoons on television.

The no-nonsense regimen works wonders. A parade of prodigies named Chang, Nguyen, and Patel takes the prizes at piano recitals and proceeds to graduate from high school with honors as valedictorian, salutatorian, and the rest of the top ten of the class, receiving full scholarships to the Ivy League colleges en route to graduate school and advanced professional training. . . .

In the view of other Americans, Asian Americans vindicate the American Dream. A publicity campaign designed to secure the acceptance of Asian Americans could hardly improve perceptions. They have done better here than they ever could have dreamed of doing in their homelands. They are living proof of the power of the free market and the absence of racial discrimination. Their good fortune flows from individual self-reliance and community self-sufficiency, not civil rights activism or government welfare benefits. They believe that merit and effort pay off handsomely and justly, and so they do. Asian Americans do not whine about racial discrimination; they only try harder. If they are told that they have a weakness that prevents their social acceptance, they quickly agree and earnestly attempt to cure it. If they are subjected to mistreatment by their employer, they quit and found their own company rather than protesting or suing.

This caricature is the portrait of the model minority. It is a parody of itself. . . .

Regrettably, the model minority myth embraced by the pundits and the public alike is neither true nor truly flattering. Instead, it is a stock character that plays multiple roles in our racial drama. Like any other myth forming our collective narrative of race, it is ultimately more revealing than reassuring. Complimentary on its face, the model minority myth is disingenuous at its heart.

As well-meaning as it may be, the model minority myth ought to be rejected for three reasons. First, the myth is a gross simplification that is not accurate enough to be seriously used for understanding 10 million people. Second, it conceals within it an invidious statement about African Americans along the lines of the inflammatory taunt: "They made it; why can't you?" Third, the myth is abused both to deny that Asian Americans experience racial discrimination and to turn Asian Americans into a racial threat.

GERMS OF TRUTH WITHIN THE MYTH

Like many racial stereotypes, the model minority myth has a germ of truth. The problem, however, is that the germ becomes exaggerated and distorted. On its own terms, the myth is not even persuasive as a description of the status of Asian Americans. In earning power, for example, the evidence points toward a disparity between what individual white Americans and what individual Asian Americans are paid—and not for lack of trying on the part of Asian Americans.

To figure out the facts, University of Hawaii sociology professor Herbert Barringer led a team that conducted the most comprehensive review of the research literature ever done. Barringer concludes that with respect to income, "in almost every category . . . whites showed advantages over most Asian Americans."[17]

Barringer proceeds cautiously because he is contesting the model minority myth. Even controlling for nativity—that is, native-born versus foreign-born—Barringer finds that Asian Americans who are native-born earn less money than white Americans who are native-born and possibly even than white Americans who are foreign-born. That means that Asians without cultural and language difficulties may earn less than white Americans who may have such difficulties. Barringer observes that "there seems to be no compelling reason to argue for parity" between Asian Americans and white Americans, but he does agree that Asian Americans "have certainly done much better with incomes than have blacks and Hispanics." He states that Asian Americans, including such ethnic groups as Vietnamese immigrants, might show "decided improvements" over time. He prefers "the most favorable interpretation," that "most Asian Americans are overeducated compared to whites for the incomes they earn."[18]

That interpretation, however, is most favorable to white Americans and not Asian Americans. Translated into practical terms, it means that white Americans are paid more than Asian Americans who are equally qualified. Either Asian Americans are not hired for the higher-paying jobs, or they are hired but are still paid less. . . .

The fact that Asian Americans are better educated than white Americans on average undermines rather than supports the model minority myth. The gap between Asian Americans and white Americans that appears with income reverses itself with education. It was consistent throughout the 1980s and 1990s. In 1980, approximately 36 percent of foreign-born Asian Americans had finished college compared with 16 percent of native-born citizens. In 1990, about 42 percent of Asian Americans had finished college compared with 25 percent of the general population. Every Asian American ethnic group, except Filipinos, attends college at higher rates than do white Americans. Chinese Americans, Indian Americans, and Korean Americans attend college at about twice the rate of white Americans. The entering classes of Ivy League schools are now as high as 20 percent Asian American, California schools such as University of California–Berkeley and UCLA as much as twice that percentage as Asian Americans become a plurality on campuses with no majority. Considering all educational institutions, Asian American overrepresentation is much lower but still significant: As of 1993, Asian Americans made up 5.3 percent of the college student body but approximately 2.9 percent of the general population. Their desire for education is increasing even as that of other groups is decreasing. Between 1979 and 1989, Asian Americans increased their numbers of Ph.D. recipients by 46 percent while whites and blacks decreased their numbers by 6 and 23 percent, respectively. By 1997, Asian Americans were receiving 12 percent of the doctorates conferred by U.S. universities, and they received more than one-quarter of the doctorates in engineering disciplines.

Although the average educational levels of Asian Americans might be taken as substantiating the model minority myth, the more plausible reading is that Asian Americans have had to overcompensate. Asian Americans receive a lower return on investment in education. They gain less money than white Americans on average for each additional degree. . . .

Moreover, Asian immigrants start off relatively privileged. This admission must be made gingerly, so that it will not be taken as corroboration of the model minority myth. In actuality, it undercuts the myth. Most Asian Americans are not rich. But some Asian immigrants are relatively fortunate compared to the many Asians who reside in Asia, and some of them are relatively fortunate compared to native-

born Americans (including, incidentally, native-born Asian Americans), even though they have not had an easy time of it in coming to the United States and even though they experience prejudice. A major study of diversity in the power elite found that almost none of the Chinese Americans who served on the boards of directors for Fortune 1000 companies were "authentic bootstrappers."[19] Almost all of them had come from well-to-do families in China, Taiwan, and Hong Kong.

University of California at Santa Cruz sociologist Deborah Woo examined more closely the media coverage of "a Korean-born immigrant who once worked the night shift at 7-Eleven to put himself through school" and who sold his company for $1 billion, as well as another Korean-born immigrant, a Silicon Valley entrepreneur who lived on ramen noodles and had to pawn his belongings to pay his phone bill, but gave $15 million to the San Francisco Asian Art Museum, "mak[ing] Horatio Alger look like a slacker."[20] Woo delved into the backgrounds of these examples of the model minority myth. In the former instance, the individual was able to start his company because he had received a government contract through a minority set-aside program. In the latter, the man was descended from the royal family that ruled Korea until the Japanese takeover of 1905, and he had been a university professor and an executive in the family business in Korea before emigrating. They are still impressive people, but they have not come from the ghetto. The sheen comes off the model minority myth once the real stories are revealed.

Asian immigrants personify "brain drain": the selective nature of immigration. More than half of the professional immigrants to the United States are Asian; Asian men are well over a majority of the professional immigrants in technical occupations. Indian doctors are the single largest ethnic group in the medical profession in this country, at about 4 percent of the total number of physicians; 11 percent of Indian men in the United States and 7 percent of Indian women hold medical degrees. Filipina women are over half the total number of registered nurses who were trained abroad; thousands more come every year. In 1990, 20 percent of all Filipino Americans listed their area of employment as health care. For many Asian ethnicities in the United States, such as Indians, the earliest cohort of immigrants following immigration policy reforms are the most qualified, and the continuing stream is less elite. Among some Asian ethnicities, such as Filipinos, the foreign-born generally make more money than the native-born. Under restrictive immigration policies, individuals who have skills that are in high demand in the United States have greater opportunities to acquire a green card. . . .

The model minority myth also masks great disparities among Asian ethnic groups. Japanese Americans and Chinese Americans are closest to equality with whites, but Vietnamese Americans and other Southeast Asian refugees languish at the bottom of the economic pyramid, along with blacks. . . .

Finally, the figures for Asian Americans are rendered unreliable by the careless inclusion of Asians who reside in the United States but who are not Asian Americans at all.[21] Hundreds of business executives with Japanese-based multinational companies spend stints of up to a few years here. Their upper-management salaries add to the average Asian American income, but they are no more representative of either Asians overseas or Asian immigrants than a white American vice president of a Fortune 500 company who was an expatriate manager in Europe would be either average of Americans or of Europeans themselves. They are part of a transnational overclass. . . .

Upon anything more than cursory reflection, the model minority myth becomes mystifying. The model minority myth is misleading not only because it takes for granted that racial groups rather than individual persons are the best basis for thinking about human lives, but also because it equates status and conduct. These most pernicious qualities of the myth are hidden in the open. Whatever else might be said about the myth, it cannot be disputed that it is a racial generalization. As such, it contains the premise that people can be arranged by racial group, and, furthermore, that the differences be-

tween racial groups are more significant than either the similarities between racial groups or the differences within them. It makes race the main feature of an individual as well as the leading division among people. . . .

The model minority myth persists, despite violating our societal norms against racial stereotyping and even though it is not accurate. Dozens of amply documented and heavily annotated government studies and scholarly papers, along with a handful of better magazine and newspaper articles supplemented by television segments and public speeches, all intended to destroy the myth, have had negligible effect on popular culture. . . .

The myth has not succumbed to individualism or facts because it serves a purpose in reinforcing racial hierarchies. Asian Americans are as much a "middleman minority" as we are a model minority. We are placed in the awkward position of buffer or intermediary, elevated as the preferred racial minority at the expense of denigrating African Americans. Asian American writers and scholars have not hesitated to call the phenomenon what it is. Novelist Frank Chin has described it as "racist love," contrasting it with "racist hate" of other people of color. DePaul University law professor Sumi Cho has explained that Asian Americans are turned into "racial mascots," giving right-wing causes a novel messenger, camouflaging arguments that would look unconscionably self-interested if made by whites about themselves. University of California at Irvine political scientist Claire Kim has argued that Asian Americans are positioned through "racial triangulation," much as a Machiavellian would engage in political triangulation for maximum advantage. Law professor Mari Matsuda famously declared, "we will not be used" in repudiating the model minority myth.[22]

Whatever the effects are called, Asian Americans become pawns. We are not recognized in our own right but advanced for ulterior motives. Michael S. Greve, a leading advocate against racial remedies, said that the controversy over anti-Asian discrimination could be used to attack affirmative action: It presented "an opportunity to call, on behalf of a racial minority (i.e., the Asian applicants), for an end to discrimination. It was an appeal that, when made on behalf of whites, is politically hopeless and, perhaps, no longer entirely respectable."[23] . . .

BACKLASH FROM THE MYTH

The model minority myth hurts Asian Americans themselves. It is two-faced. Every attractive trait matches up neatly to its repulsive complement, and the aspects are conducive to reversal. If we acquiesced to the myth in its favorable guise, we would be precluded from rejecting its unfavorable interpretations. We would already have accepted the characteristics at issue as inherent.

The turnaround is inevitable during a military crisis or economic downturn. To be intelligent is to be calculating and too clever; to be gifted in math and science is to be mechanical and not creative, lacking interpersonal skills and leadership potential. To be polite is to be inscrutable and submissive. To be hard working is to be an unfair competitor for regular human beings and not a well-rounded, likable individual. To be family oriented is to be clannish and too ethnic. To be law abiding is to be self-righteous and rigidly rule-bound. To be successfully entrepreneurial is to be deviously aggressive and economically intimidating. To revere elders is to be an ancestor-worshipping pagan, and fidelity to tradition is reactionary ignorance.

Asian Americans cannot win by winning. . . .

The model minority myth does more than cover up racial discrimination; it instigates racial discrimination as retribution. The hyperbole about Asian American affluence can lead to jealousy on the part of non-Asian Americans, who may suspect that Asian Americans are too comfortable or who are convinced [that] Asian American gains are their losses. Through the justification of the myth, the humiliation of Asian Americans or even physical attacks directed against Asian Americans become compensation or retaliation. . . .

It would be bad enough if the model minority myth were true. Everyone else would resent Asian Americans for what Asian Americans possess. It is worse that the model minority myth is false. Everyone else resents Asian Americans for what they believe Asian Americans possess. Other Americans say that their resentment is about riches and not race, but they assume that Asian Americans are rich on the basis of race; there is no escaping that the resentment is racial. Above all, the model minority myth is a case study in the risks of racial stereotypes of any kind. It is the stereotyping itself, not the positive or negative valence it assumes temporarily, that is dangerous. A stereotype confines its subjects. The myth was neither created by nor is it controlled by Asian Americans. It is applied to but not by Asian Americans.

DISCUSSION QUESTIONS

1. Is being a model minority a burden?
2. What are some of the consequences of the model minority myth for Asian Americans?
3. How would you feel about "positive stereotypes" being applied to a group that you were a member of?

NOTES

1. Richard Hofstadter, *Anti-intellectualism in American Life* (New York: Knopf, 1963), 6.
2. "Success Story: Outwhiting the Whites," *Newsweek,* June 21, 1971, 24.
3. David Grogan, "Brain Drain Boon for the U.S.: Students of Asian-American Families with Rare Genetic Gifts and a Reverence for Learning Sweep a Science Contest for the Nation's High-Schoolers," *People,* April 21, 1986, 30; Mary Shaughnessy, "When the Westinghouse Talent Scout Dealt Out Their Awards, They Gave the Kuos a Full House," *People,* June 8, 1987, 149.
4. Stephen G. Graubard, "Why Do Asian Pupils Win Those Prizes?" *New York Times,* January 29, 1988, A35.
5. "Minestrone, Ratatouille and Strudel," *Washington Post,* June 14, 1983, A18.
6. David Brand, "The New Whiz Kids: Why Asian Americans Are Doing So Well, and What It Costs Them," *Time,* August 31, 1987, 42; Martin Kasindorf, "Asian Americans: A Model Minority," *Newsweek,* December 6, 1982, 39.
7. Anthony Ramirez, "America's Super Minority," *Fortune,* November 24, 1986, 148.

Let Me Work for It!

I remember once in a sociology of education class that I was asked to describe my educational experience. At first, I was quick to say that it was very positive. Although racial remarks and jokes were passed around school, teachers and administrators paid little or no attention to them. I always felt uneasy with such remarks, but because the teachers and administrators would play ignorant to what was being said, I felt that maybe I was being too sensitive. Therefore, I learned to suck it up and was taught to view such comments as harmless.

Still, at a very young age I was very aware of racism and sexism. Both of my Vietnamese parents came to the United States when they were 20 years old. They arrived right before the Vietnam War ended, which explains the stigmatization they experienced. "VC" was a common epithet addressed to my dad along with "Gook" and "Charlie." My mom, on the other hand, struggled with gender/racial stereotypes such as being labeled mindless, dependent, and subservient. I can recall many times watching people mentally battering my parents. Numerous looks of disgust and intolerance of my parents' accent or confusion with the English language were some unpleasant cases that I experienced. Yet the snide remarks and mistreatment thrown at my parents remain the most hurtful. Many times my parents were told that their lack of proficiency in English would doom them from success and from any self-worth. They were also ostracized for holding on to their Vietnamese culture and were persuaded to assimilate to the American culture. The accumulation of these events reinforced the idea that being different, in this case Vietnamese, was negative. As far as I was concerned, my family was my only community. It was only within my family that I felt the sense of security, love, support, and, most importantly, connection. After all, I was just a "Gook" like my parents.

Yet I experienced support and love at school. I can trace this feeling all the way back to third grade. I remember how I was constantly praised for being so bright, even before turning in my first assignment. This did not send alarms to my brain. As a student, I felt great. I felt validated. But looking back on it now, there are alarms going off for me. Why? Because now I wonder if I was being labeled as a model student, a positive stereotype. Many Americans have held positive stereotypes about Asians and their work/study ethic, and making these stereotypes prior to a person's performance can create the possibility of drowning in the pressure of high expectations. Teachers have always had unreasonably high expectations for me. Although I did not experience this as pressure, I do feel that I have been robbed of the equal chance to prove myself, to see my mistakes and grow. I feel that I have so much to give, but my audience is content with what they "know" of me (which is usually built upon assumptions). I was never given the chance to work for the standing ovation; nor was I given the privilege of criticism.

At the personal level, the model minority stereotype has denied me human dignity, individuality, and the acknowledgment of my own strengths and weaknesses. I feel that I have been prejudged in this fictitious view of Asian Americans. These positive portrayals depict Asians as so flawless that they are robbed of any humanity. Some may feel indifferent to my story or ask if I really reject the positive stereotype. My only reply is this: positive and negative stereotyping are different sides of the same coin. Both invalidate individuals as human beings and lead to negative consequences.

Isabelle Nguyen

8. Daniel A. Bell, "The Triumph of Asian Americans: America's Greatest Success Story," *New Republic*, July 15, 1985, 24; Louis Winnick, "America's 'Model Minority'," *Commentary* (August 1990): 23.

9. Fox Butterfield, "Why Asians Are Going to the Head of the Class: Some Fear Colleges Use Quotas to Limit Admissions," *New York Times*, August 3, 1986, Educational Supplement, 18.

10. Spencer Rich, "Asian Americans Outperform Others in School and at Work: Census Data Outlines 'Model Minority'," *Washington Post*, October 10, 1985, A1.

11. Peter I. Rose, *Tempest-Tost: Race, Immigration, and the Dilemmas of Diversity* (New York: Oxford University Press, 1997).

12. Richard Rodriguez, "Asians: A Class by Themselves; A Formal Model for Minority Education," *Los Angeles Times*, October 11, 1987, E1. Among William Raspberry's several articles on Asian Americans are "Asian Americans—Too Successful?" *Washington Post*, February 10, 1990, A23; "The Curse of Low Expectations," *Washington Post*, March 4, 1988, A25; and "When White Guilt Won't Matter," *Washington Post*, November 4, 1987, A23.

13. Alice Z. Cuneo, "Asian Americans: Companies Disoriented about Asians: Fast-Growing but Diverse Market Holds Key to Buying Power," *Advertising Age,* July 9, 1990, S2.

14. Rose, *Tempest-Tost,* 4.

15. Ron K. Unz, "Immigration or the Welfare State: Which Is Our Real Enemy?" *Heritage Foundation Policy Review* (Fall 1994): 33.

16. William McGurn, "The Silent Majority: Asian Americans' Affinity with Republican Party Principles," *National Review,* June 24, 1991, 19. Stuart Rothenberg and William McGurn, "The Invisible Success Story: Asian Americans and Politics," *National Review,* Sept. 15, 1989, 17. After the 2000 Presidential elections, in which Asian Americans supported Gore over Bush, the editor of *National Review* changed his mind about the prospects of Asian Americans belonging to the conservative "investor class" rather than representing the liberal "impact of immigration." John O'Sullivan, "Following the Returns: Investor Class or Immigrant Tide?" *National Review,* Dec. 18, 2000, 30.

17. Herbert R. Barringer, *Asians and Pacific Islanders in the United States* (New York: Russell Sage Foundation, 1993), 265.

18. Ibid., 266–67. *See* U.S. Department of Labor, Federal Glass Ceiling Commission, *A Solid Investment: Making Full Use of the Nation's Human Capital* (Washington, D.C.: Government Printing Office, 1995) and Federal Glass Ceiling Commission, *Good for Business: Making Full Use of the Nation's Human Capital* (Washington, D.C.: Government Printing Office, 1995).

19. Richard L. Zweigenhaft and G. William Domhoff, *Diversity in the Power Elite: Have Women and Minorities Reached the Top?* (New Haven, Conn.: Yale University Press, 1998), 140–57.

20. Deborah Woo, *Glass Ceilings and Asian Americans: The New Fear of Workplace Barriers* (Walnut Creek, Calif.: Alta Mira Press, 2000), 26–30.

21. U.S. Civil Rights Commission, *The Economic Status of Asian Americans* (Washington, D.C.: Government Printing Office, 1988), 86.

22. Frank Chin and Jeffrey Paul Chan, "Racist Love," in Richard Kostelanetz, ed., *Seeing Through the Shuck* (New York: Ballantine, 1972), 65; Sumi Cho, "Redeeming Whiteness in the Shadow of Internment: Earl Warren, Brown, and a Theory of Racial Redemption," *Boston College Law Review* 40 (1988): 120; Clair Jean Kim, "The Racial Triangulation of Asian Americans," in Gordon H. Chang, ed., *Asian Americans and Politics: Perspectives, Experiences, Prospects* (Washington, D.C.: Woodrow Wilson Center/Stanford University Press 2001), 39–78; Mari Matsuda, "We Will Not Be Used: Are Asian Americans the Racial Bourgeoisie?" in *Where Is Your Body* (Boston: Beacon Press, 1996), 149–159. Matsuda delivered the talk at the 1990 dinner of the Asian Law Caucus in San Francisco, California, where she first used the phrase.

23. Michael S. Greve, "The Newest Move in Law Schools' Quota Game," *Wall Street Journal,* October 5, 1992, A12. Recognizing the divisive role Asian Americans were being inserted into, the Japanese American Citizens League withdrew its support for proposed legislation attacking affirmative action in 1989. One of the sponsors of the bill had said of the effort: "So, in a way, we want to help Asian Americans, but at the same time we're using it as a vehicle to correct what we consider to be a societal mistake on the part of the United States." Robert W. Stewart, "'Merit Only' College Entry Proposal Failing: Opposition by Japanese Americans to Admissions Policy Change Frustrates GOP Sponsor," *Los Angeles Times,* December 9, 1989, B12.

SCIENCE

READING 50

A World of Their Own

Liza Mundy

As her baby begins to emerge after a day of labor, Sharon Duchesneau has a question for the midwife who is attending the birth. Asking it is not the easiest thing, just now. Sharon is deaf, and communicates using American Sign Language, and the combination of intense pain and the position she has sought to ease it—kneeling, resting her weight on her hands—makes signing somewhat hard. Even so, Sharon manages to sign something to Risa Shaw, a hearing friend who is present to interpret for the birth, which is taking place in a softly lit bedroom of Sharon's North Bethesda home.

"Sharon wants to know what color hair you see," Risa says to the midwife.

The midwife cannot tell because the baby is not—quite—visible. He bulges outward during contractions, then recedes when the contraction fades.

Liza Mundy is a staff writer for the *Washington Post Magazine.*

But now comes another contraction and a scream from Sharon, and the midwife and her assistant call for Sharon to keep pushing but to keep it steady and controlled. They are accustomed to using their voices as a way of guiding women through this last excruciating phase; since Sharon can't hear them, all they can hope is that she doesn't close her eyes.

"Push through the pain!" shouts the midwife.

"Little bit!" shouts her assistant, as Risa frantically signs.

And suddenly the baby is out. One minute the baby wasn't here and now the baby is, hair brown, eyes blue, face gray with waxy vernix, body pulsing with life and vigor. A boy. "Is he okay?" signs Sharon, and the answer, to all appearances, is a resounding yes. There are the toes, the toenails, the fingers, the hands, the eyes, the eyelashes, the exquisite little-old-man's face, contorted in classic newborn outrage. The midwife lays the baby on Sharon and he bleats and hiccups and nuzzles her skin, the instinct to breast-feed strong.

"Did he cry?" signs Sharon, and the women say no, he cried remarkably little.

"His face looks smushed," Sharon signs, regarding him tenderly.

"It'll straighten out," says the midwife.

Presently the midwife takes the baby and performs the Apgar, the standard test of a newborn's condition, from which he emerges with an impressive score of nine out of a possible 10. "He's very calm," she notes as she weighs him (6 pounds 5 ounces), then lays him out to measure head and chest and length. She bicycles his legs to check the flexibility of his hips; examines his testicles to make sure they are descended; feels his vertebrae for gaps.

All in all, she pronounces the baby splendid. "Look how strong he is!" she says, pulling him gently up from the bed by his arms. Which means that it is, finally, possible to relax and savor his arrival. Everyone takes turns holding him: Sharon; her longtime partner, Candace McCullough, who is also deaf, and will be the boy's adoptive mother; their good friend Jan DeLap, also deaf; Risa Shaw and another hearing friend, Juniper Sussman. Candy and Sharon's five-year-old daughter, Jehanne, is brought

in to admire him, but she is fast asleep and comically refuses to awaken, even when laid on the bed and prodded. Amid the oohing and aahing someone puts a cap on the baby; somebody else swaddles him in a blanket; somebody else brings a plate of turkey and stuffing for Sharon, who hasn't eaten on a day that's dedicated to feasting. Conceived by artificial insemination 38 weeks ago, this boy, Gauvin Hughes McCullough, has arrived two weeks ahead of schedule, on Thanksgiving Day.

"A turkey baby," signs Sharon, who is lying back against a bank of pillows, her dark thick hair spread against the light gray pillowcases.

"A turkey baster baby," jokes Candy, lying next to her.

"A perfect baby," says the midwife.

"A perfect baby," says the midwife's assistant.

But there is perfect and there is perfect. There is no way to know, yet, whether Gauvin Hughes McCullough is perfect in the specific way that Sharon and Candy would like him to be. Until he is old enough, two or three months from now, for a sophisticated audiology test, the women cannot be sure whether Gauvin is—as they hope—deaf.

Several months before his birth, Sharon and Candy—both stylish and independent women in their mid-thirties, both college graduates, both holders of graduate degrees from Gallaudet University, both professionals in the mental health field— sat in their kitchen trying to envision life if their son turned out not to be deaf. It was something they had a hard time getting their minds around. When they were looking for a donor to inseminate Sharon, one thing they knew was that they wanted a deaf donor. So they contacted a local sperm bank and asked whether the bank would provide one. The sperm bank said no; congenital deafness is precisely the sort of condition that, in the world of commercial reproductive technology, gets a would-be donor eliminated.

So Sharon and Candy asked a deaf friend to be the donor, and he agreed.

Though they have gone to all this trouble, Candy and Sharon take issue with the suggestion that they are "trying" to have a deaf baby. To put it this way, they worry, implies that they will not love their son if he can hear. And, they insist, they will. As Sharon puts it: "A hearing baby would be a blessing. A deaf baby would be a special blessing."

As Candy puts it: "I would say that we wanted to increase our chances of having a baby who is deaf."

It may seem a shocking undertaking: two parents trying to screen in a quality, deafness, at a time when many parents are using genetic testing to screen out as many disorders as science will permit. Down's syndrome, cystic fibrosis, early-onset Alzheimer's—every day, it seems, there's news of yet another disorder that can be detected before birth and eliminated by abortion, manipulation of the embryo or, in the case of in vitro fertilization, destruction of an embryo. Though most deafness cannot be identified or treated in this way, it seems safe to say that when or if it can, many parents would seek to eliminate a disability that affects one out of 1,000 Americans.

As for actively trying to build a deaf baby. "I think all of us recognize that deaf children can have perfectly wonderful lives," says R. Alta Charo, a professor of law and bioethics at the University of Wisconsin. "The question is whether the parents have violated the sacred duty of parenthood, which is to maximize to some reasonable degree the advantages available to their children. I'm loath to say it, but I think it's a shame to set limits on a child's potential."

In the deaf community, however, the arrival of a deaf baby has never evoked the feelings that it does among the hearing. To be sure, there are many deaf parents who feel their children will have an easier life if they are born hearing. "I know that my parents were disappointed that I was deaf, along with my brother, and I know I felt, just for a fleeting second, bad that my children were deaf," says Nancy Rarus, a staff member at the National Association of the Deaf. Emphasizing that she is speaking personally and not on behalf of the association, she adds, "I'm a social animal, and it's very difficult for me to talk to my neighbors. I wish I could walk up to somebody and ask for information. I've had a lot of arguments in the deaf community about that. People talk about 'The sky's the limit,' but being deaf

prevents you from getting there. You don't have as many choices."

"I can't understand," she says, "why anybody would want to bring a disabled child into the world."

Then again, Rarus points out, "there are many, many deaf people who specifically want deaf kids." This is true particularly now, particularly in Washington, home to Gallaudet, the world's only liberal arts university for the deaf, and the lively deaf intelligentsia it has nurtured. Since the 1980s, many members of the deaf community have been galvanized by the idea that deafness is not a medical disability, but a cultural identity. They call themselves Deaf, with a capital D, a community whose defining and unifying quality is American Sign Language (ASL), a fluent, sophisticated language that enables deaf people to communicate fully, essentially liberating them—when they are among signers—from one of the most disabling aspects of being deaf. Sharon and Candy share the fundamental view of this Deaf camp; they see deafness as an identity, not a medical affliction that needs to be fixed. Their effort—to have a baby who belongs to what they see as their minority group—is a natural outcome of the pride and self-acceptance the Deaf movement has brought to so many. It also would seem to put them at odds with the direction of reproductive technology in general, striving as it does for a more perfect normalcy.

But the interesting thing is—if one accepts their worldview, that a deaf baby could be desirable to some parents—Sharon and Candy are squarely part of a broader trend in artificial reproduction. Because, at the same time that many would-be parents are screening out qualities they don't want, many are also selecting for qualities they do want. And in many cases, the aim is to produce not so much a superior baby as a specific baby. A white baby. A black baby. A boy. A girl. Or a baby that's been even more minutely imagined. Would-be parents can go on many fertility clinic Web sites and type in preferences for a sperm donor's weight, height, eye color, race, ancestry, complexion, hair color, even hair texture.

"In most cases." says Sean Tipton, spokesman for the American Society of Reproductive Medicine, "what the couples are interested in is someone who physically looks like them." In this sense Candy and Sharon are like many parents, hoping for a child who will be in their own image.

And yet, while deafness may be a culture, in this country it is also an official disability, recognized under the Americans with Disabilities Act. What about the obligation of parents to see that their child has a better life than they did?

Then again, what does a better life mean? Does it mean choosing a hearing donor so your baby, unlike you, might grow up hearing?

Does it mean giving birth to a deaf child, and raising it in a better environment than the one you experienced?

What if you believe you can be a better parent to a deaf child than to a hearing one?

"It would be nice to have a deaf child who is the same as us. I think that would be a wonderful experience. You know, if we can have that chance, why not take it?"

This is Sharon, seven months pregnant, dressed in black pants and a stretchy black shirt, sitting at their kitchen table on a sunny fall afternoon, Candy beside her. Jehanne, their daughter, who is also deaf, and was conceived with the same donor they've used this time, is at school. The family has been doing a lot of nesting in anticipation of the baby's arrival. The kitchen has been renovated, the backyard landscaped. Soon the women plan to rig a system in which the lights in the house will blink one rhythm if the TTY—the telephonic device that deaf people type into—is ringing; another rhythm when the front doorbell rings; another for the side door. They already have a light in the bedroom that will go on when the baby cries.

In one way, it's hard for Sharon and Candy to articulate why they want to increase their chances of having a deaf child. Because they don't view deafness as a disability, they don't see themselves as bringing a disabled child into the world. Rather, they see themselves as bringing a different sort of normal child into the world. Why not bring a deaf child into the world? What, exactly, is the problem? In their minds, they are no different from parents who try to have a girl. After all, girls can be discriminated against. Same with deaf people. Sharon and Candy have faced obstacles, but they've survived. More than that, they've prevailed to become productive, self-supporting professionals. "Some people look at it like, 'Oh my gosh, you shouldn't have a child who has a disability,'" signs Candy. "But, you know, black people have harder lives. Why shouldn't parents be able to go ahead and pick a black donor if that's what they want? They should have that option. They can feel related to that culture, bonded with that culture."

The words "bond" and "culture" say a lot; in effect, Sharon and Candy are a little like immigrant parents who, with a huge and dominant and somewhat alien culture just outside their door, want to ensure that their children will share their heritage, their culture, their life experience. If they are deaf and have a hearing child, that child will move in a world where the women cannot fully follow. For this reason they believe they can be better parents to a deaf child, if being a better parent means being better able to talk to your child, understand your child's emotions, guide your child's development, pay attention to your child's friendships. "If we have a hearing child and he visits a hearing friend, we'll be like, 'Who is the family?'" says Candy. "In the deaf community, if you don't know a family, you ask around. You get references. But with hearing families, we would have no idea."

They understand that hearing people may find this hard to accept. It would be odd, they agree, if a hearing parent preferred to have a deaf child. And if they themselves—valuing sight—were to have a blind child, well then, Candy acknowledges, they would probably try to have it fixed, if they could, like hearing parents who attempt to restore their child's hearing with cochlear implants. "I want to be the same as my child," says Candy. "I want the baby to enjoy what we enjoy."

Which is not to say that they aren't open to a hearing child. A hearing child would make life rich and interesting. It's just hard, before the fact, to know what it would be like. "He'd be the only hearing member of the family," Sharon points out, laughing. "Other than the cats." . . .

Candy usually signs with both hands, using facial expressions as well as signs. This is all part of ASL, a physical language that encompasses the whole body, from fingers to arms to eyebrows, and is noisy, too: There is lots of clapping and slapping in ASL, and in a really great conversation, it's always possible to knock your own eyeglasses off.

When she drives, though, Candy also signs one-handed, keeping the other hand on the wheel. Chatting with Sharon, she maneuvers her Volvo through Bethesda traffic and onto I-270, making her way north toward Frederick, home to the Maryland School for the Deaf. State residential schools have played a huge role in the development of America's deaf community. Historically, deaf children often left their homes as young as five and grew up in dorms with other deaf kids. This sometimes isolated them from their families but helped to create an intense sense of fellowship among the deaf population, a group that, though geographically spread out, is essentially a tribe, a small town, a family itself.

Now that people are more mobile, families with deaf children often relocate near a residential school for the deaf, where the young children are more likely to be day students. Jehanne is one; today she's waiting for them in a low corridor inside the elementary school building at MSD, petite, elfin, dimpled, with tousled brown hair and light brown, almost amber eyes. Essentially, the baby Sharon is carrying represents a second effort that they're making because the first was so successful. (Candy tried to have their second child, but a year of efforts didn't take.) At her own infant audiology test, Jehanne was diagnosed as profoundly deaf. In their baby book, under the section marked "first hearing test," Candy wrote, happily, "Oct. 11, 1996—no response at 95 decibels—DEAF!"

This afternoon, Jehanne greets her mothers and begins immediately to sign. She has been signed to since birth and, unlike her mothers, has been educated from the start in sign. At five she is beginning to read English quite well; when they're riding in the car, she'll notice funny shop names, like Food Lion and For Eyes. But she is also fluent in ASL, more fluent even than Sharon.

The women have arrived to visit Jehanne's kindergarten classroom, which in most ways is similar to that of any other Maryland public school; the kids are using flashcards to learn about opposites, conducting experiments to explore concepts like wet and dry, light and heavy. The classes are small, and teachers are mostly deaf, which is something new; years ago, even at MSD, deaf people weren't permitted to teach the young kids, because it was believed that sign would interfere with their learning to read. Now that's all changed. Sign is used to teach them reading. They learn science in sign; they sign while doing puzzles, or gluing and pasting, or coloring, or working in the computer lab.

There is a speech therapy class, but it's optional, and a far cry from the ones that Sharon and Candy remember, where laborious hours were spent blowing on feathers to see the difference between a "b" and a "p." In general, Sharon and Candy have tried not to make what they see as the mistakes their own parents did. Sharon, for example, resents having been made to wear hearing aids and denied the opportunity to learn sign, while Candy—who really wanted to try a hearing aid when she was little—was told by her father that she couldn't because it would be expensive and pointless, anyway. Trying to chart a middle course, they let Jehanne decide for herself whether she wanted to try a hearing aid; she did, one summer when attending camp at Gallaudet. It was hot pink. She wore it about a week. . . .

"Do you think this baby's hearing?" Candy asks Sharon afterward, when they are having lunch in downtown Frederick.

"I don't know," says Sharon. "I can say that I hope the baby's deaf, but to say I feel it's deaf, no."

They are talking about an old saying in the deaf community: If the mother walks into a place with loud music, and the baby moves, the baby is hearing. "If you base it on that, I do think it's deaf," says Sharon.

"I just say to myself that the baby's deaf," Candy says. "I talk as if the baby's deaf. If the baby's hearing, I'll be shocked."

"You better be prepared" Sharon tells her. "With Jehanne, I prepared myself. It could happen." Thinking about it, she speculates: "A hearing child would force us to get out and find out what's out there for hearing children. Maybe that would be nice."

Candy looks at her, amazed.

"It's not that it's my preference," says Sharon. "But I'm trying to think of something positive." . . .

In trying to know how to think about Sharon and Candy's endeavor, there are any number of opinions a person might have. Any number of abstract ideas a person might work through in, say, an ethics course. Are the women being selfish? Are they inflicting too much hardship on the child? How does one think of them compared with, say, a mother who has multiple embryos implanted in the course of fertility treatments, knowing that this raises the likelihood of multiple births and, with it, birth defects in some or all of the babies? Morally, how much difficulty can a parent impose on a child in order to satisfy the desire to have a child, or to have a certain kind of child?

A person can think about this, and think about it, but eventually will run up against the living, breathing fact of the child herself. How much difficulty have Sharon and Candy imposed on Jehanne? They haven't deafened her. They've given life to her. They've enabled her to exist. If they had used a hearing donor, they would have had a different child. That child would exist, but this one wouldn't. Jehanne can only exist as what she is: Jehanne, bright, funny, loving, loved, deaf.

And now what about Gauvin, who, at three months, already resembles his sister? He has the same elfin face shape, the same deep dimples when he smiles. On his head is a light fuzz of hair; bulkier now, alert and cheery, he's wearing gray overalls and groovy red leather sneakers. The question that will be answered this February afternoon, at Children's National Medical Center, is whether Gauvin, like Jehanne, is deaf. Whether the coin has landed on the same side twice. By now, Gauvin has had an initial hearing screening, which he failed. They considered this good news, but not conclusive. From there he was referred to this one, which is more sophisticated. The preliminaries take awhile. Sharon lays Gauvin in a crib and a technician applies conductive paste at points around his head, then attaches electrodes to the paste. He needs to be asleep for the test, in which microphones will be placed in his ears and a clicking noise sent through the wires. Through the electrodes, a machine will monitor the brain response. If the waves are flat, there is no hearing. He stirs and cries, so Sharon breast-feeds him, wires dangling from his head, until he falls asleep. The technician slips the microphone in his ear, turns on the clicking noise—up and up, louder and louder—and the two women look at the computer screen. Even at 95 decibels, a sound so loud that for hearing people it's literally painful, the line for the left ear is flat. But there is a marked difference in the right. For softer sounds the line is flat, but at 75 decibels there is a distinct wave. The technician goes to fetch the doctor, and the mothers contemplate their sleeping son, who, it appears, might be neither deaf nor hearing but somewhere in between.

The doctor, Ira Weiss, bustles in; he is a white-haired, stocky man, jovial and accustomed to all sorts of parents, hearing and deaf, happy and sobbing.

The technician points to the wave and suggests that perhaps it represents some noise that Gauvin himself was making. "No," says the doctor, "I think it's not just noise." Sharon looks up at Candy and lets out a little breath. The doctor disappears to get a printout of the results, then returns, reading it. Gauvin, he says, "has a profound hearing loss in his left ear and at least a severe hearing loss in his right ear.

"It does appear," he adds, "that his right ear has some residual hearing. There might be some usable hearing at this time. Given the mother's history, it will probably get worse over time. If you want to take advantage of it, you should take advantage of it now. Right now it's an ear that could be aided, to give him a head start on spoken English. Obviously, he's going to be a fluent signer."

At this stage, Weiss says later, a hearing parent would probably try a hearing aid, in the hope that with it, that right ear could hear something. Anything. A word, here and there. A loud vowel. Maybe just enough residual sound to help him lip-read. Maybe just enough to tell him when to turn his head to watch someone's lips. Hearing parents would do anything—anything—to nudge a child into the hearing world. Anything—anything—to make that child like them. For a similar reason, Sharon and Candy make the opposite choice. If he wants a hearing aid later, they'll let him have a hearing aid later. They won't put one on him now. After all, they point out, Sharon's hearing loss as a child occurred at below 40 decibels, which meant that under certain conditions she could make out voices, unaided. Gauvin's, already, is far more severe than hers. Bundling Gauvin up against the cold, they make their way down the corridor, and into the car, and home, where they will tell Jehanne, and Jan, and friends, and family, a sizable group, really, that wants to know. He is not as profoundly deaf as Jehanne, but he is quite deaf. Deaf enough.

DISCUSSION QUESTIONS

1. What reactions do you have to Sharon and Candy's wish for a deaf child?
2. Would you have wanted them to wish for a child who was not hearing impaired?

READING 51

Disability Definitions: The Politics of Meaning

Michael Oliver

THE IMPORTANCE OF DEFINITIONS

The social world differs from the natural world in (at least) one fundamental respect; that is, human beings give meanings to objects in the social world and subsequently orientate their behavior towards these objects in terms of the meanings given to them. W. I. Thomas (1966) succinctly puts it thus: "if men define situations as real, they are real in their consequences." As far as disability is concerned, if it is seen as a tragedy, then disabled people will be treated as if they are the victims of some tragic happening or circumstance. This treatment

---

Michael Oliver is a professor of disability studies at the University of Greenwich in the United Kingdom.

will occur not just in everyday interactions but will also be translated into social policies which will attempt to compensate these victims for the tragedies that have befallen them.

Alternatively, it logically follows that if disability is defined as social oppression, then disabled people will be seen as the collective victims of an uncaring or unknowing society rather than as individual victims of circumstance. Such a view will be translated into social policies geared towards alleviating oppression rather than compensating individuals. It almost goes without saying that at present, the individual and tragic view of disability dominates both social interactions and social policies.

A second reason why definitions are important historically centres on the need to identify and classify the growing numbers of the urban poor in modern industrial societies. In this process of identification and classification, disability has always been an important category, in that it offers a legitimate social status to those who can be defined as unable to work as opposed to those who may be classified as unwilling to do so (Stone, 1985). Throughout the twentieth century this process has become ever more sophisticated, requiring access to expert knowledge, usually residing in the ever-burgeoning medical and paramedical professions. Hence the simple dichotomy of the nineteenth century has given way to a whole new range of definitions based upon clinical criteria or functional limitation.

A third reason why definitions are important stems from what might be called "the politics of minority groups." From the 1950s onwards, though earlier in the case of alcoholics, there was a growing realisation that if particular social problems were to be resolved, or at least ameliorated, then nothing more or less than a fundamental redefinition of the problem was necessary. Thus a number of groups including women, black people and homosexuals, set about challenging the prevailing definitions of what constituted these problems by attacking the sexist and racist biases in the language used to underpin these dominant definitions. They did this by creating, substituting or taking over terminology to provide more positive imagery (e.g., gay is good, black is beautiful, etc.). Disabled people too have realised that dominant definitions of disability pose problems for individual and group identity and have begun to challenge the use of disablist language. Whether it be offensive (cripple, spastic, mongol, etc.) or merely depersonalising (the handicapped, the blind, the deaf, and so on), such terminology has been attacked, and organisations of disabled people have fostered a growing group consciousness and identity.

There is one final reason why this issue of definitions is important. From the late fifties onwards there was an upswing in the economy and an increasing concern to provide more services for disabled people out of an ever-growing national cake. But clearly, no government (of whatever persuasion) was going to commit itself to a whole range of services without some idea of what the financial consequences of such a commitment might be. Thus, after some pilot work, the Office of Population Censuses and Surveys (OPCS) was commissioned in the late sixties to carry out a national survey in Britain which was published in 1971 (Harris, 1971). Subsequent work in the international context (Wood, 1981) and more recently a further survey in this country, which has recently been published (Martin, Meltzer and Elliot, 1988), built on and extended this work. However, this work has proceeded isolated from the direct experience of disability as experienced by disabled people themselves, and this has led to a number of wide-ranging and fundamental criticisms of it. . . .

THE POLITICS OF MEANING

It could be argued that in polarising the tragic and oppressive views of disability, a conflict is being created where none necessarily exists. Disability has both individual and social dimensions and that is what official definitions from Harris (1971) through to WHO [World Health Organization] (Wood, 1981) have sought to recognize and to operationalize. The problem with this, is that these schemes, while acknowledging that there are social dimensions to disability, do not see disability as arising from social causes. . . .

TABLE 1

SURVEY OF DISABLED ADULTS—OPCS, 1986

Can you tell me what is wrong with you?
What complaint causes your difficulty in holding, gripping or turning things?
Are your difficulties in understanding people mainly due to a hearing problem?
Do you have a scar, blemish or deformity which limits your daily activities?
Have you attended a special school because of a long-term health problem or disability?
Does your health problem/disability mean that you need to live with relatives or someone else who can help look after you?
Did you move here because of your health problem/disability?
How difficult is it for you to get about your immediate neighborhood on your own?
Does your health problem/disability prevent you from going out as often or as far as you would like?
Does your health problem/disability make it difficult for you to travel by bus?
Does your health problem/disability affect your work in any way at present?

This view of disability can and does have oppressive consequences for disabled people and can be quite clearly shown in the methodology adopted by the OPCS survey in Britain (Martin et al., 1988). [Table 1 presents] a list of questions drawn from the face-to-face interview schedule of this survey.

These questions clearly ultimately reduce the problems that disabled people face to their own personal inadequacies or functional limitations. It would have been perfectly possible to reformulate these questions to locate the ultimate causes of disability as within the physical and social environments [as they are in Table 2].

This reformulation is not only about methodology or semantics, it is also about oppression. In order to understand this, it is necessary to understand that, according to OPCS's own figures, 2231 disabled people were given face-to-face interviews (Martin et al., 1988, Table 5.2). In these interviews, the interviewer visits the disabled person at home and asks many structured questions in a structured way. It is in the nature of the interview process that the interviewer presents as expert and the disabled person as an

TABLE 2

ALTERNATIVE QUESTIONS

Can you tell me what is wrong with society?

What defects in the design of everyday equipment like jars, bottles and tins causes you difficulty in holding, gripping or turning them?

Are your difficulties in understanding people mainly due to their inabilities to communicate with you?

Do other people's reactions to any scar, blemish or deformity you may have, limit your daily activities?

Have you attended a special school because of your education authority's policy of sending people with your health problem or disability to such places?

Are community services so poor that you need to rely on relatives or someone else to provide you with the right level of personal assistance?

What inadequacies in your housing caused you to move here?

What are the environmental constraints which make it difficult for you to get about in your immediate neighborhood?

Are there any transport or financial problems which prevent you from going out as often or as far as you would like?

Do poorly designed buses make it difficult for someone with your health problem/disability to use them?

Do you have problems at work because of the physical environment or the attitudes of others?

isolated individual inexperienced in research, and thus unable to reformulate the questions in a more appropriate way. It is hardly surprising that, given the nature of the questions and their direction that, by the end of the interview, the disabled person has come to believe that his or her problems are caused by their own health/disability problems rather than by the organization of society. It is in this sense that the process of the interview is oppressive, reinforcing on to isolated, individual disabled people the idea that the problems they experience in everyday living are a direct result of their own personal inadequacies or functional limitations. . . .

IMPAIRMENT: A STRUCTURED ACCOUNT

Recently it has been estimated that there are some 500 million severely impaired people in the world today, approximately one in ten of the population

(Shirley, 1983). These impairments are not randomly distributed throughout the world but are culturally produced.

> The societies men live in determine their chances of health, sickness and death. To the extent that they have the means to master their economic and social environments, they have the means to determine their life chances. (Susser and Watson, 1971, p. 45)

Hence in some countries impairments are likely to stem from infectious diseases, poverty, ignorance and the failure to ensure that existing medical treatments reach the population at risk (Shirley, 1983). In others, impairments resulting from infectious diseases are declining, only to be replaced by those stemming from the aging of the population, accidents at work, on the road or in the home, the very success of some medical technologies in ensuring the survival of some severely impaired children and adults and so on (Taylor, 1977). To put the matter simply, impairments such as blindness and deafness are likely to be more common in the Third World, whereas heart conditions, spina bifida, spinal injuries and so on, are likely to be more common in industrial societies.

Again, the distribution of these impairments is not a matter of chance, either across different societies or within a single society, for

> Social and economic forces cause disorder directly; they redistribute the proportion of people at high or low risk of being affected; and they create new pathways for the transmission of disorders of all kinds through travel, migration and the rapid diffusion of information and behaviour by the mass communication media. Finally, social forces affect the conceptualisation, recognition and visibility of disorders. A disorder in one place and at one time is not seen as such in another; these social perceptions and definitions influence both the provision of care, the demands of those being cared for, and the size of any count of health needs. (Susser and Watson, 1971, p. 35)

Social class is an important factor here both in terms of the causes of impairments or what Doyal (1979) calls degenerative diseases, and in terms of outcomes, what Le Grand (1978) refers to as long-standing illnesses.

Just as we know that poverty is not randomly distributed internationally or nationally (Cole and Miles, 1984; Townsend, 1979), neither is impairment, for in the Third World at least

> Not only does disability usually guarantee the poverty of the victim but, most importantly, poverty is itself a major cause of disability. (Doyal, 1983, p. 7)

There is a similar relation in the industrial countries. . . . Hence, if poverty is not randomly distributed and there is an intrinsic link between poverty and impairment, then neither is impairment randomly distributed.

Even a structured account of impairment cannot, however, be reduced to counting the numbers of impaired people in any one country, locality, class or social group, for

> Beliefs about sickness, the behaviours exhibited by sick persons, and the ways in which sick persons are responded to by family and practitioners are all aspects of social reality. They, like the health care system itself, are cultural constructions, shaped distinctly in different societies and in different social structural settings within those societies. (Kleinman, 1980, p. 38)

The discovery of an isolated tribe in West Africa where many of the population were born with only two toes illustrates this point, for this made no difference to those with only two toes or indeed the rest of the population (Barrett and McCann, 1979). Such differences would be regarded as pathological in our society, and the people so afflicted subjected to medical intervention.

In discussing impairment, it was not intended to provide a comprehensive discussion of the nature of impairment but to show that it occurs in a structured way. However

> such a view does not deny the significance of germs, genes and trauma, but rather points out that their effects are only ever apparent in a real social and historical context, whose nature is determined by a complex interaction of material and nonmaterial factors. (Abberley, 1987, p. 12)

This account of impairment challenges the notion underpinning personal tragedy theory, that impairments are events happening to unfortunate individuals. . . .

DISCUSSION QUESTIONS

1. Can you list some words that have changed meaning over time?
2. Why must minority groups continue to challenge definitions?

REFERENCES

Abberley, P. (1987). "The Concept of Oppression and the Development of a Social Theory of Disability," *Disability, Handicap and Society,* Vol. 2, no. 1, 5–19.

Barrett, D., and McCann, E. (1979). "Discovered: Two Toed Man," *Sunday Times Colour Supplement,* n.d.

Cole, S., and Miles, I. (1984). *Worlds Apart* (Brighton: Wheatsheaf).

Doyal, L. (1979). *The Political Economy of Health* (London: Pluto Press).

Doyal L. (1983). "The Crippling Effects of Underdevelopment" in Shirley, O. (ed.).

Harris, A. (1971). *Handicapped and Impaired in Great Britain* (London: HMSO).

Le Grand, J. (1978). "The Distribution of Public Expenditure: the Case of Health Care," *Economica,* Vol. 45.

Le Grand, J., and Robinson, R. (ed.) (1984). *Privatisation and the Welfare State* (London: Allen & Unwin).

Martin, J., Meltzer, H., and Elliot, D. (1988). *The Prevalence of Disability Amongst Adults* (London: HMSO).

Shirley, O. (ed.) (1983). *A Cry for Health: Poverty and Disability in the Third World* (Frome: Third World Group and ARHTAG).

Stone, D. (1985). *The Disabled State* (London: Macmillan).

Susser, M., and Watson, W. (2nd ed.) (1971). *Sociology in Medicine* (London: Oxford University Press).

Taylor, D. (1977). *Physical Impairment—Social Handicap* (London: Office of Health Economics).

Thomas, W. I. (1966). In Janowitz, M. (ed.), *Organization and Social Personality: Selected Papers* (Chicago: University of Chicago Press).

Townsend, P. (1979). *Poverty in the United Kingdom* (Harmondsworth: Penguin).

Wood, P. (1981). *International Classification of Impairments, Disabilities and Handicaps* (Geneva: World Health Organization).

READING 52

Cause of Death: Inequality

Alejandro Reuss

INEQUALITY KILLS

You won't see inequality on a medical chart or a coroner's report under "cause of death." You won't see it listed among the top killers in the United States each year. All too often, however, it is social inequality that lurks behind a more immediate cause of death, be it heart disease or diabetes, accidental injury or homicide. Few of the top causes of death are "equal opportunity killers." Instead, they tend to strike poor people more than rich people, the less educated more than the highly educated, people lower on the occupational ladder more than those higher up, or people of color more than white people.

Statistics on mortality and life expectancy do not provide a perfect map of social inequality. For example, the life expectancy for women in the United States is about six years longer than the life expectancy for men, despite the many ways in which women are subordinated to men. Take most indicators of socioeconomic status, however, and most causes of death, and it's a strong bet that you'll find illness and injury (or "morbidity") and mortality increasing as status decreases.

Men with less than 12 years of education are more than twice as likely to die of chronic diseases (e.g., heart disease), more than three times as likely to die as a result of injury, and nearly twice as likely to die of communicable diseases, compared to those with 13 or more years of education. Women with family incomes below $10,000 are more than three times as likely to die of heart disease and nearly three times as likely to die of diabetes, compared to those with family incomes above $25,000. African Americans are more likely than whites to die of heart disease; stroke; lung, colon, prostate, and breast cancer, as well as all cancers combined; liver disease; diabetes; AIDS; accidental injury; and homicide. In all,

Alejandro Reuss is coeditor of *Dollars & Sense.*

the lower you are in a social hierarchy, the worse your health and the shorter your life are likely to be.

THE WORSE OFF IN THE UNITED STATES ARE NOT WELL OFF BY WORLD STANDARDS

You often hear it said that even poor people in rich countries like the United States are rich compared to ordinary people in poor countries. While that may be true when it comes to consumer goods like televisions or telephones, which are widely available even to poor people in the United States, it's completely wrong when it comes to health.

In a 1996 study published in the New England Journal of Medicine, University of Michigan researchers found that African-American females living to age 15 in Harlem had a 65% chance of surviving to age 65, about the same as women in India. Meanwhile, Harlem's African-American males had only a 37% chance of surviving to age 65, about the same as men in Angola or the Democratic Republic of Congo. Among both African-American men and women, infectious diseases and diseases of the circulatory system were the prime causes of high mortality.

It takes more income to achieve a given life expectancy in a rich country like the United States than it does to achieve the same life expectancy in a less affluent country. So the higher money income of a low-income person in the United States, compared to a middle-income person in a poor country, does not necessarily translate into a longer life span. The average income per person in African-American families, for example, is more than five times the per capita income of El Salvador. The life expectancy for African-American men in the United States, however, is only about 67 years, the same as the average life expectancy for men in El Salvador.

HEALTH INEQUALITIES IN THE UNITED STATES ARE NOT JUST ABOUT ACCESS TO HEALTH CARE

Nearly one-sixth of the U.S. population lacks health insurance, including about 44% of poor people. A poor adult with a health problem is only half as likely to see a doctor as a high-income adult. Adults living in low-income areas are more than twice as likely to be hospitalized for a health problem that could have been effectively treated with timely out-patient care, compared with adults living in high-income areas. Obviously, lack of access to health care is a major health problem.

But so are environmental and occupational hazards; communicable diseases; homicide and firearm-related injuries; and smoking, alcohol consumption, lack of exercise, and other risk factors. These dangers all tend to affect lower-income people more than higher-income, less educated people more than more-educated, and people of color more than whites. African-American children are more than twice as likely as white children to be hospitalized for asthma, which is linked to air pollution. Poor men are nearly six times as likely as high-income men to have elevated blood-lead levels, which reflect both residential and workplace environmental hazards. African-American men are more than seven times as likely to fall victim to homicide as white men; African-American women, more than four times as likely as white women. The less education someone has, the more likely they are to smoke or to drink heavily. The lower someone's income, the less likely they are to get regular exercise.

Michael Marmot, a pioneer in the study of social inequality and health, notes that so-called diseases of affluence—disorders, like heart disease, associated with high calorie and high-fat diets, lack of physical activity, etc.—are most prevalent among the least affluent people in rich societies. While recognizing the role of such "behavioral" risk factors as smoking in producing poor health, he argues, "It is not sufficient . . . to ask what contribution smoking makes to generating the social gradient in ill health, but we must ask, why is there a social gradient in smoking?" What appear to be individual "lifestyle" decisions often reflect a broader social epidemiology.

GREATER INCOME INEQUALITY GOES HAND IN HAND WITH POORER HEALTH

Numerous studies suggest that the more unequal the income distribution in a country, state, or city,

the lower the life expectancies for people at all income levels. One study published in the *American Journal of Public Health,* for example, shows that U.S. metropolitan areas with low per capita incomes and low levels of income inequality have lower mortality rates than areas with high median incomes and high levels of income inequality. Meanwhile, for a given per capita income range, mortality rates always decline as inequality declines.

R. G. Wilkinson, perhaps the researcher most responsible for relating health outcomes to overall levels of inequality (rather than individual income levels), argues that greater income inequality causes worse health outcomes independent of its effects on poverty. Wilkinson and his associates suggest several explanations for this relationship. First, the bigger the income gap between rich and poor, the less inclined the well off are to pay taxes for public services they either do not use or use in low proportion to the taxes they pay. Lower spending on public hospitals, schools, and other basic services does not affect wealthy people's life expectancies very much, but it affects poor people's life expectancies a great deal. Second, the bigger the income gap, the lower the overall level of social cohesion. High levels of social cohesion are associated with good health outcomes for several reasons. For example, people in highly cohesive societies are more likely to be active in their communities, reducing social isolation, a known health risk factor. (See Thad Williamson, "Social Movements Are Good for Your Health")

Numerous researchers have criticized Wilkinson's conclusions, arguing that the real reason income inequality tends to be associated with worse health outcomes is that it is associated with higher rates of poverty. But even if they are right and income inequality causes worse health simply by bringing about greater poverty, that hardly makes for a defense of inequality. Poverty and inequality are like partners in crime. "[W]hether public policy focuses primarily on the elimination of poverty or on reduction in income disparity," argue Wilkinson critics Kevin Fiscella and Peter Franks, "neither goal is likely to be achieved in the absence of the other."

DIFFERENCES IN STATUS MAY BE JUST AS IMPORTANT AS INCOME LEVELS

Even after accounting for differences in income, education, and other factors, the life expectancy for African Americans is less than that for whites. U.S. researchers are beginning to explore the relationship between high blood pressure among African Americans and the racism of the surrounding society. African Americans tend to suffer from high blood pressure, a risk factor for circulatory disease, more often than whites. Moreover, studies have found that, when confronted with racism, African Americans suffer larger and longer-lasting increases in blood pressure than when faced with other stressful situations. Broader surveys relating blood pressure in African Americans to perceived instances of racial discrimination have yielded complex results, depending on social class, gender, and other factors.

Stresses cascade down social hierarchies and accumulate among the least empowered. Even researchers focusing on social inequality and health, however, have been surprised by the large effects on mortality. Over 30 years ago, Michael Marmot and his associates undertook a landmark study, known as Whitehall I, of health among British civil servants. Since the civil servants shared many characteristics regardless of job classification—an office work environment, a high degree of job security, etc.—the researchers expected to find only modest health differences among them. To their surprise, the study revealed a sharp increase in mortality with each step down the job hierarchy—even from the highest grade to the second highest. Over ten years, employees in the lowest grade were three times as likely to die as those in the highest grade. One factor was that people in lower grades showed a higher incidence of many "lifestyle" risk factors, like smoking, poor diet, and lack of exercise. Even when the researchers controlled for such factors, however, more than half the mortality gap remained.

Marmot noted that people in the lower job grades were less likely to describe themselves as having "control over their working lives" or being "satisfied with their work situation," compared to those higher up. While people in higher job grades were more likely to report "having to work at a fast pace," lower-level civil servants were more likely to report feelings of hostility, the main stress-related risk factor for heart disease. Marmot concluded that "psycho-social" factors—the psychological costs of being lower in the hierarchy—played an important role in the unexplained mortality gap. Many of us have probably said to ourselves, after a trying day on the job, "They're killing me." Turns out it's not just a figure of speech. Inequality kills—and it starts at the bottom.

DISCUSSION QUESTIONS

1. What explanation can you offer for why the rich are less likely to support public services in communities with a wide income gap between the rich and poor?
2. Why do you think there might be social class differences in smoking, drinking, or exercise?
3. What are all the factors that produce higher illness and mortality rates for poor Americans?

REFERENCES

Lisa Berkman, "Social Inequalities and Health: Five Key Points for Policy-Makers to Know," February 5, 2001, Kennedy School of Government, Harvard University.

Arline T. Geronimus, et al., "Excess Mortality among Blacks and Whites in the United States," *The New England Journal of Medicine* 335 (21), November 21, 1996.

Health, United States, 1998, with Socioeconomic Status and Health Chartbook, National Center for Health Statistics, www.cdc.gov/nchs.

Human Development Report 2000, UN Development Programme.

Ichiro Kawachi, Bruce P. Kennedy, and Richard G. Wilkinson, eds., *The Society and Population Health Reader, Volume I: Income Inequality and Health*, 1999.

Kevin Fiscella and Peter Franks, "Poverty or income inequality as predictors of mortality: longitudinal cohort study," *British Medical Journal* 314: 1724–8, 1997.

Nancy Krieger, Ph.D., and Stephen Sidney, M.D., "Racial Discrimination and Blood Pressure: The CARDIA Study of Young Black and White Adults," *American Journal of Public Health* 86 (10), October 1996.

Michael Marmot, "Social Differences in Mortality: The Whitehall Studies," *Adult Mortality in Developed Coun-*

tries: From Description to Explanation, Alan D. Lopez, Graziella Caselli, and Tapani Valkonen, eds., 1995.

Michael Marmot, "The Social Pattern of Health and Disease," *Health and Social Organization: Towards a Health Policy for the Twenty First Century*, David Blane, Eric Brunner, and Richard Wilkinson, eds., 1996.

Thad Williamson, "Social Movements Are Good for Your Health," *Dollars and Sense*, May/June, 2001.

World Development Indicators 2000, World Bank.

POPULAR CULTURE

READING 53

Generation EA: Ethnically Ambiguous

Ruth La Ferla

Each week, Leo Jimenez, a 25-year-old New Yorker, sifts through a mound of invitations, pulling out the handful that seem most promising. On back-to-back nights earlier this month, he dropped in to Lotus on West 14th Street for the unveiling of a new fashion line, and turned up at the opening of Crobar, a dance club in Chelsea, mingling with stars like Rosie Perez, long-stemmed models and middle-aged roués trussed in dinner jackets. Wherever he goes, Mr. Jimenez himself is an object of fascination. "You get the buttonhole," he said. "You get the table, you get the attention."

Mr. Jimenez, a model, has appeared in ads for Levi's, DKNY and Aldo, but he is anything but a conventional pretty face. His steeply raked cheekbones, dreadlocks and jet-colored eyes, suggest a background that might be Mongolian, American Indian or Chinese. In fact he is Colombian by birth, a product of that country's mixed racial heritage, and he fits right in with the melting-pot aesthetic of the downtown scene. It is also a look that is reflected in the latest youth marketing trend: using faces that are ethnically ambiguous.

Ad campaigns for Louis Vuitton, YSL Beauty and H&M stores have all purposely highlighted models with racially indeterminate features. Or consider the careers of movie stars like Vin Diesel, Lisa Bonet and Jessica Alba, whose popularity with young audiences seems due in part to the tease over whether they are black, white, Hispanic, American Indian or some combination.

"Today what's ethnically neutral, diverse or ambiguous has tremendous appeal," said Ron Berger, the chief executive of Euro RSCG MVBMS Partners in New York, an advertising agency and trend research company whose clients include Polaroid and Yahoo. "Both in the mainstream and at the high end of the marketplace, what is perceived as good, desirable, successful is often a face whose heritage is hard to pin down."

Ambiguity is chic, especially among the under-25 members of Generation Y, the most racially diverse population in the nation's history. *Teen People*'s current issue, devoted to beauty, features makeovers of girls whose backgrounds are identified on full-page head shots as "Puerto Rican and Italian-American" and "Finnish-German-Irish- and Scotch-American."

"We're seeing more of a desire for the exotic, left-of-center beauty that transcends race or class," Amy Barnett, the magazine's managing editor, said. It "represents the new reality of America, which includes considerable mixing," she added. "It is changing the face of American beauty."

Nearly seven million Americans identified themselves as members of more than one race in the 2000 census, the first time respondents were able to check more than one category. In addition, more than 14 million Latinos—about 42 percent of Latino respondents—ignored the census boxes for black or white and checked "some other race," an indication, experts said, of the mixed-race heritage of many Hispanics—with black, white and indigenous Indian strains in the mix.

The increasingly multiracial American population, demographers say, is due to intermarriage and

Ruth La Ferla writes for *The New York Times*.

waves of immigration. Mixed-race Americans tend to be young—those younger than 18 were twice as likely as adults to identify themselves as multiracial on the census.

"The younger the age group, the more diverse the population," said Gregory Spencer, who heads the Census Bureau's population projections branch.

It is no surprise that the acceptance of a melting-pot chic is greater in places like downtown New York, where immigrants and young people flood in. On a recent evening Pedro Freyre, 26, an artist of French, Mexican and Spanish heritage, was strolling there with his cap tilted to accentuate his cheekbones. "We are the new mix," Mr. Freyre said, borrowing the language of the D.J. booth. "We are the remix."

Mr. Jimenez, the model, said that being perceived as a racial hybrid "has definitely opened doors for me." He added, "suddenly there is a demand for my kind of face."

Ahmed Akkad, 44, a New York artist who is Turkish and Albanian, said that being an ethnic composite "sometimes gives you an edge, a certain sexual appeal."

But some multiracial 20-somethings view their waxing popularity with skepticism. "Back home in Minneapolis, I sometimes feel like a trophy," said Ryoji Suguro, a 28-year-old lighting director of Sri Lankan and Japanese descent. "When you're introduced, it's sometimes like, 'Oh, here is my exotic friend,'" said Mr. Sugouo, who shared cocktails with his girlfriend, who is Korean and Caucasian, at Max Fish on the Lower East Side.

Carrie Hazelwood, 30, an art dealer's assistant who is Welsh, Swedish and American Indian, is put off by advertisers' efforts to exploit mixed ethnicity. "They are just trying to cover their bases—casting as if they were solving a math problem," she said.

Mr. Diesel, 36, the star of action-adventure films like "The Fast and the Furious," once downplayed his multiracial heritage, saying in public only that his mother is Irish and his father's background was unknown. But in more recent interviews he has acknowledged that his mixed background has been an asset, allowing him to play all types of roles and ethnicities.

Among art directors, magazine editors and casting agents, there is a growing sense that the demand is weakening for P&G (Procter & Gamble), industry code for blond-haired, blue-eyed models.

"People think blond-haired, blue-eyed kids are getting all the work, but these days they are working the least," said Elise Koseff, vice president of J. Mitchell Management in New York, which represents children and teenagers for ads and television. Instead, Ms. Koseff said, actors like Miles Thompson, 13, who is Jamaican, Native American and Eastern European, are in demand. Miles has appeared on the television show "Third Watch" and will be in ads for Microsoft's Xbox video game player.

As evidence of the trend, Ms. Koseff exhibited a selection of "casting breakdowns," descriptions from television producers of roles to be filled. "Sarah, 16 to 18 years old. Light complexioned African-American. Could be part Brazilian or Dominican," read one request from CBS for its daytime serial "As the World Turns." "Zach, 12 to 14, African-American. Zach's father is Caucasian," stated another, from the producers of "Unfabulous," a pilot for Nickelodeon.

Ethnically ambiguous casting has been slower to make inroads in the fashion world. The casting of multiracial models "is just beginning," said Nian Fish, the creative director of KCD in New York, which produces fashion shows. "Fashion is taking its lead from Hollywood."

One who typifies the trend is Ujjwala, a model from India and the new face of YSL Beauty, a prestigious cosmetics brand. "Ujjwala is a woman of color," said Ivan Bart, the director of IMG Models, which represents her, "but look at her and begin to play a guessing game: Is she Mexican, Spanish, Russian? The fact you can't be sure is part of her seductiveness."

Such is the power of ethnic ambiguity that even megastars like Jennifer Lopez, Christina Aguilera, and Beyoncé Knowles have, from time to time, deliberately tweaked their looks, borrowing from diverse cultures and ethnic backgrounds. Thus, Beyoncé, an African-American, sometimes wears her hair blond; Ms. Lopez, who is Puerto Rican, takes on the identity of a Latina-Asian princess in the latest Louis Vuitton ads, and Christina Aguilera, who is half Ecuadorean, poses as a Bollywood goddess on the cover of the January *Allure,* which arrives on newsstands this week.

Their willful masquerade reflects a current fascination with the racial hybrid, according to Linda Wells, *Allure*'s editor in chief, a fascination the magazine does not hesitate to exploit. "Five years ago, about 80 percent of our covers featured fair-haired blue-eyed women, even though they represented a minority," Ms. Wells said. Today such covers are a rarity. "Uniformity just isn't appealing anymore," she said.

Global marketers like H&M, the cheap chic clothing chain with stores in 18 countries, increasingly highlight models with racially indeterminate features. "For us the models must be inspiring and attractive and at the same time, neutral," said Anna Bergare, the company's Stockholm-based spokeswoman. The campaigns contrast notably with the original marketing strategy of Benetton, another global clothing chain, whose path-breaking 1980s ads highlighted models of many races, each very distinct. These days even Benetton's billboards play up the multiracial theme. In a typical campaign, a young man with Asian features and an Afro hairdo is posed beside a blue-eyed woman with incongruously tawny skin and brown hair with the texture of yarn.

Such a transition—from racial diversity portrayed as a beautiful mosaic to a melting pot—is in line with the currently fashionable argument that race itself is a fiction. This theory has been advanced by prominent scholars like K. Anthony Appiah, professor of philosophy at Princeton, and Evelyn Hammond, a professor of the history of science and Afro-American studies at Harvard. In a PBS broadcast last spring, Ms. Hammond said race is a human contrivance, a "concept we invented to categorize the perceived biological, social and cultural differences between human groups."

More and more, that kind of thinking is echoed by the professional image makers. "Some of us are just now beginning to recognize that many cultures

and races are assimilating," said John Partilla, the chief executive of Brand Buzz, a marketing agency owned by the WPP group. "If what you're seeing now is our focus on trying to reflect the blending of individuals, it reflects a societal trend, not a marketing trend."

"For once," Mr. Partilla added, "it's about art imitating life."

DISCUSSION QUESTIONS

1. Would you agree with La Ferla that it is now fashionable to be bi- or multiracial?
2. Do you think that popular culture's current "fascination with the racial hybrid" will be long-lived or widespread? What forces would promote or discourage it?

READING 54

Patriarchy Gets Funky: The Triumph of Identity Marketing

Naomi Klein

Let's face it, when you're a story line on Friends, *it's hard to keep thinking you're radical.*
       Jay Blotcher, AIDS activist, *New York* magazine,
                                                September 1996

THE MARKETING OF ID

The backlash [from the late 1980s and early 1990s] identity politics . . . did a pretty good job of masking for us the fact that many of our demands for better representation were quickly accommodated by marketers, media makers and pop-culture producers alike—though perhaps not for the reasons we had hoped. If I had to name a precise moment for

---

Naomi Klein is a journalist. She writes a weekly column in *The Globe and Mail* and is a frequent columnist for the *Guardian.*

this shift in attitude, I would say August of 1992: the thick of the "brand crisis" that peaked with Marlboro Friday. That's when we found out that our sworn enemies in the "mainstream"—to us a giant monolithic blob outside of our known university-affiliated enclaves—didn't fear and loathe us but actually thought we were sort of interesting. Once we'd embarked on a search for new wells of cutting-edge imagery, our insistence on extreme sexual and racial identities made for great brand-content and niche-marketing strategies. If diversity is what we wanted, the brands seemed to be saying, then diversity was exactly what we would get. And with that, the marketers and media makers swooped down, airbrushes in hand, to touch up the colors and images in our culture.

The five years that followed were an orgy of red ribbons, Malcolm X baseball hats and Silence = Death T-shirts. By 1993, the stories of academic Armageddon were replaced with new ones about the sexy wave of "Do-Me Feminism" in *Esquire* and "Lesbian Chic" in *New York* and *Newsweek.* The shift in attitude was not the result of a mass political conversion but of some hard economic calculations. According to *Rocking the Ages,* a book produced in 1997 by leading U.S. consumer researchers Yankelovich Partners, "Diversity" was the "defining idea" for Gen-Xers, as opposed to "Individuality" for boomers and "Duty" for their parents.

> Xers are starting out today with pluralistic attitudes that are the strongest we have ever measured. As we look towards the next twenty five years, it is clear that acceptance of alternative lifestyles will become even stronger and more widespread as Xers grow up and take over the reins of power, and become the dominant buying group in the consumer marketplace. . . . *Diversity is the key fact of life for Xers, the core of the perspective they bring to the marketplace.* Diversity in all of its forms—cultural, political, sexual, racial, social—is a hallmark of this generation [italics theirs]. . . . [1]

The Sputnik cool-hunting agency, meanwhile, explained that "youth today are one big sample of diversity" and encouraged its clients to dive into the psychedelic "United Streets of Diversity" and not be afraid to taste the local fare. Dee Dee Gordon, author of *The L. Report,* urged her clients to get into Girl Power with a vengeance: "Teenage girls want to see someone who kicks butt back";[2] and, sounding suspiciously like me and my university friends, brand man Tom Peters took to berating his corporate audiences for being "OWMs—Old White Males."

As we have seen, this information was coming hot on the heels of two other related revelations. The first was that consumer companies would only survive if they built corporate empires around "brand identities." The second was that the ballooning youth demographic held the key to market success. So, of course, if the market researchers and cool hunters all reported that diversity was the key character trait of this lucrative demographic, there was only one thing to be done: every forward-thinking corporation would have to adopt variations on the theme of diversity as their brand identities.

Which is exactly what most brand-driven corporations have attempted to do. In an effort to understand how Starbucks became an overnight household name in 1996 without a single national ad campaign, *Advertising Age* speculated that it had something to do with its tie-dyed, Third World aura. "For devotees, Starbucks' 'experience' is about more than a daily espresso infusion; it is about immersion in a politically correct, cultured refuge. . . ."[3] Starbucks, however, was only a minor player in the P.C. marketing craze. Abercrombie & Fitch ads featured guys in their underwear making goo-goo eyes at each other; Diesel went further, showing two sailors kissing . . . and a U.S. television spot for Virgin Cola depicted "the first-ever gay wedding featured in a commercial," as the press release proudly announced. There were also gay-targeted brands like Pride Beer and Wave Water, whose slogan is "We label bottles not people," and the gay community got its very own cool hunters—market researchers who scoured gay bars with hidden cameras.[4]

The Gap, meanwhile, filled its ads with racially mixed rainbows of skinny, childlike models. Diesel harnessed frustration at that unattainable beauty ideal with ironic ads that showed women being served up for dinner to a table of pigs. The Body Shop harnessed the backlash against both of them by refusing to advertise and instead filled its windows with red ribbons and posters condemning violence against women. The rush to diversity fitted in neatly with the embrace of African-American style and heroes that companies like Nike and Tommy Hilfiger had already pinpointed as a powerful marketing source. But Nike also realized that people who saw themselves as belonging to oppressed groups were ready-made market niches: throw a few liberal platitudes their way and, presto, you're not just a product but an ally in the struggle. So the walls of Nike Town were adorned with quotes from Tiger Woods declaring that "there are still courses in the U.S. where I am not allowed to play, because of the color of my skin." Women in Nike ads told us that "I believe 'babe' is a four-letter word" and "I believe high heels are a conspiracy against women."

And everyone, it seemed, was toying with the fluidity of gender, from the old-hat story of MAC makeup using drag queen RuPaul as its spokesmodel to tequila ads that inform viewers that the she in the bikini is really a he; from Calvin Klein's colognes that tell us that gender itself is a construct to Sure Ultra Dry deodorant that in turn urges all the gender benders to chill out: "Man? Woman? Does it matter?"

OPPRESSION NOSTALGIA

Fierce debates still rage about these campaigns. Are they entirely cynical or do they indicate that advertisers want to evolve and play more positive social roles? Benetton's mid-nineties ads careered wildly between witty and beautiful challenges to racial stereotypes on the one hand, and grotesque commercial exploitation of human suffering on the other. They were, however, indisputably part of a genuine attempt to use the company's vast cultural real estate to send a message that went beyond "Buy more sweaters"; and they played a central role in the fashion world's embrace of the struggle against

AIDS. Similarly, there is no denying that the Body Shop broke ground by proving to the corporate sector that a multinational chain can be an outspoken and controversial political player, even while making millions on bubble bath and body lotion. . . . But for many of the activists who had, at one point not so long ago, believed that better media representation would make for a more just world, one thing had become abundantly clear: identity politics weren't fighting the system, or even subverting it. When it came to the vast new industry of corporate branding, they were feeding it.

The crowning of sexual and racial diversity as the new superstars of advertising and pop culture has understandably created a sort of Identity Identity Crisis. Some ex-ID warriors are even getting nostalgic about the good old days, when they were oppressed, yes, but the symbols of their radicalism weren't for sale at Wal-Mart. As music writer Ann Powers observed of the much-vaunted ascendancy of Girl Power, "at this intersection between the conventional feminine and the evolving Girl, what's springing up is not a revolution but a mall . . . Thus, a genuine movement devolves into a giant shopping spree, where girls are encouraged to purchase whatever identity fits them best off the rack."[5] Similarly, Daniel Mendelsohn has written that gay identity has dwindled into "basically, a set of product choices. . . . At least culturally speaking, oppression may have been the best thing that could have happened to gay culture. Without it, we're nothing."

The nostalgia, of course, is absurd. Even the most cynical ID warrior will admit, when pressed, that having Ellen Degeneres and other gay characters out on TV has some concrete advantages. Probably it is good for the kids, particularly those who live outside of larger urban settings—in rural or small-town environments, where being gay is more likely to confine them to a life of self-loathing. (The attempted suicide rate in 1998 among gay and bisexual male teens in America was 28.1 percent, compared with 4.2 percent among straight males of the same age group.)[6] Similarly, most feminists would concede that although the

Spice Girls' crooning, "If you wanna be my lover, you have to get with my friends" isn't likely to shatter the beauty myth, it's still a step up from Snoop Dogg's 1993 ode to gang rape, "It ain't no fun if my homies can't have none."

And yet, while raising teenagers' self-esteem and making sure they have positive role models is valuable, it's a fairly narrow achievement, and from an activist perspective, one can't help asking, Is this it? Did all our protests and supposedly subversive theory only serve to provide great content for the culture industries, fresh new lifestyle imagery for Levi's new "What's True" ad campaign and girl-power-charged record sales for the music business? Why, in other words, were our ideas about political rebellion so deeply non-threatening to the smooth flow of business as usual?

The question, of course, is not Why, but Why on earth not? Just as they had embraced the "brands, not products" equation, the smart businesses quickly realized that short-term discomfort—whether it came from a requirement to hire more women or to more carefully vet the language in an ad campaign—was a small price to pay for the tremendous market share that diversity promised. So while it may be true that real gains have emerged from this process, it is also true that Dennis Rodman wears dresses and Disney World celebrates Gay Day less because of political progress than financial expediency. The market has seized upon multiculturalism and gender-bending in the same ways that it has seized upon youth culture in general—not just as a market niche but as a source of new carnivalesque imagery. As Robert Goldman and Stephen Papson note, "White-bread culture will simply no longer do."[7] The $200 billion culture industry—now America's biggest export—needs an ever-changing, uninterrupted supply of street styles, edgy music videos and rainbows of colors. And the radical critics of the media clamoring to be "represented" in the early nineties virtually handed over their colorful identities to the brandmasters to be shrink-wrapped.

The need for greater diversity—the rallying cry of my university years—is now not only accepted by the culture industries, it is the mantra of global capital. And identity politics, as they were practiced in the nineties, weren't a threat, they were a gold mine. "This revolution," writes cultural critic Richard Goldstein in *The Village Voice,* "turned out to be the savior of late capitalism."[8] And just in time, too.

MARKET MASALA: DIVERSITY AND THE GLOBAL SALES PITCH

About the same time that my friends and I were battling for better cultural representation, the advertising agencies, broadcasters and global brands were preoccupied with some significant problems of their own. Thanks to freer trade and other forms of accelerated deregulation, the global marketplace was finally becoming a reality, but new, urgent questions were being asked: What is the best way to sell identical products across multiple borders? What voice should advertisers use to address the whole world at once? How can one company accommodate cultural differences while still remaining internally coherent?

For certain corporations, until recently, the answer was simple: force the world to speak *your* language and absorb *your* culture. In 1983, when global reach was still a fantasy for all but a handful of corporations, Harvard business professor Theodore Levitt published the essay "The Globalization of Markets," in which he argued that any corporation that was willing to bow to some local habit or taste was an unmitigated failure. "The world's needs and desires have been irrevocably homogenized," he wrote in what instantly became the manifesto of global marketing. Levitt made a stark distinction between weak *multinational* corporations, which change depending on which country they are operating in, and swaggering *global* corporations, which are, by their very definition, always the same, wherever they roam. "The multinational corporation operates in a number of countries, and adjusts its products and practices to each—at high relative costs. The global corporation operates with resolute constancy—at low relative cost—as if the entire world (or major regions of it) were a single entity; it sells the same things in the same way everywhere. . . . Ancient differences in national tastes or modes of doing business disappear."[9]

Levitt's "global" corporations were, of course, American corporations and the "homogenized" image they promoted were the images of America: blond, blue-eyed kids eating Kellogg's cereal on Japanese TV; the Marlboro Man bringing U.S. cattle country to African villages; and Coke and McDonald's selling the entire world on the taste of the U.S.A. As globalization ceased to be a somewhat kooky dream and became a reality, these cowboy-marketing antics began to step on a few toes. The twentieth century's familiar bogeyman—"American cultural imperialism"—has, in more recent years, incited cries of "cultural Chernobyl" in France, prompted the creation of a "slow-food movement" in Italy and led to the burning of chickens outside the first KFC outlet in India. . . .

It was in this minefield that "diversity" marketing appeared, presenting itself as a cure-all for the pitfalls of global expansion. Rather than creating different advertising campaigns for different markets, campaigns could sell diversity itself, to all markets at once. The formula maintained the one-size-fits-all cost benefits of old-style cowboy cultural imperialism, but ran far fewer risks of offending local sensibilities. Instead of urging the world to taste America, it calls out, like the Skittles slogan, to "Taste the Rainbow." This candy-coated multiculturalism has stepped in as a kinder, gentler packaging for the homogenizing effect of what Indian physicist Vandana Shiva calls "the monoculture"—it is, in effect, mono-multiculturalism.

Today the buzzword in global marketing isn't selling America to the world, but bringing a kind of market masala to everyone in the world. In the late nineties, the pitch is less Marlboro Man, more Ricky Martin: a bilingual mix of North and South, some Latin, some R&B, all couched in global party lyrics. This ethnic-food-court approach creates a One World placelessness, a global mall in which corporations are able to sell a single product in numerous countries without triggering the old cries of "Coca-Colonization."

As culture becomes increasingly homogenized globally, the task of marketing is to stave off the nightmare moment when branded products cease to look like lifestyles or grand ideas and suddenly appear as the ubiquitous goods they really are. In its liquid ethnicity, marketing masala has been introduced as the antidote to this horror of cultural homogeneity. By embodying corporate identities that are radically individualistic and perpetually new, the brands attempt to inoculate themselves against accusations that they are in fact selling sameness.

DISCUSSION QUESTIONS

1. What do you see as the positive and negative consequences of American marketing's adoption of multiculturalism?

2. What are the consequences of the *global* adoption of that marketing theme?

3. Do you have a most favorite or least favorite "diversity" ad? What is it that you love or loathe about the ad?

NOTES

1. J. Walker Smith and Ann Clurman, *Rocking the Ages* (New York: HarperCollins, 1997), 88.
2. *Vogue,* November 1997.
3. "Starbucks Is Ground Zero in Today's Coffee Culture," *Advertising Age,* 9 December 1996.
4. Jared Mitchell, "Out and About," *Report on Business Magazine,* December 1996, 90.
5. Powers, "Everything and the Girl," *Spin,* November 1997, 74.
6. Gary Remafedi, Simone French, Mary Story, Michael D. Resnick and Robert Blum, "The Relationship between Suicide Risk and Sexual Orientation: Results of a Population-Based Study," *American Journal of Public Health,* January 1998, 88, no. 1, 57–60.
7. Robert Goldman and Stephen Papson, *Sign Wars: The Cluttered Landscape of Advertising* (New York: Guilford Press, 1996), v.
8. Richard Goldstein, "The Culture War Is Over! We Won! (For Now)," *Village Voice,* 19 November 1996.
9. Theodore Levitt, "The Globalization of Markets," *Harvard Business Review,* May–June 1983.

Is Race Over?

David R. Roediger

The cover of a rhapsodic 1993 special issue of *Time* showed us "The New Face of America." Within, the newsmagazine proclaimed the United States to be "the first universal nation," one that supposedly was not "a military superpower but . . . a multicultural superpower." Moving cheerfully between the domestic and the global, an article declared Miami to be the new "Capital of Latin America." Commodity flows were cited as an index of tasty cultural changes: "Americans use 68% more spices today than a decade ago. The consumption of red pepper rose 105%, basil 190%." Chrysler's CEO, Robert J. Eaton, best summed up the issue's expansive mood in a lavish advertising spread:

> At the Chrysler Corporation, our commitment to cultural diversity ranges from programs for minority-owned dealerships to the brand-new Jeep factory we built in ethnically diverse downtown Detroit. And our knowhow is spreading to countries from which the immigrants came. We're building and selling Jeep vehicles in China, minivans in Austria and trucks in Mexico. We're proud to be associated with this probing look [by *Time*] at a multicultural America. We hope you enjoy it.[1]

Remarkably, *Time* sustained such euphoria amid many passages confessing to doubts, troubling facts, and even gloom. In the U.S.-led "global village," readers learned, there were more telephones in Tokyo than in the whole of Africa. The "exemplary" Asian American immigrants had succeeded, but at tremendous cost. The host population that benefited from the wonders of "our new hybrid forms" told *Time*'s pollsters that it strongly supported curbs on legal immigration (60 percent to 35 percent). By

a smaller majority, those polled also backed the unconstitutional initiatives being floated in 1993 to prevent the children of noncitizens from acquiring citizenship. One article in this issue of *Time* held that, "with a relatively static force of only 5600 agents [patrolling immigration], the U.S. has effectively lost control of its territorial integrity." Richard Brookhiser's "Three Cheers for the WASPs" fretted that liberty- and wealth-producing White Anglo-Saxon Protestants' values were being elbowed aside as the "repressed" habits of an "ice person." In one of many bows to an older language of race—one key article called intermarriage "crossbreeding"—that the issue claimed to be transcending, Brookhiser lamented that the WASP's "psychic genes" were no longer dominant and revered. The balance sheet on recent immigration was a close one for *Time*: "Though different and perhaps more problematic than those who have come before, the latest immigrants are helping to form a new society."[2]

The ability to keep smiling amid contradictory crosscurrents hinged on the image that looked out at readers from the magazine's cover. She was "Eve," the result of sending the computerized photographs of fourteen models (of "various ethnic and racial backgrounds") through the Morph 2.0 computer software program. With the aid of a multicultural crew of technicians, the program pictured serially the offspring likely to eventuate from various couples. The writers had trouble deciding how seriously we ought to take Eve and the morphing process. The exercise mapped "key facial features" with "pinpoint" accuracy. At the same time, it was portrayed as merely a playful "way to dramatize the impact of interethnic marriage which has increased dramatically in the U.S. during the latest wave of immigration," making for a society "intermarried with children." State-of-the-art technology made "no claim to scientific accuracy," but the magazine presented the results "in the spirit of fun and experiment." The crowning morph ("as in metamorphosis, a striking change in structure or appearance," a writer added) was a miracle and a cover story. The managing editor

---

David R. Roediger is a professor of history at the University of Illinois at Urbana–Champaign.

recalled, "Little did we know what we had wrought. As onlookers watched the image of our new Eve begin to appear on the computer screen, several staff members promptly fell in love. Said one: 'It really breaks my heart that she doesn't exist.' We sympathize with our lovelorn colleagues, but even technology has its limits. This is a love that must forever remain unrequited."[3]

But then again, maybe not. After all, *Time*'s cover proclaimed Eve, who was described there as a mixture of "races," (with a caffe latte skin tone) to be the nation's "new face." The beauty of that face helped to explain why the modern Eve had magazine staffers lining up to join Adam in the ranks of apple pickers. But the Eden that she represented mattered at least as much in accounting for her appeal. In connecting her face to the nation's future, *Time* implied that she is what the United States will look like at that twenty-first-century point when, as they put it, "the descendants of white Europeans, the arbiters of our national culture for most of its existence, are likely to slip into minority status." Not only did Eve reassure us that all will be well when that happens, but also she already existed in cyberspace to mock allegedly outmoded emphases on the ugliness and exploitation of race relations in the United States. The collection of morphed photos carried the headline "Rebirth of a Nation." As Michael Rogin's prescient analysis of the cover gently puts it, the title was perhaps chosen "without . . . full consciousness of its meaning." Unlike the racist film classic *The Birth of a Nation*, in which race mixing is cast as Black-on-white rape, the rebirth-in-progress was (con)sensual, even as it was chastely mediated by technology. Although associations with a fall from grace persist, Eve was decidedly presented as good news. Toni Morrison's reminder that race has often been brutally figured on a Black-white axis stuck out like a sore thumb in the special issue. Her telling warnings that immigrants have historically had to "buy into the notion of American blacks as the real aliens" in order to assimilate fully seemed a dour refusal to join the fun of Eve's cyber-wonderland. Morrison was left describing the United States as

"Star spangled. Race strangled" at the very moment when the computer could show us the end to all that. An article gratuitously attacking the "politics of separation" on college campuses underlined *Time*'s point that it is time to get over racial (and feminist and gay) politics.[4] . . .

Time [is] scarcely alone in arguing that the movement of immigrants, the demographics of intermarriage, and the global consumption of commodities associated with exotic others signal that "race" is over, or at least doomed. The influential website/social movement known as Interracial Voice touts the "intermarried with children" pattern as the key to change. Since, in the view of "Interracial Voice," "political leaders 'of color' and . . . black 'leaders' specifically" prop up the old racial order, the "mixed race contingent" is destined to usher in the "ideal future of racelessness."[5] The journalist Neil Bernstein extols "blond cheerleaders" who claim Cherokee ancestry and the "children of mixed marriages [who] insist that they are whatever race they say they are" as frontline troops "facing the complicated reality of what the 21st century will be.[6] Writing in the *New York Times Magazine*, the critic Stanley Crouch almost precisely anticipates Patterson's basic point, under the title "Race Is Over." Crouch concludes, "One hundred years from today Americans are likely to look back on the ethnic difficulties of our time as quizzically as we look at earlier periods of our history." Although his essay comments on Americans as a "culturally miscegenated people," it is lavishly illustrated with pictures like those in *Time*, serving as "previews" of the future flesh-and-blood individuals who are "Pakistani-African-American," "Russian-Polish Jewish/Puerto Rican," and "Dutch/Jamaican/Irish/ African-American/Russian Jewish." The caption of the 20 pictures is "WHAT WILL WE LOOK LIKE?"[7]

THE CASE AGAINST THE "RACE IS OVER" THESIS

It is not possible to assent to [this] vision of an automatic transition to a raceless nation. The many objections to such a view turn on two difficulties. The first of these is an inattention to change over time, and the second is an absence of discussions of power and privilege. In its conviction that everything is new regarding race, the "race is over" school tends to cut off the present and future from any serious relationship to the past. If, as Alexander Saxton argues, "white racism is essentially a theory of history," Eve announces that we are excused from paying serious attention to either racism or history. *Time*'s special issue does offer a short, rosy, and inaccurate history of immigration, but that history is written in such a distorted way as to leave no scars and set no limits. For example, the glories of U.S. multiculturalism arise, according to *Time*, from the nation's "traditional open door policy" toward immigrants. In fact, of course, the historical Open Door Policy of the United States insisted on free movement of American goods in Asia, while Asian migrants were excluded from the United States on openly racial grounds. If everything is new—*Time* writes, "During the past two decades America has produced the greatest variety of hybrid households in the history of the world"—then doing serious history can itself become a symptom of a mordant commitment to raking over old coals instead of stepping into the nonracial and multicultural sunshine. Significant in this regard is the tendency of the "postrace-ists" to keep using the hoary language of biological race as though it carries no meaning, now or in the future, to speak of crossbreeding and refer to the children of intermarriage as hybrids. Indeed, so sure are some advocates of hybridity that mixing and morphing can dissolve race that they put "race" inside wary quotation marks that (rightly) signal its scientifically spurious status but abandon all wariness when "multiracial" is invoked as a category.[8] Inattention to history leaves discussions of the transcendence of race fully saddled with the very preoccupation with biological explanations that it declares to be liquidated.

Taking history seriously also calls into question the proposition that demographic trends can easily

be extrapolated into the future to predict racial change. Not only do trends shift, but the very categories that define race can also change dramatically. The idea that "crossbreeding" will disarm racism is at least 140 years old. Demographics simply are not always decisive. Southern states in the nineteenth century with large—sometimes majority—black populations and very substantial mixing of the races were *slaveholding* states. In the recent past, California celebrated its move toward becoming a white-minority state by passing a raft of antiblack and anti-immigrant initiatives, becoming as George Lipsitz puts it, "the Mississippi of the 1990's." That the 1996 anti-affirmative action initiative's triumph occurred in a state in which the population was less than 53 percent white but the registered voters were over 80 percent white reminds us that politics matters at least as much as head counts.[9]

At the start of the twentieth century, predictions in which the changed racial character of the United States was plotted and graphed looked very much as they did in the 1990s. Reactions a century ago ranged from a sense of alarm at the threat of "degeneration," of Anglo-Saxon "race suicide," and of "mongrelization," to optimistic rhetoric regarding the creation of a new and invigorated "American race." If immigration continued and mixed marriages spread, the "pure white," "Nordic" domination of the United States was doomed. Immigration from southern and eastern Europe did continue massively for a time, but then it was decimated via political action restricting its flow. Mixed marriages grew dramatically, joining (for example) racially suspect newcomers from Poland, Greece, and Italy with each other and with older groups. But the prediction of racial change never quite became fact. Somewhere along the line, the "new immigrants" from southern and eastern Europe became fully accepted as white. It may be that, as *Time* puts it, "Native American–black-white-Hungarian-French-Catholic-Jewish-American" young people will lead the United States to an "unhyphenated whole." But the "Polish-Irish-Italian-Jewish-Greek-Croatian" offspring of the twentieth century also seemed to hold out that hope. In very many cases they ended unhyphenated, all right, but as whites. We simply do not know what racial categories will be in 2060. As Ruben Rumbaut's and Mary Waters's provocative works show, we do not know how the diverse children imagined in *Time* will be seen or will see themselves in terms of identity. Although white supremacy can certainly exist without a white majority, the question of whether such a majority might yet be cobbled together through the twenty-first century remains. These questions . . . are political ones, and even Morph 2.0 cannot answer them.[10]

The important recent work of the population specialists Sharon M. Lee, Barry Edmonston, and Jeffrey Passel underlines this point. Their projections for the year 2100 show a U.S. population 34 percent mixed race, up from about 8 percent today. (Less than a third of the latter percentage actually chose the new "multiracial" category on the 2000 census.) The Asian American/multiple-origin population, in these estimates, will rise to 42 million in the next century, rivaling in size the 56 million U.S. residents whose ancestry is "purely" Asian. Among Latinos, the 184 million persons of Latino/multiple-origin ancestry will vastly outnumber the 77 million whose ancestry is Latino on both sides. Among African Americans, lower rates of intermarriage will result in 66 million persons with African American ancestry on both sides and 39 million persons of African American/multiple-origin descent. Among "whites," the "pure" population is projected also to outnumber the white/multiple-origin one by 165 million to 90 million. Even though all of the "purities" are laughable historically, and although the new century will surely surprise us in many ways, the study's broader implications are vital. As the authors emphasize, the answer to whether there might be 77 million, or fewer, or three times that many Latinos in 2100 will be decided historically and politically, not just demographically. Particularly important will be the actions and consciousness of those whom Cherrie Moraga calls "21st century mestizos"—those "born of two parents of color of different races and/or

ethnicities." At issue too is whether the projected relative "purity" of Black-white racial categories will make that divide more rather than less salient or leave the 66 million residents with African American ancestry on both sides in a particularly exposed racial position.[11]

Eve leaves studiously vague the possibility that the "new face" of the United States might stay white. She is, the editor tells us, 35 percent southern European and 15 percent Anglo-Saxon but also 17.5 percent Middle Eastern and 7.5 percent Hispanic. Thus, in the curious racelessness that *Time* proposes, Eve remains white even as the text chatters about the nonwhite-majority nation of the future. Chicana students in my classes sometimes see Eve's picture as that of a chicana; Puerto Rican students see her as Puerto Rican; Italian Americans likewise take her as their own. When a new Betty Crocker was introduced as the "mythic spokesperson" for baking products in 1996, the General Mills Corporation's icon morphed into a figure that looks very much like Eve. Her creators announced the marketing value of the figure's ambiguity clearly: "Women of different backgrounds will see someone different: Native American, African-American, Hispanic, Caucasian."[12]

More subtle are the ways in which Eve's seductiveness blurs the line between present and future. Eve appealingly appears—but in cyberspace, not in time. She belongs in some sense to the present, insofar as she is already used to mock antiracist initiatives as anachronistic and wrong. However, Eve exists in 2050, or maybe 2060 or 2100. Those who conjure her up thus ask us to practice (or abandon) the politics of racial justice in the shadow of someone who does not exist. This problem is exacerbated by the fact that white residents of the United States *believe* that whites are a minority in the United States. In a 1996 poll, white respondents estimated whites in the United States population at 49.9 percent. The accurate figure was 74 percent. They thought that the United States was 23.8 percent African American, twice the enumerated Black population. At 10.8 percent, Asian Americans existed in the white psyche in 3½ times their numbers in the census. Hispanics were imagined to constitute 14.7 percent of the population; they represent 9.5 percent. Such misperceptions clearly fueled the anti-immigrant initiatives of the 1990s. Lovable as Eve seemed to the editors, *Time*'s special issue remained equivocal at best on favoring relatively open immigration, and its collapsing of present and future in Eve made nativist folklore credible.[13] . . .

[The] attitudinal shifts, which underpin "race is over" arguments, are suspect for three reasons. One is that racist practices may function despite reported shifts in attitude, and segregation in housing is perhaps the most dramatic example. Second, studies sometimes presume that white respondents are the experts on changing racial attitudes and practices. Polls among people of color may tell a different story. In a recent poll conducted in the Chicago area, for example, 61 percent of white respondents thought that there was "fairly little," "almost none," or no hiring discrimination against Blacks. Only 19 percent of Black respondents agreed; and 43 percent reported believing that there was a "great deal" of discrimination.[14] Finally, although racism may no longer be exhibited openly in political discourse, it is not so decisively defeated in the culture. Huge numbers of whites, for example, tell pollsters that Blacks are relatively lazy. When Charles Murray wrote a proposal for the racist tract he coauthored, *The Bell Curve,* he reportedly promised that it would cause many whites to "feel better about things they already think but do not know how to say." The huge sales of the book combine with polling data to suggest that he was not entirely wrong.[15] In justifying its own interest in *The Bell Curve, The New Republic* offered the striking editorial opinion that "the notion that there might be resilient ethnic difference in intelligence is not, we believe, an inherently racist notion."[16] . . .

A final way in which the "race is over" stance ignores existing inequalities is more subtle. In declaring race to be utterly malleable, proponents of this idea often then turn to gender and sexuality as the "real" differences on which the future is to be founded. *Time,* as Michael Rogin observes, rejected

one image produced by Morph 2.0. Because it showed a "distinctly feminine face—sitting atop a muscular neck and hairy chest," the article proclaimed, "Back to the mouse on that one." The insistence on Eve as a love object and on "intermarriage" and "breeding" as the antidotes to racial division defines a future sexual and gender universe as static as the racial frontier is dynamic. Variations on this theme play themselves out more broadly in the abandonment of attempts to build coalitions that address racism and sexism together and in the striking coexistence of usually masculine challenges to the color line with homophobic rants in hip-hop.[17]

DISCUSSION QUESTIONS

1. What do you think is the appeal of the argument that in America, "race is over"?
2. What do you think the racial categories will be in 2060? What is your rationale for this conclusion?

NOTES

1. All citations here and in nn. 2, 3, and 4 below are in *Time* 142 (Fall 1993), a special issue not in weekly sequence. On the "universal nation" and "open door," see Editors, "America's Immigrant Challenge," 3, quoting Ben J. Wattenberg; Pico Tyer, "The Global Village Finally Arrives," 87, quoting Federico Mayor Zaragoza on "superpower"; Cathy Booth, "The Capital of Latin America: Miami," 82; Robert Eaton in Chrysler advertisement at 13. On "special issues" of popular magazines, nativism, and gender, see Lauren Berlant, *The Queen of America Goes to Washington City: Essays on Sex and Citizenship* (Durham: Duke University Press, 1997), 196.
2. Tyer, "Global Village," 87; James Walsh, "The Perils of Success," 55; Bruce W. Nelan, "Not Quite So Welcome Anymore," 10–13; Michael Walsh, "The Shadow of the Law," 17; Richard Brookhiser, "Three Cheers for the WASPs," 78–79; Editors, "America's Immigrant Challenge," 6. On efforts to end "birthright citizenship" in the United States in the 1990s, see Dorothy E. Roberts, "Who May Give Birth to Citizens: Reproduction, Eugenics, and Immigration," in Juan F. Perea's important collection *Immigrants Out! The New Nativism and the Anti-Immigrant Impulse in the United States* (New York: New York University Press, 1997), 208 and 205–19 passim.

3. "Rebirth of a Nation, Computer-Style," 66; James Gaines, "From the Managing Editor," 2; Jill Smolowe, "Intermarried . . . With Children," 64–65.

4. Front cover, Editors, "America's Immigrant Challenge," 5; "Rebirth of the Nation," 66. On *The Birth of a Nation,* see Michael Rogin, "'The Sword Became a Flashing Vision': D. W. Griffith's *The Birth of a Nation,*" in Robert Lang, ed., *The Birth of a Nation* (New Brunswick, NJ: Rutgers University Press, 1994), 250–93; Toni Morrison, "On the Backs of Blacks," 57; William A. Henry III, "The Politics of Separation," 73–74. For Michael Rogin, see his *Blackface, White Noise: Jewish Immigrants in the Hollywood Melting Pot* (Berkeley: University of California Press, 1996), 7–8 and 76–79.

5. See the Interracial Voice website for September–October 1996 at http://www.com/~intvoice/.

6. Neil Bernstein, "Goin' Gangsta, Choosin' Cholita," as reprinted in *Utne Reader* (March–April 1995), 87–90, from *West,* a supplement to the *San Jose Mercury News.*

7. Molly O'Neill, "Hip-Hop at the Mall," *New York Times Magazine* (January 9, 1994), 43; Stanley Crouch, "Race Is Over: Black, White, Red, Yellow—Same Difference," *New York Times Magazine* (September 29, 1996), 170–71.

8. Alexander Saxton, *The Rise and Fall of the White Republic: Class Politics and Mass Culture in Nineteenth-Century America* (London and New York: Verso, 1990), 390; Smolowe, "Intermarried . . . With Children," 64–65 and the Interracial Voice website; Steven Masami Ropp, "Do Multiracial Subjects Really Challenge Race? Mixed-Race Asians in the United States and the Caribbean," *Amerasia Journal* 23 (1997), 1–16. On the peculiar mixture of race-transcendent claims with crudely essentialist notions of race, see also Josephine Lee's insightful "Disappointing Othellos: Cross-Racial Casting and the Baggage of Race" (Asian American Studies Workshop Series, University of Illinois, Urbana-Champaign, April, 2001).

9. See Lydia Chávez, *The Color Bind: California's Battle to End Affirmative Action* (Berkeley: University of California Press, 1998), esp. 36–37; George Lipsitz, *The Possessive Investment in Whiteness* (Philadelphia: Temple University Press, 1998), 211–34; George Fredrickson, *The Black Image in the White Mind: The Debate on Afro-American Character and Destiny, 1817–1914* (Middletown, CT: Wesleyan University Press, 1987, originally 1971), 120–22.

10. Smolowe, "Intermarried . . . With Children," 65; Stanley Lieberson, "Unhyphenated Whites in the United States," *Ethnic and Racial Studies* 8 (January 1985), 159–80 explores the most extreme case of this identification with whiteness to the exclusion of "any clearcut identification with, and/or knowledge of, a specific European origin" (159); Stanley Lieberson and Mary C. Waters, "The Ethnic Response of Whites: What Causes Their Instability, Simplification, and Inconsistency?" *Social Forces* 72 (December 1993), 421–50; see also Mary C. Waters, *Ethnic Options: Choosing Identities in America* (Berkeley: University of California Press, 1990); Ruben Rumbaut, "The Crucible Within: Ethnic Identity, Self-Esteem and Segmented Assimilation," *International Migration Review* 18 (1994), 748–94.

11. Barry Edmonston, Sharon M. Lee, and Jeffrey Passel, "Recent Trends in Intermarriage and Immigration and Their Effects on the Future Racial Composition of the U.S. Population," paper presented at the "Multiraciality: How Will the New Census Data Be Used?" conference at Bard College (September 2000) and available on webcast at http://www.levy.org; Cherrie Moraga, *The Last Generation: Prose and Poetry* (Boston: South End Press, 1993), 128. See also Joel Perlmann, "Reflecting the Changing Face of America," *Levy Institute Public Policy Brief,* Number 35 (1997); Mia Tuan, *Forever Foreigners or Honorary Whites: The Asian Ethnic Experience Today* (New Brunswick, NJ, and London: Rutgers University Press, 1998), 152–67, and Clarence Page, "Piecing It all Together," *Chicago Tribune* (March 14, 2001).

12. Gaines, "From the Managing Editor," 2; Lee Svitak Dean, "Recipe for a New Betty Crocker," *Minneapolis Star-Tribune* (March 20, 1996), 1.

13. Priscilla Labovitz, "Immigration—Just the Facts," *New York Times* (March 25, 1996); Nelan, "Not Quite So Welcome," 10–12; Editors, "America's Immigrant Challenge," 3–9; Walsh, "Shadow of the Law," 17.

14. Don Hayner and Mary A. Johnson, "In the Workplace: Most Whites See No Hiring Bias, but 82% of Blacks Disagree," *Chicago Sun-Times* (January 12, 1993), 16.

15. Alexander Star, "Dumbskulls," *The New Republic* 4163 (October 31, 1994), 11; Richard J. Herrnstein and Charles Murray, *The Bell Curve: Intelligence and Class Structure in American Life* (New York: The Free Press, 1995). Among several devastating critiques of *The Bell Curve,* see Joe Kincheloe, Shirley R. Steinberg, and Aaron D. Greeson, eds., *Measured Lies:* The Bell Curve Examined (New York: St. Martin's Press, 1996). On the continuing stereotyping of Blacks, especially as lazy, see Martin Gilens, *Why Americans Hate Welfare: Race, Media and the Politics of Antipoverty Policy* (Chicago: University of Chicago Press, 1999), 68–72 and passim, and Joe R. Feagin, *Racist America: Roots, Current Realities, and Future Reparations* (New York and London: Routledge, 2000), 110–11 and 116–17.

16. Editors, "The Issue," *The New Republic* 4163 (October 31, 1994), 9.

17. Rogin, *Blackface, White Noise,* 8; "Rebirth of a Nation," 66–67.

Black Men: How to Perpetuate Prejudice without Really Trying

Barry Glassner

Journalists, politicians, and other opinion leaders foster fears about particular groups of people both by what they play up and what they play down. Consider Americans' fears of black men. These are perpetuated by the excessive attention paid to dangers that a small percentage of African-American men create for other people, and by a relative *lack* of attention to dangers that a majority of black men face themselves.

The dangers to black men recede from public view whenever people paint color-blind pictures of hazards that particularly threaten African-American men: discussions of disease trends that fail to mention that black men are four times more likely to be infected with the AIDS virus and twice as likely to suffer from prostate cancer and heart disease than are white men; reports about upturns in teen suicide rates that neglect to note evidence that the rate for white males crept up only 22 percent between 1980 and 1995 while the rate for black males jumped 146 percent; or explorations of the gap between what middle-class Americans earn and the expenses of maintaining a middle-class lifestyle that fail to point out that the problem is more acute for black men. (College-educated black men earn only as much as white men with high school diplomas.)[1]

The most egregious omissions occur in the coverage of crime. Many more black men are casualties of crime than are perpetrators, but their victimization does not attract the media spotlight the way their crimes do. Thanks to profuse coverage of violent crime on local TV news programs, "night after night, black men rob, rape, loot, and pillage in the living room," Caryl Rivers, a journalism instructor

at Boston University, has remarked. Scores of studies document that when it comes to *victims* of crime, however, the media pay disproportionately more attention to whites and women.[2]

On occasion the degree of attention becomes so skewed that reporters start seeing patterns where none exist—the massively publicized "wave" of tourist murders in Florida in the early 1990s being a memorable example. By chance alone every decade or two there should be an unusually high number of tourists murdered in Florida, the statistician Arnold Barnett of MIT demonstrated in a journal article. The media uproar was an "overreaction to statistical noise," he wrote. The upturn that so caught reporters' fancy—ten tourists killed in a year—was labeled a crime wave because the media chose to label it as such. Objectively speaking, ten murders out of 41 million visitors did not even constitute a ripple, much less a wave, especially considering that at least 97 percent of all victims of crime in Florida are Floridians. Although the Miami area had the highest crime rate in the nation during this period, it was not tourists who had most cause for worry. One study showed that British, German, and Canadian tourists who flock to Florida each year to avoid winter weather were more than 70 times more likely to be victimized at home. The typical victim of crime in Florida, though largely invisible in the news, was young, local, and black or Hispanic.[3]

So was the typical victim of drug violence in New York City in the late 1980s and early 1990s, when some reporters and social scientists avidly implied otherwise. "The killing of innocent bystanders, particularly in the cross fires of this nation's drug wars, has suddenly become a phenomenon that greatly troubles experts on crime," began a front-page story in the *New York Times*. It is "the sense that it could happen to anybody, anywhere, like a plane crash" that makes these attacks so scary, the reporter quoted Peter Reuter from the RAND Corporation. According to the *New York Daily News*, "spillover" crime from the drug wars even affected people in "silk-stocking areas." In fact, a *New York* magazine article revealed, thanks to a crack cocaine epidemic, "most neighborhoods in

---

Barry Glassner is a professor of sociology at the University of Southern California.

the city by now have been forced to deal with either crack or its foul by-products: if not crack houses and street dealers or users, then crackhead crimes such as purse snatchings, car break-ins, burglaries, knife-point robberies, muggings, and murders." TV newscasts, needless to say, breathlessly reported much the same, with pictures at eleven.[4]

One expert eventually became skeptical of the reporting and set out to examine whether New Yorkers were truly at equal and random risk of falling victim to drug-related violence. What Henry Brownstein, a researcher with the New York State Division of Criminal Justice Services, found when he looked at data available from the police was almost exactly the opposite. About two out of one hundred homicides in New York City involved innocent bystanders, and most drug-related violence occurred between people connected to the drug trade itself. When innocent people did get hurt, Brownstein discovered, often they were roughed up or shot at not by drug users but by police officers in the course of ill-conceived raids and street busts.[5]

Drug violence, like almost every other category of violence, is not an equal opportunity danger. It principally afflicts young people from poor minority communities, and above all, young black men. . . .

Who *does* stand a realistic chance of being murdered? You guessed it: minority males. A black man is about eighteen times more likely to be murdered than is a white woman. All told, the murder rate for black men is double that of American soldiers in World War II. And for black men between the ages of fifteen and thirty, violence is the single leading cause of death.[6] . . .

THE NATION'S FOREMOST ANTI-SEMITES

. . . When it comes to race, obscure patterns become accepted as obvious and are put to use in perpetuating racial fears. Consider a scare about black men that has been directed at people like me. As a Jew, I am susceptible to fear mongering about anti-Semitism. I am not as paranoid as the Woody Allen character in *Annie Hall* who hears the word *Jew*

when someone says "did you"; but neither am I among those Jews who, never having experienced anti-Semitism personally, imagine that it vanished from the globe when Germany surrendered in 1945.

In my own life anti-Semitism has been an almost constant presence. Growing up in a small town in the South in the 1950s and 1960s, I was attacked—verbally on numerous occasions, physically a few times—and members of my family were barred from joining particular clubs and living in certain neighborhoods on account of our religion. Throughout my career as a professor as well I have endured anti-Semitic remarks from students, staff, and fellow faculty, and Jewish students have come to me for advice about how to handle bigoted teachers and classmates. My writing also brings me into contact with anti-Semites. Because I have a Jewish-sounding name, when I publish controversial articles in newspapers and magazines I can count on receiving letters that go beyond criticizing my views and accuse me of being part of an international Jewish conspiracy.[7]

So far as I can determine, on none of these occasions was the anti-Semite black. To judge by stories in the news media and reports from advocacy groups, apparently I have a phenomenally skewed sample. Blacks, we have been led to believe, are America's preeminent anti-Semites. When I conducted a search of databases for major U.S. newspapers, magazines, and network news programs for the eight-year period beginning in 1990 the vast majority of stories about anti-Semitism were on two topics: attacks on Jews in Eastern Europe following the demise of communism and anti-Semitism by African Americans. The sorts of anti-Semites I and my students most often encounter—bitter white people—received relatively little attention.

Even their most fanatical cousins went largely unnoticed. In 1993 white supremacists terrorized Jews, blacks, and other minorities in Billings, Montana, for months on end. A swastika appeared on the door of a synagogue, bottles and bricks were tossed at homes of Jewish families, racist and anti-Semitic literature appeared on windshields and in mailboxes. Yet according to a study by the sociologists

Joe Feagin and Hernán Vera of the University of Florida, only four stories on the violence appeared in the nation's news media. "In contrast," Feagin and Vera report, "during the same period more than one hundred national media stories focused on anti-Semitic remarks made by Khalid Muhammad, until then a little-known minister of the small religious group, the Nation of Islam."[8]

Indeed, the coverage of Khalid Muhammad provides a textbook illustration of how a small story, when placed in a heated media environment, can explode into a towering concern. Initially, Muhammad's description of Jews as "hook-nosed, bagel-eatin'" frauds was heard only by the few dozen students who bothered to turn out one night in November of 1993 for his speech at Kean College in Union, New Jersey. During that address Muhammad lashed out at gays, black leaders he disliked, and the "old no-good Pope," about whom he suggested, "somebody needs to raise that dress up and see what's really under there." The intense coverage and commentary that followed focused, however, on his anti-Semitism. For months it went on, with *New York Times* columnist A. M. Rosenthal and *Washington Post* columnist Richard Cohen enjoining black leaders to renounce Muhammad.[9] . . .

. . . [But] the main beneficiaries of the lavish attention directed at demagogues like Khalid Muhammad are the demagogues themselves. Nation of Islam leaders use Jew-bashing to attract the media and pull crowds. Even Louis Farrakhan has been a fixture in the press largely on account of his anti-Semitic remarks, which distinguish him from other, more mainstream black leaders. . . .

MAKERS OF THE NATION'S MOST HAZARDOUS MUSIC

Fear mongers project onto black men precisely what slavery, poverty, educational deprivation, and discrimination have ensured that they do not have—great power and influence.

After two white boys opened fire on students and teachers at a schoolyard in Jonesboro, Arkansas, in 1998 politicians, teachers, and assorted self-designated experts suggested—with utter seriousness—that black rap musicians had inspired one of them to commit the crime. A fan of rappers such as the late Tupac Shakur, the thirteen-year-old emulated massacrelike killings described in some of their songs, we were told. Never mind that, according to a minister who knew him, the Jonesboro lad also loved religious music and sang for elderly residents at local nursing homes. By the late 1990s the ruinous power of rap was so taken for granted, people could blame rappers for almost any violent or misogynistic act anywhere.[10]

So dangerous were so-called gangsta rappers taken to be, they could be imprisoned for the lyrics on their albums. Free speech and the First Amendment be damned—when Shawn Thomas, a rapper known to his fans as C-Bo, released his sixth album in 1998 he was promptly arrested and put behind bars for violating the terms of his parole for an earlier conviction. The parole condition Thomas had violated required him not to make recordings that "promote the gang lifestyle or are anti-law enforcement."

Thomas's new album, "Til My Casket Drops," contained powerful protest lyrics against California governor Pete Wilson. "Look how he did Polly Klaas/Used her death and her family name/So he can gain more votes and political fame/It's a shame that I'm the one they say is a monster." The album also contained misogynistic and antipolice lyrics. Thomas refers to women as whores and bitches, and he recommends if the police "try to pull you over, shoot 'em in the face."[11]

Lyrics like these have been the raw material for campaigns against rappers for more than a decade—campaigns that have resulted not only in the incarceration of individual rappers but also in commitments from leading entertainment conglomerates such as Time Warner and Disney, as well as the state of Texas, not to invest in companies that produce gangsta albums. William Bennett and C. Delores Tucker, leaders of the antirap campaigns, have had no trouble finding antipolice and anti-women lyrics to quote in support of their claim that "nothing less is at stake than civilization" if rappers are not rendered silent. So odious are the lyrics, that rarely do politicians or journalists stop to ask what qualifies Bennett to lead a moralistic crusade on behalf of America's minority youth. Not only has he opposed funding for the nation's leader in quality children's programming (the Public Broadcasting Corporation), he has urged that "illegitimate" babies be taken from their mothers and put in orphanages.[12]

What was Delores Tucker, a longtime Democratic party activist, doing lending her name as coauthor to antirap articles that Bennett used to raise money for his right-wing advocacy group. Empower America? Tucker would have us believe, as she exclaimed in an interview in *Ebony,* that "as a direct result" of dirty rap lyrics, we have "little boys raping little girls." But more reliable critics have rather a different take. For years they have been trying to call attention to the satiric and self-caricaturing side of rap's salacious verses, what Nelson George, the music critic, calls "cartoon machismo."[13]

Back in 1990, following the release of *Nasty As They Wanna Be,* an album by 2 Live Crew, and the band's prosecution in Florida on obscenity charges, Henry Louis Gates confided in an op-ed in the *New York Times* that when he first heard the album he "bust out laughing." Unlike *Newsweek* columnist George Will, who described the album as "extreme infantilism and menace . . . [a] slide into the sewer," Gates viewed 2 live Crew as "acting out, to lively dance music, a parodic exaggeration of the age-old stereotypes of the oversexed black female and male." Gates noted that the album included some hilarious spoofs of blues songs, the black power movement, and familiar advertising slogans of the period ("Tastes great!" "Less filling!"). The rap group's lewd nursery rhymes were best understood, Gates argued, as continuing an age-old Western tradition of bawdy satire.[14]

Not every informed and open-minded follower of rap has been as upbeat as Gates, of course. Some have strongly criticized him, in fact, for seeming to vindicate performers who refer to women as "cunts," "bitches," and "hos," or worse, who appear to justify their rape and murder, as did a track on

the 2 live Crew album that contained the boast, "I'll . . . bust your pussy then break your backbone."

Kimberlé Williams Crenshaw, a professor of law at UCLA, wrote in an essay that she was shocked rather than amused by *Nasty As They Wanna Be.* Black women should not have to tolerate misogyny, Crenshaw argued, whether or not the music is meant to be laughed at or has artistic value—both of which she granted about *Nasty.* But something else also concerned Crenshaw: the singling out of black male performers for vilification. Attacks on rap artists at once reflect and reinforce deep and enduring fears about the sexuality and physical strength of black men, she suggests. How else, Crenshaw asks, can one explain why 2 Live Crew were the first group in the history of the nation to be prosecuted on obscenity charges for a musical recording, and one of only a few ever tried for a live performance? Around this same time, she observes, Madonna acted out simulated group sex and the seduction of a priest on stage and in her music videos, and on Home Box Office programs the comic Andrew Dice Clay was making comments every bit as obscene and misogynistic as any rapper.[15]

The hypocrisy of those who single out rap singers as especially sexist or violent was starkly—and comically—demonstrated in 1995, when presidential candidate Bob Dole denounced various rap albums and movies that he considered obscene and then recommended certain films as wholesome, "friendly to the family" fare. Included among the latter was Arnold Schwarzenegger's *True Lies,* in which every major female character is called a "bitch." While in real life Arnold may be a virtuous Republican, in the movie his wife strips, and he puts her through hell when he thinks she might be cheating on him. In one gratuitous scene she is humiliated and tortured for twenty minutes of screen time. Schwarzenegger's character also kills dozens of people in sequences more graphically violent than a rapper could describe with mere words.[16]

Even within the confines of American popular music, rappers are far from the first violently sexist fictional heroes. Historians have pointed out that in country music there is a long tradition of men doing awful things to women. Johnny Cash, in an adaptation of the frontier ballad "Banks of the Ohio" declares, "I murdered the only woman I loved/Because she would not marry me." In "Attitude Adjustment" Hank Williams Jr. gives a girlfriend "adjustment on the top of her head." Bobby Bare, in "If That Ain't Love," tells a woman, "I called you a name and I gave you a whack/Spit in your eye and gave your wrist a twist/And if that ain't love what is."

Rock music too has had its share of men attacking women, and not only in heavy metal songs. In "Down by the River" amiable Neil Young sings of shooting his "baby." And the song "Run for Your Life," in which a woman is stalked and threatened with death if she is caught with another man, was a Beatles hit.[17]

JUST A THUG

After Tupac Shakur was gunned down in Las Vegas in 1996 at the age of twenty-five much of the coverage suggested he had been a victim of his own raps—even a deserving victim. "Rap Performer Who Personified Violence, Dies," read a headline in the *New York Times*. "'What Goes 'Round . . . ': Superstar Rapper Tupac Shakur Is Gunned Down in an Ugly Scene Straight Out of His Lyrics," the headline in *Time* declared. In their stories reporters recalled that Shakur's lyrics, which had come under fire intermittently throughout his brief career by the likes of William Bennett, Delores Tucker, and Bob Dole, had been directly implicated in two previous killings. In 1992 Vice President Dan Quayle cited an antipolice song by Shakur as a motivating force behind the shooting of a Texas state trooper. And in 1994 prosecutors in Milwaukee made the same claim after a police officer was murdered.[18]

Why, when white men kill, doesn't anyone do a *J'accuse* of Tennessee Ernie Ford or Johnny Cash, whose oddly violent classics are still played on country music stations? In "Sixteen Tons" Ford croons, "If you see me comin'/Better step aside/A lotta men didn't/A lotta men died," and in "Folsom Prison Blues" Cash crows, "I shot a man in Reno

just to watch him die." Yet no one has suggested, as journalists and politicians did about Shakur's and 2 Live Crew's lyrics, that these lines overpower all the others in Ford's and Cash's songbooks.[19]

Any young rap fan who heard one of Shakur's antipolice songs almost certainly also heard one or more of his antiviolence raps, in which he recounts the horrors of gangster life and calls for black men to stop killing. "And they say/It's the white man I should fear/But it's my own kind/Doin' all the killin' here," Shakur laments on one of his songs.[20]

Many of Shakur's raps seemed designed to inspire responsibility rather than violence. One of his most popular, "Dear Mama," was part thank-you letter to his mother for raising him on her own, and part explanation of bad choices he had made as an adolescent. "All along I was looking for a father—he was gone/I hung around with the thugs/And even though they sold drugs/They showed a young brother love," Shakur rapped. In another of his hits, "Papa'z Song," he recalled, all the more poignantly, having "had to play catch by myself/what a sorry sight."[21]

Shakur's songs, taken collectively, reveal "a complex and sometimes contradictory figure," as Jon Pareles, a music critic for the *New York Times*, wrote in an obituary. It was a key point missed by much of the media, which ran photos of the huge tattoo across Shakur's belly—"THUG LIFE"—but failed to pass along what he said it stood for: "The Hate You Give Little Infants Fucks Everyone." And while many mentioned that he had attended the High School of Performing Arts in Baltimore, few acknowledged the lasting impact of that education. "It influences all my work. I really like stuff like 'Les Miserables' and 'Gospel at Colonus,'" Shakur told a *Los Angeles Times* interviewer in 1995. He described himself as "the kind of guy who is moved by a song like Don McLean's 'Vincent,' that one about Van Gogh. The lyric on that song is so touching. That's how I want to make my songs feel."[22]

After Tupac Shakur's death a writer in the *Washington Post* characterized him as "stupid" and "misguided" and accused him of having "committed the unpardonable sin of using his immense poetic talents to degrade and debase the very people who needed his positive words most—his fans." To judge by their loving tributes to him in calls to radio stations, prayer vigils, and murals that appeared on walls in inner cities following his death, many of those fans apparently held a different view. Ernest Hardy of the *L.A. Weekly,* an alternative paper, was probably closer to the mark when he wrote of Shakur: "What made him important and forged a bond with so many of his young black (especially black male) fans was that he was a signifier trying to figure out what he signified. He knew he lived in a society that still didn't view him as human, that projected its worst fears onto him; he had to decide whether to battle that or to embrace it."[23]

Readers of the music magazine *Vibe* had seen Shakur himself describe this conflict in an interview not long before his death. "What are you at war with?" the interviewer asked. "Different things at different times," Shakur replied. "My own heart sometimes. There's two niggas inside me. One wants to live in peace, and the other won't die unless he's free."[24]

It seems to me at once sad, inexcusable, and entirely symptomatic of the culture of fear that the only version of Tupac Shakur many Americans knew was a frightening and unidimensional caricature. The opening lines from Ralph Ellison's novel, *Invisible Man,* still ring true nearly half a century after its publication. "I am an invisible man," Ellison wrote. "No, I am not a spook like those who haunted Edgar Allan Poe; nor am I one of your Hollywood-movie ectoplasms. I am a man of substance, of flesh and bone, fiber and liquids—and I might even be said to possess a mind. I am invisible, understand, simply because people refuse to see me."[25]

DISCUSSION QUESTIONS

1. Do you agree with Glassner that the media depicts black men as the primary source of violence in America? Do you think this has changed since 9/11? Can you provide specific examples to illustrate your position?

2. Why do you think American anti-Semitism is depicted as predominately an African American sentiment?

3. What are your own reactions to rap music?

NOTES

1. Glenn Loury, "Unequalized," *New Republic,* 6 April 1998, pp. 10–11; Janet Hook, "Clinton Offers Plan to Close Health Gap," *Los Angeles Times,* 22 February 1998, p. A20; Pam Belluck, "Black Youths' Rate of Suicide Rising Sharply," *New York Times,* 20 March 1998, p. A1. See also David Shaffer et al., "Worsening Suicide Rate in Black Teenagers," *American Journal of Psychiatry* 151 (1994): 1810–12.

2. Caryl Rivers, *Slick Spins and Fractured Facts* (New York: Columbia University Press, 1996), p. 161; David Krajicek, *Scooped* (New York: Columbia University Press, 1998); Robert Elias, "Official Stories," *Humanist* 54 (1994): 3–8; Bill Kovach, "Opportunity in the Racial Divide," *Nieman Reports* 49 (1995): 2; Franklin Gilliam, Shanto Iyengar et al., "Crime in Black and White," Working Paper, Center for American Politics and Public Policy, UCLA, September 1995; Mark Fitzgerald, "Covering Crime in Black and White," *Editor and Publisher,* 10 September 1994, pp. 12–13; Carey Quan Gelernter, "A Victim's Worth," *Seattle Times,* 28 June 1994, p. E1; Suzan Revah, "Paying More Attention to White Crime Victims," *American Journalism Review* (1995): 10–11; Bruce Shapiro, "One Violent Crime," *Nation,* 3 April 1995, pp. 437, 445–52; Bruce Shapiro, "Unkindest Cut," *New Statesman* 8 (14 April 1995): 23; Gregory Freeman, "Media Bias?" *St. Louis Post–Dispatch,* 14 November 1993, p. B4; Debra Saunders, "Heeding the Ghost of Ophelia," *San Francisco Chronicle,* 4 September, 1995, p. A19.

3. Arnold Barnett, "How Numbers Can Trick You," *Technology Review* 97 (1994): 38–44; Karen Smith, "Tourism Industry Tries to Reduce Visitors' Fears," *Ann Arbor News,* 16 January 1994, p. D5. See also Kim Cobb, "Media May Be Fanning a New Deadly Crime," *Houston Chronicle,* 18 September 1993, p. A1; Bill Kaczor, "Crimes Against Tourists Worry Florida Officials," *Ann Arbor News,* 24 February 1993, p. A7; James Bernstein, "Violence Threatens to Kill Florida's Winter Vacation Business," 2 November 1993, p. A1.

4. Henry Brownstein, "The Media and the Construction of Random Drug Violence," *Social Justice* 18 (1993): 85–103; and my own analysis of Dennis Hevesi, "Drug Wars Don't Pause to Spare the Innocent," *New York Times,* 22 January 1989, p. A1.

5. Brownstein, "The Media and the Construction." See also Maggie Mulvihill and Joseph Mallia, "Boston Police

'Sorry' for Fatal Mistake," *Boston Herald,* 27 March 1994, p. 1; Joe Hallinan, "Misfires in War on Drugs," *The Plain Dealer,* 26 September 1993, p. A17; Andrew Schneider, "Botched Drug Raid Leaves Deep Distrust," *Arizona Republic,* 14 September 1995, p. A1.

6. Ray Surette, "Predator Criminals As Media Icons," in G. Barak, ed., *Media, Process, and the Social Construction of Crime* (New York: Garland, 1994), pp. 131–58; Philip Jenkins, *Using Murder* (New York: Aldine de Gruyter, 1994), p. 156; Bureau of Justice Statistics, "Highlights from 20 Years of Surveying Crime Victims" (NCJ-144525), Washington, DC, 1993; National Center for Health Statistics, *Vital Statistics of the United States* (reports during early and mid-1990s), Washington, DC; Dave Shiflett, "Crime in the South," *The Oxford American* (Spring 1996): 136–41.

7. See also Rebecca Alpert, "Coming Out of the Closet as Politically Correct," *Tikkun* 11 (March 1996): 61–63.

8. Joe Feagin and Hernán Vera, *White Racism* (New York: Routledge, 1995), p. 79.

9. Quoted in Christopher J. Farley, "Enforcing Correctness," *Time,* 7 February 1994, p. 37.

10. Marna Walthall, "Jonesboro Teacher Says Rap Music, School Killings May Be Linked," *Dallas Morning News,* 17 June 1998, p. A5; Timothy Egan, "From Adolescent Angst to Shooting Up Schools," *New York Times,* 14 June 1998, pp. A1, 20; ABC, "World News Tonight," 16 June 1998.

11. Steve Hochman, "Rap Artist Is Jailed over Anti-Police Lyrics," *Los Angeles Times,* 4 March 1998, p. A3; Benjamin Adair, "Jailhouse Rap," *L.A. Weekly,* 13 March 1998, p. 18 (contains lyrics); Steve Hochman, "A Rapper's Risky Challenge," *Los Angeles Times,* 21 February 1998, pp. F1, 20.

12. Investment boycotts: Eric Boehlert, "Culture Skirmishes," *Rolling Stone,* 21 August 1997, pp. 29, 32; David Hinckley, "Rap Takes the Rap for Our Real Problems," *New York Daily News,* 4 June 1996, p. 33 ("civilization" quote). Tucker and Bennett: Judith Weinraub, "Delores Tucker, Gangsta Buster," *Washington Post,* 29 November 1995, C1 (contains Tucker quote); William Bennett, "Reflections on the Moynihan Report," *American Enterprise,* January 1995, pp. 28–32; Frank Rich, "Hypocrite Hit Parade," *New York Times,* 13 December 1995, p. A23; Peter Range, "MM Interview: William J. Bennett," *Modern Maturity* (March 1995): 26–30.

13. Nelson George, *Buppies, B-Boys, Baps, and Bohos: Notes on Post-Soul Black Culture* (New York: HarperCollins, 1992), p. 156; Kevin Chappell, "What's Wrong (and Right) About Black Music," *Ebony,* September 1995, p. 25. For an example of the collaboration that was used for fundraising see William Bennett, Joe Lierberman, and C. DeLores Tucker, "Rap Rubbish," *USA Today,* 6 June 1996, p. A13, which ends with a toll-free telephone number. Those of us who dialed it got a recording that invited us to press 1 for information about the dangers of rap music, 2 for literature on a flat-rate tax proposal, or 3 to contribute money to Empower America. On political alliances against rap see Leola Johnson, "Silencing Gangsta Rap," *Temple Political & Civil Rights Law Review* (October, 1993): no pages listed.

14. George F. Will, "America's Slide into the Sewer," *Newsweek,* 30 July 1990, p. 64; Henry Louis Gates, Jr., "2 live Crew, Decoded," *New York Times,* 19 June 1990, p. A23. "Laughing" quote in Kimberlé Williams Crenshaw, "Beyond Racism and Misogyny," in M. Matusda et al., *Words That Wound* (Boulder, CO: Westview Press, 1993), pp. 111–32. See also James Jones, "Gangsta Rap Reflects an Urban Jungle," *USA Today,* 2 January 1991, p. D13; Hinckley, "Rap Takes the Rap," p. 33; Nelson George, *Hip Hop America* (New York: Viking, 1998).

15. Crenshaw, "Beyond Racism." On the extent of sexism in rap and internal dialogues among rappers about the matter see Tricia Rose, *Black Noise* (Hanover, NH: Weslyan University Press, 1994), and Tricia Rose's review of *A Sister Without Sisters* by Sister Souljah, *Women's Review of Books,* June 1995, pp. 21–22. On overt homophobia and covert homoeroticism in rap see Touré, "Hiphop's Closet," *Village Voice,* 27 August 1996, pp. 59, 66. On the racist subtext in attacks on rap see Amy Binder, "Constructing racial rhetoric," *American Sociological Review* 58 (1993): 753–67; Tricia Rose, "Rap Music and the Demonization of Young Black Males," *USA Today Magazine,* May 1994, pp. 35–36; Jon Pareles, "On Rap Symbolism and Fear," *New York Times,* 2 February 1992, p. B1; Todd Boyd, "Woodstock Was Whitestock," *Chicago Tribune,* 28 August 1994, p. 36.

16. On Dole's remarks see Linda Stasi's column, *New York Daily News,* 5 June 1995, p. 3; "Dole Blasts 'Depravity' in Film, Music," *Facts on File World News Digest,* 8 June 1995.

17. Edward G. Armstrong, "The Rhetoric of Violence in Rap and Country Music," *Sociological Inquiry* 63 (1993): 64–83; John Hamerlinck, "Killing Women: A Pop-Music Tradition," *Humanist* 55 (1995): 23.

18. Milwaukee and Texas incidents: Rogers Worthington, "Gangsta Rap Blamed for Cop's Killing," *Chicago Tribune,* 10 September 1994, p. 4; Elizabeth Sanger, "Change of Venue for Gangsta Rap Debate," *Newsday,* 28 June 1995, p. 31; Chuck Philips, "Texas Death Renews Debate over Violent Rap Lyrics," *Los Angeles Times,* 17 September 1992, p. A1; Jon Pareles, "Tupac Shakur, 25, Rap Performer Who Personified Violence, Dies," *New York Times,* 14 September 1996, pp. A1, 34. Other headline: David Van Biema, "What Goes 'Round . . . ," *Time,* 23 September 1996, p. 40. Tucker continued to take on Shakur after his death: Johnnie Roberts, "Grabbing at a Dead Star," *Newsweek,* 1 September 1997, p. 48.

19. Ford and Cash songs quoted in Armstrong, "Rhetoric of Violence."

20. Quoted in "Obituary: Tupac Shakur," *The Economist,* 21 September 1996.

21. Songs quoted in Christopher Farley, "From the Driver's Side," *Time,* 30 September 1996, p. 70; Donnell Alexander, "Do Thug Niggaz Go to Heaven?" *Village Voice,* 20 September 1996, p. 51.

22. Worthington, "Gangsta Rap"; Natasha Stovall, "Death Row," *Village Voice,* 24 September 1996, pp. 29–30 (contains definition of "THUG LIFE"); Chuck Philips, "Q & A with Tupac Shakur," *Los Angeles Times,* 25 October 1995, p. F1. Songs quoted in Armstrong, "Rhetoric

of Violence." Pareles quote from "Tupac Shakur." On rap being blamed see also Jon Pareles, "On Rap, Symbolism and Fear," *New York Times,* 2 February 1992, p. B1.

23. Kenneth Carroll, "A Rap Artist's Squandered Gift," *Washington Post* National Edition, 30 September 1996, p. 25; Ernest Hardy, "Do Thug Niggaz Go to Heaven," *L.A. Weekly,* 20 September 1996, p. 51. On the content and purposes of gangsta rap see also Eric Watts, "Gangsta Rap as Cultural Commodity," *Communication Studies* 48 (1997): 42–58.

24. "All Eyes on Him," *Vibe,* February 1996.

25. Ralph Ellison, *Invisible Man* (New York: Random House, 1952), p. 1.

LANGUAGE

Racism in the English Language

Robert B. Moore

LANGUAGE AND CULTURE

An integral part of any culture is its language. Language not only develops in conjunction with a society's historical, economic and political evolution; it also reflects that society's attitudes and thinking. Language not only *expresses* ideas and concepts but actually *shapes* thought.[1] If one accepts that our dominant white culture is racist, then one would expect our language—an indispensable transmitter of culture—to be racist as well. Whites, as the dominant group, are not subjected to the same abusive characterization by our language that people of color receive. Aspects of racism in the English language that will be discussed in this essay include terminology, symbolism, politics, ethnocentrism, and context.

Before beginning our analysis of racism in language we would like to quote part of a TV film review which shows the connection between language and culture.[2]

> Depending on one's culture, one interacts with time in a very distinct fashion. One example which gives some cross-cultural insights into the concept of time is language. In Spanish, a watch is said to "walk." In English, the watch "runs." In German, the watch "functions." And in French, the watch "marches." In the Indian culture of the Southwest, people do not refer to time in this way. The value of the watch is displaced with the value of "what time it's getting to be." Viewing these five cultural perspectives of time, one can see some definite emphasis and values that each culture places on time. For example, a cultural perspective may provide a clue to why the negative stereotype of the slow and lazy Mexican who lives in the "Land of Manana" exists in the Anglo value system, where time "flies," the watch "runs" and "time is money."

A SHORT PLAY ON "BLACK" AND "WHITE" WORDS

Some may blackly (angrily) accuse me of trying to blacken (defame) the English language, to give it a black eye (a mark of shame) by writing such black words (hostile). They may denigrate (to cast aspersions; to darken) me by accusing me of being black-hearted (malevolent), of having a black outlook (pessimistic, dismal) on life, of being a blackguard (scoundrel)—which would certainly be a black mark (detrimental fact) against me. Some may black-brow (scowl at) me and hope that a black cat crosses in front of me because of this black deed. I may become a black sheep (one who causes shame or embarrassment because of deviation from the accepted standards), who will be blackballed (ostracized) by being placed on a blacklist (list of undesirables) in an attempt to blackmail (to force

No biographical information available.

or coerce into a particular action) me to retract my words. But attempts to blackjack (to compel by threat) me will have a Chinaman's chance of success, for I am not a yellow-bellied Indian-giver of words, who will whitewash (cover up or gloss over vices or crimes) a black lie (harmful, inexcusable). I challenge the purity and innocence (white) of the English language. I don't see things in black and white (entirely bad or entirely good) terms, for I am a white man (marked by upright firmness) if there ever was one. However, it would be a black day when I would not "call a spade a spade," even though some will suggest a white man calling the English language racist is like the pot calling the kettle black. While many may be niggardly (grudging, scanty) in their support, others will be honest and decent—and to them I say, that's very white of you (honest, decent).

The preceding is of course a white lie (not intended to cause harm), meant only to illustrate some examples of racist terminology in the English language.

OBVIOUS BIGOTRY

Perhaps the most obvious aspect of racism in language would be terms like "nigger," "spook," "chink," "spic," etc. While these may be facing increasing social disdain, they certainly are not dead. Large numbers of white Americans continue to utilize these terms. "Chink," "gook," and "slant-eyes" were in common usage among U.S. troops in Vietnam. An NBC nightly news broadcast, in February 1972, reported that the basketball team in Pekin, Illinois, was called the "Pekin Chinks" and noted that even though this had been protested by Chinese Americans, the term continued to be used because it was easy, and meant no harm. Spiro Agnew's widely reported "fat Jap" remark and the "little Jap" comment of lawyer John Wilson during the Watergate hearings, are surface indicators of a deep-rooted Archie Bunkerism.

Many white people continue to refer to Black people as "colored," as for instance in a July 30, 1975 *Boston Globe* article on a racist attack by whites on a group of Black people using a public beach in Boston. One white person was quoted as follows:

We've always welcomed good colored people in South Boston but we will not tolerate radical blacks or Communists. . . . Good colored people are welcome in South Boston, black militants are not.

Many white people may still be unaware of the disdain many African Americans have for the term "colored," but it often appears that whether used intentionally or unintentionally, "colored" people are "good" and "know their place," while "Black" people are perceived as "uppity" and "threatening" to many whites. Similarly, the term "boy" to refer to African American men is now acknowledged to be a demeaning term, though still in common use. Other terms such as "the pot calling the kettle black" and "calling a spade a spade" have negative racial connotations but are still frequently used, as for example when President Ford was quoted in February 1976 saying that even though Daniel Moynihan had left the U.N., the U.S. would continue "calling a spade a spade."

COLOR SYMBOLISM

The symbolism of white as positive and black as negative is pervasive in our culture, with the black/white words used in the beginning of this essay only one of many aspects. "Good guys" wear white hats and ride white horses, "bad guys" wear black hats and ride black horses. Angels are white, and devils are black. The definition of *black* includes "without any moral light or goodness, evil, wicked, indicating disgrace, sinful," while that of *white* includes "morally pure, spotless, innocent, free from evil intent."

A children's TV cartoon program, *Captain Scarlet,* is about an organization called Spectrum, whose purpose is to save the world from an evil extraterrestrial force called the Mysterons. Everyone in Spectrum has a color name—Captain Scarlet, Captain Blue, etc. The one Spectrum agent who has been mysteriously taken over by the Mysterons and works to advance their evil aims is Captain Black. The person who heads Spectrum, the good organization out to defend the world, is Colonel White.

Three of the dictionary definitions of white are "fairness of complexion, purity, innocence." These definitions affect the standards of beauty in our culture, in which whiteness represents the norm. "Blondes have more fun" and "Wouldn't you really rather be a blonde" are sexist in their attitudes toward women generally, but are racist white standards when applied to third world women. A 1971 *Mademoiselle* advertisement pictured a curly-headed, ivory-skinned woman over the caption, "When you go blonde go all the way," and asked: "Isn't this how, in the back of your mind, you always wanted to look? All wide-eyed and silky blonde down to there, and innocent?" Whatever the advertising people meant by this particular woman's innocence, one must remember that "innocent" is one of the definitions of the word white. This standard of beauty when preached to all women is racist. The statement "Isn't this how, in the back of your mind, you always wanted to look?" either ignores third world women or assumes they long to be white.

Time magazine in its coverage of the Wimbledon tennis competition between the black Australian Evonne Goolagong and the white American Chris Evert described Ms. Goolagong as "the dusky daughter of an Australian sheepshearer," while Ms. Evert was "a fair young girl from the middle-class groves of Florida." *Dusky* is a synonym of "black" and is defined as "having dark skin; of a dark color; gloomy; dark; swarthy." Its antonyms are "fair" and "blonde." *Fair* is defined in part as "free from blemish, imperfection, or anything that impairs the appearance, quality, or character; pleasing in appearance, attractive; clean; pretty; comely." By defining Evonne Goolagong as "dusky," *Time* technically defined her as the opposite of "pleasing in appearance; attractive; clean; pretty; comely."

The studies of Kenneth B. Clark, Mary Ellen Goodman, Judith Porter and others indicate that this persuasive "rightness of whiteness" in U.S. culture affects children before the age of four, providing white youngsters with a false sense of superiority and encouraging self-hatred among third world youngsters.

ETHNOCENTRISM OR FROM A WHITE PERSPECTIVE

Some words and phrases that are commonly used represent particular perspectives and frames of ref-

erence, and these often distort the understanding of the reader or listener. David R. Burgest[3] has written about the effect of using the terms "slave" or "master." He argues that the psychological impact of the statement referring to "the master raped his slave" is different from the impact of the same statement substituting the words: "the white captor raped an African woman held in captivity."

> Implicit in the English usage of the "master-slave" concept is ownership of the "slave" by the "master," therefore, the "master" is merely abusing his property (slave). In reality, the captives (slave) were African individuals with human worth, right and dignity and the term "slave" denounces that human quality thereby making the mass rape of African women by white captors more acceptable in the minds of people and setting a mental frame of reference for legitimizing the atrocities perpetuated against African people.

The term "slave" connotes a less than human quality and turns the captive person into a thing. For example, two McGraw-Hill Far Eastern Publishers textbooks (1970) stated, "At first it was the slaves who worked the cane and they got only food for it. Now men work cane and get money." Next time you write about slavery or read about it, try transposing all "slaves" into "African people held in captivity," "Black people forced to work for no pay" or "African people stolen from their families and societies." While it is more cumbersome, such phrasing conveys a different meaning.

PASSIVE TENSE

Another means by which language shapes our perspective has been noted by Thomas Greenfield,[4] who writes that the achievements of Black people—and Black people themselves—have been hidden in

> the linguistic ghetto of the passive voice, the subordinate clause, and the "understood" subject. The seemingly innocuous distinction (between active/passive voice) holds enormous implications for writers and speakers. When it is effectively applied, the rhetorical impact of the passive voice—the art of making the creator or instigator of action totally disappear from a reader's perception—can be devastating.

For instance, some history texts will discuss how European immigrants came to the United States seeking a better life and expanded opportunities, but will note that "slaves *were brought* to America." Not only does this omit the destruction of African societies and families, but it ignores the role of northern merchants and southern slaveholders in the profitable trade in human beings. Other books will state that "the continental railroad *was built,*" conveniently omitting information about the Chinese laborers who built much of it or the oppression they suffered.

Another example. While touring Monticello, Greenfield noted that the tour guide

> made all the black people at Monticello disappear through her use of the passive voice. While speaking of the architectural achievements of Jefferson in the active voice, she unfailingly shifted to passive when speaking of the work performed by Negro slaves and skilled servants.

Noting a type of door that after 166 years continued to operate without need for repair, Greenfield remarks that the design aspect of the door was much simpler than the actual skill and work involved in building and installing it. Yet his guide stated: "Mr. Jefferson designed these doors . . . " while "the doors **were installed** in 1809." The workers who installed those doors were African people whom Jefferson held in bondage. The guide's use of the passive tense enabled her to dismiss the reality of Jefferson's slaveholding. It also meant that she did not have to make any mention of the skills of those people held in bondage.

POLITICS AND TERMINOLOGY

"Culturally deprived," "economically disadvantaged" and "underdeveloped" are other terms which mislead and distort our awareness of reality. The application of the term "culturally deprived" and third world children in this society reflects a value judgment. It assumes that the dominant whites are cultured and all others without culture. In fact, third world children generally are bicultural, and many are bilingual, having grown up in their own culture as well as absorbing the dominant culture. In many ways, they are equipped with skills and experiences which white youth have been deprived of, since most white youth develop in a monocultural, monolingual environment. Burgest[5] suggests that the term "culturally deprived" be replaced by "culturally dispossessed," and that the term "economically disadvantaged" be replaced by "economically exploited." Both these terms present a perspective and implication that provide an entirely different frame of reference as to the reality of the third world experience in U.S. society.

Similarly, many nations of the third world are described as "underdeveloped." These less wealthy nations are generally those that suffered under colonialism and neo-colonialism. The "developed" nations are those that exploited their resources and wealth. Therefore, rather than referring to these countries as "underdeveloped," a more appropriate and meaningful designation might be "over exploited." Again, transpose this term next time you read about "underdeveloped nations" and note the different meaning that results.

Terms such as "culturally deprived," "economically disadvantaged" and "underdeveloped" place the responsibility for their own conditions on those being so described. This is known as "Blaming the Victim."[6] It places responsibility for poverty on the victims of poverty. It removes the blame from those in power who benefit from, and continue to permit, poverty.

Still another example involves the use of "non-white," "minority" or "third world." While people of color are a minority in the U.S., they are part of the vast majority of the world's population, in which white people are a distinct minority. Thus, by utilizing the term minority to describe people of color in the U.S., we can lose sight of the global majority/minority reality—a fact of some importance in the increasing and interconnected struggles of people of color inside and outside the U.S.

To describe people of color as "non-white" is to use whiteness as the standard and norm against which to measure all others. Use of the term "third world" to describe all people of color overcomes the inherent bias of "minority" and "nonwhite." Moreover, it connects the struggles of third world people in the U.S. with the freedom struggles around the globe.

The term "third world" gained increasing usage after the 1955 Bandung Conference of "non-aligned" nations, which represented a third force outside of the two world superpowers. The "first world" represents the United States, Western Europe and their sphere of influence. The "second world" represents the Soviet Union and its sphere. The "third world" represents, for the most part, nations that were, or are, controlled by the "first world" or West. For the most part, these are nations of Africa, Asia and Latin America.

"LOADED" WORDS AND NATIVE AMERICANS

Many words lead to a demeaning characterization of groups of people. For instance, Columbus, it is said, "discovered" America. The word *discover* is defined as "to gain sight or knowledge of something previously unseen or unknown; to discover may be to find some existent thing that was previously unknown." Thus, a continent inhabited by millions of human beings cannot be "discovered." For history books to continue this usage represents a Eurocentric (white European) perspective on world history and ignores the existence of, and the perspective of, Native Americans. "Discovery," as used in the Euro-American context, implies the right to take what one finds, ignoring the rights of those who already inhabit or own the "discovered" thing.

Eurocentrism is also apparent in the usage of "victory" and "massacre" to describe the battles between Native Americans and whites. *Victory* is defined in the dictionary as "a success or triumph over an enemy in battle or war; the decisive defeat of an opponent." *Conquest* denotes the "taking over of control by the victor, and the obedience of the conquered." *Massacre* is defined as "the unnecessary, indiscriminate killing of a number of human beings, as in barbarous warfare or persecution, or for

revenge or plunder." *Defend* is described as "to ward off attack from; guard against assault or injury; to strive to keep safe by resisting attack."

Eurocentrism turns these definitions around to serve the purpose of distorting history and justifying Euro-American conquest of the Native American homelands. Euro-Americans are not described in history books as invading Native American lands, but rather as defending *their* homes against "Indian" attacks. Since European communities were constantly encroaching on land already occupied, then a more honest interpretation would state that it was the Native Americans who were "warding off," "guarding" and "defending" their homelands.

Native American victories are invariably defined as "massacres," while the indiscriminate killing, extermination and plunder of Native American nations by Euro-Americans is defined as "victory." Distortion of history by the choice of "loaded" words used to describe historical events is a common racist practice. Rather than portraying Native Americans as human beings in highly defined and complex societies, cultures and civilizations, history books use such adjectives as "savages," "beasts," "primitive," and "backward." Native people are referred to as "squaw," "brave," or "papoose" instead of "woman," "man," or "baby."

Another term that has questionable connotations is *tribe*. The Oxford English Dictionary defines this noun as "a race of people; now applied especially to a primary aggregate of people in a primitive or barbarous condition, under a headman or chief." Morton Fried,[7] discussing "The Myth of Tribe," states that the word "did not become a general term of reference to American Indian society until the nineteenth century. Previously, the words commonly used for Indian populations were 'nation' and 'people.'" Since "tribe" has assumed a connotation of primitiveness or backwardness, it is suggested that the use of "nation" or "people" replace the term whenever possible in referring to Native American peoples.

The term *tribe* invokes even more negative implications when used in reference to American peoples. As Evelyn Jones Rich[8] has noted, the term is "almost always used to refer to third world people and it implies a stage of development which is, in short, a put-down."

"LOADED" WORDS AND AFRICANS

Conflicts among diverse peoples within African nations are often referred to as "tribal warfare," while conflicts among the diverse peoples within European countries are never described in such terms. If the rivalries between the Ibo and the Hausa and Yoruba in Nigeria are described as "tribal," why not the rivalries between Serbs and Slavs in Yugoslavia, or Scots and English in Great Britain, Protestants and Catholics in Ireland, or the Basques and the Southern Spaniards in Spain? Conflicts among African peoples in a particular nation have religious, cultural, economic and/or political roots. If we can analyze the roots of conflicts among European peoples in terms other than "tribal warfare," certainly we can do the same with African peoples, including correct reference to the ethnic groups or nations involved. For example, the terms "Kaffirs," "Hottentot" or "Bushmen" are names imposed by white Europeans. The correct names are always those by which a people refer to themselves. (In these instances Xhosa, Khoi-Khoin and San are correct.[9])

The generalized application of "tribal" in reference to Africans—as well as the failure to acknowledge the religious, cultural and social diversity of African peoples—is a decidedly racist dynamic. It is part of the process whereby Euro-Americans justify, or avoid confronting, their oppression of third world peoples. Africa has been particularly insulted by this dynamic, as witness the pervasive "darkest Africa" image. This image, widespread in Western culture, evokes an Africa covered by jungles and inhibited by "uncivilized," "cannibalistic," "pagan," "savage" peoples. This "darkest Africa" image avoids the geographical reality. Less than 20 percent of the African continent is wooded savanna, for example. The image also ignores the history of African cultures and civilizations. Ample evidence suggests this distortion of reality was developed as a convenient rationale for the European and American slave trade. The Western powers, rather than exploiting, were civilizing and christianizing "uncivilized" and "pagan savages" (so the rationalization went). This dynamic also served to justify Western colonialism. From Tarzan movies to racist children's books like *Doctor Dolittle* and *Charlie and the Chocolate Factory*, the image of "savage" Africa and the myth of "the white man's burden" has been perpetuated in Western culture.

A 1972 *Time* magazine editorial lamenting the demise of *Life* magazine, stated that the "lavishness" of *Life*'s enterprises included "organizing safaris into darkest Africa." The same year, the *New York Times*' C. L. Sulzberger wrote that "Africa has a history as dark as the skins of many of its people." Terms such as "darkest Africa," "primitive," "tribe" ("tribal") or "jungle," in reference to Africa, perpetuate myths and are especially inexcusable in such large circulation publications.

Ethnocentrism is similarly reflected in the term "pagan" to describe traditional religions. A February 1973 *Time* magazine article on Uganda stated, "Moslems account for only 500,000 of Uganda's 10 million people. Of the remainder, 5,000,000 are Christians and the rest pagan." Pagan is defined as "Heathen, a follower of a polytheistic religion; one that has little or no religion and that is marked by a frank delight in and uninhibited seeking after sensual pleasures and material goods." *Heathen* is defined as "Unenlightened; an unconverted member of a people or nation that does not acknowledge the God of the Bible. A person whose culture or enlightenment is of an inferior grade, especially an irreligious person." Now, the people of Uganda, like almost all Africans, have serious religious beliefs and practices. As used by Westerners, "pagan" connotes something wild, primitive and inferior—another term to watch out for.

The variety of traditional structures that African people live in are their "houses," not "huts." A *hut* is "an often small and temporary dwelling of simple construction." And to describe Africans as "natives" (noun) is derogatory terminology—as in, "the natives are restless." The dictionary definition of *native* includes: "one of a people inhabiting a territorial area at the time of its discovery or becoming familiar to a foreigner; one belonging to a people having a less complex civilization." Therefore, use of "native," like use of "pagan" often implies a value judgment of white superiority.

QUALIFYING ADJECTIVES

Words that would normally have positive connotations can have entirely different meanings when used in a racial context. For example, C. L. Sulzberger, the columnist of the *New York Times,* wrote in January 1975, about conversations he had with two people in Namibia. One was the white South African administrator of the country and the other a member of SWAPO, the Namibian liberation movement. The first is described as "Dirk Mudge, who as senior elected member of the administration is a kind of acting Prime Minister. . . ." But the second person is introduced as "Daniel Tijongarero, an intelligent Herero tribesman who is a member of SWAPO. . . ." What need was there for Sulzberger to state that Daniel Tijongarero is "intelligent"? Why not also state that Dirk Mudge was "intelligent"—or do we assume he wasn't?

A similar example from a 1968 *New York Times* article reporting on an address by Lyndon Johnson stated, "The President spoke to the well-dressed Negro officials and their wives." In what similar circumstances can one imagine a reporter finding it necessary to note that an audience of white government officials was "well-dressed"?

Still another word often used in a racist context is "qualified." In the 1960s white Americans often questioned whether Black people were "qualified" to hold public office, a question that was never raised (until too late) about white officials like Wallace, Maddox, Nixon, Agnew, Mitchell, et al. The question of qualifications has been raised even more frequently in recent years as white people question whether Black people are "qualified" to be hired for positions in industry and educational institutions. "We're looking for a qualified Black" has been heard again and again as institutions are confronted with affirmative action goals. Why stipulate that Blacks must be "qualified," when for others it is taken for granted that applicants must be "qualified"?

SPEAKING ENGLISH

Finally, the depiction in movies and children's books of third world people speaking English is often itself racist. Children's books about Puerto Ricans or Chicanos often connect poverty with a failure to speak English or to speak it well, thus blaming the victim and ignoring the racism which affects third world people regardless of their proficiency in English. Asian characters speak a stilted English ("Honorable so and so" or "Confucius say") or have a speech impediment ("roots or ruck," "very solly," "flied lice"). Native American characters speak another variation of stilted English ("Boy not hide. Indian take boy"), repeat certain Hollywood-Indian phrases ("Heap big" and "Many moons") or simply grunt out "Ugh" or "How." The repeated use of these language characterizations functions to make third world people seem less intelligent and less capable than the English-speaking white characters.

WRAP-UP

A *Saturday Review* editorial[10] on "The Environment of Language" stated that language

> . . . has as much to do with the philosophical and political conditioning of a society as geography or climate. . . . people in Western cultures do not realize the extent to which their racial attitudes have been conditioned since early childhood by the power of words to ennoble or condemn, augment or detract, glorify or demean. Negative language infects the subconscious of most Western people from the time they first learn to speak. Prejudice is not merely imparted or superimposed. It is metabolized in the bloodstream of society. What is needed is not so much a change in language as an awareness of the power of words to condition attitudes. If we can at least recognize the underpinnings of prejudice, we may be in a position to deal with the effects.

To recognize the racism in language is an important first step. Consciousness of the influence of language on our perceptions can help to negate much of that influence. But it is not enough to simply become aware of the effects of racism in conditioning attitudes. While we may not be able to change the language, we can definitely change our usage of the language. We can avoid using words that degrade people. We can make a conscious effort to use terminology that reflects a progressive perspective, as opposed to a distorting perspective. It is important for educators to provide students with opportunities to explore racism in language and to increase their awareness of it, as well as learning terminology that is positive and does not perpetuate negative human values.

DISCUSSION QUESTIONS

1. How is color used to indicate positive or negative attributes in advertising?
2. What words in current usage could be considered loaded?

NOTES

1. Simon Podair, "How Bigotry Builds Through Language," *Negro Digest,* March 1967.
2. Jose Armas, "Antonio and the Mayor: A Cultural Review of the Film," *The Journal of Ethnic Studies,* Fall 1975.
3. David R. Burgest, "The Racist Use of the English Language," *Black Scholar,* September 1973.
4. Thomas Greenfield, "Race and Passive Voice at Monticello," *Crisis,* April 1975.
5. David R. Burgest, "Racism in Everyday Speech and Social Work Jargon," *Social Work,* July 1973.
6. William Ryan, *Blaming the Victim,* Pantheon Books, 1971.
7. Morton Fried, "The Myth of Tribe," *National History,* April 1975.
8. Evelyn Jones Rich, "Mind Your Language," *Africa Report,* September/October 1974.
9. Steve Wolf, "Catalogers in Revolt Against LC's Racist, Sexist Headings," *Bulletin of Interracial Books for Children,* Vol. 6, Nos. 3&4, 1975.
10. "The Environment of Language," *Saturday Review,* April 8, 1967.

Also see:
Roger Bastide, "Color, Racism and Christianity," *Daedalus,* Spring 1967.

Kenneth J. Gergen, "The Significance of Skin Color in Human Relations," *Daedalus,* Spring 1967.
Lloyd Yabura, "Towards a Language of Humanism," *Rhythm,* Summer 1971.
UNESCO, "Recommendations Concerning Terminology in Education on Race Questions," June 1968.

<hr>

READING 58

Gender Stereotyping in the English Language

Laurel Richardson

Everyone in our society, regardless of class, ethnicity, sex, age, or race, is exposed to the same language, the language of the dominant culture. Analysis of verbal language can tell us a great deal about a people's fears, prejudices, anxieties, and interests. A rich vocabulary on a particular subject indicates societal interests or obsessions (e.g., the extensive vocabulary about cars in America). And different words for the same subject (such as *freedom fighter* and *terrorist, passed away* and *croaked, make love* and *ball*) show that there is a range of attitudes and feelings in the society toward that subject.

It should not be surprising, then, to find differential attitudes and feelings about men and women rooted in the English language. Although the English language has not been completely analyzed, six general propositions concerning these attitudes and feelings about males and females can be made.

First, in terms of grammatical and semantic structure, women do not have a fully autonomous, independent existence; they are part of man. The language is not divided into male and female with distinct conjugations and declensions, as many other languages are. Rather, *women* are included under the generic *man.* Grammar books specify that the pronoun *he* can be used generically to

<hr>

Laurel Richardson is emeritus professor of sociology at The Ohio State University.

mean *he* or *she.* Further, *man,* when used as an indefinite pronoun, grammatically refers to both men and women. So, for example, when we read *man* in the following phrases we are to interpret it as applying to both men and women: "man the oars," "one small step for man, one giant step for mankind," "man, that's tough," "man overboard," "man the toolmaker," "alienated man," "garbageman." Our rules of etiquette complete the grammatical presumption of inclusivity. When two persons are pronounced "man and wife," Miss Susan Jones changes her entire name to Mrs. Robert Gordon (Vanderbilt, 1972). In each of these correct usages, women are a part of man; they do not exist autonomously. The exclusion of women is well expressed in Mary Daly's ear-jarring slogan "the sisterhood of man" (1973:7–21).

However, there is some question as to whether the theory that *man* means everybody is carried out in practice (see Bendix, 1979; Martyna, 1980). For example, an eight-year-old interrupts her reading of "The Story of the Cavemen" to ask how we got here without cavewomen. A ten-year-old thinks it is dumb to have a woman post*man.* A beginning anthropology student believes (incorrectly) that all shamans ("witch doctors") are males because her textbook and professor use the referential pronoun *he.*

But beginning language learners are not the only ones who visualize males when they see the word *man.* Research has consistently demonstrated that when the generic *man* is used, people visualize men, not women (Schneider & Hacker, 1973; DeStefano, 1976; Martyna, 1978; Hamilton & Henley, 1982). DeStafano, for example, reports that college students choose silhouettes of males for sentences with the word *man* or *men* in them. Similarly, the presumably generic *he* elicits images of men rather than women. The finding is so persistent that linguists doubt whether there actually is a semantic generic in English (MacKay, 1983).

Man, then, suggests not humanity but rather male images. Moreover, over one's lifetime, an educated American will be exposed to the prescriptive *he* more than a million times (MacKay, 1983). One consequence is the exclusion of women in the visualization, imagination, and thought of males and females. Most likely this linguistic practice perpetuates in men their feelings of dominance over and responsibility for women, feelings that interfere with the development of equality in relationships.

Second, in actual practice, our pronoun usage perpetuates different personality attributes and career aspirations for men and women. Nurses, secretaries, and elementary school teachers are almost invariably referred to as *she;* doctors, engineers, electricians, and presidents as *he.* In one classroom, students referred to an unidentified child as *he* but shifted to *she* when discussing the child's parent. In a faculty discussion of the problems of acquiring new staff, all architects, engineers, security officers, faculty, and computer programmers were referred to as *he;* secretaries and file clerks were referred to as *she.* Martyna (1978) has noted that speakers consistently use *he* when the referent has a high-status occupation (e.g., doctor, lawyer, judge) but shift to *she* when the occupations have lower status (e.g., nurse, secretary).

Even our choice of sex ascription to nonhuman objects subtly reinforces different personalities for males and females. It seems as though the small (e.g., kittens), the graceful (e.g., poetry), the unpredictable (e.g., the fates), the nurturant (e.g., the church, the school), and that which is owned and/or controlled by men (e.g., boats, cars, governments, nations) represent the feminine, whereas that which is a controlling forceful power in and of itself (e.g., God, Satan, tiger) primarily represents the masculine. Even athletic teams are not immune. In one college, the men's teams are called the Bearcats and the women's teams the Bearkittens.

Some of you may wonder whether it matters that the female is linguistically included in the male. The inclusion of women under the pseudogeneric *man* and the prescriptive *he,* however, is not a trivial issue. Language has tremendous power to shape attitudes and influence behavior. Indeed, MacKay (1983) argues that the prescriptive *he* "has all the characteristics of a highly effective propaganda technique": frequent repetition, early age of acquisition (before age 6), covertness (*he* is not thought of as propaganda), use by high-prestige sources (including university texts and professors), and indirectness (presented as though it were a matter of common knowledge). As a result, the prescriptive affects females' sense of life options and feelings of well-being. For example, Adamsky (1981) found that women's sense of power and importance was enhanced when the prescriptive *he* was replaced by *she*.

Awareness of the impact of the generic *man* and prescriptive *he* has generated considerable activity to change the language. One change, approved by the Modern Language Association, is to replace the prescriptive *he* with the plural *they*—as was accepted practice before the 18th century. Another is the use of *he or she*. Although it sounds awkward at first, the *he or she* designation is increasingly being used in the media and among people who have recognized the power of the pronoun to perpetuate sex stereotyping. When a professor, for example, talks about "the lawyer" as "he or she," a speech pattern that counteracts sex stereotyping is modeled. This drive to neutralize the impact of pronouns is evidenced further in the renaming of occupations: a policeman is now a police officer, a postman is a mail carrier, a stewardess is a flight attendant.

Third, linguistic practice defines females as immature, incompetent, and incapable and males as mature, complete, and competent. Because the words *man* and *woman* tend to connote sexual and human maturity, common speech, organizational titles, public addresses, and bathroom doors frequently designate the women in question as *ladies*. Simply contrast the different connotations of *lady* and *woman* in the following common phrases:

Luck, be a lady (woman) tonight.

Barbara's a little lady (woman).

Ladies' (Women's) Air Corps.

In the first two examples, the use of *lady* desexualizes the contextual meaning of *woman*. So trivializing is the use of *lady* in the last phrase that the second is wholly anomalous. The male equivalent,

lord, is never used; and its synonym, *gentleman*, is used infrequently. When *gentleman* is used, the assumption seems to be that certain culturally condoned aspects of masculinity (e.g., aggressivity, activity, and strength) should be set aside in the interests of maturity and order, as in the following phrases:

A gentlemen's (men's) agreement.

A duel between gentlemen (men).

He's a real gentleman (man).

Rather than feeling constrained to set aside the stereotypes associated with *man*, males frequently find the opposite process occurring. The contextual connotation of *man* places a strain on males to be continuously sexually and socially potent, as the following examples reveal:

I was not a man (gentleman) with her tonight.

This is a man's (gentleman's) job.

Be a man (gentleman).

Whether males, therefore, feel competent or anxious, valuable or worthless in particular contexts is influenced by the demands placed on them by the expectations of the language.

Not only are men infrequently labeled *gentlemen*, but they are infrequently labeled *boys*. The term *boy* is reserved for young males, bellhops, car attendants, and as a putdown to those males judged inferior. *Boy* connotes immaturity and powerlessness. Only occasionally do males "have a night out with the boys." They do not talk "boy talk" at the office. Rarely does our language legitimize carefreeness in males. Rather, they are expected, linguistically, to adopt the responsibilities of manhood.

On the other hand, women of all ages may be called *girls*. Grown females "play bridge with the girls" and indulge in "girl talk." They are encouraged to remain childlike, and the implication is that they are basically immature and without power. Men can become men, linguistically, putting aside the immaturity of childhood; indeed, for them to retain the openness and playfulness of boyhood is linguistically difficult.

Further, the presumed incompetence and immaturity of women are evidenced by the linguistic company they keep. Women are categorized with children ("women and children first"), the infirm ("the blind, the lame, the women"), and the incompetent ("women, convicts, and idiots"). The use of these categorical designations is not accidental happenstance; "rather these selectional groupings are powerful forces behind the actual expressions of language and are based on distinctions which are not regarded as trivial by the speakers of the language" (Key, 1975:82). A total language analysis of categorical groupings is not available, yet it seems likely that women tend to be included in groupings that designate incompleteness, ineptitude, and immaturity. On the other hand, it is difficult for us to conceive of the word *man* in any categorical grouping other than one that extends beyond humanity, such as "Man, apes, and angels" or "Man and Superman." That is, men do exist as an independent category capable of autonomy; women are grouped with the stigmatized, the immature, and the foolish. Moreover, when men are in human groupings, males are invariably first on the list ("men and women," "he and she," "man and wife"). This order is not accidental but was prescribed in the 16th century to honor the worthier party.

Fourth, in practice women are defined in terms of their sexual desirability (to men); men are defined in terms of their sexual prowess (over women). Most slang words in reference to women refer to their sexual desirability to men (e.g., *dog, fox, broad, ass, chick*). Slang about men refers to their sexual prowess over women (e.g., *dude, stud, hunk*). The fewer examples given for men is not an oversight. An analysis of sexual slang, for example, listed more than 1,000 words and phrases that derogate women sexually but found "nowhere near this multitude for describing men" (Kramarae, 1975:72). Farmer and Henley (cited in Schulz, 1975) list 500 synonyms for *prostitute,* for example, and only 65 for *whoremonger.* Stanley (1977) reports 220 terms

for a sexually promiscuous woman and only 22 for a sexually promiscuous man. Shuster (1973) reports that the passive verb form is used in reference to women's sexual experiences (e.g., *to be laid, to be had, to be taken*), whereas the active tense is used in reference to the male's sexual experience (e.g., *lay, take, have*). Being sexually attractive to males is culturally condoned for women and being sexually powerful is approved for males. In this regard, the slang of the street is certainly not countercultural; rather it perpetuates and reinforces different expectations in females and males as sexual objects and performers.

Further, we find sexual connotations associated with neutral words applied to women. A few examples should suffice. A male academician questioned the title of a new course, asserting it was "too suggestive." The title? "The Position of Women in the Social Order." A male tramp is simply a hobo, but a female tramp is a slut. And consider the difference in connotation of the following expressions:

It's easy.

He's easy.

She's easy.

In the first, we assume something is "easy to do"; in the second, we might assume a professor is an "easy grader" or a man is "easygoing." But when we read "she's easy," the connotation is "she's an easy lay."

In the world of slang, men are defined by their sexual prowess. In the world of slang and proper speech, women are defined as sexual objects. The rule in practice seems to be: If in doubt, assume that *any* reference to a women has a sexual connotation. For both genders, the constant bombardment of prescribed sexuality is bound to have real consequences.

Fifth, women are defined in terms of their relations to men; men are defined in terms of their relations to the world at large. A good example is seen in the words *master* and *mistress*. Originally these words had the same meaning—"a person who holds power over servants." With the demise of the feudal system, however, these words took on different meanings. The masculine variant metaphorically refers to power over something; as in "He is the master of his trade"; the feminine variant metaphorically (although probably not in actuality) refers to power over a man sexually, as in "She is Tom's mistress." Men are defined in terms of their power in the occupational world, women in terms of their sexual power over men.

The existence of two contractions for Mistress (*Miss* and *Mrs.*) and but one for Mister (*Mr.*) underscores the cultural concern and linguistic practice: women are defined in relation to men. Even a divorced woman is defined in terms of her no-longer-existing relation to a man (she is still *Mrs. Man's Name*). But apparently the divorced state is not relevant enough to the man or to the society to require a label. A divorced woman is a *divorcee*, but what do you call a divorced man? The recent preference of many women to be called *Ms.* is an attempt to provide for women an equivalency title that is not dependent on marital status.

Sixth, a historical pattern can be seen in the meanings that come to be attached to words that originally were neutral: those that apply to women acquire obscene and/or debased connotations but no such pattern of derogation holds for neutral words referring to men. The processes of *pejoration* (the acquiring of an obscene or debased connotation) and *amelioration* (the reacquiring of a neutral or positive connotation) in the English language in regard to terms for males and females have been studied extensively by Muriel Schulz (1975).

Leveling is the least derogative form of pejoration. Through leveling, titles that originally referred to an elite class of persons come to include a wider class of persons. Such democratic leveling is more common for female designates than for males. For example, contrast the following: *lord-lady (lady); baronet-dame (dame); governor-governess (governess).*

Most frequently what happens to words designating women as they become pejorated, however, is that they come to denote or connote sexual wantonness. *Sir* and *mister,* for example, remain titles of

courtesy, but at some time *madam, miss,* and *mistress* have come to designate, respectively, a brothel-keeper, a prostitute, and an unmarried sexual partner of a male (Schulz, 1975:66).

Names for domestic helpers, if they are females, are frequently derogated. *Hussy,* for example, originally meant "housewife." *Laundress, needlewoman, spinster* ("tender of the spinning wheel"), and *nurse* all referred to domestic occupations within the home, and all at some point became slang expressions for prostitute or mistress.

Even kinship terms referring to women become denigrated. During the 17th century, *mother* was used to mean "a bawd"; more recently *mother (mothuh f——)* has become a common derogatory epithet (Cameron, 1974). Probably at some point in history every kinship term for females has been derogated (Schulz, 1975:66).

Terms of endearment for women also seem to follow a downward path. Such pet names as Tart, Dolly, Kitty, Polly, Mopsy, Biddy, and Jill all eventually became sexually derogatory (Schulz, 1975:67). *Whore* comes from the same Latin root as *care* and once meant "a lover of either sex."

Indeed, even the most neutral categorical designations—*girl, female, woman, lady*—at some point in their history have been used to connote sexual immorality. *Girl* originally meant "a child of either sex"; through the process of semantic degeneration it eventually meant "a prostitute." Although *girl* has lost this meaning, *girlie* still retains sexual connotations. *Woman* connoted "a mistress" in the early 19th century; *female* was a degrading epithet in the latter part of the 19th century; and when *lady* was introduced as a euphemism, it too became deprecatory. "Even so neutral a term as *person,* when it was used as substitute for *woman,* suffered [vulgarization]" (Mencken, 1963: 350, quoted in Schulz, 1975:71).

Whether one looks at elite titles, occupational roles, kinship relationships, endearments, or age-sex categorical designations, the pattern is clear. Terms referring to females are pejorated—"become negative in the middle instances and abusive in the extremes" (Schulz, 1975:69). Such semantic derogation, however, is not evidenced for male referents. *Lord, baronet, father, brother, nephew, footman, bowman, boy, lad, fellow, gentleman, man, male,* and so on "have failed to undergo the derogation found in the history of their corresponding feminine designations" (Schulz, 1975:67). Interestingly, the male word, rather than undergoing derogation, frequently is replaced by a female referent when the speaker wants to debase a male. A weak man, for example, is referred to as a *sissy* (diminutive of sister), and an army recruit during basic training is called a *pussy.* And when one is swearing at a male, he is referred to as a *bastard* or a *son-of-a-bitch*—both appellations that impugn the dignity of a man's mother.

In summary, these verbal practices are consistent with the gender stereotypes that we encounter in everyday life. Women are thought to be a part of man, nonautonomous, dependent, relegated to roles that require few skills, characteristically incompetent and immature, sexual objects, best defined in terms of their relations to men. Males are visible, autonomous and independent, responsible for the protection and containment of women, expected to occupy positions on the basis of their high achievement or physical power, assumed to be sexually potent, and defined primarily by their relations to the world of work. The use of the language perpetuates the stereotypes for both genders and limits the options available for self-definition.

DISCUSSION QUESTIONS

1. Why is it important to be cautious about the use of language if one is trying to avoid stereotypes?
2. What new words, besides Ms., have been invented to avoid stereotypes?

REFERENCES

Adamsky, C. 1981. "Changes in pronominal usage in a classroom situation." *Psychology of Women Quarterly* 5:773–79.

Bendix, J. 1979. "Linguistic models as political symbols: Gender and the generic 'he' in English." In J. Orasanu, M. Slater, and L. L. Adler, eds., *Language, sex and gender; Does la différence make a difference?* pp. 23–42. New York: New Academy of Science Annuals.

Cameron, P. 1974. "Frequency and kinds of words in various social settings, or What the hell's going on?" In M. Truzzi, ed., *Sociology for pleasure,* pp. 31–37. Englewood Cliffs, NJ: Prentice-Hall.

Daly, M. 1973. *Beyond God the father.* Boston: Beacon Press.

DeStefano, J. S. 1976. Personal communication. Columbus: Ohio State University.

Hamilton, N., & Henley, N. 1982. "Detrimental consequences of the generic masculine usage." Paper presented to the Western Psychological Association meetings, Sacramento.

Key, M. R. 1975. *Male/female language.* Metuchen, NJ: Scarecrow Press.

Kramarae, Cheris. 1975. "Woman's speech: Separate but unequal?" In Barrie Thorne and Nancy Henley, eds., *Language and sex: Difference and dominance,* pp. 43–56. Rowley, MA: Newbury House.

MacKay, D. G. 1983. "Prescriptive grammar and the pronoun problem." In B. Thorne, C. Kramarae, and N. Henley, eds., *Language, gender, and society,* pp. 38–53. Rowley, MA: Newbury House.

Martyna, W. 1978. "What does 'he' mean? Use of the generic masculine." *Journal of Communication* 28:131–38.

Martyna, W. 1980. "Beyond the 'he/man' approach: The case for nonsexist language." *Signs* 5:482–93.

Mencken, H. L. 1963. *The American language.* 4th ed. with supplements. Abr. and ed. R. I. McDavis. New York: Knopf.

Schneider, J., & Hacker, S. 1973. "Sex role imagery in the use of the generic 'man' in introductory texts: A case in the sociology of sociology." *American Sociologist* 8:12–18.

Schulz, M. R. 1975. "The semantic derogation of women." In B. Thorne and N. Henley, eds., *Language and sex: Difference and dominance,* pp. 64–75. Rowley, MA: Newbury House.

Shuster, Janet. 1973. "Grammatical forms marked for male and female in English." Unpublished paper. Chicago: University of Chicago.

Stanley, J. P. 1977. "Paradigmatic woman: The prostitute." In D. L. Shores, ed., *Papers in language variation.* Birmingham: University of Alabama Press.

Vanderbilt, A. 1972. *Amy Vanderbilt's etiquette.* Garden City, NY: Doubleday.

Let's Spread The "Fun" Around

THE ISSUE OF SPORTS TEAM NAMES AND MASCOTS

Ward Churchill

If people are genuinely interested in honoring Indians, try getting your government to live up to the more than 400 treaties it signed with our nations. Try respecting our religious freedom which has been repeatedly denied in federal courts. Try stopping the ongoing theft of Indian water and other natural resources. Try reversing your colonial process that relegates us to the most impoverished, polluted, and desperate conditions in this country . . . Try understanding that the mascot issue is only the tip of a very huge problem of continuing racism against American Indians. Then maybe your ["honors"] will mean something. Until then, it's just so much superficial, hypocritical puffery. People should remember that an honor isn't born when it parts the honorer's lips, it is born when it is accepted in the honoree's ear.

Glenn T. Morris
Colorado AIM, 1992

During the past twenty seasons, there has been an increasing controversy regarding the names of professional sports teams like the Atlanta "Braves," Cleveland "Indians," Washington "Redskins," and Kansas City "Chiefs." The issue extends to the names of college teams like the Florida State University "Seminoles," University of Illinois "Fighting Illini," and so on, right on down to high school outfits like the Lamar (Colorado) "Savages." Also involved have been team adoptions of "mascots," replete with feathers, buckskins, beads, spears, and

"warpaint" (some fans have opted to adorn themselves in the same fashion), and nifty little "pep" gestures like the "Indian Chant" and "Tomahawk Chop."

A substantial number of American Indians have protested that use of native names, images, and symbols as sports team mascots and the like is, by definition, a virulently racist practice. Given the historical relationship between Indians and nonindians during what has been called the "Conquest of America," American Indian Movement leader (and American Indian Anti-Defamation Council founder) Russell Means has compared the practice to contemporary Germans naming their soccer teams the "Jews," "Hebrews," and "Yids," while adorning their uniforms with grotesque caricatures of Jewish faces taken from the nazis' antisemitic propaganda of the 1930s. Numerous demonstrations have occurred in conjunction with games—notably during the November 15, 1992, match-up between the Chiefs and Redskins in Kansas City—by angry Indians and their supporters.

In response, a number of players—especially African Americans and other minority athletes—have been trotted out by professional team owners like Ted Turner, as well as university and public school officials, to announce that they mean not to insult, but instead to "honor," native people. They have been joined by the television networks and most major newspapers, all of which have editorialized that Indian discomfort with the situation is "no big deal," insisting that the whole thing is just "good, clean fun." The country needs more such fun, they've argued, and "a few disgruntled Native Americans" have no right to undermine the nation's enjoyment of its leisure time by complaining. This is especially the case, some have contended, "in hard times like these." It has even been contended that Indian outrage at being systematically degraded—rather than the degradation itself—creates "a serious barrier to the sort of intergroup communication so necessary in a multicultural society such as ours."

Okay, let's communicate. We may be frankly dubious that those advancing such positions really

Ward Churchill (Creek and enrolled Keetoowah Band Cherokee) is a professor of ethnic studies and coordinator of American Indian studies at the University of Colorado. He is a longtime native rights activist.

believe in their own rhetoric, but, just for the sake of argument, let's accept the premise that they are sincere. If what they are saying is true in any way at all, then isn't it time we spread such "inoffensiveness" and "good cheer" around among *all* groups so that *everybody* can participate *equally* in fostering the round of national laughs they call for? Sure it is—the country can't have too *much* fun or "intergroup involvement"—so the more, the merrier. Simple consistency demands that anyone who thinks the Tomahawk Chop is a swell pastime must be just as hearty in their endorsement of the following ideas, which—by the "logic" used to defend the defamation of American Indians—should help us all start *really* yukking it up.

First, as a counterpart to the Redskins, we need an NFL team called the "Niggers" to "honor" Afroamerica. Halftime festivities for fans might include a simulated stewing of the opposing coach in a large pot while players and cheerleaders dance around it, garbed in leopard skins and wearing fake bones in their noses. This concept obviously goes along with the kind of gaiety attending the Chop, but also the actions of the Kansas City Chiefs, whose team members—prominently including black team members—lately appeared on a poster looking "fierce" and "savage" by way of wearing Indian regalia. Just a bit of harmless "morale boosting," says the Chiefs' front office. You bet.

So that the newly formed Niggers sports club won't end up too out of sync while expressing the "spirit" and "identity" of Afroamericans in the above fashion, a baseball franchise—let's call this one the "Sambos"—should be formed. How about a basketball team called the "Spearchuckers"? A hockey team called the "Jungle Bunnies"? Maybe the "essence" of these teams could be depicted by images of tiny black faces adorned with huge pairs of lips. The players could appear on TV every week or so gnawing on chicken legs and spitting watermelon seeds at one another. Catchy, eh? Well, there's "nothing to be upset about," according to those who love wearing "war bonnets" to the Super Bowl or having "Chief Illiniwik" dance around the sports arenas of Urbana, Illinois.

And why stop there? There are plenty of other groups to include. "Hispanics? They can be "represented" by the Galveston "Greasers" and San Diego "Spics," at least until the Wisconsin "Wetbacks" and Baltimore "Beaners" get off the ground. Asian Americans? How about the "Slopes," "Dinks," Gooks," and "Zipperheads"? Owners of the latter teams might get their logo ideas from editorial page cartoons printed in the nation's newspapers during World War II: slant-eyes, buck teeth, big glasses, but nothing racially insulting or derogatory, according to the editors and artists involved at the time. Indeed, this Second World War–vintage stuff can be seen as just another barrel of laughs, at least by what current editors say are their "local standards" concerning American Indians.

Let's see. Who's been left out? Teams like the Kansas City "Kikes," Hanover "Honkies," San Leandro "Shylocks," Daytona "Dagos," and Pittsburgh "Polacks" will fill a certain social void among white folk. Have a religious belief? Let's all go for the gusto and gear up the Milwaukee "Mackerel Snappers" and Hollywood "Holy Rollers." The Fighting Irish of Notre Dame can be rechristened the "Drunken Irish" or "Papist Pigs." Issues of gender and sexual preference can be addressed through creation of teams like the St. Louis "Sluts," Boston "Bimbos," Detroit "Dykes," and the Fresno "Faggots." How about the Gainesville "Gimps" and Richmond "Retards," so the physically and mentally impaired won't be excluded from our fun and games?

Now, don't go getting "overly sensitive" out there. *None* of this is demeaning or insulting, at least not when it's being done to Indians. Just ask the folks who are doing it or their apologists like Andy Rooney in the national media. They'll tell you—as in fact they *have* been telling you—that there's been no harm done, regardless of what the victims think, feel, or say. The situation is exactly the same as when those with precisely the same mentality used to insist that Step 'n' Fetchit was okay, or Rochester on the *Jack Benny Show,* or Amos and Andy, Charlie Chan, the Frito Bandito, or any of the other cutesy symbols making up the lexicon of American racism. Have we communicated yet?

Let's get just a little bit real here. The notion of "fun" embodied in rituals like the Tomahawk Chop must be understood for what it is. There's not a single nonindian example deployed above which can be considered socially acceptable in even the most marginal sense. The reasons are obvious enough. So why is it different where American Indians are concerned? One can only conclude that, in contrast to the other groups at issue, Indians are (falsely) perceived as being too few, and therefore too weak, to defend themselves effectively against racist and otherwise offensive behavior. The sensibilities of those who take pleasure in things like the Chop are thus akin to those of schoolyard bullies and those twisted individuals who like to torture cats. At another level, their perspectives have much in common with those manifested more literally—and therefore more honestly—by groups like the nazis, aryan nations, and ku klux klan. Those who suggest this is "okay" should be treated accordingly by anyone who opposes nazism and comparable belief systems.

Fortunately, there are glimmers of hope that this may become the case. A few teams and their fans have gotten the message and have responded appropriately. One illustration is Stanford University, which opted to drop the name "Indians" with regard to its sports teams (and, contrary to the myth perpetrated by those who enjoy insulting Native Americans, Stanford has experienced *no* resulting drop-off in attendance at its games). Meanwhile, the local newspaper in Portland, Oregon, has decided its longstanding editorial policy prohibiting use of racial epithets should include derogatory sports team names. The Redskins, for instance, are now simply referred to as being "the Washington team," and will continue to be described in this way until the franchise adopts an inoffensive moniker. (Newspaper sales in Portland have suffered no decline as a result.)

Such examples are to be applauded and encouraged. They stand as figurative beacons in the night, proving beyond all doubt that it is—and has always been—quite possible to indulge in the pleasure of athletics without accepting blatant racism into the bargain. The extent to which Stanford and Portland remain atypical is exactly the extent to which America remains afflicted with an ugly reality far different from the noble and enlightened "moral leadership" it professes to show the world. Clearly, the United States has a very long way to go before it measures up to such an image of itself.

DISCUSSION QUESTIONS

1. How do you interpret the last line of the Glen T. Morris quote that begins this article: "People should remember that an honor isn't born when it parts the honorer's lips, it is born when it is accepted in the honoree's ear"?
2. What emotions do you have as you read Ward Churchill's article? Setting those emotions aside, how do you evaluate the logic of Churchill's case?

READING 60

To Be and Be Seen: The Politics of Reality*

Marilyn Frye

. . . Reality is that which is.

The English word "real" stems from a word which meant *regal,* of or pertaining to the king. "Real" in Spanish means *royal.*

Real property is that which is proper to the king.

Real estate is the estate of the king.

Reality is that which pertains to the one in power, is that over which he has power, is his domain, his estate, is proper to him.

---

*This is a very slightly revised version of the essay which appeared in *Sinister Wisdom* 17 with the title, "To Be and Be Seen: Metaphysical Misogyny."
Marilyn Frye is a professor of philosophy at Michigan State University.

The ideal king reigns over everything as far as the eye can see. His eye. What he cannot see is not royal, not real.

He sees what is proper to him.

To be real is to be visible to the king.

The king is in his counting house.

I say, "I am a lesbian. The king does not count lesbians. Lesbians are not real. There are no lesbians." To say this, I use the word "lesbian," and hence one might think that there is a word for this thing, and thus that the thing must have a place in the conceptual scheme. But this is not so. Let me take you on a guided tour of a few standard dictionaries, to display some reasons for saying that lesbians are not named in the lexicon of the King's English.

If you look up the word "lesbian" in *The Oxford English Dictionary,* you find an entry that says it is an adjective that means *of or pertaining to the island of Lesbos,* and an entry describing at length and favorably an implement called a lesbian rule, which is a flexible measuring device used by carpenters. Period.

Webster's Third International offers a more pertinent definition. It tells us that a lesbian is a homosexual female. And going on, one finds that "homosexual" means *of or pertaining to the same sex.* The elucidating example provided is the phrase "homosexual twins" which means *same-sex twins.* The alert scholar can conclude that a lesbian is a same-sex female.

A recent edition of *Webster's Collegiate Dictionary* tells us that a lesbian is a woman who has sex, or sexual relations, with other women. Such a definition would be accepted by many speakers of the language and at least seems to be coherent, even if too narrow. But the appearance is deceptive, for this account collapses into nonsense, too. The key word in this definition is "sex": having sex or having sexual relations. But what is having sex? It is worthwhile to follow this up because the pertinent dictionary entries obscure an important point about the logic of sex. Getting clear about that point helps one see that there is semantic closure against

recognition of the existence of lesbians, and it also prepares the way for understanding the connection between the place of *woman* and the place of *lesbian* with respect to the phallocratic scheme of things.[1]

Dictionaries generally agree that "sexual" means something on the order of *pertaining to the genital union of a female and a male animal,* and that "having sex" is having intercourse—intercourse being defined as the penetration of a vagina by a penis, with ejaculation. My own observation of usage leads me to think these accounts are inadequate and misleading. Some uses of these terms do fit this dictionary account. For instance, parents and counselors standardly remind young women that if they are going to be sexually active they must deal responsibly with the possibility of becoming pregnant. In this context, the word "sexually" is pretty clearly being used in a way that accords with the given definition. But many activities and events fall under the rubric "sexual," apparently without semantic deviance, though they do not involve penile penetration of the vagina of a female human being. Penile penetration of almost anything, especially if it is accompanied by ejaculation, counts as having sex or being sexual. Moreover, events which cannot plausibly be seen as pertaining to penile erection, penetration and ejaculation will, in general, not be counted as sexual, and events that do not involve penile penetration or ejaculation will not be counted as having sex. For instance, if a girlchild is fondled and aroused by a man, and comes to orgasm, but the man refrains from penetration and ejaculation, the man can say, and speakers of English will generally agree, that he did not have sex with her. No matter what is going on, or (it must be mentioned) *not* going on, with respect to female arousal or orgasm, or in connection with the vagina, a pair can be said without semantic deviance to have had sex, or not to have had sex; the use of that term turns entirely on what was going on with respect to the penis.

When one first considers the dictionary definitions of "sex" and "sexual," it seems that all sexuality is heterosexuality, by definition, and that the term "homosexual" would be internally contradictory.

There are uses of the term according to which this is exactly so. But in the usual and standard use, there is nothing semantically odd in describing two men as having sex with each other. According to that usage, any situation in which one or more penises are present is one in which something could happen which could be called having sex. But on this apparently "broader" definition there is nothing women could do in the absence of men that could, without semantic oddity, be called "having sex." Speaking of women who have sex with other women is like speaking of ducks who engage in arm wrestling.

When the dictionary defines lesbians as women who have sex or sexual relations with other women, it defines lesbians as logically impossible.

Looking for other words in the lexicon which might denote these beings which are non-named "lesbians," one thinks of terms in the vernacular, like "dyke," "bulldagger" and so on. Perhaps it is just as well that standard dictionaries do not pretend to provide relevant definitions of such terms. Generally, these two terms are used to denote women who are perceived as imitating, dressing up like, or trying to be men. Whatever the extent of the class of women who are perceived to do such things, it obviously is not coextensive with the class of lesbians. Nearly every feminist, and many other women as well, have been perceived as wishing to be men, and a great many lesbians are not so perceived. The term "dyke" has been appropriated by some lesbians as a term of pride and solidarity, but in that use it is unintelligible to most speakers of English.

One of the current definitions of "lesbianism" among lesbians is *woman-loving*—the polar opposite of misogyny. Several dictionaries I checked have entries for "misogyny" (hatred of women), but not for "philogyny" (love of women). I found one which defines "philogyny" as fondness for women, and another dictionary defines "philogyny" as *Don Juanism*. Obviously neither of these means *love of women* as it is intended by lesbians combing the vocabulary for ways to refer to themselves. According to the dictionaries, there is no term in English for the polar opposite of misogyny nor for persons whose characteristic orientation toward women is the polar opposite of misogyny.

Flinging the net wider, one can look up the more Victorian words, like sapphism and sapphist. In *Webster's Collegiate,* "sapphism" is defined just as *lesbianism.* But *The Oxford English Dictionary* introduces another twist. Under the heading of "sapphism" is an entry for "sapphist" according to which sapphists are those addicted to unnatural sexual relations between women. The fact that these relations are characterized as unnatural is revealing. For what is unnatural is contrary to the laws of nature, or contrary to the nature of the substance of entity in question. But what is contrary to the laws of nature cannot happen: that is what it means to call these laws the laws of nature. And I cannot do what is contrary to my nature, for if I could do it, it would be in my nature to do it. To call something "unnatural" is to say it cannot be. This definition defines sapphists, that is lesbians, as *naturally* impossible as well as *logically* impossible. . . .

Lesbian.

One of the people of the Isle of Lesbos.

It is bizarre that when I try to name myself and explain myself, my native tongue provides me with a word that is so foreign, so false, so hopelessly inappropriate. Why am I referred to by a term which means *one of the people of Lesbos?*

The use of the word "lesbian" to name us is a quadrifold evasion, a laminated euphemism. To name us, one goes by way of a reference to the island of Lesbos, which in turn is an indirect reference to the poet Sappho (who used to live there, they say), which in turn is itself an indirect reference to what fragments of her poetry have survived a few millennia of patriarchy, and this in turn (if we have not lost you by now) is a prophylactic avoidance of direct mention of the sort of creature who would write such poems or to whom such poems would be written . . . assuming you happen to know what is in those poems written in a dialect of Greek over two thousand five hundred years ago on some small island somewhere in the wine dark Aegean Sea.

This is a truly remarkable feat of silence.

. . . I think there is much truth in the claim that the phallocratic scheme does not include women. But while women are erased in history and in speculation, physically liquidated in gynocidal purges and banished from the community of those with perceptual and semantic authority, we are on the other hand regularly and systematically invited, seduced, cajoled, coerced and even paid to be in intimate and constant association with men and their projects. In this, the situation of women generally is radically different from the situation of lesbians. Lesbians are not invited to join—the family, the party, the project, the procession, the war effort. There is a place for a woman in every game. Wife, secretary, servant, prostitute, daughter, assistant, babysitter, mistress, seamstress, proofreader, nurse, confidante, masseusse, indexer, typist, mother. Any of these is a place for a woman, and women are much encouraged to fill them. None of these is a place for a lesbian.

The exclusion of women from the phallocratic scheme is impressive, frightening and often fatal, but it is not simple and absolute. Women's existence is both absolutely necessary to and irresolvably problematic for the dominant reality and those committed to it, for our existence is *presupposed* by phallocratic reality, but it is not and cannot be *encompassed* by or countenanced by that reality. Women's existence is a background against which phallocratic reality is a foreground.

A foreground scene is created by the motion of foreground figures against a static background. Foreground figures are perceptible, are defined, have identity, only in virtue of their movement against a background. The space in which the motion of foreground figures takes place is created and defined by their movement with respect to each other and against the background. But nothing of the background is *in* or is *part of* or is *encompassed* by the foreground scene and space. The background is unseen by the eye which is focused on foreground figures, and if anything somehow draws the eye to the background, the foreground dissolves. What would draw the eye to the background would be any sudden or well-defined motion in the background. Hence there must be either no motion at all in the background, or an unchanging buzz of small, regular and repetitive motions. The background must be utterly un*event*ful if the foreground is to continue to hang together, that is, if it is to endure as a *space* within which there are discrete *objects* in relation to each other.

I imagine phallocratic reality to be the space and figures and motion which constitute the foreground, and the constant repetitive uneventful activities of women to constitute and maintain the background against which this foreground plays. It is essential to the maintenance of the foreground reality that nothing within it refer in any way to anything in the background, and yet it depends absolutely upon the existence of the background. It is useful to carry this metaphor on in a more concrete mode—thinking of phallocratic reality as a dramatic production on a stage.

The motions of the actors against the stage settings and backdrop constitute and maintain the existence and identities of the characters in a play. The stage setting, props, lights and so forth are created, provided, maintained and occasionally rearranged (according to the script) by stagehands. The stagehands, their motions and the products of those motions, are neither in nor part of the play, are neither in nor part of the reality of the characters. The reality in the framework of which Hamlet's actions have their meaning would be rent or shattered if anything Hamlet did or thought referred in any way to the stagehands or their activities, or if that background blur of activity were in any other way to be resolved into attention-catching events.

The situation of the actors is desperately paradoxical. The actors are absolutely committed to the maintenance of the characters and the characters' reality: participation as characters in the ongoing creation of Reality is their *raison d'etre*. The reality of the character must be lived with fierce concentration. The actor must be immersed in the play and undistracted by any thought for the scenery, props or stagehands, lest the continuity of the characters and the integrity of their reality be dissolved or broken. But if the character must be lived so intently, who will supervise the stagehands to make sure they don't get rowdy, leave early, fall asleep or walk off the job? (Alas, there is no god nor heavenly host to serve as Director and Stage Managers.) Those with the most intense commitment to the maintenance of the reality of the play are precisely those most interested in the proper deportment of the stagehands, and this interest competes directly with that commitment. There is nothing the actor would like better than that there be no such thing as stagehands, posing as they do a constant threat to the very existence, the very life, of the character and hence to the meaning of the life of the actor; and yet the actor is irrevocably tied to the stagehands by his commitment to the play. Hamlet, of course, has no such problems; there are no stagehands in the play.

To escape his dilemma, the actor may throw caution to the wind and lose himself in the character, whereupon stagehands are unthinkable, hence unproblematic. Or he may construct and embrace the belief that the stagehands share exactly his own perceptions and interests and that they are as committed to the play as he—that they are like robots. On such a hypothesis he can assume them to be absolutely dependable and go on about his business single-mindedly and without existential anxiety. A third strategy, which is in a macabre way more sane, is that of trying to solve the problem technologically by constructing actual robots to serve as stagehands.[2] Given the primacy of his commitment to the play, all solutions must involve one form or another of annihilation of the stagehands. Yet all three require the existence of stagehands; the third, he would hope, requiring it only for a while longer.

The solution to the actor's problem which will appear most benign with respect to the stagehands because it erases the erasure, is that of training, persuading and seducing the stagehands into *loving* the actors and taking actors' interests and commitments unto themselves as their own. One significant advantage to this solution is that the actors can carry on without the guilt or confusion that might come with annihilating, replacing or falsely forgetting the stagehands. As it turns out, of course, even this is a less than perfect solution. Stagehands, in

the thrall of their commitment, can become confused and think of themselves as actors—and then they may disturb the play by trying to enter it as characters, by trying to participate in the creation and maintenance of Reality. But there are various well-known ways to handle these intrusions and this seems to be, generally speaking, the most popular solution to the actor's dilemma.

. . . The king is in his counting house. The king is greedy and will count for himself everything he dares to. But his greed itself imposes limits on what he dares to count.

What the king cannot count is a seer whose perception passes the plane of the foreground Reality and focuses upon the background. A seer whose eye is attracted to the ones working as stagehands—the women. A seer in whose eye the woman has authority, has interests of her own, is not a robot. A seer who has no motive for wanting there to be no women; a seer who is not loyal to Reality. We can take the account of the seer who must be unthinkable if Reality is to be kept afloat as the beginning of an account of what a lesbian is. One might try saying that a lesbian is one who, by virtue of her focus, her attention, her attachment, is disloyal to phallocratic reality. She is not committed to its maintenance and the maintenance of those who maintain it, and worse, her mode of disloyalty threatens its utter dissolution in the mere flick of the eye. This sounds extreme, of course, perhaps even hysterical. But listening carefully to the rhetoric of the fanatic fringe of the phallocratic loyalists, one hears that they do think that feminists, whom they fairly reasonably judge to be lesbians, have the power to bring down civilization, to dissolve the social order as we know it, to cause the demise of the species, by our mere existence.

Even the fanatics do not really believe that a lone maverick lesbian can in a flick of her evil eye atomize civilization, of course. Given the collectivity of conceptual schemes, the way they rest on agreement, a maverick perceiver does not have the power to bring one tumbling down—a point also verified by my own experience as a not-so-powerful maverick. What the loyalists fear, and in this I think they are more-or-less right, is a contagion of the maverick perception to the point where the agreement in perception which keeps Reality afloat begins to disintegrate.

The event of becoming a lesbian is a reorientation of attention in a kind of ontological conversion. It is characterized by a feeling of a world dissolving, and by a feeling of disengagement and re-engagement of one's power as a perceiver. That such conversion happens signals its possibility to others.

Heterosexuality for women is not simply a matter of sexual preference, any more than lesbianism is. It is a matter of orientation of attention, as is lesbianism, in a metaphysical context controlled by neither heterosexual nor lesbian women. Attention is a kind of passion. When one's attention is on something, one is present in a particular way with respect to that thing. This presence is, among other things, an element of erotic presence. The orientation of one's attention is also what fixes and directs the application of one's physical and emotional work.

If the lesbian sees the woman, the woman may see the lesbian seeing her. With this, there is a flowering of possibilities. The woman, feeling herself seen, may learn that she *can be* seen; she may also be able to know that a woman can see, that is, can author perception. With this, there enters for the woman the logical possibility of assuming her authority as a perceiver and of shifting her own attention. With that there is the dawn of choice, and it opens out over the whole world of women. The lesbian's seeing undercuts the mechanism by which the production and constant reproduction of heterosexuality for women was to be rendered *automatic*. The nonexistence of lesbians is a piece in the mechanism which is supposed to cut off the possibility of choice or alternative at the root, namely at the point of conception.

The maintenance of phallocratic reality requires that the attention of women be focused on men and men's projects—the play; and that attention not be focused on women—the stagehands. Woman-loving, as a spontaneous and habitual orientation of

attention is then, both directly and indirectly, inimical to the maintenance of that reality. And therein lies the reason for the thoroughness of the ontological closure against lesbians, the power of those closed out, and perhaps the key to the liberation of women from oppression in a male-dominated culture.

My primary goal here has not been to state and prove some rigid thesis, but simply to *say* something clearly enough, intelligibly enough, so that it can be understood and thought about. Lesbians are outside the conceptual scheme, and this is something done, not just the way things are. One can begin to see that lesbians are excluded by the scheme, and that this is *motivated*, when one begins to see what purpose the exclusion might serve in connection with keeping women generally in their metaphysical place. It is also true that lesbians are in a position to see things that cannot be seen from within the system. What lesbians see is what makes them lesbians and their seeing is why they have to be excluded. Lesbians are woman-seers. When one is suspected of seeing women, one is spat summarily out of reality, through the cognitive gap and into the negative semantic space. If you ask what became of such a woman, you may be told she became a lesbian, and if you try to find out what a lesbian is, you will be told there is no such thing.

But there is.

DISCUSSION QUESTIONS

1. Who acts as the king today to determine what is real?
2. Whose reality counts?

NOTES

1. The analysis that follows is my own rendering of an account developed by Carolyn Shafer. My version of it is informed also by my reading of "Sex and Reference," by Janice Moulton, *Philosophy and Sex*, edited by Robert Baker and Frederick Elliston (Prometheus Books, Buffalo, New York, 1975).
2. This solution is discussed in *The Transsexual Empire: The Making of the She-Male*, by Janice G. Raymond (Beacon Press, Boston, 1979).

BRIDGING DIFFERENCES

FRAMEWORK ESSAY

A book such as *The Meaning of Difference* runs the risk of leaving students with the feeling that there is little they can do to challenge the constructions of difference. Having recognized the power of master statuses and the significance of our conceptions of difference in everything from personal identity to world events, it is easy to feel powerless in the face of what appear to be overwhelming social forces.

But we did not embark on writing this book because we felt powerless or wanted you to feel that way. For us, the idea of looking at race, sex, social class, sexual orientation, and disability *all together* opened up new possibilities for understanding and creating alliances. When we started to talk about this book over 10 years ago, comparing our teaching experiences in a highly diverse university and our personal experiences of stigma and privilege, we were amazed by the connections we saw. That impression grew as we talked with students and friends who were members of other groups. Over time, we learned that understanding the similarities *across* groups opened up new ways of thinking: experiences could be accumulated toward a big picture, rather than suffered in relative isolation; people could be different but still have had the same experience; people who never had the experience might still have ways to understand it. We believe the world is more interesting and hopeful with the realization that the experience of being in "the closet" is generally the same irrespective of which status brought you there, or that a variety of race and ethnic groups are subject to racial profiling, or that women often experience the double consciousness that W. E. B. Du Bois described for blacks. When we realized how readily people could generalize from their own experience of stigma and privilege to what others might experience, we were energized.

That energy led to this book. But what should you do with your energy and insight? Or if you are feeling beaten down and depressed, rather than energized, what might you do about that?

Let us start with the worst-case scenario—that is, the possibility that you feel powerless to bring about social change, and hopelessly insignificant in the face of overwhelming social forces. Unfortunately, this is not an uncommon outcome in higher education, nor is it distinctive to this subject matter. The emphasis in higher education is more on "understanding" than "doing." Most university course work stresses detached, value-neutral reasoning, not passionate advocacy for social change.

> In the natural sciences, it is taken for granted that the aim is to explain an external order of nature. In literature, the text is an object to be interpreted. In politics, government is a phenomenon to be analyzed. Everywhere, it is intimated that the stance of the educated person should be that of the spectator. . . . In the contemporary university, one quickly learns that certain questions are out of order. One does not ask persistently about what ought to be done, for normative questions entail what are called value judgments, and these are said to be beyond the scope of scientific analysis. (Anderson, 1993:34–35, 36)

The distance from professional analyst to powerless observer is not very great; it would be easy to conclude that there is nothing you *can* do except chronicle the passing parade.

Paradoxically, however, education is also the source of much social change. We all know this almost instinctively. Educational institutions teach us our rights and our history, sharpen our thinking and decision-making, and open us to others' lived experience. Learning *changes* us, and higher education is explicit in its intention to produce that effect. The university is, after all, "an *educational* institution. As such, it is expected to have an impact on the society of which it is a part. . . . [T]he task of the university is not only to explore, systematically, the nature of the world, but also to scrutinize the practices of everyday life to see if they can be improved" (Anderson, 1993:59).

Recognizing the paradoxical nature of higher education, that it can both empower and disempower, means, in truth, that an element of choice—your choice—is involved in whether you are discouraged or inspired at the end of a course.

There is, however, another reason you might have for leaving this material feeling powerless. This has more to do with the nature of society than with the nature of education, but it again involves paradox and personal choice. Eminent sociologist Peter Berger called this the "Janus-faced" nature of human society. The Roman god Janus, for whom January was named, symbolized beginnings and endings, past and future, change and transition, and was depicted as having two faces looking in opposite directions. Berger used that image to convey that just as individuals are rarely wholly powerful, neither are they wholly powerless. In this analogy, Berger found a visual image for the truth that we are *both* the authors and victims—architects and prisoners—of social life. We *both* make society and are made by it. (And in our own spirit of powerfulness, we have edited out the sexism in Berger's prose below.)

> No social structure, however massive it may appear in the present, existed in this massivity from the dawn of time. Somewhere along the line each one of its salient features was concocted by human beings, whether they were charismatic visionaries, clever crooks, conquering heroes or just individuals in positions of power who hit on what seemed to them a better way of running the show. Since all social systems were created by [humans], it follows that [humans] can also change them.
>
> Every [person] who says "I have no choice" in referring to what his [or her] social role demands of him [or her] is engaged in "bad faith.". . . [People] are responsible for their actions. They are in "bad faith" when they attribute to iron necessity what they themselves are choosing to do. (Berger, 1963:128, 143–44)

While you do not have the power to change everything, you certainly have the power to change some things. Gandhi's paradox, discussed by Allan Johnson in Reading 62, captures this point: "Gandhi once said that nothing we do as individuals matters, but that it's vitally important to do it anyway."

So we urge you to move beyond your sense of being powerless and get on with the work of social change. We offer some suggestions for that process below, much of it drawn from work we have found both inspirational and practical.

We Make the Road by Walking

"We make the road by walking" was Spanish poet Antonio Machado's (1875–1939) adaptation of a proverb: "*se hace camino al andar,*" or "you make the way as you go."

It is also the title of a dialogue (made into a book) between two educator-activists, Myles Horton and Paulo Freire (Bell, Gaventa, and Peters, 1990).

Myles Horton founded the Highlander Folk School in Tennessee in 1932, when American racial segregation was still firmly in place. A unique school, Highlander offered racially integrated adult education—especially in history, government, and leadership—to the rural poor and working-class residents of the Cumberland Mountain communities. Horton's aim was to "use education as one of the instruments for bringing about a new social order" (Bell et al., 1990:xxiii). While many union leaders from the South studied at Highlander, the school is probably best known for its contribution to the civil rights movement. Highlander taught the methods of nonviolence and started "Citizenship Schools," which taught southern blacks to read and write, so that they could pass the tests required to vote. (Literacy tests have been used in many countries to keep poor people from voting. In the United States, they were used in southern states to keep African Americans from voting, until passage of the 1965 Voting Rights Act). Probably the most famous Highlander student was Rosa Parks, who attended Highlander shortly before her refusal to move to the back of the bus sparked the Montgomery, Alabama, bus boycott and the civil rights movement.

Paulo Freire, author of the classic, *Pedagogy of the Oppressed*, was in charge of a Brazilian national literacy program in the 1960s, before the government was overthrown by a military coup. Like American blacks before 1965, Brazil's poor were also denied the right to vote because they were illiterate. After the coup, Freire was forced to flee from Brazil, but he went on to write and develop literacy programs elsewhere. His work was distinguished by its emphasis on teaching literacy through real community issues. His belief that education must operate as a dialogue, rooted in values and committed to transforming the world, made him one of the most influential thinkers of the last century.

Apart from the example that Horton's and Freire's lives provide for the power of education to produce social change, we turn to them here for some basic lessons about transforming learning into action. First, we hope the phrase "we make the road by walking" helps you remember that *you* are the best person to know which "social interventions" will work for you. There is probably nothing more fundamental to social change than learning who you are, finding and honoring that authentic self, recognizing that it is multifaceted, complex, and *evolving*—and then making sure that the social change methods you use are consistent with that self. If you are going to pursue something as important as social change, it might as well be *you* who is doing it, not your impersonation of someone else.

"We make the road" also conveys that the road has not already been built. While there are many helpful resources, you will not find a recipe book designed for all the situations you will face, nor would that necessarily be a good idea. One of Horton's experiences with a union strike committee illustrates this point:

[Members of the committee] were getting desperate. They said: "Well, now you've had more experience than we have. You've got to tell us what to do. You're the expert." I said: "No, let's talk about it a little bit more. In the first place I don't know what to do, and if I did know what to do I wouldn't tell you, because if I had to tell you today then I'd have to tell you tomorrow, and when I'm gone you'd have to get somebody else to tell you." One guy reached in his pocket and pulled out a pistol and says, "Goddamn you, if you don't tell us I'm going to kill you." I was tempted then to become an instant expert, right on the spot! But I knew that if I did that, all would be lost and then all the rest of them would start asking me what to do. So I said: "No. Go ahead and shoot if you want to, but I'm not going to tell you." And the others calmed him down. (Bell et al., 1990:126)

So it is important to recognize that to some extent, you will need to be your *own* resource, *and* you will never have all the answers you need. Horton described two approaches to this inevitable incompleteness. First, "What I finally decided, after three or four years of reading and studying and trying to figure this thing out, was that *the way to do something was to start doing it and learn from it*" (Bell et al., 1990:40; emphasis added). And second, "*People learn from each other. You don't need to know the answer*" (Bell et al., 1990:55; emphasis added). As many of the personal accounts included in this book show, we make the road by walking.

Work on Yourself First

Challenging social constructions of difference by working on yourself first, may not seem earth shattering, but it is the unavoidable first step on Machado's proverbial "road." We think there are four main lessons on which to concentrate.

1. Increase your tolerance for making mistakes.   In his dialogue with Miles Horton, Paolo Freire remarked, "I am always in the beginning, as you"—and at that point Freire was 66 years old and Horton 82. The Reverend Jessie Jackson often reminds his listeners and himself, "The Lord is not done with me yet." Realizing how much you don't know about other people's life experience is a way to prepare for the absolute inevitability that, in trying to build connections across difference, *you will make mistakes*. You must increase your tolerance of your mistakes or risk giving up altogether, and you must try to focus on learning from all these attempts—good, bad, or ugly. As one of our colleagues often tells her students, when you are worried that you'll say the wrong thing, you wind up holding back, not extending yourself— and missing an opportunity for connection. Our advice is to just get used to making mistakes. There is no way around them.

2. Appreciate the statuses you occupy.   "Appreciating" your statuses—*stigmatized and privileged*—may sound odd, but it is the foundation that allows you to respond with more clarity to others' experiences of their statuses. By appreciating your own statuses, we mean honoring, valuing, and having some reasonable level of comfort about being white, black, Asian, or Latino; male or female; wealthy, middle class, or poor; able-bodied or disabled; straight or gay. Appreciating your status means not being ashamed of who you are.

Is there a part of your identity of which you are not proud? Is there a part of who you are that you tend to hide from people? *One of the most profound blows to oppression is claiming legitimate delight in who we are. . . .* Notice where you struggle in claiming pride in who you are. This is the preliminary work that must be done to work against all forms of oppression.

Reclaiming pride in our identities entails knowing our histories, becoming familiar not only with the side of history that causes us shame but also with the side that offers us hope. Ever mindful not to distort historical realities, it is nonetheless possible, even in the midst of the worst acts of oppression, to claim as our ancestors the few people who resisted the oppression. For example, in the present, it is useful for many people of German heritage to remember that there were heroic Germans who resisted Nazi anti-Semitism. . . . [A]long with the unfathomable devastation of the Holocaust, this minority tradition of resistance is also part of the history of the German people. (Brown and Mazza, 1997:5–6; emphasis added)

Ironically, at this juncture in American society, some level of shame seems to adhere to stigmatized *and* privileged statuses. We don't want to mislead you into thinking that getting over being ashamed of the statuses you occupy is an easy task, but recognizing the existence of shame and its dysfunction is an important first step. As Brown and Mazza suggest above, learning the *full* history of "your people"—good deeds and bad—will help you find heroes, as well as avoid false pride.

3. Learn to "sit in the fire."   For those in privileged statuses, guilt seems to be the most common reaction to discussions of prejudice and discrimination. For those in stigmatized statuses, anger probably ranks at the top. Those who occupy both privileged and stigmatized statuses are "privileged" to experience both ends of this emotional continuum! Insofar as race, sex, social class, disability, and sexual orientation are *all* on the table, *everyone* will probably have the opportunity for an intense emotional experience. That's a lot of emotion, not to mention that people have varying abilities to talk about—or even experience—those feelings. Either way, bridging differences sometimes means we must be willing to "sit in the fire" (Mindell, 1995) of conflict and intense emotion.

Regarding guilt, our advice is not to succumb to it. It is both immobilizing and distracting. Focusing on how badly *you* feel means that *you* are the subject of attention, not the people whose experience you are trying to understand.

About anger, our advice is more complicated. When it's someone else's anger, listen carefully so that you can understand it. Don't stop listening because you don't like the message or the way it is packaged. Don't take an expression of anger personally unless you are told it actually is about you. Try not to let someone else's anger trigger your own, because that will distract you from listening. Recognize that you can withstand someone's anger.

When you are the one who is angry, try not to let it overwhelm you. Try to distinguish between a setting in which you are under attack, and one populated by friends, or potential friends, who are trying to learn about your experience. Try to distinguish people who are malevolent from those who are misguided, or simply awkward in their efforts to help. Try to avoid self-righteousness. Your having been injured doesn't mean that you have not also inflicted injury. Remember that "every person is important, even those who belong to majority groups that have historically oppressed other groups" (Brown and Mazza, 1997:5).

No matter how your efforts seem to play out, remember that *the benefits of diversity derive from engagement, not passive observation. That contact will inevitably entail periods of disagreement and conflict.* Parker Palmer is a sociologist and nationally renowned expert on higher education. We quote him at length below, because he offers such a clear picture of what both frightens and draws us to engagement across difference.

> We collaborate with the structures of separation because they promise to protect us against one of the deepest fears at the heart of being human—the fear of having a live encounter with alien "otherness," whether the other is a student, a colleague, a subject, or a self-dissenting voice within. *We fear encounters in which the other is free to be itself, to speak its own truth, to tell us what we may not wish to hear. We want those encounters on our own terms, so that we can control their outcomes, so that they will not threaten our view of world and self....*
>
> This fear of the live encounter is actually a sequence of fears that begins in the fear of diversity. As long as we inhabit a university made homogeneous by our refusal to admit otherness, we can maintain the illusion that we possess the truth about ourselves and the world—after all, there is no "other" to challenge us! But as soon as we admit pluralism, we are forced to admit that ours is not the only standpoint, the only experience, the only way, and the truths we have built our lives on begin to feel fragile....
>
> Otherness, taken seriously, always invites transformation, calling us not only to new facts and theories and values but also to new ways of living our lives—and that is the most daunting threat of all. (Palmer, 1998: 36–38; emphasis added)

But what if there appears to be no diversity in the setting in which you find yourself? The odds are that that is just the appearance of things. No matter how homogeneous a group may seem, there will be layers of significant difference beneath the appearances. "Taking the time to examine [those less visible differences] can be invaluable, not only for creating a climate that welcomes the differences already present in the group, but also for laying the groundwork for becoming more inclusive of other differences" (Brown and Mazza, 1997:13).

4. Be an ally. Appreciate your allies.   We conclude this list with what we think is the most important of the lessons: Be an ally, find allies, appreciate your allies. There is nothing complicated about the concept of an ally: an ally is simply someone from a privileged status actively committed to eliminating stigma and the ill-treatment of those in stigmatized statuses. If you remember a time when you were treated unfairly because of a status you occupy and think about what you *wish* someone had done or said on your behalf, you will then understand the critical role an ally can play, and you will have a good sense of what the role calls for. Beyond that, you can learn about being an ally by asking people what would be helpful and by educating yourself about the history and experience of those in stigmatized groups.

Many of the personal accounts in this book are about having or wishing for an ally. Indeed, if "ally" were an entry in the help-wanted section of the newspaper, the opportunities would be described as "unlimited." John Larew's article on legacy admissions (Reading 38) is an example of being an ally. The article—written while he was editor of Harvard's *Crimson Tide*—sparked an extended, national discussion on legacy admissions. Larew can take considerable credit for the attention now being paid to the underrepresentation of low-income students in colleges and universities.

While Larew's article grew out of his daily experience and the media access he had as editor of the *Tide*, other ways of being an ally are available to virtually anyone, anytime—even, for example, at lunch. We single out this meal, because it is generally a public one, in which members of stigmatized categories are likely to find themselves with limited options; eat with other members of the category, eat alone, or hide. So an ally (or potential ally) might extend an invitation to share a sandwich.

Being an ally, however, is not only about what you can do on your own. It is also about joining with others in collective action. The social movements that have historically transformed the status of stigmatized groups in America, such as the women's movement or civil rights movement, included some people from privileged statuses, just as privileged allies have joined with members of stigmatized groups in innumerable more localized ways: university chapters of Men against Sexism, community groups like Parents and Friends of Lesbians and Gays, *AdBusters* culture jamming sessions, rock stars who keep concert organizers from segregating the audience by race (Burroughs, 2004:AL4), elected officials who sponsor antidiscrimination legislation, the 1960s college students who risked their lives to register black voters in the South, the Muslims in Rwanda who helped Tutsis escape from the 1994 genocide. You might consider how you could become an ally who makes a difference.

Still, *getting* allies sometimes requires *asking for help* and even telling people what you specifically want them to do. While you might wish for allies who could read your mind and then step in (and out) at exactly the right moment, it is more likely that your allies are going to be normal humans with the normal range of abilities. Those normal humans are more easily recruited to become allies with appreciation than with guilt.

> We rarely increase our effectiveness by dwelling on all of the things we still need to get right. This principle is especially important for those of us who are seeking allies. Pointing out only how the people around us have failed usually only increases their discouragement. Remembering the successes can lead to increased confidence and a greater ability to be an effective ally. (Brown and Mazza, 1997:49)

Of all potential allies, white men who are straight can be the most powerful. When a white man speaks on behalf of those in stigmatized statuses, he stands a good chance of being heard, if only because he appears not to be acting out of vested interest. His intervention can change the dynamic, provide a role model for others, and give those in stigmatized statuses a break from always being the ones to raise the contentious points. Once, on a panel about gender, we saw one of the men flag issues of sexism that the women panelists would otherwise have had to note. It seemed to us that they appreciated his intervention. In our own work settings, we have definitely appreciated the occasions when a white man has taken leadership on issues of sexual harassment, signed up for the "special interest" committee, or spoken up for the interests of people of color or white women.

Being an ally is also sometimes called for among one's friends and loved ones, that is, in more private settings where people feel free to air and cultivate their prejudices. Like Paul Kevil in Reading 64, who suggests some ways to respond in these situations, we would also urge you to be an "ally with a heart" in these settings.

> Condemning people, shaming them, and making them feel guilty are all unproductive strategies: They all increase defensiveness rather than creating an opening for change. . . . Condemning people rarely helps them to change their behavior. Instead, think about what you honestly appreciate about the person. Also consider the ways that person has made any progress, even if it's only slight, on the issue that is of concern to you. Practice telling that person the things she is doing right. Appreciation leads to action; condemnation leads to paralysis.
>
> People are often afraid to appreciate someone whose behavior they disapprove of, for fear that the appreciation will keep the oppressive behavior unchallenged. However, only by seeing what is human in the person who acts oppressively can we hope to bring about change. All of us are more receptive to suggestions to change when we know we are liked. (Brown and Mazza, 1997:3)

A Concluding Note

We opened this essay worried that our readers felt powerless and insignificant. We close with the hope that you now understand that challenging the constructions of difference is well within *all* of our capabilities. We're not likely to bring the machine to a halt, but we can certainly make a difference.

KEY CONCEPTS

Ally   someone from a privileged status committed to eliminating stigma and the ill-treatment of those in stigmatized statuses. (page **473**)

Ghandi's paradox   while nothing we do as individuals matters, it is important to take action anyway. (page **469**)

Janus-faced nature of society   that people create society, but also that society constrains people (page **469**)

REFERENCES

Anderson, Charles W. 1993. *Prescribing the Life of the Mind: An Essay on the Purpose of the University, the Aims of Liberal Education, the Competence of Citizens, and the Cultivation of Practical Reason.* Madison: University of Wisconsin Press.

Bell, Brenda, John Gaveenta, and John Peters. 1990. *We Make the Road by Walking: Conversations on Education and Social Change.* Philadephia: Temple University Press.

Berger, Peter L. 1963. *Invitation To Sociology: A Humanistic Perspective.* New York: Anchor Books.

Brown, Cherie R., and George J. Mazza. 1997. *Healing into Action: A Leadership Guide for Creating Diverse Communities.* Washington, DC: National Coalition Building Institute.

Burroughs, Alexandra. 2004. Stock Up on the Pop Tarts: Britney's in Town. *National Post,* August 12, 2004, AL4.

Mindell, Arnold. 1995. *Sitting in the Fire: Large Group Transformation Using Conflict and Diversity.* Portland, OR: Lao Tse Press.

Palmer, Parker J. 1998. *The Courage to Teach: Exploring the Inner Landscape of a Teacher's Life.* San Francisco: Jossey-Bass.

Influencing Public Policy

Jeanine C. Cogan

. . . Federal and state politics are commonly portrayed as open only to a few select stakeholders, as too complex to maneuver, and/or as too big for an individual to have an impact on. One goal of this [discussion] is to correct these misperceptions with information on and tools for how to successfully influence policy. This [discussion] reflects my experience as a policy advocate at the federal level. However, the basic principles and strategies described here can be applied to other levels of government and policy development. This [discussion] considers three topics: the players in policy development, the lifestyle of policy makers, and how you too can influence policy.

THE PLAYERS IN FEDERAL POLICY DEVELOPMENT

There are at least five central groups or stakeholders involved in influencing the legislative process: constituents, organizations or interest groups, coalitions, members of Congress, and congressional staffers. The role that each plays in the federal policy-making process is briefly described below.

Constituents

Anyone eligible to vote is a constituent. This probably includes you and many of the people you care about. As such, your primary mechanism for influencing the federal legislative process is through your members of Congress: senators and representatives. According to the American Psychological Association,[1] some members of Congress view their constituents as having the most influence on their voting decisions—more than lobbying groups, their

Jeanine C. Cogan is director of Action Based Consulting in Washington, D.C., and a former American Psychological Association congressional fellow.

colleagues, and party pressures. Because the people in their districts vote members of Congress into office, members are motivated to attend to constituent concerns. Indeed, constituent service is one of the most important aspects of congressional life.[2]

Constituents articulate their views and concerns to members through visits, letters, e-mail, and/or phone calls. In addition, grassroots activism, such as rallies and protests, is effective in mobilizing constituents within a community and to focus members' attention on specific issues. Constituents may also be a member of or become involved in organizations that work to influence policy.

Advocacy Organizations

There are numerous types of organizations and interest groups that advocate for specific policies. They cover a range of issues, including business and industry, science and technology, professional interests, labor, civil rights, public interest, and governmental interests.[3] Organizations often have a person or office responsible for advocating on behalf of their members' interests and concerns. Advocating on behalf of a large number of people across the nation can offer more political weight to a message than simply advocating on behalf of one's own interests as a constituent.[4]

Congressional staff often work closely with advocacy groups.[5] In order to move a bill forward, staffers may work with advocacy groups to identify members in key congressional districts who need to be contacted directly by their local constituents. Such grassroots support for a bill may help it gain active congressional consideration and increase its priority as an issue on the legislative agenda.

. . . To be able to exert more significant influence, advocacy groups may coordinate efforts and work together through coalitions.

Coalitions

Coalitions typically are composed of clusters of advocacy organizations that share common interests or political positions with the aim of developing strength in numbers in order to influence policy. The coalition is designed to bring diverse organizations together to lobby on national policies, promote grass-roots activism, and educate the public.[6] Members of a coalition may establish personal relationships with staff and members of Congress, which can contribute to the success of a bill or other policy initiative. Coalitions vary significantly in their membership, structure, and missions. Their constituencies and agendas may shift and adapt according to the changing policy environment and legislative focus. Membership within a coalition is typically on a group, rather than individual, basis. Coalition activities include regular meetings, federal and local outreach efforts, the sharing of knowledge and resources, and strategizing about how to optimize their influence. Working in coalitions maximizes the likelihood of successfully influencing the legislative process by allowing a large number of people to express their opinion on an issue in a short period of time.

Members of Congress

Certainly, a legislator's colleagues, the other policy makers, are another important influence. Numerous factors contribute to the decisions legislators make.[7] Three primary considerations are key in members' political decisions: (1) to satisfy constituents, (2) to enhance their personal reputations within the political world, and (3) to create good policy. All three can be accomplished when members have the skill to successfully work with and influence one another.[8] Members influence each other through direct one-on-one interaction, legislation, briefings, hearings, speeches, and the press. The well-known "Dear Colleague" letter on Capitol Hill, in which members explain legislation to their colleagues and urge them either to become co-sponsors or to vote along similar lines, is a primary strategy for influencing other members.

Members also influence each other through party affiliation and loyalty. Party politics plays a significant role in members' policy decisions.[9] Party leadership may urge members to vote in a certain way on specific legislation. Partisan politics are most apparent in party "whipping." Whipping occurs when party leadership strongly encourages members to vote in a particular way with the im-plied assumption that doing so will result in rewards. For voting along party lines, members can be rewarded with positions on more powerful committees, among other things that give them more power and clout with colleagues. This influence with colleagues may translate into a greater likelihood of successfully addressing constituent concerns, thereby improving reelection possibilities.

Congressional Staff

Until the 1950s, the U.S. Congress was a part-time institution that worked for 9 of the 24 months of a congressional session. The congressional workload has doubled in the last 30 years.[10] Currently, members work 18 months per session. The increased workload resulted from a series of decisions that enlarged congressional staff assistance, beginning in 1946 with the Legislative Reorganization Act.[11] For example, in 1967 members of the House of Representatives employed 4,000 people as personal staff. By 1990 that number had doubled. Interestingly, some scholars have argued that the increase of staff has resulted in expanded staff autonomy. With larger staffs, members are able to take on more issues and expand their workload. In turn, members need to rely more on and increasingly delegate independent authority to their staff.

Consequently, staff play a critical role in determining policy. Members rely on staff to track specific issues, write speeches, educate them on a range of topics, advise them on legislation and policy decisions, and write legislation. The autonomy and influence of a staffer depends on a range of factors including their individual personalities, the structure of the office, and the members' style.[12]

THE LIFESTYLE OF A POLICY MAKER

"To best understand the way in which federal policy is formulated, it helps to think of Capitol Hill as a community, or culture, with its own inhabitants, rules, norms, and social processes."[13] Only by understanding the culture of politicians can scientists, lobbyists, activists, or anyone else hope to influence the federal process and shape public policy.[14] Four

BOX 1

WRITE AN EFFECTIVE BRIEFING SHEET OR TALKING POINTS

1. *First identify the goal and state it clearly.* Why are you lobbying the member? What is the reason for meeting with the staffer?
2. *Summarize the research and main arguments using bullet points.*
3. *Stay focused on one topic.* If you wish to discuss more than one topic, prepare separate briefing memos (one per topic).
4. *Be concise.* Keep briefing memos to one page, if possible. If the message cannot be conveyed in a page or two, you will likely lose the opportunity to influence the staff.
5. *Make the briefing memo easy to read and visually appealing.*

BOX 2

AN EFFECTIVE BRIEFING MEMO

GOAL: WE URGE YOUR BOSS TO SUPPORT THE HATE CRIMES PREVENTION ACT (HCPA)

Why We Need the HCPA

- According to community surveys, violence against individuals on the basis of their real or perceived race, ethnicity, religion, sexual orientation, gender, disability, and other social groupings is a fact of life in the United States.
- A civil rights statute, Section 245 of Title 18 U.S.C., gives federal prosecutors the authority to investigate allegations of hate violence based on race, religion, and national origin. This avenue for federal involvement is necessary in order to address cases where state and local authorities fail to properly respond to victims' allegations. Currently such federal investigations are minimal, with typically less than 10 prosecutions annually.
- This statute is critical for responding to the problem of hate violence, yet it does not include a broad definition of hate crimes in line with more recent legislation. In 1994 Congress passed the Hate Crimes Sentencing Enhancement Act as part of the Violent Crime Control and Law Enforcement Act of 1994. In this law, hate crimes were defined broadly as a crime committed against the person:

  > "because of the actual or perceived race, color, religion, national origin, ethnicity, gender, disability, or sexual orientation of that person."

Purpose of the HCPA

- The main purpose of the HCPA is to bring Section 245 of Title 18 U.S.C. in line with this recent hate crimes definition so that federal officials can investigate and prosecute crimes motivated by hate based on the victim's real or perceived gender, disability, or sexual orientation.
- The Department of Justice (DOJ) receives inquiries from families of gay victims asking for their involvement when local authorities have failed to respond. Unfortunately, the DOJ does not have the authority to investigate such cases. The DOJ considers this bill an important measure in assisting them to properly respond to victims' concerns.

I wrote this example of a briefing memo specifically for the purposes of this [discussion]. The material is based on my advocacy work in the Public Policy Office at the American Psychological Association.

central characteristics of congressional offices are the rapid pace, the large workload, the valuing of direct experience over other data, and the need to compromise.

Political life is typically a lifestyle of unanticipated, urgent deadlines. Given these tight timelines, it is not uncommon for staffers to become "experts" on a specific topic in a few days or mere hours. Therefore, as they are searching for facts on a topic, staffers must rely on easily accessible, digestible resources—typically the Internet or talking points provided by advocates. The outcome of such quick research is often a blend of substantive and political information. Also, with the expanded congressional workload, staffers are typically stretched so thin that reading one-page summaries is all they have time to do. Extensive reports are often useless unless there is a one- or two-page summary (called talking points or briefing memo).[15] Boxes 1 and 2 explain how to prepare such documents.

Although some policy makers appreciate the importance and usefulness of considering scientific data in their decision-making process, they tend to place greater value on precedent and anecdotal evidence. It is not unusual for legislation to remain stagnant until an event occurs to galvanize members of Congress. For example, in 1998 the Hate

Crimes Prevention Act received attention, with hearings in both the House and Senate, only after an African American man was brutally murdered in Jasper, Texas. Similarly, critical gun control legislation that had been introduced each session of Congress for a number of years was not seriously considered until after the Columbine High School shooting in Littleton, Colorado, in 1999. The palpable role of real-life stories in members' policy decisions may in part reflect that they are primarily motivated to address the needs of their constituents and do so after hearing of their concerns and hardships. Additionally, research on persuasion shows that, depending on the audience, appealing to one's emotions, especially with fear-arousing messages, can be a powerful method of communication.[16] This lesson has not gone unnoticed by policy makers.

Given the nature of our two-party system of government, members must work with individuals who may have very different opinions and perspectives on an issue. As a consequence, to move a policy initiative forward one must have enough support, which often requires negotiation and compromise. This tendency to compromise may collide with the desires and expectations of constituents and advocacy groups.

Understanding the unique culture of policy makers allows you to be more effective in influencing federal policy. Given the rapid pace and heavy workloads, you can increase your effectiveness in working with congressional offices by interacting with staff in a way that shows respect for staffers' time and efforts. Additionally, when working with staff it is useful to offer both data and personal stories of affected individuals. Finally, you may be more successful working with staff if you have an understanding of the limitations of members of Congress due to the institutional tendency toward compromise.

INFLUENCING PUBLIC POLICY

There are two basic avenues by which you can shape policy. In some cases, you will want to influence leg-

islators on issues that are already on the public agenda. In others, you will want to create legislative support for an unknown or invisible issue.

Influencing Legislators on Existing Issues

As you already know, voting constituents are greatly valued in legislative offices. A constituent communicating concerns to members of Congress can play an influential role in the legislative process. The most common way in which individuals can influence policy is to register opinions on already existing bills. Interested constituents can communicate with members of Congress or work in coalitions to promote or prevent the passage of particular legislation.

Contacting Members of Congress The first step in effective communication with Congress is to determine the best person to contact. Usually, contacting your own legislator—the person who represents your congressional district—is most effective. As your elected official, this is the person who represents you and therefore must be sensitive to your views and concerns. Occasionally, however, in order to achieve a certain goal it will be more appropriate to contact other members of Congress. For example, if a member is recognized as a leader on an issue in which you have expertise or interest, then contacting that member is appropriate, even if he or she does not represent your congressional district or state.

Constituents can contact members of Congress through phone calls, letter writing, e-mail, or a visit (see Boxes 3 and 4). The purpose of the communication often determines which mode of communication to use. For example, is the communication meant to register an opinion or to educate members of Congress on a particular issue? Is it designed to establish a relationship with the congressional office? Is an immediate response and action needed?

If a bill is currently being debated, it is controversial, and/or there are other time pressures, you may be more successful communicating with members by phone. Members of Congress may inquire

CONTACT YOUR LEGISLATORS

FEDERAL LEVEL

When writing a letter to your member of Congress use the following congressional addresses:

(Your Congressperson) The Honorable First, Last Name
U.S. House of Representatives
Washington, DC 20515

(Your Senator) The Honorable First, Last Name
U.S. Senate
Washington, DC 20510

When calling your member of Congress, use the U.S. Capitol Switchboard at 202-224-3121. Constituents should ask for their representative and/or senator.

STATE AND LOCAL LEVEL

Use GovSpot at *www.govspot.com/* to identify and contact your state and local leaders. GovSpot.com is a nonpartisan government information portal designed to simplify the search for relevant government information online. This resource offers a collection of top government and civic resources such as government websites and documents, facts and figures, news, political information, and how to locate state and local policy makers.

from staff what their constituents are expressing and consider this when making policy decisions. Constituents interested in calling members should call the U.S. Capitol Switchboard at 202-224-3121 and ask for their representative and/or senator.

If you are interested in receiving a response to an inquiry or educating members of Congress, then writing a letter or setting up a visit are preferable. (For help organizing and conducting visits to congressional offices, refer to Box 4.) The most effective letters are those that are concise and focused on one issue. (An example of a sample letter is shown in Box 5.) To write an effective letter, you should follow these three steps:

1. *State the purpose.* The first paragraph should include who you are and why you are writing this particular member of Congress. For exam-

ple, "I am writing you as a constituent in your district." This is followed by the purpose of the letter. Bill names and/or numbers should be used if possible and applicable; for example, "I am writing to urge you to vote for the Hate Crimes Prevention Act."

2. *State the evidence/argument.* The purpose is followed by a rationale for the requested action. For example, "Given that so many states currently do not have laws that allow crimes to be investigated as hate crimes, the passage of this bill is necessary." Personal experiences that support the stated position can be concisely summarized as well. If you would like to make a research-based argument, then a short summary of the research or the presentation of some data can be effective.

3. *Ask for a response.* To optimize the impact of a correspondence, you should conclude by specifically asking members to reply. Responding to constituent mail is a vital role of congressional offices. The last paragraph should reiterate your concern and request a response.[17]

Effective Advocacy When interacting with policy makers, advocates may err by being overly critical without offering specific suggestions or alternatives. Making this mistake will limit your effectiveness. Most legislators and their staff want to write the best bills possible and implement effective policies. For this reason, you should view the staffer as a friend, not a foe. Many staffers will be open to your expertise and ideas (though they may not always implement them). Therefore, when possible, it is useful to offer particular strategies for implementing the goals or ideas you want to promote.

For example, if you support the overall purpose of a bill but think it has flaws, prepare talking points that outline the concerns and offer alternatives. When I served as a legislative assistant for Congresswoman DeGette, I wrote a bill that health consumers supported but health providers opposed. After introducing the bill, many provider groups were critical and some raised legitimate concerns. The groups who were most effective were those that offered alternative language for the bill. Even if they

ORGANIZE VISITS WITH ELECTED OFFICIALS

One of the best avenues to equality for LGB Americans is through establishing a personal relationship with your elected officials. Like any relationship, these relationships require cultivation over time and will involve developing ties to the elected official as well as members of their staff. A personal visit can be key to this kind of interaction. For state and local officials, this may not be difficult. If a visit to Washington, D.C., is difficult, you can arrange to visit your members of Congress when they return to their district office.

   When you schedule such a visit, it may be helpful to organize a small group of like-minded voters. Taking a delegation of interested persons with you will enhance your visit. If this is not possible, bring at least one other person with you for support.

   Your meeting will be most effective by doing the following:

- Identify the "visit team" (no more than six individuals) from your state or district who are interested in LGB issues.
- If you are from a big state and you are meeting with your senator, you may want to include individuals from several points around the state. The same is true for congressional districts and for state and local officials.
- The official's political party doesn't really matter. However, it helps if you can get someone on your team who is politically well connected or has a good sense of the local political dynamic.
- Make sure members of your team are comfortable with the process. If they are truly uncomfortable, they may detract from the overall impression you want to leave with your elected official.
- Arrange the date, time, and place for a premeeting of the visit team. Use this meeting (or at least a conference call) to make sure everyone is on board. You do not want questions or disagreements within your group during the visit.
- Arrange the date, time, and place for a meeting by contacting the state, district, or local office of the elected official you wish to meet.
- Coordinate the participants in the meeting to make sure that the visit team "sings with one voice" in making points with the elected official.
- Use the material in *Everyday Activism* to arm the team with the facts. In addition, do some research on the local situation so that you can personalize your arguments.
- Visit-team leaders should be prepared to guide and direct the meeting. After assembling at the office, team members should introduce themselves and identify the organization or institution with which they are affiliated.
- The visit-team leader should then lay out the problem and briefly outline the impact of the issue on the official's constituency.
- An open discussion should follow, with each team member providing his or her input while maintaining as much of a conversational tone as possible.
- Above all **listen.** Try to ascertain where your official is coming from. Employ active listening techniques to show her or him that you understand the concerns being raised. Try to answer objections and concerns as appropriate but don't get into a fight. Be firm and assertive but **not** combative.
- Be sure that the elected official is asked at some point to take a certain action, to support a policy initiative, or vote in a particular way on current legislation. For example:

   "Will you please assist our efforts to overturn the ban on lesbian and gay men in the military? Specifically, we would like for you to sponsor legislation to repeal the ban."
   "Will you support efforts to end workplace discrimination against lesbian and gay men? Specifically, we would like for you to co-sponsor ENDA."

- If the official expresses uncertainty about the facts, offer to provide further information to document the facts. . . .
- After the visit, send a follow-up letter thanking the official for his or her time and consideration. Include the information you offered to provide (e.g., a copy of the relevant policy brief) with your letter.

Adapted from unpublished materials originally drafted by William Baily, American Psychological Association.

AN EFFECTIVE CONSTITUENT LETTER

The Honorable John Doe
U.S. House of Representatives
Washington, DC 20515

Dear Representative John Doe:

I am a constituent and am writing to ask you to oppose the proposed amendment by Congressman Todd Tiahrt (R-Kan.) to the D.C. appropriations bill that would prevent unmarried couples from adopting children in Washington, D.C. This current bill is ill-conceived and based on a number of inaccurate beliefs about lesbians and gay men as parents.

As a lesbian mother, I live in constant fear of losing custody of my child even though I am a nurturing, committed parent. I participate actively in the school board and related activities. My ability to be a caring and effective parent has nothing to do with my sexual orientation. This current amendment further threatens my daily existence as a parent.

According to the American Psychological Association, research shows that lesbians and gay men are fit parents. Contrary to the belief that gay parents may have a negative influence on their children, when compared with children of heterosexual parents, children of gay men or lesbians show no marked difference in their intelligence, psychological adjustment, social adjustment, popularity with friends, development of sex role identity, or development of sexual orientation. Overall, the belief that children of gay and lesbian parents suffer deficits in personal development has no empirical foundation.

In sum, the characterization of homosexual parents as being a threat to children is inaccurate, therefore calling into question policy decisions based on this belief. I urge you to oppose this amendment. I look forward to hearing your perspective.

Respectfully,
Jane Smith

I wrote this as an example of a good constituent letter. The Tiahrt amendment was introduced to the D.C. appropriations bill in 1997. Although it was eliminated, a similar amendment had been introduced every year since.

agree with your perspective, legislative staffers may not have the time or expertise to find a solution for your concern. However, you can play a unique role in the legislative process by offering specific solutions and assistance to the congressional staff.

Creating Congressional Support for an Unknown Issue

In addition to influencing important policy decisions about existing legislation and visible issues, you can also help set the legislative agenda. For example, hate crimes legislation grew out of a national coordinated movement that promoted this issue as an important policy priority. Individuals and organizations met with members of Congress urging them to recognize and address this growing problem.

Finding Members to Support and Promote an Issue Members of Congress become known for their leadership in particular areas. You should research which member is likely to support and promote your issue. Given the continuing hostile environment toward LGBs, most members, even leaders on LGB-positive policies, will not showcase their work on LGB rights. So while information about members' policy priorities and accomplishments is available on their websites, you may have to look beyond their bios or issues of interest. For example, Rep. Christopher Shays (R-Conn.) has been a leading advocate for [the Employment Nondiscrimination Act]. However, his endless support for LGB protections against workplace discrimination is not obvious from his website under the heading "issues." Instead, you have to look under "press releases." Keep this in mind as you explore members' homepages and other information. The Internet address for members' homepages for the House of Representatives is www.house.gov. For the Senate, it is www.senate.gov. Members' biographies are also available by accessing the website on biographical directories of members of Congress at bioguide.congress.gov/. An excellent book, titled *Politics in America,* provides descriptions of the members of Congress and is published each year by the *Congressional Quarterly.*

Another useful avenue for learning the legislative priorities of members is to see what bills they introduced or co-sponsored through accessing the Thomas website at thomas.loc.gov. This site provides information about the bills members have introduced and/or co-sponsored, as well as the text of legislation, congressional records, committee information, and bill status and summaries.

Establishing Relationships With Congressional Staff

As you have learned already, congressional staff are critical in policy development and their influence can be substantial. Staffers serve as gatekeepers to members of Congress by deciding who receives entrée into the office. If staff advise the member of Congress to meet with a particular advocacy group, the member is likely to do so. Given this influence, advocates interested in making contact with their representatives should establish rapport with the legislative staff. To this end, you can seek an appointment by calling the legislative assistant currently working on the issue of interest. In order to increase the chances of success, you should offer an explanation for choosing this particular member and state the purpose of the proposed meeting. For example, "I am calling you because your boss is a leader on employment issues. I know she led the fight to save small businesses last year. I would like to schedule an appointment with you to discuss another important employment issue: the need for legislation to prevent work-related discrimination based on sexual orientation."

Educating Staff The primary goal of working with congressional members is to increase their knowledge and understanding of a particular topic that can lead to congressional interest and action. Because advocates tend to hold detailed knowledge on a specific topic while staffers have a little information about many topics, staffers typically welcome information. Due to the workload constraints, you should present concise summaries and clearly outlined points and goals. To facilitate this process, prepare handouts for congressional staff with talk-

ing points or briefing memos that summarize the topic. . . . As you have already seen, Box 1 provides guidelines for writing an effective policy brief and Box 2 contains an example.

Addressing Inaccurate Perceptions and Reaching a Broader Audience Given that there is so much misinformation about the lives of LGBs, one of the most important roles you can play is to correct myths and stereotypes. This is where research is particularly helpful. The American Psychological Association (APA) has created many documents based on solid social science evidence. Summaries of research that clarify the truth about LGBs' lives and experiences are readily available by accessing the American Psychological Association Lesbian, Gay, and Bisexual Concerns Office website at www.apa.org/pi/lgbc/publications/pubsreports.html/.

In addition to educating the major players in the policy process, you may need to reach broader audiences with your efforts to raise awareness and correct misinformation. Writing letters to the editor of local, regional, and national publications is one way to do this. Most policy makers pay close attention to the media in their districts, so such letters can also have an impact on policy making. In addition, many newspapers welcome well-written op-ed columns on issues of concern to their readers. The guidance provided in Boxes 6 and 7 may help you get your ideas into print.

CONCLUSION

Every day, thousands of people are actively lobbying members of Congress in an effort to influence policy. In order to defend against anti-LGB policies and to advocate for policies that are proactive in improving the lives of lesbian, gay, and bisexual people, we must remain active participants in the legislative process. From writing letters to establishing more enduring relationships with congressional staffers, we all can and do influence policy.

To some this process may seem cumbersome and complicated. However, please remember that help is always available. If you have questions about the

BOX 6

WRITE A LETTER TO THE EDITOR

- Make one point (or at most two) in your letter or fax. State the point clearly, ideally in the first sentence.
- Make your letter timely. If you are not addressing a specific article, editorial, or letter that recently appeared in the paper you are writing to, then tie your issue to a recent event.
- Familiarize yourself with the coverage and editorial position of the paper to which you are writing. Refute or support specific statements, address relevant facts that are ignored, but avoid blanket attacks on the media in general or the newspaper in particular.
- Check the letter specifications of the newspaper to which you are writing. Length and format requirements vary from paper to paper. (Generally, roughly two short paragraphs are ideal.) You also must include your name, signature, address, and phone number.
- Look at the letters that appear in your paper. Are the letters printed usually of a certain type?
- Support your facts. If the topic you address is controversial, consider sending documentation along with your letter. But don't overload the editors with too much information.
- Keep your letter brief. Type it.
- Find others to write letters when possible. This will show that other individuals in the community are concerned about the issue. If your letter doesn't get published, perhaps someone else's on the same topic will.
- Monitor the paper for your letter. If your letter has not appeared within a week or two, follow up with a call to the editorial department of the newspaper.
- Write to different sections of the paper when appropriate. Sometimes the issue you want to address is relevant to the lifestyle, book review, or other section of the paper.

Text adapted from Fairness and Accuracy in Reporting (FAIR) at www.fair.org/.

BOX 7

WRITE AN OP-ED

An op-ed gets its name because of its placement opposite the editorial page. It is longer than a letter to the editor—usually 500–800 words. Also often referred to as an opinion editorial, these are more difficult to get printed than a letter to the editor but can be very effective.

GETTING IT IN PRINT

- *Pick the right author.* Many papers will only print an op-ed from a representative of an organization or from a noted authority. A meeting with the editor can also help to establish the author as credible. Using a local spokesperson increases the local perspective or interest, especially on issues with national significance.
- *Pitch the article ahead of time.* Ideally, pitch your idea to the editor about 2 weeks before you want it to run. If you are responding to an op-ed that has just been published, contact the op-ed page editor right away to ask about a response. Even if they don't ask, offer to send a draft for their consideration.
- *Follow the guidelines.* Call your paper to find out the preferred length for an op-ed, deadlines, and any other requirements. Unless guidelines say otherwise, submit the piece typed and double-spaced on white paper with 1-inch margins. Ideally, the first page should be on your letterhead. Have a header at the top of each additional page with your name, the date, and the page number. Fax, mail, e-mail, or hand deliver the piece to the op-ed page editor.
- *Have a specific point of view and something fresh to offer.* Try to be ahead of the curve in public discussion of an issue. Let friends and peers review the piece and offer comments.
- *Follow up.* Follow the mailing with a phone call to the op-ed page editor. Be polite and respectful of his or her schedule, but try to emphasize again, as feels appropriate, why the paper should run the piece. Remember—there is a lot of competition for space on the op-ed page. If you are not successful on your first try, don't give up.

Text adapted from PFLAG at www.pflag.org/.

federal government, trained staff at the Federal Consumer Information Center will answer your questions about federal programs, benefits, or services. You can call their toll-free hotline at 800-688-9889 (TTY 800-326-2996) between 9 A.M. and 8 P.M. Eastern time or use their website (www.info.gov/).

Although this [discussion] has focused on advocacy at the federal level, the same basic principles and processes can be applied at any level. Whether you want to push for LGB-affirming legislation on Capitol Hill, in your state legislature, or with local elected officials, you will be most effective when you educate yourself and share that knowledge with those you wish to influence. Developing relationship networks can be an effective strategy for educating officials and members of their staffs regardless of the level of government. Well-crafted letters to the editor and op-ed columns can raise awareness of the issues locally, regionally, and nationally. . . . Use the lessons you have learned from this discussion and make a difference.

DISCUSSION QUESTIONS

1. Does Cogan's description of "Capitol Hill culture" fit with your assumptions about how government works? What surprised you in her description? What didn't?
2. Does the information in Cogan's article make you feel any more comfortable about pursuing "everyday activism" on issues important to you? Why or why not?

NOTES

1. American Psychological Association. (1995). *Advancing psychology in the public interest: A psychologist's guide to participation in federal policy making.* Washington, DC: Author.
2. Wells, W. G. (1996). *Working with Congress: A practical guide for scientists and engineers.* Washington, DC: American Association for the Advancement of Science.
3. Lorion, R. P., & Iscoe, I. (1996). Reshaping our views of our field. In R. P. Lorion, I. Iscoe, P. H. DeLeon, & G. R. VandenBos (Eds.), *Psychology and public policy* (pp. 1–19). Washington, DC: American Psychological Association. Truman, D. B. (1987). The nature and functions of interest groups: The governmental process. In P. Woll (Ed.), *American government: Readings and cases* (pp. 255–262). Boston: Little, Brown.
4. Ceaser, J. W., Bessette, J. M., O'Toole, L. J., & Thurow, G. (1995). *American government: Origins, institutions, and public policy* (4th ed.). Dubuque, IA: Kendall/Hunt.

5. Nickels, I. B. (1994). *Guiding a bill through the legislative process* (Congressional Research Service Report for Congress, 94-322 GOV). Washington, DC: Library of Congress.
6. Key, V. O. (1987). The nature and functions of interest groups: Pressure groups. In P. Woll (Ed.), *American government: Readings and cases* (pp. 266–273). Boston: Little, Brown.
7. American Psychological Association, 1995 (see note 1). Wells, 1996 (see note 2).
8. Drew, E. (1987). A day in the life of a United States Senator. In P. Woll (Ed.), *American government: Readings and cases* (pp. 487–497). Boston: Little, Brown. Vincent, T. A. (1990). A view from the Hill: The human element in policy making on Capitol Hill. American Psychologist, 45(1), 61–64.
9. American Psychological Association, 1995.
10. Wells, 1996.
11. Rundquist, P. S., Schneider, J., & Pauls, F. H. (1992). *Congressional staff: An analysis of their roles, functions, and impacts* (Congressional Research Service Report for Congress, 92-90S). Washington, DC: Library of Congress.
12. Redman, E. (1987). Congressional staff: The surrogates of power. In P. Woll (Ed.), *American government: Readings and cases* (pp. 452–461). Boston: Little, Brown. Rundquist, Scheider, & Pauls, 1992.
13. Vincent, T. A., 1990, p. 61 (see note 8).
14. Bevan, W. (1996). On getting in bed with a lion. In R. P. Lorion, I. Iscoe, P. H. DeLeon, & G. R. VandenBos (Eds.), *Psychology and public policy* (pp. 145–163). Washington, DC: American Psychological Association. Nissim-Sabat, D. (1997). Psychologists, Congress, and public policy. Professional Psychology: Research and Practice, 28(3). 275–280. Wells, 1996 (see note 2).
15. This is the rationale for including briefing memos throughout this [discussion].
16. For example, Wilson, D. K., Purdon, S. E., & Wallston, A. (1988). Compliance to health recommendations: A theoretical overview of message framing. *Health Education Research, 3,* 161–171.
17. American Psychological Association, 1995 (see note 1). For more information on how to write an effective letter, the reader is referred to the information brochure written by the APA titled: Calkins, B. J. (1995). *Psychology in the public interest: A psychologist's guide to participation in federal policy making.* Washington, DC: APA. Available at www.apa.org/ppo/grassroots/sadguide.html.

What Can We Do?

BECOMING PART OF THE SOLUTION

Allan G. Johnson

The challenge we face is to change patterns of exclusion, rejection, privilege, harassment, discrimination, and violence that are everywhere in this society and have existed for hundreds (or, in the case of gender, thousands) of years. We have to begin by thinking about the trouble and the challenge in new and more productive ways. . . .

Large numbers of people have sat on the sidelines and seen themselves as neither part of the problem nor the solution. Beyond this shared trait, however, they are far from homogeneous. Everyone is aware of the whites, heterosexuals, and men who intentionally act out in oppressive ways. But there is less attention to the millions of people who know inequities exist and want to be part of the solution. Their silence and invisibility allow the trouble to continue. Removing what silences them and stands in their way can tap an enormous potential of energy for change. . . .

MYTH 1: "IT'S ALWAYS BEEN THIS WAY, AND IT ALWAYS WILL"

If you don't make a point of studying history, it's easy to slide into the belief that things have always been the way we've known them to be. But if you look back a bit further, you find racial oppression has been a feature of human life for only a matter of centuries, and there is abundant evidence that male dominance has been around for only seven thousand years or so, which isn't very long when you consider that human beings have been on the earth for hundreds of thousands of years.[1] So when it comes to human social life, the smart money should

be on the idea that *nothing* has always been this way or any other.

This idea should suggest that nothing *will* always be this way or any other, contrary to the notion that privilege and oppression are here to stay. If the only thing we can count on is change, then it's hard to see why we should believe for a minute that *any* kind of social system is permanent. Reality is always in motion. Things may appear to stand still, but that's only because humans have a short attention span, dictated perhaps by the shortness of our lives. If we take the long view—the *really* long view—we can see that everything is in process all the time.

Some would argue that everything *is* process, the space between one point and another, the movement from one thing toward another. What we may see as permanent end points—world capitalism, Western civilization, advanced technology, and so on—are actually temporary states on the way to other temporary states. Even ecologists, who used to talk about ecological balance, now speak of ecosystems as inherently unstable. Instead of always returning to some steady state after a period of disruption, ecosystems are, by nature, a continuing process of change from one arrangement to another. They never go back to just where they were.

Social systems are also fluid. A society isn't some hulking *thing* that sits there forever as it is. Because a system happens only as people participate in it, it can't help being a dynamic process of creation and re-creation from one moment to the next. In something as simple as a man following the path of least resistance toward controlling conversations (and a woman letting him do it), the reality of male privilege in that moment comes into being. This is how we *do* male privilege, bit by bit, moment by moment. This is also how individuals can contribute to change: by choosing paths of *greater* resistance, as when men don't take control and women refuse their own subordination.

Since people can always choose paths of greater resistance or create new ones entirely, systems can only be as stable as the flow of human choice and creativity, which certainly isn't a recipe for permanence. In the short run, systems of privilege may

Allan G. Johnson teaches sociology at Hartford College for Women.

look unchangeable. But the relentless process of social life never produces the exact same result twice in a row, because it's impossible for everyone to participate in any system in an unvarying and uniform way. Added to this are the dynamic interactions that go on among systems—between capitalism and the state, for example, or between families and the economy—that also produce powerful and unavoidable tensions, contradictions, and other currents of change. Ultimately, systems can't help changing.

Oppressive systems often *seem* stable because they limit people's lives and imaginations so much that they can't see beyond them. But this masks a fundamental long-term instability caused by the dynamics of oppression itself. Any system organized around one group's efforts to control and exploit another is a losing proposition, because it contradicts the essentially uncontrollable nature of reality and does violence to basic human needs and values. For example, as the last two centuries of feminist thought and action have begun to challenge the violence and break down the denial, patriarchy has become increasingly vulnerable. This is one reason male resistance, backlash, and defensiveness are now so intense. Many men complain about their lot, especially their inability to realize ideals of control in relation to their own lives,[2] women, and other men. Fear of and resentment toward women are pervasive, from worrying about being accused of sexual harassment to railing against affirmative action.

No social system lasts forever, but this is especially true of oppressive systems of privilege. We can't know what will replace them, but we can be confident that they will go, that they *are* going at every moment. It's only a matter of how quickly, by what means, and toward what alternatives, and whether each of us will do our part to make it happen sooner rather than later and with less rather than more human suffering in the process.

MYTH 2: GANDHI'S PARADOX AND THE MYTH OF NO EFFECT

Whether we help change oppressive systems depends on how we handle the belief that nothing we do can make a difference, that the system is too big and powerful for us to affect it. The complaint is valid if we look at society as a whole: it's true that we aren't going to change it in our lifetime. But if changing the entire system through our own efforts is the standard against which we measure the ability to do something, then we've set ourselves up to feel powerless. It's not unreasonable to want to make a difference, but if we have to *see* the final result of what we do, then we can't be part of change that's too gradual and long term to allow that. We also can't be part of change that's so complex that we can't sort out our contribution from countless others that combine in ways we can never grasp. The problem of privilege and oppression requires complex and long-term change coupled with short-term work to soften some of its worst consequences. This means that if we're going to be part of the solution, we have to let go of the idea that change doesn't happen unless we're around to see it happen.

To shake off the paralyzing myth that we cannot, individually, be effective, we have to alter how we see ourselves in relation to a long-term, complex process of change. This begins by altering how we relate to time. Many changes can come about quickly enough for us to see them happen. When I was in college, for example, there was little talk about gender inequality as a social problem, whereas now there are more than five hundred women's studies programs in the United States. But a goal like ending oppression takes more than this and far more time than our short lives can encompass. If we're going to see ourselves as part of that kind of change, we can't use the human life span as a significant standard against which to measure progress.

To see our choices in relation to long-term change, we have to develop what might be called "time constancy," analogous to what psychologists call "object constancy." If you hold a cookie in front of very young children and then put it behind your back while they watch, they can't find the cookie because they apparently can't hold on to the image of it and where it went. They lack object constancy. In other words, if they can't see it, it might as well not even exist. After a while, children develop the mental ability to know that objects or people exist even when they're out of sight. In thinking about change and our relation to it, we need to develop a similar ability in relation to time that enables us to carry within us the knowledge, the faith, that significant change happens even though we aren't around to see it.

Along with time constancy, we need to clarify for ourselves how our choices matter and how they don't. Gandhi once said nothing we do as individuals matters, but that it's vitally important to do it anyway. This touches on a powerful paradox in the relationship between society and individuals. Imagine, for example, that social systems are trees and we are the leaves. No individual leaf on the tree matters; whether it lives or dies has no effect on much of anything. But collectively, the leaves are essential to the whole tree because they photosynthesize the sugar that feeds it. Without leaves, the tree dies.

So leaves matter and they don't, just as we matter and we don't. What each of us does may not seem like much, because in important ways, it *isn't* much. But when many people do this work together, they can form a critical mass that is anything but insignificant, especially in the long run. If we're going to be part of a larger change process, we have to learn to live with this sometimes uncomfortable paradox.

A related paradox is that we have to be willing to travel without knowing where we're going. We need faith to do what seems right without necessarily being sure of the effect that will have. We have to think like pioneers who may know the direction they want to move in or what they would like to find, without knowing where they will wind up. Because they are going where they've never been before, they can't know whether they will ever arrive at anything they might consider a destination, much less the kind of place they had in mind when they first set out. If pioneers had to know their destination from the beginning, they would never go anywhere or discover anything.

In similar ways, to seek out alternatives to systems of privilege it has to be enough to move away from social life organized around privilege and oppression and to move toward the certainty that alternatives are possible, even though we may not have a clear idea of what those are or ever experience them ourselves. It has to be enough to question how we see ourselves as people of a certain race, gender, class, and sexual orientation, for example, or examine how we see capitalism and the scarcity and competition it produces in relation to our personal striving to better our own lives, or how oppression works and how we participate in it. Then we can open ourselves to experience what happens next.

When we dare ask core questions about who we are and how the world works, things happen that we can't foresee; they don't happen unless we *move*, if only in our minds. As pioneers, we discover what's possible only by first putting ourselves in motion, because we have to move in order to change our position—and hence put perspective—on where we are, where we've been, and where we might go. This is how alternatives begin to appear.

The myth of no effect obscures the role we can play in the long-term transformation of society. But the myth also blinds us to our own power in relation to other people. We may cling to the belief that there is nothing we can do precisely because we subconsciously know how much power we *do* have and are afraid to use it because people may not like it. If we deny our power to affect people, then we don't have to worry about taking responsibility for how we use it or, more significant, how we don't.

This reluctance to acknowledge and use power comes up in the simplest everyday situations, as when a group of friends starts laughing at a racist, sexist, or homophobic joke and we have to decide whether to go along. It's just a moment among countless such moments that constitute the fabric of all kinds of oppressive systems. But it's a crucial moment, because the group's seamless response to the joke affirms the normalcy and unproblematic nature of it in a system of privilege. It takes only one person to tear the fabric of collusion and apparent consensus. On some level, we each know we have this potential, and this knowledge can empower us or scare us into silence. We can change the course of the moment with something as simple as visibly not joining in the laughter, or saying "I don't think that's funny." We know how uncomfortable this can make the group feel and how they may ward off their discomfort by dismissing, excluding, or even attacking us as bearers of bad news. Our silence, then, isn't because nothing we do will matter, our silence is our not *daring* to matter.

Our power to affect other people isn't simply the power to make them feel uncomfortable. Systems shape the choices people make primarily by providing paths of least resistance. Whenever we openly choose a different path, however, we make it possible for others to see both the path of least resistance they're following and the possibility of choosing something else.

If we choose different paths, we usually won't know if we're affecting other people, but it's safe to assume that we are. When people know that alternatives exist and witness other people choosing them, things become possible that weren't before. When we openly pass up a path of least resistance, we increase resistance for other people around that path, because now they must reconcile their choice with what they've seen us do, something they didn't have to deal with before. There's no way to predict how this will play out in the long run, but there's certainly no good reason to think it won't make a difference.

The simple fact is that we affect one another all the time without knowing it. When my family moved to our house in the woods of northwestern Connecticut, one of my first pleasures was blazing walking trails through the woods. Some time later I noticed deer scat and hoofprints along the trails, and it pleased me to think they had adopted the trail I'd laid down. But then I wondered if perhaps I had followed a trail laid down by others when I cleared "my" trail. I realized that there is no way to know that anything begins or ends with me and the choices I make. It's more likely that the paths others have chosen influence the paths I choose.

This suggests that the simplest way to help others make different choices is to make them myself, and to do it openly. As I shift the patterns of my own participation in systems of privilege, I make it easier for others to do so as well, and harder for them not to. Simply by setting an example—rather than trying to change them—I create the possibility of their participating in change in their own time and in their own way. In this way I can widen the circle of change without provoking the kind of defensiveness that perpetuates paths of least resistance and the oppressive systems they serve.

It's important to see that in doing this kind of work, we don't have to go after people to change their minds. In fact, changing people's minds may play a relatively small part in changing societies. We won't succeed in turning diehard misogynists into practicing feminists, for example, or racists into civil rights activists. At most, we can shift the odds in favor of new paths that contradict the core values that systems of privilege depend on. We can introduce so many exceptions to the paths that support privilege that the children or grandchildren of diehard racists and misogynists will start to change their perception of which paths offer the least resistance. Research on men's changing attitudes toward the male provider role, for example, shows that most of the shift occurs *between* generations, not within them.[3] This suggests that rather than trying to change people, the most important thing we can do is contribute to the slow evolution of entire cultures so that forms and values which support privilege begin to lose their "obvious" legitimacy and normalcy and new forms emerge to challenge their privileged place in social life.

In science, this is how one paradigm replaces another.[4] For hundreds of years, for example, Europeans believed that the stars, planets, and sun revolved around Earth. But scientists such as Copernicus and Galileo found that too many of their astronomical observations were anomalies that didn't fit the prevailing paradigm: if the sun and planets revolved around the Earth, then they wouldn't move as they did. As such observations accumulated, they made it increasingly difficult to hang on to an Earth-centered paradigm. Eventually the anomalies became so numerous that Copernicus offered a new paradigm, which he declined to

PERSONAL ACCOUNT

Parents' Underestimated Love

"Coming out of the closet" to my parents has been the most liberating thing that I have done in my life because having my homosexuality discovered by my parents was my biggest fear. Although I didn't grow up in a particularly homophobic environment, innately I knew that homosexuality was different and wasn't accepted because of rigid social norms and religious doctrines. I lived in anguish of being exposed and of the consequences that would come with being the queer one.

Keeping the secret from my traditional Salvadoran parents created a wedge that made it difficult for me to bond with my parents and have them participate fully in my life. I became a recluse and avoided much parental interaction to avoid questions about girlfriends. During my teenage years, girlfriends were expected from a "good and healthy" boy such as myself. I felt that my lack of interest in girls would have led to probes from my parents, and plus, I wasn't the typical macho boy who was into sports, cars, etc. . . . I was the "sensitive type." To avoid any suspicion, I limited my interaction with my par-

ents. I felt that if I opened up to them, my sexuality would be questioned and questions like "Are you gay?" would follow. Being an academic overachiever in high school made things easier for me. Whenever the question was asked of why I didn't have a girlfriend, I had the perfect excuse, "I'm too busy with school to focus on girls . . . do you want a *Playboy* or an honor student?"

During my sophomore year in college I took a bold step and moved out of my parents' house. My move facilitated my "coming out" to my parents because the possibility of being kicked out of the house when I told them I was gay wouldn't loom over me. I didn't know if my parents would kick me out, but I couldn't run the risk of finding out. One year after moving out, I "came out." Ironically it didn't come as a surprise to my parents, and frankly it wasn't a big deal! After years of living in fear of rejection and shame, my parents accepted and reaffirmed their love and support. I underestimated the power of my parents' love.

Octavio N. Espinal

publish for fear of persecution as a heretic, a fate that eventually befell Galileo when he took up the cause a century later. Eventually, however, the evidence was so overwhelming that a new paradigm replaced the old one.

In similar ways, we can see how systems of privilege are based on paradigms that shape how we think about difference and how we organize social life in relation to it. We can openly challenge those paradigms with evidence that they don't work and produce unacceptable consequences for everyone. We can help weaken them by openly choosing alternative paths in our everyday lives and thereby provide living anomalies that don't fit the prevailing paradigm. By our example, we can contradict basic assumptions and their legitimacy over and over again. We can add our choices and our lives to tip the scales toward new paradigms that don't revolve around privilege and oppression. We can't tip the scales overnight or by ourselves, and in that sense we don't amount to much. But on the other side of Gandhi's paradox, it is crucial where we choose to

place what poet Bonaro Overstreet called "the stubborn ounces of my weight":

STUBBORN OUNCES

(To One Who Doubts the Worth of Doing Anything If You Can't Do Everything)

You say the little efforts that I make

will do no good; they will never prevail

to tip the hovering scale

where Justice hangs in balance.

I don't think

I ever thought they would.

But I am prejudiced beyond debate

In favor of my right to choose which side

shall feel the stubborn ounces of my weight.[5]

It is in such small and humble choices that oppression and the movement toward something better actually happen.

DISCUSSION QUESTIONS

1. In a sense, Allan Johnson's discussion highlights the paradoxes inherent in the efforts to create social change. What are those paradoxes, and how does Johnson resolve them?

2. What would Johnson's advice be to someone who wants to make a difference in society? Can it be summarized in a sentence or two?

NOTES

1. See Elizabeth Fisher, *Woman's Creation: Sexual Evolution and the Shaping of Society* (New York: McGraw-Hill, 1979); Gerda Lerner, *The Creation of Patriarchy* (New York: Oxford University Press, 1986).

2. This is what Warren Farrell means when he describes male power as mythical. In this case, he's right. See *The Myth of Male Power* (New York: Berkley Books, 1993).

3. J. R. Wilkie, "Changes in U.S. Men's Attitudes towards the Family Provider Role, 1972–1989," *Gender and Society* 7, no. 2 (1993): 261–79.

4. The classic statement of how this happens is by Thomas S. Kuhn, *The Structure of Scientific Revolutions* (Chicago: University of Chicago Press, 1970).

5. Bonaro W. Overstreet, *Hands Laid Upon the Wind* (New York: Norton, 1955), p. 15.

READING 63

In Defense of Rich Kids

William Upski Wimsatt

My family never talked much about money, except to say that we were "middle-class . . . well maybe upper-middle-class." A few years ago, it became clear that both my parents and my grandmother had a lot more money than I realized. As an only child, I stood to inherit a nice chunk of it. I didn't know how much and I didn't know when. They did not want me to become spoiled or think I didn't have to work.

William Upski Wimsatt is an award-winning reporter, essayist, and trend spotter. Author of *Bomb the Suburbs,* he has also written for the *Chicago Tribune* and *Vibe.*

A lot of people will use this information to write me off. Oh, he's a rich kid. No wonder he could publish a book, probably with his parents' money. And why's he going around bragging about it? What is he, stupid? Some of us have to work for a living, etc.

You can hate me if you want to. I am the beneficiary of a very unfair system. The system gives me tons of free money for doing nothing, yet it forces you to work two and three jobs just to get out of debt.

On top of that, I have the nerve to sit up here and talk about it and—for some it will seem—to rub it in. Most rich people are considerate enough to shut their mouths and pretend they're struggling too. To get on TV talking about, "I got this on sale."

I didn't really have anyone to talk about it with. I knew a lot of the kids I had gone to school with were in a similar situation but we never discussed our family money, except in really strange ways like how broke we were and how those other rich people were so spoiled/lucky. Our judgments of them betrayed our own underlying shame.

And let's talk right now about motives. As soon as you bring up philanthropy, people want to talk about motives. "Is he doing this for the right reasons or is he just doing this to make himself feel good?" Well, let me tell you, I am definitely doing this to make myself feel good and—call me crazy—I believe doing what you feel good about is one of the right reasons.

Yes, I have the luxury to give my money away because I know I'm going to inherit more later in life. But don't come to me with this bullshit, "Oh, it's easy for you to give away your money because you're gonna inherit more later." If it's so easy, how come more rich people aren't doing it? How come Americans only give 2% to charity across the board, whether they are rich, poor, or middle-class? I usually give away 20–30% of my income every year. But I just got my first steady job, so this year, if you throw in the book, I'll probably be giving away more like 50%.

Hell no, I'm not some kind of saint who has taken a vow of poverty and is now sitting in judgment of you or anyone else's money decisions. But be aware, it's easy to criticize my actions when you don't have much money. If you were in my situation, who's to say you'd be any different from 99% of other rich people who keep it all for themselves. Or if they do give it away, it's to big colleges, big arts, big religion, or big service, supporting bureaucratic institutions that maintain systemic problems by treating symptoms and obscuring root causes.

Which brings me to the next very selfish reason for my philanthropy. I have a political agenda and my philanthropic "generosity" plus my sense of strategy gives me more philanthropic power to change the world than people with 50 times my income.

The deeper reason why I give away my money is because I love the world. Because I'm grateful to be alive at all. Because I'm scared about where we're headed. Because we owe it to our great-grandchildren. Because we owe it to the millions of years of evolution it took to get us here. And to everyone before us who fought to change history and make things as good as they are now. Because I know how to change history and I know it takes money. Because I get more joy out of making things better for everyone than I get out of making things materially better for myself. Because I know how to make and spend money on myself. It's boring. There's no challenge in it. And no love in it. I love helping good things happen, and supporting people I believe in. Especially people and organizations that have NO money put into them by traditional foundations and charities. I'm not talking about your everyday charities like diabetes or your college(s) that already have multi-million dollar budgets set up to fight for them.

They're new.

They don't exist yet.

They're like diabetes in 1921, the year before they extracted insulin.

They're like your college the year before it was founded.

Don't get me wrong. My father has juvenile diabetes. And I love my college too. But the money supporting the Juvenile Diabetes Foundation, and my college is already so big, their fundraising operations so effective, that giving my money to them is a drop in the bucket.

For the organizing efforts I want to support, every dollar is like a seed, helping not only to create a new kind of organization, but an organization that will be copied and that decades from now will establish new fields of work. It is the most strategic way possible to change the course of history, and the most unpopular because it's so high-risk. . . .

THE MOST EFFECTIVE THING YOU EVER DO

. . . What if we could double the number of cool rich people who are funding social change from say five hundred to a thousand? Then we could double the number of organizers on the street, lawyers in the court rooms, lobbyists in Congress. Double the number of investigative reporters. There are so many people who want to do progressive work who can't because there aren't enough activist jobs. People come out of law school to become environmental lawyers and they end up having to defend corporations because they have to pay off their student loans. Environmental groups can't afford to hire them. The same goes for radical artists and journalists, forced to get jobs in advertising and public relations.

Five hundred more cool rich people could change all that.

Five hundred cool rich people could change the political landscape of this country.

Now don't get me wrong. I'm not saying philanthropy will solve all our problems, especially not the way 99% of it is done now. I'm not saying cool rich people are any more important or worthy than any other people. Poor people are made to feel like they aren't worth anything and that's wrong. I don't want to feed into that by focusing on rich people for a while. We need billions of people from billions of backgrounds trying billions of strategies to save this planet. It's just that every serious effort to change things takes people with money who understand how to support a movement. All these naive college or punk or hip-hop revolutionaries talking about, "Fuck that. I don't know any rich people and if I do they're assholes and anyway, I don't need their money." I only have one thing to say. Wait until your community center gets shut down. Wait until your broke grassroots genius friends start burning out because they have to do menial shit all day because they don't have the time or capital to make their dreams come true.

Consider these statistics. There are about five million millionaire households in the U.S. That's approximately one out of every 50 people. So, if you are a social person (not a hermit) and you are not currently serving a life sentence in prison, then chances are you will have the opportunity at some point in your life to get to know a number of people who are, at the very least, millionaires. Most of the time you will not know they are millionaires. Half of the time, millionaires don't even realize they are millionaires. My parents didn't realize they were. People usually have their assets tied up in many different forms such as houses, trusts, mutual funds, stocks, bonds and retirement accounts.

Less than 1% of all charitable giving ends up in the hands of people who are working to change the system. As Teresa Odendahl has pointed out in her ironically-titled book *Charity Begins at Home,* contrary to popular belief, most charity money does not go to help poor children help themselves. The vast majority of money goes to big churches, big colleges, big hospitals, big arts and social service organizations which either directly cater to privileged people, or which treat the symptoms of social ills without ever addressing the root causes. . . .

Over the next 50 years, the upper-classes of my generation stand to inherit or earn the greatest personal fortune in history, while the lower classes both here and internationally will continue slipping deeper into poverty and debt.

That's where the Cool Rich Kids Movement comes in. Actually there isn't much of a "Cool Rich Kids Movement." That's just what I call the loose-knit network of maybe 100 of us young people with wealth who are in conversation with each other, and who support each other in taking small but significant actions. We are asking our parents to teach us about money. We are helping our families make responsible decisions about investments. Some of us

are getting on the boards of family foundations or helping our families to start them. We introduce each other to amazing grassroots people to break the isolation of wealth. We are just in the process of getting organized. We had our first conference last spring, sponsored by the Third Wave Foundation in New York. More are planned.

My goal is to get more young people with wealth in on the conversation. With five million millionaires in the U.S., even if we only spoke to the coolest 1% of all millionaire kids, that's still 50,000 people!

One half of the money I give away every year goes directly to grassroots youth activist organizations that I have a relationship with. (No, I don't make them kiss up to me. I just give it to them, thank them for their hard work and if they feel funny about it, I remind them that the only reason I have the money in the first place is because I've been so privileged and so many people have helped me. So it wasn't really "my" money to begin with. Oftentimes I have to *insist* that people take my money. We've all had so many bad experiences.)

The other half of my money I donate to organizing people with wealth.

That may seem strange at first.

Why give money to people who already have wealth?

From all my experience with grassroots organizations, I believe that organizing people with wealth is the most powerful work I do. And paradoxically, it is some of the hardest work to fundraise for because everybody including rich people thinks, "Why give rich people more money?" And that's why only a few dozen people in America have the job of helping rich people figure out how to come to terms with and do cool things with their money.

I think we need more of those people in the world.

So recently, I've changed my focus in a big way.

I joined the board of More Than Money. I am helping to start the Active Element Foundation, which is the first foundation that will specifically work with young donors on funding grassroots youth activism. And I'm also helping to start the Self-Education Foundation, which will tap successful people who either didn't like school or who dropped out to fund self-education resource centers which will support poor kids to take learning into their own hands. I am helping to organize a series of conferences around the country for young people with wealth, put on by The Third Wave Foundation and the Comfort Zone. . . .

I believe the most effective thing I do for the world every year is to buy gift subscriptions of *More Than Money Journal* for my privileged friends and to keep a ready supply of *Money Talks. So Can We.* for every cool young person I meet who has money. This is the most effective action I do. Any other possible action I could do, one cool rich person could hire ten more people to take my place.

But there's very little room in our culture to talk about having money and funding renegade work. Most rich people be like, "See you later." And most grassroots people be like, "It's easy for you because you're rich." There's resentment either way. People who aren't rich can play a huge role supporting us. So many of my friends who aren't wealthy act like, "Ha ha ha, going to your rich kids conference." That's not going to make me want to talk to you. If you are truly down to change the world, don't try to score points by alienating your rich friends with snide remarks. If you take the time to truly understand us and support us as people, more than likely, we will do the same for you. Rich people don't choose to be born rich any more than poor people choose to be born poor. The sickness of our society damages us each in different and complicated ways, and we sometimes forget that rich people get damaged too. Not just in a mocking way, like, "Oh, they're so spoiled." But in a real way. One of the most common ways privileged people get damaged is that we are taught not to talk about money. We put a wall around ourselves, and then it is hard for us to be honest with people who aren't rich. This makes us cold and creates a vicious cycle of not trusting and not sharing ourselves or our money.

There are only a few of us out here doing this work, which is why I have been thrust into the spotlight. It's a little ridiculous actually that I am speaking for rich kids when I haven't even inherited my money yet. But there was a deafening silence and someone needed to come out here and give us a bold public voice. Do you have any cool rich friends who may be looking for people in similar situations to talk to?

Hint: You do.

Please please please pass this along to them.

It just might be the most effective thing you ever do.

DISCUSSION QUESTIONS

1. Would you rather have money or a large number of supporters if you were seeking to create social change?
2. How much money would you want to have before you considered giving away some of it to create social change?

READING 64

Uprooting Racism
HOW WHITE PEOPLE CAN WORK FOR RACIAL JUSTICE

Paul Kivel

"THANK YOU FOR BEING ANGRY"

A person of color who is angry about discrimination or harassment is doing us a service. That person is pointing out something wrong, something that contradicts the ideals of equality set forth in our Declaration of Independence and Bill of Rights. That person is bringing our attention to a problem that needs solving, a wrong that needs righting. We could convey our appreciation by saying, "Thank you, your anger has helped me see what's not right here." What keeps us from responding in this way?

Paul Kivel is a teacher, trainer, consultant, writer, and community educator on men's lives and violence, family and dating abuse, youth violence, racism, homophobia, and raising boys.

Anger is a scary emotion in our society. In mainstream white culture we are taught to be polite, never to raise our voices, to be reasonable and to keep calm. People who are demonstrative of their feelings are discounted and ridiculed. We are told by parents just to obey "because I said so." We are told by bosses, religious leaders and professional authorities not to challenge what they say, "or else" (or else you'll be fired, go to hell, be treated as "crazy"). When we do get angry we learn to stuff it, mutter under our breath and go away. We are taught to turn our anger inward in self-destructive behaviors. If we are men we are taught to take out our frustrations on someone weaker and smaller than we are.

When we have seen someone expressing anger, it has often been a person with power who was abusing us or someone else physically, verbally or emotionally. We were hurt, scared or possibly confused. Most of us can remember a time from our youth when a parent, teacher, coach, boss or other adult was yelling at us abusively. It made us afraid when those around us become angry. It made us afraid of our own anger.

A similar response is triggered when a person of color gets angry at us about racism. We become scared, guilty, embarrassed, confused and we fear everything is falling apart and we might get hurt. If the angry person would just calm down, or go away, we could get back to the big, happy family feeling.

Relationships between people of color and whites often begin as friendly and polite. We may be pleased that we know and like a person from another cultural group. We may be pleased that they like us. We are encouraged because despite our fears, it seems that it may be possible for people from different cultures to get along together. The friendships may confirm our feelings that we are different from other white people.

But then the person of color gets angry. Perhaps they are angry about something we do or say. Perhaps they are angry about a comment or action by someone else, or about racism in general. We may back off in response, fearing that the relationship is falling apart. We aren't liked anymore. We've been found out to be racist. For a person of color, this may be a time of hope that the relationship can become more intimate and honest. The anger may be an attempt to test the depths and possibilities of the friendship. They may be open about their feelings, to see how safe we are, hoping that we will not desert them. Or the anger may be a more assertive attempt to break through our complacency to address some core assumptions, beliefs or actions.

Many white people have been taught to see anger and conflict as a sign of failure. They may instead be signs that we're becoming more honest, dealing with the real differences and problems in our lives. If it is not safe enough to argue, disagree, express anger and struggle with each other what kind of relationship can it be?

We could say, "Thank you for pointing out the racism because I want to know whenever it is occurring." Or, "I appreciate your honesty. Let's see what we can do about this situation." More likely we get scared and disappear, or become defensive and counterattack. In any case, we don't focus on the root of the problem, and the racism goes unattended.

When people of color are angry about racism it is legitimate anger. It is not their oversensitivity, but our lack of sensitivity, that causes this communication gap. They are vulnerable to the abuse of racism everyday. They are experts on it. White society, and most of us individually, rarely notice racism.

It is the anger and actions of people of color that call our attention to the injustice of racism. Sometimes that anger is from an individual person of color who is talking to us. At other times it is the rage of an entire community protesting, bringing legal action or burning down buildings. Such anger and action is almost always a last resort, a desperate attempt to get our attention when all else fails.

It is tremendously draining, costly and personally devastating for people of color to have to rage about racism. They often end up losing their friends, their livelihoods, even their lives. Rather than attacking them for their anger, we need to ask ourselves how many layers of complacency, ignorance, collusion, privilege and misinformation have we put into place for it to take so much outrage to get our attention?

The 1965 riots in Watts, as never before, brought our attention to the ravages of racism on the African-American population living there. In 1968 a national report by the Kerner Commission warned us of the dangers of not addressing racial problems. Yet in 1992, when there were new uprisings in Los Angeles, we focused again on the anger of African Americans, on containing that anger, protecting property and controlling the community, rather than on solving the problems that cause poverty, unemployment, crime and high drop-out rates. As soon as the anger was contained, we turned our attention elsewhere and left the underlying problems unaddressed. The only way to break this cycle of rage is for us to seriously address the sources of the anger, the causes of the problems. And in order to do that, we need to talk about racism directly with each other.

BEING A STRONG WHITE ALLY

What kind of active support does a strong white ally provide? People of color that I have talked with over the years have been remarkably consistent in describing the kinds of support they need from white allies. The following list is compiled from their statements at workshops I have facilitated. The focus here is on personal qualities and interpersonal relationships. More active interventions are discussed in the next part of [this discussion].

What people of color want from white allies:

"Respect"
"Find out about us"
"Don't take over"
"Provide information"
"Resources"
"Money"
"Take risks"
"Don't take it personally"
"Understanding"
"Teach your children about racism"
"Speak up"
"Don't be scared by my anger"

"Support"
"Listen"
"Don't make assumptions"
"Stand by my side"
"Don't assume you know what's best for me"
"Your body on the line"
"Make mistakes"
"Honesty"
"Talk to other white people"
"Interrupt jokes and comments"
"Don't ask me to speak for my people"

BASIC TACTICS

Every situation is different and calls for critical thinking about how to make a difference. Taking the statements above into account, I have compiled some general guidelines.

1. *Assume racism is everywhere, everyday.* Just as economics influences everything we do, just as our gender and gender politics influence everything we do, assume that racism is affecting whatever is going on. We assume this because it's true, and because one of the privileges of being white is not having to see or deal with racism all the time. We have to learn to see the effect that racism has. Notice who speaks, what is said, how things are done and described. Notice who isn't present. Notice code words for race, and the implications of the policies, patterns and comments that are being expressed. You already notice the skin color of everyone you meet and interact with—now notice what difference it makes.

2. *Notice who is the center of attention and who is the center of power.* Racism works by directing violence and blame toward people of color and consolidating power and privilege for white people.

3. *Notice how racism is denied, minimized and justified.*

4. *Understand and learn from the history of whiteness and racism.* Notice how racism has

changed over time and how it has subverted or resisted challenges. Study the tactics that have worked effectively against it.

5. ***Understand the connections between racism, economic issues, sexism and other forms of injustice.***

6. ***Take a stand against injustice.*** Take risks. It is scary, difficult, risky and may bring up many feelings, but ultimately it is the only healthy and moral human thing to do. Intervene in situations where racism is being passed on.

7. ***Be strategic.*** Decide what is important to challenge and what's not. Think about strategy in particular situations. Attack the source of power.

8. ***Don't confuse a battle with the war.*** Behind particular incidents and interactions are larger patterns. Racism is flexible and adaptable. There will be gains and losses in the struggle for justice and equality.

9. ***Don't call names or be personally abusive.*** Since power is often defined as power over others—the ability to abuse or control people—it is easy to become abusive ourselves. However, we usually end up abusing people who have less power than we do because it is less dangerous. Attacking people doesn't address the systemic nature of racism and inequality.

10. ***Support the leadership of people of color.*** Do this consistently, but not uncritically.

11. ***Don't do it alone.*** You will not end racism by yourself. We can do it if we work together. Build support, establish networks, work with already established groups.

12. ***Talk with your children and other young people about racism.***

IT'S NOT JUST A JOKE

"Let me tell you about the Chinaman who . . ." What do you do when someone starts to tell a joke which you think is likely to be a racial putdown? What do you do if the racial nature of the joke is only apparent at the punchline? How do you respond to a comment which contains a racial stereotype?

Interrupting racist comments can be scary because we risk turning the attack or anger toward us. We are sometimes accused of dampening the mood, being too serious or too sensitive. We may be ridiculed for being friends of the _____. People may think we're arrogant or trying to be politically correct. They may try to get back at us for embarrassing them. If you're in an environment where any of this could happen, then you know that it is not only not safe for you, it's even more unsafe for people of color.

People tell jokes and make comments sometimes out of ignorance, but usually knowing at some level that the comment puts down someone else and creates a collusion between the speaker and the listener. The joketeller is claiming that we're normal, intelligent and sane, and others are not. The effect is to exclude someone or some group of people from the group, to make it a little (or a lot) more unsafe for them to be there. Furthermore, by objectifying someone, it makes it that much easier for the next person to tell a joke, make a comment or take stronger action against any member of the objectified group.

The reverse is also true. Interrupting such behavior makes it less safe to harass or discriminate, and more safe for the intended targets of the abuse. Doing nothing is tacit approval and collusion with the abuse. There is no neutral stance. If someone is being attacked, even by a joke or teasing, there are no innocent bystanders.

As a white person you can play a powerful role in such a situation. When a person of color protests against being put down in an atmosphere where they are already disrespected, they are often discounted as well. You, as a white person interrupting verbal abuse, may be listened to and heeded because it breaks the collusion from other white people that was expected by the abuser. If a person of color speaks up first then you can support them by stating why you think it is right to challenge the comments. In either case, your intervention as a white person challenging racist comments is important and often effective.

What can you actually say in the presence of derogatory comments? There are no right or wrong answers. The more you do it the better you get. Even if it doesn't come off as you intended, you will influence others to be more sensitive and you will model the courage and integrity to interrupt verbal abuse. Following are suggestions for where to start.

If you can tell at the beginning that a joke is likely to be offensive or involves stereotypes and putdowns, you can say something like, "I don't want to hear a joke or story that reinforces stereotypes or puts down a group of people." Or, "Please stop right there. It sounds like your story is going to make fun of a group of people and I don't want to hear about it." Or, "I don't like humor that makes it unsafe for people here." Or, "I don't want to hear a joke that asks us to laugh at someone else's expense." There are many ways to say something appropriate without attacking or being offensive yourself.

Using "I" statements should be an important part of your strategy. Rather than attacking someone, it is stronger to state how you feel, what you want. Other people may still become defensive, but there is more opportunity for them to hear what you have to say if you word it as an "I" statement.

Often you don't know the story is offensive until the punchline. Or you just are not sure what you're hearing, but it makes you uncomfortable. It is appropriate to say afterwards that the joke was inappropriate because . . . , or the story was offensive because . . . , or it made you feel uncomfortable because . . . Trust your feelings about it!

In any of these interactions you may need to explain further why stories based on stereotypes reinforce abuse, and why jokes and comments that put people down are offensive. Rather than calling someone racist, or writing someone off, interrupting abuse is a way to do public education. It is a way to put what you know about racial stereotypes and abuse into action to stop them.

Often a person telling a racial joke is defensive about being called on the racism and may argue or defend themselves. You don't have to prove anything, although a good discussion of the issues is a great way to do more education. It's now up to the other person to think about your comments and to

decide what to do. Everyone nearby will have heard you make a clear, direct statement challenging verbal abuse. Calling people's attention to something they assumed was innocent makes them more sensitive in the future and encourages them to stop and think about what they say about others.

Some of the other kinds of reactions you can expect are:

"It's only a joke." "It may 'only' be a joke but it is at someone's expense. It creates an environment that is less safe for the person or group being joked about. Abuse is not a joke."

"I didn't mean any harm." "I'm sure you didn't. But you should understand the harm that results even if you didn't mean it, and change what you say."

"Is this some kind of thought patrol?" "No, people can think whatever they want to. But we are responsible for what we say in public. A verbal attack is like any other kind of attack, it hurts the person attacked. Unless you intentionally want to hurt someone, you should not tell jokes or stories like this."

"This joke was told to me by a member of that group." "It really makes no difference who tells it. If it is offensive then it shouldn't be told. It is sad but true that some of us put down our own racial or ethnic group. That doesn't make it okay or less hurtful."

Sometimes the speaker will try to isolate you by saying that everyone else likes the story, everyone else laughed at the joke. At that point you might want to turn to the others and ask them if they like hearing jokes that are derogatory, do they like stories that attack people?

Sometimes the joke or derogatory comment will be made by a member of the racial group the comment is about. They may believe negative stereotypes about their racial group, they may want to separate themselves from others like themselves, or they may have accepted the racial norms of white peers in order to be accepted. In this situation it is more appropriate, and probably more effective, to talk to that person separately and express your concerns about how comments reinforce stereotypes and make the environment unsafe.

Speaking out makes a difference. Even a defensive speaker will think about what you said and probably speak more carefully in the future. I have found that when I respond to jokes or comments, other people come up to me afterwards and say they are glad I said something because the comments bothered them too but they didn't know what to say. Many of us stand around, uneasy but hesitant to intervene. By speaking out we model effective intervention and encourage other people to do the same. We set a tone for being active rather than passive, challenging racism rather than colluding with it.

The response to your intervention also lets you know whether the abusive comments are intentional or unintentional, malicious or not. It will give you information about whether the speaker is willing to take responsibility for the effects words have on others. We all have a lot to learn about how racism hurts people. We need to move on from our mistakes, wiser from the process. No one should be trashed.

If the speaker persists in making racially abusive jokes or comments, then further challenge will only result in arguments and fights. People around them need to take the steps necessary to protect themselves from abuse. You may need to think of other tactics to create a safe and respectful environment, including talking with peers to develop a plan for dealing with this person, or talking with a supervisor.

If you are in a climate where people are being put down, teased or made the butt of jokes based on their race, gender, sexual orientation, age or any other factor, you should investigate whether other forms of abuse such as sexual harassment or racial discrimination are occurring as well. Jokes and verbal abuse are obviously not the most important forms that racism takes. However, we all have the right to live, work and socialize in environments free from verbal and emotional harassment. In order to create contexts where white people and peo-

---

PERSONAL ACCOUNT

Where Are You From?

As a freshman at a predominantly white private college, I was confronted with a number of unusual situations. I was extremely young for a college freshman (I was sixteen), I was African American, and I was placed in upper-division courses, because of my academic background. So being accepted and fitting in were crucial to me.

I was enrolled in a course, political thought, with approximately thirty other students, mostly juniors and seniors who had taken courses with this professor before. I was the only African American in the class. During introductions for the first class, he never got around to letting me speak, even though he went alphabetically on the list (my last name begins with a "C"). Later, I began to be aware of his exclusion of me from class discussion. By the third class, I guess he felt there was no longer any way he could avoid speaking to me. He asked me a few questions about myself—where I was from, what high school had I attended, and what was my major. His questions began to seem like a personal attack, and then finally he asked, "Why are you here?" "Where are you from?" I was quite taken aback by his line of questioning, when one of the upperclassmen (a white man) responded for me. "She's a freshman, Dr. B. Any more questions?" That guy became one of my closest friends. We have maintained contact ever since college. His response to Dr. B. totally changed the professor's way of treating me.

C.C.

---

ple of color can work together to challenge more fundamental forms of racism, we need to be able to talk to each other about the ways that we talk to each other.

DISCUSSION QUESTIONS

1. When is anger about racism appropriate?
2. What are some of the contradictions between the American ideals of equality and reality?

PERMISSIONS

Paul R. Abramson and Steven D. Pinkerton, "Is Homosexual a Noun?" from *With Pleasure: Thoughts on the Nature of Human Sexuality.* Copyright © 2002 by Paul R. Abramson and Steven D. Pinkerton. Reprinted with the permission of Oxford University Press, Inc.

Bert Archer, excerpts from *The End of Gay (and the Death of Heterosexuality).* Copyright © 2002 by Bert Archer. Reprinted with the permission of the author and Thunder's Mouth Press, a division of Avalon Publishing Group.

Ira Berkow, "The Minority Quarterback" from *How Race Is Lived in America: Pulling Together, Pulling Apart.* Copyright © 2001 by The New York Times. Reprinted with the permission of Henry Holt and Company, LLC.

Laurel Johnson Black, "Stupid Rich Bastards" from *This Fine Place So Far from Home: Voice of Academics from the Working Class*, edited by C. L. Barney Dews and Carolyn Leste Law. Copyright © 1995, 1997 by Temple University. Reprinted with the permission of Temple University Press.

Patricia Leigh Brown, "For Children of Gays, Marriage Brings Joy" from *The New York Times* (March 19, 2004). Copyright © 2004 by The New York Times Company. Reprinted with permission.

Michael K. Brown et al., "The Bankruptcy of Virtuous Markets" from *Whitewashing Race: The Myth of a Color-Blind Society.* Copyright © 2003 by The Regents of the University of California. Reprinted with the permission of the University of California Press.

Ward Churchill, "Let's Spread the 'Fun' Around" from *Acts of Rebellion: The Ward Churchill Reader.* Copyright © 2003 by Ward Churchill. Reprinted with the permission of Routledge/Taylor & Francis Books, Inc.

Jeanette Cleveland et al., "Gender Discrimination in the Workplace" from *Women and Men in Organizations: Sex and Gender Issues at Work.* Copyright © 2000 by Lawrence Erlbaum Associates, Inc. Reprinted with permission.

Charles T. Clotfelter, excerpt from *After Brown: The Rise and Retreat of School Desegregation.* Copyright © 2004 by Princeton University Press. Reprinted with the permission of Princeton University Press.

Jeanine Cogan, "Influencing Public Policy" from *Everyday Activism: A Handbook for Lesbian, Gay, and Bisexual People and Their Allies,* edited by Michael R. Stevenson and Jeanine C. Cogan. Copyright © 2003 by Routledge. Reprinted with the permission of Routledge/Taylor & Francis Books, Inc.

Marta Cruz-Janzen, "Ethnic Identity and Racial Formations: Race and Racism American-Style and *a lo latino*" from *Transnational Latina/o Communities,* edited by Carlos G. Velez-Ibanez and Anna Sampaio. Copyright © 2002 by Rowman & Littlefield Publishers, Inc. Reprinted with permission.

Heather M. Dalmage, excerpt from *Tripping on the Color Line: Black-White Multiracial Families in a Racially Divided World.* Copyright © 2000 by Heather M. Dalmage. Reprinted with the permission of Rutgers University Press.

F. James Davis, "Who is Black? One Nation's Definition" (originally titled "The Nation's Rule") from *Who is Black? One Nation's Definition.* Copyright © 1991 by The Pennsylvania State University. Reprinted with the permission of The Pennsylvania State University Press.

Barbara Ehrenreich, excerpt from *Nickel and Dimed: On (Not) Getting By in America.* Copyright © 2001 by Barbara Ehrenreich. Reprinted with the permission of Henry Holt and Company, LLC.

Yen Le Espiritu, "Asian American Panethnicity" from *Asian-American Panethnicity: Bridging Institutions and Identities.* Copyright © 1992 by Temple University. Reprinted with the permission of Temple University Press.

Anne Fausto-Sterling, "The Five Sexes: Why Male and Female are Not Enough" from *The Sciences* 22, no. 2 (March/April 1993). Reprinted with the permission of *The Sciences.*

Ruth Frankenberg, "Whiteness as an 'Unmarked' Cultural Category" from *White Women, Race Matters.* Copyright © 1993 by the Regents of the University of Minnesota. Reprinted with the permission of the author and the University of Minnesota Press.

Sally French, "'Can You See the Rainbow?' The Roots of Denial" from John Swain, Vic Finkelstein, Sally French, and Mike Oliver (eds.), *Disabling Barriers—Enabling Environments.* Copyright © 1993 by The Open University. Reprinted with the permission of Sage Publications, Ltd.

Marilyn Frye, "Oppression" and "To See and Be Seen" from *The Politics of Reality: Essays in Feminist Theory,* edited by

PHOTO CREDITS

INDEX